Old and New World Highland Bagpiping

McGill-Queen's Studies in Ethnic History
SERIES ONE: Donald Harman Akenson, Editor

SERIES TWO: John Zucchi, Editor

Old and New World Highland Bagpiping

John G. Gibson

McGill-Queen's University Press
Montreal & Kingston • London • Ithaca

© McGill-Queen's University Press 2002
ISBN 0-7735-2291-3
Legal deposit fourth quarter 2002
Bibliothèque nationale du Québec

Printed in Canada on acid-free paper.

This book has been published with the help of a grant from
the Humanities and Social Sciences Federation of Canada,
using funds provided by the Social Sciences and Humanities
Research Council of Canada.

McGill-Queen's University Press acknowledges the
support of the Canada Council for the Arts for its publishing
program. It also acknowledges the financial support of the
Government of Canada through the Book Publishing Industry
Development Program (BPIDP) for its activities.

National Library of Canada Cataloguing in Publication Data

Gibson, John G. (John Graham), 1941–
    Old and new world highland bagpiping

    Includes bibliographical references and index.
    ISBN 0-7735-2291-3

    1. Bagpipe—Scotland—Highlands—History.   2. Bagpipe—Nova
    Scotia—Cape Breton Island—History.   3. Bagpipe music—History
    and criticism.   I. Title.

    ML980.G448 2002   788.4'9'0941 15   C2001-904016-4

Typeset in 10/12 Times Roman by True to Type

Contents

Charts and Table

Preface

This book, like its predecessor, *Traditional Gaelic Bagpiping, 1745–1945,* was researched and written without any financial help from any institution. This slowed my inquiries a little and in a small number of instances precluded access. There is material held by the Public Record Office in London, for example, access to which meant hiring a local researcher, which was beyond my budget; a few texts to be found in Scotland were also all but unavailable to me in Judique, Cape Breton, Nova Scotia. I hope, however, that if there are any slight wants, they are more than compensated by some of the obscurer works and field observations that did come to my attention. The research work is by no means finished on either side of the Atlantic, although the memories that are left, like the fund of lore, are fewer and more dilute than ever on both shores. All the translations from the original Gaelic, unless otherwise noted, are my own.

I was very lucky to have settled in Cape Breton when there was still a strong echo of its rich musical past, when many of the older folk spoke English with delightfully measured Gaelic accents and phrases. I am grateful to many folk who allowed me gradually to dispel my ignorance without embarrassment.

In Scotland I was accorded many highly efficient kindnesses and services from several members of the staff of the Scottish Record Office, the National Library in Edinburgh, the National Museums of Scotland, and many other institutions. I must mention the always kind and considerate help I had from Hugh Cheape at the old and new museums of antiquities in Edinburgh; from Roy Wentworth in Gairloch; from Tearlach MacFarlane, Glenfinnan, for help with local Moidart genealogies; from Dr J.N. Hills at the Scottish Record Office; and from Bridget MacKenzie, Dornoch, and Ann MacKinnon at the Clan Donald Land Trust. Mrs Jill Kelsey at the Royal Archives and Roderick Cannon helped with the answers to several queries. I am grateful to Peter Cooke in Edinburgh who read a manuscript in unfinished form and made shrewd suggestions for its improvement and identified several sources that I should consult. I must acknowledge also the excellent work done by Keith Sanger and Fran Buisman on which I place a very high value indeed.

I have special pleasure in acknowledging the kindness of Pictonian Allan C. Dunlop, now of Halifax, Nova Scotia, who, having helped me in my work for years from his desk at the Public Archives of Nova Scotia, when retired from that work, drew to my attention a very important Canadian newspaper article that answers several queries I had and expands our knowledge of piping east of Strathspey. I am pleased also to acknowledge the kind services of Jeanne Howell at the Cambridge Military Library in Halifax. Most of the interviews conducted during the summer of 2000 in northern Cape Breton, which are used in chapter 14, are the property of Parks Canada and are used with their permission and my gratitude. These papers are lodged at the library at Operations, Cape Breton Highlands National Park, Ingonish Beach. I am grateful to David Algar, who is particularly sensitive to the human cultural history in and adjoining the park. I was also shown sensitive considerateness and cooperation by many Parks Canada people, including Tim Reynolds and Elaine Wallace. At the North Highlands Community Museum in Cape North both Kathleen MacLeod and Joliene Stockley were always helpful. Luckily, too, I had access to some of the extensive local genealogies compiled by Sheila MacEachern in Cape North and I wish to acknowledge her kindness. I must also pay my respects to the late Allie Timmons, with whom I spoke at his home in Hinkley Glen Road just over three weeks before he died on 14 September 2000. I was looking forward to seeing him again. His memory of local affairs was great and with his death the north has lost yet another lore bearer of the old school.

What I learned about piping in Washabuck, Cape Breton, was largely from the generous help of Vincent MacLean, who lives there, and of Roderick C. and Helen MacNeil of nearby Barra Glen. Where the names of Highland tunes are concerned, I always had the kind assistance of my neighbour John Donald Cameron, whose knowledge is encyclopaedic and too often taken for granted without acknowledgment.

I must also say again how grateful I am to the staff of Eastern Counties Regional Library in Mulgrave and Port Hawkesbury, and to the library staff at St Francis Xavier University, particularly Maureen Williams in Special Collections. I had also the kind help of Josephine Beaton and Father Bernard MacDonald of Brook Village; Professor John R. MacCormack, Halifax; Ronald MacDonald, Antigonish; and Professor Dan MacInnes, Lanark, Nova Scotia – all among many obliging Nova Scotians who lent me published and unpublished documents. There were uncounted others and if they, and particularly the last Gaelic speakers, are flattered to be mentioned in the text and notes, I shall be delighted and feel a debt partially repaid. With hardly an exception they had very retentive memories, and all shared a sense of cultured kindness that is the heart of the Gael. That, together with their ready acceptance of personal foibles, is what I remember from Glenfinnan far away and years ago and what binds me to them.

I am grateful also to Cel Dicks and Margaret Boudreau at Stora Port Hawkesbury Ltd, and to Peter Dunford and Michael Krüger of the Nautical Institute in Port Hawkesbury, who generously allowed me to make use of their computer equipment.

The book is about a perspective I suppose, and if that perspective is valuable, as I believe it is, then any remaining minor oversights and gaps will not detract much from this work and may be supplied by others. Should omissions exist and errors turn up, I accept the responsibility; I read it last. Neither may I allow any discredit to fall upon my editors; those I have had dealings with through McGill-Queen's University Press have been remarkably skilful people who deal carefully and scrupulously with many unusual subjects. Otherwise I hope this book adds pleasantly and provocatively to thought about the world of the traditional Gael, wherever he or she may be.

Donald ("Dan") Fortune (1906–2001) at his Glendale home with the "parlour pipes" that were bought by his father, Angus Fortune (d. 1918), in Red Island, Cape Breton, c. 1897, for Scots-born Donald McInnis (Angus Fortune's father-in-law). Both Dan and his brother Alex (Marble Mt) were piping enthusiasts. Exposure made in 1978 by the author.

The late John Angus (Jack) Collins, Scotsville, c. 1979. Nephew of the prominent Gaelic bagpiper Allan MacFarlane (1878–1938) from nearby Upper Margaree, my informant Jack Collins was a student of Scottish Gaelic affairs and shared an extensive library with his brother James in Scotsville. Photograph taken by the author.

Margaret (Blue) MacLean (1902–79). Remarkably hospitable and generous, Margaret MacLean was a Gaelic speaker and major informant on
the lives of the last Gaels in Protestant River Denys watershed, including
Big Marsh, Orangedale, and Valley Mills. Photograph taken at Mrs
MacLean's home in Melford, Cape Breton, 1978, by the author.

Barnaby Brown (Glasgow and Sassari, Italy) playing a replica of the common-stock small pipes that belonged to a member of Montgomerie's Highlanders (raised in 1757). The set was made by Julian Goodacre, English pipe maker in Peebles, Scotland. Brown's playing of unpublished Campbell Canntaireachd written *ceòl mór* (including introductory runs) adds importantly to understanding of the eighteenth-century classical music of the bagpipes. The exposure was made in Judique, 7 December 2000, by the author.

Hamish Moore, visiting Scottish traditional bagpiper, playing step-dance music on a home-made set of pipes at a Broad Cove concert in Cape Breton in 1994. Moore began his piping career as a modern piper but discovered and adopted the traditional speeds and rhythms of Cape Breton step-dance music. He is in large part responsible for reintroducing the old Gaelic traditional style that lingered longest in Gaelic Cape Breton to Hebridean Scotland. Of the two accompanying Cape Breton musicians, the guitarist is Paul MacDonald. Author's photograph.

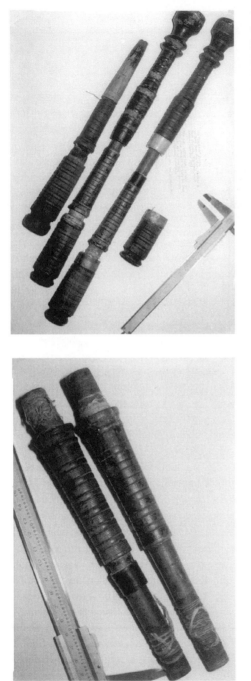

The "MacLean pipes" recovered by
the late *seannachaidh* Joe Neil Mac-
Neil from the barn at his piper friend
Mike MacLean's in Big Pond. Wood
used unknown, but probably native to
Scotland. Measurements are included
in Table I (pp. 206–10). Photograph
taken by the author, Kingsville, 1983.

The "MacLean pipes," detail of the
lower drone sections. Photograph
taken by the author, Kingsville, 1983.

A Scots-made set of bagpipes with a Glen chanter. This imported, modern set was owned and played by Hugh Gillis (stone-cutter, d. 1905) in the Catholic Margarees. With the exception of a rough replacement blow-pipe and a carefully turned replacement section of the bass drone, it probably dates to c. 1890. Exposure made in the fall of 1994 by the author.

Judique step-dancer Angus John Graham (Angie John) giving an *al fresco* performance to an unnamed bagpiper, place and date uncertain. This is an enhanced copy of the original family photograph kindly lent me by the dancer's daughter, Mary (Graham) MacDonald (Mary Archie), Judique.

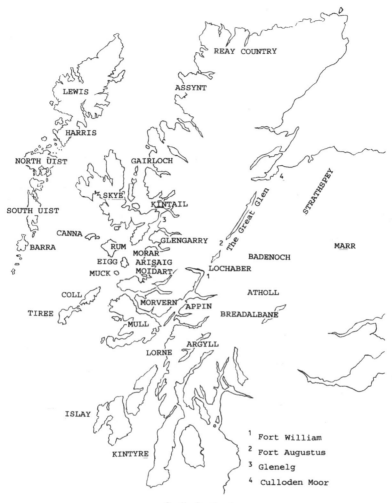

Gaelic Scotland

1 Fort William
2 Fort Augustus
3 Glenelg
4 Culloden Moor

Under Gaelic clan hegemonies I am as yet unaware of many clearly delineated patrimonial land boundaries (other than rivers and coasts). Here and there, inland, cairns mark limits; elsewhere the Ordnance Survey, while preserving a large number of Gaelic place-names and ruins, dwells upon shire boundaries. Old parish lines, watersheds, stipulatable horizons perhaps, may resolve the problem and explain the difficulties of perceived clan holdings under Gaelic polity at any given time.

Cape Breton Island, No. 1

Cape Breton Island, No. 2

Old and New World Highland Bagpiping

Introduction

This second book of mine about bagpiping brings together information about Highland pipers and piping from a large number of communities in Gaelic Scotland and from several in the disappearing Nova Scotia *Gàidhealtachd* (and sometimes from other parts of the New World where Highlanders settled from the late eighteenth century onward). The work ranges from the 1740s in Gaelic Scotland to within living memory in rural Cape Breton. It is an extensive if not exhaustive collation of data that relies generally on two kinds of sources, the written record in the Old World and the memory and lore in the New. This might suggest two distinct kinds of piper and piping, but the essential point is that as long as the piper fulfilled a High- o land function the music was of the same character, based on the same musical concepts, on both sides of the salty divide.

In the Old World this music hung on here and there into the twentieth century in the face of novel and very powerful forces for change; in the New, in rural settings, it proceeded for a little longer, beyond the reach of similar forces. The more abstract argument for the persistence of the Gaelic tradition, including very importantly the non-influence of the Disarming Act on pipers and piping, has been made in my earlier book, *Traditional Gaelic Bagpiping, 1745–1945*. This present book presumes and restates this persistence, and highlights of the argument will be woven into the introduction to Part 3, the New World section, to make the needed emphasis.

For my purpose, the subject of piping is at least twice complicated. Over the period in question, and predating it for an unknown time, there have been and there are a classical and a non-classical form. For a shorter period, but one that goes back from the present for roughly two centuries, there have coexisted two kinds of piping. The Gaelic kind is the conservative, memory-based piping that doubtless grew and changed but always within a Gaelic perception of musicality; diverging from that, there are the forms based on transcriptions of pipe music, described, for example (notably for classical piping), by William Donaldson in *The Highland Pipe and Scottish Society 1750–1950*. The two kinds of piping probably lasted together in Gaelic Scotland until bilingualism reached into the last Hebridean recesses, certainly until step-dancing succumbed. The forces of change may not have always been as withering as they are often portrayed, but there is no doubt that both kinds of piping coexisted and that the foundation was the non-literate Gaelic form.

Donaldson uses the word "tradition" to describe a piping that became profoundly influenced, and eventually troubled, by the seductive theoretical thinking of the late eighteenth century. He thus confers upon the improved and literate piping the designation "tradition." I use the term to take in Gaelic non-literately transmitted piping, that which continued to be considered tried and true in the old Scottish Gaelic world and at a remove from outside intellectualizing. *Old and New World Highland Bagpiping* deals primarily with the Gaelic perceptions of piping and the piper.

In treating piping in both the Old World and the New, this book addresses two kinds of observation, not two kinds of piper. With these two kinds of source materials presented together, you will appreciate that without understanding something of the older founding tradition it is possible, naïvely or not, to impose modern concepts of what bagpiping was (or surely must have been) in Gaelic Scotland upon observations written in English, mostly by outsiders, over more than two centuries. Misinterpretation and manipulation of those writings have dogged piping.

This book enlarges on *Traditional Gaelic Bagpiping,* broadening the foundation. It places special emphasis on the piping and pipers in Scotland in the second half of the eighteenth century, when Scottish Gaelic society was more socially coherent than it has ever been since, and follows this subject until the end of the emigrations to Canada, about 1840. It furnishes examples from almost every quarter of Gaelic Scotland of a kind of bagpiping that was, it can most cogently be argued, preliterate and thus fundamentally Gaelic and unaffected by alien concepts and constructs.

Perhaps the pipers from the Jacobite estates were more conservative and hidebound by tradition (as I define tradition) than those who lived in Hanoverian areas, but this assumption isn't particularly easy to defend. The Campbell pipers on the Breadalbane estate may have learned their music in Jacobite Keppoch, but there were more than Campbell pipers in Breadalbane. Then again preliterate Reel dance pipers appear to have been thickest on the ground in Clanranald's South Uist (where I believe Gaelic is still strong) until the early years of the twentieth century. Whatever the truth of the matter, I will indicate where improved styles and literacy have crept in rather than belabour the central point. So throughout this book there are gentle reminders that one must be circumspect about interpretation. I can't avoid touching on changes in the evolution of piping away from Gaelic tradition, but my purpose is to show that the scrupulous and careful reader of the documents may make an eloquent case for the resilient persistence of Gaelic tradition in the face of the constructed tradition. This is the New World perspective that fieldwork in Cape Breton affords the subject.

This book deals mostly but not only with civilian bagpiping and pipers; it explores piping in the context of other lineages and genealogies when there is enough information to allow the inference of their influence. It also offers critical assessment and interpretation and new data from Cape Breton, where the whole subject was conceived.

The Scottish sections of the work (Parts 1 and 2) rely on the written record, a lot of which has been quoted and requoted when enthusiastic students in their times broached the subject of piping. Unfortunately, the older, native, preliterate piping world is gone today, although invaluable memories may yet be presented from South Uist and other nooks where Gaels born in the middle of the nineteenth century are still remembered. The Cape Breton part of the book is built on interviews held in Inverness County and elsewhere, in those most culturally conservative corners of the island. Most of the best of my Cape Breton informants are now dead, and the kinds of memories that were shared with me over the last thirty years are very much harder to uncover these days. And yet, subtle intonations and assumptions in older people's conversations can still contribute details to a fascinating subject if one observes and listens carefully.

This juxtaposition of Old and New World sources allows fresh thinking – call it a New World perspective if you like – on piping. I have collated information from a wide catchment area of Highland Scotland, and the result, which is often complicated and often repetitive, offers the first opportunity to consider the subject broadly. Using this amount of material casts light on many unusual claims and beliefs about piping that have been difficult to graft onto the subject when it is studied in a fragmentary way. Sometimes I have used obscure data, giving these the chance to stand as just as important as others that, by virtue of past scholarship, have gained the patina of a modern intellectual lore. Piping literature is rife with ready acceptance of a selected portion of the facts available.

I chose a number of areas of Gaelic Cape Breton where memories of the old pipers lie, only just, within living memory. Many of those people who helped me were reaching the ends of their lives in the 1970s and early 1980s, and typically they reflected the thoughts of their grandparents, who had lived in immigrant times. Where I deal with individual pipers, I expand only on a small number of New World piping personalities. I do so with a view not just to informing (in itself of value) but to explaining my methods and to elucidating the problems that I faced in what remained of Gaelic Nova Scotia in the 1970s. That world today (October 2001) has almost completely disappeared and will be soon difficult to imagine, not so much because it was so different but because later imaginations tend to overlook similarities and to emphasize the obvious distinctions between Gael and Saxon.

If one dwells on the differences – several are now well known, including dress, bagpiping, and dancing – which for generations have been caricatures or refinements, a very unbalanced image of the Gael and his world emerges, one that has tended to spavine Gaelic cultural studies, particularly where piping is concerned.

This text ignores musical links with the piping of Ireland, certainly to the detriment of the broader subject of piping, but late medieval and later (pre-*Uillean* pipe) Irish bagpiping require independent and concentrated study for reasonable speculations and extrapolations from the Scottish analogue to appear at least plausible.[1] Even with that shortcoming, this book may offer credible ideas for the future study of piping in the Irish mother Gàidheal-tachd in the first and second halves of the eighteenth century, before cultural diversions choked off the older tradition (as it appears to have done; and the deed, I think, may have been all but done by some time in the seventeenth century).

Throughout this book I have emphasized the significance of traditional Gaelic social and cultural conservatism and of kinship in both New and Old World Gàidhealtachds. However hard to follow these complicated relationships may be, important decisions in Highland life are often only thoroughly explained through an understanding of these linkages. Gaels in Scotland were influenced in almost everything they did by their strong awareness of their place in a wide and deep web of relations, agnatic and distaff. I have tried to give a convincing overall view of traditional bagpiping as a social phenomenon for every class of Gaelic Scot. There are gaps in the record and at times I have speculated; nonetheless, my impressions, labelled as such, where they fill gaps, are founded on as solid a base as can be safely inferred from what knowledge we have from elsewhere in the Scotch Gaelic world.

Gaelic traditional society has never been bereft of its equivalent of scholars and scholarship, but in their most vital forms these relied on, and valued as distinctly superior, cultivated memory rather than ink on paper.[2] This is true also of the makers of story and song and of instrumental music, and without question an enormous amount of all of these has disappeared on the wind with scarcely a rustle or a sough. Of course, the same is true for the affairs of most rustic European peoples where essentially pre-Renaissance folk cultures died with important facets of Everyman's everyday life left with little learned remarking.[3] The last flowering of the great memory-cultivators has not completely disappeared from Cape Breton, although it is now confined more and more to the instrumental musician, and within that quite large group, more and more to the professional and semi-professional musician.[4] The great tales are no longer told and the oral historian is by and large a family historian. Biting national political comment and philosophizing in Gaelic song have gone from the New World Gàidhealtachd.

Gaelic Scotland became exposed to non-Gaels as never before after the Jacobite loss at Culloden in 1746, and I begin there. Road-building efforts in the Highlands were redoubled then, after George Wade's earlier start in the 1720s. This permitted the easier intrusion of outside soldiery for whom the mountains had been, and were, a huge barrier, physically and psychologically. But really, road building was a point of cultural contact; even if resented, it helped the Gaels begin to understand and accept the greater power of English Britain.

Along the west coast the dominance of the inner and outer Hebridean seaways by the British navy had long been possible through the cannon-broadside technology to which Gaels had only tenuous and indirect access. The size of English troop-carrying ships, shear numbers, and naval organization had left only weather conditions as incalculable; the Gael retained also the rower's edge in certain conditions. With the 1745 rising, and in its aftermath, the potential for domination became a reality. Although they were by no means tamed by superior power and organization at sea and on land, the writing was on the wall for the last traditionally conservative Gaelic-speaking people in Scotland, the ones the English and the Lowland Scots had so long feared and whom they perceived, albeit belatedly and exaggeratedly (but nonetheless with some lingering plausibility) as a threatening outlier of a roughly unified Gaelic nexus they labelled Irish or "Erse."

Piping was a vital part of Gaelic affairs in the eighteenth century, but the instrument has a much longer history. It has been attested that in Europe the basic instrument was popular for many centuries before 1745. The claims for its presence in Gaelic Scotland from the medieval period to the sixteenth century remain to be adequately defended, but now is not the time to say that an absence of literary mention means that the bagpipe was ignored by a people whose contacts in Catholic Ireland and with Christian Europe were deeper than they were to be in the eighteenth century. And who can say with what degree of refinement and sophistication the instrument was played?

Joseph MacDonald's manuscript "Compleat theory of the Scots Highland Bagpipe" (c. 1760) describes more complicated grace-note clusters (for the classical piping, which he was describing first and foremost, but also for dance music piping) than are played by almost any piper today. One speculative reaction has been that MacDonald, a young man of unmatured perspective, was describing a relatively recent and uncompleted, perhaps even experimental, development of the art.[5] However, any analogy made with the older classical Gaelic song/poetry obviously suggests that earlier there was even greater general adherence to prescribed, and complicated, Gaelic musical precepts and stricter constructional demands than existed in the mid-eighteenth century. That the bagpipe alone should have been exempted from these general notions and standards is unlikely. Angus Fraser wrote:

Music, among the Gaeil, is of the greatest antiquity, as evidenced by the metrical structure and details of their primitive poetry. And no ancient Gaelic poet ever attempted to compose, without humming a tune to regulate his accents and metres. Even in our own day, with every facility of literature and musical notation, the celebrated Burns avowed his inability to compose a song, until he could fully master the tune. The earliest notice we have of ecclesiastical singing, is that of the Culdees, or ancient Scottish Clergy; who along with the manner of holding Easter probably introduced a fresh accession of the universal music than previously prevailed in Scotland: for their teaching caused no change in poetry, their metres being the same in all ages ...

The learned Cambrensis having observed in the 12th century "that Scotland surpassed Ireland in musical science and ability, and was resorted to as the genuine source of the art."[6]

Set against that, and with the bagpipe specifically in mind, the late Alan Bruford, School of Scottish Studies at the University of Edinburgh, was apparently of a narrower perspective and an opposing opinion. He suggested in 1983 that a technically simpler piping, linked roughly to open-air, pre-engagement scare tactics and warfare, preceded the refined forms known from the eighteenth century. His query was, had piping by 1750 arrived at stasis or was it still developing when Gaelic society began to be turned into Saxon society? He adduced the fact that "the chief's bard and harper ... would certainly have been mortified to be mentioned in the same breath as the menial piper"[7] and stated that *ceòl mór* (classical piping) pipe tunes such as "MacIntosh's Lament" (which is dated in Angus MacKay's *Collection* as "About the year 1526")[8] almost certainly began as harp music and were later grafted into the top pipers' repertoire. Bruford deliberately left one to infer that harping was sophisticated and intellectual, that the piping fraternity was incapable of equally independent genius, and that, without chiefly patronage, all Gaelic bagpiping was shambling, mean musical chaos.[9] Bruford (who wrote that he composed music for the harp) at the same time lamented the lack of information concerning seventeenth-century harping, thereby betraying a prejudice.[10]

Those are the two sides of that discussion, in a very broad way, and the scarceness of factual information allows the uncanny or the unscrupulous to defend either. Where bagpiping is concerned, outside observations and opinions are difficult to assess. Chanter fingering technique, for example, is inevitably a mystery and notoriously hard for a non-piper to describe, understand, and assess. Hard enough for a piper. How is one to distinguish an *acciaccatura* from an *appoggiatura*, for example? Adverse criticism of non-modern fingering may well be challenged by the subtlety of this distinction, as well as by claims for the need for special tonal effects. The harp, with its less strident sound and more soothing music, is simpler to enjoy and is perhaps less shrouded in recondite technique. In my opinion, while there must have been repertoire borrowing, with adaptation, from one instrument to the other (perhaps even more from the harp to the bagpipe than vice versa), the natures of the two instruments, the difference in their respective ranges, and the great difference in the playing techniques for each suggest that one would be very hasty to discount parallel subtleties in pre-sixteenth-century bagpiping.[11]

In Gaelic Scotland the preference for the *clàrsach*[12] in ruling society into the early eighteenth century has bred the widespread assumption that bagpiping was rudimentary and rough skirling, especially before 1600. There are no scholarly grounds for that assumption, and although the emergence of the classical form of variational piping appears to date from the late sixteenth century, there is as yet no decent defence for its apparent completeness in variational form (which is as we have it) from that early date. Bear in mind that, with the exception of Patrick MacDonald's *Highland Vocal Airs* (1784) and various collections of fiddle music that include pipe tunes, published bagpipe music is a pronouncedly nineteenth-century phenomenon. (A similar shortage of information about the harp in Gaelic Scotland has not yet inclined anyone to think of early harpists as relatively uninventive or incompetent, at least from the twelfth century.)

How, when, where, and from what stimuli classical bagpiping emerged remain a mystery. There are outstanding suggestions that the bagpipe chanter scale was based on early Greek scales and presumably that its early music had some kind of cognate status with Greek music. There have been efforts to show links between classical piping and late medieval court music. To add to the mixture of speculation, Bridget Mackenzie offered an interesting and learned opinion in 1981. She links the structure of classical piping to Irish and skaldic poetry of the early medieval period.[13] Whether or not this structural analogue linked piping and bardism directly and continuously from early times or appeared sometime later (perhaps the early sixteenth century when classical syllabic metres were still flourishing in Gaelic Scotland) remains undiscovered, but early citations such as this from the ninth century – "Cit binni lib i cach mí / cuislennaig nó chomairi, / isí mo chobais in-díu / ro-cuala céol bad binniu" (Though you at all times take pleasure in the playing of pipers or horn-blowers, I declare today that I have heard music which could give more pleasure [translated in Murphy, *Early Irish Lyrics*]) – present formidable definitional problems concerning what word, if any, described a bagpipe as we understand it.[14]

And, if ceòl mór were indeed post-1590, there is still no defence for the assumption that non-classical piping from the Middle Ages was unclever wherever it was found. Among the important unanswered questions are, what was the vulgar dancing of the medieval and late-medieval Scottish Gael and how did it evolve,[15] what instruments were used to produce that dance music, and what reliance was put on the bagpipe as a bucolic dance-music and possibly as a rhythmic work-accompaniment instrument.

In the long, largely unknown pre-1746 period for traditional music in Gaelic Scotland, there are scattered records of pipers in military, legal, and land records. I use some of these, from primary and secondary sources, but with the warning that often such written records are unique and it is wise to recognize that generalizations from exceptional pieces of isolated data deserve circumspection. If, for example, the tune "Cill Chriosd" commemo-rates MacDonell of Glengarry's savage burning of a property in MacKen-zie's Ross-shire in 1603 (and if the tune we have has come down to us rela-tively unchanged in its variational development from that time), we might conclude that the variational form was typically sophisticated then.[16] The same may be said for a number of other tunes of the same complexity which are dated to about the same time and which, I should add, are characterized by grounds, or basic themes, on which variations may be developed. Given a more lore-based record in Cape Breton, where classical piping barely sur-vived the immigrant generations, the same warning must stand. One-off examples should be considered with caution as possible aberrancies if not striking anomalies.

Allan Bruford's opinions of Scottish bagpiping, I have to admit as well, were floated as much as tentative trial balloons as didactic statements. He per-haps anticipated a loud and hostile reaction from the piping fraternity, for whose scholarship perhaps he did not have a high opinion. However, Bruford wisely understood that a large amount of background work on eighteenth-cen-tury pipers and piping in Gaelic Scotland remained to be done, and he encour-aged it. This book makes a start on that job, at the same time as it shows, from another aspect, that the mucilage of Gaelic society in Scotland, then as now, is the kinship relationship, clannishness, which binds people together, many in thraldom but even then with important civilized compensations.

In general, I have treated piping in Gaelic Scotland under the geographical headings of the old Gaelic patrimonies in the era when loyalties were to the traditional chief. Actual ownership of the land did not necessarily dictate Gaelic social or political leadership, even if the idea of persisting political leadership was little more than a fiction. But sometimes, as in the case of the MacIntyres and the more difficult Stewarts, I have assembled what I have to say, cross-geographically, under the heading of the name of a piping family or families (apparently or actually related).

I have chosen to begin with Jacobite pipers and pipers in the Jacobite areas of Highland Scotland, tracing roots where I am able and the lovely, sad white roses.[17] It is the more romantically appealing of the two sections of Highland society; it was the more feared and persecuted and generally the more culturally conservative and, one presumes, the more hopeful. Unfortunately, piping study in those quarters sometimes demands more speculation and common-sense inference, as Jacobite family records are scarcer than Hanoverian ones. One of the policies of the Duke William of Cumberland was the finding and destroying, or confiscating, of the family documents of the leaders of the Jacobite clans. On occasion what was not destroyed on the spot (such as the Cameron of Lochiel estate papers, which were burned along with old Achnacarry House after Culloden) has since been misplaced or lost. And yet assembling plausible cultural continuities is not out of the question; the last unself-conscious fragments of Gaelic musical culture in Cape Breton play a large part in that reconstruction.

The Cape Breton and Nova Scotian Gàidhealtachd, while having retained in places vitally important cultural self-confidence, conservativeness, and self-containedness (and having influenced those Acadians and several Mi'k-maw who adjoined it rather than the other way round), has never had but a fraction of the population of the homeland. Luckily, however, music and dance that have not been subordinated to musical literacy and the classroom are common to both religious communities, the Protestant and the Catholic (with perhaps one exception in North East Margaree), and are remarkably common. Several members of countless families developed musical and rhythmical talent, and I can present my findings confident that we had here an invaluable continuance of a West Highland culture of the late eighteenth century.

The history of the bagpipe in Gaelic Scotland is short. Indeed, looked at over the instrument's known history in Europe just from medieval times, and the history of Gaelic Scotland (from c. 500), the instrument is a dramatic Johnnie-come-lately. The bagpipe is not mentioned in Highland Scotland until about the mid-sixteenth century. To some, the instrument appears to be a strident marker of the end of a civilization radically beset at last by outside powers a millennium and a half after Caesar Augustus intruded Latin and other languages upon Gaul.

The bagpipe appears in the written record at about the time of the splitting of Irish and Scottish Gaeldom by England *circa* 1600, which ended the Scottish insular and west coast mercenary system of support for Gaelic Ireland (and which marked the divergence of Scottish Gaelic as a sub-set of Irish). At about the same time a Scottish Stuart king, James VI, who had just assumed the throne of England as James I, systematized the gradual dominance of Gaelic Scotland by the effecting of the Statutes of Iona in 1603. However raggedly, this anti-Catholic, anti-Gaelic ukase sounded the death-knell of the old Gaelic-speaking aristocratic system of society and caused a breakdown in the parallel cultural class system. From about 1600 the old bardic order and the strictly metred verse it dutifully disgorged (at a price in cash and status) for its understanding rulers lost significance and the beginnings of vernacular Gaelic poetry emerged. The great harpers fell into a gradual decline, although there were still links maintained with Ireland. There are bardic resentments at the bagpipe's rise in status at this time from which some people assume a parallel improvement of its playing from unsophisticated to clever.

The Gaels, main messengers of Catholic Christianity to England and much of Europe, also faced shiftings of religious thought. The Reformation of the mid-sixteenth century caused internecine scrambles for land and power in Gaelic Scotland. Gaelic Scotland later faced chronic problems deriving from the establishment for a time of an episcopal church. This musically tolerant church was later intolerantly beaten into rump status in the post-Culloden period by a harsh, radical protestantism which, in its Christian conscience, regarded all deviance as unbearable. The Puritan excesses of the seventeenth century put paid to thousands of lives in Ireland and Scotland, widening the culturo-political chasm between the two Gaeldoms, and imposed political concepts that enfiladed the ancient society.

Through all of these changes, and on until the mid-nineteenth century, the limitations of literacy and the concomitant disregard for, and ignorance of, the non-literate ordinary people ensured that what observations are available about them and their music and dance are few, unfleshed out and often badly biased. Almost nothing is known about the instrumental music and dance of the ordinary Gael from 1550 to 1800. For this reason this book exposes a number of unfamiliar terms and concepts where piping is concerned, right shoulder, left shoulder, left hand or right hand upper, piping as step-dance accompaniment among them.

The bagpipe may actually have a long history in Gaelic Scotland that is now totally unreconstructable, because at the level of community pipers no person thought to make a record in prose or verse. It may have enjoyed typical Gaelic freedoms of expression long eradicated through nineteenth century improvement and dissatisfaction with illiterate learning and traditional Gaelic functionalisms. These freedoms of variety existed in Gaelic Cape Breton bagpiping and provide a valuable clue to everyday dance-music piping and pipers in Scotland. They were quite unlike the standardized bagpiping one finds about the world today.

Equally unknown today are the dances done by ordinary Gaels from late medieval times. We are made aware that in the second half of the eighteenth century Gaels were in love with dancing to bagpiping and to fiddling. We know what that dancing was only from Gaelic Cape Breton. What was being danced by the common folk in 1450, 1500, 1550, 1600, 1650, and 1700, however, and to what instruments, remains to be found out. It is unreasonable to extrapolate to the ordinary people from those observations we have of court dancing, there being a linguistic divide involved.

Looking at the period 1600–1800, then, in Gaelic Scotland what we do know is that the bagpipe was widely popular from Sutherland to the southwest. We do not know how many kinds of bagpipes there were or even if bagpipes were classified. We do not know if there were one-, two- or three-drone instruments or how any of these were tuned (that is, to what note or notes on the chanter). We do not know if the chanter notes were gapped the same way as they are today because so few chanters survive, especially from the earlier period. Early pictorial representations of Irish and Scottish pipers often display artistic ignorance of hole positioning, not to mention finer points of bagpipe construction. We do not know how pipers learned to play if there was any tendency to hold the bag (reservoir for air) under the left or right shoulder. Although Joseph MacDonald's manuscript asserts left hand upper on the chanter, the Blind Piper of Gairloch's chanter indicates that he and/or his descendants played right hand upper (that the evidence is the wear on one side of the chanter it has been guessed that that wear was the result of the playing of someone who kept the long nails needed to play the clarsach). The fingering that MacDonald gave as the rule may be a narrow view of an educated member of the bilingual middle class.

Until 1800 what can be said with most confidence about Gaelic classical bagpiping is nonetheless found in Joseph MacDonald's "Compleat Theory." An important point is that MacDonald made no qualitative distinction between the variational form of bagpipe music and the "Dancing musick" kind. He alluded to the "first Authors of Pipe Musick" as the creators of both kinds of music and offered, by way of comparison, only the fact that the classical form employed longer grace-note clusters.[18]

MacDonald, however, wrote that of the dance-music piping ("Jigs & Reells composed on purpose for it by the first Authors of Pipe Musick") "nothing can be more truly Highland" and that this music was played according to the "Strictest Rules of this Instrument."[19] He described the dances as peculiar to the Highlands and Isles. The examples that Barry Shears has found in Cape Breton of community, dance-music pipers suggest that there was considerable variation in fingering. Whether or not MacDonald concerned himself only with a high stratum of piper remains to be seen. If he did, typical of his class, he chose to ignore popular traditional music.

The term "hereditary" has for generations been applied to pipers of certain families, the MacCrimmons, the MacKays, and many others whose land-holdings passed down the generations in return for ceremonial (and probably also dance) bagpiping. The word does not come from any Gaelic source but nonetheless it is only right to note that most jobs were occupied hereditarily, from the chief down to the humblest cottar. The same was generally true of all rural Europe until the Industrial Revolution. The idea particularly of "hereditary" pipers now haunts the subject in Scotland, since they are assumed to have been somehow special bearers of knowledge and status.

Where the group dances of Gaelic Scotland are concerned, various forms of Reels were always more popular than Cotillons or any other foreign dances. The same was true even of Edinburgh in the 1770s, when Topham noted a Saxon Scottish predilection for Reel dancing. The Quadrille did invade Lowland society after the Napoleonic Wars but it was ignored in most of Gaelic Scotland, always in South Uist.

Until 1850, by which time family emigration to North America had run out, almost all Gaelic piping was traditional. It was ear learned. It provided music for traditional dancing such as the Reels, especially the Four and the Eight. There were no music schools. There were no Gaelic standards other than that set by Joseph MacDonald for the literate. There were no competitions. There were no pipe bands. There was no uniform.

However the whole complex – variational and dance-music piping, the traditional dancing involved, the place of the everyday piper in Gaelic society – is only exposed to us in any quantity after Culloden and then for only a few decades as the last Gaelic spontaneity in Scotland succumbed. One is ignorant of the degree of change that was going on in the Gaelic environment. One can divine no accurate duration for the tradition. Joseph MacDonald's first authors are undated and undatable. And after that half century of unacademic observation, piping falls into the hands of the improvers and becomes a forcefully powerful cultural caricature to which all Scotland clings.

Only in the isolated Gaelic communities in Nova Scotia did the older spontaneity survive long enough to be recorded, and then only just. Once out of the confines of Scotland and its English publications and attitudes about improved, literate piping, and often ill-founded imaginings about the Highland Scot, musical Gaels in Nova Scotia fell outside mythologizing, adulation, and even measured classification. There never was any praising or eulogizing literature about pipers, piping families, and piping itself in the province. There are no reports of vociferous debates or theorizings about fingering techniques or strayings from prescribed notings. The most egregious piping families to emigrate – the MacKays of Gairloch for example, Glenaladale's piper, even Donald MacCrimmon, who lived for a decade near Shelburne, go unnoticed. They were construed, if anything in particular, as normally traditional.

Those Scots, like Stewart of Garth and Norman MacLeod (*Caraid nan Gàidheal*), who deeply lamented the inevitable disappearance of the older Gaelic tradition in the first half of the nineteenth century, can be excused for overlooking the possibility that the growing British Empire might hide certain Gaelic cultural treasures for a century and a half after they wrote. Less forgiveable is the association of aspects of Gaelic cultural importance with repeated mythologizing and false adulations as happened in Scotland. Nova Scotian piping, if thought about at all by Scots, because it lacked published adulations, was seen as trivial, unaccomplished, degenerated, and unworthy of attention.

It is to put that want to rights that this book relies on a good deal of the observations of the last Gaelic-speaking pipers in Cape Breton.

PART ONE

Piping in the Jacobite Highlands from 1745

CHAPTER ONE

The MacGregors and Piping in Glengarry

There were many pipers in the Jacobite army of 1745–46, and they obviously fascinated Prince Charles (1720–88), who was still practising on a set of pipes in Florence in 1784.[1] John William O'Sullivan (1700–60) mentioned pipers in the prince's army in 1745–46 on several occasions. His "Narrative," written for King James in Rome in 1747, was based on his personal experiences of the rising.[2] Both the *Jacobite Miscellany* and the "Woodhouselee MS" mention Highland pipers during the Jacobite army's occupation of Edinburgh in 1745. There is a suggestion, however, that pipers were not uniformly distributed. When, for example, John Gordon of Glenbucket's piper defected to the English at Carlisle, the "regiment" was left without a piper for the march to Derby, but then again "regiment" was probably an exaggeration. There is no record of pipers in Lord Lewis Gordon's regiment (Stonywood's) in Prince Charles's army, although it would have been very unlikely had there been none, since the regiment had at least one fiddler. Of those Jacobite pipers who saw the business out, however, at least three were from then bilingual Angus just north of the River Tay, all of Ogilvie's regiment, which fought alongside Lewis Gordon's regiment at the battle of Falkirk. One of Ogilvie's pipers was the James Reid who was executed at York in 1746; another was Sinclair, the Arbroath town piper, who, having been taken as a Jacobite, was discharged; lastly there was Allan Stuart Donald, piper to David Ogilvie, the fifth earl of Airlie.[3]

Stiffened by the knowledge of their leader's liking for bagpipe music, all of the prince's pipers rose up and threatened to strike if the Hanoverian MacCrimmon piper captured at Inverurie on 23 December 1745, Malcolm MacCrimmon *(Calum MacCruimein)* from Boreraig in Skye (father of Red Donald and Black John), was not released. It was a gesture, which, had he known about it, would only have struck William Duke of Cumberland as ridiculously naïve. Pipers of the Athole Brigade and of the Clunie MacPhersons took part in Lord George Murray's surprise attacks on the Hanoverians'

Perthshire bases, manned by the Argyllshire militia, in early 1746. They were used to create an exaggerated impression of power, and they did their bit in forcing Lieutenant-Colonel Sir Andrew Agnew of the 21st, Royal North British Fusiliers, to retreat to his base, the Hanoverian duke of Atholl's seat at Blair. The published observation by John Home, a lieutenant in the Edinburgh Company of Volunteers in 1745, that Lord George Murray and Clunie had Athole and MacPherson country pipers with them during the Athole Raid of 1746 is one source of the claim.[4] John Buchan elaborated to say that there were twenty pipers in all.

Sir Andrew Agnew of Lochnaw (1687–1771) was himself no stranger to piping; he had a piper among the Royal North British Fusiliers at Blair. Agnew and the 21st were long besieged by Sir George Murray's Jacobites before the latter had to withdraw north for the final denouement at Culloden. Lord George was in the odd position of besieging the ducal seat of his brother, Lord James Murray, second duke of Atholl. After Culloden, when the victorious duke of Cumberland approached Blair on his way south, Agnew's piper failed to notice the approaching commander and Agnew roared in Lallans, "Blaw! blaw! ye scoondrel! Dinna ye see the King's ain bairn?"[5]

Although no Atholl pipers are named, gentlemen who chose to lead men out in the Jacobite cause from the Hanoverian duke of Atholl's Perthshire estate included Donald MacDonell of Lochgarry, Robertson of Strowan (in Rannoch), Robertson of Faskally (southeast of Blair Atholl), Charles Stewart of Bohallie (on Loch Tummel), Stewart of Kynichan (to the west of Loch Tummel), "Blairfeaty," vassals from "Bonrannoch," as well as people from Loch Voil-side, near Balquidder. Of these people, Kynichan, Bohallie, and Blairfeaty took part in the Atholl Raid, and their tenants are the most likely candidates to have supplied Atholl pipers to the Atholl Raid. In this last Jacobite success before King George's son put paid to them, the Argyll militia was all but asleep on the job. As a result, the unlucky winners came in for vengeful treatment by most of the militia after Culloden in July and August 1746.[6] Perthshire MacGregors, including pipers, may also have been present at the Atholl Raid.

Later, after Culloden, according to eyewitness Spanish John MacDonell of Scotus, all the Highland pipers in what was left of Prince Charles's army, which was bivouacked at the soon-to-be-destroyed Achnacarrie House, played "the general Cogga na si" (War or peace) as a reveille.[7]

At the level of patronized pipers, the level often referred to from the early nineteenth century as the "hereditary" pipers, the Chisholms of Strathglass had pipers, the Frasers, the MacDonalds on the mainland from Kinlochmoidart to the marches of MacLeod country in Glenelg. Keppoch had a piper. Glengarry had a piper. There was at least one Henderson piper in Glencoe. Glenaladale had a piper in Clanranald country, and there were many others elsewhere on Clanranald territory. Grant had a piper during the 1715 uprising, and no doubt there were pipers in Jacobite Glenmoriston during and after the '45. Cameron of Lochiel had his piper in 1745. Simon Fraser, author of Airs and Melodies (1816), associated the MacGillivrays of Dunmaglass with a "minstrel" called Gow in the eighteenth century.[8] The MacNeils of Barra had pipers. Family records show that the non-Gaelic Gordons had pipers (whether or not these were Gaelic speaking is unknown) and a strong interest in the instrument. Piping was popular in Lowland Scotland at the time. However, all of these pipers only represent what we imagine to have been the various pinnacles of piping in those clans. Under or perhaps just beside them were countless other unsung community pipers, pipers living on the farms of less powerful Gaels, wadsetters and tacksmen, perhaps down to the level of major tenant depending on the demography of the farmable land. The importance of the Cape Breton Gàidhealtachd is that there these community pipers and their musical descendants had a social part to play until within living memory, while, in general, the "hereditary" few associated with the classical piping form did not (not that many of the latter did not emigrate to Nova Scotia).

In Gaelic Scotland, as far as the patronized pipers are concerned, the much shorter list would be of those chiefs and chieftains and major tacksmen who did not retain the services of a piper. The piper was a feature of the Gaelic community, "retained" or not.

Showing continuity of these patronized, or hereditary, pipers is in some instances not possible, although there is seldom a reason to think that the practice of retaining a piper stopped in 1746, for however long. There was no trading/bidding system among chiefs for pipers' services in the Highlands in the early decades after 1746, but profit farming imposed new strictures on the patronizers, causing defections of old worthy musical families as better opportunities came up or as it became obvious that one should cut one's losses. Another difficulty emerged for the pipers on the forfeited and annexed estates, where old loyalties and economic ties were deliberately diverted in the change from traditional to improver farming.[9] However, there is a shortage of casual observational material dealing with these pipers, particularly in Catholic MacDonald lands, but also in largely Protestant but Jacobite Cameron country and in Glenmoriston.

Glengarry's piper, the old John MacDonald discussed below, came close to losing his traditional status at the wishes of his chief's wife, Marjorie Grant, daughter of Ludovick Grant of Dalvey. It has been argued that she spurred her husband, Duncan MacDonell of Glengarry, to evict many Glengarry people,[10] and she is said to have told the old family piper one day during the 1780s that it was a matter of surprise that he did not employ his leisure hours in doing something. The piper is said to have retorted, "Indeed, madam, it is a poor estate that cannot keep the Laird and the Piper without working."[11]

It is also tricky establishing pipers' status in the clan and exactly what was expected of them as musicians. However, evidence in *Traditional Gaelic Bagpiping* of the repertoires of many, probably the most chiefly and privileged pipers in the days before Lowland piping competitions became a serious factor in the minds of landowners, shows that there was no limit to the playing of dance and other non-classical forms. The Chisholms are said to have used MacLennans in the seventeenth century, people who may have been of chiefly stock, then Camerons and then Chisholms as their pipers. Kinlochmoidart's piper in 1790 was a MacIntyre whose family is associated earlier with clan Menzies, perhaps also with MacDonald of the Isles. The name Campbell (Mac a'Ghlasraich) is associated with the Keppoch family in Brae Lochaber during the 1745 rebellion and for long after. A Campbell and a MacGillivray are associated with MacDonald of Glenaladale. The Rankins, known also as Conduilighs, are long associated with the Duart MacLeans, and the Frasers with Lovat and others.

PRINCE CHARLES'S PIPER, JOHN MACGREGOR, AND OTHER CLANN AN SGEULAICHE PIPERS

Before looking at prominent pipers to Jacobite clan leaders I will look first at the case of John MacGregor (c. 1708–c. 1789), piper to Prince Charles Edward Stuart during the 1745 campaign. MacGregor was a piper from a Perthshire clan whose leading members were legally barred by Act of Parliament from using their name from 1633 until 1775 (although by the latter date the act was no longer enforced and the name M'Gregor crops up many times in *Survey of Lochtayside 1769*).[12] By 1745 the MacGregors had long since lost their ancestral land, in Glen Lyon and elsewhere, to Campbells in whose politics they were implicated for centuries.[13] By the mid-eighteenth century two contenders for the MacGregor chiefship had emerged and there were still several prominent MacGregor tacksmen holding land of Campbell owners, particularly Campbell of Breadalbane, whose estate stretched from Argyleshire in the west to drier, often more fertile Perthshire in the centre and east. This piper was probably affiliated to one of these MacGregor tacksmen, whatever name he went by. John MacGregor joined the Stuart army in 1745, probably with his Perthshire MacGregors, but his experiences gave him a greater claim to fame than most of them.

John MacGregor was apparently one of a storytelling and musical lineage in Perthshire. Archibald Campbell, writing in the *Piping Times*,[14] said he was a member of the family known as Clann an Sgeulaiche (Children of the Storyteller) and was piper to the chief of his people, depending on which man the piper acknowledged, either Robert MacGregor of Glencarnaig or William MacGregor (Drummond) of Balhaldy. (Balhaldy, who lived in France, was regarded as chief by the Ciar Mór branch of the MacGregors in which Rob

Roy's sons were active men.) During the '45, the MacGregors went to war for Prince Charles in two groupings, the Ciar Mór people under Balhaldy and the others under Glencarnaig. The pro-Balhaldy force was led by Gregor MacGregor of Glengyle (alias James Graham of Glengyle, nephew of Rob Roy) and James MacGregor Campbell (one of Rob Roy's sons).

In 1831 James Logan (c. 1794–1872), in his "Anecdotes of Pipers," said that members of Clann an Sgeulaiche "afforded instruction to the chief part of the pipers of the central Highlands, as those of the house of Mac Pherson, of Cluny, &c. This tribe, from their extensive knowledge of history, were termed Clan an sgeulaich, or tellers of tales, which proves that pipers were anciently qualified in that part of the bardic duties."[15]

Logan's digression into pipers "anciently" as bards is considered inaccurate today, but the idea was not new in Logan's time. The famous Blind Piper of Gairloch, John MacKay (d. c. 1754), after all, was an accomplished Gaelic bard. Both functions required what appears to the modern literate person to be a prodigious memory. There is also a glimmer of evidence from a book published in Paris in 1792 that this idea of cultural dualism had some currency earlier on. Pierre-Nicolas Chantreau, an English-speaking Frenchman who toured in Scotland in 1788, wrote in his *Voyage dans les trois royaumes,* "C'était avec la cornemuse que les Bardes qui étaient les musiciens des Ecossais célébraient les exploits ou les vertus de leurs héros." (It was with the pipes that the bards, who were the Scots' musicians, championed the exploits or the virtues of their heros.)[16]

Logan's statement that "Clan an sgeulaich" were teachers of central Highland Gaelic pipers is accurate and may have been based on the reporting of the Highland Society of London–sponsored ceòl mór competition of 1784 in the *Scots Magazine* of that year (see below). Certainly, reliable information along those lines was available to Logan both directly and indirectly. If, for example, he attended the Highland Society's competitions in any year from 1802 till 1813, with the exception of 1805, he would have heard MacGregors competing successfully in ceòl mór and possibly also piping for Reel dancing. There was presumably nothing to stop him from getting information from them. In large part, these Edinburgh competitions and their social side must have been the vehicle for a good deal of information about the Highlands and for folk like Clann an Sgeulaiche getting into English Highland lore.

Although their descriptive "sgeulaiche" celebrates their storytelling abilities, Clann an Sgeulaiche nowadays are famous in retrospect for a number of unbroken generations of bagpipers. Nothing is known about the family as storytellers. The late professor W.J. Watson located the home of these MacGregor pipers in the Vale of Fortingall: "A little way above the ford and on the left bank of Lyon is the site of Tigh Chunnairt (House of Dangers), where once the MacGregor pipers lived."[17] In its notes to the tune "Fàilte nan

Griogarach" (The MacGregors' Salute), the editors of *Pìobaireachd* say that they kept a school of piping at Drumcharry.[18]

In August of 1745 John MacGregor joined the Stuart army and became part of the Jacobite rising at Glenfinnan. He was not the only MacGregor piper to join, but he distinguished himself by becoming personal assistant and piper (and probably piping tutor) to Charles Edward Stuart.[19]

John MacGregor was wounded at Culloden but got back to Perthshire in the south-central Highlands. He was never made prisoner. Afterwards he was piper to An Coirneal Dubh (the Black Colonel), Lieutenant-Colonel John Campbell of Glenlyon, who had been a captain in the Black Watch in the Highlands during the '45.[20] The family relationship between the Glengyle MacGregors and the Glenlyon Campbells was close but characteristically one-sided; the Glenlyon Campbells gradually had appropriated traditional MacGregor lands.

When he was in his seventies, MacGregor competed in the early Highland Society competitions in the 1780s. No one knows how long he was piper for John Campbell or when he began the job. The records of the Highland Society piping competition show that he had four or five sons who were pipers, not to mention eight grandsons. All twelve or thirteen were top-class pipers, according to the notes to "Fàilte nan Griogarach" in *Pìobaireachd*, book 10. So piping and piping tutoring came down unbroken in Clann an Sgeulaiche in the Perthshire Gàidhealtachd from the early eighteenth century into the early nineteenth.

In 1745 the Black Colonel's father, old John Campbell, sixth of Glenlyon didn't enjoy much more than his title and his small Chesthill estate at the west end of Fortingall in Perthshire.[21] He had led the Breadalbane men out for the Jacobites in 1715 and was a declared Jacobite at age seventy in 1745. Glenlyon was about sixteen when his gambling, wastrel father, Robert Campbell, fifth of Glenlyon, was used to murder many of the Mac-Donalds of Glencoe in 1692. This drastic blot on this Campbell family's escutcheon guaranteed Glenlyon expiation in the form of support for King James in both risings.[22] John Campbell's family, however, reflected the Jacobite-Hanoverian split and it was the Hanoverian son who retained the MacGregor piper.

John Campbell had at least two sons who were involved in the '45. Archibald Campbell, younger of the two, was a Jacobite who "fought in all their battles."[23] His father sent him to encourage the Glenlyon men with the Jacobite army, which was under the control of "an adherent and descendant of the family, a man of judgment and mature years." (This unnamed "adherent" himself had a son who fought in the pro-Hanoverian Black Watch at Fontenoy and was later presented to King George II. He was killed at "Ticonderago.") The other son, John Campbell, younger of Glenlyon, the Coirneal Dubh and MacGregor the piper's employer, joined one of the three

Chart 1   The Glengyle MacGregor–Glenlyon Campbell Relationship

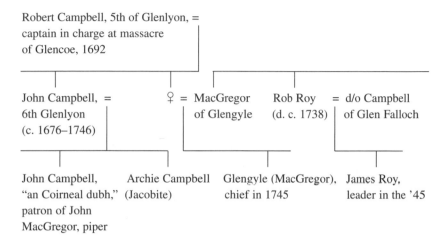

Robert Campbell, 5th of Glenlyon, =
captain in charge at massacre
of Glencoe, 1692

John Campbell, =   ♀ = MacGregor   Rob Roy   = d/o Campbell
6th Glenlyon   of Glengyle   (d. c. 1738)   of Glen Falloch
(c. 1676–1746)

John Campbell,   Archie Campbell   Glengyle (MacGregor),   James Roy,
"an Coirneal dubh,"   (Jacobite)   chief in 1745   leader in the '45
patron of John
MacGregor, piper

new companies of the Black Watch in December 1744, all of which served
in Scotland during the rising. (His company was not the one that saw its first
action at Prestonpans, which is just as well, for Cope's forces were routed
with many killed, and among the victorious enemy were the scythe- and
sword-swinging MacGregors from Glenlyon.) For this choice of sides, Old
Glenlyon, when he died in 1746, is said have been unable to forgive his son,
who nonetheless succeeded him.[24]

In the autumn of 1746, in the pre-Indemnity occupation, when the Act of
Attainder was in force, Lieutenant John Campbell, younger of Glenlyon,
was given the duty of garrisoning his own home and bringing in the rebels,
including his brother Archibald. He conveniently failed to do this and at
some time took on the ex-Jacobite John MacGregor as his piper. On 5 January 1757 Archibald, in the company of many other Jacobites, took a lieutenant's commission in the 78th (Fraser's Highlanders).[25] He was wounded
at Quebec, 28 April 1760.[26] His piper may have seen action with him. Mac-
Gregor did not suffer as a piper and neither did his son John (winner of third
prize in the Highland Society competition in 1782). The son John's date of
birth probably lies between 1728 and 1738. The closer it falls to the latter
date the more likely his piping talent developed about the time of Culloden
and the Disarming Act's first year of enforcement (excellent fingering
depends in large part on learning/practice from about the age of ten until the
early teens). Although the relationship is not recorded, the Patrick MacGregor who won first prize at the first Highland Society competition in Falkirk
in 1781, and who was a member of Clann an Sgeulaiche, may have been

another of the old John MacGregor's sons. In 1781 Patrick was piper to
Henry Balneaves of Edradour, who, Collinson informs us, was married to a
daughter of Glenlyon.[27]

MACGREGOR GENTLEMEN AND
OTHER MACGREGOR PIPERS

MacGregor family history, not uniquely, also involves piping at the gentleman level in the 1750s; the evidence is in France, however. If nothing else,
mentioning their piping in the broader perspective of MacGregor politics
shows piping for what it was, integral to the social life of Clann Griogair nan
Gleann (Clan Gregor of the Glens) in Perthshire at all social levels.

From 1633 until 1784 MacGregors, within the letter of the law, were not
allowed to use their name, so many became Murrays, Stewarts, Drummonds,
Campbells, and Grahams, the names of neighbouring farmers. This compli-
cates any modern reading of the claims to chiefship in the eighteenth century. In 1745 about three hundred men joined the Jacobite standard under
Robert MacGregor of Glencarnaig, legally Robert Murray of Lanrick, whom
they accepted as chief. Keltie implies that four hundred more considered
William MacGregor Drummond of Balhaldy the rightful chief.[28] Included in
this second group was the sept known as Ciar Mór, which according to Walter Scott was named after a foster-brother of the MacGregor chief of 1603.
The sept of Ciar Mór in its later phase included Rob Roy (d. c. 1738),
younger son of MacGregor of Glengyle. At the beginning of the 1745 rising,
Balhaldy was in France, so this second contingent was led into the fighting
by MacGregor of Glengyle and his first cousin James Roy MacGregor, the
most forceful of Rob Roy's sons.[29] They fought under the command of
James Drummond, third titular duke of Perth.

The MacGregor chief, Robert Murray of Lanrick, who had led his men
out for the Stuart cause, was imprisoned in Edinburgh after Culloden; he
died in 1758. William MacGregor Drummond of Balhaldy, who was living
at Bièvre near Paris, MacGregor of Glengyle, and James Roy MacGregor
were excepted from the 1747 Act of Indemnity, but only Balhaldy had to, or
preferred to, stay overseas; the other two appear to have met with leniency
and to have returned to Scotland by 1750.

From his letters, published in *Blackwood's Magazine,* December 1817,
James Roy MacGregor, although accused of high treason in 1746, said that
he obtained a pass from Lord-Justice Clerk in 1747 giving him immunity
from prosecution. Later, late in the year of 1753 after his trial for the infamous abduction of a Lowland woman, when outlawed for his escape from
Edinburgh Castle and living in France, he is said to have importuned from
Lord Holdernesse (secretary of state) a pass to return home. This was granted on condition that he bring with him Allan Breck Stewart, the Jacobite

widely believed to have shot Colin Campbell of Glenure in upper Appin on 14 May 1752. With this protection (but not with Allan Breck, who got wind of the plan) he visited London, where he said he received a mysterious government offer of employment in his own country from Lord Holdernesse. He said he rejected the offer because it would have compromised his honour, whereupon he was obliged to return to France. Allan Breck, according to Walter Scott, understandably threatened to kill him.

MacDonald of Lochgarry, who had deserted his lieutenant's commission in Loudon's regiment in 1745 to join, and later lead, the MacDonells of Glengarry, and who was also in exile in France as an attainted Jacobite, promptly accused James Roy of spying.[30] While Sir Walter Scott did not tap all the sources that Andrew Lang found, which appear to show an innate capacity for untruth and duplicity in MacGregor, he conceded that James MacGregor might indeed have been approached as a potential spy for the government, since he may desperately have wanted to ease the legal burden on his brother Robert, then on the verge of trial and probable execution in the abduction case. James Roy's double-dealings were transparent, and things seldom went well for him in France. Being a Jacobite in France between 1749 and 1754 (Pickle's active dates according to Andrew Lang)[31] was a bitter, suspicion-laden business.

In his last letter to William MacGregor Drummond of Balhaldy, the man he considered the chief of the MacGregors, James Roy described himself as destitute and desperate to find some form of work, breaking or breeding horses or as a hunter or fowler. In his postscript he asked Balhaldy to lend him his pipes "to play some melancholy tunes." Evidently both he and Balhaldy were pipers. James Roy's letter was written in Paris on 25 September 1754, about a week before he died of starvation.

(Sir Walter Scott, in retelling stories he had heard about Rob Roy MacGregor, the duke of Montrose's sworn enemy, wrote that at the time of his death Rob Roy MacGregor had exclaimed, "Now all is over – let the piper play 'Ha til mi tulidh' [We return no more]."[32] David Stewart of Garth later wrote that the funeral of Rob Roy occurred in 1736 and that it was the last in the Highlands of Perthshire at which a piper officiated in the old traditional way.[33] *Rob Roy* was published in December 1817 and Stewart of Garth's work in 1822.)

THE MACGREGOR PIPERS
IN THE TIME OF TRANSITION

The prize lists of pipers competing at the annual competitions (Falkirk in 1781–83 and then Edinburgh) show plenty of MacGregors until 1813.[34] With no indication that the judges were knowledgeable enough to tell good from bad playing, far less very good from excellent or anachronistic from affected (if indeed pipers indulged such fancies), there is no way to tell what this MacGregor success meant. Perhaps it is cynical but others have noted that it was just easy for them to get to the Lowlands to make some much-needed money. We are on slightly firmer ground in claiming, from an absence of evidence to the contrary, that there is no reason to disbelieve that in the eighteenth century the MacGregor and other competitors cleaved to styles of playing that they knew from the older Gaelic tradition. This was probably true for most of them for a long time subsequent, well into the time of published pipe music.

Although no MacGregor account books are extant, or pipers' receipts, the MacGregor pipers show another shrewd adaptability to the world of profit. Clann an Sgeulaiche ran a formal piping teaching institution continuously both before and after the Rankins' "college" at Kilbrennan in Mull closed its doors and the MacCrimmon one in Skye changed hands from Red Donald MacCrimmon to his brother Black John in the early 1770s. Logan, citing no authority, said that the MacGregors ran a college for piping at Rannoch.[35] The *Scots Magazine*, however, which covered the competition and presumably spoke to the winner, said that the 1784 competition winner, John Mac-Gregor of Fortingall, had already taught fifty military pipers and that he was the eldest of five sons of John MacGregor, who had taught not only him but ninety other pipers.[36] It may simply be true that the MacGregors were better situated than the Inner Hebrides to fulfil a growing need for pipers in the British army, and later, after the Falkirk and Edinburgh competitions began, in the houses of Lowland gentlemen. The idea for a non-diploma or degree-granting piping college in Gaelic-speaking Perthshire is nonetheless a Highland one.

What is unknown about the Rankins' and MacCrimmons' colleges is unknown of the MacGregors'. What they taught, to how many at a time, and at what levels of competence are unknown. What the Highland regiments' officers required of pipers, or what the MacGregors imagined them to have required or to have been satisfied with, likewise is unknown – there isn't much information on regimental repertoires of the early period. The piper's military activities, one or two per company as it was, did not cry out for any standard of technique, perhaps none of style either. There were no bands. However, we know, from MacDonell of Scotus's observation of ensemble piping mentioned earlier (Cogga na si, Achnacarrie, 1746) and from other cases later on ("MacCrummen's Lament," Falkirk, 1783; unknown, Edinburgh, 1783; not to mention, surely, many dance tunes, reels, and strathspey reels that were played by the competitors), that there was a common repertoire among Highland pipers. It may be that the MacGregors decided simply to build on this.

If the means and the method of instruction were the same in the various colleges, then the MacGregors once again were taking advantage of a new

Chart 2   An Abbreviated Genealogy of John MacGregor, Piper and Piping Teacher

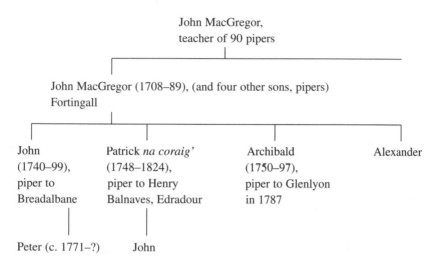

John MacGregor,
teacher of 90 pipers

John MacGregor (1708–89), (and four other sons, pipers)
Fortingall

John	Patrick *na coraig'*	Archibald	Alexander
(1740–99),	(1748–1824),	(1750–97),	
piper to	piper to Henry	piper to Glenlyon	
Breadalbane	Balnaves, Edradour	in 1787	

Peter (c. 1771–?)   John

opportunity and had perceived British military needs. If they were looking for one, they had a latter-day model instructor in John MacGregor, son of Prince Charles's piper, who, according to Angus MacKay's account, "was for some time at Dunvegan."[37]

The genealogical tree above is a truncated version of the one given by David Burns in 1982, but with an addition.[38] If it is correct, one must accept that the MacGregors were teaching pipers, in Perthshire, for decades when the two west coast colleges were in operation in the first half of the eighteenth century. Also, they were adaptable to post-Culloden circumstances, while the MacCrimmons and Conduilighs were not.

The MacGregors' apparently sudden disappearance from the Edinburgh competition winners' list has many plausible explanations. It is possible that by 1813 musical literacy and standardization of playing technique were being foisted on competitors and that the MacGregors, feeling that their talents were downgraded, dropped out. Perhaps some or many removed or were removed from their old territory and old customs and fondnesses were weakened.

With respect to the Lowland competition piping world after the war of 1812–14, a time when writing and reading pipe music from the published note were gaining an important foothold at a certain level of Highland pipers, two MacGregors made two very important contributions.

The first of these involved John MacGregor, piper to the Highland Society. Roderick Cannon states that he was one of the "Glenlyon family" (i.e., the Clann an Sgeulaiche family) and "a piper, pipe-maker and player of other instruments."[39] I still don't know how he was related to the Clann an Sgeulaiche MacGregors. In 1799 or 1800, however, he took down thirty pieces of pibroch from Angus MacArthur, piper to Lord MacDonald. Angus MacArthur died in 1800, so the Lord MacDonald in question at that time was Alexander Wentworth MacDonald (d. 1824), president of the Highland Society in 1802, who had succeeded the first Lord MacDonald, Alexander (d. 1795). Cannon, citing "the manuscript," wrote that it was from Old MacArthur's "whistling" that John MacGregor transcribed.[40] I don't know where the session or sessions took place. Either way, MacGregor captured the tunes with grace-notings in staff notation and this was a remarkable and leading achievement not properly appreciated until nearly two hundred years later.[41] Only Joseph MacDonald (c. 1760), up to that time, had done this systematically and his work may have been John MacGregor's example. If there was a link between the two, it would have been the MacGregor chief John Murray of Lanrick, also known as John MacGregor Murray, who at about the right time had strong connections with the Highland Society (presumably in London and Edinburgh).

Appropriately John Murray of Lanrick is the second influential MacGregor. His contribution, if anything, is more important than the piper's. John Murray, who belonged to the old MacGregor gentry, served as a general in the army of the Honourable East India Company and as auditor-general of Bengal. He died in 1822, the same year that he changed his name to MacGregor. He found and brought back Joseph MacDonald's manuscript study of piping, which had been written around 1760 and had been left in India when MacDonald died there, still a young man, in the service of the same company. No more potent or invaluable glimpse of piping at such an early period exists. MacDonald's manuscript is of the utmost importance for the preliterate tradition where classical and, to an intentionally less developed extent, non-classical piping are concerned. It uses staff notation for pipe music for the first time.

Did the MacGregor chief influence the obviously talented and musical piper John MacGregor in the transcribing of Angus MacArthur's thirty tunes? In 1804 the prize competition bagpipe was handed to the winner, Malcolm MacGregor, by a "Colonel A. MacGregor Murray, their Preses."[42] It was at that event that Joseph MacDonald's "On the Theory, Principle ... " was distributed to the most improved of the pipers, and it is possible that this "Preses" was the MacGregor chief, incorrectly initialled. In 1816 "Sir John MacGregor Murray ... addressed them [the competing pipers] severally in their native language, the pure Gaelic."[43]

Not having seen the thirty MacArthur tunes in the original script, I cannot compare that and the Joseph MacDonald manuscript. However, there was obviously a tribal bond between clan chief John Murray of Lanrick and the Highland Society piper John MacGregor. The date of John MacGregor

Murray's return to the United Kingdom with the Joseph MacDonald manuscript might have been a factor in more than just John MacGregor's piping and his piping literacy. He and other Clann an Sgeulaiche pipers may have had access to Joseph MacDonald's work from before the first competition. It is possible that some obvious consistency and/or brilliance of style taken from that source was enough to put them so often in the prizes.

Murray was obviously interested in piping, although no one knows the trail of his curiosity. As I've shown, he was not alone among MacGregor gentlemen to dally with the great muse of war but he is a pillar and a foundation of serious study of the earliest classical piping. Finding Joseph MacDonald's manuscript whenever he did must have been incomparably satisfying, assuming he knew its value.

John Murray of Lanrick was the first MacGregor chief since 1603, the year all MacGregors who used the name were subject to outlawry for a heinous clan crime committed within walking distance of Helensburgh. He was elevated by popular clan wish in 1784, over a challenge from the Glengyle branch (this was the same year that many of the confiscated Jacobite estates, Cluny's for example, were returned to their owners). Murray was the son of Evan, a commissioned officer in the 41st Regiment, who took the then unofficial chiefship of the MacGregors from his brother, Robert, who died in 1758. Robert Murray of Lanrick (alias Robert MacGregor of Glencarnaig) was a veteran of the '45 and imprisoned in Edinburgh for his boldness. John Murray, his nephew, was a Gaelic speaker (in 1816 he talked to the competition pipers at Edinburgh in Gaelic). He was knighted in 1795 for his services, I assume, as a general in the Honourable East India Company and as the company's chief accountant. His name pops up elsewhere in Edinburgh society, and he must have cut a dash in English and Highland society.

Undoubtedly there is a lot to be added to any biography of John MacGregor Murray, and one potential source is the records of the East India Company. Those, however, lay beyond my means and appear to have been ignored by others. Both John Murray and Joseph MacDonald were employed by the company, and while it seems unlikely, the men may have known one another in India. Whether or not, certain questions come to mind. How did Joseph MacDonald dispose of his possessions when death came a' callin' if he, just a young man, did make arrangements? If he had an executor, who was it, and most intriguing, what besides his famous manuscript existed and what happened to it?

To return for a moment to the tradition/modernist theme, I want to re-emphasize the essentially Gaelic nature of Clann an Sgeulaiche and any other non-gentleman MacGregor pipers in the second half of the eighteenth century. The typical pattern was of middle-class bilingualism veering into monoglot Englishness as the century progressed; for the ordinary person,

MacGregor and the surrounding country were Gaelic and fairly soon to fall victim to demographic change. It's not hard to imagine government attitudes and reactions to these people in 1745 and for as long as treason was suspected. Not only had many MacGregors used their Highland name (a name of which of course they were inordinately proud) in defiance of legal stricture, but they had been active Jacobites. They were widely hated as reactionary and chronically refractory. Any argument that they were effectively protected by Hanoverian patrons such as Campbell of Glenlyon, or anyone else with Georgian leanings, for anything longer than from Culloden till the Act of Indemnity, is cavilling and captious. Perthshire is close to the Lowlands and the military power of Britain. Cattle were driven through several of its glens, southward and northward, and during the Highland reivings after Culloden the shire was carefully posted and watched.

The record shows also that MacGregor and all other pipers in this strategically important area were ignored in the Disarming Act years, and they were only a rough hill-walk away from the Lowlands. Tartan wearers were sought but not pipers. Menzies's pipers and other Rannoch pipers in Perthshire will be considered later.

Until recently, the MacGregor contribution to piping has been underestimated. It extended over about a century from 1700 as far as is known. It reached from the traditional into the early days of literate-learned transmission, via John Murray of Lanrick and John MacGregor, and it involved a lot of formal or quasi-formal instruction of pipers, particularly in the Perthshire Gàidhealtachd. A stray observation, however, suggests that their influence reached further north. There was an Even MacGregor and an "Eugen M'Gregor," pipers in the employment of Fraser of Lovat, the first serving as piper and teacher of piping until about 1743 (see below).

PIPING ON THE GLENGARRY ESTATE
(INCLUDING KNOYDART)

Among the prominent and still feared Jacobite landed families who kept pipers in the early years after 1745 is MacDonell of Glengarry (patronymically, Mac 'ic Alasdair), whose final hold on an extensive estate lasted until rocky, reclusive Knoydart at last was sold in the mid-nineteenth century. By then the Gaelic-speaking population had been ravaged by leavings and clearances. The other taint associated with Glengarry is that the family is believed to have produced the infamous Pickle the Spy, Alexander MacDonell of Glengarry (known also as Young Glengarry, Alasdair Ruadh mac Iain, c. 1725–61), who secretly exposed Jacobite plotting after Culloden.[44]

As far as cultural matters are concerned in eighteenth century Glengarry, the written record is not rich[45] and is typically found outside the family. Nevertheless, what is known is valuable. The family had a hereditary piper,

John MacDonald (b. c. 1722), a veteran of Ticonderoga. MacDonald, according to the record of the Highland Society competition of 1801, piped for the family "for some generations."[46] These generations probably included John MacDonell, twelfth of Glengarry (d. 1754), known as "Old" Glengarry. They certainly included Alexander, the thirteenth, known as "Young" Glengarry (Pickle the Spy); Duncan, the fourteenth (Donnchadh mac Aonghuis 'ic Iain), Pickle's brother and the great clearer (d. 1788); and Alasdair Ranaldson (Alasdair mac Dhonnchaidh 'ic Aonghuis 'ic Iain, d. 1828), the Regency revivalist Gael.[47]

A John MacDonald, piper and tenant in North Laggan in the Great Glen, was one of a number of North Laggan men accused by the canal commissioners in 1807 of stealing cut birch wood from the lands of Laggan bordering Loch Oich.[48] If this was the veteran of Ticonderoga, he must have been about eighty-five years old and remarkably able.[49] Alasdair Ranaldson, also known to Gaels as "Alasdair Fiadhaich" (Wild Alasdair), was no lover of the canal through the Great Glen.

John MacDonell, "Old Glengary," did not soldier during the '45, but he was imprisoned and not released until October 1749. He had "disponed"[50] the estate in January 1745 to his oldest son, Alexander. The Glengarry part of the estate was not forfeited, although a part of it, Barisdale, mountain-girt in Knoydart, which was held on wadset,[51] was vulnerable and was both forfeited and annexed. As the government rightly saw matters, however, Catholic Glengarry was one of the heartlands of unsubdued Jacobite unrest. Several members of the prominent families there had raised hundreds of Jacobite soldiers in 1745.

Angus (the thirteenth chief's brother) led the Glengarry regiment in the 1745 campaign and was killed accidentally in Falkirk by a fellow-Jacobite in 1746. MacDonald of Lochgarry (who held several wadsets from Glengarry but whose Lochgarry estate, in Perthshire, was held/bought from the duke of Atholl)[52] led the clan regiment after Angus's death. Lochgarry had to go into exile in France, where he stubbornly conspired to stimulate another rising (his son John MacDonell of Lochgarry was commissioned a captain in Fraser's Highlanders on 5 January 1757).[53]

That no Glengarry was executed is on the surface a surprise. "Old" John died in 1754, and his perfidious son Alexander, "Young Glengary," succeeded him, if not at the time legally. Alexander spent twenty months in the Tower in London as a rebellious Jacobite and was set free, conditional upon his going into exile. He was served heir to the chiefship and the estate on 23 February 1758 and died in 1761. In that year he specified that his political papers be burnt and destroyed by friends of the family at his death. He was succeeded by his nephew Duncan MacDonell (Donnchadh mac Aonghuis 'ic Iain). The last of the piper's Glengarry chiefs was Alasdair Ranaldson MacDonell, who died in 1828. By that time the old piper and veteran of

Ticonderoga, John MacDonald, must have been dead several years and his musical mantle in Glengarry had passed to others, including a MacFarlane (fl. 1798), a Donald MacDonald (fl. 1822),[54] and Archie Munro from Oban among others.

The biography of the old piper John MacDonald is more gaps than detail.

Duncan MacDonell of Glengarry, fourteenth chief, was the chief under whom most of the old chief/tacksman/tenant farmer system on the Glengarry estate fell apart forever. It did so by force of rent increases, which the long-mismanaged estate desperately needed in the changing economic conditions, and through evictions.[55] Duncan, however, was typical of the new kind of chief and cultivated unusual interests, one of which was membership in the Society of the Antiquaries of Scotland in Edinburgh (formed in 1780, chartered in 1783). In 1781 he sent his piper John MacDonald to perform for the Lowland gentry at the society's anniversary. A letter exists from 13 November of that year, from James Cumming to Sir Alexander Dick of Prestonfield, relating that the piper, then quite an old man according to Cumming, had arrived safely, with the side of venison, from Glengarry. He did his bit well, playing several "pibrochs" as occasion demanded. He also played enough *ceòl beag* to charm three old Lowland gentlemen into dancing.

Cumming's letter repeats Samuel Johnson's use of the word "hereditary" in describing John MacDonald's status in the Glengarry household, a descriptive that Logan was responsible for entrenching in piping usage in 1831. In fact, many if not most rural occupations ran in families in Scotland as in Europe. Cumming, however, was perhaps not repeating others' thoughts when he talked about piping, since he had a piper of his own, from whose equipment old John MacDonald's pipes were suitably decked out for the anniversary doings. Cumming may have belonged to the Strathspey-area Cummings and been quite knowledgeable about pipers and piping. Equally well, he may have been thoroughly Lowland and have taken his lead from people like Sir John Clerk of Penicuik (1676–1755) and Hew Dalrymple in East Lothian, Lowland musical contemporaries who also kept family pipers.

Cumming wrote that at their party the old piper ran some risk of being "debauched" by the merry-making antiquarian blades, and it was through his (Cumming's) vigilance and nose for deviltry that MacDonald was steered clear of this and off to bed at his sister's home in Edinburgh. Perhaps he'd have given as good as he got, but the point is made only to fortify the supposition that Glengarry's piper was not of the middle class in Highland society. He was a veteran of Ticonderoga (1758), in which battle most, if not all, of the Gaels present were in the Black Watch. Stewart of Garth gives no officer by the name of John MacDonald in the regiment at the time, and pipers, if they played, were overlooked. With which tacksman/officer, if any, the piper enlisted is unknown, although two prominent MacDonells, John Mac-Donell, son of Jacobite Lochgarry, and Charles MacDonell, younger son of Glengarry, fought in America in Fraser's Highlanders (from which conceivably the piper could have been seconded).

Given the affection of Glengarry's people for the Jacobite cause, it would be no surprise to discover that John MacDonald had seen action as a Jacobite during the '45. However, there is no indication that he had; Cumming said nothing and there is no notice of his conviction after 1746 as a Jacobite.

MacDonald, whatever his social standing in Glengarry, played both forms of bagpipe music, ceòl mór and ceòl beag, and his music was catchy enough, and of the right speed and timing, that three Saxon Scots, none under seventy, danced the Three-some Reel to his piping. Both points are important, as they form a powerful contradiction to the long-held view that the pipers to the important Highland families concentrated on classical pipe music and never played ceòl beag, considering it demeaning. This idea got a lot of its modern impetus from Coll native John Johnston (1836–1921) in 1919,[56] but it was much earlier expressed by John MacCulloch in 1824. He observed, "[B]e it remembered, however, that it is *infra dignitatem* for a true Highland piper to play such music."[57] Glengarry was as jealous as anyone of his dignity, and it is very unlikely that he would have tolerated any radical tendencies on the part of his piper.

Before the sale of North Morar in 1769 to Simon Fraser of Lovat and of Abertarff in the Great Glen, Glengarry's estate reached westward in several mountain glens from Aberchalder's farm at Laggan, east of the Great Glen, and Collachy in the valley of the River Tarff. It included Knoydart and North Morar on the Sound of Sleat. It contained, especially in its eastern reaches, several substantial tacksman families whose holdings were threatened by the estate's impoverishment even before the North Morar portion was sold to ease the burden of debt.

A number of these tacksmen emigrated to North America in the tacksman emigrations in 1773. Three brothers, the MacDonells of Leek, Aberchalder, and Collachy (who were probably Catholics – at least their tenants were) in the relatively fertile Great Glen, all left then, on the ship the *Pearl*, with their cousin Spanish John MacDonell of Scotus,[58] a Jacobite, and other men of standing and property on the estate. They settled in the Mohawk Valley of the province of New York, just in time to fight in the British army in the Revolutionary War, be dispossessed, and shift to what became Upper Canada to the north.

About their piper-tenants nothing is known except a plausible remark to do with Spanish John. In 1777 Spanish John MacDonell of Scotus (in Knoydart) "marched" north from his farming settlement on the Upper Delaware in New York state to Schoharie near Albany with fifty-four armed Highlanders. According to John D. Monroe, they were led by a piper.[59] In Atholl the Jacobite MacDonald of Lochgarry may also have retained the services of a piper, but if so, nothing is known of him. Lochgarry lived in exile in France until 1754, or possibly 1756, with the MacGregors, Camerons, and others in that small, depressed, and frustratingly suspicious environment. His son John took a commission in Fraser's Highlanders in 1757 (78th) and went on to higher rank with Fraser's Highlanders (71st) in the American Revolutionary War. He later served in MacDonald's Highlanders. John is known to have retained a piper in his later years.

Few bother to consider that these influential MacDonells, whether tacksmen in Glengarry or elsewhere, must have had pipers among their tenants – not to have had, in their Highland world, would certainly have been most unusual, piping being so popular. Deliberately to have excluded pipers and fiddlers would have been seen as eccentricity and a dereliction of gentlemanly duties to local society. I might have called these imagined musicians "patronized," but that term was used to serve the pompous ends of the well-to-do and has been worn thin in that capacity to the point of being misleading. Henry Whyte (Fionn) (1852–1913), citing an Argyllshire Campbell story whose provenance he didn't bother to repeat, if he knew it, noted that Campbell of Craignish had a piper but Campbell of Barbreck didn't and was considered a penny-pincher for it.[60] Barbreck's meanness would have been regarded as rankest anti-culturism in Jacobite MacDonell country. Various community rituals (gatherings, welcomes, and deaths), popular pleasures (céilidhs and weddings), and work accompaniment all demanded pipe (and/or fiddle) music.

In those early community emigrations, pipers and fiddlers would never have been left behind, and with the prospect of the re-establishment of some kind of close-knit Gaelic society overseas, they would have indeed been the most propositioned and the most likely to want to go. Luckily, the assumption that middle-level Gaelic powers did patronize pipers finds critically important support in the knowledge that another cadet of the Glengarry family, MacDonald of Barisdale, had a family piper and that, a little further afield, to the southeast, a cadet family of MacDonell of Keppoch appears to have had a piper in 1745. These instances point clearly to the great extent to which people were subservient to the chief, as well as to tacksmen being associated with pipers; in most instances, one assumes that tacksmen were careful to place tenant musicians on their holdings for social as well as military reasons.[61]

Archibald MacDonell, third of Barisdale (Bàrasdal Og, born c. 1725), was more than a tacksman but less than a chief. He lost his estate to forfeiture and was attainted for his leading and recruiting part in the Jacobite army. Archibald is mentioned in John Roy Stewart's song/poem "Air Latha Chuillodair" (On/After Culloden Day) and was a first cousin of Alexander

MacDonell, 13th of Glengarry (Alasdair Ruadh). Mysteriously, Bàrasdal Og, though attainted, was not arrested and tried for treason until 1754, while his father, Coll, was arrested in 1749 and died in Edinburgh Castle.[62] Archibald was also taken in 1749 but was set free. Why it took so long to arraign him the second time is unclear.[63] However, government attitudes hardened noticeably with the murder of Colin Campbell of Glenure in northern Appin in 1752. Glenure, according to the Bighouse Papers,[64] was an uncle of Mungo Campbell, the appointed factor of the Barisdale lands and a man who long railed at "Young Barisdale's" (Archibald's) threats and brazen flouting of the Disarming Act.

At that time the government was secretly monitoring the Jacobites' Elibank Plot. As a result, a nervous apprehension was mirrored in the courts. Dr Archibald Cameron was captured and hanged in 1753 as a Jacobite messenger and coordinator, and Archibald was finally arrested.[65] Knoydart, with the presence there for a time of the bard Alasdair MacDonald (Alasdair mac Mhaighstir Alasdair), must have had the aura of a Jacobite haven.

On 12 June 1753 Mungo Campbell complained to D. Moncrieff that Barisdale "ranges up and down that country and the neighbourhood with a band of Armed men dressed as well as himself, in the Highland habite, The insolence and Tyranny of this outlaw is already well known to the Government and the military, to whom he has created a deal of trouble." Campbell also mentioned that the Barisdale rents continued to be paid to the attainted Barisdale long after 1746.[66] Stewart of Garth noted that Barisdale had 150 men with him whenever he wished. The facts of the matter are that the Disarming Act took effect, for warlike weapons, in the summer of 1748 and lasted until the autumn of 1753 and the prorogation of Parliament on 27 September. Inasmuch as Archibald MacDonell (Young Barisdale), a wadsetter, had suffered forfeiture of "his" estate, it may be that he was considered a landowner and as such, under the act of 1748 amending the Disarming Act, was entitled to a limited supply of arms.[67] However, none of his people, or himself, were entitled to wear Highland garb and the maximum number of weapons allowed to any landowner in the delineated area of Gaelic Scotland was thirty firearms, thirty pairs of pistols, and thirty swords or cutlasses for himself, his family, and servants.[68]

This was the arsenal allowed to landowners whose annual rental value was £9,000 Scots money. By what seems like a sound estimate, the Barisdale estate was worth £133.[69] Thus, after the summer of 1748 for arms, and after December 1748 for tartan clothing, Archibald MacDonell was in glaring contravention of the law and didn't appear to care. Either he was foolhardy or the government was lax in application or apprehensive about triggering a confrontation with the still-armed part of Gaelic Scotland.

In any event, at his treason trial in 1754, Archibald MacDonell was charged, found guilty, and sentenced to death. It was only months since the execution of Dr Archibald Cameron, and MacDonell must have been extremely jittery. At his trial, however, he called in his defence more than thirty witnesses, including "Donald M'Dougal, alias M'Ianoig, piper at Inverie; Allan M'Dougall, the piper's son."[70]

The piper's alias suggests that he might have come from Clanranald country to the south, since MacIain Òig is the patronymic of the Glenaladale MacDonalds in Moidart. From the researches of Tearlach MacFarlane, Glenfinnan, it appears that there were at least three families of MacDougalls within the Clanranald, all descended from various Dougals in various chiefs' families.[71] Thus, typically, a chief's son's first name became a patronymic. They were common in South Morar (Morar 'ic Dhùghail) but also cropped up in Glenforslan in Glenaladale and, subject to verification, in Inverlair in Keppoch.

The plainer fact remains, however, that MacDougall was a common Glengarry name and common enough in Knoydart. Five McDougall families were among the Knoydart emigrants who settled in Glengarry County, Ontario, in 1815.[72] Besides Donald M'Dougal, the Inverie piper, another Macdougall piper is associated with the Knoydart farm at North Kinlochdulochan (Ceann loch an dubh lochain), part of the small Scotus estate in Glengarry. Among the tenants (as distinguished in this case from the cottars) in North Keanlochdulochan in 1784 was "John Macdougall, piper." This man was piper to Ranald MacDonell, fourth or fifth of Scotus,[73] a Catholic MacDonell who had fought for King George in the '45 (guaranteeing non-forfeiture, despite Spanish John's Jacobitism) and was a clearer of people for sheep in 1784. In that year there were twenty-seven tenants and in all over three hundred people on the Scotus estate; in 1795 there were only three tenants left. Most of those who had chosen America had left in 1786.[74]

If there is any link between any Glengarry MacDougalls and the MacDougalls in the traditional MacDougall estate of Dunollie in Argyllshire, it is very tenuous. But there is one. According to Alexander MacAulay, Alan Dall MacDougall (Blind Allan), the bard and fiddler (c. 1750–1828) born in Glencoe, was a grandson of a MacDougall who had been forced to leave the Dunollie estate at the 1715 forfeiture.[75] From Glencoe Alan Dall moved to Inverlochy, where he not only ingratiated himself with Alasdair Ranaldson MacDonell of Glengarry, but left important pieces of piping information pertaining to Lochaber and Glengarry. As the latter's bard, Alan Dall travelled widely, including in Knoydart, where his name is associated with Loch an Dubh Lochain,[76] home of his namesake John M'Dougal, tenant farmer and piper.

Donald M'Dougal, alias M'Ianoig, the piper at Inverie, was Barisdale's piper in 1754, but surely pipers had been retained as a matter of course by the gentry of Knoydart. In fact, the presence of a piper to a middle-class Gael like Young Barisdale or Scotus was so commonplace in Highland Scotland

Chart 3   MacDonells of Glengarry and Barisdale

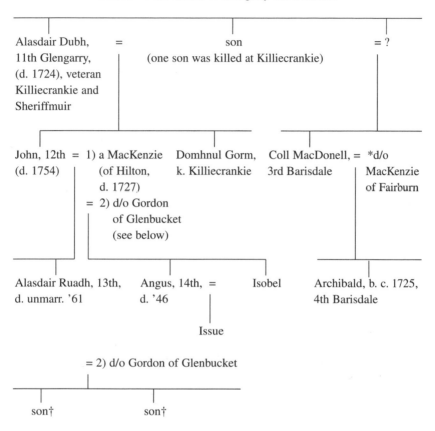

* Charles Fraser-Mackintosh, in "Minor Highland Septs – the Mac-Donells of Barisdale," gave Coll Mac-Donell as second of Barisdale and named his wife Helen, daughter of George MacKenzie of Ballamuckie, one of the officials on the west coast estates of Seaforth.

  Note also that Donald MacDonald of Lochgarry was married to Isabel Gordon, daughter of John Gordon of Glenbucket. If these are daughters of the same Jacobite "Old" Glenbucket, Lochgarry's relationship to Glengarry was one of cousinage combined with shared in-laws.

† One of these sons was Charles MacDonell, son of John, twelfth of Glengarry, by the daughter of Glenbucket. He was in Fraser's Highlanders and was killed at the taking of St John's, Newfoundland, from the French in early September 1762. The earliest conceivable date of his birth is late 1727, more likely late 1728. Presumably he was chief of the MacDonells of Glengarry from the date of Alasdair Ruadh's death on 23 December 1761 until his own, early September 1762.

that it was seldom ever mentioned. The same was true wherever piping was enjoyed in the second half of the eighteenth century, and that was through the length and breadth of Gaeldom, from Reay country to the Lowland line, from the parish of Crathie in Aberdeenshire to the Long Island.

Let me offer you a last glimpse of Barisdale, this one from a geographical perspective. An Ordnance Survey map of the area shows an "Eilean a' Phìobaire" (The Piper's Island) about four miles to the northwest of the mouth of the Barisdale River, on the south side of Loch Hourn.[77] The nearest *tobhta* (walls or remnants of walls), or what may just be the outline of a house, is shown on the mainland about half a mile northwest again, at a place called Glac nan Sgadan (Hollow of the Herrings), just east of Druim an Aoinidh (Ridge of the Steep Slope). Although it lies in some of the roughest Knoydart territory, there was the closed Gaelic herring fishery to bolster the black cattle economy (a lot of that being other people's in the case of the landlord). From a defensive point of view, when the chief was at Barisdale House, a bagpipe sounding over the water from Eilean a' Phìobaire might well have given Barisdale adequate warning of unwanted approach by water.

The other piper associated with the MacDonells, although associated with the Atholl and not the Glengarry estate in the late eighteenth century, was the boy piper John Cameron, piper to John MacDonald of Lochgarry mentioned above (son of the Lochgarry of the '45). Cameron's name appears in the record of the Highland Society piping competition in 1790.[78]

There is confusion as to who MacDonell of Lochgarry actually was. Andrew Lang described him as a cousin of Alexander, thirteenth chief. The Taylers (Alistair and Henrietta) described Lochgarry as Donald MacDonald, son of John MacDonald of Sandaig (north or west of Inverie, in Knoydart), and as a nephew of "Old Glengary," of "Old Scotus," and of "old Barisdale."[79] Showing the actual relationships between Glengarry, Lochgarry, Scotus, and Barisdale presents problems, but they were in varying degrees of cousinage. Both Glengarry's and Barisdale's marriage relationships with various MacKenzies are worth recording, since they implicate a small number of MacKenzies in the '45. They were drummed up by Archibald Mac-Donell of Barisdale.

CHAPTER TWO

Keppoch, Clanranald, and Cameron Piping

KEPPOCH MACDONELLS IN LOCHABER

The subject of piping and pipers in the Lochaber lands of the MacDonells of Keppoch (Mac Mhic Raghnaill)[1] after the Act of Indemnity in 1747 and during the period of military occupation (especially from late spring 1749) is more problematical than in Glengarry. This was a strongly Roman Catholic area and one of a number of target areas for strict treatment, including house destruction, immediately after Culloden until August 1746, perhaps extra-legally until later. The Maryburgh (Fort William) army base was very close to both Keppoch and Cameron country. The Jacobites had tried and failed to take it before Culloden. In the summer of 1747 and until late August, Fort William was garrisoned by Lee's regiment (44th Regiment), five companies of which, along with two companies of Guise's (6th Regiment), had been humiliated at Prestonpans;[2] Lee's was replaced by a hundred men each from four English regiments at Fort Augustus (Skelton's, Handasyd's, Mordaunt's, and Blakeney's). Their operations and effect are not known but that they pillaged Cameron property into 1747 cannot be ruled out. Lochiel's tenants' claims for losses, 1745–47, suggest as much.[3]

The man responsible for the post-based occupation of Lochaber, until 1748 when his regiment was reduced, was John Campbell, fourth earl of Loudoun (1705–82). He had raised Loudon's Highlanders in 1745, seen a number of his officers and men desert to the Jacobites, and then suffered the mortification of having every officer and man of the three companies of his regiment that were at Prestonpans in 1745 either killed or captured. After Culloden, two companies of Loudon's remained behind in the Highlands to recruit and to police the rampant cattle theft when the others left Scotland in May 1747. One (under a Lieutenant Campbell) was based at Ruthven, and the other was stationed at Dingwall in Easter Ross.[4]

Excesses were committed in Keppoch after Culloden, but they cannot with certainty be laid directly at Loudon's door. According to a credible source, Patrick Grant, one of the outlawed Seven Men of Glenmoriston, Loudon did not favour any depredations in Glenmoriston to the north. Still, according to Grant, Loudon's military colleagues in Glenmoriston – MacLeod of MacLeod and Sir Alexander MacDonald, who headed three parties of "the Isle of Sky militia" (the Independent Companies raised in Skye in 1745) – insisted on carrying through Cumberland's nasty, though legal, enforcement. Whether or not a red-faced sense of military ineptitude and misfortune led Loudon himself to encourage excesses in Keppoch is not known.

What is incontrovertible is that a number of Loudon's men under a Captain Patrick Grant, son of Grant of Knockando and Strathspey, behaved brutally and viciously to men, women, and children in Lochaber. Elsewhere Grant had stayed a hand that would have murdered Grant of Daldriggan but was responsible for the murder of Alexander Cameron in the Wood of Muick on Loch Arkaig-side in Cameron country. Grant's rapacity touched others also, Jacobite or not.[5] Bishop Forbes, citing the journal of Mr John Cameron, Presbyterian preacher and chaplain (at Fort William), reported this Grant to have led about two hundred men of Loudon's regiment on a predatory trip into Lochaber (including Loch Arkaig's north side) and thence into Knoydart. Men, women, and children were stripped, homes were burnt, cows driven off.[6] Whether this was the Lieutenant Patrick Grant of Rothiemurchus who served in Lord Loudon's Regiment or the "Patrick Grant Esq" identified by Garth as a captain of one of the twenty Independent Companies raised at Forbes of Culloden's instigation in 1745, is as yet undetermined. In any case, the bulk of Loudon's regiment left Britain for Flanders in May of 1747, leaving the two companies behind in the Highlands.

There is no doubt that Keppoch was a musical place in the seventeenth, eighteenth, and nineteenth centuries. Archibald MacDonell, fourteenth of Keppoch (Gilleasbuig na Ceapaich, d. 1682), wrote the song "Moladh na Pìoba" (Praise of the Pipes). Early pipers who piped for the chiefs in Keppoch are remembered in the area's poetry/song, and there is no reason to think that there were permanent breaks in the musical tradition after Culloden. Eastern Prince Edward Island (directly) and the Mabou area of Inverness County, Cape Breton (indirectly from Prince Edward Island, and directly as settlement grew), received hundreds of Brae Lochaber people from 1790–1830, and Mabou certainly has always been remarkably well supplied with fiddlers, pipers, and dancers. Many who came out remembered the army's occupation; for most it was only at a generation's remove. The effect of the emigrations may have weakened musical tradition in Lochaber, although Queen Victoria was regaled by pipers there in 1873.[7]

Few contemporary records survive, however, of pipers in Keppoch in the second half of the eighteenth century. The extent of damage and confiscation of documentary evidence in Keppoch by Cumberland's forces is unknown but probably of minor significance, since Keppoch was not owned by Keppochs but by MacIntosh chiefs and by several dukes of Gordon.

In 1691 Keppoch personally subscribed a peace bond for Sir John Campbell (Iain Glas, 1635–1716), first earl of Breadalbane; from this it is known that Coll MacDonell, fifteenth of Keppoch (Coll nam Bò [Coll of the Cows]), signed on behalf of himself and eight of his tacksmen. Assuming, reasonably, that the dignity and simple social wisdom of each tacksman demanded that a piper be among his tenants, then there were nine good pipers on the Keppoch estate.

The first mention of one, however, comes from Dòmhnul Donn, son of MacDonell of Bohuntin, a cadet of Keppoch. He was the famous reiver, character, and poet who flourished in the late decades of the seventeenth century, and who composed "Moladh a' Phìobaire" (The Piper's Praising) in commemoration of Donald Campbell, piper to Archibald MacDonell of Keppoch. The song is also known as "Slàn Iomradh dha m' Ghoistidh (Oran le Dòmhnall Donn mac Fear Bhoth-fhiunndainn do'n Phìobaire Chaimbeulach)" (Health and Fame to my Godson [A Song by Donald Donn son of Bohuntin, to the Campbell Piper]), which makes it clear to the literally minded that the piper was Donald Donn's godson.[8] As some indication of his standing in Keppoch society, Donald Campbell the piper was also Donald Donn's nephew, a son of Donn's sister.[9] According to Somerled MacMillan, the Mac a'Ghlasraich Campbells in Keppoch performed the function of hereditary pipers to Mac Mhic Raghnaill. They had a long history in Brae Lochaber;[10] one of them, a piper, was living in Inverlair on the Spean at the north end of Loch Treig around 1970.[11]

By the early nineteenth century, as the great multi-generational family emigrations changed the social face of Lochaber, the Campbell pipers dwindled in numbers on the old turf. Blind Allan MacDougall (c. 1750–1828/9) – Alasdair MacDonell of Glengarry's bard – in his song "Marbhrann do Mhac-'Ic-Ranuill na Ceapaich" (Elegy on MacDonell of Keppoch), mentions the late Keppoch's piper "Mac a'Ghlasraich." In Blind Allan's time in Lochaber, which ran from 1790, two Keppoch chiefs died, Alexander, the eighteenth, who died unmarried in Jamaica in 1808, and his brother Richard, the nineteenth, who died in 1819 of yellow fever, also in the West Indies.[12] Whichever of the two the song remembered, it attests that there were Campbell pipers into the first decade of the nineteenth century. Henry Whyte (Fionn) said that the last of Keppoch's pipers played at Culloden and that the family emigrated to Prince Edward Island, no date given.[13] No Keppoch piping tradition has yet been identified in Prince Edward Island, and certainly Mac a'Ghlasraich pipers, however they may have been related to the piper Whyte described as the last of them, were living in Keppoch into clearance times.[14]

John MacDonald, better known as Iain Lom (c. 1620–c. 1710), the pre-eminent Keppoch bard, concerned himself with power and politics and didn't mention piping or the pipes much; however, a piper figures in later Keppoch history in 1745. Donald MacDonald of Tirnadrish (Dòmhnul mac Raonuil Mhóir 'ic 'Illeasbuig [Donald, son of Big Ranald, son of Archibald])[15] led a small group of men in the ambush of government forces at High Bridge on the River Spean, northwest of Fort William, in 1745. With him was a piper, unfortunately unidentified. He may have been a tenant of Tirnadrish's or Keppoch's. It was the first action of the '45, one that Tirnadrish would live to be proud of for only a short time. He was executed at Carlisle on 18 October 1746. Tirnadrish was probably typical of Keppoch tacksmen, being a lover of piping, fiddling, and dancing. He was literate in English and also bilingual.

About twenty years later the North Uist poet John MacCodrum (c. 1700–79) left a general, stylized glimpse of Keppoch piping in his poem "Moladh Chloinn Dòmhnaill" (The Praising of Clan Donald), which may allow inference. Much hinges on when he composed the poem and then on one's understanding of stock phrasing in Gaelic. MacCodrum's output was greatest after 1763, when he was made Sir James MacDonald of Sleat's bard, and until his patron's death in 1766. From the comfort, it is presumed, of the patronage of Sir James, he penned these words: "An d'fhàg thu teaghlach na Ceapaich? / ... Le'm pìob 's le'm brataiche sròlta" (Did you leave the family of Keppoch? / ... With the pipe and with the silken banner). The bagpipe with its streamered banner is an image used by more than one bard (an earlier one being the MacLean bard Eachann Bacach, fl. 1650) and by at least one prosaic diarist, in English, of the occupation of Edinburgh in 1745, but that should not detract from MacCodrum's linking of Keppoch with piping in the early years after Culloden.

What existed of music and dance in Brae Lochaber has to be conjectured by analogy with other parts of Gaelic Scotland and from examples of musical descendants who emigrated from places like Bohuntine, Achluachrach, Killiechonate, and Tulloch in Brae Lochaber to Prince Edward Island and Nova Scotia, particularly to the Mabou area of Cape Breton in the late eighteenth and early nineteenth centuries. As has been shown in *Traditional Gaelic Bagpiping*, there was a statistically expectable presence of the Gaelic middle class in these emigrations. Furthermore, it is established, nowhere more clearly for Keppoch than in George Borrow's volume cited in Stuart MacDonald's book *Back to Lochaber*,[16] that outward material impoverishment was no fair indication of social standing in the Gaelic world.

The Keppoch chief, Alexander the sixteenth and his brother Donald were both killed at Culloden. John MacDonald (Iain Og), sixth of Bohuntine (part of lands that Keppoch held, by the sword, until 1746),[17] and his brother

Chart 4   Keppoch MacDonells and the MacDonalds from Durness

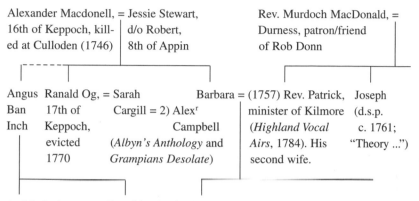

Note: This simplified composite is taken from Somerled MacMillan, *Bygone Lochaber*, Alexander MacKenzie, *History of the MacDonalds*, and Stuart Macdonald, *Back to Lochaber*. Ranald Og took a lieutenant's commission in Fraser's Highlanders in 1757. (He had married Sarah Cargill c. 1771.) Alexander Campbell did not marry Ranald Og's widow, Miss Cargill, until the mid-1790s and so had no influence on Patrick MacDonald's *Highland Vocal Airs*. Campbell interviewed Lt Donald MacCrumen in Glenelg and listened with awe to his piping of "Fàilte 'Phrionnsa." Angus Ban Inch was the older, but illegitimate, brother of Ranald Og, seventeenth of Keppoch.

Donald (Dòmhnul Glas) were banished to North Carolina as rebels. Alexander the sixteenth's son, Ranald (b. between 1733 and 1736, d. 1785), took a lieutenant's commission in the 1st Battalion of Fraser's Highlanders (the 78th) on 5 January 1757, one of two regiments that contained an abundance of former Jacobites, and which served in North America during the Seven Years' War. Contemporary documentation of the regiment and memories of everyday life in the 78th published in Simon Fraser's *Airs and Melodies* (1816) show that Fraser's Highlanders was a very musical regiment, several Highland villages in musical microcosm in fact, and it had many pipers. It is unthinkable that Raonul, chief of Keppoch, would be without a personal piper at home and overseas in service with Fraser's Highlanders.

Other possible military outlets for Keppoch pipers in general were the 89th Campbell's Highlanders (1759–65), the 81st Aberdeenshire (1778–83), and the Gordon Fencibles (1778–83) as well as Captain Hamilton Maxwell's company of the 71st (Fraser's Highlanders) of 1775.[18] All were raised, directly or indirectly, by the ducal Gordon family or relatives. The Gordons owned Keppoch until the line became extinct in 1836. Before Culloden, their power was *de jure*, since Keppoch chiefs did not accept post-Lordship landownership arrangements pertaining to Lochaber. After Culloden, Gordon power was *de facto*.

Inevitably, it became selfish and Gaelophobic. While the Keppoch Gaelic officer representation was small in the regiments (which may have precluded the
more prominent pipers from joining up), one name stands out, Lieutenant John
MacDonald of the 89th (1759), later lieutenant-colonel of the 81st (in 1783).

While nothing is known of any personal piper from Lieutenant John Mac-
Donald's tenantry who may have joined him or served him personally, there
is one excellent piece of evidence for piping in Keppoch territory in the
1780s. One of the children of Alexander MacDonell, sixteenth of Keppoch,
who was killed at Culloden, was Barbara MacDonell (a Roman Catholic).
On 28 December 1757 she married the Reverend Patrick MacDonald, minister of Kilmore Presbyterian Church in Argyll and publisher of *Highland
Vocal Airs* (1784). He was Joseph MacDonald's older brother and this was
his second marriage. Some time before 1784 Patrick MacDonald, in
response to the demands of "respectable subscribers" for "some of the
pieces, that are played on the large or true Highland bagpipe," added four
pieces of ceòl mór to the dance music pipe tunes in his manuscript.

The minister collected these tunes in Lochaber, "where he knew there was
an eminent performer upon that instrument, retained in the family of a gentleman, with whom he was nearly connected."[19] The most likely candidates
are Patrick MacDonald's brothers-in-law, Ranald MacDonell, seventeenth
chief of Keppoch, and his illegitimate half-brother, Angus Ban "Inch"
(Aonghas Bàn Innse [Fair Angus of Inch]), who ran clan affairs when
Ranald was in Jamaica. Patrick MacDonald's only near family connections
with Lochaber were with the Keppoch family. (His father, the Reverend
Murdoch, lived and worked in Sutherland, marrying a northern woman.
Alexander MacKenzie, in *History of the MacDonalds,* without elaborating,
described Patrick as a descendant of the Sleat family).[20] I have found no evi-
dence of this Skye connection.

The subject of piping in Keppoch does not fall silent in the 1820s, but I
have been interested primarily in showing what can be found out about traditional piping while the old population was relatively intact. By 1820 outside landownership had displaced local kinship loyalties in the making of
decisions in Keppoch. Then, in the long period of peace between 1815 and
the Crimean War, the expansion of sheep farming and the removals of people from their old lands left an old consciousness more dilute than it had ever
been. By the time of the potato blight in the 1840s, much of that consciousness, and with it much of the traditional music, had flown the coop.

PIPING IN CLANRANALD COUNTRY IN SOUTH UIST
AND THE MAINLAND

To the west, into the setting sun of the old Highlands, Clanranald's country,
from mainland Moidart to Hebridean South Uist and Benbecula, affords

some general information on the popularity of piping in the Gaelic middle class and a very important piece of piping history in the critical post-Culloden period. The subject of Clanranald pipers from 1700 to 1800, however, is an unsatisfactory patchwork of data; the evidence for piping in the 1740s and 1750s is less clear-cut than it is in MacLeod country, for example. The subject of the MacIntyre pipers, who are associated with Clanranald, from the account of Highland Society competitions in the late 1780s, is by no means cut-and-dried and touches on more than Clanranald holdings in the Highlands. Thus, a considerable gap exists for which not much information is available.

Initially, nevertheless, even if the record for the Clanranald estate is not filled to the brim with tales of pipers and piping, even if nothing is known about a hereditary family serving Clanranald from 1746 for a decade or two, let's say, there is a very strong case to be made for piping's having continued much as before during the Disarming Act years in both the mainland and island portions of the estate.

In Clanranald's South Uist, where traditional Reel-dance piping lasted into the twentieth century, there is at least one case of a named piper who played during the second half of the eighteenth century. In his "Marbhrann do dh'Iain Ruadh Piobair" (Eulogy on Red John the Piper), the subject of the bard Gilleasbuig na Ciotaig (Archibald MacDonald, c. 1750–1815) was his piper friend John M'Quithen.[21]

In the occupation period, Arisaig and Moidart in the mainland part of the Clanranald holding were dealt with kindly by Captain Duncan Campbell, a relative of the Breadalbane family, the family that had sent five hundred men to support the Jacobites in 1715. The theft and rapine lasted in Arisaig and Moidart only as long as it took to get the vengeful British Culloden soldiery out and to set up Campbell's benign police force.

Even given this considerate occupying force, information about piping in Clanranald country is not overwhelming during the Disarming Act years. What there is comes from three distinct sources, traditional song and lore, traveller observations, and the musical record. The rest, the speculation, is only by analogy with places of similar Catholicity and Jacobitism like Barisdale to the north.

In a song called "Banais Mhic Asgaill" (MacAskill's Wedding), John MacCodrum wrote, "Gach aon bh'air a' bhanais / A' dannsa gu grinn / Le seatadh 's an ruidhle dhùbailte / 'S iad ag glaodhaich, 'Obh, óbh, / Nach mol sibh an grìomh(sic) / Fhad's mhaireas a' phìob / 'S an t-ùrlar dhuinn'" (Everyone who was at the wedding dancing neatly setting in the double reel, and shouting, "Hurray, praise the deed as long as the pipes and the floor last us").[22] Although MacAskill is a Protestant name and South Uist was over 90 per cent Roman Catholic, William Matheson noted that the wedding that North Uist bard MacCodrum was celebrating was held in

South Uist, in the Benmore district. Matheson dated the event to around 1768.[23]

The Clanranald family aside, the observations that are available are limited to some of the main cadet families of Mac 'ic Ailein (the patronymic of the captain, or chief, of Clanranald). Certainly, lore of an earlier time linking a legendary Morar chieftain with piping and pipe composition should be mentioned.

The following story, given to Colonel Greenhill Gardyne of Glenforsa by Peter MacDonald of Sheil Bridge, Acharacle in Moidart, was known in 1909 outside Moidart:

Ronald MacAilean Og MacDonald (of Traigh in Morar, I think he was) was on his way to see Lochiel. The Camerons took a vicious bull from Loch Arkaig side, and sent him on in front of Ronald to the river Sgaitheal. The bull appeared very fierce, and Ronald said it was better to avoid him, but his gille said "I would not like them (the Camerons) to say that we ran away from him." So Ronald and the bull attacked one another in the river. Ronald killed the bull, and twisted off his two horns, and made the lad carry them. He composed a piobaireachd by the side of Lochiel, and played it for the first time when he was nearing Achnacarry Castle. When he returned home, he went to see MacDonald of Keppoch, and played the tune to him. The Laird of Keppoch asked for the tune to be a Welcome tune for himself, and Ronald gave it.[24]

That quotation defends a point of view that may have been commonly held in Clanranald country, that the famous tune which Donald MacDonald (c. 1750–1840) called "Se'n t'arm mharbh me" (later enlarged in his manuscript to "An t'arm breachd derg, se'n t'arm mharbh me" [The red speckled army, the one that killed me]) was really called "An tarbh breac dearg" or "The Red Speckled Bull."[25] Besides drawing attention to the fact that many attractive pieces of ceòl mór are the subject of endless debate as to title and composer in a world where, alas, recourse to valuable living lore is no longer possible, Peter MacDonald's story highlights one of South Morar's most famous characters, Raonul mac Ailein Oig, the warrior-leader who subdued the devilish Colunn gun cheann (Body without a head). What pipe tunes Ranald composed is open to fruitless debate, but this tune and two others, "The Vaunting" and "The Finger Lock," are associated with him and once again place piping in the sphere of the Gaelic middle class, thereby deepening its meaning for all Gaels. "Notes on Antiquities from the island of Eigg" contains an intimation that "the bones of the prince of pipers, Raonall MacAilein Oig, the author of the most celebrated pipe music in existence ... many pibrochs" lay buried in St Donan's Church in Eigg. The writer said that the stone was dated 1641.[26] Another almost phantom piper lived on Eigg at an unspecified time and is referred to by Reverend C.M. Robertson in

1898. "Another fugitive, who was ancestor of some families still living in the island, and of a man known as Am Pìobair Mór, found refuge in the same cave ('Uamh-Chloinn Diridh' near the north end of Eigg). He had fled from Rum when the inhabitants of that island were converted to Creidimh a' Bhata Bhuidhe by the proprietor, Maclean of Coll." [27]

Lore is the source of piping information on the eighteenth-century Clanranald tacksmen, French John MacDonald of Rhue and his son Archibald. French John (Iain Frangach) was a lieutenant in the Jacobite army of 1745 and afterwards accompanied Prince Charles on some of his wanderings among the mountains. As late as 1964 Iain Frangach was described by the then tenant at Rhue, Duncan MacVarish, as a great lover of the pipes, the fiddle, and the bottle. These were traits also associated with his son Archibald, who is said to have snappily got up and danced on a table in a Portree inn to divert attention when a heated argument in the company looked like it might ignite into a brawl. [28]

The second of Clanranald's people known to have been involved with piping was Angus MacDonald, grandson of Alasdair mac Mhaighstir Alasdair, the great Jacobite bard mentioned above. Angus's father had taken the farm at Lathaig on Eigg in 1765, almost certainly at an improver rent, and his son, a veteran of the taking of Quebec in 1759, was an old man when visited in 1822 by the Geneva-based mineralogist/geologist traveller L.-A. Necker de Saussure. [29] Iain MacKay described Angus MacDonald as knowing pipe airs better than "any professed piper." [30] De Saussure, although an outsider, also left a strong impression of Angus's love for pipe music. Angus Lathaig was a curious mixture of modern and old attitudes. Hugh MacKinnon's stories of him in *Tocher*, volume 10, depict him as a heartless evictor of his tenantry on Eigg, a Gael ready to flex the old tacksman's power to thoroughly untraditional ends. At the same time, the depth of his nostalgia for classical piping was poignant.

The last two tacksmen had roots as deep as anyone's in the West Highland Gàidhealtachd, but where piping was concerned in Clanranald territory, they were minor characters whose contribution to the financial or subsistence support of pipers and piping is not documented. Mentioning them at this point serves only to establish that piping was enjoyed by the local leaders and presumably by their tenants, to the humblest rank, and was not critically interrupted in the heart of Catholic Arisaig and Moidart. Angus's nostalgia for ceòl mór tends to support the belief that this music was in serious decline as a living tradition in Clanranald's estates in the early nineteenth century, although in 1822 de Saussure reported frequent pibroch playing. Maighstir Alasdair (father of Alasdair mac Mhaighstir Alasdair) lived in Dalilea in the south of Moidart and was an Episcopal minister on the Ardnamurchan peninsula to the west. Iain Frangach (d. c. 1800), the first of Rhue (in Arisaig) and Clanranald's factor in Arisaig from 1772, was a son of

Angus MacDonald, first of Borrodale, who in turn was son of John Mac-Donald of Glenaladale.

The Glenaladales (the Mac Iain Oigs), however, were major actors in mid- and later eighteenth-century Clanranald Moidart, being staunch Roman Catholics, tacksmen, military leaders, and patronizers of piping. Over the period 1742–1819 the names of only two pipers associated with the family are known, Donald Campbell and John MacGillivray (referred to either as MacGhillemhoire or MacGhille-Bhràth).[31] Donald Campbell, father of Colin Campbell, author of "Colin Campbell's Instrumental Book 1797," was at Culloden and escaped to serve as piper to Campbell of Carwhin, in Argyle. According to a grandson, a piper living on the Island of Luing in Argyllshire in the autumn of 1834, Donald was educated at Glenaladale's expense and entered his service in 1742, piping at the arrival of Prince Charles in Moidart in 1745 and, one assumes, throughout the campaign.[32] Much later, and until a few years before the piper emigrated to Nova Scotia, Alexander MacDonald of Glenaladale (d. 1815 aged 28) supported piper/poet John MacGillivray (1792–1862).

What happened to piping in Glenaladale in the twenty-five years from the date of indemnity in 1747? Did Alexander MacDonald, the Glenaladale of the '45, continue to patronize a piper and did his succeeding son, Captain John, who headed the emigration to Île St-Jean (Prince Edward Island) in 1772? The more appropriate question is, why would they not? The Mac-Donalds of Glenaladale of those days were conservative, Jacobite, Roman Catholic, Gaelic, and acutely conscious of the intricate web of social forces that bound together landowners and people in Moidart.[33] As in the case of the Keppochs, there is no record, and unless evidence turns up dealing with Glenaladale itself or with a piper or pipers who emigrated with Captain John MacDonald of Glenaladale to Île St-Jean in 1772, it may be impossible to say incontrovertibly that Donald Campbell's position was filled by another until 1772. From Captain John's own hand in 1772, we know that "the whole tribe of us Macien oigs are going off at this time to a man excepting your two Brothers & old Lochans & his Son Donald, And I will not Answer long for these."[34]

It is clear that a sizeable proportion of the 214 emigrants were of the powerful class, the Mac Iain Oigs. It was normal for gentry to have been musical, and this is a virtual guarantee that musicians formed part of the emigrant party, whether gentry themselves or tenants.

To date, the names of only about fifty of the Prince Edward Island Glenaladale settlers are known. No Campbell, MacGlasserich (Mac a'Ghlasraich), or MacGlashan has emerged and there is no "piper." Who was Donald Campbell? In the realm of speculation, the nearest geographical source of Campbell pipers to Glenaladale was almost certainly Keppoch in Brae Lochaber. It is possible that Donald Campbell, the Glenaladale piper of the 1745 rising, was from this old Keppoch stock (which came originally from Glassary in Argyle). There was at least one marriage tie between the Clann Iain Oigs and the Brae Lochaber MacDonalds/ MacDonells in 1772, and this was, according to Iain R. MacKay, between Allan "Old Lochans" MacDonald and a granddaughter of the Keppoch who was killed at Culloden.[35]

As is now well known, the Glenaladale piper who was accepted for generations as John MacDonald, piper to Glenaladale, was in fact the John MacGillivray mentioned above. He was from Mamaidh in Arisaig and emigrated to Nova Scotia in 1818. The representation of him held by the National Museum of Scotland is of a right-shoulder/right-hand-upper piper playing a three-drone bagpipe. The Glenaladale of the time who rigged out MacGillivray, Alexander MacDonald, died very young, leaving huge debts that betray a drunken, foppish, Regency spendthrift character; Bishop Chisholm of Lismore wrote to him of his reputation as a debtor and a rake.[36] The work of Neil Cameron (of the Royal Commission on the Ancient and Historical Monuments of Scotland) gives a thumbnail sketch of a young man who would have made a splendidly irresponsible crony for his superior, Clanranald.[37]

Admittedly, there is as yet no evidence that piping continued in the Glen-aladale estate for years after 1746, but Glenaladale would have been a notable exception had piping fizzled out with Donald Campbell's move to Argyle in 1746.

Going back for a moment, although to my knowledge their whereabouts are still unknown, in 1889 the Moidart priest Reverend Charles Grant Mac-Donald (Maighstir Tearlach, 1835–94) wrote that Glenaladale's piper's pipes were "still preserved in Glenfinnan."[38] Queen Victoria, who visited Glenfinnan in September 1873, met Glenaladale, a Roman Catholic, and his uncle the priest, who lived with him. The queen did not write that she had been offered a look at any historic bagpipes.[39]

As noted earlier, it is by no means implausible that the Campbell Cann-taireachd (singing)[40] used by Colin Campbell owes something to the piping and the piping repertoire of pipers living on the estate of MacDonald of Clanranald in the early eighteenth century, and as much or more to the Campbell (Mac a'Ghlasraich) pipers who were long established in the eighteenth century in Keppoch's Brae Lochaber.

Although, typically, written documentation is very scarce for the 1750–87 period for the broader estate, looking at what was the great coastal Clan-ranald estate from today's perspective, it is a truism to note that South Uist in particular was always a hotbed of pipers, of piping, and of piping lore. F.G. Rea's *A School in South Uist* offers a glimpse of the last of the old pre-literate dance-music pipers at the turn of the twentieth century, and one is forced by countless cultural analogues to extrapolate a richer past for South

Uist and other Clanranald communities. Where that conservativeness is concerned, the Protestant bard John MacCodrum[41] acknowledged that already, around 1760, South Uist contained invaluable cultural anachronisms. Captain John MacDonald of Glenaladale's correspondence to his first cousin once removed, Alexander MacDonald,[42] suggests that Clanranald was beginning to distance himself from older Gaelic attachments in 1772.[43] Where chiefly status and music are concerned, however, there is room for fickleness.

A story is extant, and hitherto unchallenged, that in around 1810 Ranald George MacDonald, eighteenth of Clanranald and in essence a London-based Englishman, was taken with the reputation of a "fiddler to the Laird of Muck" (a MacLean) and prevailed on him to move to Eigg. The source of the story was the fiddler's grandson, Donald MacKay.[44] This is a rare and very important instance of a Highland chief's retaining a fiddler. Fiddlers were common and may have been widely encouraged in one way or another in Gaelic Scotland, but they are very seldom mentioned as dignifying a chiefly presence; that position fell to the piper. A cynical explanation would be that Clanranald was keeping up appearances and mimicking Abercairney's famous patronage of Niel Gow.

If the story is true, it is only fair to point out that Ranald George was unpopular among his tacksmen: he was English, foppish, and "irrecoverable"[45] and displayed little interest in his tenantry. He was a minor until 1810 and in the not inconsiderable thrall of his tutors by one assessing.[46] The estate was being wrung to the last kelp copper with seldom a thought to compassion for tenants and folk who had lived in South Uist for generations. Ranald George, who later sold off South Uist to meet debts, had nothing to say about rack-renting. He has been described warmly by professor John MacCormack as "the Eton-educated wastrel" and for understandable reasons.

In the generation before the Eton man, however, while still not any marker of a genuine interest in Gaelic music, Ranald George's father, John MacDonald of Clanranald, is associated with a MacIntyre piper. The first MacIntyre piper recorded as being in the service of Clanranald appears in the prize lists in Angus MacKay's *Collection,* in the Edinburgh piping competition of 1787 when a Robert MacIntyre placed third. That year is also the first in which Clanranald is mentioned, although tune titles bearing the name Clanranald crop up in 1783 ("Clanranald's March") and 1785 ("Clanranald's Salute"), indicating an established connection, albeit of undetermined length, between Clanranald and the classical form. In 1788 MacIntyre was second and in 1789 he was first, but in neither case is a chiefly affiliation given. He cannot be associated with the piping of the immediate post-Culloden period. In 1787 he is described as "Piper to John MacDonald, Esq., of Clanranald."[47] It isn't established if he was in a line of pipers, far less the last of an unbroken line of MacIntyres to have held the position, although that claim has been made by several writers, including Alexander MacAulay.[48] The notes on the MacIntyres in Angus MacKay's book state that he emigrated "to America" after the death of Clanranald, around 1794.[49] This probably was so, but to date no trace of him or of his influence has been uncovered in Canada or the United States.[50] Who, if anyone, succeeded him as Clanranald's piper is unknown.

The claim that the MacIntyres were indeed pipers over a number of generations to several Clanranald chiefs is associated with the story of the famous Bannockburn bagpipes.[51] Accepted knowledge in 1987 had it that this single-drone set of bagpipes belonged to the MacIntyres of, or living in, Ulgary in Glen Moidart and that these MacIntyres were the hereditary pipers to Clanranald. Lore at the time held that the Ulgary farm was the most keenly sought in the area (a fact which a casual glimpse at its geography tends to defy). Hugh Cheape, in correspondence with Seamas MacNeill (April 1987), reported that it was thought that the Ulgary MacIntyres emigrated in 1812. No trace of them has yet come to my attention and to date I have not been able to confirm any MacIntyre-Clanranald musical link beyond that of Robert MacIntyre above.

There is information about a MacIntyre and another piper in South Uist, however. The MacIntyre piper was Donald MacIntyre (Dòmhnul Ruadh pìobaire [Red Donald the piper]), and he appears at about the same time as Dr Ross's piper John MacIntyre in Skye (see below). Donald's name is linked to a story that F.G. Rea retold in *A School in South Uist ... 1890–1913,* a recounting of his teaching experiences in that deeply Catholic and Gaelic island. It is about a man who was given the gift of piping by the fairies. Rea, an English Catholic from the Midlands who didn't speak Gaelic, didn't include the piper's name, but his scholar friend and educator in local affairs, Gael Father Allan MacDonald (1859–1905), gave a more complete version of the story, including names, in the *Celtic Review.*[52] Father MacDonald said that an old lady who lived in Rea's time, Janet MacNeil of Cachaileith, Smercleit (b. 1810), was the great-granddaughter of Dòmhnul Ruadh Mac an t-Saoir (Red Donald MacIntyre). This gives the piper a date of birth of about 1710.

The other piper from South Uist is Allan MacCormack, who left a holding on Ormaclate Castle farm in 1802. Allan, born in or not long before 1775, was the direct patrilineal ancestor of retired history professor John MacCormack, of Saint Mary's University in Halifax, Nova Scotia. In *Highland Heritage & Freedom's Quest* the professor, using incontrovertible sources, documents Allan MacCormack's holding in South Uist and charts the financial decline foisted on him and people like him by greedy estate managers who controlled Clanranald the minor's affairs. Nowhere, however, in those estate records is there reference to Allan MacCormack as a piper.

That fact is only known from family history. Surely pipers like this, unnoticed by the record keeper, were common in Gaelic Scotland and any broad reconstruction of the world of music and dance that they inhabited can now come only from this kind of personal source. There is no other memory of Allan MacCormack's bagpiping, although his biographer has imposed on him the capacity as both step-dance piper and Sword Dance and Highland Fling piper. Perhaps he is right.

Clanranald's estate in the Outer Hebrides was sold in 1838, but the Gaelic cultural tradition soldiered on. Conditions were hard until the Crofters' Act in the 1880s at last gave security of tenure to lands that were left to the common man. South Uist folk, including musical people, continued to emigrate to Cape Breton until the early 1840s. Those who remained surely passed on the same music and dance that the emigrants took overseas, but unfortunately Rea's observations of Wedding Reel dancing, for example, are insufficiently detailed for one to tell if change had already occurred by his time. Rae does not allow his reader to detect the influence of itinerant dancing masters, but equally leaves no trace of Hebridean dancing, which is known to have been intruded briefly in Barra and elsewhere in the late nineteenth century.

PIPING IN CAMERON COUNTRY
FROM LOCH LEVEN TO LOCH ARKAIG

In their triumphant march into Edinburgh after the Jacobite victory over John Cope at Prestonpans, the Camerons carried the captured colours of Cope's dragoons and their pipers played "the old cavalier air, 'The king shall enjoy his own again.'"[53] No shortage of pipers there. The three pieces of classical piping associated with the Camerons that immediately come to mind suggest the powerful significance of the bagpipe for that people: "Pìobaireachd Dhòmhnuill Dhuibh" Black Donald's Pibroch (Black Donald's Pibroch), "Fàilte Ridire Eoghann Loch-iall" (Welcome Sir Ewen Lochiel), and "'S e do Bheatha Eoghainn" (You're Welcome Ewen) – all published in modern form in the collections of the Pibroch Society (books 2, 3, and 10).

In their evidence against the active Jacobite John MacKenzie (Lord MacLeod), son of Lord Cromartie, two men in Lord Cromartie's regiment in the Jacobite army, Donald Munro and Donald Fraser, said that they "saw him frequently among the rebels at Perth [in January 1746]. From Perth the prisoner marched with the said regiment with a stand of colours to Dunblane, and some of the Camerons marched with them with colours and pipes."[54]

When parts of the defeated Jacobite army regrouped on Loch Arkaig-side in Lochiel's MacMillan country in 1746 and the pipers that Spanish John

MacDonell of Scotus remembered played "Cogadh no Sìth" (War or Peace) in unison, it is hard to imagine that there, on the estates of Mac Dhòmhnuill Dhuibh (The Son of Black Donald [patronymic of Cameron of Lochiel]), one of the pipers was not a Cameron tenant, whether a Cameron, a Mac-Martin, a MacMillan, a MacPhee, a MacMaster, a MacIntyre, or a MacKenzie. Several dispassionate observers report that the Camerons had pipers during the '45. What is called the "Cameron school" of piping, a nine-teenth-century phenomenon in pibroch playing, points perhaps to important Cameron pipers who came, perhaps as pipers, from the Cameron estate in the eighteenth century. That they did is unproveable, unfortunately. Once again, until the early nineteenth century the evidence for the Cameron tradi-tion is scant but the inferences can safely be drawn.

What, if anything, went on during the Disarming Act to touch on tradi-tional life and music on the Cameron estate is unclear. At least one published poem/song may imply a depressed Cameron musical scene, but the evidence from elsewhere in the Highlands strongly argues against this. About the time the Lochiel estate was restored to Donald Cameron (1784), the Uist bard Archibald MacDonald (friend of piper John M'Quithen mentioned above) was looking wistfully for a return to tradition when he addressed Young Donald Cameron of Lochiel in "Oran do Lochiall a tha lathair" (Song to the returned Lochiel):

'Nuair a theid Achnacaraidh air doigh, / 'S a ni Donull ann còmhnuidh le sith, / Thig cleachdan a shinsireachd beo, / 'S freag'raidh creagan na mòintich do'n phiob; / Bithidh toil-inntinn aig d'uaislean, a's spòrs, / theid mighean air fògradh, a's sgios, / Bithidh fudar ga losgadh gu leoir, / 'S daimh chroic air an leònadh san fhrith.[55]

(When Achnacarry is up and running, and Donald living there in peace, the ways of his ancestors will revive, and the rocks of the moor will echo to the pipe; your gentlemen will be content, and there'll be sport, banished discord and weariness, powder will be fired aplenty, and the stag of the hill wounded in the heath.)[56]

In the Gaelic tradition, MacDonald, not without a dose of wistful hope, upholds the chief in comely fashion, but one need not assume from the word "revive" that all of the piping tradition had died in Cameron country. The new man, a clearer of tenantry, must have disappointed the bard, but for all that piping went on.

The Lochiel estate was forfeited after Culloden and was not restored until 1784, and then to the minor, Donald Cameron, ninth of Lochiel (b. c. 1769). Like so many of his kind, he had not been fostered on the estate, did not speak Gaelic, and lacked any depth of contact with "his" people. He made his first visit north to his estate in 1790 when not a few old people were still alive whose sons had died in the Cameron regiment during the '45. Although his links with Gaelic music were tenuous, in 1793 he is known to have retained an Angus Cameron as family piper.[57] During the ninth chief's time and continuing a trend well established by then almost everywhere in the Gàidhealtachd, rents were rising and agricultural prospects for tenantry, including tacksmen, correspondingly falling. The once well-populated Cameron estate began to lose people to emigration, and eviction. The major emigration led by Archibald MacMillan of Murlaggan on Loch Arkaig to what is now Ontario, took place in 1802; small scale evictions by Donald Cameron of Clunes[58] were carried out in 1801; and in 1804 Donald Cameron, the ninth Lochiel, drove out the people of Glendessary and Loch Arkaig-side. The same chief kept a piper, but of unknown family.

"Angus Cameron, Piper to Donald Cameron, Esq. of Locheil," was second in the Highland Society piping competition in Edinburgh in 1793. In 1794 he won. This is clearly the same piper who is referred to as "Angus the piper" in a letter dated 23 March 1804 from Duncan Cameron (third) of Fassifern to Archibald MacMillan of Montreal (late of Murlaggan on Loch Arkaig-side). Recounting to his old friend the recent disruption of the resetting the Cameron tacks, he noted that "Duncan Campbell's ffarm in Stroneahun-shean" had been allotted to "Angus the piper."[59] Why a relatively unknown piper of no known middle-class pedigree or pretensions should have avoided Cameron's evictions and be allotted a named farm may seem unusual but the answer appears to be that he married above his station. He was still alive in August 1841 and then was met, for the second time, by the circuit judge Lord Cockburn.[60] Cameron, who had married "a leddy," operated the inn on the north shore of the Ballachulish Narrows (in 1819 as in 1841). The judge described Cameron's sadness at the "general decline of the art" and his reasoning that it was caused by the disappearance of "chieftains."[61]

One of the few Camerons (besides Donald, the ninth chief) known to have retained a family piper is John Cameron, tenth of Callart on the north shore of Loch Leven. From the "Account of the Competition of Pipers," 1785, a Paul MacInnes, "Piper to John Cameron, Esq., of Callert," won third prize. (In contrast, Angus Cameron, piper to Donald Cameron of Lochiel, was second in 1793 and first in 1794.)[62]

The real extent and condition of Gaelic piping on the Lochiel estate in the second half of the eighteenth century may never be assessed accurately, but inferences can be drawn from the Cameron presence, particularly of officers who raised Gaelic companies for the British Highland regiments. Bear in mind, however, that pipers in the regiments, being unofficial, are mentioned only by the way. The first Cameron regiment, the 79th (Cameron Highlanders), was formed in 1793 and is known to have had pipers, but Camerons held commissions much earlier. Cameron officers served in the 77th (Montgomerie's Highlanders, 1757), 78th (Fraser's Highlanders, 1757), 2nd

Battalion, 71st (Fraser's Highlanders, 1775), and 76th (MacDonald's High-landers, 1778), and all of these are also known to have had pipers. The following list is taken, for the most part, from lists of initial officers' commissions published in David Stewart of Garth's *Sketches*. The contradictions found in Stewart are best contended with by assuming the names in volume 2 as more nearly correct, since regiments there are treated individually, whereas in the first volume, for example, some of the history of Fraser's Highlanders is treated under a much wider heading. Stewart may not be all-inclusive, as officer replacements are not always scrupulously given for regiments with long histories. For all that, the Cameron officer presence is well distributed in most of the Highland regiments.

77th, Montgomerie's Highlanders, 1757:
Captain Allan Cameron; Lieutenant Cosmo Martin.[63]

78th, Fraser's Highlanders, 1757:
Captain Alexander Cameron of Dungallon;[64] Lieutenants Hugh Cameron, Ewen Cameron of the Glennevis family,[65] Allan Cameron, and Donald Cameron, a son of Cameron of Fassifern.[66]

71st, Fraser's Highlanders, 1775:
Captains Charles Cameron, of Lochiel, and Charles Cameron, son of Fassafern; Lieutenant Archibald Balnevis; Ensign Donald Cameron; and Adjutant Donald Cameron.[67] (I have assumed Balnevis to have been a Cameron, possibly a MacSorlie-Cameron.)

76th, MacDonald's Highlanders, 1778:
Major Charles Cameron, younger son of Allan Cameron, ninth of Callart.[68] That MacDonald's Highlanders had pipers is known from the description of one who also served as a drummer in the 76th and who settled in what became Shelburne in Nova Scotia at the end of the American Revolutionary War.[69]

2nd Battalion, 78th, Ross-shire Highlanders, 1794:
Lieutenant Donald Cameron; and Ensign Donald Cameron.

79th, Cameron Highlanders, 1793:
Colonel Allan Cameron of Erracht; Lieutenant-Colonel Philip Cameron (son of Colonel Cameron of Erracht); and Major Cameron.[70]

92nd, Gordon Highlanders, 1794:
Captain John Cameron, Fassafern.[71]

2nd Battalion, 78th, Ross-shire Highlanders, 1804:
Lieutenant William Cameron; and Ensign Alexander Cameron.

Donald Cameron of Lochiel also served as colonel in the Lochaber Fencibles (1799) and commanded the local militia, the 4th Inverness Regiment (1803). There is no reason why pipers would not have been part of both regiments.

In general, it goes almost without saying that an officer of or above the rank of captain, in a Highland regiment, took a piper or two with him for service in his regiment. The companies in Fraser's Highlanders who fought for Wolfe at Quebec had two pipers each, and there is no reason why pipers might not have been raised, privately or publicly, by any officer of or above the rank of ensign.

The strongly Jacobite nature of the chief and tacksmen of Lochiel is seen in the absence of Camerons from the officer list of the Black Watch regiment (43rd, then 42nd).[72] However, in the latter half of the eighteenth century, whether on the forfeited and factored estate or under Lochiel's Gaelic-speaking farm managers/tacksmen, it is fair to guess that piping was an important and an integral part of day-to-day life.

When Alexander Stewart heard Malcolm MacPherson play "Fhuair mi pòg 's laimh mo righ" (*sic*) in Glasgow city hall in January 1878, he said that the tune was the (ceòl mór) composition of "Ewen Macdhomhnuil Bhuidhe" (Ewan son of Yellow-haired Donald), a MacMillan from Glendessary and piper to Cameron of Lochiel. Stewart elaborated to explain that the tune had been inspired by the composer's seeing his chief kiss Prince Charles Edward's hand at a levée held at Holyrood palace a day or two after the victory at Gladsmuir (the Highlanders' name for Prestonpans).[73] The composing attribution may be incorrect, but it would be premature to challenge the name of Lochiel's piper in 1745. The MacMillans of old had fallen under the political power of the Camerons of Lochiel and only ceased to be a major presence on Lochiel's estate when they were cleared off in 1804.[74]

Somerled MacMillan's genealogies of the nearby Murlaggan MacMillans in the eighteenth century do not mention a Ewan MacMillan as such but give a Captain Ewen McGilvaile, alias Buchanan, of Murlaggan and his brother John, both sons of John, ninth of Murlaggan, a MacMillan. All were active Jacobites in Prince Charles's army. Both sons, John and Ewen, were bodyguards to Lochiel, and Ewen was in Glasgow with Prince Charles. Ewen was killed at Culloden and John injured. Murlaggan lies on the north side of Loch Arkaig not far east of Glendessary, and the MacMillans in Glendessary sprang from the Murlaggan stock.[75] In 1788 there were four MacMillan tenants in Glendessary, soon to be gone from the old home. Two went to Glengarry in Ontario in 1802 in the major pre-emptive emigration, and two moved to Camaghael near Corpach, where, according to Somerled Mac-Millan, Lochiel deposited those whose farms he wanted cleared. Of the Camaghael transplants one was Angus Ban, son of Ewen Ban, son of Donald, son of John Og, son of John, son of Duncan, son of Alan, son of Ewen MacMillan in Glendessary (the last being a younger son of Ewen, second of Murlaggan).[76] This is the only fair-haired Ewen, son of Donald, in Glendessary, from MacMillan's work, who might answer as having been Lochiel's piper in 1745–46, that is, if the piper wasn't the Captain Ewen McGilvaile, alias Buchanan, of Murlaggan, mentioned above. The other Ewen Ban MacMillan in MacMillan's text was the foster parent of the famous John Cameron (son of Fassafern) who died a colonel in the 79th at Quatre Bras.[77]

Glendessary is the northerly of two glaciated mountain glens whose rivers, the Dessary and the Pean, drain eastwards into Loch Arkaig. Passes westward to Loch Morar and Loch Nevis are rugged and difficult. Both places once supported many Highland families, and Glendessary, sequestered as it is and obviously no farmer's paradise, is mentioned twice in connection with bagpiping. In the first instance, a ceòl mór tune called "Fàilte Tighearna Oig Dhungallain" (The Young Laird of Dungallan's Salute)[78] celebrates a young laird whose estate was part of Glendessary.[79] The second, in two parts, is presented as fiction in the monthly publication *Teachdaire Gaelach* (Gaelic Messenger), by Reverend Norman MacLeod between 1830 and 1832. The two stories deal with Fionnladh Pìobaire's memories of the last Oidhche Challuinn (New Year's Eve) and Bliadhna Ur (New Year's Day), held in Glendessary.[80] Although couched in the warmth of reflection, Reverend MacLeod's observations of Glendessary are the nearest thing to a nostalgic honesty about a Lochiel tack before the collapse there of the old Gaelic agricultural system in 1802–4. They touch quite nearly on piping.

Since many pieces of ceòl mór have been published under different titles, it is noteworthy that the Dungallan tune at least retains the name Dungallan in the title. In the Campbell Canntaireachd of 1797, it is given as "Dungalan's Lament," while in Angus MacKay's *Collection* it becomes "The Young Laird of Dungallon's Salute."[81] So much for any distinction between a lament and a salute.

The importance of the Fionnladh Pìobaire stories lies in the fact that Reverend Norman MacLeod apparently was writing about a place and people he knew about personally. Although he was born in the Morvern manse, in Argyleshire (2 December 1783), he had family ties with Glendessary[82] so it is perfectly likely that he visited relatives in Glendessary before the clearance of 1804 and that Fionnladh Pìobaire was an actual character. The partial genealogy that follows does not reveal the connection with Glendessary, and to date MacLeod's "tree" referred to in endnote 82 has not been

Chart 5   Partial Genealogy of Reverend Norman MacLeod, Caraid nan Gàidheal

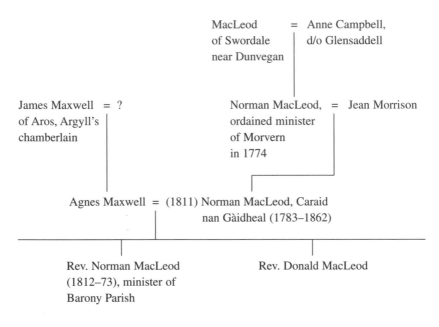

available for scrutiny. However, a valuation roll for Argyllshire shows that Glendessary Camerons persisted as landholders in Morvern into the 1770s (see below).

Reverend Norman MacLeod, minister of Morvern, was a typical Church of Scotland minister of the Moderate period in the second half of the eighteenth century; he enjoyed folk music and fiddled for the Reel dancing of his children in the manse at Fiunary. He died in 1824 having fathered sixteen children. He was also the grandfather of Reverend Roderick (Rory) MacLeod, minister of Bracadale, the man who discouraged traditional music and dancing in Skye[83] in the first half of the nineteenth century.[84] Dr Duncan Fraser reported that Rory said gleefully to one of his elders one evening, "Well John, I have burnt the last Bagpipe (or fiddle) in the parish. What do you think of that man? what do you think of that?"[85] (Note: The people of Bracadale were by no means all Presbyterians. On 24 June 1838 an Episcopal church was consecrated at Caroy, in the Reverend Rory's Presbyterian parish of Bracadale, and people were confirmed on the same day. In Scotland generally the Episcopal church had many prominent priests and members, including Reverend John Skinner [1721–1807] and William Marshall, the violinist/composer, who enjoyed and fostered tradition.)[86]

Whether or not Reverend Norman MacLeod was closely related to the Camerons in Glendessary, what he wrote about the old piper (his last name was not given but he flourished in story at least until the age of steamships plying between Glasgow and Loch Morar) is valuable in outlining a picture of the average Gaelic tack in the last days of middle-class Gaelic consciousness on the Lochiel estate.

Norman MacLeod best emphasized the warmth and friendship that had once brought tacksman, tenant, and poor Gael together in Finlay the Piper's two letters dealing with New Year's Eve and New Year's Day. He also hinted that Glendessary kept a hereditary piping family going back to long before Culloden.

A Theachdaire Ghaolaich ... B'e m'athair-sa pìobaire Ghlinne-deiseiridh, mar a bha 'athair fhéin roimhe. Faodaidh mi 'ràdh gu-n d'rugadh sinn 'n ar pìobairean; cha-n 'eil mac a rugadh dhomh mu-n gann a théid e bhàrr na cìche, nach glac feadan cho nàdurra 's a thogas am meann ris a' chreig ... Ràinig sinn an tigh-mòr ... Choinnich maighdeanan an teaghlaich sinn le dos de ribeinean air son na pìoba ... "Séid suas a Phìobaire," ars' am Maor ... Chluich m'athair "Fàilt' a' Phrionnsa;" oir ged nach robh duine 's an rìoghachd a bu rìoghaile na Fear Ghlinne-deiseiridh do'n teaghlach a bh'air a' chathair, bha bàigh aige ris a' phort so; agus is minic a chunnaic mi e 'sileadh nan deur ri cluinntinn a' chiùil nuallanaich sin, a bhrosnaich na daoin' o'n d'thàinig e ... Mar tha'n caidreamh agus an dlùth eòlas so eadar uaislean agus ìslean a' dol á cleachdadh tha modh agus sìobhaltachd a' fàgail na tìre; agus 'an àite an fhleasgaich mhodhail, shuairce, aoidheil, dhàicheil, a b'àbhaist duinn 'fhaicinn ... cha-n fhaic sinn ach an dubh-bhalach trom cheannach, gun mhodh, gun suairceas ... Fionnladh Mac-Aonghais.

(Beloved Messenger ... My father was piper of Glendessary, as was his father before him. I may say that we were born pipers; there isn't a son of mine who though scarcely off the nipple won't seize a chanter as naturally as a goat takes to the rocks ... We reached the big house ... The maidens of the family met us with bunches of ribbons for the pipe ... "Strike up Piper," says the steward ... My father played "The Prince's Salute"; for though there was no one more loyal in the kingdom to the reigning monarch than the Laird of Glendessary, he had an affection for this tune; and often I saw him shed a tear listening to that flooding music, that enspirited his ancestors ... As that familiarity and close bondedness between gentry and folk is falling out of fashion so respect and courtesy are leaving the land; and instead of the mannerly, polite, hospitable, dignified young man we used to know ... we see backward louts, without manners, lacking class.)[87]

Fionnladh Pìobaire (Finlay the Piper) is given only as Fionnladh mac Aonghuis, Finlay son of Angus, and Angus, according to Finlay, was the piper of Glendessary (perhaps Glendessary's piper) like his father and pater-

nal grandfather.[88] However, the writer places Finlay's father Angus in time
by saying of his [Angus's] preparations for that "oidhche Challuinn mu
dheireadh a chunnaic mi ann an teaghlach Ghlinne-deiseiridh, anns a' bhail'
ud thall" (last New Year's Eve that I [Finlay] saw in the Glendessary family,
in that far-off place),[89] "Thog m'athair air mu àird' an fheasgair, 'n a làn
éideadh Gàidhealach, agus claidheamh 'chinn airgid air a chrios, a thug
e fhéin a mach latha chuil-fhodair" (My father prepared himself at the
height of the evening, in full Highland habit, with his silver-hilted
broadsword on its belt, which he took out on Culloden day).[90] Finlay and
Angus may have been the actual names of Glendessary's pipers; omitting
their last name may have been disguise enough, if actually the writer sought
any.

Certainly, in the stories and elsewhere in the dialogues there is further evidence of the truth of the general presentation of Finlay the Piper as
spokesman for Gaelic tradition. In a letter from Glasgow to his wife, Finlay
describes his steamship trip to Glasgow and how he piped for Red Alexander of Coll (Alasdair Ruadh). I have no idea how many of Caraid nan Gàidheal's readers would have known of the linkage, but Morvern and Coll had
very strong marriage links with Glendessary, as the Chart 6 shows.

That three sisters of Alexander Cameron, fifth of Glendessary, married
brothers of Alexander MacLean, fifteenth of Coll, explains why MacLeod's
story has Fionnladh Pìobair' meet Red "Alasdair ruadh Mac-an-Abraich,
Tighearna Chola" (Red Alexander MacLean, Laird of Coll)[91] on the steamer *A' Mhaighdean-Mhorairneach* (The Morar Maid) on the journey from the
mouth of the narrows of Loch Morar to the Broomielaw.[92]

In 1745 the Camerons of Morvern were numerous enough to be known as
such. Cameron of Glendessary and Charles MacLean of Drimnin were the
only two landholders in Morvern. Both men held land from the duke of
Argyll, and both the Glendessary and the Drimnin people in Morvern were
singled out, particularly for Cumberland's pre-Culloden policy of destroying
property in early March 1746 (Culloden was fought on 16 April).[93] An order
from Cumberland to General John Campbell of Mamore stated that he
should "sweep in every thing" in Sunart and Morvern. This was thoroughly
carried out in Morvern under the guns of Captain Duff's HMS *Terror* on 10
March 1746 by a Lieutenant Lindsay with fifty men from the *Terror* and a
detachment of the Argyll-shire Militia under Captain Campbell. Four hundred homes were destroyed and several barns; beasts were "driven" and one
person was killed and another wounded. The duke of Argyll's reaction to this
devastation on his estate betrayed no sorrow; he managed only to regret that
it had been conducted by General Campbell's Argyll-shire Militia and not by
regular soldiers from Fort William. Mamore knew that "Cameron of
Glendisserie" was not in the rebellion, but the destruction of the property of
the Camerons raised by Glendessary's sister Jean was unmitigated by such

Chart 6   The Camerons of Glendessary and Dungallan and the MacLeans of Coll and Kinlochaline

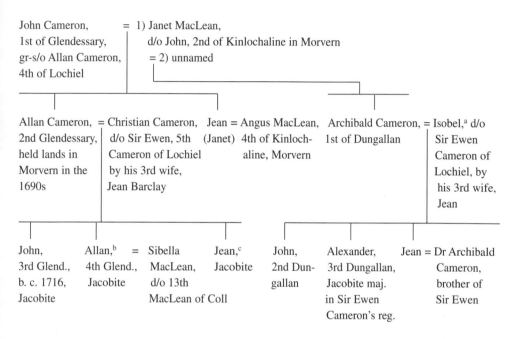

[a] Contradicted elsewhere.

[b] Captain Allan Cameron of Glendessary, JP, between 1761 and 1771, held land in Morvern valued at £746.1.0 (Scots), and in Ardgour valued at £133.6.0 (Scots). He succeeded his brother c. 1758. The bankrupt estate was sold in 1776 for £8,270.[94]

[c] Mrs Jean Cameron, daughter of Allan Cameron of Glendessary, died in 1772. Some time between 1761 and 1771 she held land in Morvern valued at £35.11.0 (Scots), and some time before 1750 she obtained a wadset of Isle of Canna from Lauchlan MacLean of Kingerloch (d. 1756). She also owned a property in Lanarkshire called Mount Cameron. (This Jean Cameron is given elsewhere, wrongly, as daughter of a Hugh Cameron of Glendessary. The above data are from Robert Chambers's *History of the Rebellion of 1745–6,* citing a pamphlet entitled "The life of Dr Archibald Cameron" [London, 1753].)[95]

Note: According to the Forfeited Estates records (PRO E68/41/1–43), Glendessary, or possibly a part of it, was held on wadset c. 1747 by an Alexander McPhie.[96]

a minor consideration. What's more, Mamore is on record as having had a plan to banish all the rebels in Morvern.[97]

The degree to which Mamore's eviction plan was effected is unknown, but Camerons persisted in Morvern. The Glendessary family may well have retained a farm on the duke of Argyll's Morvern estate long after Culloden.[98]

Norman MacLeod also used Fionnladh Pìobaire as a prominent fictional character in his *Còmhraidhean* (Dialogues). Finlay the Piper and many other

kenspeckle folk of a beloved older society illustrate the old Gaelic community life before it was overwhelmed by newer ways and imperatives. Fionnladh
Mac-Aonghais played both ceòl mór and dance music, and no matter how
much or little MacLeod knew of piping he was at pains to describe a rich piping tradition in his chosen glen on Cameron of Lochiel's estate. (Somerled
MacMillan said that Glendessary was cleared and sold in 1804.)[99]

MacLeod put in Fionnladh Pìobaire's mouth a general observation about
piping and several versions of what the author felt was the cause of its
decline. This was the disappearance of the old Gaelic middle class, the
prerequisite for membership in which, after the accident of birth, had been
the essentially Christian considerateness for the lower orders. "(Tha) là
na pìobaireachd seachad. Tha na tighearnan mòra suarach uimpe.
Tha'm bladaire ronnach a's mò 's an dùthaich cho taitneach leo ri
Mac-Cruimein." (Piping's day is gone. The important gentlefolk don't give
a fig for it. To them the meanest slavering flatterer in the country is as good
as MacCrimmon.)[100]

Piping survived of course and probably more strongly than the Reverend
MacLeod realized. However, when he was writing (between 1830 and
1832), he perceived a distinctively memorable piping past that was fading
away very rapidly, and he decently lamented. The long-drawn-out war with
France must have seemed a societal and cultural watershed. Angus Mac-
Kay's *Collection* (1838) had not yet been published when Finlay's two letters to Teachdaire Gaelach appeared, but when it was, its success can only
have emphasized for the traditionalist how alarmingly the older traditional
piping, with its oral transmission, had slipped. A Gaelic secret had been
exposed. In 1826 the annual competitions in Edinburgh began to be held
every three years, a depressing sign that confirmed the weakening gentlemanly interest, albeit at this increasingly artificial level of tradition.

What saddened MacLeod was that the old Gaelic piping world was shorn
of its naturally evolved, much-needed support element. In his opinion, the
spontaneous gentlemanly patronage of Gaelic-speaking tacksmen living
among their people, their calling for the piper's and the fiddler's music at
céilidhean and festivals, their dancing to it, their singing Gaelic songs,
telling stories, had died away.[101]

MacLeod's writing about the last New Year's Day (Oidhche Challuinn) at
Glendessary's home (no date inferrable) show without doubt that Glendessary and his family deliberately enjoyed the old Gaelic tradition. "Och!
och! b'e sin tigh a'mhànrain, 's na h-aoidheachd, ge fliuch fuar an nochd."
(Och, och, that was the house of melodies, and hospitality, although wet and
cold the night.)[102] MacLeod had known what he felt were the last days of
that Gaelic world in which piping flourished in almost all rural communities,
fostered and enjoyed by, and important to, gentleman and ordinary Gael
alike.

While Somerled MacMillan wrote that little was known of Alexander, fifth of Glendessary (b. 1760–70?), and hinted that he had a son William (who got the lease of Murlaggan in 1826 from Sir Alexander Cameron of Inverailort), Caraid nan Gàidheal in his stories mentions a name. In his telling of Finlay's memories of the last New Year's Day shinty match in Glendessary, MacLeod gives a name for his last heir to Glendessary: "Ràinig sinn Guala-nan-càrn, far an robh na h-uaislean againn fhéin r'ar coinneachadh; agus mu-n robh 'fhios againn c'àit' an robh sinn, cò 'chuir e fhéin air ar ceann ach Dòmhnull òg againn fhéin – Oighre'n teaghlach – " (We reached the Corner of the Cairns, where the gentlefolk were to meet us; and before we knew where we were, who put himself at our head but our own Young Donald – heir of the family –). The name, which may be fictional, is the same as that of Lochiel the clearer, but the text describes a local Cameron, not the chief.[103]

MacLeod's writings of Glendessary give the names of several pieces of ceòl mór that Finlay the Piper played. But "Litir o Fhionnladh Pìobaire, mu'n bhliadhn' uir" (A Letter from Finlay the Piper about the New Year) describes Finlay as a dance-music piper also. After the New Year's Day shinty game in Glendessary, Finlay's services were sought for the dancing: "'[C]'àite am bheil na dannsairean? Séid suas Ruidhle-thulachain, Fhionnlaidh.' Thòisich an dannsadh, agus bha 'ghrian a' tèurnadh sìos gu ìochdar Mhuile, agus seachd air Barra mu-n do dhealaich sinn." ("Where are the dancers? Strike up The Reel of Tulloch, Finlay." The dancing began, and the sun was sinking down to Nether Mull, and past Barra before we parted.)[104]

I am inclined to believe that this sketch of Gleann-deiseiridh was drawn from real life. When MacLeod described the older, vanishing Gaelic way of life, there is no reason not to suppose that he worked from fond boyhood memories, perhaps making composites of characters he had known.[105] When he wrote about the glen and its people in the early 1830s, almost thirty years after it had been cleared, he felt a gentle obligation to write what was at the least a touchingly oblique obituary for some people he knew or knew of, veiling in only the slightest of ways, if at all, his descriptions of the old, warm village life that he himself had known.[106] MacLeod described, in throw-away fashion, a piping heritage that continued unbroken in Glendessary from the early eighteenth century.

A last and isolated note on piping in Glendessary comes from the dimension of faerie. In *Superstitions of the Highlands and Islands of Scotland*, John Gregorson Campbell retold the story of how a "Fairy Carlin" gave MacCrimmon a brindled chanter that gave its owner unrivalled, magical piping ability. Without it the MacCrimmons may have been good but never great. According to the story, it fell into the hands of the laird of Dungallon, who gave it to his piper, whose name was MacIntyre. This is the only reference to a MacIntyre piper in Dungallon, if not the only reference to MacIntyres living on the Cameron estate.[107] Campbell said that the brindled chanter turned up later at another old Cameron farm in southern Lochaber, at Callart.

There is an interesting stray glimpse of traditional musical life, between 1790 and 1792, in neighbouring Glen Pean, which is on the Lochiel estate south of Glendessary. Allan MacMillan employed as a tutor for his family of nine the young scholar Ewen MacLachlan (1775–1822). MacLachlan went to MacMillan's one merkland of Glenpeanmore from a tutoring position with Cameron of Clunes. While at the MacMillan home, he took fiddle lessons from a man who was by profession a piper and who visited occasionally, not from Glendessary but from Morar to the west. Here, too, one finds the old connection with Morvern: MacLachlan's employer, Allan MacMillan, was the oldest son of Ewen MacMillan and his wife, who was a daughter of Donald Cameron of Peighinn a' Ghobhainn (Pennygowan) in Morvern.

CHAPTER THREE

Piping in MacLean Country

In some contrast to the case of the Camerons, piping in Protestant MacLean country, particularly in the Inner Hebridean islands of Mull, Coll, and Muck and in mainland Ardgour, is quite well recorded, in the typically informal way, in the second half of the eighteenth century. Neither is there reason to think that Morvern did not contain pipers in the 1740s and '50s, although an idea of them seems only to be deduceable from later records of the various Argyll-shire Fencible regiments that included Morvern people. To add to that, overall in MacLean country, the presence of the Conduiligh Rankins, pipers of long standing, and the existence into the 1760s of their piping "college" at Kilbrennan on Loch Tuath in Mull point to deep-rootedness of piping among the MacLeans.

In 1745 the MacLean political landscape showed the beginnings of a Jaco-bite/Hanoverian cleavage. By that year the old MacLean holdings in Mull, Morvern, and Tiree belonged to the Campbell dukes of Argyll, after a long period of resistance and contention by the MacLeans going back to the late seventeenth century. Notwithstanding the MacLean chief's being a chief only in name, the older kinship and other traditional loyalties were still common and powerful.[1] Like that of the Keppoch MacDonells, the MacLeans' history was Tory and Jacobite. Many of the MacLeans of Mull and most of the Morvern people,[2] living on what had been traditional MacLean lands, were dyed-in-the-wool Jacobites and had fought at Culloden for King James. There they suffered, and their leader, Charles MacLean of Drimnin in Morvern, was killed. They also lost property in 1746 to the systematic and legal rapacity of their almost understandably vengeful superior, Archibald Campbell, third duke of Argyll (1682–1761).[3]

Just how menacingly Jacobite the MacLeans were believed to have been is seen in the fact that their French-born and domiciled chief, Sir Hector MacLean of Duart, twenty-first chief of the clan (1703–50), when he came to Scotland, was watched and wanted before the rising began. In June of

1745, in a pre-emptive legal abduction, he was handed over to the Edinburgh legal authorities by his Edinburgh landlord and then was taken to London, where he was restrained until 1747 (the same year that Cameron of Dungallan was set free).[4]

Elsewhere on what had been the old MacLean estates, MacLean of Brolas in the south of Mull, the sixteenth MacLean of Lochbuy, and MacLean of Coll were loyal to King George, and although Coll and Brolas were prepared to take up arms in the Argyll Militia in the loyalist cause, they were not given the chance to do so by the militia's commanding officer, Major-General John Campbell of Mamore. (Mamore, under Wade, was the commander of government forces in the West Highlands.)[5] On the surface of it there obviously was little risk in resisting inducements to join the Jacobite army, since any appeal to Argyll could only have benefited the appellant. On the other hand, those MacLeans who chose to fight for King James, like the Catholic Jacobites, had a lot to fight for and a great deal to lose; a loss meant persecution and great hardship. Writing of Morvern, Major-General John Campbell noted on 7 June 1746 that "this country which is chiefly the duke of Argyll's property is intirely in my power and I have a scheme of banishing all the rebellious inhabitants of Morvern so as to have a new set of people here."[6] (A kinder attitude was shown, however. The "Valuation Roll for Argyllshire" indicates that in 1771 Allan MacLean JP, of Drimnin, son of Charles [d. 1746], held land in Morvern valued at £185.14.0. He married firstly a daughter of Donald MacLean of Brolas and secondly a daughter of Lauchlan MacLean, younger of Lochbuie. Allan was succeeded in Drimnin by his son Charles.)

So, from the 1690s, when their lands slipped out of their hands, the MacLeans were not in the strongest position to champion cultural traditionalism in Mull. From around 1692 the heartland of MacLean territory, Mull, along with Morvern and Tiree, had been taken over by Campbell of Argyll (patronymically Mac Cailein Mór[7] [son of Big Colin]) who had bought up MacLean's extensive debts. Among other things this meant that Archibald Campbell, first duke of Argyll (Campbell chief 1685–1703) and John Campbell, second duke (chief 1703–1743), if they had wanted, could have made sweeping changes in the old MacLean system of patronage of musicians and anyone else. The dukes of Argyll, however, in the 1685–1715 period, appear not to have been enemies of Gaelic tradition. The Jacobite political leanings in 1715 of the earl of Breadalbane, Argyll's relative, show remnant political uncertainty in a clan that was soon to become resolutely Whig and in favour of the Hanoverian settlement. In the inter-risings period, however, the second duke, based in Inveraray on Loch Fyne, began to shift from the traditional kin-based awarding of agricultural tacks to the revolutionary economic system that began to spur the Gaelic diaspora from Argyll from the 1730s, but MacLean musicians on the land, however much they may have been discomfited, appear not to have suffered critical dislocation.[8] (How many of the duke of Argyll's tenants had fallen into the category "kindly tenants" is unknown, but on the Argyll estates, as later on most Highland estates when economics dictated the tenanting of land, this category of tenant disappeared as an anachronism.)[9]

THE CONDUILIGH RANKIN PIPERS

On 22 April 1697 at Taymouth in eastern Perthshire, John Campbell, first earl of Breadalbane, approved the following: "Item payed to quantiliane McCraingie McLeans pyper for one complete year as prentyce fie for the Litle pyper before he was sent to McCrooman, the soume of £160."[10] (A modern interpretation suggests: "Item, paid to Conduiligh Mac Fhrangaich [Rankin], MacLean's piper, for one complete year, as apprentice fee for the Little Piper before he [the Little Piper] was sent to MacCrimmon, the sum of £160.")

John Campbell, eleventh of Glenorchy and first earl of Breadalbane, had been a Jacobite in Marr's rebellion in 1715 and did not take his cultural lead from Argyll. Pipers are associated with both the eastern and western parts of his estate in the eighteenth and nineteenth centuries, and a number of these are important to our knowledge of the preliterate classical form. In the case of the first earl, the making of his piper entailed early tuition with Conduiligh Rankin and then MacCrumen training, which the piping fraternity, probably correctly, still equates with master training. This Breadalbane Campbell cleaving to tradition may have had some minor influence in the duke of Argyll's tolerance of MacLean tradition on his more westerly estate.[11]

The old MacLean system of patronage in Mull had matured over the centuries under the MacLeans of Duart (the Mull-based chief), and in 1715 a substantial part of the MacLean middle class sided with King James. Condullie Rankin, the chief's piper (almost certainly the "quantiliane McCraingie McLeans pyper" of the quote above), is believed to have joined the Jacobites in 1715 and fought at Sheriffmuir. By 1745, however, the MacLeans were under no illusions about their legal relationship to Campbell of Argyll and were more hopeless of restoration than before, Breadalbane was loyal to King George II, and all the powerful Campbell families were Hanoverians.[12] Major-General John Campbell raised 2,776 men from his cousin's, the duke of Argyll's, estate in March 1745 to fight for the duke of Cumberland. There is no evidence that MacLean's piper, Conduiligh Rankin or not, was an active participant in the Jacobite rising of 1745, although it would have been out of character for Drimnin not to have had a piper among his men.

Turning from Mull to other MacLean homelands, one discovers that although Argyll managed to obtain land in the north and south of Coll and wanted the rest as well, the traditional MacLean owners clung determinedly to the largest part of the island until the middle of the nineteenth century. Muck, which was the holding of a cadet of the Coll MacLean family, was lost too but not until 4 June 1857 when Hugh MacLean of Coll "sold, alienated and disponed to Thomas Anthony Swinburne [Lieutenant RN, resident at Eilean Shona], his heirs and assignees whomsoever heritably and irredeemably All and haill the six merk land of the Island of Muck."[13] Hugh MacLean (1782–1861), the last laird of Coll (1828–1856), who in 1857 appears to have been living in London, was rid of Coll one year before disposing of Muck. Thus the island of Muck was the last MacLean holding to slip away, and consequently it was, perhaps, the last MacLean refuge of traditional piping. Apart from information relating to Duncan Rankin, the piper from Muck mentioned below, not much is known about Muck's importance to piping, but John Lorn MacDougall includes a number of Muck people in his *History of Inverness County* and a little of the flavour of Muck society comes across.

Lauchlin MacLean ("Lachlinn Mac Alasdair," b. 1763) emigrated to Cape Breton in 1826 with his family, including his married son Donald Ban (d. 1874), in a typically extended-family emigration. Lauchlin, a "ground-officer in Rum for thirty years,"[14] was married to a Mary MacKay, and the family settled at Foot Cape in Inverness County. According to MacDougall, Lauchlin was son of John, son of Lachlan, son of Hector, and either one of the last two named was "first of Muck."[15] The MacLeans were Presbyterians and one of their descendants, Sandy MacLean, Foot Cape, one of the best known of Inverness County fiddlers, began his musical career as a piper. Among the other Muck people to come in Inverness County were three families that settled at East Lake Ainslie. These included three MacKinnon brothers who came out in 1820. Piping was popular in this family, particularly in the persons of Big Farquhar MacKinnon, the son of one of the immigrants, and his (Big Farquhar's) nephew Little Farquhar.[16]

As for Coll, much more is known about piping there, and it is true to say that the island's place in the story of piping has been underrated.

As elsewhere in Gaelic Scotland, piping appears to have continued uninterrupted after Culloden in traditional MacLean country, in Mull, Coll, Muck, and Ardgour. What part the Conduiligh Rankin pipers played in the 1745 Jacobite rising is not known, but their teaching establishment in Mull did not close until the 1760s. There has never been any suggestion that the family was coerced by anyone into shutting the college. Argyll, if he was interested in treading on the piping tradition, appears to have allowed, or used, economic forces to govern whatever changes he anticipated in Mull. If this state of affairs is an unusual attachment to piping by the Rankins under "Luchd nam beul fiara" (Folk of the twisted mouth, as John MacCodrum called the, to him, hated Campbells of Argyll), then there are reasons.[17]

Piping has been believed by at least one student of the pipers to the MacLean chiefs in Duart to have originated some time around 1300 in Mull.[18] The eminent piping family there went by the surname Rankin and the patronymic Conduiligh. Although there is no evidence of any such antiquity, a poem cited by Neil Rankin Morrison[19] does indicate that piping thrived in Mull when the old Scotch links with Ireland were still strong. This could mean almost any time up until the late sixteenth century. In any case, the proto Conduiligh of the patronymic is said to have been an abbot at Lismore (Cuduiligh, son of Raingee), who lived in the eleventh century.[20] The Cuduilighs/Rankins were conscious of their middle-class status in MacLean country. Of all the prominent Scotch piping families, the Rankins are unique in that lore puts them into a wider British piping picture. They are linked competitively, in story, with Northumberland pipers at some undefined pre-eighteenth-century period.[21]

The first Conduiligh piper to MacLean of Duart is said to have been Cu-duiligh mac Raing. Whyte said that this individual was trained in Ireland and was the first to train bagpipers in the school of music he founded at Kilbrennan, Mull. The tradition of running a bagpiping college or institution of some kind in Mull lasted until past the middle of the eighteenth century.[22] Samuel Johnson said that the institution "expired about sixteen years ago" (i.e., c. 1757).[23] The Frenchman Barthélémy Faujas de Saint Fond, who travelled in Mull in 1784, was less precise but suggested about the same time.[24] The Rankins were definitely a socially prominent family. Their prominence in eighteenth-century Mull society, and later, and into the nineteenth century, in Coll society, springs from the fact that the abbot Cuduiligh mac Fhraing, according to Whyte, was a great-great-grandfather of the first MacLean chief.[25]

Moving beyond the early period, one can gain a better view of the Rankin pipers in the clearer light of two other observations about piping, Joseph MacDonald's (c. 1761) and Dr Neil Ross's (1925). Joseph MacDonald, renowned for not mentioning the names of pipers or tunes in his "Compleat Theory," included only the names of two centres of piping in that manuscript, Skye and Mull.[26] No one has had any difficulty accepting Skye as the principal piping centre, but Mull has been an irrational challenge to modern preconceived ideas, which dwell upon MacCrimmon primacy. (Neil Morrison was at pains to rectify this imbalance.)[27]

Dr Neil Ross, a Skyeman, was one of those Highlanders who argued in the twentieth century that the MacCrimmons of Skye were paramount. He stated unequivocally that all the other piping colleges in the Highlands, including the Rankins', were "minor offshoots of the Macrimmon College."[28] Whether or not he is correct, Ross's other stand is significant to an understanding of the Rankins' endurance as pipers and teachers in Mull. Ross, like John Johnston (from Coll) before him, was categorical in claiming that the Western Isles were the heartland of *piobaireachd*, the Gael's classical music.[29] He said that the only eastern piece of ceòl mór was the tune "Craigellachie," long associated with the Grants, a Strathspey tribe. Even if the names of tunes nowadays are a poor indicator of composer and address of composer, Ross's opinion rings true in that it underlines the importance of inner Hebridean piping, including the Rankins'. And yet the Long Island, with which few pieces of classical pipe music are associated, does not fit well into Ross's hastily concluded theory, and neither does the sizeable contribution of the Blind Piper of Gairloch in Wester Ross.

A much earlier published reference to a Rankin piper is found in John MacCodrum's song "Dìomoladh Pìoba Dhòmhnuill Bhàin" (The Dispraising of Donald Ban's Pipe), which is found in the Maclagan Collection of Gaelic Manuscripts (1755–1803) at Glasgow University.[30] MacCodrum (Iain mac Fhearchair, c. 1700–1779)[31] lived and called on his muse in some obscurity until he came to the attention of the young Gaelic revivalist Sir James MacDonald (d. 1766) and was made his official bard in 1763; then MacCodrum's career took off. "Dìomoladh" is a ten-section song debunking what MacCodrum considered the ludicrously overblown flattery by John MacPhail of an untalented local North Uist piper called Dòmhnul Bàn MacAulay. MacCodrum seems, from his use of what look like canntaireachd vocables in the song, to have been fairly well acquainted with piping and pipers. In his derision, he drew attention to the truly excellent pipers of the time whom John MacPhail had overlooked in his elaborate local praises of the inept Dòmhnul Bàn. In order of appearance in the MacCodrum's song are the pipers he considered pre-eminent, "MacCruimein, Con-duiligh, is Teàrlach."[32] Although he doesn't specify which MacCrimmon, MacCodrum's unequivocal opinion, taken from the song, was that "Air na pìobaire-an uile / b'e MacCruimein an rìgh" (Of all the pipers MacCrimmon was the king).[33]

In his notes to the text, William Matheson confidently stated that the Mac-Crimmon involved was Patrick Mor, although the text gives no clue.[34] Matheson was in as little doubt that Teàrlach was Charles MacArthur, piper to MacDonald of the Isles, and he seems to have assumed that Con-duiligh was the first name, rather than the patronymic, of the Rankin piper whom Mac-Codrum praised effusively.[35]

There is no reason to think that MacCodrum was not referring to pipers living at the time (c. 1760), and since there were probably three generations of Rankin pipers to MacLean of Duart living and active, MacCodrum may have used the term "Conduiligh" patronymically to refer to the son or grandson of Condullie Rankin, the veteran of Sheriffmuir in 1715. Although Condullie himself, if alive, was probably at least ninety by the time MacCodrum wrote the song, the poet may have been deferring fondly to his piping hey-day.

There are two genealogies of the Rankin piping family, Matheson's, which repeats the one by Reverend A. MacLean Sinclair published in 1903 in the Nova Scotian newspaper *MacTalla*[36] (and contemporaneously in TGSI), and Henry Whyte's (Fionn's), which is found in *The Rankins – Pipers to the MacLeans of Duart, and later to the MacLeans of Coll*.[37] I should note that MacLean Sinclair was a grandson of MacLean of Coll's bard, John MacLean (1787–1848), who emigrated to Nova Scotia in 1819.

Matheson's/Sinclair's genealogy gives Neil Rankin, the last of the Con-duiligh pipers (piper to Coll), as Nial mac Eachain 'ic Eoghain 'ic Eachain 'ic Conduiligh (Neil, son of Hector, son of Ewen, son of Hector, son of Conduiligh). The Henry Whyte Scottish version gives Neil as Nial mac Eoghain 'ic Eachain 'ic Conduiligh (Neil, son of Ewan, son of Hector, son of Conduiligh), noting that Neil had a brother Hector who didn't leave the traditional Mull home of the Rankin pipers, at Kilbrennan, until 1804. Whyte's version, which relies on information from a Mull descendant of the Condullie-Rankins, agrees more easily with the recorded facts and is the more credible. Where poetic lore is concerned, just inasmuch as Whyte's version makes it possible that MacCodrum could actually have been referring to Condullie Rankin himself, it is the more plausible genealogy. The Matheson-Sinclair version precludes this possibility because, as Matheson might have known, Neil Rankin can not have been born much later than 1734 to have two children listed as "of age" in the 1776 census of Coll, and this would give a plausible year of birth for his great-great-grandfather Condullie of 1654. This would have meant that he was sixty-one at the Battle of Sheriffmuir in 1715, and one hundred and six in 1760 when MacCodrum selected him for inclusion in the triad of top Gaelic pipers in the Highlands.

Whyte's Rankin genealogy was published by the Clan MacLean Association in Glasgow in 1907 under the heading "Prize Essay." He specified three of his sources: first (and formally acknowledged), "a lineal descendant of these Rankin pipers, Mr Conndullie Rankin Morison, Dervaig, Mull"[38] (a man whom Sorley MacLean described as "that great Mull seanchaidh"), and, in the body of the essay, the "late John Johnston, Coll," and "Mr John Johnston, Coll." The two John Johnstons almost certainly were father and son.[39] What's more, elsewhere, through the agency of John Johnston, the son (1836–1921), intense glimpses of and opinions about piping in Coll, plus some ceòl mór unique to the MacLeans, add controversially to the wider subject of piping. Coll piping information, as John Johnston knew and told it, is still difficult for many to graft onto accepted piping thought. (Henry Whyte's knowledge of Coll piping as found also in *The Martial Music of the Clans* [1904] probably awakened Seton Gordon's interest in John Johnston as a tradition bearer; see below.)

This attitude towards John Johnston's views is perversely thrawn in view of Joseph MacDonald's observation that Mull was one of piping's centres around 1760. If the last Rankin piper, Neil, had any influence on Coll piping, which surely he must have, having spent at least thirty years there as a piper according to Whyte, then the least that should be expected of scholarship is open-mindedness in face of John Johnston the son's feisty opinions on piping.

James Logan overlooked the Rankins in his book *The Scottish Gaël,* and the ineptitude of the writer or writers of the introductory notes in Angus MacKay's *Collection of Ancient Piobaireachd* (1838), true to form, is clearly evident in the Rankin section. This is probably no coincidence. According to Roderick Cannon's *A Bibliography of Bagpipe Music* (1980), the authorities responsible for the British Library catalogue accept James Logan's claim to the authorship of "Account of the Hereditary Pipers" and the "Historical and Traditional Notes." Logan inscribed "by James Logan" under both titles in his own copy of Angus MacKay's book, which has, since 1856, been in the possession of the British Library.[40] Logan, as the secretary of the Highland Society of London from 1835–1838, was intimately involved in the production of MacKay's famous book. The publishers were "Logan & Comp[y] Aberdeen, Inverness and Elgin."

In any case, the Rankin notes lead off with a confident rewording of Dr Samuel Johnson's wrong observation that the Rankins had been pipers to the MacLeans of Coll from time immemorial. A few truncated jottings about early Rankin genealogy, the naming of two of Conn Dauly's grandsons, and a sentence about the last member of the family to emigrate to Prince Edward Island, in 1820, are all that is offered. When held up against what a visit to Mull, or Coll, by a capable and interested researcher or journalist could have produced in the early or mid-1830s, these notes stand out as a major obstacle to knowledge about Highland bagpiping.

Samuel Johnson was wrong in saying that the Rankins were for generations hereditary pipers to Coll, but his book about his journey to the Highlands and Boswell's account of the same trip at least have been useful in showing beyond a doubt that the music of the bagpipes continued in Coll's patrimony during the hard times after Culloden. Also, from Henry Whyte's work and from the Nova Scotian MacLean Sinclair's (not to mention what Faujas de Saint Fond had to say on the subject), there is no argument but that Rankin pipers, piping, and formal piping tuition also continued in the old Mull heartland of the former MacLean estates throughout the eighteenth and into the nineteenth century.

Johnson's impact on specific, as opposed to general, piping knowledge was non-existent. In Skye he confessed that he could tell a drum from a trumpet and a bagpipe from a "guittar" but that was the extent of his knowledge of "musick." Unfortunately, neither he nor Boswell was interested enough to elicit readily available information about the structure of the music they were hearing, the techniques used in playing it, or even the names of tunes. However, Johnson was responsible for popularizing the notion of "hereditary" Highland pipers. This descriptive has been faithfully repeated ever since, often with mesmerizing and elevating effect, although in the eighteenth and nineteenth centuries most men did what their fathers did, from the tail-coated to the nicky-tammed levels of society.[41] From that earlier age when book publishing relied in many instances on upper-class patronage, the vaunted importance given to the "patronized" has clung also to piping and has relegated the everyday musician to unworthy status.

The English lexicographer's tour, and later the works of Walter Scott dealing with Gaelic Scotland, spawned countless other tours of the Highlands. Some retraced Johnson's footsteps, filling in gaps in his information and elaborating and clarifying what he had written, while others had quite different itineraries and perspectives. In the eighteenth century, none of them was much more studious regarding the intricacies of piping than Johnson, but in many of their inevitable tour books there are simple glimpses of pipers and piping in the Gaelic milieu that at least show where piping was popular and, at times, what its uses were. Johnson's (and Thomas Pennant's) interests in Gaelic Scotland legitimated those of others, and therefore, directly and indirectly, his few observations on the piper whose music he heard, say, in Coll have had some worthwhile effects in a world generally little interested in traditional folk music.

The piper Johnson heard in Coll in 1773 was Neil Rankin (Niall mac Eoghainn 'ic Eachuinn 'ic Connduiligh). He, like his ancestors, was a member of the old Gaelic middle class that claimed co-lateral descent from the originator of the MacLean clan in the late Middle Ages. Neil represented a departure from Rankin family tradition inasmuch as he was Coll's piper rather than Duart's, as his father, Hugh, and his grandfather, Hector, and their antecedents had been. The date of Neil's leaving the family farm at Kilbrennan is unknown, but his brother Hector, presumably also a piper, moved to his sister's in Greenock in 1804, a sad occasion which evoked the famous lines: "Tha'm dhìth, tha'm dhìth / Tha'm dhìth gu buileach, / Clann Duiligh 's a' phìob / Tha'm dhìth gu buileach" (My destruction, my failure, / My want is complete, / Clan Duiligh and the pipe / My want is complete).[42] Both of Whyte's informants, Condullie Rankin Morison in Dervaig, Mull, and John Johnston the son, who lived latterly at Totamore, Coll, were categorical in maintaining that Samuel Johnson was wrong in describing Coll's pipers as having for generations been Rankins of this family. One must therefore presume that younger Conduiligh sons did not stray to Coll from their Mull home, although a Duncan Rankin was piper to MacLean of Muck.[43]

Assuming that "children of age" mentioned in the Coll census of 1776 had reached twenty-one, then Neil Rankin's oldest child was born around 1754 and Neil Rankin himself probably around 1730.[44] This places his critical learning years as a novice piper in the 1740s. He also had three children who were described as "under age, Hugh, Condulli, and Janet," and the family included "[t]wo servant men and one girl ... given after those in the Castle at Breacacha."[45] Whyte's information (probably from Condullie Rankin Morison) was that Neil Rankin's wife, Catherine MacLean, was a great-granddaughter of Duncan MacLean, twelfth of Coll.[46] She was therefore first cousin once removed to the "Young Coll" whom Boswell and Johnson met in 1773 and his brother Alexander, the second last Coll (d. 1835). The piper's family lived at the best address on the island, at the chief's seat, Breacacha Castle, but the days of that privilege were on the verge of disappearing as will be seen in the case of the last of the Rankin pipers, Condullie, son of Neil (b. c. 1774).[47]

Whyte's informant said (or repeated Saint Fond in saying) that the Rankin college was on a par with the MacCrimmon college in Skye and that sometimes MacCrimmons actually attended Kilbrennan as pupils and that Rankins by times went to the MacCrimmon institution.[48] What has hitherto distinguished the MacCrimmon college is that the name and terms of tutelage of at least one of its pupils in the 1740s, David Fraser, were known beyond a doubt. (A number of others are candidates in the eighteenth century, including John MacKay, MacKenzie of Gairloch's piper; John MacIntyre, the earl of Breadalbane's "Litle pyper" [see below], in the seventeenth century; Duncan Rankin, of the Cuduiligh family; John MacKay, Raasay; Duncan MacMaster, Coll's piper in 1805; John Cumming, Sir James Grant's piper; and John MacGregor, son of Prince Charles's piper.) Something similar can be said of the Rankin pipers in Mull. Obviously the pupil that "quantiliane McCraingie" prepared and who then went on to "McCrooman" was one; the other was son of Robert the Smith.[49] By about 1760 Condullie Rankin Morison said that the college, at its dissolution, had about sixteen learners, but he named none.

Whyte (presumably citing local lore, since he did not mention McNeill's Small Isles census of 1765) expanded on the link between the Rankins and the MacCrimmons, noting that while at the MacCrimmon college Duncan Rankin had fallen in love with MacCrimmon's daughter Janet, a first-class piper. They were married while or before Rankin was piper to the laird of Muck and, according to Whyte, eventually settled on Coll at Grisibol when MacLean lost Muck.[50] However, as noted above, the presence of a couple with these names in Muck is confirmed in McNeill's census. Angus Mac-Kay's notes describe Duncan Rankin and Neil, piper to Coll, as grandsons of Conn Dauly(Conduiligh),[51] and the *Piping Times,* citing no sources, elaborated to state that they were brothers and that, although Conduiligh had not had MacCrimmon training, they had both had been trained pipers in Skye. In addition, it named the Skye MacCrimmon piping tutor as Dòmhnull Donn, called his attractive daughter Bess, and rounded out its sketch by stating that both were buried in Coll, the tutor dying there in 1807 at the age of eighty-five.[52]

The *Piping Times* article has the taint of fancy; however, if Duncan and Neil Rankin were pupils of Dòmhnul Donn, the instruction of Neil probably took place about 1750 when he would have been about fifteen. This would mean that Malcolm MacCrimmon, father of Red Donald and Black John, was not the only vaunted MacCrimmon piping teacher in the mid-eighteenth century in Skye. Add to that the presence of piping MacCrimmons at Lorgill and the picture of the MacCrimmons as teachers of piping at that time may be more extensive than is often thought.

So, during the immediate post-Culloden years, Mull had at least two Rankin pipers to the MacLeans of Duart, Hugh and Hector, sons of Hector, son of Condullie Rankin (and, if Condullie himself was alive, there would have been three). For some of those years, moreover, neighbouring Coll was the home of at least one top-class Rankin piper, Neil, son of Hector, son of Condullie. The historical indications are that Duncan Rankin, piper to MacLean of Muck, and his wife, Janet MacCrimmon, can not have moved from Muck to Grisipol in Coll until after 1773, for the tenant there, who was met by Boswell and Johnson in that year, was a MacSweyn from Skye, the former fosterer of Donald, Young Coll (d. 1774).

According to Whyte's informant (Condullie Rankin Morison), Neil Rankin's father, Hugh, lived at the pipers' farm at Kilbrennan and died there in 1783. His son Hector finally left the property for Greenock in 1804. MacLean Sinclair and Neil Rankin Morrison are agreed that it was Hugh who ended the Rankin piping college either in the late 1750s or in 1760.[53] Saint Fond's famous "Rankine" who ran the college until his death (c. 1754) may have been Con-duiligh Rankine or his son Eachan.

There has been some international scholarly one-upmanship in the quest for data about Hugh and Hector Rankin. In the *MacTalla* article of 1903 cited above, MacLean Sinclair reported from the session book for 1778 that Hugh was "na eildeir anns an sgire do'm buineadh e" (an elder in the parish he belonged to) and that he died in 1783. Whyte (1907) and Neil Rankin Morrison (1934) enlarged on Hugh's function in the church to treasurer of the kirk session for the parishes of Kilninian and Kilmore from 16 August 1780 until his death some time in 1783 after 28 September. Whyte wrote that Hector left Mull in 1804, but Neil Rankin Morrison and William Matheson (in 1938) enlarged to report that he then went to live with a sister in Greenock. At that point "Bha Muile nam mor-bheann an nis gun phiobaire de Chloinn Duilligh" (Mull of the mighty mountains was without a piper of Clan Duilligh).[54]

In this informational contest between the Old and the New Worlds, Whyte stated that Hugh, on 16 August 1780, when in his advanced years, was appointed treasurer of the kirk session of Kilninian and Kilmore parishes and that Hector took the position when his father died. Neither MacLean Sinclair nor Whyte mentions why this piece of information was included, but piping and the Presbyterian religion were not at all incompatible in the second half of the eighteenth century. Piping and fiddling and dancing were not uncommon in many kirk manses in the Disarming Act years in the Highlands. Joseph and Patrick MacDonald, both musical, were sons of the minister in Durness, Sutherland; Reverend Norman MacLeod (Fiunary), a minister of Morvern, raised a musical and reel-dancing family in the late eighteenth century;[55] Donald MacQueen, minister at Cille Mhuire, Troternish, in Skye, according to his *marbh-rann* (death verse, which may be convention rather than fact), played several instruments: "Cha tog fiodhall, na piob e, / Cha tog clarsach, na ceol e" (He'll not take up a fiddle or a pipe / he'll not take up a harp or music).[56]

Had MacLean not lost Mull there is no telling how long the college, or an equivalent, might have continued, but as Morrison and countless others have pointed out, the relationship between chief and his high-status classical piper was changing after Culloden.[57] De-Gaelicization began at the top, and Archibald Campbell, the third duke of Argyll, was a powerful national political figure and a most thoroughly Englished outsider who had no interest in Gaelic tradition. Mull's college died *circa* 1760. The MacCrimmon equivalent in Skye seems only to have died with the declining piping abilities of Black John MacCrimmon, the date unknown but probably early in the nineteenth century. People like Captain Malcolm MacLeod and later John MacKay continued to teach piping outside their own families, with some degree of formality, in Raasay, and the same was going on in Gairloch, Kintail, and Reay country and widely over Gaelic Scotland.

It is the domineering notion of "college" that has unreasonably preempted our attitudes. It connotes a formality that did not exist in all levels of Gaelic culture and seems not to have existed in Scotland to serve the would-be harper, who, in at least one case, went to Ireland to be trained. The most fascinating aspect of the college idea is that it persisted in the Clann an Sgeulaiche MacGregors in Campbell Perthshire into the nineteenth century, while it withered in Campbell Mull and MacLeod's Skye. Once Gaelic Scotland had no hope of carrying on its own parallel political consciousness behind the bristle of a military threat (supported under the Act of Union via the heritable jurisdictions), and once kin ideas no longer dominated (and friendly tenants were an unwanted indulgence and tenure for military service could no longer legally be practised), the chief deserted Gaelic society (except, some would cynically say, if it could serve him personally).[58] Over a long period, the victims in instrumental music were classical harping and bagpiping, in that order (although important echoes of bagpiping survived, forming the foundation for modern forms of competition piping, as well as the basis for arguments about the older preliterate forms). Therefore, the survival of the bagpipe and at least some of its classical repertoire owes a lot to the middle-class Gael, the tacksman whose absorption into Englishness came later. The acceptance of the superior status and power of the tacksman/laird was deeply ingrained in Gaelic society and was not to be sniffed at; even in Morvern the Camerons remained in this station after Culloden.

The Rankins were certainly high-status classical pipers and obviously not exceptions in a changing Gaelic society. Their function as teachers of (we assume) classical piping withered away. While it may be of no significance and in no way a deviance from unknown earlier Rankin practices of furnishing neighbouring chiefs with music, it is noteworthy that some time in the mid-eighteenth century an important one of them, Neil, found employment away from Mull. Coll was still MacLean territory and all indications are that until well into the nineteenth century its leaders were committed to retaining the old bonds between the people and the landowner/chief wherever possible. That commitment was best exemplified in Donald MacLean, "Young Coll" (1752–74).

Young Coll's father, Hugh, son of Donald, didn't die until 1786, but in 1771 he passed the running of Coll to his son Donald, nephew of both Sir Allan MacLean, twenty-second chief of Clan MacLean, and MacLeod of Talisker. The young laird entertained Boswell and Johnson in 1773. In that year Boswell recorded that there were only three substantial tacksmen on Coll, the bulk of the land being held directly by small tenant farmers. Young Coll had been educated in agriculture[59] and planned to introduce modern methods of farming to Coll at the same time as he sought to retain the traditionally Gaelic warm and trusting relationship between master and man. He was tragically drowned with a number of friends in 1774 and was greatly mourned; his younger brother Alexander (Alasdair Ruadh) became the laird but still there was no radical break with the older ways of life. In all likelihood all three men – Hugh, Donald, and Alexander – were patrons of Neil Rankin the piper. Samuel Johnson liked and admired Young Coll as much or more than he did MacLeod of Raasay, who was also determined to retain the warmth of the old traditional way of life.

Morison's statement that Neil Rankin gave up piping in 1806 may be correct, but by that time he either had a co-adjutor, had been replaced, or had retired from what had been the socially prestigious position as Coll's piper because the Highland Society of London first prize in 1805 was won by Duncan MacMaster, "Piper to the Laird of Coll." Neil Rankin, the last Rankin piper to a MacLean, died thirteen years later, in 1819, at Cliad where he had taken the farm.

Chart 7   The Last Condullie's Relationship to the Coll MacLeans

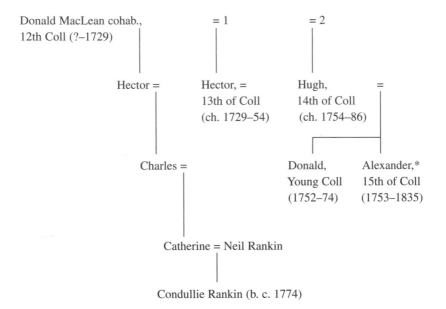

Donald MacLean cohab.,   = 1   = 2
12th Coll (?–1729)

Hector =   Hector, =   Hugh,   =
                13th of Coll   14th of Coll
                (ch. 1729–54)   (ch. 1754–86)

Charles =   Donald,   Alexander,*
                 Young Coll   15th of Coll
                 (1752–74)   (1753–1835)

Catherine = Neil Rankin

Condullie Rankin (b. c. 1774)

* This is the "Alasdair Ruadh Mac-an-Abraich, Tighearna Chola" of Reverend Norman MacLeod's story in
 Caraid nan Gaidheal.
Source: The Coll data was compiled by Dr Kenneth A. MacKinnon, Saint Mary's University, Halifax, Nova
Scotia.

"The late John Johnston [the father], Coll, who remembered him [Neil Rankin] well, said he was not very tall, but well built, and though an old man when he saw him, looked exceedingly handsome. The same authority declared that when he was a young man he was considered the most handsome piper of his time. Hugh Rankin, Neil's father, resided at Kilbrennan, Mull."[60] (The genealogical notes of Betty MacRae, Arinagour and Glasgow, show that this John Johnston, Coll, was born in 1805 at Cliad, one of Coll's major farms.)

Neil Rankin had trained his third son Condullie (b. c. 1774, d. 4 February 1852 in Charlottetown, Prince Edward Island), in piping but even before his father had given up piping, Condullie had taken the factor of Coll's advice and turned to a military career as his relatives, Young Coll and Alexander's brothers, had done.

Condullie and Young Coll were first cousins twice removed. Young Coll's brothers included Alexander, laird of Coll (1753–1835), lieutenant-colonel in the Breadalbane Fencibles; Sir Hector (1756–1849), died a lieutenant-general; Norman (1759–?), major in the 61st Regiment, served in Grenada, died of yellow fever without issue; Roderick (1761–?), died in the West Indies when he joined his regiment; Allan, captain in the 36th Regiment; Hugh (1768–?), captain in the 60th Regiment, died of tuberculosis on his return from Jamaica.[61]

In keeping with his social status, Condullie Rankin obtained a lieutenancy on 8 July 1804 in the New Brunswick Fencibles, a body that later became the 104th Regiment of Foot.[62] Piping in Coll by no means came to an end with Condullie's emigration, but its great days were numbered as the massive emigrations from the island in the nineteenth century drew near. And, if John Johnston the son is right, by 1900, and maybe as early as 1860, he was among the last to know piping tradition intimately. In any case, in both Mull and Coll, traditional patronized piping at the highest level followed its own course throughout the post-Culloden years. It fell into decay quickly in Mull, much more slowly in Coll (where Campbell land encroachment was limited), through forces of normal change in the second half of the eighteenth century.[63]

Coll in particular was the home of great piping in the second half of the eighteenth century and the first quarter of the nineteenth, and it is little wonder that John Johnston the son was so disturbed at what he saw happening to piping from around 1850 until his death in 1921. His letters to the *Oban Times* and to Seton Gordon, which will be examined later, are full of angry dismay at the virtual disappearance of traditional piping from Coll, at the passing of the old style of classical piping from the wider Gaelic scene, and at modern trends in new directions.[64]

Neil Rankin Morrison made two other interesting points in 1934. The first is that he believed that one of the Con-duiligh Rankin pipers in Mull was responsible for the famous piece of ceòl mór known as "The Finger Lock." This tune earns its title presumably from double grips on B and has been described by some as the *sine qua non* of classical pipers. It is the only piece of classical piping whose title I heard reported as the one tune that Allan MacFarlane of Upper Margaree (1878–1938) aspired to play.[65] Morrison's other point is that John Johnston the son went to Canada from Coll to teach piping, which may be true, but his main objective appears to have been different. Johnston visited, lived, and travelled in the Gaelic community in Canada, among his relatives, in order to rediscover music no longer known in his native Coll because so many people had emigrated.[66]

Addendum

Nineteenth-Century MacLean Pipers Whyte, in *Martial Music of the Clans,* noted that "[t]he clan pipers are John MacLean Johnston, Coll, Wm MacLean, Benbecula, Hector MacLean and John MacLean Johnston, Glasgow, and Archibald MacLean, Tiree. Many of the oldest Laments and Salutes of the Clan would have been lost but for the efforts of Mr. MacLean Johnston, Coll."

The John MacLean Johnston of Glasgow was in all likelihood the piper/electrician who emigrated to the United States, leaving a daughter Thelma in Philadelphia. The other presumably was Seton Gordon's old friend.

John Johnston, Coll, taught piping by ear to a Neil Cameron, a Coll native. Cameron later emigrated to Canada, where he farmed in southern Ontario. He became ill in 1935 but not before he had taught his son Allan Cameron and the Reverend Grant Muir, Embo, what he knew of piping. Unfortunately, nobody thought to interview any of them to learn what John Johnston taught and how.[67]

The "Account of the Competition of Pipers" in MacKay's *Collection* shows a number of MacLeans in the prize lists at the Edinburgh piping competitions: Donald MacLean from Kintyre was second in 1795; a boy, Donald MacLean, son of the Donald MacLean who was piper to the Highland Society of Scotland, was third in 1798; Allan MacLean, piper to Alexander MacLean Esq. of Ardgower, was second in 1806; and Allan MacLean "from Mull" was first in 1810; and "Murdoch MacLean, Pipemaker, Glasgow," was fourth in 1814 and second in 1815. The last two were not listed as attached to any laird or noble, although *Pìobaireachd* gives Murdoch as "Murdoch MacLean, pipe maker, Glasgow, late piper to Ardgour."[68]

LOCH BUIDHE PIPING

Much less is known about piping in the Loch Buidhe patrimony although the Loch Buidhe branch is said to have claimed to be the rightful leaders of Clan MacLean. In 1745 the MacLeans of Loch Buidhe were non-Jacobites. The name of one family piper, Hector MacLaine, has survived, but after 1745 pipers are only mentioned twice, to my knowledge.

In the first mention, a Donald Maclean, the son of the piper to John Maclain of Lochbuy, is included in the names of the guilty in an abduction case detailed in a court record from 15 August 1759.[69] The John Maclain of Lochbuy in question was the seventeenth to claim the title. He is described in *A History of the Clan MacLean* as a distant "kinsman" of Hector the sixteenth, who stayed out of the '45 and died *circa* 1749. By 1759 John, seventeenth Lochbuy, was badly in debt. The same source gives his date of death as 1785.[70] It is known that he had a piper in 1769: "John MacLean had his piper, and was, perhaps, the last of the Lochbuies who particularly favoured this art. John MacLean, on the garrison staff, Fort William, Bengal, writing January 29, 1799, states that thirty years before 'Hector MacLaine was piper to John Maclaine of Lochbooy, and was allowed to be the first in Scotland.'"[71]

Although Loch Buidhe was aware of the terms of the Disarming Act as they bore on him in 1758, when Boswell and Johnson met him in 1773 he made light of the old abduction case, and Sir Allan MacLean (chief of Clan MacLean, then leasing Inch Kenneth) whispered to Boswell that Loch Buidhe "could not be persuaded, that he had lost his heritable jurisdiction."[72]

If the record from the Lochbuie Charter Room documents is accurate, then it is possible that the son of John MacLean (seventeenth Lochbuy) also had a piper. That such a piper could have been unknown to the John MacLean who wrote from Bengal in 1799 is plausible, since John the seventeenth's only son, Archibald MacLean, younger of Lochbuy,[73] joined the 84th (Royal Highland Emigrants) in America, a regiment known to have had pipers.[74] Archibald MacLean's name appears in the list of officers published in the London Gazette in January 1779, and he served in 1780 and 1781 as a lieutenant in Captain Patrick Sinclair's company in the 1st Battalion.[75] This company's two drummers were Edward Carmady and William Dutton, and of the privates sixteen had Highland names. It is assumed that those who chose to remain in British America settled in Ontario (land in North America was a major inducement to enlistment). Archibald MacLean, son of Loch Buidhe, was killed in 1784 (probably in Scotland, since many of the officers returned home when the 84th was disbanded in 1783) by a Daniel Monroe.

PIPING IN ULVA

The little island of Ulva lies off the west coast of Mull, and from time immemorial, until debt forced its sale in 1778, it was the ancestral property of the MacQuarries. I include here the following short discussion of piping there, not because I know Ulva to have been actively Jacobite in 1745 but because geographically it seems better to describe Ulva's part in the piping story next to Mull's. Two schools of thought exist concerning piping of old on the island. One, John Johnston's, associates a family of hereditary pipers with the Ulva MacQuarries going back presumably unbroken from about 1835.[76] The other, Neil Rankin Morrison's, claims that Johnston is wrong. Morrison said nothing about pipers or piping on the island before it had passed out of MacQuarrie hands in 1778.

Lumping the MacQuarries of Ulva in politically with the Jacobite MacLeans is not really fair, even though the MacQuarries and various of the neighbouring MacLeans were several times intermarried and political loyalties must have been much the same for the sake of normal neighbourly intercourse.[77] The point in mentioning the controversy over the presence or not of hereditary pipers on Ulva, however, is that each school of thought has only one defender and each point of view must be viewed cautiously.

Stewart of Garth, in 1822, said that Ulva had been in the possession of the MacQuarries for six hundred years, until it was sold in 1778 by Lachlan, the indebted sixteenth chief who promptly went off, age sixty-two or three, and joined the 74th Regiment (Argyll Highlanders).[78] From elsewhere the salient points emerge that it was bought by Colin Macdonald of Boisdale, the father of Ronald Macdonald Esq., who styled himself "of Staffa" (a nearby basaltic island stump whose famous Fingal's Cave has attracted many a tourist) and who flourished until at least 1825.

In a letter to Seton Gordon, Royal Naval Volunteer Reserve, in Kingstown, Ireland, dated 6 February 1918, having just corrected Samuel Johnson's statement that Coll kept a member of a family of Rankins as hereditary pipers, John Johnston went on to say, "But the McQuarries of Ulva had a race of hereditary Pipers named McArthurs and I had the great pleasure of hearing the last of them, John McArthur, play, when I was young, but I remember it well, and knew something about Piping, even then. He was a splendit [sic] player, and if I was not seeing him, would convince me that it was my Uncle to whom I was listening to."[79]

Having had his memory jogged to satisfy Seton Gordon's youthful curiosities about piping, John Johnston again mentioned having heard the last "M'Arthur" piper, this time in a letter to the *Oban Times*, dated 10 November 1919, and it is likely that it was to this claim that Neil Rankin Morrison addressed himself in February 1934.[80]

Morrison confronted more than old John Johnston. He noted that an author of a book about Mull, John MacCormick, was the unique claimant of the belief that the MacArthurs had a school for pipers in Ulva, and he disagreed equally with that. Morrison said that tradition, as he had it, did not square with John Johnston's belief, and he went on to say that the first MacArthur to live in Ulva was Archibald MacArthur, piper to Ronald Macdonald, laird of Staffa. Walter Scott, in a letter from Ulva House on 19 July 1810, acknowledged the presence of a piper and his playing a pibroch at the mouth of the cavern at Staffa, but didn't give his name.[81] Morrison said this was Archibald MacArthur.

Morrison correctly reminded his readers that Boswell and Johnson, who spent a night as guests of the sixteenth chief on Ulva in 1773, reported nothing of any college on the island, although he did not expand on why such an institution might have been expected there. (In fact, according to Boswell, he and Johnson left after only one night, for Inch Kenneth, because they were told there was nothing worth seeing onUlva.) Something of the same presumptuous and constraining idea of Gaelic piping persists to this day, as if all were formalized. Morrison also named the piper, "a man MacLean from the Lochbuie family, Black Hector Gillies, as they called him," who was retained by Lachlan MacQuarrie, retired governor of New South Wales, when the latter re-established Ulva as MacQuarrie property in the early nineteenth century.[82]

Morrison told the world that John Johnston had met a son of Archibald MacArthur, noting that Archibald married a Janet Weir in 1801. This may be so, but confusion arises when Morrison said that Archibald won first prize, as Staffa's piper, in one of the Edinburgh piping competitions. The list of winners and placers in Angus MacKay's *Collection* shows that a John MacArthur, piper to Ronald Macdonald of Staffa, was third in 1804 and that a John MacArthur refused to accept the second-place prize in 1806.[83] The record may have got the name wrong twice – John and Archibald may have been the same man, or Janet may have been the piper's second or later wife and this John was perhaps a son of Archibald by an earlier partner – but a doubt remains that is only partially dispelled by Morrison's last salvo, to wit that he owned Archibald MacArthur's two-drone set of pipes. This, one is led to presume, gave him added credibility as an informant.

Whatever the truth may be, if the citation Matheson gave concerning the last MacArthur piper to the Sleat MacDonalds is accurate and the only male representative of that MacArthur piping family shortly after 1800 was Alexander MacArthur, then the Archibald in Ulva represents a different strain of the family, if any tie exists at all. Piping in Ulva from 1750 to about 1800 remains a mystery.

CHAPTER FOUR

Fraser, Farquharson, MacIntosh, Grant, Chisholm, and Barra MacNeil Pipers

FRASER AND FARQUHARSON PIPERS

The Frasers to the northwest and the southeast of the Great Glen and the Farquharsons in the Braes o' Mar in Aberdeenshire were both active Jacobite clans during the '45 and both paid for it. Simon Fraser, Lord Lovat, was beheaded for his part in Prince Charles's adventures, and many gentlemen of the Fraser clan were among those named to continue to be attainted after 1747's Act of Indemnity.[1] Fraser country had every right to sense the disapprobation of the British government, and Fort George was dangerously close to Fraser lands. The Farquharsons were numerically of little significance compared to the Frasers, but nonetheless two Farquharson gentlemen endured hardship after Culloden, one not being released until 1766. Farquharsons were certainly vulnerable to military occupation from Braemar[2] and the nearby eastern port city of Aberdeen. Despite the hardship, both estates maintained pipers continuously from long before 1745.

The instrumental music of pipes and fiddle was important to all Gaelic clans, and the Frasers were well supplied at all social levels. From just before the rising, the Fraser's family piper was David Fraser (1716–1812).[3] In his case, written proof exists in the form of the famous indenture of 9 March 1743 between himself and Lord Lovat, binding him to a short period of training by "Malcolm MacCrimon" in Skye, an apparent prerequisite to his official appointment as Lovat's piper. David Fraser was to replace "his Lordship's late Pyper, Even McGrigor."[4] (On 16 September 1698 one of the petitioners for expenses as witnesses against Captain Simon Fraser was "Eugen M'Gregor alias _____ pyper at Castledounie"; another petitioner was "John Chisholme brother to Alexander Chisholme violer."[5] If, as is not unreasonable to expect, at least one of David Fraser's early teachers was this Evan MacGregor, then not only did both MacCrimmon and MacGregor techniques and repertoires meet with Lovat's approval but Malcolm

MacCrimmon finishing was obviously regarded by Lovat as the finest in the Gàidhealtachd.)

Lovat put a high value on his principal piper and, anticipating the failure of the rising and the inevitable forfeiture, protected David Fraser's tenure on the estate. In his *Notes Descriptive,* published in 1892 but written between 1773 and some undetermined date after 1783, Sir Aeneas Mackintosh (d. 1820)[6] wrote of David Fraser:

The piper had a piece of Ground granted to him and his posterity, Rent free, which was secured him tho' the rest of the Estate might be sold or forfeited, for the late Ld. Lovat's piper possesses the spot formerly given him, tho' the rest of the Estate was forfeited. The present family piper has been thirty years in their service, was reckoned a good piper being bred under MacCrimmon, a famd one in the Colledge of Sky; he has two sons equally good, one with Farquharson of Invercauld the other with Grant of Rothiemurchus. The old man has held the farm of Tullochclury for all that time, no rent ever asked.[7] [The published term "colledge" in connection with bagpiping instruction may have originated with Boswell.]

Given the date of the indenture, Sir Aeneas's observation on David Fraser was made around 1773, when Mackintosh was three years chief and two years from joining the army. Presumably, this portion of the manuscript was unmodified by his later experiences as a captain in the 2nd Battalion of the 71st, Fraser's Highlanders, when he must have come into contact with Lieutenant Donald MacCrimmon (Red Donald). Mackintosh raised a company and served in the American Revolutionary War, fighting in the south at times alongside Banastre Tarleton's British Legion, in which Malcolm MacCrimmon's son Donald was a lieutenant. In fairness, there is no record of Lieutenant MacCrimmon's having played the bagpipes while campaigning with Tarleton, or later in Nova Scotia,[8] although as late as the early 1800s he was still regarded as the epitome of piping and not just by his MacLeod chief. He was literate, signing his company musters "Donald M'Crumen."

A little-considered feature of the Frasers where piping is concerned is that they, like the MacLeods, MacDonalds, the Breadalbane Campbells, the MacKenzies, and others, were a large clan whose chiefs certainly were involved, one way or another, in the support of more than one piper. The main tacksmen would also have extended a certain amount of favour to pipers and other musicians as tenants, about whom we know almost nothing.

From eyewitness and other reporting it is known that the Fraser's Highlanders who served with Wolfe at Quebec in 1759 had pipers attached to the various companies.[9] Men were raised from several parts of the Fraser estate. Besides the Lieutenant-Colonel Simon Fraser and his half-brother, Simon Fraser, the former's captain-lieutenant,[10] there were, according to

Stewart, four Fraser captains, five Fraser lieutenants, and four Fraser ensigns in 1756.[11] This suggests from five to ten Fraser pipers present from the outset. In the second Fraser's Highlanders, the 71st of 1775, seven active Fraser officers were in the initial list of commissioned officers in the 1st Battalion and three in the 2nd (in which Angus Mackintosh, twenty-third of Mackintosh, served); it is also known that pipers served in that regiment. In at least one case, on the Fraser estate a Fraser tacksman was himself a piper. Dr Henryk Minc, a member of the Clan Fraser Society of North America, has drawn attention to the fact that in 1766 William Fraser, tacksman of Wester Downie, was described as "sometimes Highland Piper."[12]

The Farquharsons were described by Duncan Forbes of Culloden as "the only clan family in Aberdeenshire."[13] They are associated with Clan Chattan. With the exception of the chief, most were Jacobites active in both risings. For King James in 1745 they went to war, with the MacIntoshes, under Farquharson of Monaltrie and Farquharson of Balmoral; the chief of the main branch, John Farquharson of Invercauld, remained discreetly in the shadows while his daughter, Anne (Farquharson) Mackintosh, raised about three hundred men for Prince Charles.[14] Anne's full brother James Farquharson, younger of Invercauld, served with the 43rd (from 1749 numbered the 42nd), the Black Watch, as a lieutenant; the members of his company, to a man, were either killed or captured at the battle of Prestonpans, all of which deflected vengeance from his father in the occupation period from early 1746. The Angus Mackintosh of the '45, twenty-second chief and Anne Farquharson's husband, was a Hanoverian.

Monaltrie is known to have had at least one piper with him at the opening of the Jacobite rising. In a deposition by a James Logie against Francis Farquharson of Monaltrie, the latter was described entering Aberdeen as a Jacobite: "The body of men came into Aberdeen with bagpipes playing, swords drawn, colours flying, and he [Monaltrie] had his sword drawn." The men were wearing Highland garb; Monaltrie was not.

After the '45, the reigning Invercauld was left alone. Farquharson of Balmoral was exempted from the Act of Indemnity but "released in 1748" according to *Prisoners of the '45*. Francis Farquharson of Monaltrie (in the parish of Crathie), also known as the "Baron Ban," was captured and given a conditional pardon, but according to the same source he was not released until 1766.[15] Socially, culturally, and politically, until Culloden the Farquharsons had looked west rather than east and their tastes, at least in pipe music, appear to have changed very little up to that time. Farquharson of Invercauld's piper was one of the sons of David Fraser, Lovat's piper. Likely born between 1740 and 1750, he learned his piping from his father in Lovat country in the 1750s on the forfeited Lovat estate.[16]

Chart 8   The Farquharsons of Invercauld[17]

John Farquharson, = 3) Margaret Murray, d/o Lord James Murray
9th of Invercauld
(neutral in 1745)

| Anne
(Jacobite) | = Aeneas*
Mackintosh,
22nd chief
(Hanoverian),
Black Watch
(d. 1770) | Lt James,
younger of
Invercauld,
Black Watch
(d. 1806) | = Amelia Murray,
d/o Lord George
Murray (Jacobite
general, 1745) | son |

*Uncle of Aeneas Mackintosh, twenty-third chief from 1770, officer in 71st Fraser Highlanders during the American Revolutionary War, author of *Notes Descriptive*, d. 1820.[18]

The Farquharsons kept up their attachment to piping until at least 1850. In 1810 and 1811 the Highland Society competition records show a John Mac-Gregor in the service of Farquharson of Monaltry.[19] Elsewhere this John MacGregor is described as a member of the famous Clann an Sgeulaiche and as having earlier been piper to the duke of Atholl.[20] David Burns, in the *Scottish Genealogist,* citing several sources, identified John MacGregor as John (1784–1861), son of Alexander, son of John McGregor of Fortingall (1708–89) (Iain mac Alasdair 'ic Iain Griogarach). In 1850 Invercauld's piper was a "P. Cotes" whose piping Queen Victoria mentioned in her diary (he piped as rowing accompaniment).[21]

Piping in Aberdeenshire and the north east of Scotland has received little scholarly attention, but in the second half of the eighteenth century it involved the Farquharsons and the Gordons (both the dukes and their successors, as well as the Gordons of Glenbucket). In 1755 the popular piper George Ingram was murdered while piping at a wedding at Ellon, in Aberdeenshire.[22]

PIPING IN JACOBITE MACINTOSH COUNTRY

While the Hanoverian laird of Mackintosh, in early 1745, raised and led one of the three new Highland companies in Lord John Murray's Highlanders (Black Watch), a larger body of MacIntoshes was recruited for the Jacobite army by his charismatic wife, Lady Anne (Farquharson) Mackintosh.[23] They numbered seven hundred according to Sir Aeneas Mackintosh in his *Notes Descriptive.* Just before Culloden, in 1746, Prince Charles spent a night at the Mackintosh seat at Moyhall, southeast of Inverness, when the active Jacobite MacIntoshes were elsewhere. Warned of the approach of Lord Loudon and five hundred soldiers, Anne Mackintosh rallied the blacksmith and six other old men to defend Moyhall: "Armed with claymore, dirk, and guns, together with a bagpipe and old pail (drum), our octogenarian little army lurked in a dense clump of brush-wood until the red-coats came up."[24] According to a report from 25 August 1747 given to bishop Robert Forbes, Episcopal Bishop of Ross and Caithness, by Mary Robertson, Lady Inches, "the stout blacksmith" killed "Loudon's piper."[25]

The famous "Rout of Moy," near the Midlairgs Burn on the Moy estate, took place at night and seven old men using the Highlanders' prime noise of war, the bagpipe, and a makeshift drum frightened off Loudon's army. The ready availability of a bagpipe and the apparent absence of a drum at Moy, even under these unusual circumstances, were typical of rural Gaelic society at the time. Pipes and bagpipes were plentiful, drums rare. Ironically, the only government casualty was Donald Ban MacCrimmon, one of MacLeod's pipers serving under Loudon, at whom surely no Gael would have deliberately directed a ball. "McCloud had his Piper killed just by his side, & was very much laughed at when he came back."[26]

At Culloden the MacIntoshes fought alongside their neighbours, the Frasers and the Farquharsons, and were mangled by Barrel's regiment (4th Foot), but "[t]he piper also escaped, is still alive, being seventy years old" (date of writing uninferrable).[27]

Sir Aeneas Mackintosh, the laird's brother's son and heir, and from 1770 until 1820 the twenty-third chief of the MacIntoshes and Clan Chattan,[28] was in an excellent position to know about chiefly, patronized pipers in his part of the Highlands. His knowledge likely extended to neighbouring Fraser and Farquharson country and to Brae Lochaber. His regiment, the 71st, Fraser's Highlanders (1775–83), had recruited several pipers. It would be improbable if he did not recruit, or condone the recruiting of in his name, a piper for his own company of the 71st in 1775.

Mackintosh, whatever depth of his involvement in piping, was exclusive in his opinions on the subject. He plumped for Skye alone as the leading source of great pipers in Highland Scotland and as generator, through its institutions, of talented pipers from elsewhere: "Frequently in the hearvast, the Reapers cut the Corn regularly to a tune [on the bagpipes], which Custom is still preserved in the Isle of Sky, where the only good pipers are reared and to be found, for there, regular Colledges are formed for instructing youth in using that Martial Instrument."[29] Inasmuch as he ignored Gairloch and Perthshire as piping teaching centres in the 1770s, one is entitled to question Mackintosh's intimate knowledge of piping and to suggest his, estrangement, so some degree, from Gaelic folk culture. Although Mackintosh wrote that "[p]ipers turn scarce, and if encouragement is not soon given, none will be found in the country,"[30] he also wrote that at weddings "the country people sometimes dance to a pipe, but oftener to the fiddle. At the commencement and finishing of each Reel or Dance the swains kiss their nymphs."[31]

This observation suggests to me that when Mackintosh wrote that pipers turned scarce what he meant was that they turned scarce in his part of the Highlands. His description of the fiddle as the Reel/dance-music instrument most enjoyed and demanded by the wider country population in his part of the Highlands owed much to trends in dancing in Strathspey. The Strathspey Reel gained rapidly in popularity in Lowland Scotland in the 1760s,[32] but just where in Strathspey it originated is unclear. The river flows in a broad strath in Grant country and from there roughly northward to the sea through English-speaking Elgin and Banff (which shires it separates). Although it is generally assumed to have been of Gaelic origin, the Strathspey Reel may have been a Saxon development or adaptation from the lower Spey region. Reels were popular in Saxon as well as Gaelic Scotland in the second half of the eighteenth century, in the cities as well as the countryside.

Despite the apparently novel dance, Mackintosh's unexpansive jottings about his own, Fraser's, Grant of Rothiemurchus's, and Farquharson of Invercauld's pipers suggest that pipers were still the musicians associated with the Highland landowner's dignity (something in which the members of the Highland Society of London were most probably interested). Mackintosh may have taken his own advice and encouraged his local piper or pipers, and unlike MacLeod of MacLeod and probably many other improver landlords, he may have given his piper a break on his rent. But where his holding in Brae Lochaber is concerned, he was, by about 1800, a typical, headstrong clearer. The piper in Mackintosh's holding at Inverroy-beg and Boline was cleared in 1802.[33] Otherwise, Mackintosh's opinion that pipers in the Highlands were a dying breed, while not isolated, was uncommon and has been challenged over and over again in the published histories and notes of various parts of the Gàidhealtachd. What's more, the continuous emigration of pipers from Highland Scotland until the middle of the nineteenth century supports the view that Mackintosh's observation was a local one and atypical.

THE GRANTS OF GLENMORISTON AND GLENURQUHART

Although the Grants in the Strathspey area of the Central Highlands were loyal to King George, the two other Grant patrimonies of Glenmoriston and Glenurquhart to the west of the Great Glen were largely Jacobite in 1745, Glenmoriston strongly so. The chief of the Glenmoriston people, Fair-haired Patrick (Pàdruig Buidhe), was attainted and his estate, while not forfeited, suffered heavily from the recriminations of the conquering hero's army. Major Lockheart of Cholmondley's regiment was the officer responsible for the murder of three men who were harrowing in Glenmoriston after Culloden. Lockheart's men committed several rapes in the glen in June 1746. Lord Loudon, Sir Alexander MacDonald of Sleat, and the laird of MacLeod authorized the destruction of the laird of Glenmoriston's house. However, the bulk of the destruction of property, particularly farm implements, was carried out by three parties of MacLeod's Skye militia, against Lord Loudon's more humane judgment.[34]

The Glenmoriston estate may have escaped forfeiture because Allan Grant, son of Patrick Grant of Glenmoriston, joined one of the three new companies of Lord John Murray's Highlanders formed in 1745 for service in the Highlands (where they stayed until they were reduced in 1748). There is no further trace of him.[35]

Several other prominent Hanoverian Grants may have interceded for the errant Glenmoriston. Colonel James Grant of Ballendalloch in Banffshire, one of the founding officers of the original Independent Companies (which became the Black Watch) around 1730, went on to become a general, dying in 1806. George Grant (brother of the laird of Grant) joined Lord John Murray's Highlanders (Black Watch) in 1739 as a major (retired or killed in 1746). Enlisting also in 1739, as lieutenants, were Lewis Grant of Auchterblair and the laird's son, Francis Grant (died lieutenant-general in 1782). Enlisting in Loudon's Highlanders on 8 June 1745 were Lieutenant Patrick Grant, younger of Rothiemurchus (a murderously vengeful Hanoverian), and Ensign John Grant, younger of Dalrachnie. In addition, twenty companies of independent Highland troops were raised in 1745 but never regimented, and among their officers were Captain Patrick Grant Esq., Lieutenant William Grant, and Ensign James Grant. MacLeod's company was one of these.[36]

All three branches of the Grants – Strathspey, Glenmoriston, and Glenurquhart – patronized pipers at the highest social/ political level, going as far back as the seventeenth century. The report of the notary public John Donaldsone to the laird of Grant in 1638 that the laird's violar, Johne Hay, and his "clairschear" had injured each other in a fight could be used, tentatively, to bolster the view that bagpiping was a relative latecomer to this part of the Scottish Gaelic world.

The Grant material, though skimpy, suggests that the mid-seventeenth century marked the turning point from strings to woodwind. One well-to-do Grant, Grant of Sheugly, who flourished, as far as one can determine, in the late seventeenth century, was himself a piper, harper, and violin player. He composed the verses to Mairi nighean Dheorsa (Grant of Sheuglie's contest betwixt his Violin, Pipe, and Harp).[37] Without doubt, pipers were a common feature of everyday life in all Grant country throughout the eighteenth century.

Glenmoriston Grants, although largely Protestant, were susceptible to the Jacobite cause, again, for whatever reasons they may have had independently, but also for one, possibly two, seemingly minor but nonetheless very strong traditional reasons. Angus MacDonell, the second son of Old Glengary (John MacDonell, d. 1754), had been fostered by Archibald Grant (Gilleasbuig an Tuim Bhealaidh [Archibald of the Broomy Knowe]), "a near relative to Glenmoriston."[38] The relationship of fosterage was powerful in Gaelic society, and everyone was aware of its many military implications. Angus MacDonell, a normal, healthy youth presumably well versed in the Highland tradition of military service, thus had natural appeal as a raiser of Glenmoriston men when the time came. He led the Glengarry soldiers to Glenfinnan, and both he and Archibald MacDonell (Young Barisdale) raised many men in Glenmoriston.[39]

The tendency to toast King James may have been the deeper in Glenmoriston for a marriage relationship with fellow-Protestant Camerons of Locheil. John Grant of Glenmoriston, Iain a' Chreagain, in 1698, married Janet, daughter of Sir Ewen Dubh Cameron of Lochiel. Another Protestant and Jacobite connection should be considered. A Cameron presence in both Glenmoriston and Glenurquhart before, during, and after the '45 may have had some significance in the political alignment of the Glenmoriston men in 1745. (No work has yet been done to link those poor Highlanders from Glenmoriston who were transported to the West Indies after Culloden with Lochiel's or any other prominent Highlander's property in the West Indies.)

Although the author of *Story and Song from Loch Ness-side,* Alexander Gleannach MacDonald (1860–1928), was naturally and probably justifiably anxious to bathe his native Glenmoriston in a favourable musical light, his treatment of piping there suffers from one major omission. MacDonald's work shows nothing of piping in his native Glenmoriston in the eighteenth century. What's more, his work elsewhere on piping lacks an intimate understanding of the subject. His 1927 publication of Joseph MacDonald's "Compleat Theory," for example, was thoroughly inadequate as a reproduction of the original in the Laing manuscript (held at Edinburgh University) or even as an effort to make some sense of the 1803 edition. However, whether this vitiates what he had to say about Glenmoriston piping is difficult to say. As a lorist, he drew on written as well as oral material for *Story and Song,* and he acknowledged the help of Dr William MacKay, author of *Urquhart and Glenmoriston* (1893). One thing to be said of *Story and Song* is that it is unable to be critical of the Glenmoriston chief in the 1770s, the Jacobite and later rack-renting Fair-haired Patrick.

The first Glenmoriston piper to appear in the easily available literature is "Donald Bayne M'Ewan vic Alaster" (recte Dòmhnul Bàn mac Eoghainn 'ic Alasdair [Fair Donald, son of Hugh, son of Alexander]), who was "pyper to the Laird of Glenmoristoun." He was one of a large number of men, prominent Frasers as well as others, named in an "Indytment" brought into court on 12 July 1698. The piper had been a member of small clan army raised by Thomas Fraser of Beaufort and his son "Captain Simon Fraser" (later the Lord Lovat who was executed for his part in the '45). In essence, the piper was part of a well-concerted scheme to thwart what the Frasers en masse saw to be a move by the Dowager Fraser (née Murray and sister to Lord James Murray and Lord Mongo Murray) to shift control of Fraser holdings to the Murrays of Athole. The dowager was kidnapped, forced into a marriage to Simon Fraser, and raped. Either this piper or Eugen M'Gregor, piper at Castle Dounie, was employed "to drown her cryes" with noise from the "great Pipe."[40]

Eugen (Aogh?) M'Gregor was deceased in 1742 and would have to have been at least eighty when he died to have been the father of Donald Bayne M'Ewan, a not too ridiculous proposition. Pipers have been known to be capable of holding the musical office until advanced in years. Donald Mac-Crimmon, after all, was about seventy-six when Sir Walter Scott heard him play in Skye in 1814, and he was still formally entertaining MacLeod of MacLeod. If a link were to be established between Evan/Eugen McGregor and Donald Bayne, then MacGregor influences on piping would be richer and deeper than so far suggested, but at the moment nothing is known about the earliest recorded Glenmoriston piper.

The next piper from Glenmoriston, Finlay MacLeod, does not emerge until the 1800s, and the little that is known about him comes from records of the Highland Society piping competitions[41] and the pen of Alexander Gleannach MacDonald. MacDonald maintained that MacLeod represented a break in Glenmoriston piping tradition, as either he or his people came from some other part of the Gàidhealtachd (presumably Assynt or Skye). However fine a piper Finlay MacLeod may have been, unquestionably he became the central figure in the latter-day tail of a Regency Highland chief, James Murray Grant JP, DL, twelfth laird of Glenmoriston, chief from 1801 to 1868. Grant, like Alasdair Ranaldson of Glengarry, maintained a bard, a piper, and a gardener, and was involved in revived Gaelicism, or pseudo-Gaelicism. Alexander Gleannach MacDonald's writings suggest that Grant enjoyed showing his own eccentric side to the world and at least tolerated, if he didn't actually encourage, exaggerated personal eccentricities on his servants' parts. Among Finlay MacLeod's friends was Archibald Munro, piper to the best-known revivalist chief, Alasdair Ranaldson MacDonell of Glengarry.

Although the following events may not adequately explain an apparent dearth of pipers from 1750 to 1800, they are significant. First, although the Glenmoriston estate was not forfeited, the glen's economy, and doubtless its social character, must have suffered desperately with the transportation to Barbados of sixty-eight men who had been at Culloden as Jacobites. They, with sixteen others from Glenurquhart, had been inveigled into turning themselves in at Inverness on 4 May 1746 in the hope of receiving understanding and leniency, if not outright clemency. Second, the rent of the glen's tenant farmers was increased dramatically by Fair-haired Patrick between 1753 and 1773, driving "seventy men out of the Glen to America" according to Lauchlan MacQueen.[42]

MacQueen, a cultured man and owner of the change-house at Anoch and a veteran of Culloden, told Boswell that his own rent had gone from £5 to £20 over that twenty-year period and that he intended to leave the next year.[43] He impressed upon Boswell that the men of the glen would bleed for the chief (Fair-haired Patrick) "if they were well used."[44] The "seventy" emigrants went to New York state in 1773 with the Glengarry emigrants, led by the MacDonell tacksmen brothers of Leek, Collachie and Aberchalder in the Great Glen, and Spanish John MacDonell of Scotus in Knoydart.[45] As Marianne McLean showed in *The People of Glengarry,* this was a typical tacksman-led emigration of the better-off tenant farmers,[46] and the Glenmoriston component was likely no different. The loss of so many families cannot but have altered Glenmoriston society dramatically yet again, although it is not known if the piper or pipers emigrated with them. Common sense, in retrospect, says that he would have been among the first to want to leave, because his status was clearly slipping, and that he would have been among the most vigorously canvassed by his friends and neighbours, who would have readily foreseen the value of his music in a far-off land.

The effects of these emigrations on the fabric of Glenmoriston in the 1770s have yet to be studied from a cultural point of view. Although the indications are otherwise, it is possible that, as in other places, the top Glenmoriston piper was offered a rent break, probably less than of yore, for the sake of tradition and chiefly face, and that an old piping family continued in the service of Grant. If the Spey-side Grants were any example, they had MacDonald pipers in the second half of the eighteenth century and John MacDonald was Glengarry's piper for several decades, presumably having taken the job in the 1750s.

Evidence of Disarming Act piping in Protestant Glenurquhart in 1763 is an interesting counterweight to the silence on the subject in Glenmoriston. Although sixteen Glenurquhart men turned themselves in at Inverness in May 1746 and were duly adjudged traitors, incarcerated in hulks, and sent off to the West Indies, Glenurquhart may not have been as Jacobite as Glenmoriston. In any case, Dr William MacKay wrote in 1893:

There has always been a piper in Urquhart belonging to the family of Grant, whose sallary has been constantly paid by a small portion of oats from each tenant. The tenants want to get free of this Tax, but it is submitted whether or not it is not better to continue it, as the Tax is small, and, being in use to be paid, it is not very sensibly felt. If you let it drop, the Highland Musick is lost, which would be a great loss in case of a civil or foreign War; and such Musick is part of the Appendages of the Dignity of the family. The commons are much pleased with this Musick, and the use of it will be a means of popularity amongst some.[47]

The piping that Lorimer was most interested in describing was ceòl mór, particularly its warrior music, which served to bind chief and man in times of emergency and ritual. Lorimer added as an afterthought that the common people liked the music and that retaining it would be a popular way to appeal to the traditionalism "amongst some." As elsewhere in the Gàidhealtachd, the farmer in Glenurquhart was beginning to feel the pinch of rising rents, and Lorimer was quite clear in noting that anyone who could be appealed to through tradition should be. He obviously saw nothing wrong with the Highland tenantry acting as soldiers in their country's wars, civil or otherwise, and paying for the means of their stimulus to face bloody death in their landowners' causes. How long this democratic form of raising the piper's salary was practised in Glenurquhart is unknown. No other examples of this sort have come to light.

Who was the piper Lorimer referred to? Was he one of a piping family deeply rooted in Glenurquhart? Unfortunately, the name of only one piper is extant in popular literature and that is Patrick Grant of Sheughly, Glenurquhart. Whether he was a hereditary piper is unknown, but according to the *Piping Times,* he was a "noted performer on the bagpipe, violin and harp in the eighteenth century."[48] Apparently he was also a poet. Patrick was a common Grant first name, so the writer in the *Piping Times* probably did not confuse this man with the Patrick Grant in Abernethy mentioned above, and indeed the reference to the harp points to an earlier date for the Glenurquhart man. The *Piping Times,* however, gave no sources.

As in the case of Glenmoriston, Glenurquhart suffered persecution after Culloden. There is a pronounced gap in knowledge of piping in Glenurquhart after 1763. The sixteen men who had fought at Culloden and had voluntarily gave themselves up to the authorities in May 1746 were deported. How much thievery and burning of property went on is unknown, although the glen's nearness to the garrison at Inverness made the population highly vulnerable to extensive and repetitive harassment and to theft of cattle and personal effects in the months of depredation before due process of law returned.

In piping terms, however, Glenurquhart appears never to have recovered from the population loss it suffered with the major block emigration in 1775. The old traditional families had cleared out, breaking forever cultural lines of contact with the older Gaelic world in the old glen.[49]

From a reading of the literature about the 1784 immigration to Douglas Township in Hants County, Nova Scotia, and to the East River in what is now Pictou County, Nova Scotia, one can reconstruct something of the Glenurquhart emigrations in the 1770s.[50] Typical of Highlanders, typical of everyone going to a relatively empty, forested continent, the people who followed the pioneers went where they had friends and relatives. The advance guard, the attractant for the bulk of the Glenurquhart folk, was the settlement of the Glengarry and other Highland families in the area west of Albany in New York province. When, out of loyalty to King George in the Revolutionary War, they had to relocate, some went where the Hector settlers had already established themselves in what is now Pictou County in the north of Nova Scotia.

At least one Glenurquhart man, Red Sorley Cameron (Somhairle Ruadh), had settled in 1773 in Albany in northern New York, presumably having sailed with the Glengarry people. Reverend A. MacLean Sinclair's notes to his list of Glenurquhart settlers on the East River in Pictou County states that Cameron had lived in Albany for three years before joining the Royal Highland Emigrant Regiment (84th).[51] Although it is not yet determined, there may have been as many as thirty families from Glenurquhart besides his at the outbreak of the Revolutionary War. With word of that initial settlement's success and the ease of obtaining productive land, the main Glenurquhart emigrations appear to have occurred in the following two years. In 1774, according to an "Additional Note" in Sinclair's manuscript, William Grant from Glenurquhart, a former lieutenant in the 42nd Regiment, brought his family along with 150 people on the ship *Moore*. The note stated that "extravagant rent had obliged him to give it up and try America."[52] The only places they would have settled, if only for protection, would have been among friends, most likely among the Glengarry people. William Grant may have been no stranger to the country, since the 42nd had lived and fought in northern New York during the French campaign of 1757–63. Then in 1775, with the war begun, the largest Glenurquhart emigration sailed from Glasgow to New York aboard the American-built ship *Glasgow*. This is one of those unknown number of emigrations that escaped official notice, although information about it appeared in Murray Logan's *Scottish Highlanders and the American Revolution* (1976).[53] The ship carried 250 emigrants (approximately fifty families) to the port of New York, from which the immigrants clearly intended to head north for the Mohawk Valley and settle among Highland friends.

Their plans were thwarted in a miserably hard fashion. Having had foreknowledge of the ship's sailing from Scotland, Lieutenant-Colonel Allan McLean ordered the impressment of all capable men upon their arrival in New York. A sixty-four-gunner carried out the kidnapping, and the Glenurquhart people were taken to Halifax, where the men dutifully enlisted, forming a sizeable block of the 2nd Battalion of the Royal Highland Emigrants Regiment. As inducement, they had been promised land in Nova

Scotia and they got it. McLean, the bold perpetrator of this impressment, was the Mull man who had recently obtained an important commission to raise and command Gaelic immigrants settled in North America for service in the army. To give him some post-hoc-et-ergo-propter-hoc due, the stubborn resilience of the 1st Battalion of the Royal Highland Emigrants was the main reason the American attack on Canada failed during that war.

In any case, after Lorimer's mention of a publicly funded Glenurquhart piper in 1763, the long silence about piping in that glen was the result of the emigrations to the New World of the bulk of the old families, the people who had been prosperous under the Gaelic régime (presumably, the piper went with them). Allowing an average of five people per family, one can conclude that over eighty families emigrated from Glenurquhart. This might not have depopulated the glen entirely, but it must have come close to that. Alas, though there are traces of piping both in the Douglas settlement north of Halifax[54] and in Pictou County on the East River, as yet none go back to immigrant times in enough detail to indicate who the prominent piper or piping family in Glenurquhart was *circa* 1770.

PIPING IN STRATHGLASS

Strathglass is part of a watershed dominated by the rivers Beauly, Farrar, and Affrick, which drain east-northeastward into the Beauly Firth and thence into the North Sea a few miles west of Inverness. In the eighteenth century it was a Jacobite area controlled by two families, the Chisholms in the south and the Frasers in the north. The chiefs of both clans maintained family pipers as a normal part of their respective customs, which did not dissolve, in the case of the Chisholms, until the 1790s, when the temptation to profit from sheep farming threw tradition onto the dung heap (the piper to various Lords Lovat from 1743, David Fraser [see above], did not die until 1812).

According to the venerable and traditional Strathglass piper and piping authority George Moss (1903–90), there were two prominent piping families in the Strathglass "of old,"[55] the Camerons, who were the Chisholms' pipers, and the Frasers, at least one of whom, David, was Lord Lovat's piper in 1745. By "of old," Moss meant before the Act against the Heritable Jurisdictions. The Camerons' service as pre-eminent Chisholm pipers is believed to have been much more ancient, although next to nothing is known about the early generations of Cameron pipers.

According to Moss, the first Cameron to serve as piper to a Chisholm chief came to Strathglass from Lochaber some time in the 1500s. This man started a line of hereditary pipers to the Chisholms that Moss all but implied endured without a break until some time after the defeat at Culloden (he did not know the exact year of the rupture of chief and piper).[56] In all that time, more than two hundred years, the first name of only one piper to the Chisholm chiefs has survived from Scottish sources and even that name is not at all certain. According to John Prebble, the piper to the Chisholm at the time of Culloden was Little John (Iain Beag), who played his music on the magical Chisholm pipe chanter, the "Maiden of the Slipper" (Maighdean a' Chuarain) that broke spontaneously at the death of any Chisholm chief.[57] George Moss, a man on intimate terms with Strathglass piping and other history, could not mention the name of any of the Camerons in the Chisholms' service and said nothing about any Iain Beag, last name unknown, who flourished around 1745.

The name of one other early (1715) piper to the Chisholms has been suggested, although George Moss neither mentioned nor discussed him. John MacLennan (Iain mac Ruairidh) is described in a less than reliable work as having been, in his superannuated years in the early 1700s, piper to Chisholm of Chisholm. John MacLennan was the son of the chief of the MacLennans, Rory (Ruairidh), who was killed fighting with Alexander MacDonell (Col Ciotach) and royalist leader Graham of Montrose at the Battle of Auldearn in 1645. Apparently, John MacLennan had been a general in the army before taking the appropriately respected and genteel position in the Chisholm household "several years prior to 1721."[58] MacLennan must have been born some time near the time of his father's death if he was still piping well enough to enhance a chiefly house in the early eighteenth century. Ronald G. MacLennan, author of *The History of the MacLennans,* cited no reference but wrote, with what inevitably appears to suggest incontrovertible primary sources, that John MacLennan received £20 Scots per annum for his services as piper and paid ten merks for his croft.[59] Presumably there was either a break in the Cameron line at this point, someone not yet suitably trained perhaps, or Chisholm had more than one piper and offered a worthy but financially embarrassed MacLennan a sinecure.

According to Moss, when the Camerons left the service of the Jacobite Chisholms, they moved west to Strath Conon in loyal MacKenzie country. Moss gave them no official piping status among the MacKenzies and no one until Donald Cameron (c. 1811–68) became "[p]iper to Lord Seaforth in Brahan Castle, near Dingwall." George Moss wrote that Donald Cameron "had 3 sons, Colin, Keith, and Alexander (Sandy). A good deal of my knowledge of traditional piping, came from the latter."[60] In Strathglass, the evidence strongly suggests that the position of piper to the Chisholms was taken over by a local Chisholm, presumably one from that wide pool of piping and other musical talent that goes largely unsung (John and Alexander Chisholme having had musical work at Frasers' Castledounie in 1698 [see above]).

From a North American point of view, the following excerpt from Angus MacKay's book goes some way to vindicate the credibility of the author(s) of that part of the "Historical and Traditional notes on the Piobaireachds": "Kenneth Chisholm, the last family Piper, was taught by John Beag MacRae, Piper to the late Lord Seaforth. He [Kenneth] went to America, where he was accidentally killed by the fall of a tree."[61]

All the contradictions, inaccuracies, and omissions in the text in Angus MacKay's book are counterbalanced from time to time by peculiar little accuracies like this one. Kenneth Chisholm was indeed killed by a falling tree in America. A genealogical history of Antigonish County compiled between 1885 and 1892 by a Gaelic-speaking Roman Catholic priest, known locally as Sagart Arasaig (Father Ronald MacGillivray, b. 1836), confirms it but doesn't date the fatality. The *Piping Times* of August 1968 was less diffident; in its occasionally published "Notices of Pipers," it said confidently (evidence unadduced) that he died in America around 1820.[62] Unfortunately, Angus MacKay's book does not mention the Chisholm chief to whom Kenneth was the last family piper. The last pro-Gaelic chief was Alexander, An Siosal Bàn (Fair-haired Chisholm, d. 1793). He was succeeded by his younger brother William, who presided over some very heartless clearances in Strathglass. William was an unlikely man to indulge tradition, but more than one of his kind have been shown to manipulate tradition for status ends. In any case, William was a man tenants would have felt little sorrow seeing leave for the New World.

The phrase "last family Piper" suggests a continuity of pipers maintained by Chisholm of Chisholm to the time of Kenneth Chisholm's emigration. That is a position which George Moss, when approached generally on the subject in May 1980, presumed to be the case as a matter of course. Moss did not claim that chiefs' pipers uniformly continued to be from the Gaelic middle class after Culloden and its aftermath, but he allowed this suggestion to stand, and where the Chisholms are concerned, the point of view finds confirmation from Nova Scotia.[63]

Sagart Arasaig MacGillivray wrote:

John Chisholm, the father of Alexander Ruadh Chisholm, was a gentleman of means in Strathglass, Scotland. He had a small estate in the country, but lost it before his son, Alasdair Ruadh, came to this country. He was a near relative of the Laird of Strathglass of the time. Alasdair Ruadh lived for some time with the Laird in the capacity of *Ciobair*, and his brother Kenneth was piper to the Laird. This Kenneth Chisholm, piper, was a powerful man; he could march six miles playing the bagpipes all the time ... This Alaistair Ruadh came out to Pictou about the year 1791 and came down to the Cape and settled where his people are to this day. His brother Kenneth joined him after a few years.[64]

George Moss remarked on the unusualness of Kenneth as a Chisholm first name but by no means excluded it.[65] Actually, Moss gladly accepted Sagairt Arasaig's genealogical information. His only critical comment on Sagart Arasaig's work was that Alasdair Ruadh was almost certainly not a "ciobair" to the pro-Gaelic Chisholm chief of 1791. He suggested that a typist's error, or a lack of understanding of how large-scale commercial sheep farming was introduced in Chisholm Strathglass, or both, a century later in semi-urban Antigonish, had allowed this word to go to the printer unchanged. Moss said that the word intended was *pìobair* (piper).

Moss's reasoning was based on the knowledge that Alexander Chisholm (An Siosal Bàn), the twenty-third chief[66] of the clan, was compassionate towards his tenantry, was fond of Gaelic tradition, and stoutly resisted the blandishments of Lowlanders to buy or lease the estate, to drive the Gael off and the sheep on. His wife and his daughter, Mary, were also staunchly in favour of keeping the old agricultural demography of Chisholm Strathglass, but they were less able to plug holes in the dykes when Alexander died in 1793 and his brother William took over. Sheep paths then invaded the heather hills and the farmed fields, and by the middle of the Victorian century Chisholms were almost as rare as Kowalskis in Strathglass.

The other point worth reiterating is that, in the eighteenth century, Highland emigration was almost always a family affair, very often an extended family affair, as well as a community affair. The underlying hope was of re-establishing relatively self-sufficient agricultural communities overseas. Alasdair Chisholm would have been atypical had he not brought a wife and family with him; he was probably head of one family among several collaterally related families to emigrate to Nova Scotia in *circa* 1791. His age is unknown but it would by no means have been unusual had he been in his fifties, since his parents and his own adult children sailed with him. The same may well be true for Kenneth, his brother. Without a formal record of Kenneth's birth date, it is impossible to say.

Where the Seaforth MacKenzies are concerned (referred to in Angus MacKay's note, above), the first actual Lord Seaforth, as distinct from the earl of Seaforth, was created in 1797 (Francis Humberston MacKenzie [d. 1815], cousin of Kenneth, earl of Seaforth, who raised the Seaforth Highlanders in 1778), but the designation "Lord Seaforth" was applied to the earls of Seaforth quite normally – by Stewart of Garth, for example – since it was commonly used for noblemen of lower degree than a duke. If for some reason a stricter interpretation has to be put on Angus MacKay's note, it is possible that Little John MacRae (Iain Beag) was Francis Humberston MacKenzie's piper for many years before, as well as after, his accepting the titles "Lord Seaforth" and "Baron Kintail." All that can be said is that Iain Beag MacRae may have been piper to one or more of the following: Colonel Kenneth MacKenzie, the earl of Seaforth from 1771, who died in 1781 en route to India with his regiment; Colonel Kenneth's cousin Thomas Frederick Humberston MacKenzie, who moved to the colonelship of the Seaforths (from the 100th Regiment) and to proprietorship of the MacKenzie estate and who died in India in 1783 aged twenty-seven; and Thomas's brother, Francis Humberston MacKenzie, Lord Seaforth and Baron MacKenzie of Kintail (d. 1815).

There is little evidence to suggest, at this time, that Kenneth Chisholm and his brother Alasdair Ruadh, both relatives of the chiefs of Clan Chisholm, did not represent Chisholm piping at its top level as early as the 1760s. And if Prebble's "Iain Beag" was a Chisholm, one can reasonably conclude that the pipers to the Chisholm chiefs came from within the clan for several generations in the eighteenth century.

PIPING IN THE MACNEILS' BARRA

The man who piloted Prince Charles Edward Stuart's ship *Du Teillay* into Eriskay in 1745 was the piper to MacNeil of Barra. "When they were near the shore of the Long Isle, Duncan Cameron was set out in the long boat to fetch them a proper pilot.[67] When he accidentally met with Barra's piper, who was his old acquaintance, and brought him on board. The piper piloted them safely into Erisca (about July 21st)."[68] However, there is doubt as to the piper's name.

The Cape Breton outline of the pipers to MacNeil of Barra, published originally in 1926 by A.J. MacKenzie (Eairdsidh Sheumais 1861–1939) of Rear Christmas Island, begins with Rory MacNeil. MacKenzie offered no dates for Rory the piper but stated that he was "descended from famous pipers" and played a bagpipe for which the laird of Barra had spent £70. In gratitude for a valuable service by Rory the piper, MacNeil of Barra took Rory's son John into his service as "attendant," and later John's sons Calum and Donald enjoyed the same privileged position (and then Donald's son Murdoch Beag).[69] The lore into which A.J. MacKenzie tapped has it that two grandsons of Rory MacNeil the piper, Rory and Hector MacNeil, emigrated and settled in Piper's Cove, in the parish of Christmas Island in Cape Breton. What is more, these two grandsons were brothers of Calum and Donald. MacKenzie's knowledge was sustained orally by the descendants and neighbours of the descendants of these two grandsons of Rory MacNeil. According to Cape Breton oral history, no piper to the laird of Barra ever settled in Cape Breton. If he had, that sort of fact could not have escaped local memory.

On the other hand, the twentieth-century Barra tradition bearer, John MacPherson (the Coddy), in *Tales from Barra,* said that the prince's pilot was "Calum the piper" who lived in Gigha, a small island off the northwest coast of Barra. The Coddy told John Lorn Campbell that Calum the piper,

Chart 9   Rory MacNeil the Piper and His Descendants in Barra and Nova Scotia
(from the Cape Breton source, A.J. MacKenzie)

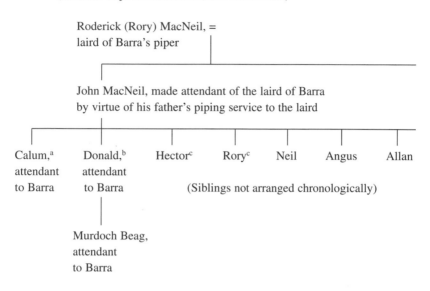

Roderick (Rory) MacNeil, =
laird of Barra's piper

John MacNeil, made attendant of the laird of Barra
by virtue of his father's piping service to the laird

Calum,[a]	Donald,[b]	Hector[c]	Rory[c]	Neil	Angus	Allan
attendant	attendant					
to Barra	to Barra	(Siblings not arranged chronologically)				

Murdoch Beag,
attendant
to Barra

[a] Calum, according to A.J. MacKenzie, was with Lieutenant Roderick MacNeil, younger of Barra, in Wolfe's campaign in Quebec in the Seven Years' War (and so in Cape Breton a little earlier with his regiment, Fraser's Highlanders). He married and had children, at least some of whom emigrated. If the Coddy is in error, then this Calum appears to be the focal point of the confusion. The fact that A.J. MacKenzie also called Calum MacNeil "Calum Pìobaire" offers another hint as to the confusion.

[b] Donald's son, Murdock Beag, followed in his father's position as "attendant" to the Barra laird.

[c] Rory and Hector, the emigrants to Pictou in 1802 who later settled at Piper's Cove, Cape Breton. A.J. MacKenzie called Hector "Hector Piper."[70]

presumably as well as playing his minor part in the opening of the 1745 campaign, fought alongside Lieutenant Roderick MacNeil (younger of Barra)[71] in Wolfe's Quebec campaign. According to the Coddy, the piper then returned home but later emigrated to Cape Breton with his seven sons, settling at Piper's Cove.[72] The depopulation of Barra in the nineteenth century perhaps denied the Coddy the sort of direct family lore available to MacKenzie in the Christmas Island area, where so many Barraich settled. While there is no reason to doubt that a piper to Lieutenant Roderick Mac-Neil of Barra, Calum MacNeil, was at Quebec and that he returned to his native Barra, it is less certain that he emigrated in 1802 to Pictou, finding his way the next year to Christmas Island, as has been suggested.[73]

A.J. MacKenzie's version is that Calum MacNeil was one of seven brothers, all sons of John MacNeil, son of Rory MacNeil, the celebrated Barra piper. It was Calum's two brothers, Rory and Hector MacNeil, who emi-

Chart 10   The Family of Calum Pìobaire MacNeil

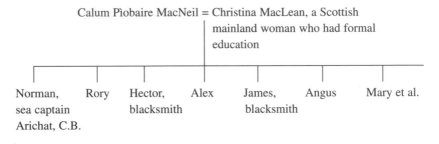

Calum Pìobaire MacNeil = Christina MacLean, a Scottish
mainland woman who had formal
education

| Norman, sea captain Arichat, C.B. | Rory | Hector, blacksmith | Alex | James, blacksmith | Angus | Mary et al. |

Note: There is no word of Calum's having emigrated but indeed several of his family settled in Cape
Breton. MacKenzie named six sons. The Coddy said that his Calum had seven.
Source: MacKenzie, *The MacKenzies' History of Christmas Island Parish*.

grated from Barra to Pictou, Nova Scotia, late in 1802, moving in 1803 to
Cape Breton. (If Gaelic naming of the first male child after his father's father
was used in this case, then Rory, son of John, son of Rory, was the first male
child in the family.)

Archibald MacKenzie's *The MacKenzies' History of Christmas Island
Parish* makes it clear that not all of the 370 Catholic Barra people (about
seventy-five families) who emigrated in August 1802 to Pictou shifted to
Cape Breton. A greater number of families stayed in mainland Nova Scotia,
went to live among fellow Catholics in Prince Edward Island, or went elsewhere. At least one who was relatively well off and influential, the grandson
of the first chief to be included in the abbreviated genealogy (see below),
went to Prince Edward Island.

A.J. MacKenzie's genealogical work on Christmas Island parish includes
a section under the heading "'Calum Pìobaire' MacNeil, 'Page, or Attendant'" to the chiefs of Barra. After his service overseas in Cape Breton and
Quebec (1758–59) with Lieutenant Roderick MacNeil, Calum first served,
in Barra, the late lieutenant's father, the chief until he died in 1763, and then
the lieutenant's son Roderick, the next chief, going with him to the American Revolutionary War (regiment unspecified).

Who the piper was to the Roderick MacNeil who got the Crown grant to
Barra in 1688 is by no means clear, but MacPherson in *Tales from Barra* said
that the composer of the pipe music "Colonel MacNeil's Salute – Sealladh
nan Ruairidh, sealladh thog mulad dhiom" (View of the Rories, a perspective that lifted the sorrow from me) was Donald MacKinnon, MacNeil of
Barra's piper, and that the date of the composition was before 1700 (the year
the MacNeils ceased to live in Kisimul Castle, the "sealladh" implying
chiefly residence there). In the '45, Roderick's younger son Roderick

Chart 11   MacNeil Chiefs of Barra

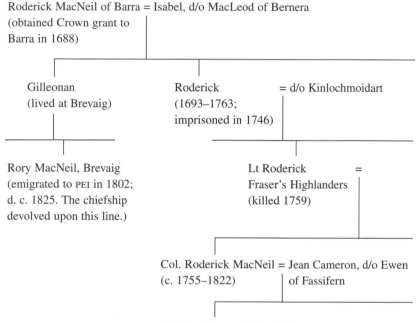

Roderick MacNeil of Barra = Isabel, d/o MacLeod of Bernera
(obtained Crown grant to
Barra in 1688)

Gilleonan   Roderick   = d/o Kinlochmoidart
(lived at Brevaig)   (1693–1763;
                             imprisoned in 1746)

Rory MacNeil, Brevaig   Lt Roderick   =
(emigrated to PEI in 1802;   Fraser's Highlanders
d. c. 1825. The chiefship   (killed 1759)
devolved upon this line.)

                    Col. Roderick MacNeil = Jean Cameron, d/o Ewen
                    (c. 1755–1822)   of Fassifern

                    Lt-Gen. Roderick MacNeil
                    (c. 1788–1863; retained a piper; bankrupt in
                    1827; sold Barra in 1838 to Col. Gordon of Cluny)

(1693–1763) was imprisoned, like Sir Hector MacLean from Mull, for his known Jacobite sympathies, but nothing is known of the principal Barra piper's activities during the rising.

A.J. MacKenzie stated that Rory MacNeil, the prince's pilot in 1745, was the most prominent in a long line of pipers, a fact that need not be inconsistent with John MacPherson's presentation of Donald MacKinnon as a family piper pre-1700. Intrusions into James Logan's, and earlier writers', "hereditary pipers" skein may have been common. The name Mac-Kinnon is associated with Protestant Skye, not Roman Catholic Barra, although a Catholic, musical MacKinnon family could, by 1700, have had deep roots there; Catholic MacKinnons are among the early settlers at Christmas Island parish, elsewhere in Gaelic Nova Scotia, and presumably also in Prince Edward Island.[74] None of the Barra MacKinnons in Cape Breton, for all that, are known to be directly associated with any Barra MacNeil piping family, although a widow, Mairead MacKinnon (a daughter of Hector Piper MacNeil), came to Christmas Island with her children.

A.J. MacMillan, in *To the Hill of Boisdale* (1986), gave her "Mairead MacNeil (Eachann Piobair)" (Margaret MacNeil [Hector the piper]) as the wife of Eachunn mac Iain Oig MacKinnon (Hector son of Young John MacKinnon), a man who died in Barra (having presumably lived all his life there).[75] At this stage, no family connection has been made between John MacPherson's Donald MacKinnon piper to MacNeil, Eachunn mac Iain Oig MacKinnon, and the MacKinnon pipers in Prince Edward Island in the nineteenth century,[76] or antecedents of the Burnt Piper (Am Pìobaire Loisge) MacKinnon in Inverness County, Cape Breton.

Two points remain. First, assuming that these "attendants" were pipers, then the number of MacNeil piping generations to the MacNeils of Barra may end with "Murdock Beag, s/o Donald, s/o John, s/o Rory Piper" (Murchadh beag mac Dhòmhnuil 'ic Iain 'ic Ruairidh Pìobaire), whose life, given a normal span, should have reached until Lieutenant-General Roderick MacNeil sold Barra to Gordon of Cluny in 1838.[77] Were this the case, then the playing of the bagpipes in Barra was continued uninterruptedly from the early eighteenth to the early nineteenth century in this MacNeil family.

Second, for Barra as for almost everywhere in traditional Gaelic Scotland, the link with hundreds of years of cultural past was broken by the emigrations, voluntary and forced, that came upon the Gael. In Barra the emigration of 1802 took with it the older son Gilleonan of the laird of Barra, Roderick MacNeil, to Prince Edward Island. Gilleonan, described as inept, was the ancestor of later nineteenth-century lairds of Barra who lived in Prince Edward Island. This was not the first emigration from Barra, and it was by no means unique in being multi-class and made up of large multi-generational families. What had happened to Glengarry, Glendessary, Glenurquhart, and Skye and many other Highland communities in the 1770s happened over and over again in Barra between 1780 and 1830 until, as the Coddy wrote, only the tacksman of Vatersay remained of the class that had once defined and been such an integral part of Highland community life.[78] That Lieutenant-General Roderick MacNeil's prize-winning piper in 1832 was a MacInnes and not a MacNeil suggests a break from fidelity to old ties.

John Lorn Campbell, casting a jaundiced eye on Barra's nobility, noted that Colonel Roderick (c. 1755–1822), grandson of the Roderick MacNeil who had been pre-emptively imprisoned as a dangerous potential Jacobite in 1746, was the last proprietor of the island to regret that Barramen were leaving. He may have been, but it was during his reign that the first massive emigrations from Barra occurred. Looking back with sympathy for the powerless Barra people, one finds it hard to believe that the regretful MacNeil proudly described himself as a melieuratier (improver). Procrustes would have smiled.

The work of de-peopling that Colonel Roderick left unfinished fell to the lot of his lieutenant-general son, a full-time improver who Campbell insinuated was a rugged Protestantizer. Gordon of Cluny's evictions of 1851 rounded out almost a century of persecution which changed Barra for ever. Traditional music and dance in Barra cannot but have lost a large portion of their vigour.

CHAPTER FIVE

Raasay MacLeods, Glencoe MacDonalds, Appin Stewarts, and Cluny MacPhersons

PIPING IN MAC GHILLE CHALUIM MACLEOD'S RAASAY

The MacKay pipers from Raasay, particularly in the person of Angus (c. 1813–59), son of John (c. 1767–1848), son of Rory of the family known as Clann mhic Ruairidh (the family of Rory, or the Rories), have had a profound impact on modern bagpiping, classical and light music. John MacKay, however, was firmly in the Gaelic piping tradition, and the family thus presents piping scholarship with a fascinating, but very speculative, study in the shift to modern literate bagpiping.

Angus MacKay's *Collection* (1838) defined modern classical piping for generations and is still a source of discussion and dispute. The MacKays have been described by several writers, none of whom have limited themselves to the few confirmable facts.[1] Even if it does require some speculation, however, Raasay can be put into a historico-demographic perspective that helps in assessing the MacKays' part in the story of bagpiping. And the MacKays, if one uses a share of the plausible speculation already reused again and again, can be situated in an interesting network of relationships of relevance to modern piping.

The Raasay MacLeods and their people were Jacobites in 1745 and remained Gaelic traditionalists until the last Mac Ghille Chaluim[2] Jacobite chief, John MacLeod (c. 1714–1786/87), eleventh of Raasay, died. Once the heritable jurisdictions were outlawed in 1747, there were in some parts of the Highlands inadequate juridical procedures as late as 1773, but in a law-abiding, Christian society, closely interwoven by kin relationships and with a traditionally Gaelic chief, this was no insurmountable obstacle. Johnson and Boswell were in Raasay in September 1773, and the conservative Latinist Johnson was delighted, at last, to find the conservative "patriarchal life" he had come to the Highlands to find. All the work he witnessed – rowing, "wawking," and reaping – was done to the accompaniment of Gaelic singing. There was dancing, to the "fidler," the night they arrived, and Boswell wrote simply that dancing was a nightly affair in the chiefly family.[3] Obviously the Church of Scotland minister serving Raasay was no enemy of tradition or kept his thoughts to himself.[4] Despite the chief John MacLeod's cultural conservatism, even in his time, in Raasay, there began the process of organized, voluntary depopulation, similar to that of nearby Skye. Citing Alick Morrison's *The MacLeods – The Genealogy of a Clan,* James McLeod mentioned a Murdoch MacLeod from Raasay "and other MacLeods from Raasay and Skye" emigrating "to North Carolina along with Flora and Alan MacDonald of Kingsburgh."[5]

Although the evidence I have at my disposal is in isolated fragments, it suggests that there probably was one important shift from older cultural times in Raasay with the fading away of Episcopalianism on the island. From *Fasti Ecclesiae Scotorum,* the appointment of the first Presbyterian minister for Portree (which included Raasay), Reverend Hugh MacDonald (1703–56), dates to 1727, leaving the earlier, different religious preference of the Raasay folk undescribed. However, James Boswell, MacLeod of Raasay, and Samuel Johnson visited the "old chapel" on 9 September 1773, and Boswell's use of the term "chapel" indicates an Episcopal church.[6] Also, as they were being rowed along the coast of Scalpa, the island south of Raasay, Johnson jokingly (and in the presence of the Presbyterian minister of Snizort, Reverend Donald MacQueen) suggested Boswell buy the chapel and found a good school and an Episcopal church there. In the text, Boswell bracketed Captain Malcolm MacLeod's response that "he would come to it."[7] The vigour of Episcopalianism in Skye and in mainland Gairloch, Kintail, and Reay country society persisted into the 1720s and later. In the 1720s, for example, it was still impossible for the Presbyterian minister for Gairloch, for example, to take up his charge there. Stewart of Garth wrote that "in many parishes, the Presbyterian clergy were not established till the reigns of George I and II" and that before this "for several ages after the Reformation they evinced a strong predilection to the Episcopalian form of worship."[8] Positive Episcopalian attitudes to folk culture and that church's part in preliterate Gaelic cultural retention in the eighteenth century are unstudied, although David Daiches associates the Episcopal church with the fostering of traditions in the northeast.[9]

As in Skye, Kintail, and elsewhere in Gaelic Scotland, the voluntary emigrations from Raasay in the 1770s were followed by improvement, dismay, misery, clearance, and the realization that the old life was no longer liveable. Raasay was finally sold to an outsider, George Rainy, in 1846.[10] He cleared it, but in fact the population had been leaving for two decades, ever since the death of James MacLeod, twelfth of Raasay (c. 1761–1824), a man, in the opinion of John MacKay's piper, of weakening attachment to the Gaelic way of life. James R. McLeod's recent articles and references show that a large

number of Raasay people went to Prince Edward Island and that consciousness of their Raasay roots persisted doggedly among them. John MacKay (c.
1767–1848), piper to James MacLeod, twelfth of Raasay, left for a piper's
job at Drummond Castle when his employer, the twelfth chief of Raasay,
died in 1824. (He had already won the top prize at the Edinburgh piping
competition in 1792.)[11]

When he left Raasay, John MacKay was in his late fifties. His oldest son,
Donald, had already left Raasay for service with Ranald George MacDonald
of Clanranald.[12] Certainly in the last quarter of the eighteenth century, when
John MacKay learned his piping, the piping world was thoroughly non-
literate; Joseph MacDonald's "Compleat Theory" had not yet been discovered in Bengal, and John MacKay, as late as 1821, was using the old
traditional method of transmitting classical piping. By the 1820s, however,
gentleman-inspired change, centred in the Lowlands and in London was
championing new classical bagpiping. Although one of the bard Sorley
MacLean's paternal uncles, Alasdair MacLean, was a piper in Raasay, it is
fair to say that the end of vigorous traditional Raasay piping came not long
after the end of the Napoleonic Wars. Perhaps that shift was more decisive
in the Raasay MacKay pipers than in any other piping family.

Three-quarters of a century earlier, if we believe (and infer accurately
from) what the writer in Angus MacKay's *Collection* wrote, at least one
piper went with the hundred men raised on the island to fight for King
James in 1745 and that was Captain Malcolm MacLeod of Bràigh, mentioned above (later of Aire, hence the name Fear Aire [the Laird of
Aire]).[13] Boswell and Johnson met him in his brogues, purple camblet
kilt, tartan hose, and blue bonnet and considered him the bearded *beau
idéal* Highlander. They heard him singing Gaelic songs and saw him
dancing as a fit sixty-two-year-old. Malcolm MacLeod (who died in or
after 1782) was a brother-in-law and cousin of the Jacobite John
MacLeod, eleventh of Raasay.[14] He was a great-grandson of John
MacLeod, first of Rigg in Trotternish, Skye (John was a younger son of
the fifth MacLeod of Raasay). Captain Malcolm was a tacksman who, like
other Raasay gentlemen, was hunted as a Jacobite fugitive by men of
MacLeod of MacLeod's independent company in 1746. He is believed, on
what should be excellent authority, to have composed "Cumha Phrionnsa
Thearlach" (Lament for Prince Charles), a pleasant, unchallenging tune.[15]
Nothing is known of when, how, and from whom he learned his piping,
but lore concerning him says that he kept company with John MacKay,
the Blind Piper of Gairloch (Iain Dall mac Ruairidh, d. c. 1754).[16] If he
piped for Boswell and Johnson they wrote nothing about it. Apart from
the Raasay MacKay source, probably Angus MacKay (c. 1813–59) himself, there is no confirming evidence that Captain Malcolm MacLeod was
even a piper.

Angus MacKay is also the source of the story that Captain Malcolm MacLeod was teaching piping to at least two youngsters on Raasay in the mid-1770s. One is unnamed, the other was Angus MacKay's father, the orphan John MacKay (Iain mac Ruairidh) whom Captain MacLeod is believed to have raised.[17] Even without this piece of information it is almost inconceivable that there was no Highland piper with the Raasay men in 1745–46.

The origins of the MacKays in Raasay are unknown, but the family descriptive "Clann mhic Ruairidh" suggests that a Ruairidh was the first, probably John's father. According to James McLeod, "Tradition maintains, and Angus [MacKay] confirms, that the progenitor of the MacKays of Raasay was John's father, Ruaraidh, a man from the Reay country 'who received his training from his countryman and namesake the Piobaire Dall of Gairloch.'"[18] If so, he probably moved to the island in the early or middle decades of the eighteenth century. MacKay is a Reay country name but one that has had roots in Gairloch since the early seventeenth century. However, if there is any relationship between the Raasay and Gairloch MacKays, it remains unknown.

Neither Ruairidh nor John MacKay left any record, and the chain of traditional lore is long dead in Raasay. Those interested in the subject are left to circle and pick at a number of unsubstantiated bits of data of unascertainable reliability, most of which have a nostalgic patina. Most of these originate, one way or another, with John's famous son Angus MacKay. At first glance he seems to be a reliable source for his own family information, but unfortunately he was mad and delusional when he was still writing towards the end of his life. Alistair Campsie, in 1980, drew attention to the significance of Angus MacKay's late-life insanity from 1854 to 1859.[19]

Another central supposition in Campsie's book is that Angus MacKay, delaying the publication of his *Collection,* took a job as piper with Campbell of Isla and Shawfield in 1837, in Isla, in order to gather music from the manuscript of the Campbell Canntaireachd held by, or in, Isla, or to learn how to read the manuscript which he, MacKay, perhaps had obtained from MacGregor Murray.[20] Worse, according to Campsie, was that Angus MacKay, in helping himself to the manuscript tunes, invented names for three tunes and, with no grounds, attributed another to Patrick Og MacCrimmon and John Dall MacKay (the Blind Piper of Gairloch). He stands accused by Campsie as well of wrongly describing tunes via their new titles, thereby forcing pipers to interpret wrongly the underlying sentiment (marches being different in expression from laments and salutes).[21]

Campsie intensified his argument by repeating the words of John Francis Campbell (Iain Og Ile), author of *Canntaireachd: Articulate Music,* that Angus MacKay "knew little of the system used by Campbells in Lorn, by MacArthurs and MacCrummens in Skye."[22] Not only does John Francis

Campbell's as yet incomprehensible treatment of *canntaireachd* in his book incline one to disbelieve this claim, but John Ban MacKenzie, one of John MacKay's pupils in Raasay in 1821, reported that John MacKay's sister sang the canntaireachd to the tune the piper was playing by way of guidance for the pupil.[23] John must have known it and how could John's son Angus not have?

Where non-classical bagpipe music is concerned, Angus MacKay's publishing record ostensibly does little to deflect Campsie's accusations. In 1843 Angus MacKay, "piper to Her Majesty," corrected and improved the sixth edition of William MacKay's (no relation) *Complete Tutor for the great Highland Bagpipe* (first edition, 1840), and evidence suggests that he had revised the now missing fifth edition.[24] Then, when Angus MacKay's *The piper's assistant, a collection of marches, quicksteps, strathspeys, reels & jigs* was published in 1843, most of the contents, and the pagination, were taken from William MacKay's *Complete Tutor.*[25] (It should be borne in mind that neither Campsie's nor Angus MacKay's book claimed to present scholarship to their readers. Not enough is known about William MacKay, and any relationship he may have had with Angus MacKay to suppose the latter was greedy or malicious.)

With respect to the source of the ceòl mól in his *Collection*, while Angus MacKay acknowledged input from "some literary friends who assisted him in researches for the historical portion of the work," there is no knowing who they all were, or how reliable. One can only surmise what MacKay contributed.[26] Archibald Campbell's "History of Angus MacKay" cites Angus MacKay as having given his father's wife's name as "Margaret MacLean or Marearad nion Aonghas," and it seems charitable to believe he at least knew his own mother's name.[27]

No one has yet challenged Angus MacKay's sanity in 1838, or in the 1840s (Seumas MacNeill gave him "teeming intelligence" as a boy of about thirteen when he had "presented at the Highland Society's competition an example of his attempt to write piobaireachd in staff notation"),[28] but according to Campsie, who was implying befuddlement, when MacKay gave his father's wife's name (above), he was in a Lowland lunatic asylum. The citation that Archibald Campbell used is expanded: "he [John Mac-Kay] was overheard by Fir Aire [Malcolm MacLeod], who taught him thereafter sent him to the College of the MacCrummens and to the Mac-Kays of Gearloch; and he married Margaret Maclean or Marearad nion Aonghas."[29]

There is no corroborating record that John MacKay was in Gairloch or in MacCrummen country, but if he had been, then his piping tutors would have been Red John MacKay (Iain Ruadh) in Gairloch[30] and possibly Black John MacCrimmon (Iain Dubh) at Boreraig, although other MacCrimmons on the MacLeod estate may have been teaching piping at the time, as Angus

MacIntosh implied in *Notes Descriptive* (see above). However unsatisfactory Campsie's work may be, he did piping a service by unearthing the records of Angus MacKay's lunacy and asking when it began and how his written legacy should be assessed.[31]

James McLeod repeated William MacLean's flattering and incorrect line that John MacKay was "the bottleneck through whom has come all that we know about *piobaireachd*." If that attitude is to be refuted, as it should be, one should include in one's refutation the mental condition of the transmitter of John MacKay's music, his son Angus.[32] With the exception of John Ban MacKenzie, the great nineteenth-century piper who learned ceòl mór by ear from John MacKay in Raasay in 1821, the definable Raasay MacKay influence has been Angus MacKay's and that invariably through staff notation. The differences between his ceòl mór and that explained in Joseph MacDonald's "Compleat theory" suggest either a regional limitedness to MacKay's work, deliberate simplification or adaptation, or perhaps a more general slipping from complexity to simpler fingerings and understandings of Scottish Gaelic classical piping in the early decades of the nineteenth century. (John Ban MacKenzie's piping is remembered for its general brilliance and not for any eccentricity of style or fingering, although he seems not to have learned the latter from John MacKay, whose habit, John Ban MacKenzie said, was to hide his fingers when teaching.[33] Perhaps what was sought was fidelity to the ear rather than the eye. Or perhaps, although it is hard to imagine how differently a *tuludh* or a *crunludh* might have been fingered, John MacKay may have felt guarded about his own skills. Perhaps, too, he may have wanted to hide the fact that his fingering differed from that in the standard set in 1803 by Joseph MacDonald in *A Compleat Theory of the Scots Highland Bagpipe*. The prize-awarding committee in Edinburgh in 1804 offered copies of a treatise, which they called "On the Theory, Principle, and Practice of the Great Highland Bag-Pipe Music" [accepted as Joseph MacDonald's work, although he was named John MacDonald, brother of Reverend Patrick MacDonald], to the performers who had "made the greatest improvement.")[34]

Relying on the writing of Angus MacKay in 1854, James McLeod pointed to the presence of a married sister, perhaps two, and a niece of Angus MacKay's in Prince Edward Island. McLeod reproduced the jotting that MacKay's sister "Kitty Og married John Munro and has one son alive at Kyleakin, Isle of Skye."[35] Munro, probably even more than MacKay, is not a common Highland name outside eastern Ross-shire and is seldom met with in piping's titles or other documentation.[36] However, an Archibald Munro (b. c. 1800), no known relative, achieved prominence in Kintail and Glengarry as a piper and is believed, from the lore sources available, to have been taught piping by John MacKay at Eyre in Raasay (see below). When he served Colonel John MacRa of Ardintoul as piper, it is noteworthy that

Munro was serving a nephew of John MacKay's piping patron, James MacLeod, twelfth of Raasay.

In the same article and its references, McLeod extends the breadth and depth of the MacKay pipers' family links with Prince Edward Island. McLeod also added to the genealogical file in noting that the great piper John Ban MacKenzie was married to a Maria MacKenzie from Applecross, granddaughter of John MacLeod, eleventh of Raasay (Malcolm MacLeod's brother-in-law and cousin).

Angus MacKay learned to be a modern, literate piper, and his publications influenced modern piping greatly. His father, it seems, was typically traditional. Unfortunately, one cannot safely infer that John MacKay played dance-music piping as well as the ceòl mór that he is known to have taught, although his son Angus improved, arranged, and composed a lot of non-classical pipe music. However, MacLeod of Raasay indulged his fancy for dancing, to fiddling, in 1773, so there may have been no stigma attached to bagpiping for the same function in Raasay.[37]

As elsewhere in Gaelic Scotland, the reaction of the traditional fraternity in Raasay to various modernizing influences in music and dance must be regarded in light of the emigrations. The Raasay population was thoroughly, but not totally, cleared from *circa* 1825. What lingered of traditional piping, fiddling, and dancing is now undiscoverable, but the idea that almost nothing survived the anti-cultural chastenings of radical Presbyterian clergy and others from the early 1800s touched the best Raasay thinker, Sorley MacLean, in the twentieth century.

In an overwhelmed, depopulated island, powerful Gaelic consciousness survived, particularly in the Raasay MacLean family that included song and story collector, Calum MacLean (author of *The Highlands*) and his brother Sorley, the pre-eminent Gaelic bard of the twentieth century. On their father Calum's side, they claimed descent from a Uist MacLean. At least one of that line, their great-grandfather John MacLean, did not emigrate from Raasay as his cousins did in and after the 1830s. John MacLean's son Malcolm was a singer-bard who, according to Sorley MacLean, was related to the Raasay MacKays (not all of whom emigrated either). Sorley and Calum MacLean's father's brother, Alasdair MacLean, Glasgow, was a piper and there were two pipers on their Nicolson mother's side, but no memory of their style and preferences in piping were recorded by the nephews.[38] According to Sorley MacLean, their mother was a great-granddaughter of a Soirle Nicolson (Somhairle mac Iain mhic Eóghainn [Sorley, son of John, son of Ewan]), also known as Somhairle na pìoba (Sorley of the pipe), who was a piper in the British army in the [Iberian] Peninsula and was at the retreat from La Coruña in northwest Spain.[39]

Sorley MacLean wrote of Raasay Gaelic tradition as follows: "But I now realise, when it is too late, that I myself exaggerated the Evangelical suppression of traditions in Raasay, thinking that the Free Church and Free Presbyterian churches had destroyed traditions that had really gone underground. I think now that there existed in Raasay, when I was young, more tradition, especially clan traditions, than I had suspected."[40]

What Sorley MacLean might have learned had he known what to ask when he was young is unknown, but where piping is concerned, a correspondent and friend of his was surprised to find that he had no knowledge of John Ban MacKenzie, John MacKay's pupil at Aire, or of Donald Cameron, Seaforth's famous nineteenth-century piper. Sorley MacLean's regret indicates a possible survival of knowledge of Raasay tradition into the twentieth century.[41] Raasay shows us no nineteenth-century equivalent of John Johnston in Coll, who was fascinated with traditional bagpiping, but even had one existed, the will to penetrate his or her thinking profitably apparently did not exist.

A known part, if perhaps not the only part, of Raasay piping tradition went to its grave in Skye in 1848. Old John MacKay (Iain mac Ruairidh), father of Angus MacKay, settled for his last years in Kyleakin, Skye, and died there. He may have had a grandson, son of John Munro, as a neighbour there as well as Donald MacRae, the Kintail military piper who won the first prize in 1791 and also chose Kyleakin to retire to (in July 1835 he was in his eightieth year). Nothing is known, or inferrable, about John MacKay's nonclassical piping; nor is it known that he ever played that music, although it is difficult to believe that his son Angus MacKay came to that popular repertoire only as an adult.

PIPING IN GLENCOE

The MacDonalds of Glencoe, patronymically the MacIains, holders of land from the Appin Stewart family, were active Jacobites in 1745. John Buchan claimed that Glencoe was Roman Catholic and he was supported in the belief by John Prebble, but neither writer consulted or paid attention to the evidence for enduring Episcopalianism in that region.[42] When Episcopal Bishop Forbes visited the diocese of Argyll in 1770, he confirmed 446 people in the district of Lochaber and Ballachulish.[43] Citing the *Old Statistical Account,* Loraine MacLean described the parish of Appin in 1791 as containing "four or five Papists" and "[g]reat numbers of Episcopalians, with four places of worship in the parish, viz. Lismore and Appin, Glenco and Kingerloch."[44]

Among the Glencoe officers in King James's lost cause were two Hendersons, one of whom, Donald MacErich, was a piper, if not the piper.[45] According to John Prebble, an earlier Henderson piper, known once as "Big Henderson of the Chanters," had mustered at Dail Magh-Comair (Mucomir) at the south end of Loch Lochy in 1689 with the Glencoe men and the

Chart 12   Father A.D. MacDonald's Genealogy of the MacDonald/MacHenry
Relationship in Glencoe

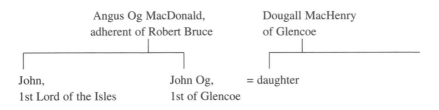

Jacobite clans who fought with Dundee at Killiecrankie.[46] He was still
Alasdair MacDonald's, Mac Iain's, piper in 1692 and escaped the massacre,
later settling in Ardnamurchan. (In 1951 Calum MacLean, Raasay, wrote of
meeting a descendant of this fugitive, Alex Dan Henderson.)[47] On the basis
of these two Henderson pipers, the family has been described as being the
"hereditary" piping family in Glencoe.

The commissioned rank of the Henderson piper of 1745, not in itself a
remarkable fact (see Captain Malcolm MacLeod of Braigh, above), is partially explained by the extremely long pedigree of Hendersons in Glencoe,
one that goes back to the early eleventh century, when the property, according to Father Alexander D. MacDonald (1907–56) of Mabou, was theirs. The
MacDonalds of Glencoe were "descended from John, a son of Angus Og
by a daughter of Dougall MacHenry, then the chief man of Glencoe. He
was thus a brother of John, First Lord of the Isles ... The MacHenrys were
in Glencoe as early as 1011."[48] Presumably younger sons of Dougall
MacHenry, or of his brother(s), kept the line going.

Mention of Donald MacErich (Henderson) in the list of Glencoe officers
fixes at least one piper there in 1745–46. The presence a generation later of
Allan MacDougall (Ailean Dall MacDhùghail, b. c. 1750),[49] bard and fiddler, is an indicator that traditional music continued in the late 1740s and
beyond, presumably until Glencoe society and culture succumbed, in the
nineteenth century, to emigration and economic change. Despite an understandable animosity between the Glencoe folk and some of the Campbell
clan over the massacre in 1692, Alasdair MacDonald (MacIain) turned himself in in 1746 to General John Campbell of Mamore,[50] an officer trusted,
according to the author of *Argyll in the Forty-Five,* by the Glencoe chief.[51]
MacDonald also prudently handed in his people's arms in May 1746, anticipating the duke of Cumberland's harsh reprisals.[52] The chief was released
from the Edinburgh Tolbooth 11 October 1749, the same year as Robert
MacGregor Murray of Glencarnaig and the same day as Cameron of Dungallon and John MacDonell "Glengarry,"[53] when the non-Gaelic–speaking

occupying forces were thought to have a clear vision of their legal mandate. No criminal activity of any significance was recorded from Glencoe in the military post reports 1749–50.

On 7 August 1749 a sergeant and a small party of troops belonging to Colonel Herbert's regiment were stationed at Glencoe to enforce the Disarming Act provisions against holding weapons and wearing Highland clothing.[54] Piping, like fiddling, storytelling, and song, having no part in their mandate, doubtless went on much as was normal – naturally, unselfconsciously, taken for granted. Unfortunately, nothing further is yet known about Glencoe's bagpiping in the eighteenth century. (Allan MacDougall did not mention any Glencoe piper although he did praise a Keppoch and a Glengarry piper in his published book in 1828.)[55]

Tacksmen had lands at Achnancon, Inverrigan, Achtriachtan, Brecklet, and Strone in Glencoe itself. One also had lands outside, at Dalness, tucked away in Glen Etive at the southern feet of the two "Herdsmen" (paying rent to a Campbell but owing allegiance to the Glencoe chief). Given that their fighting strength in 1745 generally ran at about 150 men (according to Duncan Forbes of Culloden), it is fair to assume that one or more of these subsections of the Glencoe people had a piper.

The other possible source of information about Glencoe pipers in the second half of the eighteenth century is the army, but any information there can only be inferred owing to a lack of recorded piping data. Glencoe only briefly held the eye of Scotland, in 1692. By the time of the Napoleonic Wars the chief had expanded his farming interests to a tack in Keppoch; he was one of the clearers in Keppoch, and, like many another chief, by mid-century he and his pride and importance as a Gael were parted.[56]

PIPING IN THE STEWARTS' ARGYLLSHIRE AND PERTHSHIRE

The main Stewart estates in eighteenth-century Gaelic Scotland were in Argyllshire and Perthshire, all long-enough established to have shown a distribution of Stewarts at all social levels. In Argyllshire the leading family was the Stewarts of Appin, with cadets going by the place-name designations, Ardshiel,[57] Invernahyle, Auchnacrone, Fasnacloich, and Ballachulish. (Other Argyllshire Stewart families were associated with Lorn and Balquhidder and an outlier at Belladrum in Banffshire [dates unknown]). In Perthshire, Stewarts held land at Grandtully, Ardvorlich, Dalguise, Ballechin, Kynichan, Bohallie, Blairfeaty,[58] and also at Inverchomrie, in Rannoch,[59] and at Benmore.[60] All these estates carry names that are obviously Gaelic in origin, and by the eighteenth century the majority of the tenantry and most of the laird class were Gaelic speaking, with John Roy Stewart the soldier-bard and Allan Breac Stewart prominent in popular memory.[61]

Although the Athollmen and Cluny MacPhersons had several pipers with them for the Atholl Raid on the Campbell-occupied bases in Perthshire in early 1746 (see above), no pipers are named or associated with any of the main Stewart tacks north of Loch Tay, and this shortcoming exemplifies the Stewarts generally and many other clans at the time. Pipers were a *sine qua non* and generally taken for granted.

With exceptions, the Stewarts were Jacobites.[62] From the fifty, mostly civilian Stewarts listed among the ordinary prisoners taken at and after Culloden, one can deduce that the main regiments in which they served were John Roy Stewart's, Stewart of Ardshiel's, Lord George Murray's, Lord Lewis Gordon's (Stonywood's), Gordon of Glenbucket's, MacGregor of Glengyle's, Lord Nairn's, and Glengarry's.[63] Among other regiments known from English records to have had pipers (some named and of those none obviously Stewarts) the following contained Stewart soldiers: Glengyle's, the duke of Perth's,[64] his brother Lord John Drummond's, Ogilvy's, and Lord George Murray's in the south, as well as Lord Nairn's and Gordon of Glenbucket's in the north. For all that, the nearest one comes to being able to propose that an actual Stewart tenant piped is to extrapolate from the knowledge that Captain James Stewart of Lord George Murray's regiment in 1745–46 had a piper, John Ballantine, in his company.[65] At a step removed is Charles Stewart (son of John Roy Stewart), officer veteran of Culloden and Quebec (1759 and 1760), who almost certainly had a piper with him while serving under James Wolfe.[66]

Although it is to stray further beyond the bounds of this work, it is interesting to note that, in the thirteen North American colonies, only one soldier was listed as a piper, and he was in Banastre Tarleton's British Legion.[67] His name was John McKay, and at different times he is listed as a drummer, a private man, and a serjeant. He enlisted 13 August 1778 in Captain John MacKenzie's company, where he is given as a piper. In the summer of 1779 both he and Lieutenant Donald McCrumen began service in Captain Charles Stewart's "Scotch Company Infantry British Legion Commanded by The Right Honble Lord Cathcart."[68] The speculation concerning this John McKay's family links with the famous MacKay pipers to the MacKenzies of Gairloch (Mac Eachuinn Gheàrrloch) is to be found elsewhere.[69] The identity of the Charles Stewart of Tarleton's British Legion has yet to be discovered.

From 1763 until the classical piping competitions at Falkirk (1781, '82, and '83) and Edinburgh from 1783,[70] piping on Stewart estates, to my knowledge, is only vaguely and generally mentioned in the written record. Then, at the second competition in 1783, in Edinburgh, a Paul MacInnes from Fasnacloiche in Argyll, a prominent Stewart of Appin tack, played "Pìobaireachd na Pairc" (The Park Pibroch).[71] In the mid-eighteenth century MacInnes was an Appin name.[72] Paul MacInnes, who won a suit of Highland clothes and some cash, was given no patron or affiliation with any organization, although in 1785 he was piper to Cameron of Callert on the north shore of Loch Leven in Lochaber.[73] The names of various other Stewarts and Stuarts appear in the "Account" in Angus MacKay's *Collection,* until the competitors Alexander Stewart from Kinloch Rannoch and an Archibald Stewart from Rannoch round them out in 1838.[74] More to the point, no piper representing a Stewart/Stuart landholder (with the possible exception of Duncan Stuart, piper to the Right Honourable Lord Mountstuart in 1791),[75] is mentioned in the "Account."

The decline in Gaelic society's vigour in Appin is tentatively chartable from observations of the ruling people's recoiling from Gaelicness. The situation in Appin, however, was also greatly influenced by the murder of Colin Campbell of Glenure by person or persons unknown on 14 May 1752 and that event's aftermath. To begin with, however, a possible first sign of a chief's withering interest in Gaelic tradition is found in one of the post reports of the occupying soldiery in 1750, two years after the Disarming Act took effect in the summer of 1748. Captain Henry Patton of Guise's regiment, stationed at Head of Loch Rannoch, reported on 23 July 1750 that "This Moment the party at Kinloch Leven have Brought me a Black belong to Mr. Stewart of Appin, dressed in tartan Livery, turned up with yellow; and to-morrow I send him to the nearest Justice of peace."[76] Gaelic chiefs' and chieftains' investment in property in the West Indies from the first half of the eighteenth century was not inconsiderable. Stewart of Appin's having a black servant may have been a mark of involvement in modern, non-Gaelic society.

The Stewarts of Appin had fought under the chief in 1715, but in 1745 Dougald Stewart, tenth of Appin, was a minor and the Stewarts were led out for King James by Big Charles (Stewart) of Ard Shiel (Teàrlach Mór Aird Seile, Charles Stewart fifth of Ardshiel, d. 1757).[77] Ardshiel was attainted and forfeited his holding for his fidelity to the Jacobite cause, and his estate was plundered and re-plundered by government troops in 1746. (If Ardshiel held his land by wadset, then, as with Young Barisdale, wadset holding did not exempt one from forfeiture in 1747.) According to Robert Bain, the ninth chief of the Appin Stewarts sold the Appin estate, and Duncan Stewart, sixth of Ardshiel became the tenth chief in 1769. The estate of Ardshiel, was returned to the chief in 1782.[78] In 1752 Colin Campbell of Glenure, a grandson of Sir Ewen Cameron, fifth of Lochiel, left Fort William to evict a number of tenants from the Ardshiel estate, of which he was factor (he was also the forfeited estates factor for Callart and the part of Lochiel's estate in Mamore that Lochiel held from the duke of Gordon). Serious disruption for some of the traditional Appin families thus began early, and the malign influence of the factor of the forfeited estates is here obvious.[79]

That bagpiping had once been common in Appin – and supported by the Gaelic middle class there – emerges from the publication of the gist of a conversation between an old piper and a judge in 1841. In that year, the circuit judge Henry Lord Cockburn travelled to Ballachulish, where he spent the night at the inn run by the former competition piper Angus Cameron. Lord Cockburn had stayed previously at Cameron's inn on the north side of Loch Leven in 1819. Donald Cameron (b. c. 1776), once piper to Donald Cameron, ninth of Lochiel, told the judge that there had been a "general decline of the art [of piping]" and that "there was not now one single *real* [italics published as Lord Cockburn's] piper – a man who made the pipe his business in the whole of Appin."[80] Cameron attributed the decline pointedly to the disappearance of the old chieftains and their castles and gatherings.[81] The learned judge had advanced other reasons for piping's decline, as it had never occurred to him that Gaelic cultural decline was class linked.

In 1845 there was still a "Stuart" laird of Ballachulish, whose brother, John Stuart, "a Chancery barrister," lived at Kinlochleven. In that year, however, Fasnacloiche was occupied by a Lord Ivory. At Callert, Sir Duncan Cameron had built a new Callert House.[82]

Where family or clan-associated classical pipe tunes are concerned, the information field is no more fertile. A tune published until the title "Bratach Bhàn nan Stiùbhartach" (The Stewarts' White Banner) is found in *Piobaireachd*, book 7.[83] The notes appended show that this is the name that Angus MacKay, son of John, Raasay, gave the tune *circa* 1838, pursuant presumably to personal fancy. They show also that *circa* 1822 Donald MacDonald called it "Cumadh Dubh Shomhairle – a doleful lament for the death of Samuel, a celebrated Piper" and in the early 1790s the Campbell Canntaireachd called it "Samuell's Black Dog" (which would have been "Cù Dubh Shomhairle" in Gaelic); the author of the note in *Piobaireachd,* book 7 noted that the latter was "obviously a mistaken translation of Donald MacDonald's name" (that is, of the name which Donald MacDonald used, which in modern orthography would have read "Cumha Dubh Shomhairle").[84]

PIPING ON THE CLUNY MACPHERSON ESTATE

A family of MacPherson pipers in Badenoch, claiming a pupil/teacher relationship with Red Donald MacCrimmon in Glenelg in the early nineteenth century, played a large part in the resuscitation of classical piping in the nineteenth century.[85] In the eighteenth century, on the other hand, the story of Cluny MacPherson piping is much more obscure and much less documented. Nonetheless, there are occasional estrays to be used and inferences to be drawn that point to a continuous presence of bagpipers on the Cluny estates from 1745.

The Cluny MacPhersons (Clann Mhuirich Cluanaidh) formed a major part of the congeries of clans known as Clan Chattan in the district of Badenoch along the upper waters of the Spey. Although the area was roughly used after Culloden, a little more is known about their chiefly piping than is about the Stewarts', at least between 1745 and 1751. The Cluny MacPhersons are also a people, like the Chisholms, Dungallan Camerons, and others, with a magic chanter story. The Cluny MacPhersons were Jacobites in 1745 and fought successfully at Falkirk and in the Atholl Raid against Campbell Militia–held forts in the south of the Highlands in 1746. It is almost certain that pipers from MacPherson country were present when Andrew Agnew and his North British Fusiliers (21st Regiment of Foot) were frightened back to Blair Castle.[86] Not being present at Culloden, the Cluny MacPhersons only lost those arms that they chose to hand in in 1746 and after. (On 4 June 1746 MacPhersons handed in some arms to Lord Loudon.) However, as in Keppoch and Lochiel, the old family house was destroyed some time after Culloden.[87]

Ewen MacPherson of Cluny (died in Dunkirk, 1756)[88] broke his officer's oath and deserted the Hanoverian army for the cause of King James in 1745, thus doubly imperilling himself.[89] After Culloden, in hiding, he was still a man in charge of a well-armed small civilian army known for its firmness and resolution under trained British military fire. Cluny was therefore an obvious rallying point for any future Jacobite military business in Gaelic Scotland. It is no surprise that his capture was a high priority after Culloden and that that priority ensured year-round attentions by the occupying British soldiery, normally barracks-based during the winter months.[90] Hector Munro with eighty men of the 34th Foot unsuccessfully hunted for Cluny in Badenoch from 1751 to 1753,[91] a failure made the more pathetic in that during the summer of 1752 James Wolfe, who was at Fort Augustus,[92] deliberately stationed Trapaud[93] and his men at Laggan to get the job done. When Cluny finally left the Highlands in 1755, it was at the bidding of Prince Charles, not because of British military pressures.

Two valuable sources for chiefly piping in Cluny's country exist. The first comes from a letter from John MacPherson of Strathmashie to Bishop Forbes, dated 1 May 1750. "In Benalder of Badenoch," in 1746, with Cameron of Locheil, Lochgarry, Dr Archibald Cameron, and Breakachie, there was "one Allan Cameron, a young genteel lad of Calard's [Callert] family, who was principal servant to Locheil, and four servants, belonging to Cluny, particularly James McPherson, his piper."[94] Then, in a revealing letter dated 22 October 1751, from Colonel Crawfurd in command at Fort William, to Churchill, Crawfurd wrote that (Cameron of) Glen Nevis, his brother Angus Cameron, MacDonald of Lochgarry, Lochgarry's brother or half-brother Angus MacIain, and Young Glengarry went to talk with Cluny at Dalwhinnie in Badenoch in 1749. Presumably Crawfurd's source for this information was Young Glengarry (Pickle the Spy). Presumably Pickle, or whichever informant, either did not learn where Cluny was hiding (at Benalder) or chose not to expose him to Crawfurd. Cluny talked to Lochgarry and Young Glengarry but told Glen Nevis to wait till he (Cluny) called him, "tho he [Glen Nevis presumably] sent repeated messages by Clunie's Piper, and a young Brother of Clunie's."[95]

Direct musical references pertaining specifically to the MacPherson family are scarce from the occupation period, although nearby analogues, especially the Grants' pipers in Strathspey, all but guarantee widespread piping in MacPherson territories. Also, there were MacPherson officers in the Black Watch (43rd, 42nd) and in Montgomerie's (77th) and Fraser's (78th) Highlanders, all of which had company pipers.[96]

Where chanter stories are concerned, the MacPhersons had their "feadan dubh" (black chanter), which they said had descended to them from heaven.[97] At some undetermined time the Cluny MacPherson chief lent it to a neighbouring Grant who needed extraterrestrial help. It was returned, then reborrowed, and eventually found its MacPherson home in 1822.[98] James Logan in 1831 paraphrased a letter that he had received from Ewen MacPherson, Esq., of Cluny (who had succeeded his father Duncan in 1817).[99]

Duncan MacPherson (b. 1750, d. 1 August 1817), son of Cluny of the '45, was raised by his guardian, his father's brother, Captain John MacPherson of Fraser's Highlanders (5 January 1757), a regiment known to have had a strong attachment to Gaelic traditional piping. Duncan himself took a major's commission in the Fraser's Highlanders (1st Battalion, 71st, 1775) of the American Revolutionary War.[100] His interest in tradition is not indicated in military sources, but the ball that he held at Pitmain in 1784 to celebrate the return of the Cluny estate was dominated by Scotch Reels. The event was witnessed by Colonel Thornton. Also, one of the last honours accruing to Duncan MacPherson publicly was the winning of the Edinburgh classical piping competition's fifth prize in July 1817 by "John MacPherson, Piper to Colonel MacPherson of Cluny."[101]

Although Aeneas Mackintosh may have been right about pipers turning scarce in the Spey area of the Gàidhealtachd in the last quarter of the eighteenth century, and although there may have been a preference, even in Cluny MacPherson's country, for the violin over the bagpipes at that time, these notions are challenged in a number of places. Here is one example: at the level of the community piper, John MacKenzie (Eileanach, 1803–86), son of the Sir Hector MacKenzie of Gairloch whose piper left for Nova Scotia in 1805, wrote of a piping incident in his diary. When he was travelling on the coach from Inverness to Edinburgh *circa* 1816, the coach's "guard," a familiar old friend Eileanach called "dear Donald" (Mackintosh), asked the passengers if they would mind leaving Pitmain, the usual stop/change place half a mile south of Kingussie, a little late for the leg to Dalwhinnie. He wanted to join in the wedding celebrations of a cousin of his in Kingussie. "So, all the passengers being fonder of their fun than of their meat, we soon despatched our dinner and, pioneered by Donald, reached a house in the village and were made more than welcome by the marriage party we found dancing to the pipes. And we agreed that, as was right and proper in Strathspey, we had never seen such famous dancing, nor have I ever seen the like since. All seemed trained dancing masters."[102]

PART TWO

"Hereditary" or Chiefs' Pipers in Hanoverian Scotland

CHAPTER SIX

Piping in MacCrimmon and MacDonald Skye and in Strathspey (Grants)

THE MACCRIMMONS AND LIEUTENANT DONALD MACCRIMMON, PIPER TO MACLEODS OF DUNVEGAN

The MacLeods in Skye retained, for an unknown number of generations, the most famous name in Scotch bagpiping, the MacCrimmons,[1] although how justified or unjustified the elevated MacCrimmon piping reputation is is debatable. Joseph MacDonald never mentioned any MacCrimmon and put Skye second in the two piping centres that he did mention.[2] He was probably also not deluded in thinking that his Reay country was very significant to Gaelic bagpiping. On the other hand, Aeneas Mackintosh of Mackintosh in *Notes Descriptive,* while not mentioning the MacCrimmons either, made Skye the epicentre of all Scottish bagpiping in or after 1773.

Earlier, by 1700, there were several MacCrimmon families in Skye, in Glenelg on the marches of Matheson country[3] and probably elsewhere. Today the name has almost disappeared from its old haunts, and there is not enough trustworthy information about most of the retrospectively famous piping people to dispel some of modern piping's most fertile imaginings about them. Campsie's *The MacCrimmon Legend* tried, humorously but at times convincingly, to lance the awed notions held by modern pipers about the MacCrimmons and that is the book's achievement.[4] Apart from major shortcomings, to some of which Alan Bruford drew public attention,[5] Campsie gave no hint that he had had exposure to remnant traditional Gaelic piping, and he too would have been slow to understand positive aspects of piping of a different brilliance than his own.[6]

Since almost nothing is known of the fingering techniques of the MacCrimmons, it is impossible to set up any MacCrimmon as paragon of that aspect of piping. Alexander Campbell wrote that Red Donald's fingering seemed peculiar to himself, but we don't know with whose he compared it. From the eighteenth century the source of the idea of the dominance of technique in classical bagpiping (now long extended to include the remainder of piping's repertoire) springs, apparently, from Joseph MacDonald's manuscript of *circa* 1760. Certainly MacDonald's diagrams of modern fingering and left hand upper are the earliest of their kind. Neither appears to have been prescribed in preliterate piping.

Fingering variants recorded in Highland Scotland during the nineteenth century, probably including Red Donald's, show there to have been different ways of making the notes, but noone knows the reasons. Otherwise, much else that MacDonald described may or may not have been the stuff of competition in the years after 1804; we don't know because no descriptions of the playing exist. Sticking unfailingly to one technique, until fairly recently, has come to preclude other understandings of traditional piping, especially when the same technique standards are applied to dance-music piping, where speed and timing, depth of repertoire, and the need for unbroken music must, if necessary, subordinate technique.

James Logan's simple model for "the piper" as dignified land-rich gentleman-tacksman, however obviously narrowly limited and derogatory of the majority of community pipers, does apply in the case of many of the MacCrimmon pipers to various MacLeods of MacLeod. Red Donald Mac-Crimmon (Dòmhnul Ruadh MacCruimein, d. 31 July 1825, aged 87),[7] about whose life more is reliably recorded than of any other MacCrimmon, held tacks at Boreraig and Shader and at Trien in Waternish,[8] as well as a farm (tack?) in Glenelg. His older brother Black John (Iain Dubh, d. 1822, aged 91) also held the Boreraig tack. Accepted thought is that these MacCrimmon brothers were sons of Malcolm (Calum), son of Pàdruig Og.[9] Malcolm (1690?–1767?) and Pàdruig Og (d. 1730) were also pipers to MacLeod chiefs and held land from MacLeod. It has long been assumed that the "college of piping" that Samuel Johnson said was "not quite extinct" in 1773 had been run at Boreraig by Red Donald until 1772 or '73 and by his brother Black John in Johnson's time in the Highlands.

There were many other MacCrimmons, pipers and non-pipers, with whom other MacLeod properties are associated, in Skye and Harris, making the family a large and prominent one. The MacCrimmon cairn on the bounds of Glenelg and Lochalsh marked on the 1885 Ordnance Survey one-inch-to-the-mile sheet gives evidence of the MacCrimmon presence on what had been the mainland part of MacLeod lands.[10] Unfortunately, speculating on the relationships even of many of the eighteenth-century ones to one another is seldom helpful.[11]

In the 1760s and on into 1770 Donald MacCrimmon held Boreraig and Shader from MacLeod, in Skye, not far from Dunvegan, and kept up the college of piping associated with his family for at least thirty years. He was a member of the Gaelic middle class and, following his father, Malcolm, was the chief's piper. The Highland Society of London from the 1780s till the early 1800s, under chiefly MacLeod promptings, considered him the acme of the art.[12] Pipers everywhere believe that his music, like that of several of his ancestors, was important as a statement of his inherent and acquired genius as a player, and of his chief's taste. Most pipers assume this taste was exclusively for classical piping, that unusual, isolated form of Celtic court and martial music, played on an instrument that was disappearing in Ireland and variant forms of which were rapidly being reduced to derogated, rustic status in England and in urban Europe.

This assumption has a weak foundation, since there is a demonstrable interest within this class of eighteenth-century Gaelic society in Reel dancing.[13] If there is any truth to the assumption, then it is linked to the Highland Society of London's self-imposed mandate to stimulate classical piping. That important mandate doubtless influenced most strongly would-be Highlanders and Scots who resented being considered North Britons and who were searching for a distinctive identity. From those reactionaries began the long process of the elevation of ceòl mór to near mystical status.[14] Ceòl mór grew to be something learned only by technically correct, tried and true adult pipers capable of comprehending profound subtleties of expression. It is therefore strange that, from 1781 to 1838, the classical piping of several boy pipers merited prizes in the Edinburgh competitions, and that Joseph MacDonald's book was offered to pipers who had made the most improvement. As Gaelic self-confidence weakened in Scotland throughout the nineteenth century, this idea of the mystic genius of ceòl mór vis-à-vis the less-inspired, prosaic inventiveness that nonetheless produced songs like "Nead na circe fraoiche," "Cabar Féidh," and a hundred other memorable songs, infected an uninoculated, vulnerable society. In other spheres one finds people like Sorley MacLean coming to realize too late that not all accepted knowledge ought to have been so readily accepted (see above).

Lore suggests Donald MacCrimmon was from a teaching and composing family of long standing. The records of the Breadalbane estate for 1696 show "McIntyre ye pyper" being given "forty pounds scots as his prentisewhip with McCrooman."[15] Later, under Breadalbane's signature, the apprentice's name is given as John MacIntyre. Forward a century, Ruairidh Halford MacLeod reported that "the daughter in law of MacCremman," Marion Mackinnon, wrote a letter on 11 December 1793 to the Highland Society of London stating that "MacCremman is now settled in the ancient colege for Pipe Music in the Isle of Skye, and is ready to instruct pupils." MacLeod stated that Lieutenant Donald MacCrimmon was then at Boreraig, his old home[16] (to which he had moved from a tack that ran from 1792 to 1811 in Trien, Waternish, Skye), and added elsewhere that MacCrimmon declared himself ready to teach piping to Alexander MacArthur in 1797.[17] He played and taught piping in Glenelg around 1814 when he was about seventy-six, although, according to Walter Scott, he deliberately chose not to pass his piping knowledge on to any of his sons.[18] His older brother, Black John, passed the piping gift along to one of his daughters and, outside the family, to Angus MacPherson (b. 1800), to Angus Munro of Oban, to the father of Simon Fraser (b. 1796), and probably in his earlier days to more than that. He also shared, some say, more than two hundred tunes with Captain Neil MacLeod of Gesto (d. 1836), who chose to publish twenty in *Pibereach or pipe tunes, as taught verbally by the McCrimmen pipers in Skye to their apprentices. The following as taken from John McCrimmon, piper to the old Laird of MacLeod, and his grandson the late General McLeod of McLeod, at Dunvegan* (1828).

In 1745 MacLeod of Dunvegan was a Loyalist. Red Donald's father and paternal uncle both piped for King George's army during the 1745–46 uprising, the latter being the only fatality at Moy in 1746 referred to above. Assuming Red Donald to have been born around 1738, he must have begun learning the instrument in the mid- to late 1740s. His older brother, Black John (b. c. 1730), must have started earlier. Both future pipers unquestionably were developing their craft during the immediate post-Culloden years.

Genealogically the MacCrimmons have been the subject of books by Poulter and by Poulter and Fisher. Elsewhere, dealing specifically with Red Donald, Alexander Campbell's reminiscences of his piping, published in *Albyn's Anthology* (1816), and other remarks in "A Slight Sketch of a Journey" make an enticing beginning, and Ruairidh Halford MacLeod's two articles in the *Clan MacLeod Magazine* provide a foundation, for an understanding of Red Donald and for further enquiry. What we have learned of Donald MacCrimmon's seven years in what is now Shelburne County, Nova Scotia, from 1783 till 1790 casts no light on him as a piper. No neighbour's diary has come to light offering any memories of his playing any instrument and he certainly had a lot to lament; his southern plantations were gone and his farm in Nova Scotia was pathetically infertile. In Nova Scotia he ran a ferry across Jordan Bay, but his name is one that is forgotten nowadays, like many another Loyalist's.

There is no record of Donald MacCrimmon's piping anywhere in the New World, in North Carolina or Nova Scotia, although he claimed to have been present at the battle of Moore's Creek Bridge and it is known that pipers were present.[19] He was gone from Scotland for seventeen years from 1773 until 1790. Nevertheless, the Highland Society did not want any other MacCrimmon or a MacKay, a MacArthur, a MacGregor, or a Rankin (or anyone else whose ego might have been flattered by the offer of a "professorship" of piping) to teach at a projected new college of piping in the Highlands. They wanted Donald MacCrimmon and to get him they defrayed the cost of his and his wife's and three of his four children's passages back to Scotland in 1790, when he was just a step ahead of the Shelburne sheriff.[20] His piping reputation was obviously still high after a trying set of experiences in the New World.

Why the Highland Society's project failed is unclear. In 1814 the subject seems still to have been a lingering sore point with MacCrimmon, one he preferred not to enlarge upon when talking to Alexander Campbell. The Crown owed Donald MacCrimmon better than he got and so did the duke of Kent (after the Regency, King George IV), who, according to Donald's son Patrick's will, owed Donald's estate £492.10.0.[21]

Lieutenant Donald MacCrimmon's decision not to instruct his children in the art of piping was certainly based on ideas conceived at about the time of the early tacksman emigrations, in the early 1770s, when he gave up Boreraig, possibly earlier. Although he taught various pupils when he was an old man, the overall disposition of parts of the once extensive MacLeod estate, during his lifetime, must have confirmed the rightness of his decision to let the Gaelic past slip into nostalgia. In 1799, only a few years after he had returned to Boreraig, several substantial Skye tacks quite close to Dunvegan, including Boreraig, Glendale, Hamar, Galtrigall, Skinidin, and Colbost, were sold by MacLeod. MacCrimmon may have returned to Trien, Waternish, but his teaching is more closely associated with his later home, Glenelg, and it too was on the market. Glenelg, once an important MacLeod holding on the mainland side of the cattle route to southern markets, according to John Prebble, was sold by MacLeod in 1798, then resold in 1811, 1824, and 1837, each change in ownership forcing more of the ordinary Gaels off the land.[22] What degree of tenant security pipers like Lieutenant MacCrimmon and his pupil Alexander Bruce had in the area is unknown.

The idea that what is known as classical piping began with one or more MacCrimmon ancestors, of Red Donald and his brother Black John has had currency for generations. There's no proving or disproving it, but the mystique of originating genius and of composing giftedness clings to the name MacCrimmon. Many people accept a facile corollary that piping was somehow rude and simple in earlier Highland Scottish society, during the times when the harp was the chief's chosen classical instrument. This also is an assumption, and it doesn't say very much for the players of and composers for bagpipes over their long existence of hundreds of years in many parts of Europe, including Gaelic Ireland and Gaelic and English Scotland. Poor piping, after all, has always been easy to identify.

While there is a temptation to think that ceòl mór must be linked with wider European classical music of the sixteenth, seventeenth, and eighteenth centuries, at least one old piper and student of the instrument, John Johnston, who died in Coll in 1921, believed that a traditional tune that he played was from the fourteenth century (springing from the same inter-clan fight at Perth that, according to one story, encouraged God to bestow upon the MacPhersons their famous chanter). What Johnston presented is obviously a piece of ceòl mór, although shorter than almost all tunes known since 1800. John Johnston had no trouble with the fact that it contains both *tudhludh* (*taorluath*) and *creanludh* (*crunluath*) variations, thought by many to be MacCrimmon inventions and relatively recent (and perhaps, in some people's thinking, to be the subtle novelty that helped the pipe overtake the harp as the chiefs' preferred musical instrument).[23] There is no reason, however, that these tudhludh and creanludh fingerings have to be relatively recent. In any case, John Johnston claimed that the tune he knew commemorated, and was contemporary in composition with, the Battle of the North Inch of Perth in 1396. A contemporary report of the event doesn't mention bagpipes being played, but bagpipers were commonly overlooked in the eighteenth century.[24]

However much one may imagine within the MacCrimmon family a lineage of talented pipers reaching back the seven generations Alexander Campbell wrote about after his visit to the old piper in Glenelg in October 1814,[25] the only generation of which we know anything much more than a name with any certainty is the last one, which included Lieutenant Donald and his older brother Black John. No bagpiping peculiar to either of them is identifiable today, although lots of pipers have at times felt convinced by their vaunted lines of tutorship that they were playing like the great ones. This is not to say that the MacCrimmons were not highly distinctive in ways about which we know nothing. They both taught and lines leading to them are constructible, but there can never be a guarantee of faithful duplication of their musical foibles or exceptionalness. Some of the tunes they played are known, by title in the case of Donald and by title and by the canntaireachd left by MacLeod of Gesto in the case of Black John. The latter's canntaireachd, however, can only have been a rough outline of his actual music, a shorthand, lacking personal playing eccentricities, giving no speed or timing.

While both men are thought to have restricted their bagpiping to the classical repertoire, no contemporary made such a claim. Gesto was on intimate terms with Black John and took many classical pieces down from him. Red Donald was heard playing ceòl mór as a man in his sixties and seventies by Norman MacLeod (later Reverend) in 1799,[26] Walter Scott in 1814, and Alexander Campbell in October 1814.[27] They all wrote about the experience, Campbell most glowingly, although, since as far as we know he was untrained in piping, his opinion is unassessable. One could only play "Pibroch of Donuil Dubh" as Campbell wrote it in *Albyn's Anthology* if one had a knowledge of the published modern form.[28] Campbell's description of the overall effect and of piper's fingering is well known now, but he appears not to have found the courage to ask MacCrimmon anything about his peculiar fingering. Campbell did not find MacCrimmon ready to enlarge on piping and learned more later on from Donald MacCrimmon's pupil Alexander Bruce at the Glenelg public house where he was staying. MacCrimmon had invited Bruce in to play for Campbell (before he himself produced his prelude and then "The Prince's Salute"), and from Alexander Bruce, Campbell learned "many interesting particulars regarding the mode of training pipers by his celebrated Preceptor which I have taken notes of and may hereafter prove useful."[29] Among the sadnesses of piping's tale is that Campbell's notes have not been found and that nothing survives from Alexander Bruce, if he wrote anything, about a learning experience that in later life he surely must have dined out on. So, because Campbell had the temerity to suggest that MacCrimmon's fingering was in a class by itself, one is inevitably left to try to guage Campbell's competence as a non-playing judge of Mac-Crimmon's fingering.

Alexander Campbell (1746–1824), pupil of the Italian castrato Giusto Tenducci (presumably in Edinburgh, where Tenducci made several visits), episcopal organist and singing teacher, and Gaelic speaker from Tombea (about twenty miles northwest of Callander), must have been exposed to Keppoch piping in Brae Lochaber, if not in his home community. Four or five years after Ranald MacDonell of Keppoch died, in 1785, Campbell married his widow and lived in Keppoch from 1806 until 1810.[30] The Mac a'Ghlasraich Campbells were pipers in Keppoch at the time, and in 1798 a MacFarlane piper in Glengarry's retinue is mentioned by Allan MacDougall (Ailean Dall Dughalach), whom also he knew.[31]

Campbell travelled and collected Gaelic material as early as 1784;[32] he was aware of Patrick and Joseph MacDonald's work and knew that Patrick MacDonald was well on in years in 1815. He acknowledged help from Sir John Sinclair (Ulbster), Sir John MacGregor Murray (of Lanrick), Ranald MacDonald of Staffa, and Lewis Gordon, secretary to the Highland Society.[33] He also was in contact with David Stewart of Garth.

What Walter Scott, the crippled Edinburgh writer (and singing pupil of the same Alexander Campbell), wrote of the man who had raised men on his own broad acres in Anson County, North Carolina, who had fought with Tarleton in the American south, who had apparently evaded capture by the Americans at Yorktown in 1781, and who had lost two comfortable fortunes (the first, his tack in Skye, which he quit *circa* 1771; the second, a large acreage in what is now North Carolina), not to mention an eye, smacks of ignorance of Highland affairs and of condescension (perhaps also of an initial social rebuff by the piper). The following famous paragraph is taken from J.G. Lockhart's biography of Scott: "MacLeod's hereditary piper is called MacCrimmon, but the present holder of the office has risen above his profession. He is an old man, a lieutenant in the army, and a most capital piper, possessing about 200 tunes and pibrochs, most of which will probably die with him as he declines to have any of his sons instructed in the art. He plays to MacLeod and his lady, but only in the same room, and maintains his minstrel privilege by putting on his bonnet so soon as he begins to play."[34]

Some of the numerous MacCrimmons on the MacLeod holdings were unquestionably celebrated pipers in Skye, Harris, and perhaps Glenelg (before Lieutenant Donald settled there). Certainly in Skye many were teachers of the finer points of piping. However, there were other pipers and fiddlers in Skye in the eighteenth century. Red Donald and Black John have so much dominated all thinking about MacLeod piping in the later eighteenth century that other MacCrimmons of the family, and non-MacCrimmons, have been overshadowed. What Walter Scott went on to say about MacLeod piping at Dunvegan in 1814 has deepened the mystique surrounding Donald and Black John: "MacLeod's present piper is of the name but scarcely as yet a deacon in his craft. He played every day at dinner."[35]

I.F. Grant identified this "deacon" as Donald Donn MacCrimmon, and that indeed may have been his name, although in piping circles the name Donald Donn, on the basis of one source of questionable reliability, is immediately associated in piping circles with the seventh son of the famous Pàdruig Og (d. c. 1730). This Donald Donn would have been a man very ripe in years by 1814. The *Piping Times* said that the piper Scott heard was another Donald, Donald Donn's paternal grandson, Donald (Dòmhnul mac Coinnich 'ic Dhòmhnuill Dhuinn [Donald, son of Kenneth, son of Donald Donn]).[36] Donald and his father, Kenneth, were both from Lorgill on the west coast of Skye at some distance from Dunvegan. A record from 1768 attests to their presence there. Both were pipers and, if the story is right, cousins to Red Donald and Black John. They swell the number of MacCrimmon pipers during the Disarming Act times to four.

On the basis of Scott's observation, many people have believed that around 1800 there were the great MacCrimmon pipers, old but still remarkably effective, in the long, long shadow of a golden tradition, and there were the rest. The "deacon" that Scott heard has been assumed to have been among the rest and to have been forever inferior as a piper, unbrushed by the genius of his famous cousins.

The MacCrimmons, what's more, sold or gave their piping talents outside the MacLeod holdings. Ruairidh H. MacLeod, searching in the MacDonald Papers, came on a Farquhar MacCrimmon who was "an innkeeper and piper in Sleat in 1746,"[37] and according to Angus MacKay's notorious notes in his *Collection,* there was a John MacCrimmon, son of Pàdruig Og by his second wife, who was piper to MacKenzie, earl of Seaforth.

MacLeods, beyond a doubt, were avid supporters of music, of pipers, violers, fiddlers, and, one must assume, harpers, as long as the traditional Gaelic life lasted. Lines written by Màiri nighean Alasdair Ruaidh (Mary, daughter of Red Alasdair) in the late seventeenth century sum up a MacLeod chief's interest in music, an interest that endured in his descendants into the second half of the eighteenth century, although then tempered by the new demands of profitability: "An fhìdhleireachd 'gam / Chur a chadal, / A' phìobaireachd / Mo dhùsgadh maidne" (Fiddling putting me to sleep, piping my morning call).[38]

Writing of a slightly later period, the opening years of the eighteenth century, I.F. Grant noted that MacLeod, through his tutor (estate manager) Contullich, supported pipers and fiddlers in the neighbourhood. MacLeod's violer in 1706, for example, was James Glass. He received his "customary allowance." In the same year MacLeod was paying "Ronald Pyper" in Minginish. In 1707 and 1709 the "pyper in Harris," Hugh MacLeod, was being paid. A piper was also employed in Bracadale, and two payments were made to unnamed pipers in 1710. It was the done thing and during his tutorship Contullich defended his behaviour by mentioning the fact.[39] Music and dance were popular in MacLeod's holdings through the kirk's moderate days, into the days in the early years of the nineteenth century when ex-fiddler Donald Munro was one of the puritan revivalists. The story of the suppression by religious bigots of Neil MacLeod of Gesto's book about the MacCrimmons, implicating the putative source, Black John MacCrimmon, is found in Collinson's *The Bagpipe*.[40] The curtailing factor is the tacksman-led emigrations from MacLeod's estate from around 1770, largely to the Carolinas. These were well organized by middle-class Gaels, and they involved large numbers of families threatened with a rapidly falling standard of living as rents were dramatically raised, often before old tack agreements had run out. Red Donald left and with him, and other tacksmen, who knows how many other good musicians.

MacLeod, living as he did in the northern part of Skye, controlled the flow of cattle from the Long Island to Southern markets. The drove roads through Skye and through mainland Glenelg had to be secure from reivers, and it made sense to ensconce militarily capable tacksmen along the route, where there was farmland that was appealing enough for them.

MacCrimmons are associated with the Boreraig area and with other places along the drove roads in Skye and also in Glenelg, a MacLeod mainland holding till 1798. He who controlled Glenelg controlled the cattle crossing at Kyle Rhea and the high passes to the east. He had to contend with several mainland thieving clans, not least of which was Barisdale. At least at times there were also MacCrimmons in Harris.

If the MacCrimmons were dominant in the piping of the eighteenth century, they were insignificant in the nineteenth. Lore nonetheless stubbornly accords them a pre-eminent place in the story of Scotch bagpiping. The skimpy written record, in Gaelic and English, is far from unkind but unfortunately leaves more questions than answers and affirmations.

MACDONALDS OF THE ISLES, IN SKYE AND NORTH UIST

The MacDonald estates occupied a large part of Skye, including Sleat in the south, and the most northerly peninsula of Trotternish. They also included North Uist in the Outer Islands. They supported a large population, among whom in the second half of the eighteenth century were many pipers, as elsewhere many more than are known about, including several in North Uist. How these musicians compared with one another in the mind of the local Gael is unknown, although MacCodrum isolated the three discussed earlier. All three were associated with the Inner Hebrides, Skye, and Mull (but perhaps including Harris and Glenelg), and these names fit nicely into nineteenth-century published ideas about prominent eighteenth-century pipers. Matheson believed that MacCodrum's "Teàrlach" was Charles MacArthur, and today MacArthurs are believed to have been by far the most prominent on the whole MacDonald estate. Apart from MacCodrum's three pipers, however, in the pre-Culloden decades there is one case of a gentleman piper-composer associated with Vallay, a tiny island to the north of North Uist, and perhaps also with Airds in Trotternish.

Angus MacKay's writer(s) made this note above the relevant tune in the *Collection:* "William Macdonald Esqr of Vallay" was the gentleman who composed "Failte Ridir Seumas na'n Eilean" (Sir James MacDonald of the Isles' Salute).[41] In the "Historical and traditional notes on the Piobaireachds," the writer expanded on the circumstances of the tune's conception in 1664.[42] Elsewhere, in Angus MacKay's manuscript collection, one of the tunes included is headed "Cumha Tuitear Chlann Domhnuill, Lament for the MacDonald's Tutor. The Tutors of the MacDonalds of the Isles were the MacDonalds of Vallay."[43] Henry Whyte (Fionn) claimed that the tutor being commemorated was William MacDonald of Aird in Trotternish (Skye), not of Vallay.[44] William, a son of Sir Donald MacDonald of Sleat, was tutor to Sir Alexander MacDonald (d. 1746) during that chief's minority. William MacDonald was a veteran of Killiecrankie (1689) and died in 1730. Since Sir Donald MacDonald, fourth baronet of Sleat (d. 1718), had only one son, the Sir Alexander in question, William MacDonald must have been the son of the fourth baronet's father, Sir Donald MacDonald, third baronet, and consequently an uncle of Sir Alexander.

Blending Angus MacKay's and Whyte's information leaves one with the important confirmation that, from time to time, as in the case of the MacCrimmon and Rankin families (and as in the field of Gaelic poetry where middle-class Gaels composed), classical Gaelic bagpiping had composing and playing exponents in the gentleman-tacksman class, in this case, on the estate of MacDonald of the Isles in the mid-seventeenth century. Whyte in the same place ("Historic, Biographic and Legendary Notes to the Tunes") added that William MacDonald had a son, Ewen MacDonald of Vallay, who, "was a famous piper and composer of pipe music."[45] According to Donald Fergusson, when Ewen MacDonald of Vallay, the piper-composer, died, a tune in his memory, "Marbhrann do Fhear Bhallaigh" (Eulogy on Vallay), was composed by "piper, harper and fiddler Donnachadh macPhadruig" (Duncan, son of Patrick [MacPhail], d. c. 1795 aged 107). Duncan MacPhail apparently was a North Uist man.[46] Fergusson also stated that Ewen of Val-

Chart 13 Abbreviated Genealogy of Some of the MacDonald Baronets of Sleat

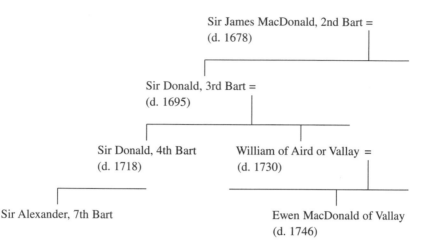

Sir James MacDonald, 2nd Bart =
(d. 1678)

Sir Donald, 3rd Bart =
(d. 1695)

Sir Donald, 4th Bart   William of Aird or Vallay =
(d. 1718)   (d. 1730)

Sir Alexander, 7th Bart   Ewen MacDonald of Vallay
                                           (d. 1746)

lay left Skye in 1733 to be factor in North Uist, serving there until 1746. Fergusson named one Angus MacDonald (Aonaghus mac Dhomhnuill 'ic Iain Duibh [Angus, son of Donald son of Black John], one of the old North Uist MacDonald family of Sìol Mhurchaidh (Children of Murdoch), as the last piper and a fine one, who could play the "Lament for the Laird of Vallay" all the way through. Angus was a veteran of the Napoleonic Wars and the subject of a poem in Fergusson's book.

It is not inconceivable that this gentleman, Ewen MacDonald of Vallay, was piping after the '45, nor that he was the Fear Bhàlaidh referred to in John MacCodrum's song/poem "Diomoladh Pìoba Dhòmhnaill Bhàin" (Dispraise of Donald Ban's Pipe). MacCodrum began his fifth verse "Cha tug thu taing idir / Do Bhriogardaich Theàrlaich / Mach o Fhear Bhàlaidh / Bhith ghnàth air a thì"[47] (You gave no thanks at all / to the twittering of Charles / but for Vallay / to be following his fancy[?]).

In his outrage, mock or not, MacCodrum said that the "bard" only deigned to include the name of one of the three top pipers of the time, Teàrlach, in the context of his having been a favourite of Fear Bhàlaidh, the gentleman of Vallay. As already mentioned, Matheson identified Teàrlach as Charles MacArthur, the most famous of the hereditary pipers to the MacDonalds of the Isles. Tradition said that Charles attended his first chief, Alexander MacDonald, when the latter attended St Andrew's University between 1726 and 1729. If Alexander was a minor at the time, then his "tutor" was the William MacDonald discussed above and Charles MacArthur and William's son Ewen were of much the same age and doubtless acquainted. Charles MacArthur piped during the Disarming

Act years (1748–53), and so must have the younger MacDonald of Vallay.

Vallay is a very small island off the north coast of North Uist, lying in a bay between Griminish Point and the community of Sollas.[48] Trotternish is the most northerly part of Skye and the Aird is within walking distance of Hunglader, where the MacArthurs are believed to have held a farm. Even conceding that Fergusson's data and sources may be less than thoroughly tested, North Uist was clearly a much more musical place than many people imagine.

Three MacIntyre pipers show up in Skye, at least one of whom piped in 1745, and probably afterwards, the others having flourished earlier in the century. These will be treated after the Breadalbane segment for the sake of an easier continuity.

Apart from the MacCrimmons, the MacArthurs are widely accepted as one of the other major piping families about whom lore exists over a number of generations. They were based in the Skye and in North Uist in the eighteenth century and earlier on in Islay and Uist, but they are commonly associated with a farm holding in Trotternish in the north of Skye. Records of them and their genealogy(ies) in Skye and in North Uist in that period are incomplete and the subject of argument. One of the few sources, *Clan Donald,* affords what appears to be a fairly credible framework.[49] Information in that work, and elsewhere, points to a long association of MacArthur pipers and Mac-Donald chiefs in Skye and the Outer Islands and possibly to an earlier bond in Islay. Undoubtedly several of them played the pipes during the Disarming Act days. They are believed by most pipers to have been one of the top-three teaching families of Highland pipers in the eighteenth century and probably earlier. The zoologist Thomas Pennant, while touring in Skye in 1769, was given "a repast" and "treated ... with several tunes" by Sir Alexander Mac-Donald's Mac-Karter piper; he said that the "Mac-Karters" had a college of piping and were the chief pipers to the MacDonalds of Skye.[50]

The most important MacArthur piper during the Disarming Act years was Charles, a contemporary of John MacCodrum, the MacDonald bard. He is given in *Clan Donald* as son of the Angus MacArthur who piped at Sheriff-muir in 1715 in his capacity as piper to Sir Donald MacDonald of Sleat.[51] According to William Matheson, apparently on his own authority, Charles MacArthur was piper to three MacDonald chiefs, Sir Alexander MacDonald, presumably seventh baronet, and his two successors, Sir James, eighth baronet (1741–66), and his (Sir James's) brother, Sir Alexander, ninth baronet, who died first Lord MacDonald in 1795. Matheson wrote, "Charles had the advantage of being under the tuition of Padruig Og MacCrimmon (?1645–?1730) for eleven years."[52] This claim, even if it is a mistaken interpretation of the Roman numeral for Arabic 2, may still be an exaggeration. The author of the notes on the MacArthurs in Angus MacKay's *Collection* said that he was perfected a piper by Pàdruig Og MacCruimein, and perfecting already competent pipers seems to have been the real teaching work of the MacCrimmons; as in the case of David Fraser, this was undertaken in a matter of months. MacArthur lived through the post-Culloden period, and Thomason's *Ceòl Mór* (c. 1896) attributes to him "Lament for Sir James MacDonald."

William Matheson said that it was he, Charles, whom Pennant met in Skye in 1772 and whose recumbent stone lies, with its carved inscription unfinished, in the Kilmuir graveyard.[53] The *Piping Times* states that the piper whom Pennant heard was the same one that Dr Johnson heard at Armadale Castle in Sleat in 1773, Angus MacArthur, son of John Ban, Charles's brother.[54] It seems fairly safe to say that it wasn't the innkeeper, Farquhar Mac-Crimmon mentioned above.

Unless there are two Charles MacArthurs, and that is the plausible theory of the author(s) of the notices of pipers in the *Piping Times*,[55] Charles MacArthur must have lived, and bagpiped, into a ripe old age, and unlike any MacCrimmon or MacKay of Gairloch, he must have deigned to enter the piping competitions in the Lowlands. The Highland Society lists of competitors and prize winners in Angus MacKay's *Collection* includes a Charles MacArthur in 1781 who was piper to Archibald Montgomerie, the earl of Eglinton (d. 1796). How this Charles MacArthur got into Montgomerie's service is straightforward, but why isn't, nor when. Margaret Montgomerie, Archibald's sister, was married to Sir (later Lord) Alexander MacDonald of Sleat (d. 1795), hence the link between a Skye MacArthur piper and a Montgomerie.

Montgomerie was a non-Gael but popular among Highlanders; he raised the 77th Highland Regiment with no difficulty, his commission dating to 4 January 1757, his officers' to a day later. They served in the Seven Years' War, and according to Stewart of Garth, the regiment contained "30 pipers and drummers."[56] It is conceivable that Charles MacArthur, entrenched in middle age, began his connection with Montgomerie as a private soldier-piper or simply as the colonel's personal piper during the Seven Years' War. There were no officers answering to his name in Montgomerie's Highlanders, but the Black Watch model of gentlemen and tacksmen serving as rank and file might not have entirely faded away by 1757.[57] If MacArthur was the piper who, as *Clan Donald* said, accompanied his chief to St Andrew's University between 1726 and 1729 and later piped for three MacDonald chiefs, then what happened to take him out of secure, high-status MacDonald service and make him piper for the earl of Eglinton, in or out of the British army? If he had a son or a nephew called Charles MacArthur, a younger man, sufficiently less impregnated with Hebridean pipers' pride to enter a pibroch competition in Edinburgh, then some of the apparent anomalies would be laid to rest. In any case, one or perhaps two Charles MacArthurs piped during the Disarming Act years in Skye and one of them taught piping.

If we turn back the pages for a moment, we see a spasm of irateness and a quirk of poetic fortune show MacArthur pipers in Uist at an early period. Two pipers, Ian and Dòmhnull Mhic Artair, are mentioned in a short poem called "Seanachas sloinnidh na pioba bho thus" (*sic*) (that is, Seanachas sloinnidh na pìoba bho thùs [The story of the geneaology of the pipe from the beginning]), which is attributed to the Clanranald (MacDonald) hereditary bard/historian Niall mór MacMhuirich.[58] Derick Thomson gave Niall Mor's dates, tentatively, as 1552–1613 and added that his grandfather, Donald MacVurich, probably was a landholder in Kintyre in 1541.[59] The MacArthurs, too, are thought to have come originally from the south of the Scottish Gàidhealtachd, from Proaig in Islay, where they are said to have been armourers and pipers to MacDonald of the Isles. Islay and Kintyre, once MacDonald strongholds, lie at a latitude lower than Edinburgh's. They are also near one another, making the MacArthurs and MacVurichs neighbours, which would go some way to explain the MacArthurs' presence, however unwanted, in the MacVurich home in Uist.

The poem in question is no celebration of glorious piping, and in contrast to contemporary MacMhuirich court poetry, it is written in the vernacular of its time. Thomson described it as humorous rather than cruel. Niall was just back in Uist from bardic training in Ireland at the time, showing the ravages of smallpox. He was stretched out asleep near the fire when John and Donald MacArthur came into the house, pretext unknown, and proceeded to tune their pipes. Niall didn't like piping and his outrage found outlet in this apparently spontaneous, unpremeditated poem. (His father, Lachlan, who heard his son's outburst, is said to have reflected that his time in Ireland had been well spent.) Others have suggested that the MacVurichs' power and influence were in decline at the time and that their resentment of pipers, pipes, and piping sprang from jealousy.[60]

Doubtless there were always MacArthur pipers from this early date, but there is no evidence for a continuity between the John and Donald trapped in MacVurich's crude vituperation in the late sixteenth century and the eighteenth-century people in Skye or elsewhere in the Highlands, although the two first names crop up at the later period.

The writer of Angus MacKay's notes said that Charles MacArthur, the greatest of the eighteenth-century pipers, had two brothers, Iain Bàn and Neil.[61] *Clan Donald* only mentions Iain Bàn; he was Sir Alexander MacDonald's official piper in North Uist and received a salary of £33.6.8 in 1745 for the service. His son Angus (Aonghus mac Iain Bhàin) was piper to Lord MacDonald and died in London in 1800, last MacArthur to the chief of Clan Donald. (Alexander, ninth baronet, was created peer of Ireland in 1776; he died in 1795 and the title of Lord MacDonald fell to his eldest son, Alexander Wentworth MacDonald, who died unmarried in 1824.) Thirty of Angus MacArthur's pieces of pibroch were taken down by John MacGregor, forming the first collection of classical piping. Neil may not have been a piper but his son John was, trained by his uncle Charles MacArthur. He settled in Edinburgh and was piper to the Highland Society of Scotland.

Charles MacArthur himself had at least two sons, Donald and Alexander, and the latter was a piper. Donald is believed to have drowned taking cattle from Uist to Skye. Alexander is said to have emigrated to "America," although in 1797 Ruairidh Halford MacLeod stated that Red Donald MacCrimmon was willing to teach an Alexander MacArthur piping. To date, no definite trace of him in the New World has come to light, but Matheson noted of Alexander that, "[s]hortly after 1800, he petitioned Lord MacDonald to appoint him his piper, describing himself as the only male representative of the family then living."[62] This perhaps suggests that he had successfully managed to avail himself of the tutoring of Lieutenant Donald MacCrimmon – what better recommendation to lay before Lord MacDonald.

All of these men, Charles, Iain Bàn, Alexander, John, and Angus MacArthur, piped during the years 1747 to 1782, in Sleat, Trotternish, and North Uist. A number of them, like the MacCrimmon brothers, must have been in their most formative learning periods during the Disarming Act years.

Apart from those sources, there is a folk-tradition witness to MacArthur pipers, John MacDonald, a Skyeman who died in 1835 at the age of 107. He was from Glenhinisdale in Trotternish, a mile or two north of Kingsburgh in Skye, and spent a lot of his time there with Allan MacDonald, seventh of Kingsburgh, and his wife, Flora MacDonald. His acquaintance with the MacArthur pipers presumably goes back to the 1730s. John was the father of Donald MacDonald, the Lawn Market (Edinburgh) piper and pipe maker whose published books of pipe music of 1822 and 1828 went into several editions. John MacDonald was interviewed by a divinity student, Alexander MacGregor,[63] in and around 1831, and to use MacGregor's words, "It was a favourite theme of his to dilate upon the musical proficiency of the MacCrimmons, the family pipers of the Macleods of Dunvegan, and likewise the MacArthurs, the hereditary pipers of the Macdonalds of the Isles. He acknowledged that the MacCrimmons were more famed for their musical talent, but still that they could not surpass the beautiful and systematic performances of the MacArthurs."[64]

No one knows how numerous the MacArthur pipers were or the extent of their influence as pipers in the Gàidhealtachd outside of Skye. John Johnston, the old Coll piping devotee, knew of MacArthur pipers in Ulva; he had heard the last of them, John MacArthur play, but he suggested no relationship between them and the Skye pipers.[65] Johnston placed them firmly in the older ceòl mór tradition whose passing he so ardently lamented. Much nearer the present, Pipe Major William Gray wrote in the *Piping Times* that Charles MacArthur had two nephews settled at Ulva who were pipers to Boisdale and (Reginald MacDonald of) Staffa.[66] Gray's source is unknown, but Staffa had a piper in 1810 called Archibald MacArthur; a reproduction of him appears in *Kay's Edinburgh Portraits* for that year. Walter Scott heard a piper play in Staffa's company in 1810 at the cavern (Fingal's Cave, on Staffa), and he may have been the same MacArthur.

The Skye MacArthur family farm in the 1770s was either at Peighinn a' Ghobhainn (the Smith's Penny-land), about three miles as the crow flies slightly east of north of MacDonald's eighteenth century seat at Monkstat in Trotternish, or at Hungladder nearby to the west. *Clan Donald* says that the MacArthurs had held land in Hunglater in Trotternish, "from time immemorial," worth eighty-three merks in silver in 1733. The terms on which it was held from MacDonald are known for *circa* 1770. The name of the holding suggests that the occupants were also smiths. The family was certainly prominent in the classical piping scene in the second half of the eighteenth century.

Looking again at Angus MacKay's *Collection,* we see that in 1781 at the ceòl mór competition sponsored by the Highland Society of London, held at the Mason Lodge in Falkirk, Charles MacArthur, piper to the earl of Eglinton, played four pieces and won the second prize of thirty merks. Next mentioned is John, a grocer in Edinburgh who had earned the sobriquet "Professor" for his teaching of piping. He was piper to the Highland Society of Scotland, lived and taught piping in Edinburgh in the 1780s, and appears in the competition lists for 1783. With reference to the Piobaireachd Society, finally there is Angus MacArthur, the last hereditary piper to MacDonald mentioned above.

The chances are excellent that old John MacDonald had heard them all play the pipes. At least one of them was in Skye during the early 1770s. Like so much in piping, MacGregor committed little to paper. Thomas Pennant visited the house of "Sir Alexander Mac-donald's piper" in Skye in 1772. Pennant didn't name the man. Matheson states that it was Charles; the *Piping Times* says that it was Angus, son of John Ban. In any case, in Skye the piper seems to have had a better deal from MacDonald than Donald MacCrimmon had from MacLeod at much the same time. MacArthur had his land free for the service and that at a time when rents in Skye were high and rising. The piper lived in what Pennant said was a four-room house, "like many others in this country."

While *Clan Donald* doesn't elaborate much on piping, it does say that the Sleat MacDonald chiefs kept a piper in "each of their three baronies of Sleat, Trotternish, and North Uist."[67] For 1723 (elsewhere 1733) the Sleat piper

Chart 14   Short Genealogy of the MacArthurs, as Generally Accepted

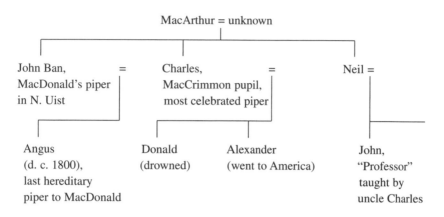

was Malcolm MacIntyre, who held his lands free for the service. According to the MacDonald Papers, in 1745 two Trotternish pipers, Iain MacIntyre and Neil MacCodrum, served as pipers in the two MacDonald independent companies of the four raised by MacLeod in 1745.[68] In 1746 the innkeeper in Sleat was Farquhar MacCrimmon, a piper. Pipers were plentiful on Mac-Donald holdings as they were in MacLeod country. Their numbers and the family name of most of the other pipers in these areas after 1747 are unknown. How much the tacksmen emigrations of the 1760s and '70s, as well as the later major population shifts to the New World affected pipers great and small on the MacDonald estate is also unstudied, but large numbers of families from MacDonald holdings in Skye went to North Carolina before the outbreak of the American Revolutionary War in 1776.

We should now go back to within months of Culloden, to November 1746. Sir Alexander MacDonald died at Glenelg barracks in that month, and his remains were taken to Kilmore in Sleat, "where he was accorded what was perhaps one of the most sumptuous funerals ever witnessed in our island. All the pipers of note were there, and, a mighty concourse of mourners."[69] Alexander Nicolson reported the rumour that the funeral had cost the huge sum of £2,645 and noted that MacDonald of Ord had seemed nostalgic when he discussed the wild affair, which took the lives of three men and caused the serious injury of another fifty (thus apparently were successful funerals gauged). However much Sleat may have been Hanoverian, there are enough examples shortly after Culloden of undiscriminating violence by the occupying forces in parts of the Highlands to make the reference to "pipers of note" very much corroborative of the fact that pipers were not persecuted.

THE GRANTS IN STRATHSPEY

The Grants were Protestants, with a small number of Roman Catholic exceptions among the ordinary folk in Glenmoriston and maybe also in Glenurquhart. Grant landholdings included the heartland on the strath of the River Spey as well as land to the west of the Great Glen in Glenmoriston and Glenurquhart. In 1745 they were split politically between Hanoverians and Jacobites. The main family of Grants who inhabited the broad strath of the River Spey were loyal to the Hanoverians,[70] and for them the continuity of piping and pipers before and after 1746 is reliably stated, and repeated, without contradiction. In fact, the importance of the Hanoverian Grant family as patronizers of piping in the eighteenth century is very much under-estimated and typically treated in isolation from the subject as a whole, despite the fact that the Spey valley and probably the Grants' musicians there are credited with having introduced strathspey timing to the Gaelic musical repertoire, despite some very important lore and record, and despite Richard Waitt's painting from life of Grant of Grant's piper, William Cumming, in 1714.

The Glenmoriston branch, on the other hand, was Jacobite *pur laine,* and even though, according to Keltie, the estate was not forfeited, the natives of that long east-west glen (a number of whom had sheltered Prince Charles) had to put up with suffering and disruption immediately after Culloden, particularly with the transportation of nearly seventy men to Barbados. In the case of the Glenmoriston portion of the clan, some might argue that they were the closer to traditional Gaelic ways, and more in the sphere of influence of the Jacobite MacDonells and less in that of the loyal Grant chief or the nearby loyalist activist Forbes of Culloden (d. 1747). As in Catholic Jacobite Keppoch and Protestant Jacobite Cameron country, the record of piping in Glenmoriston during the critical years is unreconstructable and obscure.

In Strathspey a piper to the Grant chief is mentioned in 1624. Citing a letter from John Grant of Glenmoriston, chamberlain and baron-bailie for the laird of Grant, at the time at Baile MacCathan (MacCathan's farm), the local historian William MacKay noted that the bearer of the letter would have with him, in custody, the person who killed "your serwand Donll Pyper."[71] Almost certainly the John Grant of Glenmoriston involved was the third Grant of Glenmoriston, Iain mór a' chaisteil (Iain mac Phàdruig 'ic Iain [Big John of the castle (John son of Patrick son of John)]). He had added to the Glenmoriston seat at Invermoriston and was married to a daughter of the laird of Grant.[72] The chief of the Grants in Strathspey at the time was another John Grant, Sir John Grant, son of John Grant (d. 1622), buyer of Rothiemurchus from the Shaws, and Lillias Murray.[73] The piper's surname is unrecorded, but he may have been a Cumming, that being the name of the hereditary pipers to the Grants for at least three, probably more, generations until the 1780s or '90s.[74]

In fact, the musicians' function may have been a dual one, for James Logan, no source adduced, in *The Scottish Gaël,* described the Cummings of Freuchie as hereditary fiddlers to the Grants.[75] The Cummings appear to have been patronized for their skills on both instruments. If this is so, it is a feature of Gaelic society whose importance is seldom recognized, let alone given much attention in modern Scotland, but which finds a very substantial number of parallels, in a non-patronized way, in rural Gaelic society in nineteenth- and early twentieth-century Gaelic Nova Scotia, where pipers were often fiddlers too.

The Reverend W. Forsyth, writing in 1900, nearly seventy years after Logan, said that the first Cumming was Alex Cumming, piper and violer to the laird of Grant in 1653.[76] In citing (in the same place) his stipend of twenty marks Scots per annum, Forsyth probably relied on the Seafield Papers (Seafield was the seat of An Granndach, the Grant chief, the earl of Seafield), but whether Forsyth's cue came from James Logan's popular work or from the local lore available to him is unknown. Cumming is described as from Freuchie (the site of Castle Grant) in the parish of Abernethy and Kincardine, the Jacobite John Roy Stewart's territory.

The *Piping Times* offers additional Cumming data, but with no source citations, giving the last hereditary Cumming musician living at Freuchie as Red John (Iain Ruadh); he was a "regular performer on the bellows-blown or Lowland pipe and the fiddle." His date of death is given as between 1750 and 1760.[77] This claim may be correct; he may have been the last hereditary piper to live at Freuchie and he may have predeceased his father, William, who by then may have quit piping. However, indications are that at least some sort of Cumming-Grant relationship, if not the old piper father-to-son one, endured until well into the nineteenth century. A John Cumming, piper to Sir James Grant of Grant (1738–1811), was one of the unsuccessful competitors in the 1784 Highland Society competition in Edinburgh. Then, *In the Shadow of Cairngorm,* Forsyth put the death date of the last of the Cumming musicians in the parishes of Abernethy and Kincardine at about 1869, when another John Roy died.

Following Red John Cumming in the *Piping Times*'s alphabetical notices of pipers is his father, William Cumming, whose dates are listed as 1687–1762. He is described as an excellent piper, piper to the Grant chief, and the piper whose portrait was painted by Richard Waitt. This oil-based painting, completed in 1714, was one in a collection of portraits by Waitt, commissioned by the lairds of Grant between 1714 and 1725.[78] The piper is holding the instrument under his right shoulder, and his right hand is the upper one on the chanter. In a photographic reproduction of the original Waitt's perceptiveness appears, at first glance, to have been stunted, especially when it came to pipe chanters and drones. The colour of the wood may be an accurate representation and the lathed ornamentation of the various pieces may also be true to what he saw, but there are apparent anomalies in the construction.

Tuning slides (which must have existed) for the drones for any bagpipe or for bellows pipe drones are indistinguishable in this representation. The chanter is apparently unconical in bore under the finger holes, with belling only of the terminal. In this it may resemble or actually be from a Lowland set or from a contemporary parlour set of pipes. Red John is supposed to have played a bellows set, one he received, presumably, from his father. Parts of this set may have been adapted to more current fashions in the early eighteenth century. The blow-pipe is remarkably slender and short. The piper's fingers are crooked rather than held straight on the chanter, and the upper (right) hand seems barely to be a fair representation of a piper's hand. This may have been because Cumming was not actually playing the instrument at the time the representation of the fingers was made; alternatively, and more important, however much it conflicts with our notion of how the best pipers are believed to have covered the chanter holes, Cumming may have played like that, as some old traditional community pipers did in Cape Breton into the twentieth century.[79] Why would Waitt have so adeptly represented the piper's livery outfit while making so many apparent errors in the man's musical instrument and in his fingers?

Livery appurtenances apart, one general impression is obviously uncontestably right. The instrument William Cumming is playing is a three-drone set with both tenor drones emerging from a common stock. With the technical ignorance of pipes and piping that we assume Waitt the painter to have displayed, it is most unlikely that he would have imagined a common stock for the tenor drones. The famous Glen set, now proved to have been made in the early eighteenth century but which masquerades as a much older instrument, was a two-drone set using a common stock. It isn't impossible either that the "Grant piper" was playing an old traditional two-drone bagpipe to which the third, the base drone, had been recently added.

From a Disarming Act point of view, the most cogent piece of corroborative data pertaining to the Grants is that, according to family records, in 1753, the last year when arms were proscribed to all but the larger landowner, the year also of the critical and last Jacobite scare, and the year that Dr Cameron was hanged at Tyburn and Barisdale faced execution, a resident piper at Castle Grant was receiving £40 per annum for his music.[80]

It is evident that the chief of the Grants retained a family piper during the Disarming Act years, with no fear of recrimination, and throughout the eighteenth century.[81] The *Piping Times*'s list of Cumming pipers is clearly incomplete, for whatever reason. Until the present, for those followers of Collinson's theory who know about Grant pipers at all, the fact that the hereditary Cumming pipers appear to have come to a halt around 1760 has been used speciously as an argument that the Disarming Act killed off piping, albeit more slowly in some places than in others. In actual fact, that evidence and the presence of the various west coast colleges in the 1760s show again that there was no persecution of pipers and piping.

Whatever financial arrangement Grant arrived at with his musicians in the days of improved estate management, patronage of the Cumming family does not appear to have disappeared at the convenient rough date of 1760 any more than MacLeod of MacLeod's did of John MacCrimmon in Skye after Donald MacCrimmon left for North Carolina around 1771. Unless there are ulterior motives for promoting falsehood, the best that can be said is that the closure of the MacCrimmon, the Rankin, and the MacArthur colleges of piping has prompted people with preconceived ideas to assume that patronized piping (and for some almost all buccolic piping itself) went the way of the colleges.

How healthy dance-music piping was in Grant territory is not known, but since "Strathspey" dance timing is known to have grown in popularity from about 1750 in Lowland Scotland, there is an almost unassailable case to be made for traditional dance music's vitality in Hanoverian Grant country coeval with the £40 per annum piper. The several cases of "violers" brought before the kirk courts in the 1750s in the united parishes of Abernethy and Kincardine, "in the shadow of Cairngorm," and reprimanded or punished, were always associated either with public sabbath breaking and/or rioting/disorderliness. Actual music was not the object of the clerical campaign. The *Form of process in the Judicatories of the Church of Scotland; with relation to Scandals and censures* (1707 and the unchanged 1771 edition) shows that the Church of Scotland was concerned "to apprehend, correct and absolve or not, swearers, cursers, fornicators, drunkards, promiscuous dancers etc." The 1645 act against "Lykewakes" and the 1649 act discharging "promiscuous dancing" appear to have been combined into an *Act against Lykwakes, Penny Bridals and promiscuous Dancing* in 1701.[82] As Forsyth noted, in the 1750s a number of local violers in Speyside were apprehended. Their punishments appear to have been light, and the overall kirk attitude to music and dancing softened demonstrably as "moderate" views came to dominate not long afterwards.

Among the first feuars of Am Baile Ur (Newtown, now Grantown-on-Spey) on the Spey in 1768 was Angus Cumming, piper, according to Forsyth. As far as other names go, Aeneas Mackintosh's *Notes Descriptive* tell us that "Grant of Rothiemurchus's" piper was one of the sons of David Fraser, Fraser of Lovat's piper. Elsewhere we find a Patrick Bàn Grant, celebrated piper of Abernethy in Strathspey with whom the following lines are associated: "Cluich Tulach gorm, righ na'm port, / Na tulaichean a's drochaidt Pheart; / A's damhsaidh sinn le'ur uile neart / Ruidhle mor Strath

Spea" (Play Tulloch Gorm, king of tunes, / the hills and bridge of Perth; / and we'll dance with all our might / the great Strathspey reel.

The James Cumming who was secretary of the Society of Antiquaries in 1781 may not have belonged to the Strathspey piping tradition but he kept his own piper.

If the record of pipers at late eighteenth-century Highland Society competitions found in Angus MacKay's *Collection* is reliable, then the Cummings ended their long tenure as Grant pipers some time between 1784 and 1795 when Peter MacNeil took over (although he might have been a second piper or have represented only a temporary break). In fact, the Grants continued to retain a piper whose job was hereditary long into the nineteenth century. Alexander MacDonald, author of *Story and Song from Loch Ness-side* (1914), said that the pipers in question were "of a family of MacDonalds who were hereditary pipers to the Seafield for generations. The last of them settled at Abriachan, where his descendants still flourish. It may be interesting to mention that his MS of pibrochs, which is said to have been in the MacCrimmon notation, was in evidence for some time after his death."[83]

The manuscript that Alexander MacDonald talked about has not come to light, and no teacher-pupil relationship involving Grant's MacDonald piper and either Donald or John MacCrimmon is known to have existed.

A piece of chanter lore fixes the Hanoverian Grants even more firmly in the Gaelic piping world. They are linked with one of the Highlands' magic pipe chanters, one that had come, its owners believed, directly from heaven. James Logan, in his book of 1831,[84] paraphrased a letter that he had received from Ewen MacPherson, Esq., of Cluny (who succeeded his father Duncan on 1 August 1817). According to the story in the letter, a Grant chief of some earlier time had borrowed from the MacPhersons their famous "feadan dubh," or black chanter, to inspirit his young men who were thoroughly dejected because they hadn't been able to stymie a raid on their cattle by three brave MacDonald men. Before borrowing the magic chanter, Grant had deepened his men's despondence, and the clan's, by publicly ridiculing the young Grants involved. The chanter wielded its mystical power and was duly returned. Later, however, it was reacquired by the Grants and was in the possession of the Grant of Glenmoriston in 1822 when at last it was presented to James Logan's correspondent, Ewen MacPherson of Cluny. Alexander MacDonald left this piece of lore untouched.

CHAPTER SEVEN

Piping in Glenorchy/Breadalbane, in Islay, and in MacDougall and MacIntyre Territory

PIPING IN CAMPBELL GLENORCHY/BREADALBANE AND ELSEWHERE IN ARGYLLSHIRE

While Skye has received repeated attention as a centre of piping, Breadalbane has seldom been considered in the same detail or at the same length. This is a critical oversight in any overall study of Highland piping, since various Glenorchy and Breadalbane Campbells were important patrons of bagpiping, particularly various earls of Breadalbane from the late seventeenth century.[1] The recorded piping names connected with the estate, chronologically, are McIndeor, MacIntyre, Campbell, MacGregor, and MacDougall. Highland Society competition records from the later eighteenth century show that Breadalbane at times kept two pipers, perhaps reflecting older and separate traditions in the western and eastern parts of the estate. Given the extent of the holding and the large population, there may have been more than two associated with the earl's household, not to mention countless unrecorded community pipers.

The part of Scotland, known in English as Breadalbane and in Gaelic as Bràghad Albainn (the Breadth of Scotland), in which this major Campbell holding lay stretches from Argyllshire's salt water lochs in the west to two miles east of Tay Bridge in Perthshire in the south-central Highlands. Breadalbane is in the southern Highlands and relatively accessible to Saxon economic ideas and agricultural practices. Not surprisingly, estate records for the mid-eighteenth century show many of the tacksman class, like Glenure and Barcaldine, and junior officers down to the rank of ensign, as well as factors, to have been habitual correspondents in English. The general population in the eighteenth century, however, was solidly Gaelic speaking[2] and, in general, culturally indistinguishable from the rest of Gaelic Scotland. In 1822, according to Stewart of Garth, the population of the estate was 13,537.[3]

Piping goes back at least to before 1561 in Glenorchy, and the records of the Breadalbane family show piping in the mid-seventeenth century in Breadalbane. Using the Scottish Record Office's extensive holding of Breadalbane material, Keith Sanger uncovered references in Lady Glenorchy's household book (presumably kept in and referring to Taymouth) to a visiting piper and his man and to a visiting fiddler and his man in 1662, no names and addresses given. Then, in 1669, two unnamed pipers and their men are mentioned in the same source. Who these pipers were and who the fiddler was are not on record.[4]

As the record begins to name pipers in Breadalbane, three problems have to be faced: first, Breadalbane may have had an east-west piping dichotomy; second, one important piping name there, MacIntyre, is associated not just with early Breadalbane but also with the Hebrides and the Perthshire Gàidhealtachd; and third, Breadalbane is associated with the Jacobite piper, Donald Campbell, whose (and whose antecedents') origins are obscure but who went to the Breadalbane estate after having piped for Alexander MacDonald of Glenaladale during the 1745 campaign. The east-west problem is not particularly complicating, but study of the MacIntyres requires sizeable digressions into other Highland estates.

It is thought that there were two MacIntyre pipers in Breadalbane in the third quarter of the seventeenth century and the beginning of the eighteenth. In Skye the evidence suggests that pipers of that name flourished in the first half of the eighteenth century, and in Rannoch MacIntyres are thought to have been the hereditary piping family to the Menzieses throughout the eighteenth century. D.P. Menzies's *"Red and White" Book of Menzies* (1894) contains a photograph of a one-drone bagpipe, and the author claims it was played at Bannockburn (1314) by an early MacIntyre whose hereditary piping line did not die out until about 1840 (this is the fairy pipe associated with Clanranald's MacIntyre pipers in Ulgary, Moidart). The MacIntyres were replaced by MacGregors.

Sir Robert Menzies (1706–86) declined John Cope's invitation to join the Hanoverian army when Cope occupied Menzies lands by Loch Rannoch at the beginning of the '45. Menzies was lame and did not fight for the Jacobites; instead he delegated authority to do so to "Ian Vohr Meinerich" (Big John Menzies, of Shian), a veteran of 1715. Ian Vohr and several Menzieses of Pitfodels in Aberdeenshire (most of whom were officers in the French army) fought at Culloden. For their parts in the rebellion, the estates of Gilbert Menzies of Pitfodels and John Menzies of Shian (at Glenquiech) were confiscated. (Glenquiech was eventually obtained by Campbell of Breadalbane.)

Whether all these MacIntyre pipers (including Red Donald in South Uist in the early eighteenth century, the Roman Catholic MacIntyre pipers who emigrated from South Uist to Cape Breton in the 1820s,[5] and the Robert who piped for Clanranald in the 1780s) sprang from one family is unknown and may never be. The notes in Angus MacKay's *Collection* confine themselves to "The MacIntyres, hereditary pipers to Menzies of Menzies," in Perthshire. These notes claim, with plausibility for the late eighteenth and early nineteenth centuries, that they were hereditary holders of the office and so enjoyed high status among the patronized pipers of the eighteenth-century Highlands. Unfortunately, the notes in Angus MacKay's book are unreliable.

The MacIntyres' homeland in the eighteenth century, and perhaps going back as early as 1300, was in Argyll.[6] However, their most celebrated bard, Duncan Ban Macintyre (1724–1812),[7] in a poem/song, part of which is cited below, maintained the hoarier tradition that the family was originally from the Inner Hebrides. The introductory notes on the hereditary piping families in Angus MacKay's *Collection* claim that the MacIntyre pipers were originally from the Isles, and other sources citing seemingly stray MacIntyres in the Isles appear to confirm this.

Whether or not the Argyll MacIntyre family (whose leader, James MacIntyre of Glen Noe, Duncan Ban Macintyre posted as clan chief in the mid-eighteenth century) was an offshoot of the Hebridean clan (or vice versa) has yet to be established. In the case of the MacIntyres who piped for Menzies in Perthshire, it seems more reasonable to concede the possibility that they were an offshoot of the Argyll family, since Menzies and Breadalbane territories abutted one another and the piping families for whom there is traditional information are roughly contemporaneous.[8]

Overall, judging by their patrons, the best-known MacIntyre pipers' allegiances in the eighteenth century were Hanoverian and Protestant, but hints of Jacobitism, or perhaps just fashionable nostalgia, can be found in the title of a piece of ceòl mór attributed to one of them, "My King has landed in Moydart." Also, the South Uist piper was in all likelihood a Roman Catholic, since non-conformity was extremely rare in that island after the re-Catholicizing trend that came from Ireland in the early seventeenth century, and there is as yet no reason to say that he wasn't of old South Uist MacIntyre stock and didn't have piper descendants or relatives who went to Cape Breton in the 1820s.

For the MacIntyre pipers in general there is a growing body of recorded data and lore, from estate records and from song. This information shows them to have piped in a number of Highland patrimonies, and it would probably be better to assemble this data under the rubric "MacIntyre pipers" than to treat the MacIntyre pipers separately by estate. One obvious reason to choose the scheme also used in Angus MacKay's prefatory notes would be that piping, however much the genealogical information may be incomplete, did run in families, just as musical talent, it is generally believed, tends to run in families. In what's left of Gaelic Cape Breton it is widely believed that talent at music and dance are inherited characteristics. Whether or not that is true, musical talent and knowledge of technique and repertoire were in all likelihood jealously guarded for as many generations as possible because it was economically advantageous to do so. For the time being, however, the MacIntyres will be discussed within the estate framework, starting with Breadalbane (assuming it to have been a possible base of operations) and going on to the MacDonalds' Skye estate and then to the Menzies holdings in Rannoch.

What follows is an aggregate of several pieces of information, presented chronologically, about MacIntyre pipers. These men may all ultimately be shown to have been related to one another, but at this point, any genealogical linkages between various of them are imagined (possibly excepting what was published in Angus MacKay's book). MacIntyre pipers served several masters on a number of Highland estates over about two centuries. They are associated with the first Campbell earl of Breadalbane (five hundred of whose people were out with Mar in the Jacobite movement in 1715 when the earl was nearly eighty). The two Disarming Act piping MacIntyres who flourished in Skye until 1745 have been mentioned above. Then there is the Red Donald MacIntyre (Dòmhnul Ruadh Mac an t-Saoir) in South Uist, subject of a fairy-related story in the 1890s mentioned above in the section dealing with Clanranald.

The MacIntyres in the eighteenth century, according to Duncan Ban MacIntyre's song "Rainn Gearradh-Arm" (Verse on Arms), looked to the senior male of the Glen Noe family as chief of the clan:[9] " 'S rìoghail an eachdraidh na chualas / Riamh mu'd phàirtidh; / 'S lìonmhor an taic, na tha suas dhiubh, / Na'm biodh càs ort; / Tha gach buaidh eile dh' a réir sin, / An Gleann-Nodha féin an tàmhachd: / Pìob is bratach is neart aig Seumas, / An Ceann-cinnidh nach tréig gu bràth sinn." (Majestic is the record, aught ever heard / about thy people, / those of them now living would lend their ample aid, / wert thou in peril; / all other symbols of like virtue / in Glen Noe itself are stablished: / bagpipe, banner, power hath James, / the chieftain who will never fail us.)[10]

The Seumas (James) referred to was the chief, James MacIntyre, a scholar who lived from about 1725 to 1799. Gillies's collection contains three poems attributed to him, all critical of Samuel Johnson. In his appended notes to *The Songs of Duncan Ban Macintyre,* Angus MacLeod said that Duncan Ban had visited James MacIntyre, so the reference to "Pìob a's bratach ... aig Seumas" may be more than licence; MacIntyre probably did have a piper during the Disarming Act years.[11] MacLeod also mentioned that James MacIntyre's wife was a daughter of Duncan Campbell of Barcaldine, elder brother of Colin Campbell of Glenure (1708–52); Glenure, though much older than Duncan Ban, was his foster brother, so Duncan Ban had family ties of an adoptive sort with Glen Noe's wife.

According to the Campbell of Mamore manuscripts, the "local Macintyres" were giving trouble to the Hanoverian garrison at "Castle Keilchurn," which was under the command of Captain Colin Campbell of Skipness in early April 1746.[12] Some idea of the MacIntyre threat can be gauged from the fact that Kilchurn, by the end of January 1746, had twelve officers and two hundred men under Skipness.

The farm Gleann-Nodha (Glen Noe) is a west-running valley in Nether Lorn opening onto Loch Etive's eastern shores north of Ben Cruachan. The MacIntyres never owned the farm but are associated with the holding from about 1300 until the last of them died in 1808. They are said to have held it initially from the Stewart lord of Lorn and later from the Campbells of Glenorchy, one of whom married the Stewart heiress to the property. (The eleventh Glenorchy Campbell became the first earl of Breadalbane in the late seventeenth century and the first of a number of earls whose patronage of piping was very important throughout the eighteenth century.) In the same song Duncan Ban included the piece of MacIntyre legend that associated the progenitor of the family with "Colla cheud-chathaich Spàintich" (Coll of the hundred Spanish-bladed warriors) and rooted the Sleat MacIntyres in Skye in the medieval period.[13]

Thus, part of the family, even if its distant origins may have been in the Isles, had, by 1700, extremely deep roots in Lorn as holders of land from the Campbells of Glenorchy, of whom Sir John (c. 1635–1716; death date elsewhere specified as 19 March 1717), eleventh "Glenurchy," became the first earl of Breadalbane on 13 August 1681.

However one interprets Sir John Campbell's later public career in Scotland's politically and religiously turbulent period following the Revolution of 1688–89, including the massacre of Glencoe, he was unquestionably astute politically and able to contend with complex personalities and policies in English Scotland adeptly. At the same time, his estate records show that he had a typical concern with Gaelic tradition; among other things, for example, one of his pipers received professional training from a Rankin in Mull and a McCrooman, possibly in Skye.

In October 1675, according to Keith Sanger, John Campbell while still of Glenorchy instructed John Campbell of Innergeldie to "give Donald Roy pyper fortie pund Scotts to learn his trade and give him four pund Scotts to buy him cloaths."[14] In the accounts for 1675 a plaid was purchased for "Donald Roy MacIntyre pyper," thereby fixing the full name of Glenorchy's musician, who was in some degree a learner at the time. There are indications that Donald Roy MacIntyre may have lived in Perthshire. Innergeldie, which is given elsewhere as Innerzeldies,[15] is in the central Perthshire parish of Comrie in the eastern part of the very large Glenorchy estate; furthermore, in 1675, Glenorchy's seat had been for over a century at Taymouth, also in Perthshire. There's one last snippet about Donald Roy MacIntyre: he and his wife, Margaret Dunster, petitioned the second earl of Breadalbane for a continuance of their meal allowance in 1722 and in that petition they declared themselves as having served the family "since ever we were capable" and as being "very old and infirm."[16]

The next MacIntyre piper to be recorded is the now-celebrated character in the mid-1690s whose surname is only mentioned in the famous citation from a written order from the first earl of Breadalbane to his second cousin and chamberlain, Campbell of Barcaldine. This order is found in the Campbell of Barcaldine papers: "Give McIntyre ye pyper fforty pounds scots as his prentises(hi)p with McCrooman till May nixt as also provyde him in what Cloths he needs and dispatch him immediately to the Isles."[17] Not only did this quote establish a "McCrooman" as an important teacher of piping at the time, but it also focused attention on the importance of the MacIntyres in the piping profession. That the chamberlain was based on the south shore of the sea loch, Loch Creran in Argyllshire, within a few miles of Loch Linnhe, may suggest that this MacIntyre piper was from Argyllshire, although there is no proof of this. Rory Halford MacLeod gives the date of the earl of Breadalbane's instruction to Barcaldine as 1698; Keith Sanger has another opinion, on the basis of a cross-referencing entry in the Breadalbane accounts, signed by the earl at Taymouth on 22 April 1697: "Item sent with John MacIntyre the pyper at your Lordships desyre to be given McCrooman pyper in the Isles, £40," and "Item payed to quantiliane McCraingie McLeans pyper for one complete year as prentyce fie for the Litle pyper before he was sent to McCrooman, the soume of £160."[18]

While one is inevitably tempted to assume that John MacIntyre and the "Litle pyper" were one and the same, it is not certain, on a large estate, that this would be so.[19] However, the second item does subordinate "quantiliane McCraingie" (Conduiligh mac Fhraingich or Rankin) as a tutor of piping to the McCrooman of the time, who may have been Pàdruig Og, as Angus MacKay's notes published in 1838 state was the case.

The residences of the earliest unnamed Glenorchy pipers of the 1660s are unknown. Donald Roy MacIntyre may have lived in Perthshire, but the tack of Breadalbane's second cousin and chamberlain at Balcardine is in the west of the very large estate, which suggests that John, over whom this second cousin had control, may have always lived in the west. If John and the "Litle Pyper" are the same person, both of his piping teachers were Hebrideans, which would have been most convenient for someone living on west coast salt water. From 1705 John certainly did live in Nether Lorn. His main job was as piper to one of the earl of Breadalbane's sons, Colin Campbell (1679–1708). Colin Campbell held the tack of Ardmaddy, and at least since his time and until well into the nineteenth century Ardmaddy was one of piping's focal points, its piper ranking with Joseph MacDonald in Sutherland and the MacCrimmons in Skye as a contributor to modern knowledge of traditional Gaelic classical piping. John MacIntyre's duties for Colin Campbell in Ardmaddy were subject to being overridden by Breadalbane's requirements for pipe music, but as Sanger found out, there is only one record of Breadalbane's having used his services, in 1709, at "Castle Kilchorn," which is also in Argyll.[20] Ardmaddy lies on the east side of Loch Etive a few miles north of the MacIntyre tack of Glen Noe and is the preferable of the two holdings only inasmuch as it commands Glen Kinglass, which has easy walking/riding access to inland Glenorchy. Glen Noe is much nearer Kilchurn to its east, but the pass westward is much more mountainous.

The second Breadalbane piping family was the Campbell family; Donald Campbell, Glenaladale's piper during the '45, his son Colin, and his grandson Donald all lived as pipers at Ardmaddy in Nether Lorn, which had gained a reputation as the home of a top piper. What had happened to the MacIntyres as pipers in Nether Lorn by the time of the Disarming Act is unclear, although their Jacobite sympathies, as evidenced in their harassment of Kilchurn, may have alienated them forever from the powerful Campbells.

The first of these, Donald Campbell, established Breadalbane with piping at Ardmaddy in Argyllshire during the Disarming Act years. He is a very consequential figure in the history of piping. While not a lot is known about him, his son Colin was, in his contribution to ceòl mór repertoire, intensely important to modern classical piping. In the 1790s his achievement was to write down, or to have written down, in modified pipers' words, nearly 170 pieces of ceòl mór from the singing known as canntaireachd, which was the essential means of transmission. This particular canntaireachd, also known as the "Nether Lorn" canntaireachd, was chosen by the Pibroch Society for use in its various publications of pibroch in the twentieth century, and according to Frans Buisman, "Campbell transformed it considerably so as to make a system of notation that is immediately understood in writing, – that is, without the actual chant."[21] The differences between Colin Campbell's and Joseph MacDonald's grace-notings, particularly in introductory runs, again confirm the idea that much had been lost since Culloden. On the other hand, one might consider that embellishments that were known by all serious pipers at the time did not need to be included in any mapping of the basic tunes themselves.

As for what is known about Colin Campbell's father, Donald Campbell, piper to Alexander MacDonald of Glenaladale before and during the '45, there are three easily accessible sources, two from the family and the third from the notes published in MacKay's *Collection*.

The first family source is Donald Campbell's grandson Donald Campbell (Dòmhnul mac Cailein 'ic Dhòmhnuill), discussed above. Campbell was interviewed by a *Glasgow Herald* reporter on 12 September 1834. According to Campsie's transcription, the headline described him as "The Piper of Nether Lorn," at that time piper to the Marquis of Breadalbane and living in Ardmaddy in Argyll. (His brother John [Iain mac Cailein 'ic Dhòmhnuill], prize-winning piper [1819], is known to have died in 1831 aged thirty-six in the service of Campbell of Shawfield and Isla [cadet of the Argyll Campbell family], so Donald's year of birth is probably in the early 1790s, when his paternal grandfather may well have been not long turned sixty.) In any case, Donald, the Gaelic-speaking piper, said in 1834 that he was the grandson of the piper who attended the party that welcomed Prince Charles when he landed at Kinlochmoidart. The report goes on:

The grandfather was at that time eighteen years of age, and piper to Glenalladale. He had – as a document we saw shews – been educated by Glenalladale, and, in 1742 entered his service as piper. Prince Charles, the evening of his landing, put in his hand three guineas for his performance. During the whole campaign, he looked upon him with regard, and, on the march, would frequently make up to him, desiring him in Gaelic, to blow the pipes – 'seid a phiop.'

A day or two after the fatal field of Culloden, he gave him a chanter as a token of remembrance, which the grandson now has shown us. It is rather rude, and had undergone some repair, which has not improved its tone.

After the Prince's army had been defeated, Glenalladale's piper was taken under the protection of Carwhin, who was an officer in the Argyllshire Militia with whom he staid the rest of his life, as family piper at Ardmaddy. His son succeeded to his calling, and in turn, trained his own sons to be pipers.[22]

The second family source is Miss Ann Campbell, Oban, a great-grand-daughter of Glenaladale's and Carwhin's piper, and, according to A. Campbell's note on the "Campbell Canntaireachd MS" in *Pìobaireachd*,[23] a daughter of the Donald interviewed in 1834 at Ardmaddy. It was from her that Sheriff John Bartholomew of Glenorchard obtained Colin Campbell's (Cailean mac Dhòmhnuill's) two invaluable manuscript volumes of "canntaireachd" in 1909. She told Bartholomew that her great-grandfather had been a piper; he had been in the service of Glenaladale at Culloden and had helped the wounded man off the field. Afterwards he took service with Campbell of Carwhin.

Angus MacKay's notes on "The Campbells, hereditary pipers to the Campbells of Mochaster," declare that the first of them "of whom there is an authenticated account was Donald, who was sent by Colin Campbell of Corwhin to take lessons from Patrick òg MacCrummen in Skye. He remained with him a considerable time and was esteemed a performer of merit, as was his son Caillan Mòr or Great Colin, whose son John, late Piper to W.F. Campbell, Esq. of Shawfield and Isla, was also an excellent Piper. This man died at Woodhall in 1831."[24]

Using the earlier family source then, Glenaladale's piper in 1745 was born in 1726 or 1727. The education referred to was probably in piping and took place, one must assume, before 1742, when Donald Campbell was in his early teens. (The document proving that Glenaladale had educated Donald has never come to light.) There is no mention of who his teacher was, but a MacArthur or a MacCrimmon in nearby Skye is not altogether implausible as a candidate.[25] Ann Campbell's version adds to the notes in MacKay's *Collection* in giving a heroic role to Donald at Culloden. In a footnote in his *Reminiscences*,[26] Joseph Mitchell says that MacDonald of Borrodale, later of Glenaladale, had the bagpipes that were played at Culloden by Glenaladale's piper, lending some plausibility to Ann Campbell's addendum, although it is possible that Mitchell never actually saw the instrument.[27] It appears that Ann Campbell repeated the anonymous report in Angus MacKay's notes that Donald Campbell had been taught his piping by Patrick Og MacCrimmon. This is impossible if one accepts, on no evidence, that Patrick Og died around 1730 (it is interesting that, given his presumed importance to piping, no rhyme or other memorial of the death of Patrick Og has survived). It is tempting to believe the opening line in Angus MacKay's notes concerning the Campbell pipers: "This family, ... there is reason to believe, were long known in the Highland musical world, before they are recognised as hereditary Pipers to the Campbells of Mochaster in Argyleshire."[28]

These piping Campbells, whose piping line, from current knowledge, began with Donald in the service of MacDonald of Glenaladale, continued in the profession without a break, father to son, from the 1730s until at least the 1830s. With Prince Charlie's personal piper, John MacGregor, tucked away in the haven of the tiny estate of Campbell of Glenlyon in Perthshire, and Donald Campbell with Carwhin, it is worth noting a similarity between the Breadalbane and Glenlyon families; both had been involved in the turmoil of the revolution, Glenlyon having had an opprobrious part in the Glencoe massacre and Breadalbane staunchly denying any complicity, although he certainly was a major national political figure of the times. Later, in 1715, both sided with Mar's Jacobites (Breadalbane was admittedly in his dotage). The relocating of the pipers John MacGregor and Donald Campbell to Campbell country in 1746, suggests a lingeringly sympathetic understanding on the part of the first earl of Breadalbane's son, the second earl, John Campbell (1662–1752), of the positive aspects of Jacobitism; indeed, on his deathbed in the 1740s, Glenlyon is said to have shunned the shrewd one of his sons, the one who joined the 43rd (Black Watch) during the '45. The fact that both pipers thrived as pipers in Campbell country proves that they flitted south for the sole purpose of avoiding capture, simply as Jacobites and not as players of a musical instrument.

Donald, the piper to the first marquis of Breadalbane (John Campbell, 1762–1834), lived, like his grandfather, at Ardmaddy in Nether Lorn. Donald is believed to have followed his father, Colin (author of "Colin Campbell's Instrumental Book 1797"), as piper in the same service, to the same family of Campbells, confusingly given as Campbells of Mochaster, Corwhin (Carwhin) and then as marquis of Breadalbane. In fact, these are all of the same patrilineage. To start, with Colin Campbell of Carwhin (1704–72) was a descendant of the Colin Campbell of Mochaster (d. 1678), who himself was the younger son of Sir Robert Campbell, ninth of Glenorchy.

During the '45, Colin Campbell of Carwhin was in command of the Glenorchy company of the Argyll Militia. His son John, born 1762, became, through extinction in the main Breadalbane line in 1782, fourth earl of Breadalbane, and at the coronation of King William IV in 1831, marquis of Breadalbane and earl of Ormelie.[29] He died in 1834 having always been associated with the Campbell piping family in the Argyllshire part of the estate and a number of others in Perthshire. He was patron probably of Culloden veteran Donald, certainly of his son Colin and of his grandson Donald (the interviewee in 1834). He is associated also with MacGregor and MacDougall pipers. Although John Campbell's son John (c. 1796–1862), the second marquis of Breadalbane, kept a piper for thirty years (John Ban MacKenzie), his actual sympathy for traditional Gaelic culture was shallow; he was a notorious clearer of Glenorchy and the Loch Tay/Glenquaich area Highland population in the 1830s and '40s.

As far as is known, the Carwhin/Breadalbane/marquis of Breadalbane pipers from 1746 to 1834, and later, included Donald Campbell (Dòmhnul), Colin his son (Cailein mac Dhòmhnuill), and Donald, son of Colin, son of Donald (Dòmhnul mac Cailein 'ic Dhòmhnuill). Then there is John Ban MacKenzie (who played the introductory salute at the 1832 Edinburgh competition and won the gold medal in 1835). John Campbell, the younger brother of the last listed Campbell (Donald, son of Colin, son of Donald), was piper to W.F. Campbell of Shawfield and Isla and the champion piper in the Highland Society competition in 1819. He was the vehicle for their father's manuscript "Colin Campbell's Instrumental Book 1797" coming to light first in the early 1800s (1815, 1816, or 1818). John Campbell (d. 1831) was also one of the critically important culture bearers whose "teaching" of Gaelic and Gaelic affairs fired John Francis Campbell's (Iain Og Ila's) fascination with things Gaelic, particularly stories.

At that time the Highland Society in Edinburgh was earnestly encouraging the intelligible writing of ceòl mór but it turned down the Campbell work; around the year 1816 either no one in the society understood canntaireachd or no one recognized the document's value. About a decade before Colin Campbell produced his famous manuscript at Ardmaddy on

Loch Etive-side, a dichotomy in Breadalbane piping appears in the written record. Edinburgh competition results for 1783 and 1784 show that the second piper to the earl of Breadalbane was Donald Fisher. The Highland Society competition for 1789 shows that the third prize in Edinburgh that year went to "John MacGregor, junior, son of John MacGregor, first Piper to the earl of Breadalbane." The status of the Campbell pipers in 1789 is unclear, but it is obvious that upon donning the mantle of earldom, Carwhin felt obliged to continue the previous earl's commitment to this John MacGregor, confirming him as his first piper. This indicates that he was keeping up the age-old Breadalbane custom of supporting pipers in both the Perthshire and Argyllshire parts of the estate and not that he had any part in invidious designations like "first" and "second."

At any rate, it wasn't until 1909 that two volumes of Colin Campbell's manuscript work of about 170 pibrochs became extant, along with the notes from the donor, Ann Campbell. It appears that there was a third volume of Campbell canntaireachd as well. To Dalyell's dismay, the Highland Society chose to disregard this volume in 1818, when it was offered to them by Shawfield and Isla's piper. Sir John MacGregor Murray[30] understood the value of such a document and bought the single volume on offer from John Campbell. MacGregor was obviously very keen to ensure the safety of what he considered a threatened form. Unfortunately, that actual volume has subsequently been lost.

The two volumes, presumably those that Miss Ann Campbell gave Bartholomew in 1909, were known to exist in the early 1800s, long before 1838, the year Angus MacKay's *Collection* was published. They were said by Dalyell, in 1818 (Dalyell's date), to have been in the possession of their author, Colin Campbell (Cailean mac Dhòmhnuill), who was/had been piper to John Campbell, fourth earl of Breadalbane (formerly of Carwhin). Alastair Campsie assumed that because John Campbell, the younger brother and piper to Shawfield and Isla, had brought the one volume to the Highland Society competition, he had the other two volumes.

Campsie's suspicion that the material remained in the possession of Shawfield and Isla, in Isla, when John Campbell the piper died young in 1831, hinges on his realization that Angus MacKay adjourned out of what he knew would soon be a prosperous and tempting piping limelight, in suspiciously timely fashion, to act as piper to Shawfield and Isla. Campsie hinted broadly that Angus MacKay took this obscure position in order to appropriate the contents of the Campbell manuscripts for inclusion in his well-advertised book.[31] This set of assumptions may be correct inasmuch as Angus MacKay may have hoped desperately to find the manuscripts and was prepared to take any job in Campbell country to get close to them. Perhaps Isla was close enough for him. However, although Colin was probably dead by the mid-1830s (having been born, one assumes, around 1750), his son

Donald was the senior piper in the family and continued at Ardmaddy as a piper on the estate of both the first and second marquis. The publication of Angus MacKay's *Collection* was certainly delayed, but the degree of his success in finding the manuscripts and in plagiarizing from them is debatable. Eventually, Colin Campbell's collected canntaireachd did reach the world intact, through Donald's daughter Ann, Oban. What happened to the chanter Prince Charles gave to Donald in 1746 is anyone's guess.

The manuscripts are held today by the National Library of Scotland, and they have been used extensively by the Piobaireachd Society over nearly a century in its various volumes of pipe music. Criticism of the way classical piping has been selected and presented from the few available sources for publication by the Piobaireachd Society makes up the latter part of William Donaldson's recent book. For generations the classical forms have been learned, initially at least, from the written page, not by ear. Alongside Donaldson's scathing criticism of the contrived evolution of classical piping and of the Piobaireachd Society, and of its gentlemen antecedents, lies the encouraging work in interpreting the Campbell Canntaireachd of Barnaby Brown, who has introduced to the world a number of deliberately overlooked tunes from the old manuscript. Other work, Allan MacDonald's for example, also shows that for the first time in many years classical piping enthusiasts are searching for the music's honest roots.

For my purpose, there remains the problem of the origin of the music found in the pages of "Colin Campbell's Instrumental Book 1797." Colin Campbell wrote the vocables of about 170, a remarkable repertoire, by the standards of modern piping, of ceòl mór. Joseph MacDonald wrote of two strains of bagpiping (classical and dance music) and did not mention canntaireachd.

Concerning the tunes recorded in Colin Campbells manuscripts, what influence had his father on the content? Donald, if born around 1728, would have been seventy-two in 1800, not a great age. He may easily have overseen the work to the point of singing and playing tunes for inclusion. To date, he is the only known teacher of his son Colin. What ceòl mór style and repertoire did Glenaladale's piper pass on to his son Colin? A Mac a'Ghlasraich Campbell foundation is a not unreasonable beginning. Then, if Glenaladale had in mind for his piper what Simon Fraser of Lovat had for David Fraser and sent Campbell to Skye, then his finishing instruction perhaps came from a MacCrimmon or a MacArthur. All that is to deny the possibility that the Jacobite piper adapted to and learned piping in Campbell country and passed that on to his son Colin. The answers will probably never been teased out of the welter of speculation.

Where the Mac a'Ghlasraich Campbells in Keppoch are concerned, Somerled MacMillan stated that they came to Keppoch from Argyllshire in 1497.[32] MacMillan said that they had appealed on at least one occasion in two hundred and more years to Argyll to mediate problems they were having in Keppoch. Citing *Argyll in the Forty-Five,*[33] MacMillan added that after Culloden thirty Glasserichs living in Keppoch claimed to have been forced "out" for Prince Charles. They sent an envoy to "Lord Glenorchy" (John Campbell [1662–1752], second earl of Breadalbane), asking to be allowed to submit their arms "to a Campbell" and his lordship diplomatically directed them to the nearest commander, who happened to be Colonel John Campbell, the Lord Loudoun of Lord Loudoun's Highlanders (raised in 1745).[34]

Another speculation might be based on the observation that, of all the Jacobite pipers in Prince Charles's army, the two who benefited through the personal kindness of the prince during the '45 were John MacGregor from Perthshire and Donald Campbell, Glenaladale's piper. If Charles frequently demanded Donald to "seid a phiop" (blow the pipes), then Donald must have been known to the prince's personal piper, John MacGregor. If there was a fraternal bond between the two pipers, it is hard to imagine that before and after Culloden they had not discussed contingency plans to cover the problems they would face if the cause failed. The older returned to his home county; Donald Campbell, who was young enough to have been John MacGregor's son, took the pipe chanter the prince gave him and went to pipe for Carwhin. The date he left Glenaladale is unknown, but circumstances point to a time soon after the Battle of Culloden, before the amnesty and before Duncan Campbell's reputation as a kindly occupier of Arisaig and Moidart was established (assuming that he had the responsibility of Glenaladale). Glenaladale was staunchly Catholic and Jacobite and offered no back doors to Argyll.

The last famous piping name associated with the Breadalbane Campbells is a MacDougall, first name unknown, who according to Alexander MacAulay was the "marquis of Breadalbane's" piper in the period 1750–60. He was a wood carver and joiner according to MacAulay. His son Allan MacDougall (b. 1764 on the Breadalbane estate) continued his father's service as piper and was piper at Taymouth Castle in 1781; he later started the famous MacDougall family pipe-making business in Perth in 1792 (subsequently in Aberfeldy). Another son, Donald MacDougall (b. c. 1770), emigrated with wife and family to Canada in 1817.[35] MacAulay's potted history cites no sources and its credibility, for some, will be weakened by the knowledge that John Campbell (1696–1782), third of Breadalbane for thirty years from 23 February 1752, died as he had lived, an earl, not a marquis. He was predeceased by all three of his sons. His successor was his distant cousin John Campbell of Carwhin (1762–1834), who was made the first marquis of Breadalbane and earl of Ormelie in 1831. On the other hand, a "Donald McDougall, his wife, and five children, his sister Janet, her husband Malcolm Fisher, and their family" emigrated from Loch Tay in 1817 to

Glengarry County, Ontario. Donald McDougall and his brother-in-law Malcolm Fisher had shared a farm at Callelochan on Loch Tay.[36]

ISLAY PIPERS

In the period 1737–40 eighty-three families (423 people) left Islay in a three-stage emigration, led by a Captain Lachlan Campbell (d. c. 1747) from Islay. Eventually an unknown number of them managed to arrange title to lands in northern New York province, but little more is known about them except that their presence encouraged some of Montgomerie's Highlanders (77th) to settle there as well, in 1763. It is unknown whether the emigrants included a piper or pipers, but Islay was by no means left piperless.

Piping in Islay continued demonstrably from about 1760, and certainly was a common céilidh pleasure there during the boyhood years of folklorist John Francis Campbell (Iain Og Ile, 1821–85). There is no reason to believe that there was any break in piping's tradition in that part of Argyllshire until the middle of the nineteenth century, although remarks about folk life there in the eighteenth century are fragmentary and fortuitously offered. In the family of the Campbells of Shawfield and Islay, John Francis's father being the last of the line to own Islay, traditional piping went on in its native Gaelicness at least until the death of John Campbell, the family piper, in 1831.[37]

In 1860 John Francis Campbell included a story called "A Bhaintreach" (*sic*) in volume 2 of *Popular Tales of the West Highlands*. This particular tale had been collected for Campbell by his old tutor Hector MacLean (1818–1893), schoolmaster in Ballygrant, Islay, from a "Hugh Mac in deor" of Bowmore in Islay, an old piper nearing eighty in 1860. Hugh Mac in Deor (Mac an deòir [Dewar]) was the son of a man who Campbell said was considered to have been an excellent piper in his day. This earlier Mac in deor was probably born between 1750 and 1760. Dewar family piping in Islay lasted for three known generations, since Hugh, according to John Francis Campbell, had a son Dougald Mac in Deor (no dates) who was "allowed to be one of the best pipers in the island."[38]

The Campbells of Shawfield and Isla may have had a long association with Gaelic pipers living on the Islay estate, but no record of that appears until John Campbell crops up as family servant and piper. Campbell (c. 1795–1831) cannot have entered Islay's service much before 1815, but he was obviously a prepossessing Gael of many traditionary talents. As the owner of his father's (Colin Campbell's) famous "Instrumental Book" of canntaireachd, he was a major link in pibroch's literary history. John Campbell won the Edinburgh competition first prize in 1819.[39] Genealogically he was Iain mac Cailein 'ic Dhòmhnuil (John, son of Colin, son of Donald), a brother of Donald, piper to the Marquis of Breadalbane (see above).

The generally ignored aspect of John Campbell the piper is his capacity as a traditional teller of tales. To the forefront of John Francis Campbell's mind, when he realized that he had an imperative to record Gaelic tales, came memories of the Gaelic stories told by the family piper, John Campbell, the man who was entrusted by the boy's abnormally enlightened father to ensure that his son become a native speaker of Gaelic. Along with the language, the piper passed on, or exposed the future Eton pupil, lawyer, traveller, courtier, artist, linguist, folklorist to, many of Gaelic society's insights, céilidh skills (including dance steps), dignities, and refinements, a heritage which had long since ceased to be important to any Campbells of Shawfield and Islay but which John Francis cherished. He wrote: "Highland stories, then, have been despised by educated men, and they are as yet unchanged popular tales. It so happened that a piper was the instructor of my babyhood. He was a stalwart, kindly, gentle man, whose face is often before me, though he has long since gone to his rest. From him I first heard a few of the tales in this collection. They had almost faded from my memory ... so I began at the beginning of 1859 by writing to my Highland friends."[40]

John Campbell knew stories. The MacGregor pipers in Perthshire were the Clann an Sgeulaiche discussed above. From the MacGregors' title James Logan was satisfied "that pipers were anciently qualified in that part of the bardic duties."[41] A version of Logan's opinion was voiced much earlier, in 1792, by Pierre-Nicolas Chantreau, who was in Scotland in 1788–89. Citing no authority, he wrote that it was with the bagpipes that the bards, who were the musicians of the Scots, celebrated the exploits or virtues of their heroes.[42] Logan's and Chantreau's views are not held by many Gaelophiles today; even allowing for the famous bard/piper, John MacKay, the blind piper of Gairloch (Iain dall MacAoidh), there is insufficient evidence to support the idea. However, two MacCrimmons have been associated in published literature with storytelling; if not exactly making Logan's and Chantreau's case, this at least opens the door to seeing some if not all pipers in a wider cultural context. The two storytellers were Johanna MacCrimmon of Berneray, a Skye-born woman who was descended from the "celebrated pipers. Her father, grandfather, and uncles were pipers." In 1859 she gave Hector MacLean (Ballygrant, Islay), a version of "The Two Shepherds" story, called "The Bauchan," which she had learned from her grand-uncle, Angus MacCrimmon.[43]

It is thus not premature to note that some important eighteenth- and nineteenth-century Gaelic pipers considered it important to be able to tell the old Gaelic tales; the practice, however, in no way diminished what have long been imagined to have been their exaggerated notions of their own superiority as pipers first and last.

Postscript: Although pipers must have been common on the estate of the dukes of Argyll in the eighteenth century, there is to date no record that either John (second duke, d. 1743) or his brother Archibald (third duke, d. 1761) kept a family piper at Inveraray. Both men were born in the south of England, and the third duke (the "King of Scotland") certainly spent many summers in Inveraray, building the new castle. However, he had continuous problems with his own local Highland tenants' illegally grazing their beasts on his estate, and, when working on the new building or in his quarries, cheating his overseers. His social bonds with his people were minimal, and he was treated as an outsider by most of them. His successor, the fourth duke, his cousin General John Campbell of Mamore (c. 1694–1770), inasmuch as he was colonel of *inter alia* the Royal North British Fusiliers, was aware of military piping, but there is no report of his retaining a piper at the Inveraray seat.[44] His son, John (1723–1806), the fifth duke of Argyll, also a military man with service in the 21st (Royal North British Fusiliers), is on record as opposing the decision to abolish the staff rank of "piper major" in the Royal Regiment of Foot (the Royal Scots) in 1764, but that is the known extent of any sympathy he may have had for Gaelic instrumental music. The records of the Edinburgh piping competitions from 1781 until 1838 make no mention of any piper to the duke of Argyll.

THE MACDOUGALLS IN KILMORE AND KILBRIDE IN ARGYLLSHIRE

Although the sources are secondary, the indications are strong that piping and pipemaking in the small MacDougall estate of Dunollie in Argyllshire continued from the 1740s until the early nineteenth century. The Rankin pipers/piping teachers in Kilbrennan on Mull, because of their proximity and renown, have overshadowed the MacDougalls in their homeland and made an assessment of their contribution to traditional piping difficult. The Mac-Dougalls' importance as pipemakers in Perthshire, through Allan Mac-Dougall (in the late eighteenth century, and then most prominently in the nineteenth century through Allan's son John (Iain mac Ailein) and his son in turn, Duncan (Donnchadh mac Iain 'ic Ailein), point strongly to an unde-scribed earlier history of wood turning and pipe manufacture in MacDougall country, if not in Allan's father's generation then in an earlier one.

The unnamed piper, Allan's father, whom MacAulay allows the reader to suppose was a native of the Dunollie estate, and who went as piper to Breadalbane between 1750 and 1760, illustrates the continuation of piping during the occupation. In the absence of information, it is significant that he obviously passed his knowledge of woodturning to his son. The art of turn-ing must have been something he began to learn in the 1750s if not earlier.

Offering no documentary evidence, MacAulay wrote from South Uist[45] that Allan MacDougall's brother Donald (b. c. 1770) emigrated with a wife and family to Canada in 1817. Nothing as yet is known about Donald Mac-

Dougall. If he was a good piper, it is not implausible that he was related to the Donald MacDougall piper who emigrated to South West Margaree, Inverness County, Cape Breton. The latter was a member of *teaghlach Dhòmhnuill 'ic Alasdair* (the family of Donald, son of Alasdair) who emigrated from Arisaig to Cape Breton in 1828.

According to MacAulay, there was more than one family of MacDougall pipers to the MacDougalls of Dunollie since the first hereditary one, the family of Big Alasdair (Alasdair Mor [MacAulay's dates, 1635–1709]). He described them as holding land at Monagh Leigh and running a piping school at Kilbride known as "taigh nam pìobairean" (house of the pipers). Seton Gordon, in *Highland Summer,* reiterated MacAulay's earlier notes with minor variations and drew into the matrix, and extended backward in time, documentation taken from Angus MacKay's manuscript notes. According to the Pibroch Society publications (books 1 and 6,) MacKay's manuscript is the only source for an early nineteenth-century pibroch called "Cumha an Chaiptein MacDhùghaill" (Captain MacDougall's Lament). The tune was believed by MacKay and confirmed by a MacDougall authority to commemorate the death at Ciudad Rodrigo in 1812 of Captain Alexander MacDougall, younger of Dunolly (b. c. 1785). The man who composed the tune, according to the MacKay manuscript, was "Ronald MacDougall, the family piper." What Seton Gordon added, ingenuously, was that Ronald MacDougall was "almost the last of the hereditary MacDougall pipers to the chiefs." Of the college, he wrote that Ronald Ban MacDougall, grandfather of Ronald Mór, the last hereditary piper, was the last to preside. This suggests that the middle of the three last hereditary MacDougall pipers was the composer of the tune and that his father was the last of the keepers of the MacDougall school. If so, then one or perhaps, and more likely, probably two of them were piping in the early 1750s.

What may be inferred from MacAulay's article is that ignorance of Mac-Dougall piping on the Dunollie estate during the Disarming Act years is the result of the primary disruption on the holding, forfeiture for active Jacobitism during the 1715 uprising. It is a moot point, since the MacDougall estate was returned to them either as a bribe not to, or a reward for not, joining the '45. The more obvious answer is that few records have yet been found or consulted. MacAulay chose not to cite his sources for the data he did offer. He laid much personal hardship at the door of the 1715 forfeiture, noting for example that Alasdair Ranaldson MacDonell of Glengarry's bard Allan Dall MacDougall (b. c. 1750–1829) had been born in Glencoe, grandson of a family that had to leave their Dunollie homeland after the '15. In his next line, MacAulay introduced the MacDougall piper who went to serve Breadalbane between 1750 and 1760; not only did he not know the piper's name but he did not make it safe to assume that this piper was even a native of the Dunollie estate.

If, as MacAulay implies, many families were forced out of Dunollie after 1715, it is noteworthy that MacDougalls were among the emigrants to Glengarry County, Ontario, from such one-time Jacobite havens as the Glengarry estate and from North Morar in the 1780s. MacDougalls also emigrated from Knoydart to Glengarry County and from places such as Barra, Eigg, Mull, Arisaig, North Morar, and Moidart to Inverness County, Nova Scotia, in and after 1815. Allan Dall's Glencoe MacDougalls have been mentioned, as have the Loch Tayside emigrants after 1815. These latter may have included the unnamed MacDougall piper's son Donald, mentioned above.

Alexander MacAulay didn't say where his information came from, but a latter-day vindication of the "MacDougall piper to the MacDougall chief" idea appears in the lists of winners in the 1784 Highland Society competition: a Dugald MacDugall, piper to Dugald MacDugall Esq., of Gallanach, won third prize. Gallanach was a cadet family of the MacDougall chiefs; the property lies a little more than five miles southwest of Dunollie.

THE MacINTYRES IN SKYE AND RANNOCH

It is appropriate now to turn again to the once very musical Isle of Skye and the MacIntyre piper theme. Dr Roderick Ross in 1959 cited the genealogical work of his father, Dr Neil Ross, on the subject of a John MacIntyre, "the composer of 'Menzies Salute,' 'My King has landed in Moidart' and other piobaireachds. This John MacIntyre was a son of MacIntyre, a farmer in Totachocar, near Dunvegan Castle. He was great-great-grandfather of Mrs Norman MacLeod (grandmother of Dr Neil Ross, his mother's mother, Catherine MacSwan). The famous piper was her great-grand-uncle.[46]

If you allow thirty years per generation and assume that Dr Roddie Ross was born in 1920, then his father, Dr Neil, would have been born in 1890, Dr Neil's maternal grandmother (Catherine MacSwan/Mrs Norman MacLeod) in 1830, and her great-great-grandfather, John MacIntyre the piper, in 1710. (If the quotation is correct and John MacIntyre was Catherine MacSwan's great-grand-uncle as well as her great-great-grandfather, then there must have been a marriage between a grandchild and a great-grandchild of John MacIntyre.) At the time, depending on how the above quotation is read, he or his father may have held a farm in Totachocar (*Tobht' a'chocaire* [the cook's house]), not far north of Dunvegan.

The Ross information comes from neighbours of the MacCrimmons in Skye and from others in Skye who were profoundly interested in piping. Because it reflects traditional family history, an area in which Highlanders are famous for being remarkably accurate, there is no reason it should not be taken as correct. It establishes John MacIntyre, a piper living and possibly farming on the lands of MacLeod of Dunvegan as an adult in the 1730s.

By virtue of the tune attributed to him, "My King has landed in Moidart," he may have continued living there until the arrival of Prince Charles Edward Stuart at Loch nan Uamh in 1745. The information also shows some connection between John MacIntyre and the Menzies chief in Perthshire. If John lived to the age of fifty, his name must be added either to the number of Skye pipers or to the Menzies family pipers who practised their art during the post-1748 period.

Still in Skye, a Neil MacIntyre was a paid piper in Waternish in MacLeod's Skye on 9 January 1720.[47] Then, in 1723 (according to *Clan Donald*) or in 1733 (according to Keith Sanger), a Malcolm MacIntyre is said to have held Tarskavaigmore in Sleat rent free as (one of) Lord MacDonald's piper(s). Lastly, there is an Iain MacIntyre who piped for one of MacLeod's Independent companies raised in 1745. If by any chance this was the John MacIntyre who was piper at Ardmaddy on the Breadalbane estate in and after 1705, he must have been about sixty-five years old in 1745. Sanger posed the question "Is it possible in this climate, that John MacIntyre, or his descendants returned to Skye, scene of his earlier tuition?" but has no answer. The fact is that there are to date no relationships linking John, Neil, Malcolm, and Iain MacIntyre in Skye. All that can be said with confidence is that there certainly was no shortage of MacIntyre pipers in Skye in the eighteenth century.

We turn now to Rannoch and the notes in Angus MacKay's *Collection* headed "The MacIntyres, heredity pipers to Menzies of Menzies." These begin:

These Pipers lived in Rannach, but they were originally from the Isles. Donald Mòr, the first of whom we have any account, was Piper to Menzies of Menzies. His son John learned with Patrick òg at the college of Dunvegan, and is known as the author of the "Field of Sheriffmoor," a fine Piobaireachd composed on that battle, 1715. His son Donald Bane followed the same profession, and left two sons Robert and John. Robert became Piper to the late MacDonald of Clanranald, after whose death he went to America.

John died about three years ago in Rannach, leaving a son Donald, who has a farm called Allarich at the top of Loch Rannach.

Unless there was more than one John MacIntyre taught by Pàdruig Og MacCrimmon in Skye, the John described by Angus MacKay's note-writer as a pupil of Patrick Og is almost certainly the same man Breadalbane sent to "McCrooman" in the mid-1690s. It is equally tempting to believe that he was also the "Litle pyper" whose year of piping training with "quantiliane McCraingie McLeans pyper" cost Breadalbane £160. Extending the fancy to include what Dr Roderick Ross added, he composed, among other tunes, the tune "My King has landed in Moidart." His date of birth, based on the Breadalbane source, was probably between 1675 and 1680. This makes it probable that his interest in the 1745 rising was nostalgic rather than active, wherever he was piping. This date of birth, together with an absence of information about him from before the 1715 Jacobite rising in the Breadalbane records, would make a period of service with the Menzieses perfectly possible, and also a later move to Skye, but the genealogical picture is surely much more complicated than that.

As a final rider to the speculation, the minor Perthshire laird John Menzies of Shian, in the company of John Campbell of Glenlyon, sent the fiery cross around Loch Tay in 1745, in an effort to raise Breadalbane men for Prince Charles. They had some success, despite the second earl of Breadalbane's strict orders to the contrary and the lively disincentives of local ministers.[48]

Reconciling the information in Angus MacKay's notes and the Breadalbane and other records of the MacIntyres would put a strain on already stretched and contorted credibility, but in the 1960s, in the days before the Breadalbane material had been discovered and all that was readily to hand was Angus MacKay's Menzies material and the results of the Highland Society competitions between the same covers, Alexander MacAulay made the effort to twist the two threads into a durable worsted. His theory was that "Donald Mor, piper to Menzie of Menzie around the closing years of 1700," was the progenitor of two lines of MacIntyre pipers, the Clanranald and the Menzies.[49] While this is speculation and quite unsubstantiated, what MacAulay implied strongly in his piece of wishful thinking was that piping was never snuffed out in either chief's household. That much he doubtless got right.

CHAPTER EIGHT

Sutherland and Gairloch, Seaforth, and Gordon Piping

SUTHERLAND AND GAIRLOCH IN ROSS-SHIRE

Sutherland and Ross were both Gaelic shires included in the list to be disarmed after the last Jacobite war, and that there was piping during the weapons provision of the Act in both places is irrefutable. Beginning with Sutherland, Joseph MacDonald and his brother Patrick, minister's sons, were both raised there, in Durness, and both were thoroughly steeped in Gaelic traditional piping and fiddling. Their most receptive years were in the late 1740s and early 1750s. The Reverend Angus MacKay, writing in 1906, said that Reverend Murdo MacDonald (1696–1763) taught music at the manse in Durness (where he ministered from 1726 to 1763) to Hugh MacKay, sixth Lord Reay, who held the title from 1768 to1797.[1] Elsewhere it is stated that Kenneth Sutherland (Coinnich Sutharlan), tacksman at Keoldale (Cealdail) in Durness and sometime land steward for Lord Reay for the Balnacille (Baile na Cille) estate, taught the violin to several of Reverend Murdoch MacDonald's children.[2]

The Sutherland bard Rob Donn MacKay (1714?–1778) composed two laments for the Reverend Murdoch MacDonald (Maistir Murcha Mac Dhonuill), but mentioned neither the pipes nor the violin in either of them. Still, in the shorter of the two *marbhrainn* (death verses), written at the request of the deceased's son, the Reverend Patrick MacDonald, the bard wrote, "'S caomh leam na fuinn bhiodh tu seinn ann ad' fhardaich" (I love the airs you'd be singing in your home).[3] This line hints at the Durness minister's musicality.

Elsewhere Rob Donn refers to a friend of his, George MacLeod, as "piobair fir an tigh," which Neville T. McKay translated as "piper to the chief." McKay added that the penal legislation, which he clearly hadn't read carefully enough, obviously didn't have much effect in MacKay country.[4] Where actual weapons were concerned, Hew Morrison, in the introductory notes to the third printing of *Orain le Rob Donn* (1899), described Rob Donn and others as inveterate hunters in Reay country in the 1740s and '50s. In fact, according to Morrison, MacKay of Bighouse had to have the bard removed from his home in Bad na h-Achlais to Allt Coire Fhreasguil some time between the mid-1740s (at my guess) and 1759, the reason being that the bard was becoming too fond of helping himself to venison on the hoof. Rob Donn's defiant and feared satirical ripostes apparently could no longer protect him.

The most telling instance of the illegal gunning down of deer involving Rob Donn in Reay country occurred just after the de-weaponing clause became a dead letter (27 September 1753). The evidence is found in the bard's song contrasting the conditions of the death of a poor Highlander called Eòghann who lived in squalor at Polla by Loch Eribol and Henry Pelham's vice-regal demise; the song is accurately dated to within a few days of Pelham's death, 3 March 1754, and it is known that the poet was on one of his many private deer-hunting forays at the time. Obviously, if there was a military presence in Sutherland from 1748 to 1753, no government soldiers were enforcing the Disarming Act there.

Although Hew Morrison gave English titles for Rob Donn's songs and offered notes in English to each title, and although he suggested that the Reay Gaelic dialect had been polished (giving an example of the improvement in his introduction), the depth of the traditional kinship network in Rob Donn's Reay, the depth of the Gaelicness of life conveyed by the Gaelic songs, is splendid. The poet was an assessor (not a powerful position) of the Church of Scotland under his friend Reverend Murdoch; he was also a Free Mason, we are safely to infer from his funeral obsequies. Not surprisingly, there is a moral and intellectual quality to his *bàrdach* that has a limiting effect on couthier observations. Nonetheless, he cast two songs as pibrochs[5] and was on friendly terms with George MacLeod, Lord Reay's piper. MacLeod was one of the two men in December 1766 who were designated collectors of kirk session fines. At that time he was a "Sheriff-Officer." The bard sang of the piper MacLeod in two songs dealing with the piper's pre- and post-matrimonial dealings with his wife, Catherine MacKay (first lines: "'S toigh le Seòras Leòdach mise" [I'm fond of George MacLeod] and "Tha mac a'chìobair 'n a chlò" [The keeper's son's wearing his homespun]).[6] The absence of a marbh-rann (death verse) to the piper, by the bard, could simply mean that the verse was lost; otherwise one is left to assume that George MacLeod outlived Rob Donn, which is unfortunate.

There is at least one piece of evidence that proves that Rob Donn himself composed a pipe jig, among other airs. John MacKenzie, the editor of *Sar-Obair,* noted in his footnote to the Rob Donn song "Am Boc Glas" (The Grey Buck) that "[t]he tune is excellent, and may justly be entitled the first of the Sutherlandshire pipe jigs. It was the poet's own composition. He also composed several other popular airs of great merit."[7] Several tunes in the Simon Fraser collection are attributed to Rob Donn.

The Reverend Murdoch's younger son, Joseph MacDonald, was exposed to piping in his boyhood and teenage years from the early 1750s and is believed to have been a competent player. He was a prodigious, precocious, and remarkably adept analyser of ceòl mór *circa* 1760. The painting of a traditionally clad Highland piper on his manuscript of "Compleat Theory" was thought by R.L.C. Lorimer in the 1960s to have been a self-portrait. Joseph MacDonald never divulged who taught him his classical piping, and although he celebrated Skye and Mull as the pre-eminent piping centres *circa* 1750, piping went back much further than that in Lord Reay's country and he must have known it.

The most famous piping family from Sutherland, of course, is the famous MacKay family now associated with Gairloch to the southwest. The pipers Donald MacKay and his younger brother Rory were born in Lord Reay's country in the last quarter of the sixteenth century. According to lore, in 1609 Rory, a favourite of the MacKay chief's, for safety's sake and to avoid embarrassment to his chief, had to flee to Gairloch. Donald, who had had connections earlier on with the MacKenzies of Gairloch, joined his brother there some time afterwards. Both pipers were living at "Telladil" on Loch Maree around 1650, apparently on the same farm, but lore has it that Donald went home to Sutherland, so at least his name is associated with piping in later seventeenth-century Reay country. John MacKay, second Lord Reay (c. 1612–80), who succeeded his father, Donald (Dòmhnul Dùghal Mac Aoidh), in 1649 and who likely was Donald MacKay the piper's last chief, is known to have retained the services of a "pipier," a "clarsor," and an "amadan" (fool).[8]

In the mid-eighteenth century, Joseph MacDonald's life and that of Rory's famous piper/bard son, John MacKay (Iain Dall mac Ruairidh), the Blind Piper of Gairloch, overlapped by about fourteen years, given the accepted date of death of the Blind Piper as 1754. More's the pity that the author of "Compleat Theory" did not live long enough to discuss his sources and to have published his knowledge of the pipers who flourished around 1750.

Also from the early seventeenth century is another notice of a piper in the neighbouring Sutherland estate to the south. In this case, Sir Robert Gordon, tutor to John, earl of Sutherland (a minor), paid to "Donald Maccrummin pyper" "20 bolls of victual meal" in 1624 and "13 bolls, 2 firlots of meal" in 1625. This citation and another[9] (which mentions "Donaldo McCruimien lie pyper"), indicate a MacCrimmon presence in Sutherland and in Ross, which of course has led to speculation that the classical piping in Lord Reay's country stemmed from Donald MacCrimmon. Joseph MacDonald's mention of Skye's having been so important to piping prompted speculation that

Reay piping adopted Skye standards. While this is quite possible, there is no evidence that it is so. Incidentally, at about this time the MacCrimmons seem to have been both numerous and adventurous; stray members of the family turn up in Strathardle (piper), in Glenorchy (apparently a criminal), and in the north of Scotland.

Between 1761 and 1768 the piper to George MacKay, through the length of his seven years as fifth Lord Reay, was a MacLeod (given as Donald in the *Book of MacKay*) and he was paid £21.6.8 for his service.[10] If he was a young man at the time, he must have begun his piping in the late 1740s and early 1750s.[11] If the number of times the story has been repeated are anything to go by, it is also widely accepted that the Blind Piper's paternal grandson, Red John MacKay (Iain Ruadh mac Aonghuis 'ic Iain Dhoill 'ic Ruairidh [b. Gairloch c. 1753, d. Nova Scotia, date unknown]), went/was sent to Lord Reay's country to learn to play the "small pipes." No date has ever been put forward for this experience. Given his approximate date of birth, he was probably not much over twenty when his father, Angus, died. He was privileged, receiving a formal education away from Gairloch, at Thurso and Inveraray, and was both literate and bilingual. With a formal education in English, he may have been unprepared to take on the piping office in Gairloch[12] in the 1770s. It may then have been the wish of the Gairloch chief, Sir Hector MacKenzie, that Red John get the "small pipe" training, whatever that was, in the north. It may also be possible that George MacLeod was his tutor, as has been suggested elsewhere. The question of the small pipes has been raised in *Traditional Gaelic Bagpiping*.

Where the MacKay pipers are concerned, the loss of the brothers Donald and Rory MacKay by Lord Reay turned out to be a huge cultural gain for the MacKenzies of Gairloch. John MacKay, the Blind Piper, whatever he actually composed of pipe music, is considered the only challenger to the Mac-Crimmons in that department, and if he did make just "Cumha Phàdruig Oig" (Lament for Patrick Og), no praise is unwasted. If he also made "Crosanachd an Doill" (The Blind Piper's Obstinacy), his remarkable range of imagination as a composer will always be celebrated. And, according to Bridget Mackenzie, his poetry, at times closely related in structural form to the classical form of piping, is just as brilliant. Nobody knows when the Blind Piper quit piping but he lived through Culloden and the aftermath, pensioned off and visiting friends, they say. His son Angus, however, is the main Disarming Act piper in Gairloch. His name appears in the Gairloch rentals in 1752.[13] At that time he held two pecks of Cairbeg[14] and two pecks of the quarterland of Engdalmore. For Cairbeg he is described as "Angus Makay the Piper Tenant, of Rent pays 60 Marks of Crown rent."

In 1759 Angus Mackay obtained a twenty-five-year tack to last from Whitsunday 1760 until 1785, from Sir Alexander MacKenzie, ninth of

Gairloch, "as his piper."[15] The land included four pecks of Carmore and Cairbeg and half the grazing of "Dirichhin," all of which is near the chiefly seat of Flowerdale. In 1770, the year of Sir Alexander's death, Angus Mac-Kay signed his name to the following statement of his standing on the estate: "[F]or past years his Master allowed him in name of Salary as his piper yearly the Sum of Three pounds five shillings and nine pence Sterling."[16]

There has never been any claim that the Gairloch MacKay pipers ran a college of piping, but there is no reason to believe that at least Angus did not pass on his piping to others, outside his family.[17]

The late chief of the MacLennans, Ronald G. MacLennan of MacLennan, was proud to report that a Duncan MacLennan (b. c. 1752 at Mellon Charles) was taught to play the pipes by Angus MacKay of Gairloch. This piper MacLennan joined the Seaforth Highlanders (78th Regiment), presumably at their raising in 1778, since the chief said that in 1779 Duncan piped at the head of fifty recruits. The MacLennans lived about seventeen miles roughly north of the MacKay pipers in the parish of Gairloch, and the families must have come to know one another well, as Angus MacKay's only daughter, Ann, married a Donald McLennan from the parish around 1777[18] (by which time Angus was probably deceased).

The other pupil of Angus MacKay's learned piping at an earlier period. He was the fiddler/piper Roderick Campbell (Ruairidh mac Thormoid [Roderick, son of Norman]), probably born a decade earlier than Duncan MacLennan, in the 1740s. Such detail such as there is about him comes from John H. Dixon's *Gairloch* (1886), and there is little reason to dispute it. Dixon, an outsider but one whose piper[19] won the 1880 piping competition at the Northern Meeting, was a good interviewer, and it is known that the grandson of an older brother of Roderick was living in Gairloch in 1886, so, directly or indirectly, the information is likely to have been his. Roderick Campbell lived at Cuilchonich near Aultbea and Mellon Charles, on the north shore of Loch Ewe, about fifteen miles north of Angus MacKay's farm. He drowned while a young man, crossing the River Ewe.

According to the piper Angus MacKay's grandson, John MacKay JP (Iain mac Iain Ruaidh 'ic Aonghuis), Angus MacKay died soon after Sir Alexander, presumably in the early 1770s. This corrects the long-held idea that Red John was mature and well established in his profession when his father, Angus, died.[20] The JP's statement is backed up by the minutes of the sett of 1780, which show no Angus MacKay but do show a John MacKay holding two pecks of "Engadale ffuil" and 1/2 peck of "Fasvicenvue" (Fas mhic Iain Bhuidh [Yellow John's homestead?]), both near Flowerdale; he too signed his name and undoubtedly is Angus's son.[21] Then there's a change: in 1785 (when Angus's tack ran out) John was in one of the two farms in Talladale, a considerable distance from Flowerdale House, the Gairloch family's seat.

The decade 1770–79 is an interesting time in Gairloch piping. In his reminiscences, John MacKay JP said that Sir Alexander MacKenzie and his piper, friend, and religious inspirer Angus MacKay "both died comparatively young. The Laird first, my grand-father attending him on his deathbed."[22] Sir Alexander died in April 1770 and by 1780 there is no longer an Angus MacKay in the Gairloch record. In 1773, according to one Nova Scotia source, the impoverished piper mentioned above, John MacKay, joined the passengers of the ship *Hector,* bound from Loch Broom for Nova Scotia, and had his passage paid by those aboard who preferred his music to the cost of his one-way ticket. The central question is just how closely he was related to the chieftain's piper.

Squire John MacKay JP said nothing about any relative having been among the Hector settlers in Nova Scotia, but when his "Reminiscences" are read carefully, they cannot be interpreted as precluding such a possibility, even a relative as near as a paternal uncle. On the other hand, whoever wrote the notes on the MacKays of Gairloch in Angus MacKay's *Collection* had no doubts whatever; according to this source, the piper Angus MacKay, son of the Blind Piper, indeed had a brother called John and he emigrated to "America." Writing about the Blind Piper, Angus MacKay's author stated: "He left issue two sons, Angus and John. The first succeeded his father as family Piper, and left his son John Roy in the same situation. However, submitting to the changes which took place in the Highlands on the abolition of ancient systems, he emigrated to America about the year 1800, whither his brother John had proceeded 60 years ago. He had two sons, who also were Pipers, and who accompanied their father across the Atlantic."[23]

There is reason to take a closer look at this account of the hereditary pipers in Angus MacKay's *Collection* because this time the writer is accurate about the obscure detail that John Roy had two sons, pipers, neither of whom made any name for himself in nineteenth-century Scottish piping, or piping anywhere. The writer was accurate also about the second emigration and its being *circa* 1800. In fact, John Roy, with his piping sons, Angus (Aonghus mac Iain Ruaidh 'ic Aonghuis 'ic Iain Dhoill) and John (later JP in New Glasgow, Nova Scotia), and several daughters, landed in what is now Pictou County in 1805. Given that the "Account of the Hereditary Pipers" could have been written earlier by some years than the date of publication of the *Collection,* since publication was delayed, this John may indeed have been aboard the *Hector*. (The "his" in "whither his brother," above, of course has to refer to Angus [Aonghas mac Iain Dhoill], not his son John Roy [Iain Ruadh mac Aonghais 'ic Iain Dhoill]).

But the point to be made is that the credibility of Angus MacKay's authority is all but made unshakeable in this case. Angus MacKay's father, John MacKay, Raasay, was a piping pupil, almost certainly, of Red John,[24] the John MacKay who took his family to Nova Scotia in 1805. The person best positioned then to know all this, and to have written it down, or at least have dictated it, surely was Angus MacKay (*Collection*) himself.

MacKenzie of Gairloch, like the MacKenzies of Seaforth, stayed out of the '45, although some men chose to fight for Prince Charles. The prime suspect as raiser of these men was Archibald MacDonell (Young Barisdale) from Knoydart, who recruited soldiers further north even than Gairloch. Hanoverian repercussions in Gairloch, for all that were minimal. Piping was unaffected one way or another. However, judging by the distance the Blind Piper's grandson John (Iain Ruadh) found himself from Flowerdale House in 1785, piping's status in the eyes of the chief may have slipped a notch or two between 1745 and 1785; all the earlier MacKays had lived a walk away from the chief at Flowerdale House, but now Red John had a long row down Loch Maree[25] before he took to the footpath. This apparent relegation of John MacKay is consistent with the exposure of the Gaelic Highlands to the new economic system. Sir Hector (1758–1826) was a keen improver. As has become obvious about at least one level of piping, by the 1760s the so-called colleges were closing and by 1785 they had closed. Despite all the demands of the British military, from 1757, for pipers and their classical and other music, the truth appears to be that sophisticated Gaelic military music was no longer as highly valued on Highland estates. Something of the stuffing of the old Gaelic chiefs' militarism had gone out of the Highlands with the dissolution of the heritable jurisdictions after Culloden; the classical piping form thereafter withered even more noticeably than before. Joseph MacDonald's youthful fears for the future of ceòl mór were justified. Gairloch, however, held on until 1805, the year that the last hereditary piper, Red John, cashed in his not inconsiderable assets and sailed for Pictou County, Nova Scotia. Sir Hector never cared to retain another piper, although there were many on the estate as late as the 1880s according to Dixon.

The most notable thing about the MacKenzies and piping from about 1610 to 1805 on the wider estate is that the MacKays of Gairloch dominated the scene so thoroughly, through the genius of John MacKay, the Blind Piper, that little is known about piping on the rest of what was one of Gaeldom's most extensive estates, capable of raising a small army of its own.

To the north on the mainland, Assynt was another MacKenzie holding (until 1741, when the estate was sold), a part of the world that went to war for the Jacobite cause in the '45 under its MacKenzie chief, the earl of Cromartie. The story of piping in this region is unreconstructed, but an interesting and important piece of supporting evidence has emerged from the second half of the eighteenth century.[26] The song/dance tune "Moladh Chabair-Feidh" (Praise of the Deer's Horns), composed by Tormod Bàn Mac Leoid (Fair Norman MacLeod) in immediate post-Culloden era, was a bagpipe reel that quickly became the MacKenzie signature tune it remains. MacLeod was inspired to write it in bitter, cutting reaction to the plundering of his native Jacobite Assynt by Munro of Achany on the orders of the earl of Sutherland. (This poetic response rather than an armed retaliation may point to Sutherland's having acted within the boundaries of prevailing military occupation law.) John MacKenzie's notes to the song assert that both the words and the melody were MacLeod's, that it was "one of the most spirit-stirring airs that can be played on the bagpipe," and that it was a tune thought important enough to merit a variation of the everywhere-popular reel.[27] John MacKenzie (1806–48) said that the tune was so popular in many parts of the Highlands that it was not danced as a "common reel but as a sort of country-dance. We have seen 'Cabar Feidh' danced in character, and can bear testimony that, for diversified parts, for transitions, mazes and evolutions, it yields not, when well performed, to any 'Cotillon brent new from France.'"[28] (For the principal non-dance use of the tune, see the Seaforth Highlanders, below.)

What MacKenzie meant by a "country-dance" is impossible to say. What he meant to convey by the term "Cotillon" is also open to some debate, since the word was used to signify a Quadrille in some parts of the English-speaking world. The dance in question seems to have been a faster dance than a cotillion and to have had the complexity of a Quadrille.

Elsewhere in Sutherland there are indications also that the prominent Gunn family in the north retained a piper or pipers but space does not permit any description of them.

PIPING ON THE MACKENZIES OF SEAFORTH ESTATE IN KINTAIL IN SOUTHWEST ROSS-SHIRE

Although two old sets of bagpipes are associated with Clan MacRae, one possibly of late seventeenth-century origin, the survival of traditional piping in Kintail into the 1780s is not well documented. However, threads of tradition's continuity into that decade and probably on into the first quarter of the nineteenth century in the Catholic enclave of Ardintoul (Ard an t-Sabhail) can be gleaned but only by drawing together what information is available from about 1715 to about 1825 and letting the spaces paint themselves in.

Political and religious turmoil, particularly from around 1690, when the Episcopal church was proscribed in Scotland, intensified instabilities in deeply episcopal and anti-Whig Kintail and guaranteed enthusiastic MacRae support for the earl of Mar and King James in 1715. A new Seaforth was a lukewarm Hanoverian during the '45, and improvement rents and the tacksman emigrations they would cause were about twenty years in the future. Later emigrations in the 1830s ensured that by 1899, when the Reverend

Alexander MacRae's *History of the Clan MacRae* was published, local community lore to which he had access had apparently fallen silent about piping in the second half of the eighteenth century. Piping lore lingered, however, beyond the reach of the Reverend MacRae, in the Kintail military fabric and was used by MacKay Scobie in 1924 in *Pipers and Pipe Music in a Highland Regiment*. This material, which is word of mouth rather than from records in the early period, dates to 1778 when the first Seaforth regiment was raised (see below) and concerns pipers born, for the most part one assumes, after 1745.

Boswell and Johnson passed through Kintail in a day on their way to Glenelg. No gentleman entertained them and all the MacRaes they met at Achnasheal were uneducated, unprepossessing monoglot Gaels; hence, not having any expectations of learning anything edifying or exceptional, they picked up nothing about piping there. The surviving songs of the Kintail MacRae bard John MacRae (Iain mac Mhurchaidh) of the 1760s, '70s and '80s say nothing about piping there or in America where he went around 1770.[29] The earliest source is Angus MacKay's 1838 *Collection*, and it is typically unreliable. For all that, the *Collection* is the likeliest origin of still widely repeated stories of a Kintail piper and composer called Finlay Dubh Mac Rae whose piping life is said to have included military service in both Jacobite rebellions and who is thought to have passed his gift and knowledge on.

Finlay Dubh's tracks in MacKay's book have to be examined in light of what the geologist Sir Roderick Impey Murchison knew in 1850, independently, of an incident that took place at the Battle of Sheriffmuir, and in light of other written evidence, including what Farquhar MacRae, Dornie, told the Reverend Alexander MacRae of Kintail about place-names he remembered in the 1890s.

In the headings of his scores Angus MacKay claimed authorship of three pieces of ceòl mór for Finlay Dubh MacRae, "Spaidearachd Dhiuc Pheairt" (The Duke of Perth's March) (1745), "Blar Sliabh an t-Shirra" (The Battle of Sheriffmuir) (1715), and "Failte Uilleam Dhuibh Mhic Coinich" (Black William MacKenzie's Welcome) (1715).[30] For the last tune, Gaelic words are given for the ground (*ùrlar*), which at least suggests that the title in this case was correct. The appendix notes on one of the other three tunes, however, immediately undermine that confidence, for there "Blar Sliabh an t-Shirra" is attributed to "John MacIntyre, one of the Brae Rannoch family who was then Piper to the Menzies of Menzies."[31]

Nonetheless, Finlay Dubh is probably more than a figment of the imagination, for when Roderick Impey Murchison visited the field of Sheriffmuir in 1850, he and his companion hunted for the rock on which a piper had played, so they had heard, during the battle.[32] Murchison had not gotten this information from Angus MacKay's book. Although not raised in Kintail and not a Gaelic speaker, Murchison was a great-grand-nephew of the Donald Murchison who had denied the Seaforth rents to the commissioners of the forfeited estates for years after the 1715 rising. Roderick Murchison's source for the piper on the rock story may have been his own family, but undoubtedly this sort of story would have been céilidh material in Kintail even in Angus MacKay's day. Whoever the piper was, the author of MacKay's note either hadn't known about him or chose to exclude the event, and Murchison never mentioned the piper's name.

Elsewhere, in the *Piping Times* of May 1978, Fionnladh Dubh is categorically claimed to have been piper to William, fifth earl of Seaforth (from the late seventeenth century until 1740), and in 1978 a two-drone (tenor) set of pipes, minus the chanter, reputedly played by Fionnladh Dubh at Sheriffmuir and Culloden, was in the possession of the son of the late Captain Alex Matheson, owner of Brahan, the Seaforth MacKenzie seat. The writer of the *Piping Times* article, Finlay MacRae, said the drones were "made of laburnum or some similar wood and mounted in bone," both native materials. For the rest of his data he gave no sources, written or oral, but suspicion must fall on Angus MacKay's book.[33]

Angus MacKay's notes in the *Collection* are the source of two further glimpses of the mysterious Finlay Dubh/Fionnladh Dubh, both plausible. The information accompanying the tune runs as follows: "'Spaidsearachd Dhiuc Pheairt'. The Duke of Perth's March. Composed by Finlay Dubh MacRae. 1745."[34] There is also this descriptive text: "After the battle of Culloden he embarhed [*sic*] for France, but he died on his passage, the 13th May 1746. Finlay the Piper joined to follow the fortunes of the white rose, along with MacRae of Ceandaloch, and they are said to have been the only persons who went from Kintail."[35]

The reliability of this information is strengthened in that the actual date of the duke's death is given, which suggests a written source or an eyewitness (as yet undiscovered). The mention of the only other Kintail man to fight as a Jacobite in 1745 also rings with some truth inasmuch as there were only eleven MacRaes (no Finlays) listed in the prisoners of the '45, five from Cromartie's regiment. The difficulty arises with Ceandaloch, which doesn't exist on modern maps and is not included in the map of MacRae country that Farquhar MacRae, Dornie, provided to the Reverend Alexander MacRae in the 1890s for his book. The Dornie man's information is distinctive in that it contains many local village place-names shown nowhere else. Ceandaloch is not mentioned either in rental lists for 1718 or in Reverend A. MacRae's book published about a decade later. The place-name Bundalloch, on the other hand, is common to almost all of those documents and is probably the place Angus MacKay's writer was referring to.

Very little else is repeated about Finlay Dubh MacRae the piper and composer except that he taught a Charles Munro the pipes. Munro became piper to Sir John MacKenzie (unidentified) and later emigrated "to America," where no trace of him has been found. It is unknown whether Finlay Dubh taught his children piping or even if he had children. Many Finlay MacRaes appear in the *History of the Clan MacRae* but none in connection with the bagpipes.

His men having suffered trying consequences for their Jacobitism in 1715 and again after the Battle of Glenshiel in 1719, the ruling Seaforth did more than keep his horns in during Bliadhna Thearlaich (Charles's Year).[36] In fact, Kenneth, Lord Fortrose, raised soldiers for King George, if not in great numbers. In 1745 at least two Independent companies were raised in Kintail by the MacKenzie chief, one under Captain Alexander MacKenzie, the other under Captain Colin MacKenzie of Hilton. In the first, the lieutenant was John Mathison and the ensign, Simon Murchison. In the second, the lieutenant was Alexander Campbell and the ensign, John MacRae. Both Murchison and MacRae are names that go back a long way in Kintail and southern Lochalsh. There is no reason to believe that these loyal companies did without the customary piper, so in all probability Kintail pipers were on both sides in 1745.

The next and more trustworthy information source on Kintail piping is I.F. MacKay Scobie's *Pipers and Pipe Music in a Highland Regiment* (1924). The author was a commissioned officer in the Seaforth Highlanders during the Great War and a piper himself. He tapped into a valuable vein of piping lore from the Seaforth estate passed down in his regiment from the pre-record period during the Disarming Act years. While the Gaelic language survived, valuable oral history survived and in the Seaforths there was a strong Gaelic-speaking component even into the 1880s. In 1778 Kintail contributed a disproportionate number of soldiers to the Seaforth Highlanders, so many in fact that the mutiny at Leith in September of that year was known everywhere as "The Affair of the MacRaes," not of the Seaforths. MacKay Scobie's essential information begins with the raising of the first Seaforth Highlanders (78th) in 1778, and the author alludes, with greater credibility than the writer or writers in Angus MacKay's *Collection*, to the persistence of a rich piping tradition among the MacRaes after the '45.

MacKay Scobie never mentions Finlay Dubh. He does, however, intimate that there was traditional piping in Kintail in the 1760s and 1770s. From his work in the regiment's oral history the military piper Red Donald MacRae (Dòmhnul Ruadh MacRae) emerges and with him two salient, but isolated, facts about the old piping in Kintail. Red Donald (b. c. 1755; d. after 1848)[37] was a native of Applecross and second in the line of head pipers of the Seaforths, his term running from 1784 to 1789; according to MacKay Scobie, he learned his piping at a "school" in Kintail run by MacRae pipers. MacRae won the Highland Society of London's prize pipe in 1791 and competed at the triennial competition, at the age of seventy-nine, in 1835. When he left the army he lived in Inverness, Raasay, and Kyleakin (Skye) over the swirling narrows from Lochalsh. MacKay Scobie's is the only published mention of a school of piping, whatever that was, in Kintail, one which, if it existed, must have been in operation when Boswell and Johnson travelled through Glenshiel.

MacKay Scobie is also unique in having associated the MacRaes in Kintail with a named bagpipe, the "Maighdean" (Maiden). If he is correct, this gives the macRaes a valuable musical imprimatur, for the MacRaes would make up the third party in a bagpiping triumvirate: the MacCrimmons, having the "Oinseach" (Dwelly translates this as the Bagpipe/Foolish Woman/Idiot); the Conduiligh Rankins, "A' Bhairisgeach" (Dwelly translates "Bairisg" as a fool); and the Kintail MacRaes, their "Maighdean." MacKay Scobie may have confused the name of the MacRaes pipe with that of their neighbouring Chisholms' chanter, the "Maighdean a' Chuarain" (Maiden of the Slipper). After all, over the generations the Kintail MacRaes had several marriage relationships with Chisholms of Strathglass, a member of which clan, Captain Archibald Macra Chisholm, owned the MacRaes' "Feadan Dubh Chintaille" (Black Chanter of Kintail) from 1847 to 1897.

The interpretation of the history of Seaforth-patronized piping that follows from Angus MacKay's notes is that after William, fifth earl, died in 1740 or 1741, Finlay Dubh's Jacobite sympathies became an embarrassment to an owner who had no intention of risking his newly regained mountains and valleys for King James. Finlay's death en route to exile in France conveniently averted further embarrassment. The new earl and his Lowland Stewart wife, according to Angus MacKay, retained the services of a John MacCrimmon, son of Pàdruig Og (putative teacher of the Blind Piper of Gairloch) and brother of the Donald MacCrimmon who was killed at Moy in early 1746.[38] It is extremely unlikely that a son of Pàdruig Og, an almost hallowed name in piping, by his second wife, according to Angus MacKay, was Seaforth's piper before "Finlay Dubh MacRae," but in any event there's not a wisp of lore anywhere to corroborate Angus MacKay's claim that Seaforth had a piper called John MacCrimmon. It is the more surprising that a son of the almost legendary Pàdruig Og would have gone unsung when John MacRae, the Kintail bard was coming into his own in Kintail in the 1760s, unless this MacCrimmon had no particular talent.[39]

How much social disruption through tack changes and rent adjustments there was in Kintail during the rule of Kenneth, who died in 1761, is unknown. His son, Kenneth (1744–81), the man who raised the first Seaforth Highlanders, was certainly responsible for poverty and hardship where there had been none before, according to John MacRae the bard, whose brother was one of those left destitute (*falamh*) in the early 1770s. The bard called Kintail and Lochalsh "Dùthaich bhochd na h-éiginn" (Poor land of distress) and remembered bitterly what had been done to the inhabitants, no matter their social class, by the gentry: "Mollachd air an uachdaran / A chuir fad' air chuaintean sinn" (A curse on the gentry / Who drove us o'er the seas).

What worked against the Kintail MacRaes in particular was their strong anti-Williamite episcopalianism. To them, Whiggery and Presbyterianism went hand in hand; they detested and despised both. Many learned MacRaes were episcopal clergy and they were influential over their people, both as Jacobite encouragers and, after about 1690 (in the person of Alexander MacRae [Alasdair mac Iain]), as leaders of many people to the Roman Catholic Church. Had it not been for this deep attachment to episcopalianism, their part in the 1715 and 1719 risings would not have been so emphatic, nor the official reaction so sharp. The Kintail Episcopal church was destroyed from the sea by a Hanoverian ship's guns in 1719, but even though the kirk had its first Kintail minister appointed in 1730, a Presbyterian church was not built till 1758. Politically and legally, Kintail bristled in 1721 when a small army under Donald Murchison marched to Glenaffric ready to fight at Ath nam Muileach. Their purpose was to deny the Kintail rents to the agents of the commissioners of the forfeited estates who were foolhardily marching west from Inverness to enforce the law. It can have come as little surprise when George I sanctioned the building of the barracks at Glenelg in 1722.

In the estate of Gairloch to the north there was a similar sense of outrage at imposed Presbyterianism but less concerted reaction, and the transition to the new religion, all in all, was smoother. There, the piping tradition went on relatively undisturbed. Much less is known about traditional piping in Kintail, but it is unthinkable that Gairloch would have had a piper and the senior MacKenzie family, in whom was vested much greater power and prestige, had not. And, at the tack level, Kintail must have cleaved closely to tradition as long as rents were bearable, which seems to have been till about 1770.

The next known MacRae piper in the eighteenth century, a piper to the earl of Seaforth, was John Beag, according to the appended notes in Angus MacKay's book. In a little apostrophizing in the notes to the tune MacKay calls "Fàilte an t-Siosalaich" (The Chisholm's Salute), John Beag is remembered as the piping tutor of Kenneth Chisholm, the last family piper to the Chisholm chiefs in Strathglass. There is no telling when John Beag lived, but it appears that he and Red Donald MacRae were contemporaries, both enjoying success around 1790.

While there is no claim anywhere that John Beag was a member of a hereditary MacRae piping, that is the guess of many people who look for musical lineages and continuity in Kintail. By his first wife, Red Donald had two sons, Alexander and John, both pipers. If John was John Beag MacRae, the date of his tutoring of Kenneth Chisholm would have to have been much later than the mid-1790s, the rough date given by the Nova Scotian genealogis Sagart Arasaig for the Chisholm piper's leaving for Nova Scotia. On the other hand, if John Beag was a son of Finlay Dubh, the Chisholm and MacRae stories would mesh nicely in time. (A stray John MacRae is mentioned by Dixon[40] as having been a judge of piping at the Edinburgh competitions with John MacKenzie [17 July 1806–19 August 1848], compiler of *Sar-Obair.* Dixon describes him as John MacRae of Raasay.)

Remarkably, Angus MacKay's note about the accidental death of John Beag's pupil Kenneth Chisholm (he was killed by a falling tree in "America") is correct. This lifts one's hopes again about the note writer's research accuracy and strengthens the case that John Beag really was Seaforth's piper and Kenneth Chisholm's piping tutor. The actual title of earl of Seaforth was not renewed until 1771, when Kenneth MacKenzie became the sixth earl. He raised the Seaforth Highlanders in 1778, but his head piper (and the only piper that we know of while he was colonel) was Roderick MacKenzie. The sixth earl of Seaforth died in 1781 on his way to service in India, and the next Seaforth was the earl's relative Thomas Frederick Humberston MacKenzie (c. 1756–83). Thomas was followed by his brother Francis Humberston MacKenzie in 1783. The latter became Baron Seaforth in 1797 and was president of the Highland Society of London in 1788. It would have been *de rigueur* for him to have retained a piper, and thus he looks to be the best candidate as patron of John Beag MacRae.

The last of several native MacRae pipers to be discussed here is the prominent Colonel Sir John MacRa of Ardintoul (1786–1847), first of the 79th or Cameron Highlanders, then military secretary to his cousin Francis Rawdon, marquis of Hastings and Lord Moira (1754–1825). Although he was born later than the Disarming Act period, MacRa made an important contribution to Highland piping and inferences can be drawn about the continuance of traditional piping in eighteenth-century Kintail from what is known of the Ardintoul family.

Sir John MacRa came from much the same mould as Sir John MacGregor Murray, the discoverer in Bengal of the Joseph MacDonald manuscript. Like Murray, MacRa served for many years in India. While there, in 1816, he made a copy of a copy of the manuscript history of the MacRas written by the Reverend John MacRa (d. 1704); he also taught Indians to play the pipes. He was a piper and a maker of bagpipes according to *History of the Clan MacRae.* The same book informs us that the black chanter of Kintail, "one of the heirlooms of the 'High Chiefs' of Kintail" was given by the last earl of Seaforth (presumably Francis Humberston MacKenzie, who died in 1815 without surviving male issue) to Colonel Sir John MacRa.

According to the Reverend Alexander MacRae, who saw the black chanter in the 1890s, it was the oldest, much-repaired part of a set of bag-

Chart 15   The MacRaes of Ardintoul

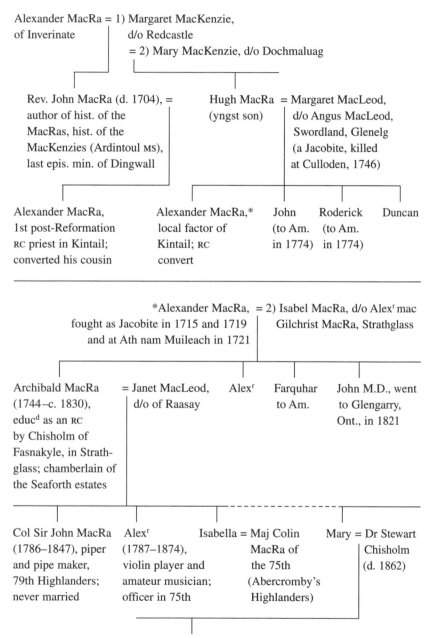

Alexander MacRa = 1) Margaret MacKenzie,
of Inverinate | d/o Redcastle
= 2) Mary MacKenzie, d/o Dochmaluag

Rev. John MacRa (d. 1704), =
author of hist. of the
MacRas, hist. of the
MacKenzies (Ardintoul MS),
last epis. min. of Dingwall

Hugh MacRa = Margaret MacLeod,
(yngst son) | d/o Angus MacLeod,
Swordland, Glenelg
(a Jacobite, killed
at Culloden, 1746)

Alexander MacRa,
1st post-Reformation
RC priest in Kintail;
converted his cousin

Alexander MacRa,*
local factor of
Kintail; RC
convert

John
(to Am.
in 1774)

Roderick
(to Am.
in 1774)

Duncan

*Alexander MacRa, = 2) Isabel MacRa, d/o Alex^r mac
fought as Jacobite in 1715 and 1719 | Gilchrist MacRa, Strathglass
and at Ath nam Muileach in 1721

Archibald MacRa
(1744–c. 1830),
educ^d as an RC
by Chisholm of
Fasnakyle, in Strath-
glass; chamberlain of
the Seaforth estates

= Janet MacLeod,
d/o of Raasay

Alex^r

Farquhar
to Am.

John M.D., went
to Glengarry,
Ont., in 1821

Col Sir John MacRa
(1786–1847), piper
and pipe maker,
79th Highlanders;
never married

Alex^r
(1787–1874),
violin player and
amateur musician;
officer in 75th

Isabella = Maj Colin
MacRa of
the 75th
(Abercromby's
Highlanders)

Mary = Dr Stewart
Chisholm
(d. 1862)

Captain Archibald MacRa Chisholm, 42nd Regiment
(1824–97), piper and judge at northern meetings; married but no issue

pipes once owned by Sir John. Sir John gave the pipes to his cousin Captain Archibald MacRa Chisholm of the 42nd (d. 1897), who in turn, in 1895, gave it to his cousin and fellow officer in the Black Watch, Lieutenant Colin William MacRae of Glassburn, also a bagpiper (grandson of Major Colin of the 75th Regiment and his wife, Isabella MacRa, see below).

The MacRaes of Ardintoul, from the conversion of Alexander from episcopalianism by his first cousin, Reverend Alexander MacRa, at least until the death of Archibald around 1830, were Roman Catholics. This was no impediment to their local progress in the eighteenth century: Alexander was the factor and his son Archibald (1744–c. 1830) the estate chamberlain. According to the *Old Statistical Account,* about a third of Kintail was Catholic (c. 1790), a fact that may have had some bearing on the tacksman emigrations of the 1770s and on the tide of emigrations that the author Reverend A. MacRae said took place after 1831.

Colonel Sir John MacRa was in India from 1813 until 1823 with Lord Moira[41] and he knew how to play the pipes at that time. It is not known where he learned and from whom, but he must have been influenced by piping in Raasay. His mother, Janet MacLeod (daughter of the John MacLeod, eleventh of Raasay, who entertained Boswell and Johnson) was no stranger to pipe and fiddle music and dancing, which were plentiful in her father's home. James MacLeod twelfth of Raasay's piper *circa* 1790–1823 was John MacKay, son of Rory (Iain mac Ruairidh), Eyre. Sir John retired from the army in 1826, the year that Lord Moira died. By that time John MacKay and most of his family had packed their bags and moved to the more lucrative opportunities in Lowland Scotland. Sir John lived in his retirement "chiefly at Ardintoul and Raasay." He must have witnessed the evictions of almost every Raasay man, woman, and child.

The year Colonel Sir John MacRa was born, 1786, was the year his mother's brother James MacLeod (d. 1824) became chieftain of Raasay. James became the patron of the piper John MacKay who lived at Eyre, and a niggardly patron in MacKay's opinion. By the time he was ten, Sir John must have been well acquainted with Iain mac Ruairidh, his family, his music, and, if he had any in the 1790s, his pupils.

According to a number of sources,[42] one of those pupils was Archibald Munro (c. 1800–56), piper to Walter Scott's friend Colonel Alasdair Ranaldson MacDonell of Glengarry. Accepted knowledge about Munro says that he was a native of Ross-shire, "a MacCrimmon product" through John MacKay in Eyre, Raasay, and some time after Glengarry's death in 1828, piper to one Colonel Sir John MacRa of Ardintoul in Kintail. Angus MacKay's notes to the tunes in his *Collection,* give Archibald Munro the position as Glengarry's piper and describe him as the composer of "Cumha Mhic Alasdair" (Glengarry's Lament). Munro competed in the 1824 competition as Glengarry's piper and was apparently still in the office when Glengarry died in 1828. Munro was a close friend of Finlay MacLeod, the piper to Grant of Glenmoriston. In 1835 an Archibald Munro, "from Oban" according to Angus MacKay's summaries of the competition results, took third prize in the Edinburgh competition.

Given the Ardintoul MacRas' ties to Raasay and Colonel Alasdair Ranaldson MacDonell's written encouragement to the Highland Society of London, *circa* 1815, to hire Lieutenant Donald MacCrimmon in Glenelg as the unquestionable choice for professor of piping, there is a case to be made for Munro's having served the MacRas first and then Alasdair Ranaldson rather than the other way round. A plausible argument is that Archibald Munro was native either to Raasay or Kintail. In that case, his early talent as a piper would naturally have been fostered by the Gaelic traditionalist Ardintoul MacRas (Archibald and Colonel Sir John), Kintail tacksmen, by sending him to the Raasay family piper, Iain mac Ruairidh, for his first professional tuition.[43] Later, after he was promoted to be Glengarry's piper, the possibility exists, at least until 1823 (when MacCrimmon was imprisoned in Inverness for debt and Iain mac Ruairidh had moved to the Lowlands), that Archibald Munro had piping tuition from MacCrimmon himself at Glenelg. MacCrimmon had pupils at Glenelg, and Glengarry's pride would have ensured that his piper have the best training available from the man Glengarry considered to be Gaeldom's best. Much hinges on the date that Archibald Munro was hired by Glengarry, and that date is unknown. The accepted version, which has Munro serving Sir John MacRa on his yacht after Glengarry's accidental death in 1828, is challenged by the Abertarff (Fort Augustus) parish records, which show his marriage there in 1830 and the baptisms of his two daughters there in 1832 and 1835. Other sources associate Munro with MacRaes in Port Clair, between Fort Augustus and Glenmoriston, and describe him as a "cutterman" (revenue cutters in this case, presumably operating on Loch Ness against *fir nam poit dubha* [the moonshiners]).

The idea that Sir John MacRa was a Roman Catholic bastion of traditional Gaelic piping into the nineteenth century is speculative but worth stating nonetheless. By the time he was old enough to learn the chanter, the Highland Society of London competitions in Edinburgh had been a spreading influence in Scotland for ten to fifteen years and there is circumstantial evidence that he interested himself in the society's affairs. MacRa's later (probably self-admitted) contribution, the adding of the bass drone to the older two- or three- (tenor) drone instrument that was common outside the northern Gàidhealtachd, was a factor in the Highland Society of London's decision, in 1821, to disallow competition on the two-drone set. Assuming his involvement with the Highland Society, one can reasonably say that he had no aversion to reel-music piping for dancing, which was a feature of the Edinburgh competitions until the mid-1820s.[44] The person most likely to have influenced Sir John's piping was John MacKay of Raasay. Through him he must have absorbed some of John MacKay of Gairloch's style, technique, and repertoire, which belonged in the older tradition of the Blind Piper and thus conceivably of Sutherland. Another speculative suggestion is that Sir John learned his piping in his own family from his father, Archibald.

Kintail suffered for its religious contrariness after 1715. Sackville's little bout of mean-spiritedness after Culloden rubbed salt in the wound. When the rents were raised as tack changes took place around 1770, the reaction of many tacksmen, like those of Glengarry and Skye, was to emigrate to the Carolinas. MacRae and Murchison, for that matter, are not uncommon names among the Loyalists who fought in the American Revolutionary War (see *inter alia* the Loyalists' claims for losses), but the actual extent of emigration in the 1760s and '70s to that "America" and later on to the more northerly British territory has yet to be properly explored. How many tacksmen left is not known and neither is the number of pipers among or with them, since lore in the Carolinas is dead and the records of the time few, far between, and not informative culturally. However, all the indications are that piping continued in its traditional ways in Kintail throughout the eighteenth century. The survival of the tradition is strongly attested to in the Seaforth Highlanders, raised in 1778.[45]

PIPING IN GORDON COUNTRY IN THE NORTHEAST

Lochaber was fairly solidly Jacobite in the 1745, and thus the Highland inhabitants of the Inverlochy estate did not share the politics of their feudal superior, Cosmo, sixth marquis of Huntly and third duke of Gordon, who was a Hanoverian. Records uncovered by Dr B.L.H. Horn of the Scottish Record Office nevertheless show that Cosmo, at the year of his death, 1752, retained a piper, name and place of origin unknown. Accounts show this piper to have been paid ten merks Scots a year, less than the duke's "scavenger" got, although some rental and/or other adjustment on his behalf may have escaped the record. He was used, presumably among many other things, to lead the haymakers. The third duke is known to have been generous to the pipers of visiting gentlemen.[46]

In keeping a piper the third duke was continuing a custom and preference indulged in by his father, Alexander Gordon (b. c. 1682), the Roman Catholic and Jacobite fifth marquis of Huntly and second duke, who had fought as a Jacobite at Sheriffmuir in November 1715. This makes it all the more tempting to suppose that his Jacobite brother, Lord Lewis Gordon of the '45, had a piper or pipers during the Jacobite campaign; Lord Lewis raised two regiments for the service of Prince Charles.[47] It is then also quite plausible that a third brother, Lord Adam Gordon (1728–d.s.p. 1801), had a piper from the estate with him in his Independent company raised 3 September 1745 in the service of King George (Stewart of Garth calls him Lieutenant Adam Gordon in *Sketches*, 2:334). Lord Adam Gordon was president of the Highland Society of London in 1784.[48]

Cosmo Gordon's successor, Alexander Gordon (c. 1743–1827), seventh marquis of Huntly and fourth duke,[49] is known from "the household books for 1776" to have retained a piper "from Huntly" (there was another "from Glenbuchat" for some part of whose income he also may have been responsible).[50] There are two other sources that indicate his appreciation of piping.

The first source is taken indirectly from John MacDonald's published autobiography. In 1778 the Argyllshire schoolmaster/piper John MacDonald, newly enlisted (4 June 1778) in the duke of Gordon's North Fencibles, arrived in Elgin: "[T]hat very evening ... I was despatched to the Duke of Gordon's house ... ten weeks, to play the pipes ... Before I left the duke's house I received two guineas as a present from His Grace for my music."[51] From Reverend Angus MacKay's citation in *The Book of MacKay* of MacDonald's longhand manuscript, it is deducible that MacDonald spent his time with the hospitable fourth duke between September and November 1778, since the piper implies that he was among the men who then marched from Elgin to Fort George, where the regiment took up quarters for the winter.[52] Neither Bridget MacKenzie's citing of MacKay's published version of John MacDonald's *Autobiographical Journal* (1906)[53] nor MacKay's citing of the original manuscript in his *Book of MacKay* (1906) mentions any specific bagpipes, so one assumes MacDonald played his own pipes while living at the duke of Gordon's house.

The second source is an article published in 1849 in the Toronto *Globe*.[54] It states that "a pair of bagpipes ... which are believed to be among the best ever manufactured, were made about a hundred years ago, for the Duke of Gordon, father of the last Duke."[55] The father of the last duke of Gordon was Alexander, the fourth duke, who had been so generous to John MacDonald; he was only sixteen in 1759 but patriotic withal.[56] The newspaper story states that after the bagpipes had been "in His Grace's possession for some years, they were lent to Capt. Simon Fraser, when about to proceed to America as a Captain of the 78th Regt., and they were used at the taking of Quebec, in 1759." If this data is correct, then the recipient was Simon Fraser of Inverallochy, who was the only one of six Simon Frasers gazetted captain in the 78th (Fraser's Highlanders); he was gazetted 11 January 1757.[57] The regiment arrived in Halifax, Nova Scotia, in June 1757. This also means that Alexander, the fourth duke, was some years younger than fourteen when he bought the instrument, or had it bought for him, and that the purchase was probably made during the years when the Disarming Act was being enforced (1748–53).

The future disposition of the bagpipes introduces new data on the MacRae pipers. At the end of the Seven Years' War, the pipes were returned to their owner at Gordon Castle "and after being long used there were made a present of, about 60 years ago [c. 1789], to Donald McCrae, father of the present owner, by the marquis of Huntly, as a prize, at the annual competition of Pipers at Edinburgh."[58] According to the *Globe* article, McCrae, "having joined the 42nd Regiment, as Pipe Major, carried his valuable instrument to the wars, and there played the same inspiring notes at the landing at Egypt, under Sir Ralph Abercrombie, as had been done under the walls of Quebec."[59]

After the short peace McCrae joined "the new 78th [2nd Battalion, Ross-shire Highlanders, 1804] having been raised chiefly on the estate of Lord Seaforth ... taking his pipes with him." He played them at the battle of Maida in southern Italy in 1806.[60] According to the newspaper article, "the 78th was afterwards engaged in many of the battles in Spain and Portugal. At the battle of Corunna [16 January 1809], McCrae was wounded and left on the field – but careful of his valuable pipes, he dispatched them by a comrade to a place of safety."[61] The *Globe* article concludes: "These pipes have been in thirty-two engagements. In 1826, they were transferred by the veteran to his son, the present owner, who now holds a situation in the Custom House, Kingston. His father yet lives in Scotland, and is now in his hundreth [*sic*] year." The owner of the bagpipes in 1849 was his son "Mr Alexander McKenzie Fraser McCrae."[62]

Although I do not know where the bagpipes were made or who presently owns them, they were almost certainly a two-drone set. It's unfortunate that John MacDonald had nothing to say on the subject in his autobiography.

The earlier piping and dancing celebration in Aberdeenshire at the news of the exoneration of Lord George Gordon (1751–93), leader of the infamous anti-Catholic Gordon riots in the 1770s, has been touched upon elsewhere; it also took place during the fourth duke's tenure.

Where the ducal family is concerned, there is another piping reference connected to the family. In 1779 the duchess (Jane Maxwell, "the Queen of the North") gave an unidentified piper tip of five shillings. Unfortunately, according to Dr Horn Alexander, the fourth duke kept no wage books and nothing is known of the incomes of pipers living on the estate. Besides piping, however, Alexander (d. 1827) was all of his life friend and patron of William Marshall (1748–1833), the great fiddler-composer whose welfare and career the fourth duke of Gordon assiduously fostered, so his considerateness of other traditional musicians probably was a byword.

Thus, there is no reason to think that on the Gordon estates in Lochaber, as in Banff and Aberdeen shires, community pipers were ever scarce from the early eighteenth century until deep into the nineteenth. In fact, strong pro-Highland sympathies appear on the part of an early Gordon in the first half of the seventeenth century, and probably not for the first time. Lewis Gordon, third marquis of Huntly, at age thirteen raised Gaels in the Braes of

Mar with whom he cut a dash. In 1644 he married a Highland daughter of Grant of Freuchie by whom he had issue, including George, fourth marquis and first duke of Gordon (b. c. 1650).

In the later eighteenth century the Gordon family's piper was used to accompany the haymakers, pointing to a more menial status for one piper than the land-rich gentlemen and semi-gentlemen pipers on MacLeod's estate and elsewhere enjoyed. Nothing is known, however, of what John MacDonald the Skerray schoolteacher and piper in Bighouse's company played for the duke of Gordon, but MacDonald was literate in English, *et ergo* bilingual, and doubtless properly aware of classical music for the bag-pipes. Perhaps the fourth duke of Gordon's long-standing generosity to William Marshall (and the army commissions later granted to three of his sons) shows that the ducal line of Gordons latterly favoured stringed music.

And yet, when the eighth marquis of Huntly and fifth and last duke of Gordon died without issue in 1836, his successor as titular head of the clan, George Gordon, earl of Aboyne (1761–1853), who became ninth marquis of Huntly,[63] is associated with the piper Angus M'Innes in Inverroy in Lochaber in 1840. A later marquis of Huntly retained the services of the piper Alexander Cameron (1848–1923), son of Donald Cameron (1810–68).[64]

There is an impression that the degree of "classicism" in Highland bag-piping declined as one travelled eastwards. That may be so (there surely were Lowland tastes in folk music and piping to which the ducal Gordon family paid respect), but for long enough the Gordons and the Farquharsons in Aberdeenshire were the most easterly of Scottish piping enthusiasts who had patronized the Gaelic folk musician over several generations.

PART THREE

New World Piping in Cape Breton

CHAPTER NINE

The East Bay Area of Cape Breton and the MacLean Pipers in Washabuck

As I have written elsewhere, in the Old World Gàidhealtachd, tradition, where it was confident and defiant, ignored and/or struggled against forces of change. In instrumental and vocal music, this change – call it improvement if you like – expressed itself as changing perceptions of the importance of literacy and the tempered scale.[1] In dance, the introduction of outsiders' dances was combined with the invention of refined variations of once-traditional dances.[2] Where piping is concerned, competition and monetary reward were intruded as incentives from the time of the 1795 Edinburgh piping competition. Similar competitions spread through the Highland Games phenomenon in the nineteenth and twentieth centuries, touching a large number of pipers even in out-of-the-way corners.[3]

Here I have to isolate the indignant argument I hear in my imagination that indeed pipers piped for dancing in Scotland in rural areas of the Gaelic Highlands until well into the twentieth century and often it was for Reel dancing, not Quadrilles or English long dances. Indignation will just as strenuously emphasize that not all of these rural pipers relied primarily upon the written note to learn their music. Many may have been ear players. Thus, it might be claimed quite honestly that these were community pipers who could have differed little or not at all from pipers in Cape Breton's Gaelic-speaking communities. However, there is a vital distinction: Cape Breton dance setting steps in all communities where there is dancing (and that means nearly all of them) are invariably step-dance setting steps. Until evidence is found that the same dancing existed in Highland Scotland, traditional step-dance music in Cape Breton is definable as distinct.

When Calum MacLeod from Dornie,[4] gold medallist in Gaelic at Edinburgh University, came to Cape Breton, he had never seen these steps done.[5] When Frank Rhodes visited to research what became a chapter in the Fletts' book *Traditional Dancing in Scotland*, he found the steps unlike what he knew to exist in Scotland, although he found similar Reel figures and what he took to be old circular forms of the Highland Reel.

It is a lot more than splitting hairs to say that the differences in speed and timing required to play the same tunes for step-dancing as for a Scottish Reel or other modern dance are sizeable. Until the 1970s I often heard it said by non-Cape Bretoners that the Highland folk of Cape Breton learned these steps in Canada from Irish immigrants (perhaps also to some extent from the Irish community in greater Boston, although nobody said that to me). There was never any elaboration. This is an absurd argument, since the Irish presence in rural Nova Scotia is not large, it is diffused, and, in one important area, it became unmistakably Scotch.[6] More recently, those in Scotland who understand the distinction have been inclined, more productively, to examine where and until how recently step-dancing existed in Scotland, and not just Gaelic Scotland.

In the most Gaelic corners of Highland Scotland, the old ways survived behind the barrier of an ancient infixing and aspirating language, rich in idiom, into a time when they were disowned by many ignorant Scots as alien and almost invariably substandard, no matter the criteria. The first two parts of this book have as their premise that piping in those Gaelic areas went on being traditional until the changes became unavoidable or until there were simply not enough representatives of the old ways left to maintain the ship on course. At the same time, Gaelic tradition in the rural New World found itself largely ignored and capable of self-generation. There too, however, it was challenged; as early as the mid- to late nineteenth century, modern Scottish concepts of traditional Gaelic culture existed in the urban and industrial areas of the Maritime Gàidhealtachd and corroded the older preliterate tradition contiguous to them.[7] Even in the most sequestered corners of Gaelic Inverness County, some people were conscious of being citizens of the great British Empire. However, this consciousness was adhered to voluntarily and generally by a small percentage in the community; it was not imposed from outside and there were few social structures, like competition or upper-class sanction, to promote it. Thus, in the rustic areas where something of an agricultural/fishing subsistence persisted within a Gaelic family and community consciousness, where there was often resentment when children who spoke only Gaelic were educated in English,[8] the older tradition stood on its own feet until the twentieth century.

While perhaps 1845 is a late date for the emigration to Nova Scotia of highly conservative Gaelic tradition bearers from places like South Uist, Moidart, and the Morars, the influences for change in North America itself have to be given some thought. Under the fast-changing economic circumstances in North America (marked to a great extent in the United States by the American Civil War), which were so intensely dominant in urban places, Gaelic and its associated music and dance seem to have had a lifetime of vigour in rural North America for about a century. Very little or nothing of traditional cultural value has survived in the Carolinas, where immigration began in pre-Revolutionary War times. In Prince Edward Island immigration from the West Highlands began in the 1770s, roughly half a century before the zenith of Gaelic immigration to Cape Breton in the 1820s. Today in Prince Edward Island's essentially rural environment (but one that has had superior economic potential in potatoes), the language has almost disappeared and with it much of folk tradition, to the point that Islanders now turn to the last traditional fiddlers in Inverness County (such as Alex Francis MacKay) for cultural models. Work I did for Parks Canada in Victoria County, Cape Breton, in the summer of 2000 revealed that there are no Gaelic speakers left in that county north of Smoky.

The last, fast-weakening stronghold of the language, Gaelic thought and values, fiddling, and some of the old dancing is concentrated now in Inverness County. But even there all who are interested in such things are constantly reminded that if only they had been old enough or had done the work fifty years ago, how much would have been understood and preserved. That is an old, old song but I can vouch for its accuracy over the last thirty years in Inverness County. In the mid-1970s I experienced this in a cultural sense when witnessing the will of an old man in his nineties. I asked him if he remembered Kennie Bolliken (MacQuarrie) the piper. There was a pause while he registered what was a totally unexpected question from what to him was a most unlikely quarter. He seemed to take on a quieter mood then he told me what he remembered from his boyhood about Bolliken in River Denys, and he confessed that he had never thought he would ever find anyone who would ask about those old rural times, so great and many had been the changes. Gaelic is in a condition of its last rapid decline. The number of speakers in Cape Breton is probably down to a few hundred. Step-dance fiddling is becoming more and more a commercial enterprise as the old communities become commercial satellites of the nearest industrial centre and the electronically connected world.

The principal part of this book (Parts 1 and 2) deals with pipers in the Old World Gàidhealtachd of Scotland and relies almost exclusively on the written record. Most of this is secondary material, and the value of some of it is difficult to assess. However, the record contains observations of a coherent, rural Gaelic society, the one that was transplanted to Nova Scotia, often by communities. The rest of the book (Part 3), dealing with New World piping anachronisms, relies first and foremost on human memories because contemporary published and unpublished written cultural observations are scarce and seldom adequately detailed. All of my interviews were conducted in English. I met no one who could not speak the language.

In Scotland the Gaelic Highlands were made fascinating in Europe for many reasons, but four obvious advertisers among the many were Charles Stuart, Samuel Johnson, Walter Scott, and Queen Victoria. No mystique attached to colonial and dominion Scotch Gaelic society in Canada while it was at its most vibrant, so there is no similar corpus of traveller literature there to be tapped. Scottish Gaelic was spoken all over Canada in the nineteenth century, and it is surprising how little this linguistic presence and its society have been studied.[9]

The great importance of Cape Breton lies in its retention of a variant on familiar Highland music and a kind of dance, both of which have died away in Gaelic Scotland. There are glimpses of Gaelic story and song elsewhere in the New World, but now almost exclusively on the tape recordings made of the last lore bearers.[10] It is surprising just how close the Gaelic world came to losing Cape Breton's cultural anachronisms without anyone's bothering to take a look.

I met none of the last generation of traditional Gaelic pipers in Cape Breton about whom I have already written at any length (Allan MacFarlane, Little Farquhar MacKinnon, Angus Campbell Beaton, Black Angus MacDonald, and Archibald Beaton), and this may raise skepticism. I did, however, visit Alex Currie with my wife, who is a step-dancer and the daughter and great-granddaughter of step-dancers. Currie played the chanter and she danced because his timing was right.[11] Where *Traditional Gaelic Bagpiping* is concerned, I avoided including Alex Currie because he lived within walking distance of Sydney River and Sydney, both industrial centres. I don't for a moment think that Currie's South Uist–based traditional music was necessarily corrupted by nearby urban and suburban tastes, but I had to present the strongest argument possible, since my own knowledge and discernment might not be sufficiently subtle. Those pipers I did include, therefore, lived in remoter areas of the island where their grandparents' conservative tastes were most likely to be indulged. Also, Alex Currie's repertoire and his style are much more the subject of others' researches than mine.[12]

In Part 3, I hope to address that skepticism as well as provide a glimpse, by way of other traditional Scotch Gaelic bagpipers and many kind informants, of an old Highland consciousness under threat for a century and now almost disappeared from Nova Scotia. The last chapter deals with the Mac-Dougall pipers, and one or two others, who lived in northern Inverness and Victoria Counties. These concluding pages show the rapidness of Gaelic's decline and something of a richness that has slipped away, recorded but by few.

Rather than try to offer an encyclopaedic collection of biographies of Cape Breton traditional pipers, which would be a very large project, I have presented material from a few geographical areas. I have not scrupled so much this time about the nearness of industrial areas. The areas break down two ways: first, where there was a pronounced urban-industrial influence and second, where the urban influence was remote. I have no reason to believe that these are untypical of their types anywhere in Gaelic Nova Scotia. Since there has long been an overestimation of the power of the Free Church Presbyterian clergy to eradicate dance music from the Presbyterian Gael's Saturday night, I have drawn attention to the bagpipe's popularity in the Presbyterian areas, whether isolated from, conterminous with, or intermingled with Catholic communities.

The number of pipers in Gaelic Cape Breton was large in the first three or four generations of Gaelic settlement in Nova Scotia and Cape Breton. The instrument clearly held a place of major cultural significance for the Gael, enjoying a popularity greater than that of any other instrument, even the violin, if one were to compare the numbers of published references to immigrant and early pipers and fiddlers.[13] If this is an accurate assessment and if piping has declined as the violin (always popular, in my opinion) has taken up the slack, then the introduction of the organ and the piano (*clàrsach mór*) from around 1870 may share some responsibility for the shift. They added accompanying noise over all the violin's flexible range, making the violin with the organ or piano an attractive combination for dances at home or in a hall. Their adoption may also have strongly emphasized the bagpipe scale's old-fashioned and inflexible gapping to the latter's detriment. Old violins are seldom found gathering dust in barns; old cracked sets of drones have been.[14]

My early decision not to tape-record my interviews was based on a fear that informants might be intimidated, as I would have been in their place; that decision rested more importantly on a desire to learn about Gaelic society in the traditional way, by memory. In some cases, I was thus remiss in obtaining and taking down preferred information which at the time struck me as insignificant or less important than something else told to me. Discovering how to maintain a discreet professional distance in interviewing improved with time. Diffidence at times limited the people I visited and the questions I asked, and how I regret that now; to compensate I sought as many informants as I could and sometimes I re-interviewed.[15] I regret not having had a broad and deep enough curiosity much earlier than I had, but that's life. Important memories of before 1895 were open to me in the 1970s and my fascinations were much too limited, and often ill-directed, to take advantage of information people had but which they took for granted and to the grave.

Where the older Gaelic bagpiping was concerned, a few who played in the older style were still living in the early 1970s and a small number of amateur tape recordings of the piping of the deceased are extant. Unfortunately, I didn't know about the pipers or the tapes at the time, so it was from an old amateur tape recording of an older musician's piping that I recognized an unusual style of playing familiar tunes.[16] In 1976 I had been living in or near Inverness County for four years when I heard an old tape of Angus Campbell Beaton (Aonghas Iagain Raonuil) playing the bagpipes.[17] He was from Mabou and his strathspey and reel timing in particular stood out as distinctive. It was Cape Breton step-dance timing and that was the first time that I had heard it played on the bagpipes.

Beaton had died in 1971 in Mabou, and although I couldn't hear his or any of the other best-remembered local pipers' live music, if informants remembered their piping for individual step-dancing, for the old traditional Scotch Four (which comprised simple travelling steps and step-dance setting steps to Strathspeys and Reels), and/or, to a lesser extent perhaps, for the third or later figure of the Square Set (Reels),[18] then there is no doubt that the timing of all these pipers was the same and Beaton could never be described as a unique adaptive anomaly. To support the thesis, I could take a less direct approach and attempt to discover whether there were step-dance pipers who were also traditional step-dance fiddlers, since that heightened the likelihood that the same speed and timing were used for both instruments.

In 1976 I had all but lost my earlier hope of finding some relic of classical bagpiping in the Nova Scotia Gàidhealtachd, and I might have counted the hearing of Beaton's music as of little significance. The tape was not of good quality, and I might have ignored it had Angus Beaton not sounded to be a good piper by modern standards of fingering technique[19] and drone tuning. Local people, as far as I could discover, were unaware of anything traditional about his music, although all of them were accustomed to listening to modern Scottish bagpiping and knew it as non-step-dance associated.[20] When I played Beaton's best reel to an Inverness County–born member of the Celtic Studies Department at St Francis Xavier University, for example, it brought no special response until I drew attention to the essential difference in timing.[21]

For all the tentativeness of my earliest curiosities, what I gradually discovered was that rural Gaelic-speaking, ear-learned pipers had been much more numerous than I and most people had thought, and that their strathspeys and reels in particular, in speed and timing and function, were step-dance music. The piper's local prominence, what's more, had faded largely unnoticed, yielding to the fiddler. Bagpipes and bagpipers had probably been as important in an earlier Nova Scotia Gàidhealtachd as fiddlers had become after violins had become easy and cheap to buy. I soon found, furthermore, that pipers who were also fiddlers were not at all uncommon, although I have yet to compare the numbers of those who began with each instrument. In addition, there had been chanter players, men and women, well distributed in Gaelic communities, for whom I presume acquiring a set of bagpipes had been impossible.

PIPING AND PIPERS IN THE EAST BAY AREA

The major informant for this section is Joe Neil MacNeil (1908–96), the last of the *seannachaidhean* in Cape Breton, known to many Cape Bretoners as "Mechanical Joe."[22] I begin with Joe Neil MacNeil's recollections of his old friend the Rear Big Pond piper Neil R. MacIsaac, and I then place Joe Neil's memories of pipers more generally in the East Bay area and southwards next to those of Hugh MacSween and Joe Lawrence MacDonald, whose cultural knowledge concentrated on the little farming communities to the north (Beaver Cove, Boisdale, Ironville, Frenchvale, Leitche's Creek, MacAdam's Lake, Gillisville). I also rely on interviews conducted in the Sydney area in 1998. For the southern area, I draw from Joe Neil MacNeil's *Tales until Dawn* (Sgialachdan gu Latha 1987), and for the northern area, from Father Allan MacMillan's genealogical study *To the Hill of Boisdale* (1986). Both of these areas were readily exposed to the influences of an industrial, coal-mining town, Sydney, and its industrial satellites.

Neil R. MacIsaac (1887–1973), Rear Big Pond

I never met Neil R. MacIsaac or heard his piping. My first and most remark-able informant was Joe Neil MacNeil, and rarely these days does one have such a knowledgeable informant (and never one whose mother tongue is Gaelic). It was often flattering to find my own thoughts spontaneously con-firmed, unprompted, but I remember having misgivings nonetheless. Joe Neil had the remarkably honed memory of the old Gaelic storyteller, and his capacity to present information on the same topic, more than once, sponta-neously or in response to gentle suggestion, in something almost akin to a spoken subchant involving repetition,[23] sometimes suggested to my out-sider's literately trained mind a cultured presentation not completely divorced from sophistical rote. Sometimes I noticed that points were unex-plorable beyond the teller's stopping point, and I was disappointed that I was seldom able to begin to speculate where pipers, or almost anything else, was concerned.[24] Joe Neil, however, was bilingual and literate in both English and Gaelic, and on general topics I wondered if the lore and literate worlds needed to be separated.[25]

Most of my other informants' responses, on Allan MacFarlane and Little Farquhar MacKinnon and many other pipers, for example, were obviously ingenuous, unstudied. They were prompted by an easily detectable pleasure in finding, often for the first time, someone who was curious about a subject that they believed important, even in a modern world that ignored or dis-dained their values and memories.[26] Almost none of these informants were able to read Gaelic, and some were poorly read in Gaelic subjects in English and thus reflected convincingly, in my opinion, conservatively traditional community thoughts and standards. Joe Neil, who knew so much, was a different kettle of fish.

And yet I knew that Joe Neil had only his own memories of Neil R. MacIsaac to go on because no one had written about MacIsaac at any length or at all. My additional notes about Neil R. MacIsaac and his family were made much later when most of the best sources had died. Fortunately, Dr John Shaw and Father Allan J. MacMillan, to whose books I often refer, tape-recorded their conversations with Joe Neil, and thus his voice may be heard and his contribution examined. I have used Joe Neil MacNeil's *Tales until Dawn* in its English translation. John Shaw was the translator and editor.

Joe Neil was delighted to encounter interest in the Gaelic world he knew. His generosity extended to educating everyone whose curiosity was profound and disinterested. His visits were really tutorials. His contribution to Gaelic studies is set and celebrated by Gaelic cultural scholarship in these acquisitively nostalgic times, and his information must be adjudged reliable as almost no one else's.[27] Neil R. cannot but have been a very talented piper. He was born in Ben Eoin in one record, Big Pond in another; they are the same place to me. It was a time when Gaelic was still common speech and piping was strongly favoured. There were many besides Neil R., if perhaps none, in Joe Neil's opinion, as good.[28]

Although Joe Neil had heard many Gaelic-speaking pipers when he travelled in Cape Breton, learning stories and telling them and bringing along the fascinated, Neil R. MacIsaac from Ben Eoin/Big Pond was his favourite.[29] MacIsaac, a left-shoulder and left-hand-upper piper, was Joe Neil's bagpiping touchstone. Joe said that he could immediately tell if another piper had been taught by him by the character of his music. Joe heard MacIsaac play countless times in many céilidh (including dance) atmospheres. Joe, going to a well-coddled memory, told of a time they were both at a home in Barra Glen; it was about three-thirty in the morning and MacIsaac made for his instrument box. Joe thought he was going to put the pipes away after what had been a long informal session, but instead "he put up the pipes and began to play again." Joe emphasized to me again that he had heard Neil R. play so often that he should have known his full repertoire, and yet at that early-morning session MacIsaac played three or four tunes that Joe Neil was surprised to realize he had never heard played by anyone before. "Music was not coming from the pipes but from the walls, the ceiling."[30]

In the same conversation, Joe Neil told me that Neil R. used to play a tune called "Neil Ramsay Buchanan," which had been the prize-winning tune at a competition in Scotland in the 1920s. It has been played by the pipe major of the Glasgow Police pipe band, a man Joe Neil thought might have been a MacAskill. Joe told me that Sandy Boyd, the Largs-born, John Mac-

Coll–taught piper who lived for many years in Cape Breton, did not know the tune and that no one in the Glasgow Police could give it to him (Joe Neil) when he was in Scotland.[31] Practised facts like this lingered in Joe Neil's memory along with the last extended repertoire of ancient Gaelic lore and a host of other genealogical and historical pieces of information reflecting a broad fascination with Scottish Gaelic affairs.

He frequently talked about Neil R. MacIsaac's seemingly endless repertoire of tunes: "[H]e would play to no end, he was unlimited."[32] Older traditional fiddlers in what remains of Scotch Cape Breton all have the ability to play a very large number of tunes, one naturally leading into another seemingly endlessly, in spontaneous playing situations like the traditional céilidh.[33] Clusters of tunes and key changes are obviously quite confidently established in subconscious patterns of memory. MacIsaac conformed in this, and for Joe Neil to get him to replay a fancied tune, he had to be able to reproduce some phrase or phrases. (Joe Neil told me that on one occasion when such a tune caught his attention, MacIsaac's fingers were hidden from him and so he couldn't commit some of the fingering to memory to help him to retain something of this one tune among many.)[34] There was typically variation in the order of the tunes he played. I don't know if he felt as free as some traditional fiddlers to make changes in notes and grace-noting while playing.[35]

MacIsaac, when he learned to read and write pipe music, extended his faculty for memorizing by remembering where tunes and their various settings had been published and when he had heard them played. He knew all the local pipers and used to list a dozen to Joe Neil just from the Woodbine area in the rear of East Bay, which indicates what today would seem a surprising popularity of the instrument there.[36] To start with, however, MacIsaac, like his father, Rory "Shim" (Roderick J.), and nearly all rural pipers of his time, was ear learned. According to Joe Neil, Neil R. "was playing hundreds of tunes by ear before he learned music."[37] He had been born into a Gaelic-speaking piping family, son of Rory MacIsaac, whose English, according to Joe Neil, "was not so very good,"[38] and had lived in an area of Cape Breton where, though near the industrial area of Sydney, traditional Gaelic piping was still clearly very popular. A story told to me by one of Rory Shim's grandsons, Dannie Campbell (b. 1913), indicates the strength of Gaelic in places where now there is none. One of Rory Shim's brothers, Mike "the Lantern" MacIsaac, lived "in the rear" and had only a little English; he visited through the woods, lantern in hand.[39] I found no death record for Rory Shim but his grandson Dannie remembered him clearly.

Campbell told me that Neil R. was a Gaelic speaker and that he was witty and "well able to tell you when to leave."[40] He lived alone but took pride in his appearance. He enjoyed fishing. Dannie Campbell said that Neil R. was often visited by Black Jack MacDonald, Joe MacAdam (a Sydney piper who worked for the Canadian National Railways), Francis MacKenzie, Peter Morrison, and Rod Nicolson (a veteran of the First World War), all pipers.[41]

Neil R. also taught piping. Among his pupils was Stephen MacNeil, a first cousin once removed, Bernard Stephen Gillis, one of Stephen's nephews,[42] and Cecilia Campbell, a granddaughter. Joe Neil said nothing about the influence of musical literacy on Neil R., whether he altered his fingering or the notation in his mind's eye. He more than most must have been aware of local variant forms of tunes.

As a community Scotch piper, where Neil R. MacIsaac may perhaps have been distinguished from people like Black Angus MacDonald, Melrose Hill, and Angus Campbell Beaton, Mabou, is in his having lived near the modern musical influences of an industrial centre. There is a faint case to be made, at present indirectly through Joe Neil, that MacIsaac was exposed, probably almost from the beginning of his adult piping life, to a slightly more dilute taste in Scotch tradition than the pipers from Upper Margaree and Mabou in Inverness County. Father Allan MacMillan, who is (February 2001) in the later stages of preparing his book on the area, remarked that Gaelic had declined more quickly in the East Bay area than in Boisdale.[43]

Joe Neil was nonetheless categorical in saying that Neil R. was well aware of the distinction between modern and step-dance strathspeys, the latter which Joe Neil distinguished simply as "dancing strathspeys."[44] MacIsaac played both types of music, in itself unusual. A measure of the shift away from tradition is to be noted in Joe Neil's saying that he had only seen the Scotch Four danced three times, and Joe Neil had been raised in MacIsaac's neighbourhood.[45] He said that in the East Bay area the Scotch Four dramatically lost its popularity after 1900.[46] And yet he confidently told me that "Tulloch Gorm," "The Braes o' Mar," and "Christy Campbell" were commonly played on the pipes for the Scotch Four, that it was danced as often by four men as two couples, and that the dancers stamped at the end of the strathspey section (which Joe Neil said was called the "break down").[47] For all that, Joe Neil told me that he remembered old women in Big Pond who would not dance a Quadrille.[48] As far as step-dancing is concerned, Joe Neil remembered his piping for step-dancing at many summer picnics and out-door frolics at East Bay, where as in Inverness County, the custom was to set up two stages. He also piped for the multi-figure Square Set on uncounted occasions into the 1950s,[49] which may mean piping for step-dancing in the reel figure(s), a feature of the Quadrille that emerged around 1950.[50] Alex Currie (1910–97), the left-handed ear-learned piper who lived north of East Bay's latitude by a few miles, certainly played step-dance reels for Square Sets, whether or not in earlier decades of the century they accompanied step-dancing.[51] I sat in his kitchen and heard him play them on the chanter and watched my wife step-dance to his strathspeys and reels.[52] Tapes of his piping exist and some of his music has been transcribed by Barry Shears in three collections. According to Joe Neil, Neil R. MacIsaac also differentiated band tunes and in a way that suggested a loss of Gaelicness too.

Neil R.'s father, Rory Shim MacIsaac, certainly was less influenced by non-Gaelic trends. He stopped piping when news of the death of his piping son John P. in the Great War reached him in 1915, but Joe Neil knew enough about his playing, presumably from Neil R., to say that he was a right-shoulder piper who, by Joe Neil's deduction rather than memory when I asked him, played right hand upper on the chanter. Joe Neil retained strong memories of Rory's fiddling and in fiddling Rory bowed with his right hand. When he played the fiddle, he had the habit of making puffing sounds as if he were blowing. He was by no means exceptional in Cape Breton Scotch traditional circles in playing both instruments, or in his handedness on each. At Kempt Head, Boularderie, John Francis MacDonald, of the "Post" family, grandson of Donald "Post" MacDonald, who had left Barra at age sixteen, played both instruments, but I have no knowledge of his handedness on either.[53] Allan MacFarlane and Black Angus MacDonald, the latter from Melrose Hill, were among many piper-fiddlers in Inverness County. In buying a modern set of bagpipes, Rory MacIsaac also conformed to the fairly common practice of many other traditional Cape Breton pipers. The set of Henderson bagpipes he bought around 1904 remains in the family. Another interesting note is that Rory MacIsaac, whose grandparents were immigrants from the Scottish Gàidhealtachd, maintained a correspondence with a woman called Rona MacIsaac in South Uist as well as with an unnamed piper in Scotland.[54]

In our discussions of musicians and dancers, Joe Neil often restated the common belief among rural Scotch people in the Cape Breton Gàidhealtachd that aptitude in music and dance is inherited.[55] He told me that Neil R.'s and his family's skill in Scotch music came from his father Rory MacIsaac's maternal grandfather, who was a Gillis immigrant to Cape Breton.[56] This suggests at least one South Morar provenance for Rory and Neil R. MacIsaac's musical talent. The MacIsaacs, many of whom came to Cape Breton from the Island of Eigg, have been linked, through Neil R.'s family, with either Mùideart or Morar.

My notes never mention what Sandy Boyd might have thought about Neil R.'s piping, and the fault is mine for not having tried to elicit an honest opinion. Joe Neil's positive assessment of Neil R.'s piping was based on his broad and sophisticated knowledge of piping and his sense of honesty, which implied inclusion of clever, modern pipers like Sandy Boyd. It is also the case, however, that MacIsaac's name was not mentioned to me spontaneously by any of my Inverness County informants.

PIPING AND TRADITION SOUTH OF EAST BAY

The information that Joe Neil gave me about Cape Breton and bordering Richmond County pipers of the old Gaelic school comes from four interviews conducted in November 1978 (date missing), on 30 November 1979, on 27 July 1980, and on 30 May 1982, although we met on several other occasions as well. Apart from the Gaelic-speaking ear piper John MacDonald from Boisdale[57] and Joe (Hughie) MacIntyre from Glace Bay (27 July 1980), about whom Joe Neil added nothing important, all of those following lived and piped south of the latitude of East Bay and within a twenty-mile radius of it reaching to Hay Cove, Richmond County, in the southwest. Besides piper-fiddler Little Angus MacKinnon (see note above), whom Neil R. MacIsaac mentioned as one among many from Woodbine, there are eight other local pipers whom Joe Neil talked about to me in more than a passing way: Dan C. MacDonald from the Woodbine area (27 July 1980), Dan Uisdean MacDonald from Soldier's Cove (30 November 1979), a MacMahon from East Bay (27 July 1980), Donald Stewart (30 November 1980), Jonathon MacPhee (November 1978), John MacLean (30 November 1979), Murdoch MacMillan (30 May 1982), and Angus MacNeil (30 May 1982).[58]

Joe Neil had heard Dan C.'s piping and described it as not up to Neil R. MacIsaac's standard. If Neil R. was as good as Joe Neil claimed, then not being up to his standard may not have meant being a bad piper (tapes of Joe Hughie MacIntyre's piping when he was not an old man reveal fingering subtlety and a good standard of playing technique by modern lights). Dan Uisdean was an ear-learned piper and a distant relative of Black Jack MacDonald, one of the Cape Breton Highlanders' pipe majors during the Second World War. Joe Neil heard him piping on a visit to his home. If he himself had not come from there, his people were from Antigonish County. MacMahon, first name unknown, was remembered only inasmuch as he imported an ebony set of bagpipes in 1905 and Joe Neil remarked that the ebony tended to crack if left a while without being played. This set went to a MacDonald and then to Joe Neil's friend, the piper-fiddler Michael MacLean.

Murdoch MacMillan was a piper and fiddler from Johnstown, Richmond County. He died around 1940.[59] Joe Neil heard him playing the fiddle, not the bagpipes but reported that Neil R. MacIsaac had called him "a sweet piper" but one who didn't have many tunes. Murdoch MacMillan was a grandson of piper Neil mac Iain 'ic Mhurchaidh 'ic Dhòmhnuil (Neil, son of John, son of Murdoch, son of Donald), who had immigrated from North Uist. Neil married a MacNeil from Piper's Cove and was probably a convert to Catholicism. Joe Neil hinted that he had been an army piper.[60] Angus MacNeil the piper lived at Hay Cove and all Joe Neil recollected was his *sloinneadh*, Aonghus mac Fhionnlaidh (Angus, son of Finlay).

I assume that none of these pipers was a ceòl mór piper. Joe Neil did not enlarge specifically on their talents or on their particular value culturally to their communities; he was not ready to indulge the spontaneous and ingenuousness comments of the observant but unknowledgeable, who if at their ease often painted stories rich in social detail and background that allowed one to draw more inferences about the character, if not the quality, of the piper's music. On the other hand, Joe Neil's memory for sloinneadhs was brilliant.

There remain the three other Cape Breton pipers whom Joe Neil mentioned. While typically he didn't create a social milieu for any of them as musicians, whether from his own or others' memories, they were from the beginning the more interesting to me. Donald Stewart, who settled on the south side of East Bay "towards Mira," was an immigrant piper from Scotland.[61] Joe Neil knew nothing of his origins or piping status in Scotland or of his piping repertoire and technique. Then about seventeen miles to the southwest of East Bay, at Irish Vale, the Scots immigrant piper John MacLean settled. He arrived in 1831, and Joe Neil remembered meeting his son in 1923. What distinguished John MacLean was that he was a ceòl mór piper. His pipes survived at least until October 1983 (see below). The other immigrant piper he told me about, Jonathon MacPhee, came to Cape Breton in the 1830s and was also a ceòl mór piper. In his riper years "Mechanical Joe" shared a house with Mike MacLean, a one-time piper. MacLean's mother was descended from Jonathon MacPhee.[62] If these classical players' music was strikingly different from modern, competition ceòl mór playing, there is no record of it. Joe Neil never hinted that he knew anything about the form. He never named or discussed any piece of ceòl mór.[63]

THE MACLEAN PIPES

On 1 October 1983 Joe Neil MacNeil brought me ten pieces of an old set of bagpipes, which I photographed, measured, and described. There was no chanter or bass drone, and there were signs on all the pieces of an attempt or attempts to blacken the wood. Two pieces were made from wood, or woods, different from that used in the other eight.

Joe Neil said that he had heard the set played as a two-drone set by a MacMullen man in Cape Breton, but told me that the complete set had had three drones and that the bass drone had been lent out and not returned. The set was found in Mike MacLean's barn in Big Pond when Joe Neil was doing carpentry work, but his knowledge of the pipes and his hearing of MacMullen's playing them predated their rediscovery.

This set was brought to Cape Breton *circa* 1831 by John MacLean, one of the men believed to have been a ceòl mór piper. Joe Neil identified John MacLean as Iain mac Caluim Oig 'ic Iain 'ic Lachlainn (John, son of young

Table 1   The "MacLean Pipes"

	Tenor Drone 1 (top section) (cm)	Tenor Drone 2 (top section) (cm)
Length	20.545	20.490
Length of lower ferrule	2.015	2.065
Diameter of wood under top ferrule		
a) upper	3.485	Ferrule
b) lower	3.515	unremoveable
Diameter of belling		
a) upper	4.080	4.115
b) lower	4.020	4.025
Diameter of widest part of drone shaft (belling and cord containment excepted)	2.955 (12.775 from top)	2.880 (13.595 from top)
Diameter of narrowest part of shaft (grooving excepted)	2.025 (7.9 from top)	2.065 (7.8 from top)
Max. diameter of cord containment		
a) upper	3.11 (4.96 from top)	3.235 (4.93 from top)
b) lower	3.17 (5.9 from top)	3.26 (5.94 from top)
Min. diameter cord groove	2.38	2.4
Diameter shaft above lower ferrule	2.825	2.795
Diameter of wood under lower ferrule		
a) upper	2.17	2.16
b) lower	2.03	2.045
Bore diameter		
a) top (no ferrule)	1.575	1.560
b) bottom (ferrule on)	1.71	1.76
Bore (approx.)	1.190 (taken 2.8 from top)	1.195 (taken 3.0 from top)
Length of central bore (approx.)	10.145	9.490
Cracks	One major one running approx. 9.5 cm from bottom	One major one running approx. 15.5 cm from bottom, and a lesser one of similar length.
Ferrules	Top one broken; lower in good condition and snug fit. Both of bone	Top one unremoved. Both show signs of paint. Both of bone
Paint	All except lower ferrule show paint, although over 90% has been worn off	Paint detectable on all wood and bone surfaces
Mutilation		Three grooved sections have been removed (see photos)

Table 1   (continued)

	Tenor Drone 1 (slide part) (cm)	Tenor Drone 2 (slide part) (cm)
Length (approx.)	21.91	21.52
Length of slide	9.355	9.105
Length of main section	9.31	9.34
Length of stock insert	3.26	3.08
Average diameter of slide (non-ferruled part)	1.59	1.63
Diameter of slide just above main section	1.725	1.755
Length of taper on slide (for ferrule)	1.64	1.64
Slide grooving from top	0.315–4.075	0.450–3.780
Max. diameter main section (i.e., at the bottom)	2.9	2.925
Min. diameter main section (at top, grooving excepted)	2.145	2.140
Diameter low part of stock insert (0.645 up from bottom)	1.875	1.675
Bore 1.64 from top	0.815	0.800
Bore 1.64 from bottom	1.035	0.980
Bore at bottom	1.135	1.055
Approx. length of wide bore to take reed	?	3.700
Ferrules	None	One on the slide, of unidentified substance, colour black
Grooving	Very shallow where ferrule would be	
Reed hole	Off-centre	More nearly centred

Calum, son of John, son of Lachlan), an immigrant from Barra. His teacher, or one of them, in Barra was a man Joe Neil only heard described as "an gille bàn" (the fair-haired lad).

The pipes were used in the MacLean family until 1905, when the immigrant's grandson John S. MacLean laid them aside in favour of a new Hen-

Table 1   (continued)

	Tenor Drone 1 (stock) (cm)	Tenor Drone 2 (stock) (cm)
Length (approx.)	9.4	8.97
Length of ferrule area (approx.)	1.255	1.160
Length of main section (ferrule, groove and flange excepted)	6.765	6.200 (upper end of the main section ends within the pattern, a part having been turned down, perhaps to accommodate the ferrule)
Length of groove and flange	1.38	1.575 (approx.)
Min. diameter main section (1.365 down from top)	3.165	3.220
Max. diameter main section (1.465 from bottom)	3.465	3.495
Max. diameter lower flange	3.390	3.215
Taper at ferrule	2.370-2.165	Unmeasurable
Ferrule	Bone	Bone ferrule present but appears to be a misfit, being too long. Ragged nature of the end of the wood under the ferrule suggests truncation
Cracks	One major one, visible inside and out for length of stock	One major crack, visible inside and out for length of stock
Flange	Chipped to lowest groove plus one lesser chip	Flange has two chips, one as deep as the grooving

derson set acquired from Scotland. John S. lent the pipes to Mike MacLean in Big Pond.

Joe Neil's information was limited to the areas he was most acquainted with, but if one were to extend one's net, one would come across many more pipers. As an example, another immigrant piper, Alexander MacLeod, an

Table 1   (continued)

Dimensions of the Third Stock	(cm)	
Length (approx)	7.085	
Length of ferrule section	1.465	
Length of main section	4.435	
Length of groove & flange section	1.180	
Diameter at upper end of ferrule section (ferrule removed)	2.370 ⎫	the taper is even
Diameter at lower end of ferrule section	2.455 ⎭	
Diameter near top of main section	3.115	
Diameter near lower end of main secn	3.450	
Max. diameter of flange	3.330	
Bore at top, ferrule removed (approx 1.64 from top)	2.000	
Bore 1.64 from bottom	1.865	

The grooving on the wood at the ferrule is almost undetectable. Ferrule end is described as the top end. There is one major crack, visible inside and out but not extending for the length of the stock. Stock was turned from one piece of wood, of apparently the same type as that of the drones and other stocks.

ancestor of Danny MacIntyre's who settled off the French Road, is mentioned in the *Piping Times* of November 1968. No further information about him exists.[64]

PIPING AND TRADITION NORTH OF EAST BAY

For a roughly similar area of Cape Breton County to the north of the East Bay latitude, an area encompassing Beaver Cove on the south of St Andrew's Channel in the west and Frenchvale and Leitche's Creek in the east I had two informants, Hugh MacSween (Eoghan Eachuinn Dhòmhnuil Iain mac Eoghainn, 1903–88) in East Bay[65] and Joe Lawrence MacDonald (Joseph mac Iain ghobha 'ic Iain 'ic Lachlainn, 1910–97) in Boisdale.[66] I also drew on Father Allan MacMillan's book *To the Hill of Boisdale.*

I met Hugh MacSween on 25 August 1980 at East Bay. He told me that his great-great-grandfather Eoghan had left Barra, married, with a Scots-born son, Iain.[67] He landed and settled for a time in Prince Edward Island before coming to Cape Breton. After a spell at Kempt Head in the south of

Table 1   (continued)

Blow-Pipe Parts	(cm)

Mouth piece

The mouthpiece has been roughly sawn off at its top. The piece looks like a home-made addition.

Length (approx.)	9.545
Max. diameter (lower end)	2.250
Min. diameter (at top)	1.330
Bore from top down for approx. 7.165 cm	0.900
Bore of lower 2.380 cm	1.650

(Note: Three cracks in the lower end extending up for about 2.7 cm have altered the bore and diameter.)

Blow-pipe

Length (approx.)	12.310
Length at mouthpiece insert section	2.060
Length of main section	7.000
Length of stock insert	3.270
Min. diameter (upper end)	2.240
Max. diameter (lower end)	2.880

(Note: Stock insert portion has been whittled. Bore is irregular, at places oval. One piece of wood, uniform in colour but more reddish than that of the drones and stocks. It is also more porous and the pattern of the grooving is different.)

Stock

Length (approx.)	11.880
Length of main section	8.140
Length of groove & flange	2.260
Length of flange (approx.)	1.500
Min. diameter of main section	3.040
Max. diameter of main section	3.470
Diameter of flange	3.540
Bore at top (approx.)	1.985
Bore at bottom (approx.)	1.865

The stock is made of the same wood as the drones and other stocks and is similarly patterned. The top approx. 0.4 cm of main section has been removed. There is one major crack. The three blow-pipe parts have been coloured. None has a ferrule.

Boularderie Island, he took up a six-hundred-acre land grant "on a hill" in Beaver Cove where he and his wife, a MacKinnon, are buried. Iain married a Nicholson and fathered Donald (b. Beaver Cove), who in turn married

Elizabeth MacLean and fathered Hector, Hugh MacSween's father. Hector (the Eachun of the sloinneadh) married an Agnes MacNeil from Boisdale, whom Hugh identified as the daughter of Sandy MacNeil, son of Rory, son of Allan, a pioneer to the Iona area of Cape Breton and a former major in the British army.[68]

The MacSweens moved to MacAdam's Lake after the storm of 1873 and settled among Gillises, MacVarishes, MacPhees, and Curries, all of whom were well represented there in 1914. From his mother, Agnes, Hugh Mac-Sween heard the Gaelic song that the immigrant piper Lachlan MacIntyre of MacAdam's Lake made for his wife. This MacIntyre had immigrated from South Uist. His son Duncan, also a piper, died around 1914 and is buried at East Bay. Duncan's son Red Mick was a Gaelic speaker and ear piper who piped for Square Sets.[69] Hugh MacSween also remembered from his parents the name of the local piper, Big Donald MacIntyre (Dòmhnul Mór mac Aonghuis 'ic Dhòmhnuil 'ic Thormoid),[70] who piped the Scottish mission priest Reverend Archibald Campbell sj from East Bay to Boisdale in 1907. Big Donald was from the Rear of Boisdale and was not related to Lachlan.[71] Big Donald's son Little Donald (Dòmhnul Beag), also an ear piper, piped for step-dancing and Square Sets according to Hugh MacSween.

I asked Hugh MacSween casually who the good step-dancers were in MacAdam's Lake and he mentioned Hughie Steele and Peter Currie. He said Steele was "dead twelve, fifteen years" and that Peter Currie was "another Roman Catholic from South Uist." Peter's son Paddy had been a piper, and Paddy's brother Alex Currie (1910--97) was a piper living in Upper French Vale. On 23 August 1980 Joe Lawrence MacDonald told me that Alex Currie, "one of the bears," was a non-Gaelic speaker whose people came from MacAdam's Lake. From my own meeting with Currie I know that he used several Gaelic words and expressions but with a lack of clear understanding and within an English frame of thought as far as I could judge.

Notwithstanding Father Francis Cameron's statement (1976)[72] that there was no step-dancing in the Square Set in Boisdale in the 1940s and Joe Neil MacNeil's judgment that the Scotch Four had withered away as a living ceilidh dance in the wider East Bay area by the twentieth century, Hugh MacSween's prompt, easy, and ingenuous answer to my leading question about step-dancers indicates that step-dancing was still popular in the 1940s and that it is fair enough to assume that the term "dancing" even near to the industrial area, in Gaelic areas in the MacAdam's Lake of the 1940s, was synonymous with step-dancing. (Hugh MacSween, a blacksmith, moved from MacAdam's Lake after a fire in 1947.)

Joe Lawrence MacDonald's credentials as an informant are more remarkable. His knowledge, what I learned of it, was essentially local, but because of its depth and integratedness he was a valuable documenter of the shift from tradition in a language and way of life. He knew that such changes as he observed could only be collected and were no longer imbued with quiddity. He was born into a Gaelic-speaking family in 1910 to parents who discouraged the use of anything but English, although they used Gaelic to keep secrets from their children.[73] This trend towards English was common throughout Cape Breton in the first half of the twentieth century, but there were still many core Gaelic areas and often at only a short distance from little places where, for one reason or another, change was rapid.

Even if Boisdale was more conservative than the area around East Bay, in Boisdale at least three factors worked against the retention of the Gaelic language: the influence of urban English-speaking Sydney, about eighteen miles away; the building of a Canadian National Railways line through Boisdale and Beaver Cove in the mid-1880s; and, according to Joe Lawrence, the presence of an unidentified North Carolinian from about 1915 who discouraged the use of the language.

Joe Lawrence learned Gaelic from an uncle and aunt (brother and sister) who moved into his home from Rear Beaver Cove around 1920 after a bad frost[74] when he was ten. In those days, when Boisdale was moving into a modern North American consciousness, Rear Beaver Cove was a thriving Gaelic community of thirty-nine families and two schools and many traditional musicians. Analogues are traditional Glencoe and the nearby coal-mining and modernizing town of Port Hood, as well as the many communities within walking distance of places like Inverness, Port Hastings, Port Hawkesbury, and Marble Mountain.

Joe Lawrence's mother, Mairead Gillis, had a musical brother, John Gillis, who piped and played the chanter. He made his own chanters and used a grass for a reed. When he played for dances, he fiddled. Joe's father's mother was a Campbell whose brother Dòmhnul Bàn Fìdhlear (Fair Donald the Fiddler) lived in Rear of Boisdale. Joe Lawrence never met or heard Dòmhnul Bàn and assumed that he'd died in the early 1900s. Another Gaelic-speaking Rear of Boisdale piper he talked about was Johnnie MacLean (Johnnie Chaluim Ruaidh), who died in the 1950s, or perhaps in 1960, aged about eighty.[75] MacLean was an ear player who probably made some acquaintance with written pipe music later in life. Joe Lawrence saw people step-dancing to his piping and classed his playing above Allan MacFarlane's, which he had probably heard when the piper lived at Christmas Island in the late 1930s. Joe Lawrence also remembered Tony MacDonald, son of John, and drew my attention to his gravestone in the Boisdale cemetery, which offered the information that he had died 13 February 1971, aged sixty-three, and had been a corporal in the Canadian army. He said that Tony MacDonald was from Soldier's Cove, had known only a few words of Gaelic, had been taught his piping by Black Jack MacDonald (Cape Breton Highlanders), and had served in the army in the Second World War. Joe Lawrence had heard him piping.

Some time in 1980 before 23 August, Rod MacNeil, Barra Glen, had drawn my attention to a set of bagpipes made in Rear Beaver Cove, and Joe Lawrence was able to expand on them. He told me that they had been made by a member of the musical family of Nicolsons in Rear Beaver Cove. He did not know the first name of the maker or that of many others of the Nicolson family. Despite the surname and its immediate association with Presbyterian Skye, these Nicolsons were from Barra and all were Roman Catholic and, of course, Gaelic speaking. They were known locally for nearly a century, from 1821 until 1905, as traditional musicians, pipers, fiddlers, and Gaelic singers. Joe Lawrence said that at a céilidh in Rear Beaver Cove four or five Nicolson pipers would pass the set around, playing in turn. Those names of other Nicolsons that he remembered included Dr John Nicolson, then professor at the College of Cape Breton; Rod (deceased), a fiddler and Gaelic singer; and George, who made violins. No Nicolsons lived in Rear Beaver Cove in August 1980; many of those who once lived there are buried in Boisdale.[76]

Both Hugh MacSween (on 25 August 1980) and Joe Lawrence MacDonald (who confirmed MacSween's information independently on 26 August 1980) said that the first Nicolson in Rear Beaver Cove was Sandy (Alasdair), who had at least three sons, George (Seòras), John (Iain), and Hector (Eachun). George, born in Beaver Cove, was the father of Monsignor Dr P.J. Nicolson, VG, president of St Francis Xavier University. John, son of Sandy, through a son Patrick, was grandfather of the John of the College of Cape Breton referred to above. Joe Lawrence mentioned other sons of a John Nicolson (presumably John, son of Sandy), Angus, Neil, Hugh, and Ronald, all of whom lived at Barrachois. On Barrachois Mountain there were William and Paul Nicolson, and at Long Island, Malcolm, Hugh, Angus, and Father John Hugh Nicolson of Mount Carmel parish in New Waterford.[77]

The last musical family that Joe Lawrence mentioned was the Campbell family from "music hill" about two miles east of the Catholic church in Boisdale. Rod Campbell, son of John, was a fair piper who also fiddled, and his brother Hughie Patrick played the fiddle. Both were Gaelic speakers.

Father Allan MacMillan's *To the Hill of Boisdale* mentions a number of other musical Gaels in and in the vicinity of Boisdale. One of the more tantalizing is Big Norman MacIntyre, a popular fiddler who disappeared without trace after a local *reiteachadh* (betrothal party). MacIntyre's sloinneadh was Tormad Mór mac Alasdair 'ic Dhòmhnuil 'ic Thormaid (the last Tormad is the one referred to in the "lineage of Tormad" mentioned below). MacMillan had access to no musical detail but the fact that Alasdair was born around 1789 in South Uist suggests quite strongly that Big Norman (Tormad Mór) was also born in Scotland.[78] Since few immigrant fiddlers are named in the record, this is an important historical addition in an area of Highland culture that has not been recorded in detail. Although there was clearly no radical deviation in traditional music and dance styles from 1800 to 1830 in Cape Breton, the relative scarcity of mention of fiddlers in those years permits the contrary-minded to posit other sources than Scotland for the musical forms with which they are unaccustomed.

Apart from those noted above, MacMillan mentioned four other MacIntyre pipers from the same lineage of Norman. Two are unnamed sons of Scots-born Donald MacIntyre (Dòmhnul mac Iain Mhóir 'ic Dhòmhnuil 'ic Thormaid [Donald, son of Big John, son of Donald, son of Norman]). They were born and raised at or near Island Point, Boularderie.[79] The others are Donald "piper" MacIntyre (Dòmhnull mac Dhòmhnuill Mhóir 'ic Aonghais 'ic Dhòmhnuill 'ic Thormaid) and Angus MacIntyre (Aonghas mac Dhòmhnuill 'ic Eoghainn Bhig 'ic Eoghainn 'ic Thormaid).

Two of the remaining pipers flagged by MacMillan were sons of immigrant Gaels. The first was Michael D. Campbell, also known as "Sleepy Mick" (Mìcheal mac Alasdair 'ic Nìll), who was from Boisdale and who played small pipes (no definition given).[80] The other was Duncan MacCormick (Donnchadh mac Dhòmhnuill 'ic Nìll) in Upper Leitche's Creek.[81] Then there is Rod Campbell (Ruairidh mac Iain 'ic Dhòmhnuill, from Boisdale mentioned above)[82] and Duncan MacIntyre (Donnchadh Pìobaire) of northside East Bay.[83]

Hector Campbell (Eachann Nìll Thearlaich, 1888–1976), the Gaelic storyteller and sometime piper from Hillsdale in Judique parish, was born in Boisdale, but discussion of his piping and his storytelling belongs elsewhere; his conservative influences were in Hillsdale rather than Boisdale. The minor point to be made, however, is that his father Neil (1851–1923), from Hillsdale, had taken up part-time work on the railway, where he met Flora O'Handley of Boisdale.[84]

In defence of giving prominence to pipers and piping in the most rural areas of Cape Breton, I should add what Father Allan MacMillan told me 11 May 1998. Apparently, Gaelic withered faster in the east and south than in the Boisdale area, by virtue of its nearness to Sydney and relative ease of access. His eagerly anticipated second book deals with the family histories of the East Bay and south folk, including the MacIsaacs, MacPhees, and others. Father MacMillan told me that Rory Shim was named for his mother's brother, Simon Gillis, with whom he lived for a time. I told Father Allan that Joe Neil had told me that the MacIsaacs' music had come down to the MacIsaacs from the Gillises, and Father Allan tended to agree. Rory Shim had learned a lot of music while living with his uncle Simon.

THE MACLEAN PIPERS IN WASHABUCK, VICTORIA COUNTY

From the unpublished MacLean family history "The Pioneers of Washabuckt" by Alex D. MacLean,[85] dated 15 September 1940, two immigrant bagpipers, perhaps learner pipers, the brothers Peter (Peadar) and Roderick (Ruairidh) MacLean, sailed with their parents and other siblings on the ship *Ann*, bound from Barra to Sydney, Nova Scotia. The date for sailing and arrival, 1817, was given as categorically as was the captain's name, Simon Fraser, by Vincent MacLean of Washabuck (b. 1944).[86]

The immigrant MacLean family settled in Washabuck on the south side of St Patrick's Channel, a short sail south of Baddeck. Details of the head of the family, Lachlann MacLean (d. 1848), are scarce, but his home in Barra is identified in Washabuck MacLean lore as having been on the east side, at Leanish, and he is believed to have been of a smith (*gobha*) family there.[87] Vincent MacLean's story runs that these, his MacLeans, had been gobhas, or smiths, to the Duart MacLeans in Mull and had had their choice of land in Barra when they moved, date unreported, cause unknown. Leanish was within sight of Mull, hence their choice. The descriptive "piper" does not come up in MacDougall's *History of Inverness County* or in Stephen R. MacNeil's *All Call Iona Home;* however, family lore states that Lachlann MacLean bought a set of bagpipes at a stopover in Tobermory, Mull, for his son Peadar.[88]

I have no indication that Lachlann MacLean played the pipes in Scotland, or that any of his sons did for that matter, or that any of them had had to leave a favourite set with some putative patron-owner, tacksman, or laird in Barra. However, the purchase of a set of bagpipes suggests that one or more of the men were either fairly competent or aspiring pipers. Alex D. MacLean, a patrilineal great-great-grandson of Lachlann, suggests, perhaps wryly, that the acquisition of the set had to do with his concept of his expanded dignity in the New World.[89] The fact, however, stands out that Lachlann MacLean had enough ready cash to buy the set after the not-inconsiderable cost of shipping a large family to the New World.

Lachlann MacLean's ticket of land location for two hundred acres is dated 12 July 1825, and according to it, the anticipated future grant was contingent upon "his being fairly settled and [having] erected thereon a House" (which surely he must have done between 1817 and that date).[90]

There is no record of how Peter and Roderick (the youngest son) learned to play the pipes or what their repertoire consisted of. After Peter drowned in 1827, piping became the function of Roderick. He became what Alex D. described as "truly the family piper." The same writer stated, one presumes on reliable authority, that Roderick piped at his brother Neil's funeral (Neil MacLean, son of Lachlann, was Alex D. MacLean's great-grandfather), at one of his sister's funerals, and also at the funerals of three of his own filial grandchildren. The best Alex D. offers us about the piper's repertoire is that he played "the dirge" at these funerals. A photograph or perhaps a combination photograph/etching of Roderick MacLean holding his set of bagpipes has been published in Shears's *Gathering of the Clans Collection.*[91]

When Roderick MacLean died, his pipes were donated to Reverend Alexander F. MacGillivray, who had become, in 1873, parish priest of near-by Iona.[92] The donation apparently was made as a "customary offering for Masses for the respose [*sic*] of his soul."[93] It seems that such an heirloom would have surely stayed in the family had there been continuing interest in playing, not just in the family but in the growing community. The priest, though from Iona, had charge of the small Roman Catholic community in Baddeck (a largely Presbyterian settlement then as now); he later parted with the bagpipes to an Inverness County MacDonnell, a stonemason in Baddeck. Alex D. MacLean was aware that MacDonnell had had them in Baddeck about 1898 and that the set later became the property of his son. Neither MacDonnell has been identified, and the instrument has never been located with certainty.

Although piping has recently enjoyed an important renaissance in the Washabuck and Iona area, it is a post–Second World War phenomenon that was initially linked to the inroads of modern piping and the decline of Gaelic as the first language among the people.[94] And yet well within living memory, and while the language was in decline, the Iona-Washabuck area was very musical in the older, spontaneous, ear-learned way, a typical Catholic rural Gaelic community in Cape Breton on the cusp of English but reluctant and unable to part with a friendly old céilidh essence. The immigrant piper Roderick MacLean's great grandson, Johnnie "Washabuck" MacLean (son of "Red" Rory, son of Donald, son of Roderick), was a well-known fiddler in Cape Breton. He married the daughter of a brother of Alex Currie, the French Vale step-dance piper, and their son John MacLean is one of the island's emerging traditional-style pipers.[95] Alex Currie told me how well his grandnephew in Halifax piped long before I heard him play; I have no evidence that Currie saw the modern technique melded with his own sense of timing, or even the potential for that, but whatever the case, he had a generous appreciation for the modern piping of Sandy Boyd and others like him.

Something of the same Gaelic-linked retentiveness and natural, unselfconscious musicality is found in the MacLean paternal aunts and uncles of my informant Vincent MacLean (b. 1944), Washabuck. John in Detroit is a fiddler; the late Joe W. (Joe MacLean) of Sydney was a very well known, talented, and recorded fiddler; Theresa (over eighty years old), Sydney, is soon to produce a compact disc recording of her fiddling. (She is married to the Glen Morrison piper, Peter Morrison, and their son Vincent Morrison is a piper in Ontario.)[96] In that generation, music and step-dancing were typically unsheddable, although the way of life and language had changed or were quickly changing. The same is true of many other areas of Cape Breton.[97]

However, in piping in the Iona area, as I have said, there are more recent and interesting turns in the direction of the older tradition, particularly in the persons of John MacLean (Johnnie Washabuck's son) and Paul MacNeil from Barra Glen, both of whom play step-dance music on the bagpipes.[98] John MacLean's primary model was Alex Currie of French Vale.[99]

The pattern was, however, that fiddling and step-dancing maintained a strong hold in the rapidly de-Gaelicizing world, but piping did not. Surely the inroads of the modern technical form were at least partially responsible. More than the language declined in the first half of the twentieth century, as evidenced elsewhere in Alex D. MacLean's writing. For example, he wrote that on 23 August 1934, at a special celebration in the pioneer cemetery, two pipers were engaged to take part; they were "Pipe Major Alexander A. Mac-Donald of Inverness county and Piper Hugh McKenzie of Christmas Island," both of whom "were on hand with their pipes and brave figures they looked attired in their Highland costumes."[100]

Later in the document Alex D. wrote that "[t]oday in all the Washback district there is no one who plays the bag pipes."[101] The writer wistfully lamented the dying away of funeral bagpiping in Washabuck, adding that the "parish of Mabou, Inverness county is one place where this practice is still kept up."[102]

CHAPTER TEN

Piping and Tradition in the Margarees, Inverness County

An anonymous Antigonish *Casket* writer noted of South West Margaree in 1896 that "[t]here was never any scarcity of musicians here. Violinists and bagpipe players could be counted by the dozen, and many of them excellent performers at that. I have often seen as many as eight, ten and twelve musicians at a wedding."[1] The article lists the fiddlers and pipers, dividing them by instrument and into earlier and later categories (including some in the later period who played both instruments). The earlier pipers named are "Donald McDougall, Hugh Gillis, his brother Donald Gillis, Ranald McLellan, Neil Jamieson, Duncan Gillis, [and] John McDonell."

Donald McDougall was almost certainly the Arisaig immigrant of *circa* 1828 mentioned as one of the "teaghlach Dhòmhnuil 'ic Alasdair" (the family of Donald, son of Alexander) by J.L. MacDougall.[2] Neil Jamieson was Nial mac Lachlainn, Piper's Glen, of Canna stock. I speculate below about John MacDonell and the brothers Hugh and Donald Gillis but have not established who Ranald McLellan and Duncan Gillis were.

The later pipers mentioned in the *Casket* article are "Peter Gillis and his brother Dan, Hugh McIsaac, Angus and Patrick McFarlane, John and Charlie Jamieson, Jim H. Gillis, Malcolm D. McFarlane, Allan McFarlane and Simon McLellan. Many of these can play on more than one musical instrument, and I know two or three young ladies in the parish who could play very sweetly on both the violin and bagpipes."[3]

D.D. MacFarlane (Dòmhnul Dhùghail, 1861–1950), if he was the writer of the *Casket* article, remembered many musicians who had been born in Scotland and had emigrated to Canada. The series is a schoolteacher's jottings of the early days of Gaelic settlement in the southwest. D.D. MacFarlane lived long enough to witness the decline of one of the culturally richest Gaelic communities in the county and to remark as a matter of course as well as accidentally upon some of the changes.[4] Apart from *Margaree.Doc* "The Parish of South-West Margaree ..." and the *Casket* articles, only his diaries have survived.[5] These provide terse genealogical and social information of local value and here and there the micro-climatological and agricultural observations of an observant man. Whatever else he may have written was most probably destroyed in a house fire in the early 1950s not long after his death.

Many of the pipers that MacFarlane named remain a mystery to me, but at least he included them and one may trust in his subtle taste for tradition, even though he was in many a way an improver. MacDougall's *History of Inverness County* offers few descriptives with the names, and I am uncertain of his reasons for mentioning as pipers those people who are so called. Were they the best and if so what were MacDougall's standards, or were they the only pipers MacDougall had heard?[6] Had my concentration been sharper twenty-six years ago when Gaelic consciousness was more alive than it is today, I would have learned more about such things.

As an addendum, I must mention that this chapter is headed as it is because I have found out nothing about the traditional music of the Scottish Gaelic part of the Protestant community of North East Margaree. I visited the area and have read its local history but found no references to music or dance. This may be a critical shortcoming of my research methods, but in all of my conversations with Catholic Gaels from the neighbouring Margarees, no hint of an instrumental music tradition emerged from what's called the North East. In a Cape Breton Protestant (Congregational, Baptist, Presbyterian, Methodist) community in which there were several Skye MacDonald families, it would be abnormal for no music and dance to be remembered, one way or another, and this is the only such musically bereft area I have come upon.

ALLAN MACFARLANE (1878–1938), UPPER MARGAREE, AND THE JAMIESONS OF PIPER'S GLEN

A brief study of Allan MacFarlane from Upper Margaree forms part of an important but condensed chapter in *Traditional Gaelic Bagpiping*; here I will include further information about him.

Generally, while none of the people I interviewed about MacFarlane were as assertively knowledgeable as Joe Neil MacNeil was about the MacIsaacs,[7] in the case of Allan MacFarlane I had an unusually large number of informants, including relatives, and consequently I found out more about him than about most other local pipers. The gathered material was unusually cross-referenced just as any similar work in the East Bay area would have yielded a mass of material about Neil R. MacIsaac. When I tried to find out who was or were MacFarlane's teachers or models in piping, no one could be sure, but in the process the names of several other pipers and piping families in or near his native Upper Margaree came up; many of them will be discussed in this section.

From my many interviews, musical impression of Scotsville, Upper Margaree, South West Margaree, Egypt, Piper's Glen, and Kiltarlity began to emerge, evoking the days of the horse and the scythe and a strong neighbourliness bound up in the embrace of Catholic belief. The distance between Scotsville and South West Margaree is about eight miles. Kiltarlity and Piper's Glen/Egypt are west and east respectively of the Margaree Valley and are on mountain land and not as easily accessible. The whole conglomeration was linked with more distant communities like Kenloch, North East Margaree, and Middle River by hill paths through the forest of mixed deciduous and softwoods, little used today. Typically the social nature of these subsistence-farming communities was characterized by a complicated interweaving of marriages at the turn of the century, when the people were still not entirely detached from pioneer consciousness. Although there was plenty of evidence of resolute and loyal pro-Britishness, it was still possible and not uncommon for people to speak only Gaelic. Education was in essence an English education. MacFarlane was one of many poorly educated Gaels whose first language was Gaelic.

The general feeling of my informants was that Allan MacFarlane was an exceptionally good piper, on a par at least with the technically trained Sandy Boyd, John MacColl's pupil from Largs, whom all of them had heard from the late 1940s. John Angus (Jack) Collins, Scotsville, was MacFarlane's nephew, and Malcolm Bernard MacNeil (1916–78), who lived on MacRae Street in Sydney in 1977, lived in the same house as MacFarlane in the latter's last years. Jack Collins, who had amassed a small library of Gaelic and Scottish books, had worked for forty-five years in the United States but retired to live in Scotsville. He lived with his brother James and both indulged a powerful predilection for Gaelic affairs. Bernie MacNeil had been an adopted son of the Francis MacNeil family in Christmas Island when MacFarlane was living his last years there.[8]

The MacFarlane family is mentioned in a number of local genealogies of Antigonish and Inverness counties: in Reverend Duncan J. Rankin's, *A History of the County of Antigonish, Nova Scotia* (1929), in R.A. MacLean's *History of Antigonish* (based on Sagairt Arasaig's *A History of the County of Antigonish, Nova Scotia,* 1890–92), and in J.L. MacDougall's *History of Inverness County* (1922). All of these genealogical works are written in English and were in some degree prompted by the unhappy realization that Gaelic consciousness was being threatened as the last Scots-born immigrants were dying and as modern industrial society slipped surreptitiously into the glens. However limited in reading appeal they may be to non-relatives, they offer a unique understanding of ordinary Gaels, particularly their marriage patterns over four or five generations in the New World. Occasionally they point out the Gaels' links with known and unknown people in Scotland. An unusual feature is that they record much more thoroughly the Catholic communities than the Presbyterian (and, post-1925, United Church) communities in Antigonish and Inverness counties. Whatever their shortcomings, these books are valuable to the Gaelic world where Catholic Everyman is seldom discussed.

By contrast, most of the genealogies constructed in Scotland dwell on the families of the literate and prominent with a bias (one common enough in the New World also) on the agnate side. The ordinary folk were generally overlooked, as they were by English writers of Tudor and Elizabethan Ireland, to the point where the reader could be forgiven for wondering if any such existed. For that reason, these North American recitations of names and marriages, laboriously constructed, with an occasional glimpse of a musician or storyteller or other success or exception in life, are an important balance. They prove in the sharpest way that there were well-peopled communities in Gaelic Scotland where often now there is emptiness.

Study of Allan MacFarlane's family is constrained by the Scottish writer's preoccupation with the prominent. Charles Fraser-Mackintosh MP, who wrote and spoke about the MacDonells of Scotus in Knoydart,[9] had nothing to say about the daughter(s) of "John of Crowlin," a younger son of Eneas MacDonell, third of Scotus (dead by 1753). It is from Nova Scotian work that we know that one of them, a sister of the famous "Spanish John" (who emigrated to Upper Canada), married Dougal MacFarlane, Allan Mac-Farlane's patrilineal immigrant ancestor. In Ray MacLean's first volume of the history of Antigonish County, she is described as Margaret MacDonell, a daughter of "Fear Chrolem." If there was any detail about the daughter of "John of Crowlin" who married Allan MacFarlane's immigrant ancestor, Fraser-Mackintosh ignored it.

From that same largely male perspective (for the sake of brevity), but with Margaret MacDonell and Mary MacFarlane added, Allan MacFarlane's family tree and claim to Gaelic gentility is charted below.

Although information from John Neillie MacLean of East Lake was referred to in *Traditional Gaelic Bagpiping,* his importance in the establishing of Allan MacFarlane's significance as a piper was not enlarged on there. His contribution in 1979 carried special weight because he spontaneously offered the information that Allan MacFarlane had played the bagpipes for step-dancing and for step-dancing in the old Scotch Fours and that he also piped for Square Sets. I had neither broached the subject of piping for any kind of dancing, far less step-dancing, nor hinted in any way at what I suspected. This is not to say that other informants were either mean or secretive. Most did not anticipate any depth of interest and many had probably forgotten such details in any case and needed to be carefully reminded.

Chart 16   Allan MacFarlane's Family Tree

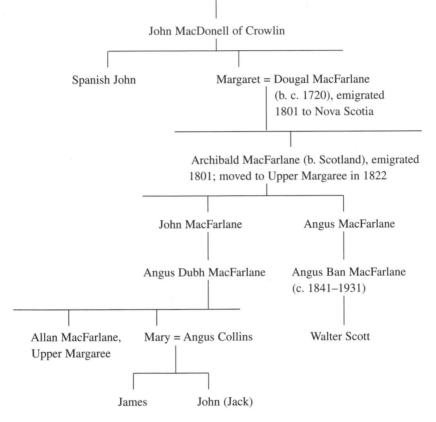

Eneas (Aonghus) MacDonell
of Scotus

John MacDonell of Crowlin

Spanish John

Margaret = Dougal MacFarlane
(b. c. 1720), emigrated
1801 to Nova Scotia

Archibald MacFarlane (b. Scotland), emigrated
1801; moved to Upper Margaree in 1822

John MacFarlane   Angus MacFarlane

Angus Dubh MacFarlane   Angus Ban MacFarlane
(c. 1841–1931)

Allan MacFarlane,   Mary = Angus Collins   Walter Scott
Upper Margaree

James   John (Jack)

John Neillie MacLean was born and raised a Presbyterian and in 1979 attended the United Church of Canada at Lake Ainslie (East Side), a little to the north of his farm.[10] According to Archie MacPhail (b. 1900), Scotsville, John Neillie MacLean's brother Malcolm was a good Scotch fiddler who played for Scotch Fours and four-figure Quadrilles.[11] MacPhail also said that their mother (née MacLean) was a sister of the mother of Protestant fiddler Sandy MacLean from Footcape.[12]

While John Neillie and others were staid and conventional, the old school-teacher Clarence Moore was opinionated and questioning. He lived with his wife in a tiny house at the side of Lake Ainslie and was a Gaelic speaker.

Several local people recommended that I visit him, since he was very well informed on local Scotch affairs; they hinted at his outspokenness. I cycled to visit him first on 9 May 1979.[13] He knew who I was but didn't invite me in because he and his wife were preparing to go to the funeral in Belle Côte of one her aunts, Annie (MacKay) Munro. Thus, on that occasion we managed only a brief conversation, mostly about Allan MacFarlane.

Clarence Moore, although unwilling to discuss Little Farquhar MacKinnon (Fearchar Beag) the piper because he knew him to be untrained, alluded briefly to clerical disapproval of music in the area. He told me that Little Farquhar had to take his chanter to the woods to practise in the good weather to avoid recriminations from a local minister. He also said that it was widely thought that Farquhar played a set of pipes that had been played at Waterloo.

With Allan MacFarlane it was a different matter. Clarence Moore did not know if MacFarlane had been taught piping by anyone, but he knew that MacFarlane was a first-class piper and worthy of discussion. He mentioned MacFarlane's speech impediment, his hatred of the tune "The Road to the Isles," and the time when he got his new set of pipes. The last involved an event at the hall at Headlake, which was also the local school.[14] The teacher's desk in those days (1920s?) was on a dais. When Allan, who had one leg a little shorter than the other, went in, he bumped into the dais and let out a string of curses and then got started. Clarence said he played for Scotch Fours and other dances that night, and when it ended there was a céilidh at George MacKinnon's place nearby.[15]

Moore remembered dancing the "Lancers" in his young days. As that was a somewhat less commonly used name in rural Inverness County than "Square Set," I asked him if the terms were roughly synonymous and he said they were. He went on to say that at those old dances "pretty soon somebody would be calling for the Scotch Four and if there was a piper around, that was danced."[16] Moore was one of only two of my many informants on Allan MacFarlane or anyone else, piper or fiddler, or both, to link the Scotch Four and the bagpipes so intimately. The other was John Angie MacDonell, Inverness, who is discussed below. If Moore's was a fair statement, then the advent of the Square Set/Lancers from the 1880s was not only responsible for the decline of the once thoroughly Gaelic two-couple dance (a *sine qua non* at Scotch marriages), but also for the slippage of the bagpipe as a common folk dance instrument.

When Allan MacFarlane got a modern set of bagpipes, he paid much less attention to the violin but he was a good fiddler. According to Walter Scott MacFarlane, a second cousin (see genealogical chart), Allan had fiddled at a competition in Baddeck with Tina Campbell (piano).[17] In the late 1970s I saw what I was told was the older set of bagpipes that Allan MacFarlane had owned, and I wondered what had urged him to part with such a beautiful old set of drones. They were turned from a lighter wood than most modern sets, and no effort had been made to stain them. The turnings were of an older style not unreminiscent at first glance of the Culloden set drawn in Dalyell's *Musical Memoirs;* beside the fact that they lacked the chanter, I know little more about them.[18] Walter Scott MacFarlane told me that Allan MacFarlane sold the set to a Jimmy MacLellan from Kiltarlity (d. 1977).[19] MacLellan apparently only had one or two tunes and was no piper. He took the bagpipes with him to Roxbury, Massachusetts, in 1925, where they stayed in a box for half a century. A visiting relative was given them and they are still in the family.

A story that I heard from Walter Scott MacFarlane and later from Jack Collins indicates a piper and another set of bagpipes from Piper's Glen. The pipes belonged to an Angus MacLellan (Aonghus Sheumais Ruairidh),[20] nephew of Red Angus MacLellan, who lived on the mountain as the road dipped into Piper's Glen.[21] Walter MacFarlane remembered that before he was married he was at a milling frolic at Angus Allan Gillis the fiddler's farm, high above the valley of the Margaree on its east side. Allan Mac-Farlane was there and had borrowed Angus MacLellan's bagpipes. He took them on a buggy ride to the Collins's in Scotsville where there was beer, and stayed away long enough for the owner to wonder what was going on. He could hear his pipes being played but there was no other sign of them. Jack Collins dated the frolic to 1922 or 1923. Angus MacLellan and his family's connection with piping is treated below.

Walter Scott MacFarlane's memories included many old Gaels born in the first half of the nineteenth century, among them his father, Angus Bàn (see Chart 16). On 20 April 1977, when he was eighty-two, Walter Scott told me that his father had been born and had lived and died in Egypt Road in Upper Margaree quite close to Allan MacFarlane's home and that he'd made his own set of bagpipes. Walter remembered seeing him and Hughie Gillis playing them "on the steps" of the house in Upper Margaree a hundred yards east of where the Sloy Brook joins the Margaree.[22] Angus Bàn also made songs, including one that lamented the departure of one of the piping Jamiesons and his family from Piper's Glen, a sequestered and narrow glen deep in the forest hills east of Upper Margaree.[23] A soil map classifies the land as "rough mountain."[24] There is no doubt whatever that Allan MacFarlane was a traditional step-dance piper. Equally it is beyond doubt that he learned to read and write pipe music and has to be classified as a literate traditional piper, like Archie Beaton (Gilleasbuig Aonghuis Fhionnlaidh Mhóir) and Angus Campbell Beaton (Aonghus Iagain Raonuil).[25] Bernie MacNeil remembered seeing him, in his last two or three years, going through his copy of one of the works of J. Scott Skinner (probably *The Scottish Violinist*), looking for pipe tunes, but his ability to use written music to his own advantage goes back to his early days in Upper

Margaree. (The Glace Bay piper Joe Hughie MacIntyre also used Skinner as a source of new tunes.)

Even Walter Scott MacFarlane had no idea if Allan (Allachan) MacFarlane had any piping teacher although there were plenty of pipers in the area, including the Jamiesons, Angus MacLellan in Piper's Glen, Angus Bàn Mac-Farlane (c. 1841–1931, Allachan's father's first cousin) in the Upper Margaree area, Hugh Gillis in Scotsville (d. 1905), and the MacDonells in Kiltarlity and in "Gleann Mór."[26] It was his opinion that MacFarlane was self-taught and that is the consensus. On the other hand, Walter Scott Mac-Farlane knew beyond a doubt that Allan could read pipe music, which, typically and without qualification, he regarded as a praise-worthy achievement for a rural Highland piper. He described him as having been "one of the first" traditional musicians in the area to learn to read music, adding that Allan was the first piper or violinist in the community to own one of Scott Skinner's books. John Angus Collins didn't know if anyone had taught or helped his uncle learn to read music, but he was proud that a man who had had so many physical and educational disadvantages not only mastered those difficulties but taught other pipers and fiddlers as well.[27]

According to Jack Collins, Allan MacFarlane taught the local fiddler Angus Allan Gillis (Aonghus mac Alasdair 'ic Eoghainn 'ic Aonghuis 'ic Eoghainn) to read violin music (elsewhere James D. Gillis [1870–1965] is given the credit). Barry Shears learned that the bard and teacher Malcolm H. Gillis[28] (Calum Eoghainn) of nearby South West Margaree had a son, Malcolm, who was taught piping by Allan MacFarlane, although the bard himself played the pipes and the fiddle and taught some basic musical concepts at the local school in the early years of this century.[29] While who taught whom is moot, what is more important is that there were countless informal interpersonal musical influences at work in Upper and South West Margaree. Interestingly, too, schoolteachers in South West Margaree like Malcolm Gillis and D.D. MacFarlane (whose diaries show that he supplied for the bard when the latter was travelling), while promoting the Cape Breton/North American version of Victorian improvement, in English, were deeply immersed in the older traditional Gaelic world.

One of those influences was the presence, presumably at least since the mid-1870s, of modern tropical-wood bagpipes. Although MacFarlane's first bagpipes were made by an accomplished turner, he eventually replaced them with a modern set. Archie MacPhail[30] dated the acquisition to around 1917 and remembered being at the welcoming céilidh for the new set. MacFarlane played the pipes in the corner of a room for the dancing, then, laying the pipes aside, he took up where he had left off with the fiddle. Archie MacPhail was one of many who told me proudly that MacFarlane was equally good on either instrument. In any case, the era of Scottish-made, pre-dark-wood pipes was fast disappearing, and the day of the home-made set with it. The impetus behind Allan MacFarlane's importing a modern Scottish set is unknown, but there was at least one modern set in his neighbourhood, possibly from as early as 1873. The chanter bears the name David Glen, and the set, ivory-mounted and now minus only the blow-pipe and the blow-pipe stock, still exists.

Another Glen set, now owned by Barry Shears, Halifax, was first owned by the teacher and piper Jimmie Dubh Gillis in South West Margaree. Jimmie Dubh left them to the fiddler/step-dancer Angus Allan Gillis, from whom they went to Francis MacDonald (Black Watch of Canada piper) and thence by sale to Barry Shears.[31] These sets, if both David Glens, were made in Edinburgh no earlier than 1873, the year David Glen took over his father's pipe-making business.[32]

Whoever influenced Allan MacFarlane's fingering and perhaps helped him learn to read pipe music, Allan certainly thought himself a good enough piper when he went to Maine and elsewhere to compete in piping competitions.[33] It is revealing, however, that at a Sydney, Nova Scotia, competition in the 1930s the military piper Black Jack MacDonald won the march section while MacFarlane won in the strathspeys and reels.[34] In my opinion, it is quite likely that the judge's or judges' ears were attuned to traditional speeds and timings and that MacFarlane was superior where traditional dance rhythms were concerned.

Assuming that Frank Rhodes was right in dating the introduction of the Quadrille/Lancers in rural Inverness County to around 1890, Allan MacFarlane had the essentially Scottish strathspey and reel rhythms and speeds laid down in his mind at about, or just before, the time that the new dance was gaining its foothold. His repertoire probably included Highland jigs in the early days, but if not, jigs were all he needed to add to play for Square Sets. Unfortunately, no one remembered his piping for the Scotch Four prior to 1900 but there were many who recalled his doing so afterwards. MacFarlane piped for Fours and Sets and for individual step-dancing at picnics, frolics, concerts, and "garden parties" all over the island but particularly in the Margarees at places like Widow Lord's.

In the Scotsville/South West Margaree communities there appears to have been almost no published pipe music for as long as Gaelic was the common tongue. However, one tenuous link between published pipe music and South West Margaree should be noted. William MacKay, of the Inverness Militia in Scotland (in 1811) and who later, in 1820 and 1840, was piper to the Celtic Society of Scotland, was awarded prizes for writing pipe music (ceòl mór)[35] on the staff in 1820, 1822, and 1823. Captain Allan MacDonald, an immigrant to South West Margaree, had also been in the Inverness-shire Militia. This is all apropos of the fact that the only published book of nineteenth-century light pipe music to turn up from Scotland in Gaelic Inverness

County, perhaps in Gaelic Cape Breton, is what appears to be William MacKay's *The complete tutor for the great Highland bagpipe with a compendious selection of marches, quick steps, strathspeys, reels & jigs.* I assume that it was brought to Cape Breton in the nineteenth century. The edition is not yet known, but it appears to be a second and to be the only known copy. At one time it was the property of Ranald Beaton (Raonul Màiri Bhàin, 1859–1961), piper and fiddler in Port Hood.

THE JAMIESONS AND MACLELLANS
FROM PIPER'S GLEN

The immigrant Jamieson family was from Canna and one of not many Canna families to settle in Inverness County.[36] At the time Angus Bàn MacFarlane's lament was composed, the family was represented by a shoemaker and piper son Neil Jamieson (Néil mac Lachlainn [Neil, son of Lachlan], 1837–1931), his wife, Ann,[37] and his children Iain, Sìne, Teàrlach, Eachann, Flòiri, Seumas, Mary Jane, May, and Seàrlot, all of whom were pipers according to the MacFarlane song.[38] I have learned nothing of the siblings' or their father's competence as pipers and the earliest memory I managed to evoke was from 1900.

Walter Scott MacFarlane recollected a visit made by Neil, his wife, and some of the family around 1900. He remembered first hearing "Blue Bonnets" and then seeing the tall old piper with the black whiskers. Neil Jamieson used to be a regular visitor to the MacFarlane home, where he was given the use of Walter Scott's mother's sewing machine, the only one in the area, to sew uppers. Neil later moved his family to Glace Bay. The old Jamieson farm, according to Gerry MacFarlane, Troy, Inverness County, lay between the post office at Keppoch and Dan Stewart's place. It was cut over for pulp wood in 1945,[39] meaning perhaps a forty-year vacancy.

Neil's daughter, Sìne (Jane), a piper, married a local man, Archibald MacLellan (Gilleasbuig Dhòmhnuil Ruairidh Chùl), a first cousin of the piper Angus MacLellan (Aonghus Sheumais Ruairidh), and his brothers John H., the chanter player and fiddler, and Malcolm, the singer-storyteller. Malcolm MacLellan was the father of John Neillie MacLellan (b. 1925), a Gaelic speaker and my principal informant on the MacLellan pipers of Piper's Glen and Egypt.[40] Malcolm MacLellan did not play an instrument, but according to John Neillie, Malcolm's father, James (the Seumas Ruairidh of the sloinneadh), was a chanter player.[41]

John Neillie said that he remembered hearing Sìne's piping and that her piping brother Hector (Eachunn) had a very musical family. Hector's family attended a performance by Boston musicians in Broad Cove one summer, and according to John Neillie, it included fiddlers, piano players, and pipers. John Neillie described the Jamiesons as unilingual English speakers who had lost contact with Gaelic and were curious about it. He remembered Allan MacFarlane's piping, too, from the 1920s and early 1930s in Upper Margaree, and from the most impressionable and retentive mind of a youngster. Once again MacFarlane is described as an exceptional piper.[42] In all of these cases no piping function was ascribed or alluded to by John Neillie MacLellan in our telephone conversation or later; it was enough that they were pipers and numerous.

Angus MacLellan the piper was one of two piper brothers (in a family of six children) who both must surely have been strongly influenced by their cousin, the Jamieson wife of Archy MacLellan (Gilleasbuig Dhòmhnuil Ruairidh), and her people.[43] What's more, the strong bagpiping ambience of Piper's Glen must have influenced everyone living there. The other brother was John H., whom John Neillie described as a chanter player and fiddler. John H. made his own chanters out of a wood John Neillie did not identify but which almost certainly was druman(ach) (elder/*Caprifoliaciae sambucus*), since the pith could be easily removed;[44] he used a straw from the barn for a reed. Angus, initially a self-taught piper, was also a schoolteacher who taught in western Canada, in Dunakin, Inverness County (for two years in the late 1930s), and in Egypt and Whycocomagh.[45]

At Whycocomagh Angus assisted Alex the piper MacDonald (Alasdair Iain Alasdair Alain); John Neillie told me (17 June 1998) that the experience improved his playing and that Alex the piper was reluctant to have to let him go. Like fellow-teachers D.D. MacFarlane and Malcolm Gillis he took an interest in Gaelic affairs, teaching himself to read and write the language as well as pipe music. He bought himself a modern set of bagpipes which his brother's son, John Neillie MacLellan, said were subsequently owned by George Ingraham, Kenloch, Inverness County. John Neillie's conversation did not expose pipers further back in his MacLellan lineage, but when asked about pre-modern bagpipes in the family, he said that Angus "picked up an old set for John H." I have no more information about these pipes.[46]

Angus MacLellan followed education policy, and parental wishes, and taught in English. He was married to Mary Ann (MacLellan) Spillane, a sister of John Neillie's mother, both sisters being born MacLellans. It was her second marriage and a son is living in Boston.[47] John Neillie added a number of other pipers, including a cousin at one remove, "Archie A." MacLellan (Gilleasbuig Andra Ruairidh), from adjoining Egypt. Archie A. died at Vimy Ridge just before the Great War ended. The wider MacLellan family was apparently well represented by step-dancers as well. Another Piper's Glen piper whom John Neillie described as "pretty fair" was Sandy MacDonell (d. c. 1968), and he said that piping was popular in the MacDonell family in "Gleann Mór."[48]

John James MacKenzie (b. 1916, South West Margaree, was the only informant who, when prompted by his youngest brother, John Archie (aged sixty-four), offered a glimpse of the real function of piping in Piper's Glen and Egypt. He recollected Angus MacLellan's piping for dances and house parties, which undoubtedly indicates step-dancing, and for picnics "in the old days." According to John James, Angus had left for Boston late in life.[49] The late Lauchie Dan N. MacLellan, Dunvegan, mentioned an Angus MacLellan, address unspecified, who piped for step-dancing.[50] According to MacDougall, Rory MacLellan was from Eigg,[51] but any speculation about his relationship to Catholic MacLellans included in McNeill's Eigg census of 1764–65 is impossible. The Eigg Catholic MacLellan families were much smaller than the families of the first two, three, sometimes more immigrant generations, and given the shortage of children's names in the census, even knowing the order of their birth is insufficient to allow guesses about future nomenclature.

John Neillie MacLellan told me (8 June 1998) that most of the MacLellans were dancers and that there were fiddlers among them as well, but the overall impression of the instrumental music of Piper's Glen is that it was bagpipe music, often simply using home-made chanters with grass reeds. In later days, after the Second World War, Calum Sheumais Ruairidh's home was a ceilidh house, Calum having had a retentive memory for story and song.[52] All the Gaels are gone from Piper's Glen today, but memories of them and their descendants and the ceilidhs of another age are still fresh elsewhere on Cape Breton and further afield.

THE MACDONELL PIPERS FROM KILTARLITY AND INVERNESS

Kiltarlity, now almost empty, lies to the west of Upper Margaree on the same "rough mountain" soil as Piper's Glen (and nearby Egypt and Keppoch). The Scotch farmers at Kiltarlity included Presbyterians and Catholics in the first decade of the twentieth century.[53] The MacDonells living there appear to be treated by J.L. MacDougall but under the broader heading "South West of Margaree" and then, in a subsection, under the heading "MacDonell." He says nothing either of the name Kiltarlity or of piping, although it seems that the first MacDonell family is the one associated closely with piping.[54] Among several MacDonell families in "South West of Margaree," the first of them that MacDougall described in 1922 is Ronald Ban's and the genealogy is taken to the grandchildren, including Alexander, James, and Penelope, all children of Donald, son of Ronald Ban. According to MacDougall, Ronald Ban immigrated from Morar in 1826. D.D. MacFarlane had already noted in addition that all but the youngest of his children (unnamed) were born in Scotland.[55] See the abbreviated geneaology for the MacDonells in Chart 17.

Chart 17   The MacDonells, an Abbreviated Geneaology

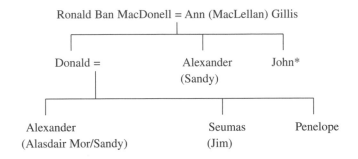

Whether or not he was relying on MacDougall's work, Duncan Alex Beag MacDonald described the first MacDonell piper from Kiltarlity that he had heard as "Alasdair Mór Dhòmhnuill 'ic Raonuil" (Big Alex, son of Donald, son of Ranald). He also told me that this MacDonell family was from Keppoch.[56] While Alexander, son of Donald, son of Ronald MacDonell, is probably sufficient identification, the recurrence of an unusual first name is helpful. One of Ronald Ban's daughters was Penelope and this name crops up again in the grandchildren of Alexander. Otherwise, those MacDonells I spoke to gave names in familiar English and stopped at the brothers Sandy and Jim (Duncan Alex Beag's "Alasdair Mór" and "Seumas"; J.L. MacDougall's Alexander and James). That these were sons of Donald, son of Ranald (Dòmhnul mac Raonuil), seems certain.

Duncan Alex Beag MacDonald also mentioned that Alasdair Mór (Big Alex) had a brother Seumas (Jim),[57] whose descendants were the Deepdale MacDonells, including (through Jim's son Hughie Dan, the Gaelic storyteller)[57] the piper Harold Joseph MacDonell and his piping brother Jimmy and (through Jim's son Robert) their cousins Robert, Father Angus, and Neil, all pipers. Duncan Alex Beag heard Alasdair Mór play the pipes in 1921, when he was a boy of five. John Angus Collins, Scotsville, saw him around 1916, describing him as a tall but old man who he thought had not lived much longer.[59] Piping was thus clearly popular in the MacDonell family for at least three Gaelic generations, beginning with Big Alex/Sandy (Alasdair Mór) some time in the second half of the nineteenth century. Walter Scott MacFarlane never mentioned the MacDonell pipers in Kiltarlity to me, and I learned only something of the nature of their music and nothing of their technique. Observations, critical, though non-pejorative, of ear-learned pipers were only voiced about John Angie, who was probably more conspicuous than others.

Chart 18   Kiltarlity MacDonell Family Tree

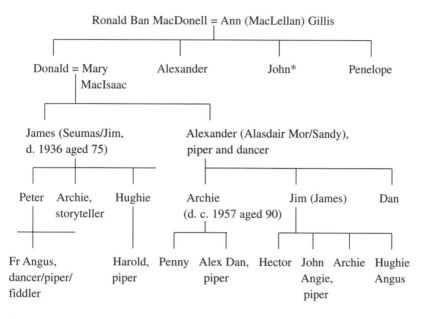

Note: Ranald Ban's sons Donald and John were probably born in Scotland.

    I was given two rural memories of the last of the Gaelic MacDonells in Kiltarlity, Isabel MacMillan's and Grantie MacDougall's. Isabel (1903–98), from Twin Rock Valley, remembered the brothers Dan, Archie, and Jim, all sons of Sandy. Grantie MacDougall (c. 1918–95),[60] from Scotsville, only remembered Dan.[61]

On Alasdair Mór's (Sandy's) side, in 1980 I spoke to John Angie Mac-Donell, the Cape Breton Highlanders piper mentioned in *Traditional Gaelic Bagpiping*,[62] and to his brother Hector, both sons of Jim, son of Sandy Mac-Donell of Kiltarlity. I also spoke to their cousin Penny (daughter of Archie, son of Sandy), who talked about a set of bagpipes Alasdair Mór had made and played.

By 5 July 1980, when I met John Angie in Inverness, he had been forced to give up piping because of bronchial problems (he died 17 November 1980). He told me that he understood Gaelic but blamed his schooling in English in Inverness for not being fluent. He was an ear-learned piper like his brothers Archie and Hughie Angus. He played by ear until he was twenty and admitted that later on he found it hard not to revert to his earlier habits; he played right-handedly. George Sutherland, his old pipe major in the Highlanders, said he could take a tune from the book but considered him an ear piper. His father, James John MacDonell, encouraged him to learn pipe notation and he took lessons from the Dundee Scot Sandy Russell in

Inverness. Unprompted, John Angie said that he "never lost his timing," and when I asked him what Sandy Russell's piping was like, he told me he piped "like he was going to a fire."[63]

John Angie also told me he often played for Scotch Fours that embodied strathspey and reel timing, to which the dancers step-danced. He added that the pipes were preferred for that dance in Inverness, a surprising remark since Inverness was a hustling coal-mining company town and railway terminal, attracting foreigners like Sandy Russell and many others, including local and hinterland Gaels, to the mines. One could say it was Inverness County's latter-day, smaller version of Sydney.[64] The Sydney example given by Joe Neil MacNeil suggests that tradition failed in urban and suburban environments. Nonetheless John Angie said that the Scotch Four was popular, particularly at the old Highland Games that were held in Inverness in the late 1920s.

However, John Angie described the Scotch Four as danced by eight people and lasting as long as the dancers had steps. Perhaps he was confused or was describing a hybrid of tradition and modern ideas because he elaborated to tell me emphatically that the Scotch Four was not a "figure dance" like the Square Set and that it had no callers as all Square Sets danced in Inverness had.[65] Whatever his "Scotch Four" was (and the dance has to be put somehow into the category "traditional Gaelic" because it had step-dance setting steps), it lost popularity during the Depression. No one I talked to in the county has ever said the Scotch Four had eight dancers. John Angie's dance may, however, represent a variation of the Scotch Four, what might be called a double four (although I have never heard the term), as the term "single four" may be a modern retronomer based on the Scotch Four in areas where tradition was weakened, memories of the traditional Four and Eight having waned under outside influences.[66]

John Angie told me unasked that he had often piped for Square Sets in South West Margaree and that in 1947 or '48 he had piped at the Fireman's Ball in Inverness for a Saratoga Lancer (for which he told me he played jigs and a march called "Lord Alexander Kennedy").

Where his family was concerned, John Angie said that his mother, a MacKinnon from MacKinnon's Brook north of Mabou Coal Mines in the Beinn Bhiorach (Pointed Hill) area, played the chanter and his father, Jim, was a piper. Jim was born in Kiltarlity where he was schooled in Gaelic.[67] He learned to pipe right-handedly, by ear, and never played by note; he also step-danced. His son described his timing as great and said that he piped for step-dancing. He married around 1900 when he was twenty-one and had a job with the railway at Inverness. After serving in the Great War, he worked in the Inverness coal mine. He died around 1947, aged sixty-eight.

John Angie's father's father, Sandy (Alasdair Mór), also was a piper and an ear player. John Angie heard him play and thought he played left-handed. What he did remember was that he "had all his tartans attached to the bass drone" and that he spoke very little English. Sandy, who was born, lived, and died in Kiltarlity, went blind in his old age. John Angie also thought that Sandy's father (Donald) was a piper and that the family had probably brought a set of bagpipes out with them, although he didn't know of any such set. He also thought that his MacDonells were from Glengarry in Scotland.

From John Angie MacDonell's memory the following Gaelic speakers, all ear pipers, played the bagpipes for Scotch Four dancing, specifically strathspeys and reels: Jim MacDonell (John Angie's father), Fred MacKinnon, Joe and John MacKinnon, Little Farquhar MacKinnon, Neil MacLellan (Upper South West Margaree?), Red Jimmy MacIsaac, Willie "the piper" Gillis, and Sandy MacDonell.[68] John Angie said that in his own family, apart from the step-dancing of his father, Jim, Jim's aunt in Deepdale was a step-dancer. John Angie's family knowledge extended to his grandfather and to this step-dancing aunt (whom he did not name). However, he described the piper Harold in the following terms: Harold's paternal grandfather and John Angie's father, Jim, were first cousins. My chart shows that they were first cousins at one remove; however, knowledge of this sort of relationship shows that Donald's presence was known, even if he was unnamed.

Although John Angie's relatively limited knowledge of his family history and his use of English names without a second thought reflect non-Gaelic notions of the extended family,[69] his cleaving to ear piping for step-dancing was very traditional. George Sutherland's recollection that he was an ear piper is balanced by John Angie's impressions of army piping from 1939 to 1946 in the Cape Breton Highlanders. For him it was "the same thing over and over, you got so sick of it."[70]

Other Catholic Margaree-area pipers, such as Malcolm H. Gillis (Calum Eoghainn), the bard/piper/fiddler, and the immigrant MacDougall piper, are mentioned in *Traditional Gaelic Bagpiping*, as are the differing influences upon Gaelic tradition of Sandy Russell and Sandy Boyd. A measure of the yielding of the Gael to modern ideas of piping as the Second World War slipped into background memory is captured in the juxtaposing of the piping of Harold MacDonell and that of Hamish Moore, the Scots piper, at a Broad Cove concert in 1994. Harold MacDonell, the local piper and a breath away from the richest, memory- and ear-based Gaelic piping tradition in any Gàidhealtachd, was dutifully garbed in modern Highland dress and played in the style he had so competently mastered from the tuition of Sandy Boyd. Hamish Moore, bagpipe maker and a retired veterinary surgeon from Edinburgh, who realized that modern piping had strayed from those often-claimed Gaelic roots, sat down to play; he wore jeans and an earring, played a (three-drone) set of pipes he had made himself, and turned out step-dance music. Moore was appropriately introduced as a visiting Scots piper, and his performance was enthusiastically received. Later I drew public attention to the fact that when Barry Shears had done the same some years earlier, there had only been polite, largely uncomprehending applause.[71] While the impetus to resurrect the older fashion could only have come from Gaelic Cape Breton, somehow any revival, at that moment, seemed to require the imprimatur of a Scotsman. This is not an uncommon theme in New World piping, but one that, if extended to violin playing and dancing, will be disastrous for the last of Gaelic tradition in Nova Scotia.

For all that, Sandy Russell's impact on John Angie MacDonell's piping was much less easily detected than Sandy Boyd's on Harold MacDonell's.

To return to D.D. MacFarlane's early pipers, the last point (a speculative one, but plausible in light of the amount of piping in the wider family) is that the John MacDonell who has an asterisk against his name in Charts 17 and 18 is the early piper mentioned by MacFarlane. If he is, then he was an immigrant piper and one who, unfortunately, did not survive in the memory of my latter-day MacDonell informants.

The piping brothers Hugh and Donald Gillis are more difficult to identify, there being several families in the South West–Upper Margaree area in which sons with those names appear. However, in Donald (Irish) Gillis's family there was a Hugh and a Donald and the Hugh was a piper. Regrettably, no memory of Donald as a piper appears to have survived, although there is a record of Hugh the piper and a published obituary. While this may seem to confuse the subject, Archie MacPhail told me about an Eoghan Pìobaire mac 'Ill' Ios' (Hugh Piper Gillis) from Scotsville. He was one of two musical brothers whose mother, Archie MacPhail (b. 1900) told me, had been a Coady. MacPhail mentioned an old set of pipes that had belonged to Eoghan, and told me how I might find them.[72]

These bagpipes, which I did locate and which to my knowledge are extant, are owned by a family descended from Hugh Gillis, stonecutter, whose obituary in the Antigonish *Casket* shows that he died in Louisburg in 1905.[73] Hugh had a brother Donald, and the two were sons of immigrant Donald (Irish) Gillis (b. c. 1810) and Catherine MacGillivray. Although Hugh's obituary does not allude to piping, an entry in D.D. MacFarlane's diary for 25 January 1905 reads "Burial of Hugh Gillis – piper – mason Scotsville, who died at Louisburg on the 22nd. Remains taken home."[74] The *Casket* obituary states that Hugh left three sons and one daughter, but fails to name them; however, among his children were a Peter and a Dan Gillis who may be MacFarlane's pipers of the later period. Another son, Alex, son of Hugh Gillis, was a piper who played right hand upper on the chanter; around the time of the Great War Alex Gillis was working for the Winnipeg fire department. Another of his sons, Duncan, went to Utah around 1885 and died there.

Unfortunately, I was not able to speak to Gaelic singer James Gillis (age ninety-one), Gillisdale, who lived with his niece Marie Moran in Port Hood. I had been advised by Christie (Cameron) Gillis (age eighty-three) Scotsville, that Mr Gillis's knowledge of the Scotsville Gillises might extend to knowing whether the David Glen bagpipes had belonged to Hugh Big Peter or to Hugh Donald Irish, both of whom had brothers named Donald.[75]

PROTESTANT CÉILIDH PIPERS
FROM THE SCOTSVILLE AREA

A hitherto undescribed Protestant piper in Fearchar Beag's neighbourhood was Robbie Campbell, a traditional piper who went to Boston about the time of the First World War and never returned. Isobel MacMillan of Twin Rock Valley in the rear of East Lake Ainslie remembered him (personal interview, 29 October 1994). She said that he had lived near the home of Neil Allan MacLean (1897–1992) in the rear/north of Scotsville and had played the pipes sitting down. Isobel MacMillan, the daughter of Allan Cameron of Kiltarlity, a strict Sunday sabbath keeper, was a non-dancer, and the thing she remembered most vividly about Robbie Campbell's piping was that he beat time, vigorously, with both feet. She said he'd have been about forty when she saw him piping.

An idea of the time when Campbell left for Massachusetts is deducible from Grantie MacDougall's knowledge of the old Campbell farm. As far back as MacDougall (b. 1918) could remember, it had been vacant and going back to forest. The most detailed memory of Robert Campbell the piper, however, was Archie MacPhail's. MacPhail said that before Campbell went to Boston he had worked at the Scotsville barites mine. He remembered him piping all day at the céilidh celebrating the opening of the mine *circa* 1910. Archie MacPhail, who was as fascinated with pipes and piping then as he is today, had sat near Campbell throughout the day. Campbell played an old three-drone set, provenance and present holder unknown. MacPhail once visited the Campbell home in Boston and remembered there having been two sons. Campbell was a fast piper and, from what Archie MacPhail implied, roughly on a par with Little Farquhar MacKinnon as a player.[76] Lastly, transmitted through the memory of Archie MacPhail to Barry Fraser, it emerges that the Campbell family was musical, particularly in the person of the unnamed immigrant believed to have been a fiddling pupil of Nathaniel Gow (Niel Gow's son).

Kenneth MacKay is another Scotsville Protestant piper about whom it is now extremely difficult to learn anything. Last memories of him date to the early 1900s. Like Campbell, he was a céilidh piper, and the story persists that the Presbyterian minister of his time would not baptize his children because of their father's unsuitability as a Christian father.

The Protestant MacLeans in Scotsville added at the minimum two pipers to the area's instrumental musicians, not to mention a number of Gaelic singers and composers and step-dancers. To call this family prototypical of Moderate Church of Scotland immigrant families before the Disruption (1843) would perhaps be to exaggerate, but their love of music and dance was quite commonly shared in most of the Protestant communities. The MacKinnons who settled at Cobb Brook south of Scotsville, for example, were as musical and for as long as the MacLeans; the family included the Reverend A.D. MacKinnon, himself a step-dancer.[78] Ministers and others who tried to curb musicality often did so for the reason given Archie MacPhail by his Campbell grandfather: "Where there's a fiddle there's liquor."

The immigrant Malcolm MacLean from Mull was a dancing master in Scotland. He was married to a Tiree MacLean who claimed relationship with the immigrant bard MacLean (author of "An Coille Gruamach" [The Melancholy Forest]). Malcolm MacLean emigrated in 1826 with three or four family members, according to Neil Allan MacLean, his great grandson.[79] Neil Allan, himself a well-known Gaelic singer in Inverness County, remembered his paternal grandfather's youngest brother, John M., who played the pipes and the fiddle, but not the piper Murdoch (possibly Scots born) who was lost at sea. Although he (Neil Allan) didn't dance, he was well aware of the Scotch Four and told me that all of his MacLean family danced (presumably antecedent generations).[80]

Neil Allan's son Hugh Don believed that there had been more pipers in the community in earlier generations and mentioned a Campbell piper from Kiltarlity, first name unknown, who had moved to Boston. He also said that some of the Scotsville MacLeans, including Neil Allan's father, Alex MacLean, learned step-dancing from a MacDonell woman (who married a Gillis) living in Kiltarlity.[81] Herein is the only hint that the immigrant dancing master Malcolm MacLean may not have taught step-dancing, although it is possible that he chose not to teach his children in the New World. The range of setting steps taught by the various immigrant and other dancing masters in Gaelic Cape Breton remains undescribed and only by inference can they be placed into the step-dance tradition.

CHAPTER ELEVEN

Piping in the Glendale Area, River Denys Mountain, Melford, Big Marsh, Orangedale, and Valley Mills

PIPING AND TRADITION IN THE GLENDALE AREA

Most of the information that I gathered on pipers and piping in Catholic Glendale and River Denys Mountain and in the Protestant communities in the River Denys watershed represents the earliest research work I did. While it was collected from 1976 to 1978, however, important additions and corroborations were made as late as 1998. Once I'd grasped the probable significance of Gaelic Cape Breton piping, my task became to broaden the fieldwork. The underlying problem was how to present the information most convincingly to Scottish readers, especially to scholars.

During the greater part of my lifetime, people interested in piping were content to discountenance as inferior any piping other than the prescribed Scottish forms. I never heard a good word in Scotland about Scottish tinker pipers, who, it was invariably said, played much too fast, or about Breton, Italian, and Greek pipers. They all lacked grandeur. Only Scotland had evolved a classical form. Certainly no one I knew paused to think that piping might be considered in more ways than the technical. This narrower attitude has now been weakened. There is a growing place for eccentricity of fingering and for step-dance piping in Scotland.[1] In *Traditional Gaelic Bagpiping* a number of the prominent pipers who came to Canada are included. I perceive them as members of the preliterate tradition, which of course they were (including Lieutenant Donald MacCrimmon), but their inclusion somehow also authenticates and gilds those pipers I found who had occupied no position of privilege in Scotland.

That was why, after 1979, having moved from Melford (once known as Gladstone and/or Victoria Line) to Kingsville, which adjoins Glendale to the south, I concentrated on an enquiry into the MacKay pipers of Gairloch, Scotland, and Pictou County, Nova Scotia.[2] I also read the available official documentation dealing with Banastre Tarleton's British Legion regiment, in which Donald MacCrimmon fought throughout the American Revolutionary War, as well as the Nova Scotia and New Brunswick Loyalist papers and records.[3]

Concerning my earlier fieldwork in the Glendale area, my informants were James MacKay (1913–92), Kingsville; Patrick MacEachern (Pàdruig Aonghuis Sìne, b. 1917) and his mother, Bella (4 January 1882–December 1981), both of Glendale; Allan Dan MacInnis (c. 1887–1980) and his nephew Dan Fortune (1906–2001); Glendale, John (b. 1914) and Neil Williams (1918–97) and Albert "Bornish" MacDonald (also known locally as Albert Johnnie Angus, b. 1919), all of Melford; and Margaret (Blue) MacLean (1902–79), Orangedale and Melford. I have not always tried to obtain precise dates for the pipers and others discussed. Sometimes such information wasn't available, but generally speaking I was painting a broad cultural picture of an older time of which I was vouchsafed the sort of unusual glimpse one normally sees and savours only in childhood, when everything is large and impressive.

When I lived in Melford, I lived next to Margaret and Edna MacLean, all of us between the Williamses' and Albert MacDonald's farms. The Mac-Donald farm had belonged to a MacLennan and had been the sometime home of Red Gordon MacQuarrie, an ear piper and fiddler and member of the Cape Breton Highlander's pipe band during the Second World War.[4] I was given warm glimpses of old Melford by Neil and Johnnie Williams and Albert MacDonald. They described where the old homes and schoolhouse had stood, where the dusty old road had wended its summer way, where the ice had been stored between its sawdust layers in the shade from the sun, who brought the mail, who visited to sing and hear songs sung. The Williamses' father, Angus Williams (Aonghus Iain, d. 1947 aged sixty-nine), had been firmly rooted in the Gaelic singing tradition, despite his un-Gaelic surname. All kinds of traditionalists showed up, including pipers like Sandy Malcolm MacDonald and Kennie Matheson. Johnnie Williams is still in the habit of singing Gaelic songs into his tape recorder and presenting copies to friends and collectors.[5] In the 1970s the Williamses still kept a horse[6] and made their rows for potatoes with a horse-drawn plough. Johnnie, who is eighty-six, still keeps a few sheep (nine of which he sheared on 14 June 1998 but that year he used John Shaw's old tractor to make the rows).

Albert "Bornish" MacDonald (Ailbert mac Iain 'ic Aonghuis na beinne) shared with me his memories of Bornish, Inverness County. His patrilineal ancestors emigrated from Bornish in South Uist in the 1830s.[7] They settled between Glendale and Judique, on the "rough mountain" land that has been empty of Gaelic-speaking folk for nearly half a century (electricity was not extended to the mountain community). In 1978 Albert owned an old home-made set of bagpipes but had never been more than a tentative ear player.[8]

John Duncan MacLeod (b. 1929) and his wife Florence, Glendale, also gave me glimpses of the Catholic Glendale Mountain people. The Blues were Presbyterian immigrants from Coll, and from Margaret MacLean I obtained strong impressions of the old agricultural world of Presbyterian River Denys. Her recollections of Allan MacFarlane are included in *Traditional Gaelic Bagpiping* but other local piping information is included here.

Among informants I talked to in 1998 are Alex Matheson and his sister-in-law Mary (MacPherson) Matheson, Billy the fiddler's wife, both living in the old home at Big Marsh. Their memories are considered in detail below.

Donald MacInnis (1838–1924) from Moidart and His Small Pipes

On 2 May 1978 I interviewed and photographed Allan Dan MacInnis (b. 1887) and his nephew Dan Fortune in Allan Dan's home in Glendale.[9] Although Allan Dan was ninety-one and blind, he was still active and had a good memory and a thirst for images of Moidart, where his father, Donald, had been born in 1838.[10] According to Allan Dan, Donald MacInnis had been baptised in Castle Tioram, the last Clanranald holding in the Highlands after Ranald George had rid the family of the estate, and had been brought by his father, John, to Cape Breton in 1844 in a wooden ship sailing from Tobermory. He said also that John, whom he did not remember, is buried at West Bay Road and that Donald MacInnis and his wife are buried in Glendale.[11] Allan Dan said nothing of his father's Gaelic song-making ability[12] but knew him as a piper.

Donald MacInnis, according to Allan Dan, learned to play the pipes by ear in Cape Breton from an immigrant Scots piper Black Donald MacDonald (Dòmhnul Dubh MacDhòmhnuill), who lived with his brother Angus Ewan MacDonald (Aonghus Eoghain) on the mountain west of Glendale.[13] Black Donald also taught two MacEacherns who lived "on the other side of Big Jim's in Glendale" to play the pipes (see below). Allan Dan went on to describe the MacEacherns as good pipers and good for step-dancing. Black Donald returned to Scotland, date unknown.[14]

When I spoke to Allan Dan MacInnis again on 5 May 1978, he said that Black Donald was retained as a piper by Queen Victoria.[15] Offering a little more detail, he said that Black Donald had a brother Duncan (Donnchadh) who lived on River Denys Mountain and that it was from this place that Black Donald had returned to Scotland. Allan Dan elaborated further saying that Duncan had two sons, Angus Duncan (Aonghus Dhonnchaidh) and Donald Duncan (Dòmhnul Dhonnchaidh), and two daughters. Angus was "lame" but was a "great horse man." Allan Dan said that Lame Angus settled in Maple Brook to the east of Glendale and drove the mail. He married when he was about sixty and died an old man in his eighties. Allan Dan was at his wake.[16]

So local lore has it that there were three immigrant MacDonald brothers, the piper Black Donald, Angus Ewan, and Duncan, but so far I have been unable to confirm that any of them settled in Inverness County. Several Angus MacDonalds are given as settlers at "River Dennis Mountain" in MacDougall's *History*, but there is no way to distinguish them. James MacKay's genealogies, which contain Maple Brook family information, are equally unrewarding and the government censuses yield nothing illuminating.

However, Patrick MacEachern immediately knew of Lame Angus, whom he confidently styled Aonghus Dhonnchaidh 'ic Aonghuis Bhàin (Angus, son of Duncan, son of Fair Angus). He said that Lame Angus was a MacDonald and had lived (first) on an old, long-grown-in road up Glendale Mountain that led westward from near the farm of Dan Hughie MacInnis in Glendale over to Centennial near the St Lawrence shore several miles away. According to Patrick, Lame Angus died in the winter of 1935, a very hard one (he was probably born in the 1850s). He drove the mail, which he picked the at the Boyds' change house in Glendale and then transported over to Mabou and Glencoe; this was before the railway went through West Bay Road from Sydney to Port Hawkesbury in the 1880s.[17] Patrick remembered seeing Lame Angus when he was living in Maple Brook but never him driving the mail.[18]

The subject of Donald MacInnis's piping is enhanced, and complicated, by the presence of an old and incomplete three-drone set of bagpipes that was in Dan Fortune's possession in 1978. Dan called the set "parlour pipes" or "small pipes." He had been given them by Allan Dan, who had played the bagpipes and the chanter himself but was a better fiddler. Dan Fortune, at that time (1978) a beginning piper, said that the set (presumably as he showed it to me) was bought for five dollars by his father, Angus Fortune (1865–1918), around 1897 from someone in Red Island, Cape Breton, and given to Donald MacInnis, his father-in-law or father-in-law to be. However, Donald MacInnis is known to have piped long before getting this set. Allan Dan MacInnis and Dan Fortune said that he piped at Militia Point at Malagawatch Harbour on Bras d'Or Lake at the time of the Fenian scare in 1866 and at the occasion of the first mass said in the Glendale church in 1877.

Dan Fortune recollected returning in the summertime to Glendale from Marble Mountain (where his father worked) or haymaking, and hearing his grandfather Donald MacInnis playing the pipes.[19] My typed notes indicate that Black Donald helped Donald with his piping after Donald got the Red Island set, but that is unconfirmable now. Allan Dan told me that his father had piped for step-dancing, "Scotch Fours, Jigs, [and] Reels" and mentioned the reel tune "Lord MacDonald"; he said nothing of the Square Set or Lancers.

Dan Fortune's bagpipes lacked a chanter, and the bass drone was not a match for the two tenors that were plainly turned without ornamentation. The blow-pipe and the two lower sections (stock excluded) of the bass drone were of a lighter wood than the rest of the instrument. One part of the bass drone was stained a darker colour, as visibly evident from wear on the tuning slide. The chanter stock was smaller than that of a modern full set of bagpipes. The big drone stock aperture was too large for the drone. When the set was sent to Scotland for an assessment of its maker and origin, it was returned unassessed, no interest having been taken.

Allan Dan told me that he had made his own chanters of *drumanach*, which he knew in English as elder. When I remarked that I had never seen a home-made chanter, he said they lasted a long time if taken care of.[20] He also recollected his mother's distaste for the odour of burning *smior* (pith) as he drove red-hot metal lengthwise through a piece of drumanach. Since conical boring is not feasible using drumanach, Allan Dan was referring to practice chanters or possibly cylindrical-bore chanters for bagpipes (of which I have found no record in Cape Breton). He added that he made his own reeds, using ash wood for pipe reeds and oats for the practice chanter. My original underlying wish to find out whether any local people had made pipe chanters went neglected.[21] The subject of drone reeds never came up but it is not a large step from boring elder for a chanter to boring a reed and fashioning the appropriate tongue, if cane were not readily available.

Albert MacDonald's bagpipes were home-made in Cape Breton, and MacDonald associated them with a man called "Pheadar Iain 'ic Eachuinn" (Albert invariably used the aspirated form of the first name). Pheadar Iain is discussed in the Judique section below). Originally a three-drone set, these pipes had only two matching tenors when I saw them on 8 May 1978. These were made of light-coloured wood, and horn was used on one drone. There were three stocks, the worse for splitting, and Albert knew there to have been a bass drone. When he played them, Albert borrowed a chanter from Kennie Matheson. Matheson claimed that the chanter had been played at Culloden in 1746. Red Gordon MacQuarrie played this old set and reported it difficult to tune. Sometime after 1978 Albert MacDonald sold the old pipes to Floyd (Hector Hughie) MacDonald, Creignish, Nova Scotia.[22]

Piping in the Gilleasbuig Bàn MacEachern Family

While Allan Dan MacInnis said that the mysterious Scottish piper Black Donald MacDonald had taught two MacEacherns who had lived near Big Jim's place,[23] the local genealogist James MacKay, Kingsville, did not tell me anything about this, and he was unfailingly generous with his knowledge. He did, however, identify, independently and unprompted, three

MacEachern pipers who had lived on adjacent farms on MacEachern Road, which lies westward across the valley of the River Inhabitants at the eastern slope of the Creignish Hills. These were Sarah (Mór nighean Dhòmhnuill 'ic Ghilleasbuig Bhàin) and her brother Angus (Aonghus mac Dhòmhnuill 'ic Ghilleasbuig Bhàin) and their first cousin Hugh (Eoghann mac Aonghuis 'ic Ghilleasbuig Bhàin).[24] None married, and Angus and Hugh died early in the twentieth century, just far enough back for confirmation of Allan Dan's opinion of them as good step-dance pipers to be unconfirmable.

I was unable to unearth any memories, critical or otherwise, of the piping of Angus and Hugh and discovered little about Sarah's, but other information has come down. Jimmy MacKay remembered that "Mór" (Sarah) did not own a set of pipes but used to borrow a set from the River Denys Mountain piper Sandy Malcolm MacDonald (1860–1947), about whose piping nothing appears to have survived. Otherwise she played a chanter. What Jimmy MacKay did not say of her music suggests that she was not very accomplished.[25] Angus was known as "Dory" Angus MacEachern. The story that Patrick MacEachern told of him did not involve piping but rather his survival for eight days and eight nights in a dory off Louisburg, presumably fog-bound, back in the days when schools of one-man dories were used in the cod fishery. Patrick, who remembered seeing Angus in 1923 on one of his infrequent visits home, said that he spent a lot of time at sea and in fishermen's haunts when ashore. Patrick knew of Hugh MacEachern as Hughie "the black boy"; he was aware that he had played the pipes but had never met him.[26] Nobody mentioned Angus's having had a set of bagpipes, but Jimmy MacKay said that Angus's cousin Hugh (Eoghann mac Aonghuis 'ic Ghilleasbuig Bhàin) may have had a home-made set.[27]

For all this dubious evidence, there was a broad vein of music in the MacEacherns. Hughie "the black boy" had a brother Duncan MacEachern whose children included the fiddler-composer Dan Hughie MacEachern (1913–96), Queensville; the fiddler John Willie (1901–70), Queensville; and the fiddler Alex Joe (1907–76), Boston and New York. Two of Dan Hughie's books of fiddle compositions were published during his lifetime, and he was the finest traditional exponent of "Tulloch Gorm" in the county that I have ever heard.[28]

Patrick MacEachern (b. 1917), whose memory is now one of the most remarkable in Glendale, has no knowledge of Black Donald MacDonald, the immigrant Scottish piper. That is not, however, to deny the latter's existence. Although unlikely, it is not inconceivable that this Black Donald MacDonald was the same Donald S. MacDonald from River Denys who taught Hector Campbell of Hillsdale to play the pipes.[29] Neither should J.L. MacDougall's and Jimmy MacKay's genealogies be taken as all-inclusive, since there are gaps in both. Neither includes the MacCuish family or the Buchanan man mentioned to me by Neil and Johnnie Williams. Sometimes

gaps occurred for want of willing informants, sometimes because the writers were sensitive to neighbours' possible embarrassments, and sometimes
simply because there was a Catholic-Protestant divide that was seen as
unwise to cross.

With the exception of Donald MacInnis and his small pipes, piping memories in Glendale are strays of an indeterminate standard. Whether or not this
is because of an early decline of the Scotch Four I have not discovered.
Jimmy MacKay remembered seeing the dance done to fiddling at a local
wedding.[30] An important event remembered by a number of people was a
picnic held in the 1930s involving outside pipers, not local people. Johnnie
Williams dated it to 1930, the year that Father Angus MacNeil began his
work in the parish. Johnnie told me that he and his younger brother Neil and
their mother were at the picnic. What stayed in their memories, and in Albert
MacDonald's, was the little pipe band that played on that occasion. It was
made up of Allan MacFarlane (Upper Margaree), Alex the piper MacDonald
("the Indian teacher" from the Margarees), an unidentified Beaton, and a
MacCuish piper "from Pictou," also unidentified.[31] Johnnie speculated that
this MacCuish was a son of Churchill MacCuish and noted that he was a
"cousin" of Finlay MacCuish from Maple Brook. There were three drummers with the band, one of whom was Roddie Gillis from Port Hawkesbury.
Johnnie recollected the MacCuish piper piping for his cousin Finlay's step-
dancing and another member of the pipe band playing for a large group of
step-dancers. Long gone from the Glendale area, the MacCuishes were
Protestants who kept their own cemetery on their own land.

The MacKays' home in Kingsville, within easy buggy distance of the
church, was, and still is, a céilidh house for the area, and while it is associated with the best of the old traditional fiddlers (Dan Rory MacDonald, Dan
Hughie MacEachern, Big Ranald MacLellan, Joe MacLean, and Theresa
MacLellan, as well as Alex Francis and Peter MacKay from the family), it
was also a stopping place for pipers like Black Angus MacDonald, Melrose
Hill, and later the Scots piper Sandy Boyd. Jimmy MacKay had kept an old
home-made chanter from the elder days, made by Angus MacEachern
(Aonghus mac Dhòmhnuil 'ic 'Ill'easbuig). When Allan MacFarlane piped
in the band in 1930, he stayed with a neighbour of the MacKays', D.R.
MacEachern (now deceased).

There is little reason to presume that bagpiping faced any antagonism in
Glendale. It was a mission of Creignish and Judique until 1875, and elsewhere that peripheral status within the Roman Catholic realm may have
permitted traditional tastes to go untouched a little longer than in some fully-
fledged parishes.[32] After 1875 the forces that touched tradition indirectly
were the temperance movement fostered by Bishop John Cameron, which
enjoyed some patchy success, the growing keenness for English education,

and the inroads of the Quadrille in one or other of its forms.[33] The 1930 gathering/picnic that had included the little pipe and drum band probably had only a passing influence.

One interesting summer event in the rural life of the area was what a 1986 issue of the *Cape Breton Mirror* called the "Highland Games."[34] This event was held in Kingsville, which adjoined Glendale to the south, in the early years of this century and seems to have been the only one of its kind. Patrick MacEachern dated the games from some time not long after 1901 up until shortly before 1920. He told me that the event was organized by Simon P. Gillis from Margaree, himself an athlete.[35] Patrick's first choice of word for the occasion was, as might be expected, "picnic," but he said that there were tug-of-war and stone- and hammer-throwing competitions, which suggests that the *Mirror*'s classification of Highland Games was accurate. The site, MacEachern told me, was Alex MacEachern's vacant farm,[36] which included flat valley-bottom land. It is now owned by Alex Dougal MacDonald, having been acquired earlier from Alex MacEachern or an assign by John B. MacLellan.[37]

The newspaper article includes a photograph showing the winner of all the sporting events, Dr Hoodie MacDonald, the wrestler from East Lake Ainslie, beside one of the young fiddlers of the day, Mary (Beaton) MacDonald from Beinn Bhiorach, known in Gaelic as Màiri Alasdair Raonuil and in English as Mary Hughie.

PIPERS AND PIPING ON RIVER DENYS MOUNTAIN

Today the eight miles that MacDougall described "in that space extending from Dennistown to Melford"[38] are empty of people and the only building in use, besides the occasional summer camp, is the Catholic Church of Saint Mary of Scotland, where mass was first said in 1841. Overgrown basements mark the old homes. The maple forest is in places becoming a spruce forest for the purposes of a local pulp and paper company, and a fire tower stands guard. But once, according to several Glendalers and Melford people, and as government cadastral and soil maps show, many families farmed on the poor soil and there was a school. The Aodh MacDonalds arrived from Ormacleit, South Uist, in about 1822. Thirty families settled in 1833, again from South Uist, including Angus MacDonald's, which included John "Bodach" Bhornais, age about ten.[39] MacDougall gives only a cursory listing of the original settlers; he noted that many of them were from South Uist with others from Eigg and other islands in the Hebrides. The MacAskills and MacQuarries on River Denys Mountain were Catholics. (There were two Presbyterian MacAskills on Eigg in 1764–65, and no Catholics; there was only one other Protestant MacAskill, in Canna, in McNeill's "Census of the Small Isles"; and there was one Catholic "McGuary" in "Laig in Eigg papists.")[40]

Albert MacDonald said that from his grandfather Angus MacDonald's (Aonghus na beinne's) home on the Mountain pipers could be heard from three neighbouring farms, from Big Ronald MacDonald's (Raonul Mór's), the MacAskills', and the MacLeods'. Johnnie Joe MacDonald (b. 1920) of River Denys independently told the same story but without the names of the pipers or piping families.[41] Many if not all of the immigrant generation's male representatives are included in MacDougall's *History of Inverness County* but with no descriptions other than their names. Among them are "Ronald MacDonald (Mor)," "Kenneth MacAskill," and "John MacLeod." MacDougall supplied no genealogical information under these headings.[42] In these and other cases of River Denys Mountain pipers, the people left the area early and now there are only a few second-hand memories of them. For all that, there appear to have been more memorable pipers on River Denys Mountain than in Glendale, perhaps because traditional bagpiping was always strong among South Uist people. Most of the Glendale settlers were from Moidart and Arisaig, although four pioneer families were from South Uist.[43]

Big Ronald lived on the other side of the Mountain road from Angus MacDonald, though not directly opposite. He was an immigrant ear piper. His son Donald played the chanter, and his grandsons through Donald, Dannie Donald Big Ranald and John Alex Dannie Big Ronald both played the fiddle; Dannie played the chanter as well and John Alex the bagpipes. They were all ear players on all these instruments. Ronald Mor's people, according to Albert MacDonald, moved away from the original homestead early on, first further eastward towards Melford but still on the mountain, and then to a farm whose semi-wrecked little house stood for decades below the mountain, on the west side of the Trans-Canada Highway roughly between Albert MacDonald's farm and Carmeline's at the Melford crossroads.[44]

Concerning the MacAskills, Albert could not say whether it was Kenneth or Malcolm, or both, who played the pipes. His memories on the subject came only from his father, John Angus (d. c. 1962 aged eighty-nine). The MacAskills left River Denys Mountain early.[45] However, Albert's father remembered visiting them as a young boy (presumably in the late 1870s or early 1880s) and told of their working in the "burnt field" hoeing potatoes. I neglected to speak to old Angus "Bornish" MacDonald in the 1970s about the family, and so any personal memories he may have had of the MacAskills' and the community's pipers and piping have gone to the grave unrecorded.

John MacLeod, according to Albert MacDonald an immigrant piper, settled on River Denys Mountain behind Albert MacDonald's home. MacDougall described the MacLeod land as "on the second concession of lots extending from River Dennis Road."[46] According to Neil Williams (30 July

1980), MacLeod was married to Scots-born Isabel Henderson, sister-in-law of John Williams, Melford. My attention was first drawn to John MacLeod by Albert MacDonald in 1977 and my interest increased after Neil Williams mentioned him independently on 30 July 1980. The MacLeods lived on Big Ronald's side of the Mountain road at a farm Albert MacDonald called "Baile Iain mac Leòid" (John MacLeod's farmstead). Albert, recalling what his father told him, said that there were three pipers in the family, one a woman. The 1861 census of the area shows a John MacLeod as the head of a family of eight, five males and three females, including parents; the 1871 census lists John MacLeod (84) and Euphemia (60), both Catholics and Scots born, and John (24), Angus (22), Malcolm (19), Mary (20), and Margaret (28), all born in Nova Scotia.[47]

At least two other pipers settled on River Denys Mountain, a MacQuarrie and a MacDonald. They settled close to one another near where the fire lookout tower stands today, but the MacQuarries soon moved away to Antigonish County. Representatives of both families also went to greater Boston and kept up their acquaintance there.[48] They were Catholics, and the immigrant MacQuarrie piper was remembered by Albert MacDonald as "Big John" MacQuarrie, grandfather of Angus MacQuarrie (living), then warden of Antigonish County.[49] Patrick MacEachern of Glendale was also aware of Roman Catholic MacQuarries on River Denny Mountain who had gone on to Antigonish early. The MacQuarries, from Eigg, were post-1853 emigrants whose stay on River Denys Mountain was short enough to go unrecorded.[50] McNeill's census (1764/65) shows Donald McGuary as head of a family of six. Piping has continued in this family to the present, and that tradition and some family history are dealt with in *Traditional Gaelic Bagpiping* and elsewhere.

The neighbouring family of MacDonalds, established by the immigrant Malcolm MacDonald (b. in Eigg c. 1818),[51] included the piper Sandy Malcolm MacDonald (1860–1947), whose brother, the Reverend Duncan MacDonald (1848–1930), according to Neil Williams, also piped. Old Sandy Malcolm, according to Albert MacDonald, "was a bit of a piper."[52] The set of bagpipes that he had and which Sarah MacEachern (Mór) borrowed appear to have been taken to Boston by Sandy's daughter Margaret (Neil Williams, 28 March 1977). I do not know their present whereabouts. I also have a stray note, perhaps taken down from Albert MacDonald, that Sandy Malcolm's old pipes were a two-drone set.

THE CATHOLIC MACMILLANS IN MELFORD
AND THE PROTESTANT MATHESONS AT BIG MARSH

According to Albert MacDonald, a family of three MacMillan brothers lived in Melford, all Gaelic speakers and one of whom was a piper. Albert remembered his father calling them Ruairidh "Gobha" (Rory the smith), Angus "Mac an t-seann duine" (Angus the old man's son), and "Peadar mac 'Ill' Mhaol" (Peter MacMillan). Albert did not know which brother had played the pipes but was sure he would have been an ear player. A brief genealogical sketch of the family is in *Genealogical History of Glendale* (p. 80). The MacMillans were Catholics from South Uist. Mary MacMillan (c. 1843–1947), a spinster woman Albert MacDonald did not like, was asked during an interview before her admittance to a home if she'd been married, to which she replied, "That's ahead of me yet" (Albert MacDonald, c. 25 March 1977).

Donald MacMillan (c. 1845–1915), son of immigrant Angus MacMillan, was styled Dòmhnull Fhionnghaill (Donald Fionngal) after his mother, which suggests that his father died young. He was married to Mary Mac-Donald, daughter of Angus na Beinne MacDonald and thus Albert Mac-Donald's aunt. Mary died in her eighties, during the Second World War. According to Catherine Effie (MacMillan) White, her father, Donald Fionn-gal, was a good step-dancer.[53] Catherine Effie knew nothing of piping in the MacMillan family and told me that the only piping she heard from her home in Upper River Denys was Kenny Matheson's. She also knew about her grandmother Fionngal but not about Fionngal's husband Angus MacMillan, not even his name. But an interest in Gaelic traditional music persisted; two of Catherine Effie's brothers played the violin – John, who died in Ontario *circa* 1955, and John Donald, a left-handed fiddler and Second World War veteran who was living in the Camphill Hospital in Halifax in 1980.

The best-remembered piper in the Protestant Matheson family was Kenneth Matheson (Coinneach Dhannaidh), who died in 1962 aged eighty-two. He was an ear player. Johnnie and Neil Williams remembered his visits to their father Angus Williams's home in Melford and his playing Malcolm Sandy MacDonald's bagpipes, which they called the "alumium" pipes. Neil Williams told me (23 November 1976) that Kenneth Matheson often used to tune Albert MacDonald's pipes. Kennie also played the fiddle and had two in the house, but he preferred the bagpipes and had a lot of tunes. Neil Williams described him as a tall, good-looking man who never played the pipes at picnics, preferring to play at céilidhs. Neil also said that to begin with Matheson borrowed Malcolm Sandy's bagpipes but that later he got his own "big brown set" "on the lake [Ainslie]." He had a brother who played, but not as well as he did. Kennie Matheson was a Gaelic speaker, as are his children, although the Williamses said that he didn't practise the language. The big brown set had "an awful noise to them," according to Neil Williams.[54]

The immigrant Matheson was Dougal (Dùghal, c. 1788–1865), who was born in Lochalsh, Scotland, and emigrated in 1821.[55] His wife was

Catherine MacIntosh (d. 1886 aged eighty-four) from Applecross, who first
came to Prince Edward Island. In Cape Breton the couple moved from Malagawatch to Big Marsh in the River Denys watershed. Alex Matheson (b.
1909) knew nothing about music in either family, and sad to say there appear
to be no linkages with MacCrimmon (Glenelg), MacRae, or MacKenzie piping (Kintail) in the old country.[56] However, Dougal's son Daniel was a piper.
He died in 1925 at the age of ninety and is clearly remembered by his grandson Alex. Daniel held the bag under his right shoulder and played with his
right hand upper on the chanter. He began with a home-made chanter, but
then he (or possibly his brother Kenneth) bought a two-drone set somewhere
in the United States. Kenneth, a blacksmith, was also a piper; he later took
the pipes to the United States and they were never brought back to Cape Breton. Alex never saw his grandfather's brother or the two-drone set. After that
set had gone, Daniel borrowed bagpipes. Alex vividly remembered his having to put his head between the drones of sets tied in for left-shoulder pipers
so that the bass drone on the outside did not make the set completely
unwieldy.[57]

The ease and spontaneousness with which Alex Matheson conjured up
this odd picture of his grandfather playing the pipes caught me by surprise.
Later it occurred to me that we should reconsider the old opinion that two-
drone pipes were inferior to the "great" Highland bagpipes. The argument
that two-drone bagpipes allowed the chanter to be heard more clearly or that
they were simply easier to blow/play is a familiar one (and indeed two
drones make less volume), but even more significant is the fact that an
instrument with two tenor drones might have been played as easily and as
well by either right- or left-shoulder pipers. Modern band bagpiping all but
demands left-shoulder pipers only,[58] but older traditional bagpiping was in
essence a social phenomenon and thus more flexible. For most people, the
bagpipes were a céilidh instrument, and if the two drones and the blow-pipe
were tied in appropriately, both left- and right-shoulder pipers could be
accommodated.[59] So, when the Edinburgh competition organizers decreed in
1821 that all competing pipers should play a three-drone (including a bass
drone) bagpipe – good intentions and the natural desire for standardization
aside – the effect was that two-drone piping was discouraged. Furthermore,
this "improvement" may have helped drive a deeper wedge between competition and folk. Submerged in the change have been fingering and musical
expression.

Alex Matheson told me that there never were Highland Games in the Big
Marsh and River Denys area of Cape Breton. At the time I interviewed him,
no one wore tartan, although he told me almost eagerly that the earlier generations must have.[60] He was strongly of the opinion that most of the Matheson family came out to the New World knowing step-dancing and well
steeped in traditional Scotch music. Alex and his sister-in-law (and distant

cousin) Mary (MacPherson) Matheson are very famliar with family and local history and well informed on local Catholic family and Scotch history as well.

I asked Alex if there had been any clerical discouragement in the Big Marsh–River Denys area and he said no, implying a moment later that the minister kept out of the debate over music and dancing. This observation is almost identical to Neil Dan MacInnis's remarks to me around 1978 about music and dance in his Glenville home; in the early years of this century, any visiting minister would discreetly leave when the music was to begin. Alex emphasized, too, that traditional dancing had its own teachers in the Cape Breton Gàidhealtachd (he did not specify anyone, let alone the MacLean immigrant dancing master in the Scotsville area). When I raised the subject of the Disruption and post-Disruption earnestness, I evoked no reply.

Alex Matheson mentioned that Daniel piped for dances and had included the Scotch Four and the Eight-Hand Reel, even though he didn't step-dance himself.[61] Alex said that he (Alex) used to dance a few steps, but since he also told me that he had never seen an Eight-Hand Reel danced, I couldn't be sure that he was distinguishing reliably between the Eight-Hand Reel and the Square Set, both of which feature similar travelling movements for four couples. When I began to make a distinction between slow, classical piping and dance-music piping, Alex said that his grandfather Daniel was very interested in what I had called "ceòl mór" and had played it, as he did his dance music, by ear.[62]

Daniel Matheson's wife was a Margaret MacLennan from River Denys; the rest of her family went out west. Alex Matheson did not know if there was traditional music in the family, but there were three pipers among Daniel Matheson's six sons and one daughter, the Kenneth mentioned above and widely remembered, Dougal, and John D. The last two went to Utah, Dougal to Salt Lake City in 1913.

Kennie Matheson stands out in local memory as the most prominent Matheson piper largely because the rest had either died or gone away. The Williamses were obviously right in saying that he made use of Sandy Malcolm MacDonald's bagpipes until he got his own set, and for a Melford resident, their provenance of "on the lake" is near enough to South West Margaree to pass a general examination.[63] Alex Matheson told me (2 July 1998) that the old three-drone set his father bought eventually he got from Alex MacDonald, "the Indian teacher" in Whycocomagh, for twenty-five dollars. The set had a David Glen chanter which Alex said was so worn that Kennie got a replacement from Sandy Malcolm, also a David Glen. This set, with its two chanters, both extensively reinforced with hempen ringings, remains in the family. The bass drone has been repaired but the set is repairable.

PIPERS AND PIPING IN PROTESTANT RIVER DENYS, ORANGEDALE AND VALLEY MILLS

Although Protestant clerical attitudes in Inverness county show signs of flexibility to music and dance, if not to alcohol consumption, there were instances of condemnation. James MacKay, Kingsville, told me that at a dance in Port Hastings years ago a Presbyterian MacLean man step-danced to a piper and the local minister intervened. The minister remonstrated with the man about the evils of dancing, and MacLean replied: "Nuair a chluinneas mi pìob chlanna na Gàidheal theid mi dhannsa; tha mi coma co chì mi, agus rud eile dheth; olaidh mi dram is tha mi coma co a chì deifir ann." (When I hear the pipe of the Gael I'm going to dance; I don't care who sees me and anything else about it; I'll drink a dram and I don't care who cares.)

Not all Protestant step-dancers, or pipers and fiddlers, were as assertive, but in all Inverness County Protestant communities, with the exception of North East Margaree, traditional music and dance were popular, generally outwith the presence and knowledge of many of the stricter clergy. Most of the information I have from River Denys and Orangedale was given me by Margaret A. (Blue) MacLean when she was living in Melford in 1977. Her interviews contain more significant material about step-dancing than piping in those Presbyterian communities, but she also talked about pipers known and remembered.

Perhaps the most memorable of them was Angus Hector MacLean (Aonghus Eachuinn), who lived near Munroe Bridge on the south side of Denys Basin. He is buried at Malagawatch and all of his family, nine boys and three girls, were dead in 1977. Unfortunately, apart from his genealogy, nothing of his piping was told me either by Margaret MacLean or by the piper's great-grandson, Reverend Langley MacLean (telephone interview, 16 March 1977). Of his large family, only John Eddie played the pipes, but Dan and Jimmie step-danced.[64] A little more is known about the Presbyterian piper Hector Lachlan MacLean (Heckie Nìll Dhòmhnuill), who died around 1950. Heckie piped and fiddled for step-dancing at céilidhs in people's homes, and he played in the old schoolhouses in the Orangedale (Seal's Cove) and Valley Mills area. Hector MacLean owned a modern brown set of bagpipes that he had bought for himself, although not in Scotland. They have a David Glen chanter. He made his own reeds. MacLean also played the fiddle.

There was some clerical disapproval of music and dance in River Denys, but nonetheless both were popular and firmly in the Gaelic tradition, with the Scotch Four and Eight-Hand Reel enjoying widespread popularity in the nineteenth century. Angus Hector MacLean, the author of *God and the Devil at Seal Cove,* noted that dancing and occasional drinking "didn't improve [his family's] status as church-people."[65] He added that a number of teenagers were struck off church rolls for attending a dance.[66] For all that, piping and step-dancing were the highlight of many a céilidh according to Margaret MacLean.

KENNIE "BOLLIKEN" MACQUARRIE, QUEENSVILLE OR LEXINGTON

Jimmie MacKay, Kingsville, was the first to tell me about the old piper Kennie Bolliken (MacQuarrie), religion unspecified.[67] The name "Bolliken" is probably from the Gaelic *ballachan*, (little fellow). He was an illiterate Gaelic-speaking piper of no piping sophistication anyone recognized at that late date (late nineteenth century), rather the opposite, for he had had no contact with anything other than day-to-day Gaelic life. That made him interesting as a traditional piper. There is no known photograph of him and not enough name detail to point with certainty to any record (birth, death, or census). Bolliken, however, in those early days of my curiosity in the mid-1970s, was one of only a few late nineteenth-century Gaelic bagpipers I was aware of and that made him the more important. Faint hope quickly became forlorn when Bella MacEachern, Glendale, told me that she knew nothing about him or his music. She had been working in Boston around the turn of the century, and as it turns out, Bolliken died in 1902 aged about forty-five. Ann Ferguson, a retired schoolteacher living in Port Hawkesbury who has compiled genealogical data for an area near "Clearing Bholliken" in the Queensville-Lexington area, also did not know who he was.

Since then the only notice of Kenny Bolliken MacQuarrie to turn up is in the Sydney *Daily Record* of 18 August 1902. On page 5, there is a notice with this heading: "Scotch Piper Killed at West Bay. Kenneth McQuarrie, of Inverness, run over by engine Saturday night. Asleep on the rail." Kenneth MacQuarrie was described as "an old piper, better known in Inverness as 'Old Bolligan.'" The shunter had left the River Denys ballast pit and had run over the piper on its way to Point Tupper, beheading him. "The unfortunate man was about 45 years of age, and belonged to Port Hastings. He was well known in that part of the country, and occasionally visited Sydney."[68] That roughly confirmed what I had heard locally, although the place of the accident would have been more correctly given as West Bay Road, an important station on the Sydney line; many local farmers delivered pit props there for the mines in industrial Cape Breton. West Bay is not on the railway line. The newspaper notice only adds a date of death; there was no family information. The line had not been open for more than a few years in 1902.

Bolliken had the reputation of being a boozing ne'er-do-well who lived in a shanty at "Clearing Bholliken" at the south side of Queensville and who didn't really seem worth considering as a piper. Then, on 16 August 1978, visiting Edna and Margaret MacLean, neighbours in Melford, I was asked to witness the will of an old friend of theirs, Colin MacLean from Mull, near Orangedale. He was nearing ninety. Colin MacLean's memories went back to the mid-1890s quite comfortably; his father had died in 1910 and his grandfather in 1854. In fact, his father had been born in Scotland and had emigrated in 1843. This meant that Colin MacLean and Allan Dan MacInnis of Glendale were the two Nova Scotia Gaels closest to the old country that I met in all my questings. To MacLean's surprise I brought up the subject of Kennie Bolliken, and to mine he remembered the old piper. Kennie Bolliken had been part of a large intimate skein of Gaelicness that Colin MacLean had grown up with, before cars, before electricity, in self-sufficient farming times that were gradually being touched by the railway and the Boston states and the harvest excursions out west.

As it happened, Bolliken was the first piper Colin MacLean had heard as a boy. He heard him playing in the 1890s outside the MacMasters' place in Orangedale (where Sadie MacDonald lived in 1978, next to the Orangedale railway station, roughly to the south), and he vividly remembered that Bolliken had a pint bottle tied around his neck to collect change for a drink. Colin and the boys he was with saw Bolliken as an old man and naturally thought he was a great piper. MacLean went on to tell me a story that for him summed up Kenny Bolliken. Once, when the piper was really drunk, someone plunged a knife into the bag of his pipes, but Bolliken was too detached from reality to get angry. Bolliken's was a life of dissipation and the stories about him tend to be humorous.

That and similar stories are all that remain of Kennie Bolliken to date. There is nothing about his fingering or his repertoire, how he learned, what sort of pipes he played, if he piped for Scotch Fours or step-dancing. Colin MacLean had nothing to say on any of those topics. I should not have bothered to write about him except that I wanted to show that a single-minded curiosity can work the wrong way. I missed the much more important opportunity to learn other things from Bella MacEachern. Bella, you see, was one of the few old Gaels left who had been in Boston before the Great War, a time when there were still hundreds of Cape Breton Gaels living and working there who had been in the first wave of migrants to the Boston states.

I did not realize until many years later that the Boston clubs had been an important influence in the introduction of the relatively modern Quadrilles and Lancers to rural Gaelic Nova Scotia from about 1890. When I recognized their significance, it was too late to find firsthand memories. Nowadays there are only memories of memories of pre–First World War Boston, making it more difficult to document an important aspect of modern Gaelic dance culture.

CHAPTER TWELVE

Pipers, Piping, and Cultural Glimpses of West Lake Ainslie

West Lake Ainslie Gaelic-speaking society in the nineteenth century, although smaller numerically,[1] compares better with South West Margaree's and Mabou's than with Glendale's inasmuch as it contained a strong, low-level, British-army-officer presence (one possibly *soi-disant*) from the earliest days of Highland immigration. Those military families along with others of some distinction in the nineteenth century appear, typically, to have endorsed Gaelic folk culture, joining in and taking it quite for granted.

There were several bagpipers in West Lake, one of whom, the immigrant Allan MacCormack from Ormacleit in South Uist via Prince Edward Island, has been mentioned elsewhere.[2] Others, to be dealt with here, are Alexander Dubh MacDonald, an immigrant from Moidart, and, within living memory, the brothers Frederick and Angus D.F. MacDonald. A cultural picture of West Lake Ainslie would include the necessary glimpses of traditional fiddlers and step-dancers and there is the valuable analogue of nearby Upper and South West Margaree.

As in the case of the more populous South West Margaree,[3] any proposition that older Gaelic traditions had their normal vigour in West Lake Ainslie, perhaps even with an edge over intruding modern forms, should take into account that West Lake Ainslie was, throughout the immigrant years and long beyond, a mission. It had a physical church building from the 1830s but with an itinerating priest resident elsewhere.[4] From 1825 until the late 1860s or early 1870s, West Lake Ainslie was a mission of Broad Cove Chapel. Then it became a mission of the fiddle-confiscating priest in Mabou, Father Kenneth J. MacDonald (parish priest at Mabou, 1868–94), who built the present church at West Lake and in whose name a Lands and Forests land-grant map shows a sizeable acreage at Lake Ainslie Chapel.[5] According to a local history, from 1893 until 1896 there were three resident priests at West Lake: Father Francis MacRae, 1893; Father Charles MacDonald, 1894–95; and Dr Alexander Chisholm, 1895–96. From 1896 West Lake parishioners had the ministrations of parish priests from Brook Village, start-ing with Dr Chisholm, who had moved there in August.[6]

Besides land papers and census, death, and church records, as well as J.L. MacDougall's *History of Inverness County* and Father A.D. MacDon-ald's *Mabou Pioneers*, I had access to one unpublished and almost unknown document written by a native. This was Frederick MacDonald's "Manuscript-book" (begun in September 1912). This almost entirely hand-written work has genealogical value, and also, like Squire John MacKay's "Reminiscences of a Long Life [at New Glasgow, Pictou County]" (writ-ten in 1868 and later) and Dr Hugh N. MacDonald's *Macdonald and Mackinnon Families* [at East Lake Ainslie] (1937), it has a rustic, quasi-British, almost middle-class aura that is telling. It is the work of a young man and is described by him (or someone else who might have typed on its first loose page) as "composed of marriages. deaths. at West lake Ainslie. & other places. And other events. by Fred Mac Donald. Esq. of West Lake Ainslie." Until June 1998 the book and various other records were kept in the family in southwest Scotland. I have the material on loan from Julia Little, Dumfries, Scotland.

The "Manuscript-book" touches lightly on domestic affairs at West Lake, but MacDonald (1891–1973) deals with folk culture only selectively and shallowly and in a few sentences.[7] He completely ignores, for example, his younger brother Angus's and others' bagpiping and only notes that he him-self was transferred within the Nova Scotia Highland Brigade from the 85th Nova Scotia Highlanders (which he had joined) "to the 219.th pipe band in September [1916]" before going overseas.[8] He does not mention Angus MacDougall, the "superior dancer" described by J.L. MacDougall,[9] and says nothing of the violin or the dances that country people danced to lighten their hearts and see folk properly married.

West Lake Ainslie was, as it remains in late 2001, a rural community, albeit in dramatic decline agriculturally and in population from a century ago. Frederick MacDonald gave its population in 1901 as 391 and in 1911 as 296 (his figures for the same years for East Lake Ainslie were 621 and 517).[10] He also gave the number of families as thirty in 1871, when he said the new church was built.[11] MacDonald was bilingual but his "Manuscript-book" is mostly in English. He uses many Gaelic *sloinnidhean* (Gaelic nam-ings) for clearer identification purposes (at times with differing spellings of the same names). Generally, the last named of the sloinneadh is that of the immigrant and Gaelic appears to be used in deference to well-known High-land characters who had sailed the ocean (D.D. MacFarlane's diaries stop at the same point). A few paragraphs in Gaelic also appear on part of a sepa-rate sheet and in a hand-printed form. These few lines deal with the family connection with the Clanranald family in "Ormaclait," known as the Aodhs (immigrants to River Denys Mountain). MacDonald's work deals in large part with his own family's and the neighbourhood's genealogies, giving many vital statistics, but there is as well (*inter alia*) "A Brief Sketch of Lake Ainslie" (undated, pages 40–7). Here he wrote about "piling frolics," the telling of *sgeulachdan* (tales), and the singing of Gaelic songs. He paints a picture of a roadless, bridgeless, forested land, of the fertile *coille dhubh* (burnt land), the *corran* (sickle), and the *clach bhratheanadh* (hand stone quern or grain grinder), the latter among the simple tools available to the sturdy pioneers in those early days. He even remarks that many of the Brahan Seer's forecasts had come true for West Lake Ainslie.[12] Indeed, he wrote, there now was

Drochaid air gach allta;
Muillean air gach abhainn
Agus tigh geal air gach cnoc.

A bridge on every stream;
A mill on every river
And a white house on every knoll.[13]

For whatever reason, MacDonald did not indulge a fancy and describe a few West Lake céilidhs, naming a few fiddlers, pipers, and dancers. He does, however, give the names of his earliest schoolteachers, several weeks' worth of data about his shopping habits, and his own record of the passing of Haley's Comet (which he first saw at West Lake Ainslie, 22 May 1910) and of Malcolm H. Gillis (Calum Eoghainn), the South West Margaree published bard (d. 23 September 1929), who had courted Frederick D.F.'s mother Mary.

In his work MacDonald naturally emphasizes his pride in the two prominent elements of his family, its double connection to the Tulloch MacDonalds (seventeenth-century descendants of the chiefly Keppoch family). The separate half sheet in his manuscript explores the family's linkage through his mother's mother "do Dhòmhnullaich Chlann Raonuill. 'Teaghlach mhic 'ic Ailein.' an ormaclait, Uista chinn-a-deas" (to the MacDonalds of Clan Ranald. Family of Mac 'ic Ailein[14] in Ormacleit, South Uist). In his father's line, MacDonald presents only two extended lineages, without elaboration. One gives his father's sloinneadh as "Domhul Fhearchair 'ic Dhomhuil 'ic Ruaridh" (Donald, son of Farquhar, son of Donald, son of Roderick); the other, "as told by my father," is "Domhul Fhearchair 'ic Dhomhuil 'ic Ruaridh, 'ic Aonghais 'ic Alasdair" (Donald, son of Farquhar, son of Donald, son of Roderick, son of Angus, son of Alexander).[15] On his mother's Tulloch side, he has much more detail, often proudly repeated.

West Lake was only a small farming community, but its settlers enthusiastically cleared the forest for the plough despite problems for many in obtaining final security of title.[16] The community contained a noticeable number of people who had some education and training, as well as others who had relatively large landholdings; all of these can only be thought of as belonging to the old traditional Gaelic middle class and what Stewart of Garth called the old tenantry, implying honourableness. Prominent among them is Frederick MacDonald's ancestor "Captain" Angus Tulloch Mac-Donald (1790–1843), from Tulloch on the north bank of the River Spean in Lochaber. He was the son of another "Captain" Angus Tulloch MacDonald (b. 1759). Reverend Alexander D. MacDonald in the *Mabou Pioneers* allots the son the rank of ensign in the 6th West Indies Regiment;[17] Angus Tulloch had a land grant of five hundred acres at West Lake Ainslie, for which he had applied in 1818.[18]

Of considerable cultural importance where this class of immigrant is concerned is Captain Angus Tulloch's sister Mary Tulloch (b. 1795). She married immigrant John Beaton (son of Finlay Beaton, b. Achluachrach in 1766), who had been born at Glen Spean, Lochaber, in 1794.[19] Achluachrach is about three kilometres west of Tulloch on the north bank of the Spean.[20] Around 1975 one of the last great old Gaelic-speaking traditional Cape Breton fiddlers and step-dancers, Mary (Beaton) MacDonald[21] (born and raised at MacKinnon's Brook north of Mabou Coal Mines), told me how she had learned her step-dancing and strongly implicated Mary "Tulloch" MacDonald in the transmission of Gaelic traditional step-dancing.[22]

Mary first learned her steps at home from her mother, Peggy (MacIsaac) Beaton, but also from their neighbour Alexander J. Beaton, who regularly visited her home to teach Mary and her old sister Jessie the fiddle and afterwards to teach their mother extra step-dance steps. Old Alex, born in 1837 at MacKinnon's Brook, was a son of Mary Tulloch (MacDonald) Beaton.[23]

The other captain, Angus MacLellan, emigrated to Antigonish and moved as a married man with a family to West Lake Ainslie. There he settled near what J.L. MacDougall called the "Tulloch estate."[24] MacDougall noted some genealogy and that "they could read and write some, and talk plenty English of a special brand."[25] The British army lists that I read show no officer Angus MacLellan. He may have been a ship's captain or have held a foreign commission.

Then, still seemingly from the better-off segment, there was Angus Bàn MacDougall, a Moidart man who emigrated to Nova Scotia, settling first in Antigonish before resettling at West Lake Ainslie. By his first wife he had six sons and three daughters, and by his second he had one son. Four of his sons, including the one half-brother, took over four 200-acre lots from their father.[26] Angus MacDougall thus disponed or left at least 800 acres, not a prince's ransom perhaps but enough to indicate a successful man.

MacDougall is an old Moidart and South Morar name. The Mac-Dougalls are descended from a number of Dougals in the Clanranald chiefly family (in the case of South Morar the progenitor was from Dougal, sixth of Clanranald).[27] Tearlach MacFarlane suggested that if Angus was from Moidart, he was probably of the Glenaladale MacDougall family. A Dougal "the weaver" MacDougal (b. c. 1772) lived in Glenaladale; his brother Archibald (b. c. 1785) died, leaving two grandsons (brothers Archie and Angus "the piper" MacDougal) at Eignaig on the mainland of Moidart opposite Eilean Shona. It is possible that Angus Bàn MacDougall was one of the weaver's brothers. MacFarlane's imagined that these Glenaladale MacDougalls were shepherds, gamekeepers, and crofters – non-acquisitive people – which could explain the immigrant Angus Mac-Dougall's comparative wealth in that he might have been dealing in cattle.[28]

The Calendar land record for Cape Breton and the data dealing with Angus Bàn MacDougall[29] in the census for the west half of Lake Ainslie in 1841, when compared to J.L. MacDougall's *History of Inverness County*, display a variance in the information. This points up inherent problems in relying on memory in a work of the size of MacDougall's (he appears not to have consulted available statistics in this case).[30] Other discrepancies between J.L. MacDougall and the 1841 census aside, the names of those four sons, Duncan, John, Allan, and Alexander MacDougall, are common to both lists of names.

The cultural connection, again in dance, is first found in J.L. Mac-Dougall's *History*. Angus Bàn's grandson, Angus, son of John, son of Angus Bàn, is briefly discussed as a "superior dancer ... invited to every frolic and wedding."[31] The dancer's father found his bachelor son dilatory in meeting his home duties and turned away with a ready phrase the Broad Cove priest's praise of a talented son. This might indicate that this particular parish priest was fond of traditional pastimes.

At least two other pioneers obtained large acreages as well, John Mac-Donald (Iain mac Alasdair) around 1814[32] and John Walker, the latter settling at the mouth of Hay('s) River and the former having first emigrated to Prince Edward Island.

According to Reverend MacDonald's *Mabou Pioneers*, John Walker had been a bailiff in Scotland to the laird of Staffa and had married one of the laird's daughters. John Walker is given as being from "Uist."[33] According to the death records in Nova Scotia for 1864–76, a John Walker, son of Donald and Flora, died at Lake Ainslie on 2 February 1867. John Walker was 108 years old and had been born in South Uist (presumably in 1758 or '59).[34] The *Mabou Pioneers* also described John's brother and fellow settler at West Lake, Angus Walker, as being from Mull. Family historians (MacDougall and MacDonald and Agnes Walker) agree that while still in Mull, Inverness County, Angus married a Catherine MacDougall, who had converted late in life to Roman Catholicism; a daughter, Effie, was born to them in Scotland in 1828 or '29.[35] Angus bought a two hundred-acre farm at Upper West Lake Ainslie from a widow MacEachen.[36]

According to the record of deaths in Inverness County for 1864–76, an Angus Walker, born in Scotland the son of Donald and Florie Walker, died 31 December 1872 aged eighty-five (i.e., he was born *circa* 1787).[37] This gap of almost thirty years in birth dates between two brothers casts doubt upon the accepted theory of two immigrant brothers in MacDougall's and MacDonald's genealogies.[38]

In any event, bailiff to the laird of Staffa was a position of social and economic prominence that would certainly have implied literacy and probably bilingualism. The one MacDonald known as "Staffa" was Ranald MacDonald (c. 1778–1838), son of the notorious Colin MacDonald, second of Boisdale (the vicious anti-Catholic landlord who precipitated the 1772 Captain John MacDonald Glenaladale emigration to Prince Edward Island). Walter Scott, in writing of his visit to Ulva in 1810, referred to his host (Ranald, son of Colin) as "Staffa."[39] Ranald, who became an advocate in 1798, succeeded his father in "Ulva, and other lands in Mull in 1800,"[40] but notwithstanding putative greater religious tolerance on his side than on Colin his father's, Staffa did not marry until 1812, when old John Walker would have been over fifty (Frederick MacDonald's "Manuscript-book" shows that old John had a grandson, John Walker [Iain mac Alasdair], born around 1834).[41]

Colin, the Protestant businessman of Boisdale who bought Ulva on 8 June 1785 and who died in 1800, however unlikely, offers a better candidature for father of Walker's wife. He was twice married and had six recorded daughters (none of whom married a Walker according to *Clan Donald*). I presume that had any daughter married a Roman Catholic the couple would have had ample reason to emigrate *instanter*. No matter, the claim for Walker status in Mull and at West Lake Ainslie remains provocatively not proven.[42]

I do not have accurate dates of settlement at West Lake Ainslie for the two Walker brothers, but perhaps a generation has been skipped in the case of old John Walker in the Inverness County genealogies. The Walkers in question, however, were Catholics; John was certainly a South Uist man, and it is no surprise to find an Angus Walker among the Father/Bishop MacEachern emigrants who came to Prince Edward Island in 1790.[43]

Apart from the minor niggling problems of proving this or that casual claim, there is no doubt that several men of some substance settled at West Lake Ainslie in the first three decades of Queen Victoria's century. From the beginnings of White society in that region, there were pipers, one of whom, Alexander Dubh MacDonald, was literate in 1837.

Allan MacCormack was the first non-Native man to inhabit West Lake Ainslie and he was from South Uist, via Prince Edward Island. According to John R. MacCormack, a descendant, Allan was a piper. The story of the

MacCormacks in Ireland, Scotland, and the New World is the subject of MacCormack's *Highland Heritage & Freedom's Quest*. Professor Mac-Cormack shows that Allan MacCormack, his patrilineal great-grandfather, had left a fifty-acre tenant's farm "at Ormaclate"[44] and thereon "on the Ormaclate Castle farm" *circa* 1802 to settle in Prince Edward Island.[45] Also of interest from the same source is that Allan MacCormack's first wife was a "Miss MacIntyre, d. c. 1807."[46] Having noted that Allan Mac-Cormack's neighbour at Ormaclate was an Angus MacIntyre, the writer speculates that Allan MacCormack was married, prior to 1802, to one of Angus's daughters.[47]

Now it is only fair to note that nothing of Allan MacCormack's piping is known either in the records of South Uist, of Prince Edward Island, or of West Lake Ainslie. There is no set of pipes, no music, no lore at West Lake. John R. MacCormack's association of Allan's piper's status at Ormaclate Castle farm with the claim that he was "a member of the Clan [Clanranald] élite"[48] would only have been considered valid by members of the old tradi-tional Gaelic social orders who, by Allan MacCormack's adult years in South Uist, were nearly powerless and increasingly economically abused.[49] Allan MacCormack may have been a brilliant piper living on what was a greatly diminished tenant's holding, but as John R. MacCormack has so clearly pointed out, Allan enjoyed no benefit or status in the eyes of Clan-ranald or his functionaries as a piper. Ranald, chief of Clanranald, had died in 1789 and the South Uist holdings were run on behalf of his son, a minor, by an Edinburgh tutor group that had no demonstrable interests in promot-ing anything other than monetary gain.

Whatever his piping talent, Allan MacCormack lived in a part of Inver-ness County where traditional music and dance became ubiquitous as the settlers swarmed in, whether in the nearby Presbyterian Scotch community of East Lake Ainslie or in the mostly Catholic Margarees, Mabou or Broad Cove. His son Allan Jr married Mary Kennedy, whose uncle Archie Kennedy from Broad Cove was a step-dancer and whose brother, Dr Alexander Kennedy of Mabou, was another. Allan Jr's son Allan Y. MacCormack (d. 1949), a steel-plant carpenter in Sydney, was a Gaelic speaker, a fiddler, and a notable step-dancer who also danced the Sword Dance.[50]

While Mary Tulloch MacDonald contributed in a signal way to the fos-tering of Gaelic traditional dance at some sort of now-dead formal level, there is less to link the Tulloch pipers Frederick D.F. and Angus D.F. Mac-Donald with tradition. They were brothers and were born in the 1890s. Liv-ing long into the twentieth century, they both served in the Great War as mil-itary pipers. While there have been more informants about both men than about Mary Tulloch, and more traces of them than of her, there has been so far little to suggest that they did not desert the demanding but flexible para-meters of tradition for the improved literate form(s) of bagpiping. Modern piping, bagpipe and drum bands, and literate teaching and learning of piping during the Great War were potent forces. But it must be borne in mind that turn-of-the-twentieth-century improved bagpiping, judging by the example of one early Willie Ross recording, could be much closer to traditional speeds and rhythms than modern competition bagpiping has become.

I learned about the piper Angus D.F. and Frederick D.F. MacDonald first from their second cousin Albert Johnnie Angus MacDonald, Melford, in the mid-1970s. He and they had a member of the Aodh MacDonald family from Ormacleit in South Uist in common. Although Angus was still alive at the time and living in southwest Scotland, I did not take the opportunity to correspond with him. For all that, some of Albert MacDonald's memories contribute to what unfortunately can now only be a general picture of the brothers. From him, for example, I learned that Frederick and Angus piped at the funeral of the Melford Glen grist- and saw-miller Donald "the Glen" MacDonald in 1919 or 1920 (known also as Donald Gillis MacDonald and Dòmhnul Mór Aogh, a son of Aodh).[51] Albert told me that Danny Fortune had heard a record that Angus D.F. made of his own piping (unconfirmed). Angus, according to Albert, would have been a note piper.

Angus D.F. MacDonald, the younger of the two brothers (21 November 1893–25 September 1978), was born at West Lake Ainslie. His father, Donald Farquhar (D.F.) MacDonald (b. Brook Village, 1863), was not to any of my informants' knowledge a piper, but Angus's nephew Ainslie MacNeil (May 1941–2001) told me that D.F. played the fiddle.[52] Apparently, D.F. had high expectations of his sons and a deep-seated Calvinist work ethic that likely prompted the boys to leave home.[53] MacNeil also told me that Angus D.F. played the pipes and the fiddle and that he piped for Square Sets at the Brook Village parish hall. This was not a guarantee of traditional step-dance timing because there probably was no step-dancing in the Square Set at the time. That does not preclude the use of step-dance timing and rhythms since probably no musician raised in tradition, and perhaps no more than a few with formal training, could have known anything else.

When I asked Ainslie MacNeil which local, rural, Inverness County, Gaelic-speaking pipers might have influenced Angus D.F.'s piping aspirations, he told me that Angus admired the piping of John Angie MacDonell, Inverness, but even more so that of John Angie's father, Jim (Seumas mac Alasdair), presumably when Jim was still in Kiltarlity, only a fairly short boat trip and walk from West Lake Ainslie. Angus thought that Jim Mac-Donell was a very good piper, and the evidence suggests that Jim MacDonell, like his son John Angie, was an ear-learned, step-dance piper. This is one link between Angus D.F. and step-dance piping; another could be his and his brother Fred's reported ability to play "Calum Crubach anns a' Ghlean," a popular Inverness County step-dance strathspey.[54]

Angus D.F.'s career included piping in the 85th's pipe band in the First World War. After a postwar period working for the Halifax police department, he took a job in 1925 in Kingston. There he served for thirty years as caretaker and curator of the Fort Frederick Martello Tower, which Sir Archibald Macdonell had converted into a military museum in 1923. A Kingston *Whig Standard* article about him described "His Famous Lecture" about the old tower and its contents and remarked on his "distinct Scotch burr."[55] In July 1941 both Angus D.F. and Fred D.F. were members of the Stormont and Glengarry pipe band, which came first in the pipe band competition at the Antigonish Highland Games.

Frederick D.F. MacDonald (1891–1973), the older brother, joined the 85th Cape Breton Highlanders as a piper in October 1915, leaving his job with Petrie's Manufacturing Company in Sydney, Cape Breton. After the war he became an American citizen and lived in Detroit, but he renounced his U.S. citizenship in order to join Britain's anti-Nazi cause in the Second World War, serving as a piper with the Stormont, Dundas and Glengarry Highlanders. He died in Kingston, Ontario, having retired from an aluminium plant there in 1964. Presumably his early interest in the bagpipes brushed off on his brother Angus D.F., but nothing is known about early teachers or models in the West Lake Ainslie area for either man.

Two letters to (C.53645) Piper Fred MacDonald of the Glengarry Highlanders Pipe Band (Ninth Brigade, Third Division, Canadian Army Overseas, England) from Hugh MacPhee of the Gaelic section of the BBC (British Broadcasing Corporation) in Glasgow have survived. The first, dated 19 January 1942, invites the piper to the north on Monday, 16 February, to record a talk in Gaelic for the BBC's Gaelic-speaking listeners. The other letter, dated 27 February 1942, thanks the piper for his efforts and includes intimation of a cheque to be received in a day or two and a transcribed comment "from a fellow Clansman on this side": "I enjoyed the half-hour programme on Wednesday evening of this week and certainly not least your Canadian friend. I think that recording could bear repetition at some suitable date. His Gaelic is good and I liked the way he told history and the manner in which he finished it. He gave his family's history with confidence which showed that he was not afraid of finding one of them hanging from a tree either by the neck or the tail!"[56]

Gaelic clearly was the mother tongue of at least some of the D.F. family in the 1890s. In the MacCormack family the years around 1890 marked the deliberate change from Gaelic to English. John R. MacCormack described his paternal grandparents, Angus MacCormack (1833–1909) and his second wife, Catherine MacLellan (1859–1944), as having been literate in both Gaelic and English and their unmarried daughter Jessie Isobel (1891–1989) as the last West Lake Ainslie MacCormack to speak Gaelic. All of that generation were taught to speak English from infancy.[57] By contrast, Francis "Dixie" Walker (b. 1932), Hay's River, told me that he heard only Gaelic at home until about 1945, when his parents began to use English only.[58]

The other immigrant bagpiper to settle at West Lake Ainslie was Alexander Dubh MacDonald from Glenuig in Moidart (in the old Clanranald estate) via Prince Edward Island and Antigonish County. I am indebted to Josephine Beaton, Brook Village, for drawing my attention to him and to a reference to him in the Antigonish *Casket* of 21 September 1944. Unfortunately, not much more is known about his piping than is known about Allan MacCormack's. In fact, Alexander Dubh himself remains very much a mystery. Had not a few records existed, he would have gone unnoticed as a musician altogether.

The first piece of evidence about Alexander Dubh is a letter in his own hand ordering "2 cotton shirts [for] 5 shillings cash" from William McKeen Esq. On that document he signed himself "Alexander McDonald Piper." The order is from "Hay River, Lake Ainslie" and is dated 22 January 1837. The piper wrote that he was going to Antigonish for a carpenter to finish the chapel (most likely that chapel at West Lake Ainslie, the building of which presumably was under his control).[59] The second is the reference in the *Casket* article. The writer reported that Alexander Dubh MacDonald had been heard piping for a Reel by Bishop MacEachern on Prince Edward Island.[60] The third glimpse of Alexander Dubh occurs in Colin S. MacDonald's "The Alastair Dhu MacDonalds of West Lake Ainslie": "The pioneer at West Lake Ainslie was Alastair Dhu Mhic Alasdair Vich Dhomniull Vich Iain [Alasdair Dubh mac Alasdair 'ic Dhòmhnuill 'ic Iain (Black Alexander, son of Alexander, son of Donald, son of John)], and his father belonged to Kinlochmoidart, on the authority of James (Peigi) MacLellan of Centreville, who was brought up at West Lake."[61] Alasdair Dubh's father settled at Georgeville, "while the son located first at South River and eventually at West Lake Ainslie ... and was also a good piper. One of his sons, John (Mor) the carpenter, settled at Little Mabou."[62]

Alexander Dubh the piper falls outside the attention of the person who wrote about the Denoon MacDonalds in the 21 September 1944 *Casket*, but if the family described there was the piper's, one must assume that Alexander Dubh did not stay long in Antigonish County. The *Casket* describes the family of Alexander MacDonald and Catherine MacIntyre as giving issue to six sons and five daughters, not including an Alexander (but including a John who settled at Chimney Corner, Margaree, and who later moved to a Denoon property he had purchased in Antigonish County.[63] This family emigrated in 1790 to Prince Edward Island and thence to the Gulf Shore (Antigonish County), where they bought a property from a John MacNeil, Georgeville.

The *Lucy*'s passenger list kindly shows that an Alexander ("Alexander M'Donald Glenuig, tenant") emigrated to Prince Edward Island, with his wife and six of a family, on 12 July 1790 (the *Lucy* was one of three ships taking emigrants from the Clanranald estate that summer).[64] In the family were three full passengers (i.e., over 12 years), two between 8 and 6, one between 4 and 2, and two under 2.[65] According to "The Clanranald Mac-Donalds of Kinlochmoidart," the family (number unknown) moved from the Mount Stewart district of Prince Edward Island to Georgeville in Antigonish County in 1810, buying a farm there from a John MacNeil.[66] Alexander's son Alexander Dubh the piper was born in Scotland *circa* 1786.[67]

The piper came to West Lake Ainslie around 1821 but appears to have moved away. Frederick MacDonald was unaware of Alexander Dubh's connection with West Lake Ainslie's first church and wrote that it "was built in the year 1835 by Rev William McLeod. P.P."[68] The piper's wife's name is unknown. The only other pointers to him in the county are his daughter Mary (b. 1825), who married and settled down at West Mabou, and his son John the carpenter, who moved to Colindale.[69] Alexander Dubh MacDonald, the West Lake Ainslie piper, also went by the cognomen "Denoon" but only retrospectively.[70] He was not ashamed to identify himself to McKeen the merchant as a piper.

Josephine Beaton informed me that the piper had cleared a farm near the site where the church was built at West Lake Ainslie. She speculated that he returned to Antigonish County. She referred to his son John the carpenter as "John Mór" and said that another of the piper's sons moved to the Chapel Road, leaving descendants (she identified Angus Dan, living in 1998, as one of them).[71] A bilingual piper who was literate in English and a dance-music player sums up our knowledge about Alexander Dubh.

West Lake Ainslie thus contained at least two immigrant pipers from Clanranald country, one temporarily. We know that a piper Robert MacIntyre also left Clanranald employment for America and that the Glenaladale piper John MacGillivray from Arisaig settled at Highfield, Antigonish County, in 1818. We know also that piping continued in Clanranald's Eigg deep into clearance times in the MacKinnon and MacQuarrie families, piping representatives of both settling on the land in Antigonish County. The once great Clanranald estate disappeared as a social and political entity before the middle of the nineteenth century, never to reappear except in mists of nostalgia. By that time a large part of its tenantry, musical and otherwise, was dispersed hither and yon.

The presence of pipers and of traditional Gaelic music and dancing in Keppoch[72] is just as clearly obvious in the record, if one reads widely and collates the data. So in my opinion it would not be unfair to fill the large cultural chinks in Frederick D.F. MacDonald's "Manuscript-book" with a general observation of cultural doings in nearby South West Margaree. The

Antigonish *Casket* writer cited above described in 1896, a musical world with dozens of fiddlers and pipers, some of them excellent players, and their regular appearance in rich numbers at weddings. Perhaps West Lake Ainslie had fewer musicians but surely it was in essence the same experience there.[73]

Where dance is concerned, the South West Margaree cultural analogue is useful also. While I have yet to check John R. MacCormack's sources for his assumption that "Allan [MacCormack] frequently piped a tune in the forest clearing while Angus [Bàn MacDougall] gave an expert rendition of the Sword Dance or Highland Fling" and his statement that "[t]he two musical traditions were to coalesce,"[74] the South West Margaree example suggests to me that there were gradations within one tradition rather than different traditions. What conceivable argument could be made for Allan MacCormack's piping having been anything but traditional, living as he did in the cultural heartland of Catholic South Uist. How could Angus Bàn from almost equally sequestered Moidart represent anything noticeably different?

What makes South West Margaree of the late nineteenth century important is that while it was a typical Cape Breton Gaelic community in many ways, with pipers and fiddlers plentiful at weddings and céilidhs, it presents a more complex picture than the straightforward and perhaps oversimplified perceptions we had of most Cape Breton Gaelic communities in the 1970s. The evidence lies in the *Casket*'s short published history of the parish and in some remarkable memories. The striking features of the complications are the apparent anomalies in the dance, the existence of some kind of cultural stratification in dancing, and the influence of the Catholic Church. Why Allan MacFarlane aspired to play "A' Ghlas Mheur" (The Finger Lock) may always be debatable, but a short look at those apparent anomalies, particularly the dance forms, will cast Gaelic South West Margaree, and surely also many more Highland communities in Scotland and the New World (perhaps now including West Lake Ainslie's), in a new light.

The old social stratification of Gaelic society in Scotland survived in Cape Breton and, what's more, may have been mirrored in cultural gradations. These gradations may only have differed inasmuch as some contained some formality in approach and presentation. Into this category I am inclined to put the dancing and dances taught in the dancing schools that existed for most of the nineteenth century but had practically disappeared from living memory by 1994.

The first suggestion that gradations in dancing existed crops up in an intriguing reference to the "Gille Calum," (Sword Dance) in a *Casket* series of article in 1896. Citing "Mr MacDougall's clever sketches of Inverness ... some years ago in the Casket," the writer quoted "that clever barrister and fascinating writer" as follows: "It was nothing for those able pioneers to carry three bushels of salt on his back for eight or ten miles, and dance 'Gille Calum' after getting home with as much cheer and spirit as if life had no burdens at all."[75] It is unknown whether this Gille Calum was the version with which we are familiar, where swords placed cross-wise on the ground are danced over, or whether it was a conservative colonial form of the sword-swinging "Mac an Fhorsair" dance, which Stewart of Garth said had disappeared by 1822.[76] Nonetheless, this quotation suggests a buccolic untrained status for the Sword Dance and little or no connection with formal ritual picked up at a dancing school, unless there were only subtle distinctions between what the dancing school taught and what survived spontaneously.

The Fletts are sure that the Gille Calum was a Gaelic dance rooted in tradition.[77] It was first included as a diversion in the Highland Society piping competitions in 1832, fifty-one years after the competition began, suggesting a minor popularity at least among the early piper/dancers vis-à-vis the Reel, which was by far the dance of choice. In 1832 it was called "That ancient Ghille Challaim or sword dance over two naked swords."[78] This dance was also associated with bagpipe accompaniment.[79] There is no reason to assume that it wasn't old and traditionally Gaelic, the sword having been used longest as the basic weapon in Scottish Gaelic society in Britain. And consider that the South Morar dancing teacher Alexander Gillis was the South West Margaree pioneer who came out in 1826, some years before the dance could have been gussied up for the stage and an Edinburgh audience. There is, however, no corpus of references to the dance in contemporary Gaelic poetry or to the "Makinorsair" mentioned by Stewart of Garth.

Nowadays in Scotland and Nova Scotia the Gille Calum is exclusively a stage dance, and for a century and a half it has been a stalwart feature of the Highland Games. From my experience, it was never a feature of the spontaneous céilidh in either the Scottish or Nova Scotian Gàidhealtachd and I tapped memories of the immigrant world. This makes its appearance in immigrant Cape Breton an apparent anomaly and J.L. MacDougall's observation of its having been done spontaneously in Highland homes in South West Margaree a rare and very valuable one.[80] MacDougall didn't even describe the dance, assuming, I think, that his readers would be familiar with it, and he seldom indulged any drooling deference to pseudo-Scottishness. That makes me think that MacDougall's Gille Calum had not suffered any non-Gaelic choreographic or setting-step modernizings. (This stage dance alone might be a fairly unchanged reflection of late eighteenth-century forms, perhaps including "Mac an Fhorsair," yet to be found described in greater detail in the written record of the time.)

John R. MacCormack's inclusion of the Highland Fling is another matter, one that may vitiate his two sentences about Allan MacCormack's dance-music piping in pioneer West Lake Ainslie. None of my Gaelic-

speaking informants born in the last quarter of the nineteenth century mentioned this dance in connection with céilidhs either, but this time there is
no MacDougall reference and hardly anyone else's in Nova Scotia to force
serious reflection.[81] The modern stage dance known as the Highland Fling
bears almost no likeness to step-dance steps done in what remains of Gaelic Cape Breton (and there are no obstacles like placed swords to dictate
anything). There are no references to it in the Gaelic literature of the late
eighteenth century and only a handful in the English written record from
the period, which they describe the dance as a small punctuating part of a
Reel. The modern Highland Fling seems to be a contrived dance from outside the Gaelic tradition; it certainly displays none of the intimate connection between musician and dancer found in all good step-dancing. If it
existed in Gaelic Nova Scotia, as a step let's say of reel/Reel dancing (as
it appears to have been in Scotland), it went unremarked and we are left
with John R. MacCormack's unique example.

CHAPTER THIRTEEN

Reverend Archibald Campbell's Observations of Piping in Judique

The Reverend Archibald Campbell (c. 1849–1921) was a snuff-using Scottish Jesuit priest who made an extensive mission in Gaelic Nova Scotia in 1907. His writings about his travels and parish work there offer some tantalizing glimpses of piping. He wrote two articles in Gaelic in 1908 under the titles "Dùthaich na Saorsa" (Land of Freedom) and "Tìr an Aigh" (Land of Joy),¹ not many pages, simple, often gratefully flattering, and untranslated; in fact, the articles are seldom read these days, although echoes of the stories still are heard, in English.

Though perhaps not of great significance, the articles do register nostalgic delight and show the importance of the piper in six or seven of the many Catholic Highland parishes in the Gaelic-speaking northeastern corner of Nova Scotia that Campbell visited. Undoubtedly, too, there were plenty of pipers in other parishes he visited – South West Margaree, Inverness, East Bay, Arisaig, for example.

Campbell didn't make any pointed or critical assessments of the céilidhs and gatherings, except for humorously repetitive asides about one Campbell pipe tune that he was forever hearing ("Bha mi air banais am Bail' Inbhiraora" ["I was at a wedding in Inveraray," better known as "The Campbells Are Coming"]). In general, his writing shows no bias where cultural matters are concerned; neither was he very descriptive, which suggests to an optimist that he was familiar with what he saw.² However, although the mission work taxed his waning strength, he had the warmest memories of his visit to this New World Gàidhealtachd.

As late as 1980 I met older Gaels like the late John D. MacMaster, Long Point, Inverness County, who remembered the priest's visits. And where Judique is concerned, a local non-clerical diary entry names the four local pipers involved in greeting and bidding farewell to the Scottish priest (Campbell himself only gave partial names of two pipers he met). There are probably no more living memories and just as irretrievably gone is that old rural world that Campbell found, not long before it was infiltrated by the iron horse and Yankee baseball. The old railway station in Judique, like so many of the big old barns, has long since been torn down; no more the *Judique Flyer*, the rails are gone, and few are the folk who speak Gaelic.[3] Campbell would scarcely recognize the place, with its new stone church. And yet ninety-two years ago, without having to satisfy any temptation to flatter, he wrote that "blessed Gaelic" in Nova Scotia, and especially in Cape Breton, was as pithy and as seasoned as any in the Highlands.[4]

Campbell's Gelic name was Gilleasbuig mac Dhòmhnuill 'ic Eoghain (Archibald, son of Donald, son of Ewan). He was the descendant of a convert to Catholicism from Ballachulish in Appin. His base of operations in Scotland was Glasgow. When he arrived in Antigonish, Nova Scotia, he was given the appropriate academic and clerical greeting. The following Sunday at St Andrew's Church, where he preached, the clergy in attendance told him that there wasn't the least flavour of English on his Gaelic and that indeed his Gaelic bore the true tang of the peat (*fior bhlas na moine*). He was pleased and proud to hear this praise, and obviously was pleasantly surprised to be met in Antigonish by a third cousin, a MacDonald, chief inspector of schools, a great-grandson of one of his great-grandfather's brothers.[5]

Campbell's words have the same surprised delightedness at finding the Old World nestling in the New, sheltered, protected still, that Alexander MacKenzie's have in his recollection about meeting the Blind Piper's patrilineal great-grandson Squire John MacKay (from Gairloch) in New Glasgow about two score years earlier.[6]

FOUR JUDIQUE PARISH PIPERS IN 1907

Although Campbell's first stop was not Judique, let's begin there anyway and with a long-dead parishioner Angus MacDougall's diary entry for 27 July 1907. That was the day that Campbell stepped off the train at the station just north of where fiddler Hugh A. (Buddy) MacMaster's home is today,

in the oldest Gaelic speaking parrish in Cape Breton and was Received by The Good People of the Parrish with a Cead Mile Failte [Hundred Thousand Welcomes]. They were Headed by four Hiland Pipers who Played in wright good style the appropriate Hiland airs the Campbells are Comeing and many other Welcom and favourate Airs.

And from the same source when he left Judique for Inverness,

on the 3rd inst., ... the send off Given the Good Father was fully equal to his Reception the Pipers and the Whole Parrish accompanying him to the station.[7]

MacDougall luckily gives the pipers' names and ages: Donald McLellan (73), Angus McDougall (73), Niel Campbell (60), and "Fadrick" McEachen (60), all from the parish of Judique. He also wrote:

It is Generaly beleived that the report Which Father Campbell will make of the Parrish of Judique As well as of Every other parrish which he has visited in the diocese Will be an Eyeopener to our brethren In the land. May our Good people ever Preserve the Faith and traditions of their Fathers.[8]

In those days of stronger priestly influence, incentives to ensure rousing turnouts and good attendance at the mission included bunting, flags and processions and music, story and song, now and then dance, just as the priest described it.

All of the Judique pipers MacDougall mentions were born in the lifetimes of thousands of immigrant Gaels, although not one of the four was an immigrant. Their number and their ages point to the parish's deeply imbedded interest in bagpiping in the Victorian century, an interest found in most Gaelic-speaking Scotch communities. But their ages also point to the shift from tradition. Judique is now associated much more with stepdancing and fiddling than with bagpiping. When thinking of traditional music in Judique before the Second World War, most people would come up with fiddlers rather than pipers, people like Little Jack MacDonald, Hughie "Tàl" MacDonald, at whose farmhouse Little Jack was raised, and Dan R. MacDonald, although there were many more; and today Hugh A. (Buddy) MacMaster is internationally accepted as one of the greatest of the older fiddlers living.

There is piping there today but its flavour is modern and at a remove from the essentially preliterate forms that must have greeted Father Archibald Campbell in 1907.[9] I think, too, that there was, typically, a hiatus when the older pipers died away in Judique, perhaps with the local exception of Hector Campbell (Neil's son) Hillsdale, who may not have been intimidated by the rise of modernism and literately learned bagpiping.

I'll discuss the Judique mission pipers of 1907 in the order that Angus MacDougall presented them. Donald McLellan (c. 1834–1912) almost certainly was the son of an immigrant Gael. He had a farm in Hillsdale (formerly Beinn Noah [Noah's Mountain]) that lay on a west-facing hill inland from the north of Judique and with a view as splendid as any of the setting summer sun across the Saint Lawrence and Cape George. The house that was a hospitable place in the 1930s was there for as long as neighbour Robert Gillis (b. 1922), Hillsdale Road, remembers, back into the mid-1920s, and still stands.[10] There's still a barn, although it was built in the 1930s to replace a smaller, older one.

John L. MacDougall's *History of Inverness County* has a small sub-section called "John MacLellan and family, Hillsdale,"[11] and inasmuch as Donald the piper knew himself a cousin of John's there is a kinship relationship adding to the fact that the families were neighbours in Hillsdale. John's property is known today as Gussie Campbell's home and farm, abutting to the south of the piper's farm. Robert Gillis told me that both MacLellan families had come together to Judique parish from the Brook Village area long before 1900, and he seems not to have been too wide of the mark.[12]

The general thought is that both strains of Hillsdale MacLellans descend from Donald MacLellan, who emigrated with his family, including John (c. 1804–82), to West Lake Ainslie in 1818 from Morar, by and large the MacLellan mountain homeland in Scotland. This suggests that Donald the piper's line descends from another son of Donald who, unfortunately, is overlooked in John R. MacDougall's book.

According to MacDougall, John MacLellan (b. Scotland c. 1804), the son of Donald MacLellan and Ann Gillis, married one of Captain Angus MacLellan's daughters (Margaret), West Lake Ainslie.[13] They moved to Hillsdale in 1841 where he rose to local prominence and, having become a justice of the peace, sported the title "Squire" MacLellan.[14] The bare bones of this are found in the 1871 census. That census also shows a Donald MacLellan (aged thirty-six, i.e., b. 1834 or 1835) and his wife Mary (twenty-five), both born in Nova Scotia. This is Donald the piper and she is his second wife and mother of all his children. Besides a six-month-old son at the time (Alexander John), two other people are listed, a Scots-born widow Mary (sixty-five, i.e., b. Scotland 1805 or 1806), presumably the piper's mother, and a Mary MacLellan (forty), born in Nova Scotia, presumably an older unmarried sister. The piper's father's first name is unknown.

What is known about Donald the piper is that he died five years after Father Campbell's mission to Nova Scotia, on 27 May 1912. The death is recorded most interestingly in the diary of a neighbouring MacIsaac whose patrilineal grandson Duncan Dan D. MacIsaac (1907–87) typed it from the original longhand version (retaining the whimsical spellings). Donald the piper was married three times, first to a sister of Judge Nicolas Meaghar from Brook Village, next to a Miss Gillis (1871 census gives Mary), and lastly to Catherine Kennedy, John Kennedy's daughter from Glen Road in Antigonish County.[15]

No one in the piper MacLellan family after the mission piper Donald is remembered as having played the bagpipes. His son Dannie Donald the piper (d. May 1952 aged seventy-nine) played no instrument and did not step-dance;[16] he worked on the railway. Also, I've never heard Donald MacLellan's name in connection with any céilidh or picnic or dance in Judique or elsewhere in the early years of the twentieth century, which of course is not to deny the possibility that he piped at all of those affairs.

On 10 January 1998 Dannie Donald the piper's son Donald A. (Angus) MacLellan died aged eight-two, the last and youngest of seven siblings (not including a foster sister Mary Gillis).[17] Locally he was known as "Donald A." or more exactly as "Donald A., Danny, Donald the piper," but he didn't add much to the subject of his grandfather's piping. He said that the piper MacLellans came to Hillsdale from West Lake Ainslie. As far as traditional piping goes, only the term "piper" clings to the family.[18]

John D. MacMaster, Long Point (the local Raleigh man), told me in 1978 that he remembered seeing Donald MacLellan and described him as an ear piper who had played at the head of a bishop's procession more than seventy years earlier (before 1908). He described the bishop of the time visiting the various Highland parishes by horse and buggy with the old piper leading the way. The only other titbit John D. vouchsafed was that MacLellan once played a tune in the bishop's presence the words of which were both scurrilous and possibly insulting:

Cuir do shron 'sa thòn a'choin dhuibh,
Cuir do shron 'nam thòn-sa
'S gheibh thu airgead is òr[19]

No one has ever claimed that the piper played the tune on purpose and insultingly and it is unlikely that any musician would have deliberately risked the old bishop's rage. On the other hand, Bishop John Cameron (1827–1910) was a committed and partisan Conservative and a Liberal piper from Hillsdale might have been tempted to share an in-joke with musical friends, knowing the bishop would not understand the words to some pipe tune. There is a variant of the story to be considered later.

Lastly, about Donald the piper MacLellan's bagpipes, Robert Gillis said that he was sure there had been a set in the house that had not been prominently on display but rather had been kept in an old case. Robert's sister Mary told me that throughout her years growing up in Dannie's family she never saw a set. Robert believed that one of Donald A.'s sons would have the bagpipes to this day, but Donald A. MacLellan's daughter-in-law Jessica (Rankin) MacLellan told me that they were thrown out while Donald A. was away working in the mines in Elliot Lake, Ontario, something that he repeatedly told his family he always greatly regretted.[20]

Where the second mission piper is concerned, the death of Angus McDougall is at least included in the Antigonish *Casket*,[21] but that apart, there is even less offered about his piping in the parish. According to his obituary, he was born 14 May 1834 and lived and died (19 February 1919) at "Rear Judique Intervale" at his father's old home. The obituary calls him "an old and familiar landmark." He was married twice and had eight children. The obituary goes on:

His home was a fount of hospitality and good cheer, his general disposition attracting thereto many warm friends. If trouble came to him, he would seek solace in his favourite musical instrument – the Highland Pipes. Only a few days before the end, when his son William reached his bedside, after thirty-one years' absence, he asked that the Pipes be given him and he played with enthusiasm. A profound Catholic humbly received the last rites.

What else remains is statistical corroboration of the old piper. The 1871 census gives Angus MacDougall (75) as the head of the eighty-third household enumerated; his wife is Elizabeth (75) (both b. 1795 or 1796 and in Nova Scotia); in the same house are Angus (36) and four children, including William (5) and Joseph (5). Among others, an Ann (28) also lives there.[22] The 1891 census gives Angus MacDougall (57) and his family, which includes Ann (50) and eight children, including William and Joseph.[23] Although comparing the censuses shows apparent inconsistencies in ages, and it is not inconceivable that Angus the piper was a son of Donald (given as a son of Neil in MacDougall's *History of Inverness*), this Angus is the only one with a son William who had either a twin or a brother (Joseph) very close in age.

J.L. MacDougall, under the subtitle "The MacDougalls of Judique Intervale," gives a short genealogy of Neil, son of Patrick MacDougall (Eigg). Neil (d. 1845) fits the bill, having emigrated in 1791, settling first in Pictou, where he married Flora MacEachern, and later moving to Judique Intervale.[24] His son Angus married an Elizabeth MacInnis, daughter of Robert who had been in Captain John MacDonald's emigration to Prince Edward Island in 1771–72.[25] It is unfortunate that MacDougall didn't make some cultural remark about a fellow-MacDougall. I have found no appropriate Patrick MacDougall, Eigg, among either the Catholics or the Presbyterians in the census of the Small Isles made by Neill McNeill in 1764–75.

Neil Campbell, the third mission piper, according to Angus Innis MacDougall's "Memorandum Page," was sixty when the mission priest arrived in Judique on 27 July 1907 (b. 1846 or 1847). Like Donald the piper MacLellan, he was from Hillsdale, or Beinn Noah. Also like MacLellan, he was the son of a Scots-born immigrant. This Neil Campbell is given in the 1871 census as aged twenty-four and in the 1891 census as forty-three.[26] (Enumeration dates varied decade to decade.)

Genealogical work on his family has been done by Sister Margaret Mac-Donell (St Francis Xavier University, Antigonish) and Father Allan MacMillan, Boisdale (PP, Judique, 1999–) and can be found in shortened form in a sketch in *Luirgean Eachainn Nìll – A collection of folktales told by Hector Campbell*, edited by Margaret MacDonell and John Shaw. MacDonell cited family lore in saying that the Campbell family was from Muck; Neil's father, Charles, left there perhaps as early as 1835 after marrying Mary MacEachen from Eigg.[27] Both families were near neighbours and important culture bearers in the New World. It is by no means too adventurous to claim that the Campbells either accompanied the MacEachens from Eigg, attracted them, or were attracted by them to Beinn Noah/Hillsdale – more likely attracted.

There is no indication that Neil, like the others, was anything other than an ear piper, but no specific memory of his playing and its function in the community (apart from his regaling Archibald Campbell SJ) has come to my attention. Sister MacDonell, from nearby St Ninian (called by some Upper South West Mabou, and by others Rear Judique Intervale), acknowledged that Neil was a piper and his son Hector (Eachainn Nìll, b. 20 August 1888) as well. In connection with Hector Campbell, she wrote that he got help with his piping from a Donald S. MacDonald from River Denys,[28] from his neighbour, piper Fred MacEachen, and "possibly from his own father."[29] Hector, by a number of reports, including Sister MacDonell's, was not a particularly good piper, but nothing is known about Neil's ability. It is quite possible that Neil played more in the style of Eigg than of Muck. As a youngster he had worked on the railway in the Boisdale area, where piping was very popular. While there he married Flora O'Handley and cannot have been unaware of Cnoc a'Chiùil (Music Hill) and of several very able Campbell and other musicians in the area, in Campbell Lake, Rear Beaver Cove, and Rear Boisdale.[30]

There is no doubt that Neil Campbell was steeped in old-style, almost certainly ear-learned, piping, as well as fiddling and storytelling and all other aspects of transplanted Gaelic tradition. Not only were his MacEachen neighbours profoundly Gaelic – especially John and his son Hector, both remarkable storytellers[31] and socially very close to the Campbells – but in 1871 Neil's household contained a Scots-born Mary Campbell, aged sixty, surely his mother.[32] Her musical influence, if any, would have also favoured Eigg.

Where "Fadrick" MacEachen is concerned, for many years I wondered about him. Why had he been given persistently what appeared to me to be a vocative form (of Pàdruig, or conceivably Peadar) in nominative and accusative oral contexts? I knew from Albert Johnnie Angus MacDonald (b. 10 March 1919) in Melford that Fadrick had made a number of sets of bagpipe drones.[33] Albert himself had a set, which he showed me.[34] These pipes were old, cracked, and obviously hand-made without sophisticated equipment. They were stained black with at least some bone ferrules, and it was suggested that they might be of apple wood, not known for its resilience under Cape Breton's temperature range (roughly −20°C to +30°C). The terminals were not noticeably belled. My notes from 1980 report four such sets, but come with a doubt. Albert said that another set was then in the possession of Jim Alex Cameron in Hillsdale, Judique (now dead). In rechecking with Albert MacDonald on 16 February 2000, I learned that he knew of only three sets made by Fadrick MacEachen and that the set Albert had owned had "drifted over" to Melford and somehow into Albert's hands many years ago. Albert told me that they were the first bagpipe drones that "Red" Gordon MacQuarrie had ever played and that Gordon had reported that they were not too bad but hard to tune.[35]

When asked, Albert told me that the piper's first name was a Gaelicization of Frederick and no vocative of Pàdruig (Phàdruig, which is pronounced pretty much as "Fadrick" with a long "a"). Frederick MacEachen was from Hillsdale. The 1871 census shows a John MacEachen (aged sixty-six) and his wife Sarah (forty-five), both born in Scotland. Their home is listed as number 131, three from Neil Campbell's (128). This family includes the only Frederick MacEachen in the Judique area (the name is very rare among Highlanders in Cape Breton). According to the 1871 census, Frederick was twenty-one, born in 1849 or 1850, in Nova Scotia; his brother Hector was twenty-three, also born in Nova Scotia.[36]

Albert, while he had never heard Fadrick play the pipes, remembered seeing him at a wake at Iagan Iain[37] (Johnnie John) MacLellan's on the River Denys Mountain when Albert was a youth in the early 1930s. An aunt, age unidentified, of Johnnie John MacLellan's had died and Fadrick arrived in a friend's or neighbour's horse-drawn buggy to pay his respects. Albert remembered that he was a bit unsteady when he got down, not having been accustomed to riding in a buggy. Fadrick did not play the pipes on that occasion.

Another link to Fadrick is the late Duncan Dan D. MacIsaac (1907–87) mentioned above. His son-in-law, the Gaelic-speaking musician and authority on Scottish violin music John Donald Cameron (b. 1937), Judique, recollected (15 February 2000) driving through Hillsdale with Duncan and being told about Fadrick the piper and of his piping the tune "Cuir do shron 's a' thòn." Duncan did not sing the tune clearly enough and John Donald was left wondering exactly how it had gone. His wife, Rose Cameron, remembers her mother singing Gaelic words to the tune (a 6/8 in A on the violin), and John Donald knew that Peigi "the millar" MacIsaac might have been able to throw more light on the subject but he didn't have the opportunity to ask her in her last days.[38] Whatever incident or incidents spawned the dog's arse song/pipe tune, it was memorable enough that there is still humorous speculation about it in Judique.

The two pipers Campbell almost identified by name, both in Inverness County, were "am piobaire MacNeil" at Creignish and "Aonghas Dubh am piobair" (Black Angus the piper). The latter greeted the priest midway between Camus Farsuing (Broad Cove) and Mabou in 1907. Black Angus piped at the head of a mile-long tail of about two hundred buggies full of thoroughly Gaelic descendants of immigrants for the most part from Glen Spean and Glen Roy in Brae Lochaber.[39] Earlier on, the piper MacNeil had led the priest's procession out of Creignish at the end of the week's mission and over the Creignish Hills to Glendale parish limits "a'cluich gu mireagach 'Baile-Inbhìraora'" (*sic*) (merrily playing "The Campbells Are Coming").[40]

Black Angus (MacDonald) has been described in *The History of Traditional Gaelic Bagpiping*. The piper MacNeil's identity poses a problem, but for the sake of the stories I have about him I prefer to assume he was the man widely known in lower Inverness County as Am Pìobaire Mór (The Big Piper), Stephen B. MacNeil.[41] MacNeil (2 August 1851–19 October 1940) was the grandson of a Scots immigrant; from 1899 he was a watch and clock repairer, later adding photography to his quiver, at his shop on the railway side of Granville Street, Port Hawkesbury, within easy enough train or wagon range of Creignish.

In 1980 Malcolm J. MacNeil, a piper from Piper's Cove, told me about a piper Steaphan Mhicheil Mhurchaidh (MacNeil) (Stephen, son of Michael, son of Murdoch).[42] Barry Shears calls him Stephain Mhicheil Murchadh Domhnull Og (Stephen, son of Michael, son of Murdoch, son of young Donald) and describes him as a first cousin of the piper and Great War veteran Captain Angus MacNeil.[43] Shears cites family lore for Stephen's having trekked over the winter ice from his native Gillis Point to get piping lessons (I presume this happened in the early 1860s). Shears offers the suggestion that Donald MacIntyre, the piper in Boisdale, was the likeliest tutor for a serious learner of piping, and he may be right, but it would have been a very long, hard walk in winter.

Stephen B. MacNeil stands out in Cape Breton Gaelic society because he was literate in his mother tongue of Gaelic as well as in English. According to a grandson (his daughter Annie Gillis's son Greg Gillis [b. 1920]), in the 1920s he was one of the last two people in Port Hawkesbury to be both literate and scholarly in Scottish Gaelic.[44] MacNeil taught for a time at the MacIntyre Lake road school at Duff Brook and taught his wife (a MacNeil from Boularderie West) to read and write English. That sense of schoolishness and learning through literacy touched his piping as well. Whatever theory there was he absorbed.

When Stephen's son Francis A. (Frank) decided to learn to play the fiddle, the old piper got him a violin locally and ordered several books of fiddle music from Scotland, where he had bagpiping dealings. Literacy was important in his scheme of Scottish music, although he had no love whatever for fiddling.[45] He is believed to have composed a pipe tune called "Spaidsearachd Mhic Neil" (MacNeil's March), surely among others. According to Shears, he played ceòl mór, which would have been appropriate to a person of his character.[46]

MacNeil was a popular piper at picnics, weddings, gatherings of many sorts, and, inevitably, at funerals.[47] At the centenary at Christmas Island of the first appearance of a Catholic bishop on the shores of Bras d'Or in 1815, MacNeil piped the crowd across the Grand Narrows railway bridge. There is no record of his having piped for traditional step-dancing and there's no telling if he could have. A photograph of him in Stephen R. MacNeil's "Centenary of the first landing" shows the piper playing left hand upper with the bagpipe held under his left shoulder. An obituary says that he was uniformly generous with his music (which means locally that he played willingly for others), and this apparently does not unduly flatter him. Greg Gillis said that people used to visit his shop on Granville Street regularly and listen to him play. Laconic he may have been, not a man of many words, but he shared his music. It was his wife who drove the lads with the flasks away when too much musical informality rattled her nerves. Gillis, a natural teller of stories, also chose to tell me, however, that on one – only one – fine day each year, a day chosen for its languid calmness, his grandfather would play the pipes in his backyard for the benefit of the wider community, a condescension he knew suited the instrument.

Gillis said that by 1980 nothing was left of the old piper's music records, his watches, or his pipe music, and he had had a good collection of pipe music, including a book with many titles in Gaelic.[48] In fact, the old piper, preparing for death, gave his music books and manuscripts to Donald MacLean, son of Hector, in North Sydney. Donald was a nephew of St. Francis Xavier physics professor Reverend Dr P.J. Nicolson, and when the latter saw that MacLean was making no use of the old piper's books, he arranged for their transfer to Father Raymond MacDonald, another grandson of Stephen B. MacNeil.[49] Father MacDonald said that Stephen MacNeil had impressed upon his wife that she should not sell his bagpipes for less than $125, adding that the piper had a set of Henderson pipes to which he had added a MacRae chanter. After he died, his widow sold the pipes to Father Vincent MacDonald, pastor priest of Mulgrave, who had pleaded that his nephew James (?) MacDonald needed a set. According to Father MacDonald, James (?) MacDonald served with the Cape Breton Highlanders.

Few books of pipe music have survived from the nineteenth century in Inverness County, and few indeed were the pipers who used them. Stephen

B. MacNeil was one; another was the irrascible Raonul Màiri Bhàin in Port Hood; but of these two, it was MacNeil who chose the path of modern piping.[50]

One of the many stories that gild Stephen B. MacNeil's memory even yet has to do with a Protestant minister (MacNeil from Gillis Point near Iona, of course, was a Catholic). The minister enjoyed pipe music and was forever trying to get Stephen MacNeil to visit the manse. Well, one day the piper put on his dark suit and dark hat, and set off for the manse. The minister greeted him effusively. At last! he must have thought. The piper put down his pipe box and the minister took his hat and coat, anticipating an evening of music. Straightaway Stephen took the pipes out of the box, tuned the drones, and played a tune. The moment it was finished he put the pipes away, asked for his coat and hat, and made to leave. The minister, having expected a longer visit and a lot more music, delicately remonstrated, saying that he had heard him play many, many tunes before but that he'd never heard that one before. What was it called he wanted to know. "Tòn a'Mhinisteir" (The Minister's Arse) came the piper's reply.

Otherwise MacNeil maintained a position of outward gentility, wearing a suit as everyday wear. His wife did the barn work and rode herd on excesses going on around her husband. He was a big heavy man, and one of those troublesome little things that happened again and again to him, for which he was not responsible, involved his entry into church. The floor of the church had loose boards here and there, and when he lumbered up the aisle to the pew on Sunday morning, they squeaked embarrassingly. On one occasion his wife had had enough. Before she left for church, she took his shoes away and hid them. Then, at the quietest part of the mass, a reverent hush o'er the congregation, in walked Stephen B. He was wearing his bedroom slippers and he set off at a deliberate pace up the aisle, past his wife who was sitting in the back, to the front pew, using his ample weight to greatest advantage on the quirky old floor.

Archibald Campbell SJ's articles leave no hint of scatological pipe tunes but looking back it would have been appropriate for the priest in Creignish to call on Stephen B. to pipe Campbell on his way to Judique (where he was met by an even larger number of wagons and two pipers, playing his family tune).

It is unknown who the Glendale pipers were and likewise we don't know who provided the music (and on which instrument) for the Reel of Tulloch that was danced on the green sward outside the church not long after Archibald Campbell had arrived from Creignish. To my knowledge, Campbell's is the only published mention of this dance having been done in Gaelic Cape Breton. Whatever it was, it was obviously danced spontaneously, by both old and young. The priest likened it to a wedding.[51]

While he was at Glendale, Campbell visited the mountain church, St Margaret of Scotland, which served many families who had settled to the westward of Glendale on the plateau lands (now empty). Here he talked to Alexander Chisholm (aged about ninety-two) who had left Strathglass for Cape Breton when he was about twelve (c. 1827).

Dh'innis e dhomh gu'm fac e e-fhein agus athair agus a shean-athair agus a shinn-sean-athair cearta comhla air air na buird a'dannsadh ruidhle an Strath ghlais mu'n d'fhàg e an t-seann dùthaich.

(He told me that he saw himself and [his] father and his grandfather and his great-grandfather precisely [and] together on the boards dancing a reel in Strathglass before he left the old country.)

Campbell mentioned good céilidhean on his travels in Nova Scotia, at Catholic Lismore in Antigonish County and at Presbyterian Baddeck in Victoria County, Cape Breton. It was Maighstir Ruairidh (Reverend Roderick MacKenzie, 1857–1925, pp Iona) who organized the Baddeck visit to the home of a prominent Catholic Baddeck merchant, John E. Campbell (1859–c. 1935). There they had music and dance and stories, and the mission priest wrote that it was the host and his wife who were the best dancers but that he'd give the honour to the wife.

John E. Campbell was married to Mary Ann MacNeil (b. 1860), a daughter of John, son of Little Murdoch MacNeil (Washabuck); Mary Ann was also a daughter of Ann, daughter of Rory, son of Neil MacNeil, and on the distaff side she was a niece of Neil MacNeil, "the millionaire" who was the great benefactor of St Francis Xavier University. John E. and Mary Ann's house was built by her millionaire uncle, and today it is part of Giselle's in Baddeck. Campbell's store, now long gone, was on the town's main street. On her mother's side, Mary Ann (MacNeil) Campbell was a descendant of the piper MacNeil family dealt with earlier.[52] Today (20 February 2000) there are no memories of either John E. Campbell or his wife having been musically or dance oriented.

The mission priest Archibald Campbell, thought that Gaelic was in no danger of dying out in the Nova Scotia Gàidhealtachd in the short term. He confidently wrote without risk of denial ("gun chunnart gu'n àichear e")[53] that the parish of Judique he found in 1907 was as Gaelic as any other on the face of the earth. He was also impressed by the intensity of devotion to the Catholic faith. They are there, he wrote, as attached to the faith as they are to the British Empire.[54] The pending failure of that mighty empire was not easy for him to envisage in 1907. Dr Alexander MacDonald, who gave the farewell address for Campbell, saw the future more clearly, though still from a Christian priest's point of view, when he said, "Am measg ùpraid an linn so, is ro-fhurasda d'ar n-oigridh di-chuimhn a dheanadh air na gaisgich a thàinig air fogradh gu Creideamh an àthraichean a ghleid[h]eadh d'an sliochd."[55] (In the midst of the troubles of this age, it is so easy for our youth to forget the heroes who came through exile preserving the Faith of their fathers to their posterity.)

Catholicism has changed in the diocese of Antigonish, as clerical power has been balanced by that of the laity and influenced by powerful scientific discoveries, but the great empire is gone, replaced by something of a different character and with different strengths and freedoms and weaknesses. Gaelic is on its last legs in northeastern Nova Scotia, and the commercial spirit that some believe corrupts freely given music has deeply penetrated a depressed society living in a very beautiful corner of the world. If the Christian church was the vehicle for the spread of institutionalized caring, shifting responsibility from the individual to the state, then there is a nasty irony in the fact that the emergence of a vibrant, acquisitive tourist and "hospitality" industry in what once was Gaelic Nova Scotia is driving the last nail in the coffin of an ancient, dignified, and in many ways honourable way of life.

CHAPTER FOURTEEN

Some Pipers in Northern Cape Breton

THE MacDOUGALLS

Dan Rory (1885–1957) and his father, Rory MacDougall (c. 1853–1936),[1] were both Gaelic-speaking pipers and well-known characters in northern Cape Breton, from Lowland Cove and Meat Cove in the north of Inverness County to Ingonish Ferry in the southeast in Victoria County on the Atlantic. Both men were also fiddlers, and Dan Rory step-danced and made songs. Both were bilingual Gaelic-English and Roman Catholic. Mike MacDougall (1928–81), Dan Rory's son by his second wife, Mary Ann Whittey,[2] was the most recent prominent musician in the family. Mike lived in Ingonish and earned an enviable reputation far and near as a fiddler. Tape recordings of his music are still widely available. His Whitty mother did not speak Gaelic and neither did he or any of his full siblings. Mike's widow, Peggy (Margaret Francis Donovan), living in Ingonish, told me that Mike was always more appreciated as a fiddler in Bay St Lawrence than in his native Ingonish.[3]

Mike's father and paternal grandfather, although they died and were buried in Ingonish, were both from the more strongly Catholic parish of Bay St Lawrence in the north.[4] As far as I am able to assess the matter,[5] there was more step-dancing and Gaelic traditional, ear-learned Scotch music on the fiddle and the bagpipes in Bay St Lawrence than anywhere else in the north of Victoria County. It was in the northerly communities – Lowland Cove (long empty) and Meat Cove (both just across the county line in Inverness County), Bay St Lawrence, Aspy Bay, and Sugarloaf – that Gaelic lasted longest[6] although in the Pleasant Bay area and the Big Intervale Cape North communities, Gaelic was still spoken into the 1950s.[7] When referring to the language, almost everyone I spoke to in the summer of 2000 pronounced it "Gallic," including George Whitty (b. 1907), Mary Ann Whitty's brother, and thus Dan Rory the piper's brother-in-law.[8]

There are two sets of records about the MacDougall pipers' family in the North Highlands Community Museum in Cape North, and these offer slight differences in places and dates. The earlier set is handwritten and held in ring-binders labelled by family, starting with the pioneer; the second is held in computer memory. For my purposes, the differences are not significant.

The first of these MacDougalls to live in Bay St Lawrence was pioneer Donald MacDougall, born in Christmas Island, Cape Breton, in either 1802 or 1803. His wife was Mary (no last name given), born in Scotland in 1821. There is no record of his, or their, musicality or non-musicality, and local lore is silent about them. They had six sons, including Roderick (Rory, b. 1851), and three daughters. In the ring-binder all the children are described as having been born in Bay St Lawrence. The computer record shows that, chronologically, the first, fourth (Roderick), fifth, and eighth were all born in Bay St Lawrence, while the second, third, sixth, and ninth were born in Sugarloaf. The seventh was born in Aspy Bay.[9] Although there are no Mac-Dougalls in Aspy Bay or Sugarloaf today, within living memory they were abundant there and some of their farmhouses still stand below the forested scarp slope of the Aspy fault, facing the rolling Atlantic.

Donald MacDougall, the pioneer in Bay St Lawrence, is the Donald in Rory Donald Hector MacDougall mentioned in Stephen Rory MacNeil's *All Call Iona Home*.[10] MacNeil had written that MacDougalls had settled in Washabuck but that he had difficulty tracing them, since many had left that area early.[11] What one is led to deduce from their landing place in the New World, and to some extent from early marriages and long-held memories of Barra, is that the MacDougalls were Barra people. The Iona and Washabuck area is peopled mainly from that island.[12]

Stephen Rory MacNeil wrote that Rory Donald Hector (the piper) of "Ingonish lived for a short time in Upper Washabuck. He married Mary (Thomas, Johnnie) MacKinnon, Iona Rear (see 456) and had a son Daniel. 404."[13] The museum records all agree that Rory's wife was Mary MacKinnon, but the handwritten document describes her as Mary MacKinnon of MacKinnon's Harbour in Mabou.[14] Inasmuch as the first Highland settler in MacKinnon's Brook, Cape Mabou, was Hugh MacKinnon from Barra, the earlier record is plausible.

Of the music of the two generations of pipers, Rory MacDougall's would have been the closer to Highland Gaelic, probably Barra, tradition. He was born and reached adulthood long before square dancing became popular (and it was every bit as popular in the north of Cape Breton as elsewhere), which means that his dance music would have been for Reels and step-dancing. Nowhere is there any description of his repertoire or his fingering, but several of the older people in Bay St Lawrence, Aspy Bay, and Sugar-loaf, as well as in the Ingonish area, remember him.

Joe Curtis (b. 1922), Bay St Lawrence, is a grandson of a sister (Annie MacKinnon) of Mary MacKinnon, Rory MacDougall's wife. Joe remembered Rory and just as clearly his (Rory's) brothers Mike and Angus, all born, Curtis said, in Bay St Lawrence. He had recollections also of two of Rory's sisters, one who married a Chaisson and the other, Betsy, who had a spinal deformity.[15] Annie MacKinnon was married to a Brown. They lived in Bay St Lawrence, and Joe spent a lot of time in their home when he was a boy. He remembered sleeping in her bed and her saying her night prayers, always in "Gallic," which he couldn't understand. Because she often talked about Barra, Joe took it for granted that her MacKinnons were Barra folk. He said that Annie may have come out from Scotland and that she settled in Iona, Cape Breton.[16]

While Joe remembered Rory clearly enough, he unfortunately did not remember his piping, and indeed the shortage of memories of his piping suggests that he quit the instrument early in this century, perhaps around the time of the Great War. What Joe Curtis did remember was his fiddling. Joe described Rory as "here today, gone tomorrow."[17] When Rory went to fiddle at a home or a hall, he took with him a pair of red shoes and always changed from his normal shoes to the red ones when it came time to play. Fiddling was not uncommon in the family; Rory's brother Angus had two sons, Jack and Donald, who played the fiddle as did Mike's son Hector.[18] Joe talked about a feud between Rory MacDougall and a Burton family in Bay St Lawrence that got serious and came to a head with one of the Burtons taking a shot at the piper/fiddler. From this Rory MacDougall earned the local nickname "Three-ball Rory."[19]

Joe Curtis told me that on the basis of some of the old local place-names he had concluded that the MacDougalls were pioneers at Bay St Lawrence. They settled along the coast to the east of Bay St Lawrence at a place once called "MacDougall's Settlement." Joe described walking along the shore and finding an original MacDougall basement, long since grown over. Nearby was a track cut up the slope from the sea to allow vessels to be drawn up. He told me, too, that what is now called "Dead Man's Pond" in Bay St Lawrence was earlier known as "MacDougall's Pond."[20]

As the museum records show, Donald the immigrant's oldest son, Alexander (Sandy), stayed in Bay St Lawrence, where all his family were born. Many of the rest of Donald's family appear to have spread out to nearby Aspy Bay and Sugarloaf a few miles southeast through Bay Road Valley. Many later moved away altogether, some to the United States. Yet another local place-name, MacDougall's Cove, is marked on maps of St Paul's Island; it's located to the northeast of Money Point (the northeastern tip of Cape Breton). I have not discovered how the cove was named, but the most likely reason is that MacDougalls fished there.[21]

Joe Curtis had danced in many Square Sets. He mentioned the following fiddlers in this order: Angus Chisholm, Margaree Forks (sometime Cape Breton Highlands National Park warden in the 1930s or 40s), and local men Mossy MacKinnon, Hector Mike MacDougall, and Hector MacDonald (from Bay Road Valley and in Joe's opinion the best local step-dance fiddler by far). However, all through our conversation I was eager to know if he had seen the Scotch Four-Hand Reel. After doing my best to allow him to bring the topic up himself, I asked him what was danced at a Scotch wedding in Bay St Lawrence when he was a lad. Were there any two-couple dances done at those occasions? Straight away he remembered having seen one, and his wife Margaret chipped in with confirmation. Both were eager to expand on the recollection as though this was a topic they had both let slip from their minds and were delighted to rediscover.

Joe told me that when he was seven, in 1929, John J. MacNeil married Janie MacNeil and Joe was left at his grandmother Annie (MacKinnon) Brown's house in the charge of a young woman who was caring for the old lady. He wanted to go to the wedding party and prevailed on the nurse to take him. There he saw two couples, the bride and groom and the best man and his partner, dancing "the Wedding Reel."[22]

On the topic of old Gaelic customs in Bay St Lawrence, Joe spontaneously mentioned George "the piper" at the end of a reminiscence, quite obviously without having intended to broach the subject of piping. There is as little information specifically about piping in this story as there is about Rory or his son Dan Rory, but the incident Joe talked about confirms the existence of another bagpipe player in Bay St Lawrence (to be discussed below) and emphasizes the sad passing away of Gaelic life from the community.

Joe told me that when he stayed with Annie (MacKinnon) Brown, his thoroughly Gaelic grandmother, Angus George MacNeil and his brother Sandy George MacNeil used to visit the old lady. They were all Highlanders and of Barra descent living in times when English was beginning to dominate, and they celebrated the older ways with a lovely little ritual. Each man greeted the old lady at her door in the same manner. Each in turn would hold Annie Brown's hands and then with hands raised they would sing a verse of a Gaelic song, swaying in rhythm, their arms moving gently. They went in and she would offer them a tea, as was customary. Joe said that the MacNeil brothers died in the 1930s, old men in their eighties. When asked who they were, he realized that they were George MacNeil the piper's sons. "There's another piper for you!" he said.[23]

Joe Curtis said that George MacNeil lived by "Piper's Brook," which he also called "George the piper's Brook." He told me that the older folk in Bay St Lawrence still use those names but that they are unknown to the younger people.

I had already known about a piper MacNeil in Bay St Lawrence; he is mentioned under the heading "Pioneer MacNeil, the Piper" in *Cape North and Vicinity Pioneer Families* (1933) by the Reverend D. MacDonald. He settled first at Big Intervale, a Presbyterian farming community southwest of Dingwall and Cape North, but moved on to Bay St Lawrence to be among his fellow Catholics. MacDonald did not name the piper but described his son George as carrying the mail from Bay St Lawrence to Ingonish once a week, on his back, later from Bay St Lawrence to Neil's Harbour "or the Half Way House."[24]

To return to the MacDougalls, Joe Curtis did not have much information to offer about Rory's son Dan Rory. He knew Dan Rory to have been a fiddler as well as a piper. Joe said that in Bay St Lawrence Dan Rory was known as "Dykie Rory," which sounds to be an anglicization of the Gaelic diminutive Dòmhagan or Little Donald. Otherwise all Joe Curtis told me was that Dan Rory had a brother Douglas who moved away to the United States but later returned and settled in Bay St Lawrence, where he died and is buried.[25]

The other person up north to whom I was referred for memories of old Rory MacDougall was Howard Chaisson. I found him working in an outbuilding of his beautifully wooded, oceanside farm lying to the east of the highway in Aspy Bay. Like Joe Curtis, Howard Chaisson (b. 1922, d. 11 November 2000) was a veteran of the Second World War. He was unilingual English and so, he told me, was his father, George.[26] Howard's mother was Catherine MacDougall, daughter of Alexander (Sandy) MacDougall, the first son of the immigrant Donald MacDougall, and Margaret Burton. Catherine was a niece of Rory the piper. She spoke a few words of Gaelic but didn't speak the language fluently,[27] surely because her mother had not spoken Gaelic. Rory the piper used to visit his home territory often enough. His brother Angus lived near the Chaissons' in Aspy Bay, and in the 1920s and 1930s Rory stopped in at his niece's and at other homes of relatives in the neighbourhood. Howard remembered him from his childhood and in retrospect thought that he had stopped in to be properly fed and then moved on. Howard said, with typical Cape Breton rural understanding of foibles, that Rory was a "harum-scarum." Musical ability still forgives what others might consider critical weaknesses. Although other memories assert that Rory was a "Gallic" speaker, Howard said he also spoke English.[28]

Howard described Rory as a piper, fiddler, and step-dancer but could enlarge on none of those talents.

The rest of what I learned about Rory and Dan Rory MacDougall came from the Ingonish area, directly and indirectly, from George Whitty, Bette (Donovan) MacDougall, Maurice Donovan, and Marjorie (MacIntyre) Donovan.

George Whitty (b. 19 August 1907), Ingonish Beach, was Dan Rory Mac-
Dougall's brother-in-law. He knew both of the MacDougalls, but Dannie
intimately.[29] Although George Whitty's life and Rory's had a long overlap,
George told me that he never saw or heard Rory playing the bagpipes. The
subject of Rory's fiddling and step-dancing never came up. All that George
could recollect was seeing the old man sitting on a chair with a set of bagpipes on his knee. He thought that Rory's was not the same set as his son
Dan Rory's and was quite sure that Dannie was by far the better piper. Dannie piped for square dances and "kitchen rackets."[30] He also piped at the out-
door picnics held by St Peter's Catholic Church, and George told me that
there was one outdoor stage.[31] It is also common knowledge among the older
generations, and interested younger folk, that Dan Rory piped at the opening of Cape Breton Highlands National Park and, according to Roland
Hussey (a younger man), at the beach afterwards.

Whitty said that there were three "sets" (he meant what elsewhere are
called figures) in the local square dances before the First World War. He
mentioned Jack Whitty as a well-known prompter.[32] When I asked if and
when step-dance setting steps were used in Ingonish area Square Set dancing, George Whitty said that there wasn't much step-dancing. Then, when I
described the step-dancing done to the reel figure in most of Inverness County and elsewhere in Cape Breton (a style of square dancing that began after
the Second World War, partners stepping facing each other), he said that
there was partner step-dancing but not facing one another.[33] The haziness of
Whitty's reply left me wondering about the subject.

Having given him ample opportunity to mention the next topic himself, I
asked George Whitty if there had been any "two-couple dances" in the Ingonish area when he was a youngster. He told me that there hadn't been. I never
used the word "Reel," so I may not have jogged his memory enough, but not
wanting to send ideas and then be told what it was imagined I wanted to
hear, I left matters there. From this and another's thoughts (included below)
I believe that any Reel dancing there might have been in either the Irish or
the Scotch communities in the wider Ingonish area had become extinct by
the Great War.

George Whitty said that Dan Rory had very little formal schooling but
described him as "smart," associating this not just with his capacity to cope
in his world but also with his untaught ability to compose songs. Whitty also
said that Dan Rory played the bagpipes and the fiddle and that he step-
danced. Whitty remembered him piping and fiddling for dances at the hall
of St Peter's Catholic Church, where he himself had been baptised while the
building was still the church (until 1913).[34] As far as Dannie's lifestyle went,
Whitty told me that he was a woodsman. He married twice, and by his first
wife, Christie (Christena) MacLean from Washabuck, he fathered Tommy,
Dan R., Mary, and Allan. By his second wife, George Whitty's sister Mary

Ann, he also had issue, Mike (fiddler), John, Tim (a fiddler and step-dancer), Christy, and Gabriel.[35]

There are photographs of Dannie MacDougall playing the bagpipes, perhaps the best of them in the second volume of Barry Shears's *The Gathering of the Clans Collection* (page viii). He was a left-shoulder, left-hand-upper player, exactly as George Whitty described him from his mind's eye.[36] George also told me that Dannie sat down to play the pipes, and when I asked directly whether Dannie beat his feet to his own music, George Whitty said, "Yes my dear."

Many of my informants in Cape Breton were unready to admit that a piper they knew was ear learned, that was the badge of incompetence and they felt embarrassed to confess as much so sometimes gave round-about answers. Anticipating that George Whitty might be embarrassed to answer the direct question "Did Danny learn to play by ear?" I delayed asking. I was surprised, when I finally did, that George was not in the least put out by the question. He said that Dannie was an ear piper and that when he passed on music, it was just by ear. George also was the first to tell me that Dannie played a three-drone, "black and white" set of bagpipes, adding that the piper always maintained that his was a pure ivory set. George remembered lots of ribbons. The pipes were destroyed in a house fire in Ingonish Beach,[37] but photographs confirm Whitty's memories of them.

If anything, George Whitty was more impressed by Dan Rory's ability to compose songs than by his other musical talents. He recited two verses of a scurrilous Dan Rory song about a local long-dead politician; he (George Whitty) himself was mentioned in the song, dancing in his red rubber boots. Like all the piper's songs, this one was in English. (I found no one who had collected Dan Rory's songs, but certainly there are fragments available.)[38] George Whitty, smiling at the thought, remembered that in the song Dan Rory called the politician a liar, cheat, thief, and rogue. The aggrieved had sought justice in the court. The judge sat the composer down on a chair in the middle of the courtroom and bade him sing the offending song. As it happened, the magistrate was a fellow Liberal; he chuckled and the case was thrown out.[39]

Bette (Donovan) MacDougall (b. 1923) is the widow of Dan Rory's son Tim (1921–84). We talked at her home in Ingonish Beach on 20 June 2000. She remembered Rory MacDougall only as a big, black-hatted man she feared, but she knew a lot about her father-in-law, Dan Rory. Like his father, he travelled around a lot; she said he was "like bad weather, he was everywhere at one time or another." Among those he visited was Hector MacDougall the fiddler in Bay St Lawrence, presumably his first cousin. Of his music for local hall dances, Bette said that when he piped he had no accompaniment but when he fiddled he was more often than not accompanied by a guitar.

She mentioned Sanford and Jack Whitty as prompters. The square dances were made up of three or four "sets."

Dan Rory died of throat cancer in 1957, and his bagpipes went to his widow, Mary Ann. Mary Ann gave them to their most musical son, Mike the fiddler, and when he died (1981), they were given to his brother Tim, who in turn gave them to another brother, Martin (it was in his home that the pipes were destroyed in a house fire). Tim piped a little by ear. Like his father he also played the fiddle and step-danced. Tim's and Mike's teacher for fiddling (and in Tim's case, also for piping) was their father, Dan Rory. They would play the violin in the bedroom while the old man sat listening in the kitchen. When they went wrong in a tune he would knock on the wall. Sound was all, technique was self-acquired.

Mike MacDougall became well known as a fiddler but Tim also fiddled in public. He played at the old Stardome Hall in Dingwall with guitarist Ralph Williams. None of the family spoke Gaelic except Dan Rory, although his music and sense of Highland timing persisted into the next generation. Mary Ann (Whitty) MacDougall sang at least one "Gallic" song, but Bette knew that none of the Whittys were Gaelic speakers.

Another remarkable memory of local affairs covering eight decades of the twentieth century belongs to Maurice Donovan (the St Peter's baptismal register for 28 October 1883 to 14 July 1918 gives Maurice as b. 3 November 1904, baptised 9 November, son of John Donovan and Emma MacDonald), who now lives at Highland Manor in Neil's Harbour. He still harbours a sharp ill-feeling against the Cape Breton Highlands National Park because his family farm had once been where holes nine and ten of the golf course are now and they had no option but to sell. He described himself as having become a "black Tory" from the date of their eviction/compulsory purchase. We spoke on 14 and 24 June 2000. In this tight little world of relationships, Maurice Donovan is Bette (Donovan) MacDougall's and Peggy (Donovan) MacDougall's (Mike's widow's) uncle. He remembered Dan Rory MacDougall piping for Square Sets at the old St Peter's Church/hall in Ingonish Beach and at the opening of the park. At the latter event, Maurice told me proudly, a military piper who was present confessed that he'd be ashamed to pipe in the presence of such an accomplished piper. Dan Rory piped at his brother-in-law George Whitty's wedding on 5 October 1931 and in general missed as few marriages as possible. Of his travelling habits, Maurice said that Dan Rory was one-third in Ingonish, one-third in Iona, and one-third in Bay St Lawrence.[40] Maurice also remembered the piping of Dan Rory's father, Rory MacDougall, and said that it would have been hard to say who was better. He offered no description of either's music or technique. As to what Dan Rory did in life, aside from music, Maurice said that he "fished lobster, chewed tobacco and snared rabbits and partridges."[41]

Maurice Donovan also told the story of a "horse trader" in days gone by who used to visit the Ingonish Beach area regularly. His first stop was at Dan Rory MacDougall the piper's, and for a small sum the piper would pipe the man down the dusty roads at the head of his wares to catch the people's attention. I asked Maurice who the horse trader was, and without missing a beat he said it was a Farquharson, although he had no idea where he was from.[42]

When we spoke again ten days later, Maurice, anxious to make the correction, said that it was not Dan Rory but his father Rory who had piped for the horse trader. This time he was less than certain that the trader was a Farquharson, thinking he might have been a Ferguson. In any case, Rory was hired for fifty cents or a dollar and the horse trader did indeed lead a string of horses. When the subject turned again to Dan Rory, Maurice described him as a "walking music box." He recollected the titles of four of Dan Rory's songs, "The Lobster Factory," "The Bay," "The Harvest Song," and "The Cook's Song," and the song George Whitty had sung to me about the grasping politician. Of that individual, Maurice said, "He shaved the horse's tail."[43]

Marjorie (MacIntyre) Donovan (b. 1913), South Ingonish Harbour, great-granddaughter of immigrant Roderick MacIntyre, is my last informant on the MacDougall pipers. She was a sister-in-law of Thomas MacDougall (d. 1935), Dan Rory's son by his first wife, Christena MacLean from Iona (d. 1920), and consequently knew that family well. On her own account, her paternal grandfather, Allan MacIntyre,[44] was born in Washabuck around 1848[45] and settled down with his Donovan wife to farm and fish in the Ingonish Ferry area, about where the Castlerock building is today (2000).[46] My informant spent her childhood there. Her knowledge of her extended family history is extensive; what I use of all that she told me comes from a personal interview at her home on 4 August 2000.

Marjorie Donovan remembered Rory MacDougall partly because he used to visit her maternal aunt (Jenny [Ross] Donovan, wife of John J. Donovan), but she never heard his piping. She was adamant that the bagpipes that burnt in the house fire were the same ones that Rory played, which could suggest a purchase from Scotland or possibly the United States. She also knew Dan Rory's first wife, Christena MacLean, who had cared for her (MacLean) father in his old age and had inherited land from him (which eventually went into a fishing boat for Dan Rory). Christena knew Allan MacIntyre, presumably in Washabuck parish, so she and the informant had a strong social connection as well. A similar social bond may have linked the MacIntyres and the MacDougalls.

Dan Rory kept two sons from the first marriage, Dan R. and Thomas (who married Elsie MacIntyre). Of more interest perhaps was that, according to

Marjorie, Dan Rory was an only child and that he and Rory lived in Whitty's Intervale, where George Whitty (above) grew up (now known on maps as Power River, a gravelly and stony strip of river-bottom land, long forsaken). In any case, Dan Rory piped at Marjorie's wedding.

The remainder of what Marjorie told me is of general interest culturally but touches here and there on Dan Rory MacDougall. It is a familiar picture of the older society but with slightly less Scotchness than Joe Curtis remembers for Bay St Lawrence.

Marjorie Donovan told me that while her offspring are musical, none of the earlier MacIntyres that she knew of were particularly musical. However, she step-danced as a child and remembered Dan Rory and his son Tommy step-dancing (Tommy also sang). Her father, Urban "Vyno" MacIntyre, used to take her to St Peter's hall in Ingonish Beach and that way she learned to dance the Square Set. She said it was all Square Sets in those times, and her description of local marriages suggests that Reel dancing did not exist, not even as integrals of Scotch marriages in the south part of Ingonish Beach. I asked her about weddings that she remembered, and she said that they were not big affairs. "You saw the couple married, then had a breakfast and that was it."

She remembered the Square Sets danced in the old hall in Ingonish Beach, the outline of which to the northwest of and abutting the graveyard is still visible. There was a platform where the altar had once been, and the dancing was done in what had been the body of the church. The fiddlers she remembered were Dan Rory and his son Mike MacDougall. She said that the Whittys were all good dancers. She remembered Allan Williams the caller. In her time there was a New Year's Ball and an Easter Ball, and there were regular bean suppers and pie socials, all in or associated with the parish and the old hall. There was a 1st of July picnic when the coastal steamer the *Aspy* brought in people from Glace Bay, Sydney, and North Sydney. There was also a Labour Day picnic. These affairs were held next to the hall on land that since 1983 has been the graveyard extension.

Elsewhere I have noted that, by about the time of the Second World War, the Square Set in rural Cape Breton communities appears to have broken free of its original character to include step-dance setting steps in the reel figure. In communities that were less pronouncedly Gaelic, the term for the fast (reel) figure was the "break-down," so I asked Marjorie Donovan if they step-danced in the break-down and she said they did. She remembered that Tommy, Dan Rory the piper's son, step-danced in the break-down when he was sixteen, at the old hall. Marjorie Donovan said that this was around 1940, but the record shows almost certainly that Thomas MacDougall turned sixteen in 1926.[47]

From her and George Whitty's memories, one can see that step-dancing and its music, on both the bagpipes and fiddle, continued, independent of

Reel dancing, long into the twentieth century in the Ingonish area. Surely one would think that Irish tunes crept into the local musicians' repertoires, but I have not extended my inquiry in that direction. Equally, I am unaware of any Irish Reel dancing survivals in the area, or even prominent Irish speakers or musicians. The Scotch contribution of pipers and fiddlers in the Ingonish area is not inconsiderable.

THE MacKINNONS

Another very Scotch family in the north of Cape Breton was a compound MacKinnon family, in many of its parts very musical and lore oriented. Actually, a few MacKinnon families settled in the north,[48] but the one that included Rory the piper and Angus the step-dancer had a disproportionate cultural influence locally. Many of that family live vividly still in local memory. According to one of his grandsons (John A. MacKinnon, b. 1935), (John) Alexander MacKinnon was a Protestant.[49] Rory MacKinnon was both a piper and a memorable storyteller.

Where the musical MacKinnon family is concerned, there is sometimes confusion between lore and recorded data, but if unwritten memory is accorded its prominence, a not unimportant picture of music and dance in the north emerges. The North Highlands Community Museum data base (NHCM/db) shows two brothers, "Pioneer Archibald MacKinnon" (b. 1841 at Meat Cove) and "Pioneer John Alexander" (b. 1851 at Mabou or Judique), sons of pioneer Archibald MacKinnon (b. c. 1820, d. in or before 1871, place of origin unstated).[50] The son Archibald, religion uncertain, married an Ann Fraser (b. 1836)[51] and had issue. The other son, John Alexander MacKinnon, religion uncertain, married twice, first to Mary Catherine MacDonald, Meat Cove, a Catholic, and second to Elizabeth Fraser, Pleasant Bay, a Protestant.[52] The sons of the first marriage who are remembered locally are John, Stephen, Angus, David, and Archibald; those of the second are David, Duncan, John Alex, and Rory. Among these two families were several musically talented people, including Rory the piper (known locally as "Ciosag")[53] and Angus the step-dancer (known as "Mossy-Face" or "Old Mossy-Face"). The last child born to John Alexander MacKinnon and Elizabeth Fraser was Christie, born in 1907, so John Alexander MacKinnon the pioneer in the north is still remembered by the older people. He is often referred to as "Sandy the flea."

Both Catholic and Protestant MacKinnons settled in Cape Breton, some of the former from Eigg and Barra, some of the latter from Skye, Harris, and Muck. Music and step-dancing are common to both groups.[54] Sarah Jennings categorized Sandy as being "from Inverness."[55]

The museum data base shows that three of Sandy's first wife's children were born in Pleasant Bay on the St Lawrence coast (John, 1871; Stephen,

1872; and Mary, 1874), but the family is associated with Black Point to the east of Meat Cove. Sandy's family by Lizzie Fraser is associated with Lowland Cove, where Frasers were quite numerous once upon a time. But Frasers also lived at various times in Fishing Cove and Pollett's Cove, and there was, I suspect, a transitory nature to the settlement of those places. They appear to have been in essence tiny, to some extent seasonal, fishing communities crooked in the palm of an ancient granite massif. Apart from Pond Intervale, now known as the Grande Anse Valley, these coastal inlets had almost no fertile river-bottom land to encourage subsistence farming. The museum data base gives Elizabeth Fraser as from Pleasant Bay, but Sarah Jennings told me that "Lizzie" was a daughter of Murdoch Fraser from Pollett's Cove; possibly both are right. Sarah elaborated to say that Sandy MacKinnon and Lizzie began married life in Pollett's Cove, later settling in Lowland Cove.[56]

Lowland Cove has been empty of people for decades,[57] but Black Point for a shorter time, having been sytematically cleared in the late 1960s and early 1970s. Black Point was a predominantly Protestant Highland community. There remains bitterness at the breaking up of the community in the name of progress. One local person felt strongly that the forced removal of the settlement destroyed what remained of a valuable linguistic and cultural integrity.[58] Rory the piper was long gone from Black Point when the clearance occurred.

The less thorough genealogical material held in folders at the North Highlands Community Museum (NHCM/f) shows that Alexander MacKinnon's family by "Catherine MacDonald" includes an Angus MacKinnon, and helpfully gives his nickname, "Mossy Face." This earlier source adds another child born to Sandy MacKinnon and his first wife in Pleasant Bay (the first-born, Jessie [1869–1967]). Joe Curtis said that the MacKinnons were "back and forth."[59] Mossy-Face is generally thought to have been born in Black Point and his sister Mary was born there (NHCM/db, 1874). Mossy-Face played the fiddle and step-danced but is best remembered for his dancing.[60]

Sarah Jennings (b. 1917) and Lawrence Petrie recollected that Mossy-Face had a bad finger that had to be held down by an elastic when he played the fiddle. They both talked of the old man with great fondness, so it was surprising to find that four out of the five young people I met at the museum in Cape North had never heard of him (the fifth, Joel Burton, was a relative). Lawrence Petrie told me that from time to time he would ask the step-dancer to pass a judgment on another step-dancer. Often the answer would come, "Good for threshing oats!" One of Joe Curtis's last memories of old Mossy-Face is a sad one. Joe was driving the snow plough one winter and passed Mossy-Face hurpling slowly along the side of the road. Joe said he was moved to sadness knowing what those feet had once been capable of.[61]

Mossy-Face had a full brother Stephen (NHCM/db, b. 1872), who also step-danced.

Alexander MacKinnon's other family, by Elizabeth Fraser, included Rory the piper who was born in Otter Brook.[62] His stone in the Bay St Lawrence Roman Catholic cemetery dates him 1898–1968 and his wife Sarah "Cassie" (d/o Johnnie Fraser and Kitty MacLennan) 1907–82. Other sons of Sandy and Elizabeth Fraser include David (b. c. 1889), John Alex (b. 1892) and Duncan (b. 1900). Besides Rory, Duncan played the bagpipes a bit and David piped and fiddled, although nobody outside the family told me this. There was no report of John Alex's playing any instrument.

A photograph of Rory the piper and his bagpipes is reproduced in Barry Shears's *The Cape Breton Collection of Bagpipe Music*.[63] This and other photographs show that he played the bagpipes under his right shoulder with right hand upper on the chanter. Shears reports that Rory the piper was visited by the song collector Helen Creighton, who recorded him telling stories and playing the bagpipes. Shears states that Rory learned the pipes from his half-brother Red John MacKinnon and other local pipers.[64]

One of my earliest set of reminiscences about Rory the piper came from Andrew "Allie" Timmons (1927–14 September 2000) from Hinkley Glen Road in Red River, north of Pleasant Bay. Allie, who appeared to be in good health (despite the fact that he would live only twenty-five days longer), had a remarkably good memory and had spent almost all of his life in the area, his father Jim having kept the Cape St Lawrence light (from 1927 until the early 1940s). Allie said that Rory the piper spoke Gaelic, though none of his children do. He made his own bagpipes from apple wood in "the Lowlands" without the use of a lathe. These pipes had three drones (which Allie called "reeds") and had a sheep-skin bag.[65] Allie Timmons also called Rory a great storyteller, and he was not the first to pass the observation. Whether or not Rory was aware of any Scotch tradition of pipers being storytellers is almost certainly irrelevant; he was simply a natural storyteller who had a loud voice and who loved the bagpipes.

Allie remembered hearing the sound of the chanter from Rory the piper's home in the Lowlands in the 1930s and knew that Rory had played that instrument before making himself bagpipes. The piper's repertoire as Allie described it was "old Scotch tunes, not the tunes you hear on the pipes today."[66] Where Rory's homes were concerned, he moved from the Lowlands to Black Point and thence to Sugarloaf. Allie repeated the opinion usually held by older folk that pipers had been common in the early days (implying that their numbers had melted away with the decline and disappearance of Gaelic) and that home-made bagpipes and fiddles had not been at all unusual either. Allie, it turned out, unfortunately did not have a tape recording of Rory MacKinnon's piping, as had been suggested to me by one of his nephews. Neither did he know what had happened to Rory's bagpipes over the years or where they were.[67]

Christie Ellen (MacKinnon) Burchell (b. 1940), the old piper's daughter, lives in Sugarloaf on a farm. Opposite her home is a red house, obscured by bushes in the summer, which was where Rory lived when, later in life, he moved to Sugarloaf. Christie and I talked about her father at her home on 29 July 2000. Rory was illiterate in letters and notes. He spoke a little "Gallic" with his wife Catherine "Cassie" Fraser, typically "to keep things ahide on the children," as the saying goes in Cape Breton. Cassie was a Catholic. As for his piping, Rory was completely self-taught. He did not play the fiddle. Christie said that he whittled his first pipes from "an apple tree limb" and made the bag out of deer hide, which he seasoned with molasses. Date? Around 1948. Christie told me that Rory's "half-brother" Dave also played the pipes but didn't have his own set, so he often borrowed Rory's. She also acknowledged Rory's "brother" Mossy-Face the step-dancer.[68] Christie also twice spoke of her father playing the chanter. This instrument and the original set appear not to have survived, and the photographs of Rory and his bagpipes are of the new set he bought later. Christie remembered when the new set arrived at the post office in Bay St Lawrence in the 1950s. Rory had trustingly sent $148 in answer to an advertisement in the *Free Press*, that farmer's magazine," and was obviously thrilled to get them, although they took two years to come.[69]

Starting with the more nearly related memories first, Christie did not know, or surmise, that her father ever piped for any dancing at all, let alone step-dancing. She has a mental picture of him piping in the field outside the red house in the summer and of lines of cars pulling over to listen to him.

In terms of Rory's life and work, however, she said that before he got married he fished for some time in Fishing Cove, the lonely, cliff-girt river mouth to the south and west of Pleasant Bay (once the home of at least one family of Frasers)[70] that now lies in the national park. He also fished three seasons from Pollett's Cove.[71] Christie remembered living in the old schoolhouse in Cape St Lawrence built by Allie's father, Jim Timmons, in the days when Jim's son Freeman had taken over the light-keeping; they were there from 1939 to until about 1942. Then they moved to Black Point for a year and lastly to Sugarloaf in either 1946 or 1948. Rory bought the Sugarloaf property, and Christie marked the improvement over the place in Cape St Lawrence by telling me that at Sugarloaf they had a cow, a horse, and pigs, whereas at Cape St Lawrence they had only a cow. When he lived at Cape St Lawrence, Rory fished at the Lowlands and grew his potatoes at "Big Johnnie's field," which was in "the backlands" about a mile or so inland. When necessary, he used to snowshoe to Pleasant Bay on home-made snowshoes.[72]

John A. MacKinnon (b. 1935) knew more about his father's piping than did his younger sister Christie. He remembered that Rory piped for "kitchen rackets" at Black Point and for dancing at the schoolhouse (now burned down). John A. confirmed that his father had been born at Otter Brook. Rory could dance a bit and certainly spoke Gaelic, though perhaps not all that well. He made snowshoes and moccasins and entertained his children with little dancing men. He fished swordfish like many another.[73]

Douglas MacKinnon, Rory the piper's daughter Tina's son (by Sandy MacKinnon, a relative), told me that his maternal grandmother, Cassie, had told him that pioneer John Alexander MacKinnon had been a piper. Douglas is the only person to volunteer this information and I did not ask anyone else. Douglas also specified that Rory piped at the Sugarloaf schoolhouse for step-dancing. Rory, he said, talked loudly for effect but that it amounted to nothing.[74]

Old Rory was one of those rare folk in his time who were pretty much untouched by formal education and lived to a large extent by older preliterate values. He seemed to cope well enough with difficult conditions. His oldest son, John A. MacKinnon, brought out two other aspects of the piper. First, Rory was intensely superstitious. He always left a house by the same door he entered, a custom that has not died out in rural Inverness County yet. Women were of course absolutely taboo from any vessel. Along the same lines, Rory claimed to be able to cure warts. He heated a piece of chalk in the oven, perhaps rubbed it in soot, and, making the sign of the Cross on the wart, said a Gaelic prayer. People believed that this worked and many turned to him for help. Goodness knows what other cures he may have known. Nobody has begun a file on his cures, or on those of other local Highlanders in the north of Cape Breton. He also invoked spirits to attract fish. John A. described one fishing trip when nothing was going right. Rory took the dory to a certain spot, got out, and walked to a spring where he gathered a pailful of water. He then dropped money into the spring (*uisge airgid*) and returned to the dory and blessed it with the special water. Back out on the ocean he caught a six-hundred-pound swordfish.[75]

Rory's other talent was storytelling. Two stories of his that I heard are of a Faustian nature, with Rory the main character. Both contain a message about self-control, I suspect primarily for youngsters. Christie his daughter said that the following tale was a "ghost story."

It was wintertime and Rory had set out from Lowland Cove on snowshoes for Pleasant Bay, a walk of many miles over rough and exposed mountain country. Exhausted, on his way back with supplies through the driving snow, he stopped in at a house. There in the warmth of a wood fire and the gentle oil light he found the men playing cards "as a pastime" and having each a few drams. Though perhaps not dissipated, they were not guarding their tongues and they were gambling. Rory was invited to join them.

After a while "a knock came on the door" and there in the storm outside stood a well-dressed man looking surprisingly unruffled and unaffected by conditions. Without a question, of course, he was invited in out of the snow. Hospitality in Highland society has for centuries been completely *de rigueur*. The unknown newcomer joined the table and they contentedly resumed their gambling. The well-dressed man began to win and after a while he seemed uncannily unable to lose. The men at the table got more and more frustrated and their language got rougher and rougher.

Rory became suspicious. On a whim he peeked under the table cover and there to his horror he saw the cloven hoof of the goat. When he could find a moment, he made a sign to the woman of the house and she slipped upstairs and returned with a bible. In an instant the stranger in the fine clothes disappeared in a dramatic puff of smoke.[76]

I heard the other story of Rory's from Marie (MacIntosh) MacKinnon of MacKinnon's Hill by Smelt Brook, Victoria County, 5 August 2000. Marie could rhyme off a few Gaelic curses and lewd suggestions that she had learned from an old woman in the neighbourhood, but she (Marie) did not speak the language. In fact, Marie's English was probably more affected by the Newfoundland English spoken at nearby White Point than by Highland English. She used "I be's" and "you be's" and one unusual term that's in the story of Rory and the shoes which follows. She said that Rory used to tell this story and that it had been published.

A small group of men, Rory among them, were in a shack deep in the backwoods. They had been hunting and trapping and they were drinking. There was a lot of foul language, language of the very worst sort. Rory MacKinnon was poor and needed shoes.

Later, when Rory found himself alone in the cabin nursing those temporary ailments that go with carousing, an impeccably dressed man appeared before him. He told Rory he would give him a pair of shoes that would never wear out, an offer which Rory, in his present condition, appreciated. He jumped at the offer.

"But," the stranger added, pausing,"there is a price."

"And what would that be?" Rory asked.

"You must in return give me your soul," the man said.

Thinking it all a joke and that somehow he should never actually fall victim to such a bizarre bargain, Rory took the shoes. The moment they were in his hands, to his profound dismay, the well-dressed stranger disappeared with a crack, leaving a weird acrid odour on the cabin air. To a superstitious man like Rory, forebodings and misgivings loomed.

But the days passed, then the weeks and months, and at last long years and clumps of years, and other things jostled in his mind for attention. He was getting old. And indeed the shoes never did wear out; they never as much as showed a sign of wear and Rory had always been hard on his footwear. Over the years he had grown used to them and took them for granted.

Then one day, when the old piper was standing by the old woodstove in the backwoods shack warming himself, there came a knock at the door. He couldn't imagine anyone so deep in the wintry forest, as he was the only trapper left in MacEachern's glen, but Rory answered the knock and there, to his dismay, was the well-dressed stranger. Rory's blood ran cold. The stranger had changed not one whit, not a grey hair, not a wrinkle; the clothes were exactly the same, the manner polished, detached, commanding.

"I've come to take my side of our bargain," he said to Rory. "The shoes have lasted just as I said they would. Now I shall have your soul."

Rory looked the man over from head to foot and there, bearing out his worst fears, he saw that the man was but half-shod and the unshod foot was not a foot but a cloven hoof. Everything came back to him.

In a flash Rory lifted the lid of the firebox, whipped off the eternal shoes, and began to stuff them into the flames. The devil, for of course the devil it was, made a rush to save the shoes from the flames, but Rory, by preternatural power, managed to consign him as well as the wear-free footwear to the old woodstove.[77]

SANDY MaCLELLAN AND DAN RANALD MaCPHEE

The last old-style piper about whom I accumulated some information in the summer of 2000 was Sandy MacLellan, born at Meat Cove 10 April 1883 to Alexander MacLellan and Mary Powers.[78] An Alexander Sandy MacLellan is buried in St Joseph's Cemetery in Bras d'Or with dates 1874–1939.[79]

My first glimpse of him was given me by a young man, Robert Durando (b. 1965), in August 2000.[80] Robert, a great-grandson of the piper, is accumulating information about him and also teaching himself to play step-dance pipe music on a bellows-blown bagpipe. He told me he was using the singing of his grandmother, Mary Theresa (MacLellan) Burton (b. 1914, Sandy the piper's daughter), then living at Glen Nevis. Robert said that two of his great-grandparents were step-dance and céilidh pipers, Sandy MacLellan from Meat Cove and Dan Ranald MacPhee. Sandy MacLellan was almost certainly the son of the pioneer to Meat Cove Alexander MacLellan (b. 1836).[81] Mary Theresa, however, never met or knew her father's father's name.

Robert said that Sandy MacLellan used to sit down to play the pipes, beating time with his feet in a typically Cape Breton fiddler fashion. Sandy distinguished himself by occasionally standing up and step-dancing while playing the pipes. Robert said that he had this information from a number of people who knew the piper. Mary Theresa confirmed that he was a step-dance piper.

Sandy the piper, raised a Catholic, went to Alder Point when he was about seventeen and at the time could only speak Gaelic. Alder Point's attraction, even to people from the distant Lowlands and Meat Cove, was the "old Toronto mine" at Bras d'Or. In Alder Point Sandy married Protestant Ellen Jane MacDonald. He had five or six daughters and two sons, all of whom could "dance." I asked Mary Theresa what "dance" meant and she replied, "You dance with your feet. You stand on the floor and go to it."

Mary Theresa and her son-in-law, Hughie Durando (b. 1936), said that Sandy was completely ear learned as a piper. He played on the outdoor stages of local picnics, at "garden parties," and for dances (all step-dances) and weddings. He was unaccompanied. At home he piped on the patio for his children's step-dancing. He is remembered in the same quarter as piping on a boat on the "Alder Point Gut," now known as St George's Channel. He also had a piping student, Peter Powers, who was a neighbour.[82] Hughie Durando recollected that the two pipers occasionally used to pipe their way towards each other along the shore of the channel, alternating tunes.[83]

Hughie Durando used the names "MacLennan" and "MacLellan" interchangeably, so when he mentioned that there were MacLennan neighbours, as well as Powers, in the Alder Point area, it was tempting to think that Alder Point had been a place where Lowland Cove and Meat Cove MacLellans went around the turn of the century.

A photograph of Sandy MacLellan shows that he held his fingers straight on the chanter. No one knew where he got his bagpipes, although Hugh Durando suggested that they were a battlefield set from the First World War. They are still kept in the family. Mary Theresa said that Sandy died young as the result of an ulcerated tooth. The cemetery record appears to contradict this.

Dan Ranald MacPhee, the other step-dance piper mentioned by Robert Durando, was Hugh Durando's grandfather through a daughter Catherine Anne MacPhee. Hugh was uncertain where Dan Ranald was born, perhaps in or near Benacadie Pond, but was sure that Dan Ranald and his wife, Ann MacLean (d. c. 1939, aged c. 65),[84] were Gaelic speakers. Dan Ranald moved to Bridport, where he worked on the railway. Apparently he was an ear-learned piper. He was dead before 1936, according to Hugh.

Catherine Ann was a step-dancer and she sang Gaelic songs. Hugh Durando told me that Catherine Ann had a sister Janie, the baby of the family, who had married a Harold "Buddy" Slauenwhite. He said that they were still living and owned an old set of bagpipes. When I phoned them I was told that

Dan Ranald had never played the bagpipes and that Janie had no bagpipes.

Since I finished my summer work in the north of Cape Breton in 2000, two of my informants have died, Allie Timmons and Howard Chaisson, neither very old men. By the time summer comes again there will be fewer still of the old school left, whether of English, Irish, Scottish, Newfoundland, or Magdalen Island origins (the autochthonous people are long gone), and the older, poorer, subsistence-oriented life of home-made entertainments and neighbourly dependence will have receded further into the mists. In the lifetime of Maurice Donovan, George Whitty, or anyone a little over ninety, a great deal can change and many things disappear forever, like the caribou.

In December 1914, agents Bryant and Paul got off the ss *Aspy* at Bay St Lawrence. The men worked for "the Federal Detective Agency" and were on their way to arrest a "gang" of armed robbers in the hinterland of Meat Cove. They picked up their guide, a local man and Gaelic speaker, at Wreck Cove in a motorboat, then came ashore in heavy surf at Meat Cove. The muddy roads could not take a team, so they had to tramp over roads and fields until they reached the "last house in Cape Breton" at one-thirty in the morning. The next lap was about four miles further along a dirt road, and that took another hour, but at this address they captured one of the wanted men, who went without a struggle. There followed another four-mile tramp to yet another home. Here the dog barked, and agent Paul approached the door.

"I stood outside listening but could not hear anything but Gaelic and that was beyond me," Paul is reported to have said.[85]

Today there are very few, if any, homes in Cape Breton where a family could all use Gaelic. I don't believe that Gaelic is the first language of a single family, and I am almost certain that there is no unilingual Gaelic speaker alive in Nova Scotia, probably in North America. The last census indicates that almost every Gaelic speaker in Cape Breton was beyond the age of child-rearing; none of them had passed the language on. There are certainly no Gaelic speakers in the north of Cape Breton. In 1914 there were thousands, from Meat Cove to the western marches of Colchester County in Nova Scotia. So much can change in a lifetime.

Conclusion

This work on piping in both Scotland and Cape Breton, long as it is, is obviously incomplete. It does, however, state that piping in the Gaelic communities on both sides of the Atlantic was much the same at the times when piping was an integral part of Gaelic-speaking communities. While the terms "dancing" and "step-dancing" were synonymous, as they still are in the post-Gaelic Scotch communities in Cape Breton, the music was the same in certain identifiable ways, no matter the instrument. A large amount of work remains to be done in Scotland to discover just what happened to step-dancing in the Scottish Gàidhealtachd (and elsewhere in Europe).

Unfortunately, it appears to be too late to explore community or district variations in techniques and repertoires, and perhaps in speed of playing, in piping in Nova Scotia. The Gairloch tradition, whatever it was, is gone from Pictou County. Tape recordings of old pipers like Alex Currie and Joe Hughie MacIntyre in Cape Breton offer a starting point from which we can begin to understand traditional piping, but they can only point tantalizingly to a rich and widespread musical tradition that has sadly disappeared. There are no answers to questions about the distinctiveness of piping on Canna (the Jamiesons in Piper's Glen in the Margarees), on Eigg (the MacQuarries and MacKinnons in Antigonish County and in Cape Breton), on Muck (the MacKinnons at East Lake Ainslie), in Clanranald country (the MacDougalls, MacLellans, Campbells, and Gillises), and in Keppoch (the Beatons and the Campbells in the Mabou area and the MacDonells further north). We have a corpus of post–Second World War fiddling records from Gaels in Cape Breton whose roots were in Lochaber and Moidart and elsewhere but perhaps not enough to extrapolate to piping. Fiddling repertoires have expanded dramatically as the literate accumulation of tunes has become commonplace, since the last war.

However old Rory MacKinnon may have played, his kind is gone. Allie Timmons, who was no more than an unskilled listener to piping, noted acutely that Rory's repertoire was distinctively conservative and bound intimately to Gaelic tradition.[1] Douglas MacKinnon, the piper's grandson, told me that Rory played only fiddle tunes, which he picked up by ear.[2]

Hugh Cheape, in his review of William Donaldson's *The Highland Pipe and Scottish Society*, summed up the current state of things by noting that "the stranglehold of the social élite has loosened," adding that pipers "with a fierce enthusiasm for their art ... are keener than ever to interpret and sustain the music of the Great Highland Bagpipe, which arguably is now happening more imaginatively and musically than at any time since the early nineteenth century."[3]

Cape Breton so far does not play a large part in the resuscitation of the classical piping form. A few Cape Breton step-dance pipers use some fingerings long associated with pibroch – the "dre" and the trill on F, for example – but as far as we know, these were only used in dance music.[4] Pibroch playing was not an enduring feature of immigrant farming communities in the Nova Scotian Gàidhealtachd, but important linkages between the two forms (dance and pibroch) are emphasized in some Cape Breton piping. On the other hand, over the last few years the piping world has turned with quickened pulse to Cape Breton to learn about dance-music bagpiping. The same is happening with step-dancing and fiddling. A glance at the curricula at Sabhal Mór, Ostaig, and at Ceòlas in South Uist proves the point.

Cape Breton piping has become important and how quickly have so many "Cape Breton"–style pipers emerged from so many unexpected corners of the world! The very least one can say is that there is a rapidly decreasing tendency to derogate those who prefer to play with what George Sutherland (Cape Breton Highlanders) called "leaky fingers." Subtler step-dance timings are returning to piping. The importance of having a large and flexible repertoire is now recognized by all those who play for Four-Hand and Eight-Hand Reel dancing. Thus are one's labours rewarded.

Glossary

BAILIE – An agent (esp. land) or land administrator.

BÀRDACH – Poetry.

CADET – A younger son or branch of a family.

CANNTAIREACHD – The singing system of transmitting pipe music in preliterate times.

CÉILIDH (*pl.* CÉILIDHEAN) – A Gaelic social event involving, often, music and dance, story and song.

CEÒL BEAG – Small music; a modern term for non-classical pipe music.

CEÒL MÒR – Great music; a modern term for classical pipe music.

CHANTER – The fingering part of a bagpipe.

CIOBAIR – A game-keeper.

CLAIRSCHEAR – A harp player.

CLANN AN SGEULAICHE – The Children of the Storyteller.

CLÀRSACH – A Gaelic Scottish harp.

CREANLUDH or CRUNLUDH (modern spelling) – An advanced and complicated note embellishment in traditional and modern classical piping.

DRONE – A reeded pipe whose note is adjustable by length.

DRUMANACH – Elder wood.

EAR LEARNED – One who has learned music by ear.

EAR PIPER – A piper whose music was learned only by ear.

EISTODDFOD – A modern Welsh public singing and poetry event.

FALAMH – Empty, deserted.

FEUAR – One who holds land for the annual payment of a feu.

FINISHING – An equivalent of master-class musical training.

GÀIDHEALTACHD – The Gaelic-speaking community.

GILLE CALUM – A Scottish Gaelic dance long-since modernized.

GOBHA – A smith or blacksmith.

HANOVERIAN – One who supported the government of the house of Hanover.

HEREDITARY PIPERS – A modern term describing the tendency for piping to be retained in families.

HERITABLE JURISDICTIONS – Inheritable legal power.

IMPROVER – One whose motive for development of natural resources was predicated on personal profit.

JACOBITE – A follower of King James or his heirs.

LALLANS – A variety of English spoken in Lowland Scotland.

LITERATE – Learned by means of written sources.

MARBH-RANN (*pl.* MARBHRAINN) – Death verse, eulogy.

MELIEURATIER – An improver.

MERK – An old Scots coin worth 13/4d. Scots or $13^1/_3$d. sterling.

MERKLAND – Land and/or occupation valued at a MERK.

MOD – A modern Scottish Gaelic public singing event.

PATRONIZED PIPERS – Pipers whose security of tenure was in some degree guaranteed.

PECK – An old Scottish land value.

PIBROCH – A piece of pipe music, a term now used exclusively for classical piping.

PÌOBAIR – A piper.

PÌOBAIREACHD – A piece of piping (PIBROCH – see above).

PRELITERATE – Not reliant on writing for transmission of data.

RACK-RENTING – Unreasonably greedy rents.

REITEACHADH – A marriage contract; the party enjoyed at a betrothal.

SEANNACHAIDHEAN – Storytellers and lore bearers.

SETT – An allotting of an estate's large farms.

SGEULACHDAN – Stories or tales.

SIUBHAL – A following movement based on the theme of a PIBROCH.

SLOINNEADH – A naming identifying a person in his or her family.

TACK – A major farm holding on a Scottish Gaelic Highland estate.

TACKSMAN – The holder of such a farm (a TACK) who had rights to sublet.

TOBHTA – A roofless ruin with walls standing in whole or in part.

TRADITION(AL) – Cleaving to conservative, long-term community usage.

TUDHLUDH (also TULUDH) – A classical piping grace-note embellishment less complex than the CREAN/CRUNLUDH (the "ludh" was the little finger).

TUNING SLIDE – That part of a bagpipe drone that could allow shortening and lengthening of a drone.

UILLEAN – Elbow; a descriptive of a droned pipe whose air was given by a bellows squeezed by an elbow.

ÙRLAR – A ground, or theme, of a piece of classical pipe music; the base for the SIUBHAL and later variations, including the TUDHLUDH and CRUNLUDH.

VIOLAR – A player of a viol (a forerunner of the violin class of stringed instruments).

WADSET – A type of landholding in Gaelic Scotland gained in return for the long-term loan of a large sum of cash – not unlike a pawning transaction.

WADSETTER – One holding land by this type of tenure (WADSET).

Notes

INTRODUCTION

1 Steven G. Ellis's observation that "a pan-Gaelic perspective would be more appropriate to the late medieval period than the separate study of Ireland and Scotland as nations in the making" is a shrewd one (Ellis, *Tudor Ireland*, 16). Whether or not his statement that "the influence of Gaelic Scotland on Ireland was clearly substantial" is valid for instrumental music in the same period remains to be discovered (ibid., 12). The spread of the three-sided harp from Gaelic Scotland to Gaelic Ireland suggests this direction (see Sanger and Kinnaird, *Tree of Strings*).

2 James MacPherson, collector and editor of the Ossian stories, is known to have received and given a receipt for four or five old Gaelic texts from "Neil M'Murrich," the last of the South Uist bards. The transaction was witnessed by M'Murrich's interviewer, Reverend Angus Mac Neil of "Hovemore" in South Uist in 1763/64. M'Murrich also told his interviewer that he had read in another, more lengthy manuscript, which had been lost. These losses apparently caused no outcry in Gaelic Scotland, perhaps because memory was more important to cultural retention than the written word. (Angus Mac Neil, letter to Dr Blair, in *inter alia* Grant, *Thoughts on the Origin,* 389–92.)

3 Charles Rearick's *Beyond the Enlightenment,* while dealing with the emergence of French folk scholarship in the early nineteenth century, charts an historiography from Giambattista Vico (1725) through James MacPherson (1760–63) then the Grimms (1812–22) to the French school (Thierry, Barante, Ballanche, Fauriel, Michelet et al.). Much was collected but much was overlooked. Even today there are gaps in the fields of study of professional anthropologists in white European rustic cultures such as Gaelic Scotland's (although the techniques of the archaeologist are now being used to explore relatively recent physical remnants of various Highland communities).

4 Accepting payment of one form or another for one's musical contribution is

and has been normal in Scots Gaelic society for centuries, but the departure from the céilidh, where music, song, story, and other social contributions were unrelated to any concept of gain or exploitation, has resulted in another level of professionalism that offers little or no support to the remaining warmth of social life.

5 MacDonald, "Compleat theory of the Scots Highland Bagpipe," passim. Mac-Donald did not suggest that pibroch and dance-music piping were novel developments but neither does his description of the "first authors" of both classical and dance-music piping (that is, one and the same people) suggest antiquity. By 1760, when MacDonald wrote, there may already have been some decline. He undoubtedly sensed that ceòl mór was in rapid, uncorrectable decline.

6 "Ceol-Suaicheantas Morair Bhraidh'-Albainn. The distinguishing Family Tune of The Lords of Breadalbane. An ancient Gaelic Melody," unpublished MS held by Edinburgh University Library, George Square. Attempts to identify and recall this part of the Angus Fraser MSS (Gen. 614) in 1996 failed; a librarian located Angus Fraser's work but was unable to separate this portion of it. Angus Fraser was a natural son of Simon Fraser (1773–1852), the editor/collector of *The Airs and Melodies.* Sanger and Kinnaird's work implies a spread of the three-sided harp from Scotland to Ireland in medieval times (see *Tree of Strings,* passim).

7 Bruford, "The Rise of the Highland Piper," first page.

8 MacKay, *Collection,* 162.

9 I have heard a recording of a modern group singing medieval French music and using, from time to time, the bagpipe, and the fingering could only be described as unimaginative.

10 Correspondence from Alan Bruford, archivist, School of Scottish Studies, University of Edinburgh, to Ann Heymann, Minneapolis, 1 March 1986. I am very grateful to Dr Bruford for a copy of this letter, together with a copy of "The Rise of the Highland Piper."

11 Bruford, "The Rise of the Highland Piper." Harp tuning lies outside my area of knowledge, but scale gappings similar to the early bagpipe's may have been employed.

12 The records of clàrsach and harp players in Scotland have been published in *Tree of Strings* by Keith Sanger and Alison Kinnaird.

13 In the conclusion to her important article "On the relation of Norse skaldic verse to Irish syllabic poetry" MacKenzie, a prominent authority on Scottish bagpiping and particularly on the bardic and bagpiping output of John Mac-Kay, the blind piper of Gairloch (Iain Dall Mac Aoidh), wrote: "Pipe music also has some devices which remind us of skaldic technique, such as the breaking up of two or more melodies, which are then intertwined as if to form a third ... Another device is 'rogue' linking; all the phrases of a *piobaireachd* tune are matched up in repetition or echo except (usually) one or two, one of which is then developed as a rogue in the next section. This is

close to the 'rogue' linking in both skaldic and Irish poetry. Both Welsh harp music and *piobaireachd* have forms with a short recurring refrain or repeated variation, very similar to the *stef* in the skaldic *drápa*. *Piobaireachd* also has a variation using substitution, comparable to the *ofljóst* technique of the skalds. // *Piobaireachd* was composed in the same circumstances as court skaldic poetry. Its purpose was the same ('occasional'); the social background was the same; the tradition of impromptu composition was the same; the composer had the same relation with his overlord, the same prestige, the same rewards, the same travels. All that Professor Turville-Petre says (*Scaldic Poetry*, p. xvi) is equally true of the Hebridean clan piper. The clan system was destroyed in the eighteenth century, but the classical music survived."

14   See Deirdriu's "Lament for the Sons of Uisnech," a ninth-century song in Murphy, ed., *Early Irish Lyrics,* xviii.

15   The modern Irish musician and musicologist Seán Ó Riada (1931–71) noted on no stated authority that "so-called [dance] music, [was] imported for the most part into this country in the 17th and 18th centuries" (Ó Riada, *Our Musical Heritage*, 50). Assuming Irish dance to have much longer roots, if there were analogies with sung poetry, what dance parallels existed alongside the old syllabic system of classical poetry, and what ones coexisted with the later emerging lyric *amhran* system in the fifteenth and sixteenth centuries? And does a near absence of mention of dancing in the sagas mean that the Norse didn't dance?

16   Keltie, *History of the Scottish Highlands*, 2:157 (where a footnote cites "*Gregory's Highlands,* 301–303"). See also Piobaireachd Society, *Pìobaireachd*, book 2, 57–9, and Bridget MacKenzie, *Piping Traditions,* 63–5. In an earlier example, a complaint was made in 1592 against Alastair Stuart of Ardvorlich and others for theft of cattle. The defendants were charged with having come onto the complainants' lands "with twa bagpypis blawand befoir thame" (Haldane, *The Drove Roads of Scotland,* 9, citing RPC [Register of the Privy Council], 1st series, 5:28). John Johnston's claim to have known the tune celebrating the clan battle of the North Inch of Perth in 1396 (Keltie, *History of the Scottish Highlands*, 1:66) is discussed elsewhere.

17   Even here I have had difficulties and I ask the reader to indulge my whim. For example, because there was a MacLean group at Culloden I have treated the non-Jacobite Loch Buidhe piping, the little that there is of it, in the Jacobite section dealing with the MacLeans, where geographically they belong. I don't know if Ulva people were Jacobites or not but I have discussed them also with the MacLeans to avoid too much geographical fragmentation.

18   MacDonald, "Compleat Theory of the Scots Highland Bagpipe," Laing MS 111, 804.

19   Ibid.

CHAPTER ONE

1 Daiches, *Charles Edward Stuart*, 319.
2 Tayler and Taylor, *1745 and After.* (In essence, this was the "narrative" of John William O'Sullivan, one of the seven men of Moidart and a man hated by Lord George Murray. O'Sullivan's MS forms part of the Stuart Papers held at Windsor Castle.)
3 Allan Stuart Donald was with Ogilvie at Culloden. The piper's great-grandson, George W. Donald, born near Forfar in 1820, became a locally well-known Lowland song-maker. (Rogers, *The Scottish Minstrel.*) Both Reid and Sinclair may have been closer to a Lowland tradition of piping than the Highland one, whether or not they were Gaels.
4 Home, *History of the Rebellion in Scotland in 1745*, 148.
5 Agnew, *Hereditary Sheriffs of Galloway*, 2:323.
6 Leneman, *Living in Atholl*, 230–1.
7 MacDonell, *Spanish John*, 42.
8 Fraser, *Airs and Melodies*, 104, in note to tune no. 80. In Gaelic, Gow would have been "gobha" (blacksmith).
9 Originally fifty-three Jacobite estates were surveyed. Of these, forty-one were taken over by the Barons of Exchequer. Most of them were sold at public auction but thirteen remained. The thirteen Jacobite estates forfeited or, in other words, inalienably annexed to the Crown were Barisdale, Cromarty, Lovat, Perth, Struan, part of Kinlochmoidart, Monaltry, part of Arnprior, Locheil, Ardsheil, Callart, Lochgarry, and Cluny. Of these, the first eight were operated by unpaid commissioners who were first appointed in 1755. The other five were first held of subject superiors (such as Colin Campbell of Glenure for Ardsheil, Callart, and parts of Cameron of Lochiel's estate) and after 1770, when the Crown purchased these superiorities, commissioners assumed the running of them from the Barons of the Exchequer. In the five were Locheil, Ardsheil, Callart, Lochgarry, and Cluny, as well as the remaining parts of Arnprior (in Stirlingshire) and parts of Kinlochmoidart (Youngson, *After the Forty-Five,* passim). Lovat's estate was returned in 1774, the rest, according to Youngson, in 1784.
10 Fraser-Mackintosh, *Antiquarian Notes,* 124–5; and McLean, *People of Glengarry,* 121.
11 "Account of the competition of Pipers," in MacKay, *Collection,* 17 n.
12 (Farquharson), *Survey of Lochtayside 1769,* Scottish History Society, series 3 passim.
13 For a treatment of the client-superior relationship between MacGregors and Campbells, see MacGregor, "A Political History of the MacGregors before 1751" (PhD thesis); and (anonymous) "Rìgh gur mór mo chuid mhulaid."
14 Campbell, "The MacGregor Pipers of the Clann an Sgeulaiche," in *Piping Times* 2, no. 10 (July 1950).

15 Logan, *The Scottish Gaël,* 2:289.

16 Chantreau, *Voyage,* 3:85–6, cited in Bain, *Les Voyageurs français en Ecosse,* 46.

17 Watson, "Place names of Perthshire," *Transactions of the Gaelic Society of Inverness* (*TGSI*) 35:281 (talk given 11 April 1930).

18 Comunn na Piobaireachd, *Piobaireachd,* book 10, 287.

19 Ibid. The other known MacGregor piper was Glengyle's, James Campbell Mac-Grigor, who was made prisoner by the Hanoverian forces, tried for treason at Carlisle, and transported on 21 November 1748. (See Seton and Arnot, *Prisoners of the '45,* 94, 95.)

20 For Campbell of Glenlyon's service in the 42nd, see Stewart, *Sketches,* vol. 2, appendix no. 111, *inter* lx and lxi. James Campbell, alias MacGregor, listed as a piper of Glengyle's Regiment, composed mainly of MacGregors from Perthshire, was transported as a traitor after Culloden, but this was bad luck rather than selective revenge against MacGregors or pipers. As Walter Scott noted, most of the MacGregors returned to their old lives after Culloden (Scott, "Author's Introduction," in *Rob Roy*).

21 "Contemporary Letters on the Rebellion of 1745. Prefatory Notes by the Editor of the 'Northern Chronicle,'" in "Selections from the Family Papers of the MacKays of Bighouse," *TGSI* 21:149.

22 By 1745, apart from Glenlyon and one or two other, minor Campbells, Clan Campbell was resolutely, if not always courageously, Whig and Hanoverian.

23 Stewart, *Sketches,* 1:263 n.

24 Ibid., 1;263.

25 Ibid., 2:65. Lt Campbell of Glenlyon is likely to have served in Capt. John Campbell of Ballimore's company of Fraser's Highlanders.

26 Campbell, *Lairds of Glenlyon,* 279.

27 Collinson, *The Bagpipe,* 180.

28 Keltie, *History of the Scottish Highlands,* 2: 245–50.

29 Rob Roy MacGregor, born c. 1660, was a younger son of Donald MacGregor of Glengyle, a lieutenant-colonel in King James VII's army. Note that Charles Fraser-Macintosh described Col. Macgregor of Glengyle, who was at Dingwall on the day Culloden was fought (with Col. Coll MacDonell of Barisdale [of Glengarry's regiment] and MacLeod of Raza), as "Rob Roy's son." See Fraser-Mackintosh, "Minor Highland Septs – the Mac-Donells of Barisdale," *TGSI,* 13:89 (1886–87).

30 The Jacobite Elibank Plot, originally planned for 10 November 1752, was a leaky one. It was postponed and finally aborted after the arrest on 23 March 1753 of one of the messengers, Dr Archibald Cameron, who was hanged at Tyburn the same year. Andrew Lang's comparison, made in the 1890s, from the two extant sets of records, left by "Pickle" and "Young Glengarry" (Alasdair Ruadh), shows that they were the same person. Lochgarry, the other messenger to the Highlanders, had led the Glengarry MacDonells during the '45. He was

an unshakeable Jacobite who after Culloden, with a band of loyal followers, had killed a dozen redcoats who were driving off his cattle. James Mohr (*sic*) MacGregor, as Lang called him, was also certainly treacherous, as Lang proved (Lang, *Pickle the Spy,* 234–5, 240–7).

31 Lang, *Pickle the Spy.*

32 Scott was careful to make the appropriate disclaimers about his Rob Roy stories, noting in his "Author's Introduction" that he was "far from warranting their exact authenticity." He, or his publisher, was by no means so scrupulous in apologizing for his lack of knowledge of Gaelic or its orthography. The tune Rob Roy asked for in 1738 (recte "Cha till mi tuilleadh" [I shall return no more]) has for years been accepted as the gloomy, eve-of-action creation of Donald Ban MacCrimmon before he left with a MacLeod militia company to fight the Jacobites in 1746. It has gone from being called "Cha tile mi tuil" in 1797, to "MacCrummen will never return" in 1838, and to the current "Lament for Donald Ban MacCrimmon." (Campsie, *MacCrimmon Legend,* 175, 180.)

33 Stewart, *Sketches,* 2:xiii (appendix). Stewart devoted five pages of his appendix (xiii–xviii) to expatiating on Rob Roy.

34 "A Circumstantial Account of the Competitions for the Prizes" (given also as "Account of the competition of Pipers"), in MacKay, *Collection.*

35 Logan, *The Scottish Gaël,* 289.

36 Report of the piping competition held in Edinburgh in October 1784, *Scots Magazine* 46:552–3 (October 1784).

37 "Account of the competition of pipers," in MacKay, *Collection,* 15.

38 Burns, "John McGregor of Fortingall and his descendants," 109.

39 Cannon, *The Highland Bagpipe,* 76.

40 Ibid., 76. Cannon cites "Transcripts of entries in the minute book of the Highland Society of London, copied by Campbell." There is more recent scholarship pending.

41 I am indebted to Peter Cooke for drawing the importance of John MacGregor to my attention.

42 "Account of the competition of pipers," in MacKay, *Collection,* 17.

43 Ibid., 18.

44 Lang, *Pickle the Spy,* passim. Alexander MacDonell (Young Glengarry) is reported as captain in Lord John Drummond's regiment in a list of prisoners captured in one of Drummond's transports by HMS *Sheerness,* 25 November 1745. (See Blaikie, *Itinerary,* footnote in the first page of the "Postscript Lochgarry's Narrative." The same footnote refers also to Young Glengarry's statement that he had been imprisoned in the Tower of London for twenty-two months, citing Stuart Papers, B.H. App. clxxxv.)

45 The record of piping in Catholic Glengarry, Morar, Glenaladale, Moydart, and Keppoch, not to overlook largely Protestant Cameron country, for the period in question, is diffuse and difficult to discover and assemble.

46 "Account of the competition of pipers," in MacKay, *Collection,* 17.

47 Alasdair Ranaldson was in a powerful clique that patronized and promoted
    Gaelic life, language, and culture. He was a friend of Sir Walter Scott and
    David Stewart of Garth, but a slightly unbalanced, unpleasantly imperious
    proto-caricaturist of a bygone age. He played his tartan part in welcoming King
    George IV to Edinburgh in 1822 and posed for Henry Raeburn, armed in the
    full garb of his ancestors.

48 Fraser-Macintosh, "Glengarry's piper and the canal commissioners in 1807,
    etc.," in *Antiquarian Notes,* series 2, 149–55.

49 The "Account" for the July 1801 competition at Edinburgh gives his age as
    "near four score." See "Account," in MacKay, *Collection,* 17.

50 In Scots Law to dispone meant to convey or to assign (OED).

51 McLean, *People of Glengarry,* 17, 221 n. The wadset held by Archibald Mac-
    Donell of Barisdale for his part of Knoydart clearly constituted something near
    enough to ownership, in government eyes, allowing it to expropriate by forfei-
    ture and annexation.

52 According to *Clan Donald,* Donald MacDonald was a paternal grandson of
    Ronald MacDonell (ninth of Glengarry and second of Scotus). He was cham-
    berlain of the Glengarry estates in 1733, from which he held wadsets for land.
    He bought the lands of Innerhadden in Rannoch from James, duke of Athole, in
    1736 and Lochgarry in 1738. (The estate of Lochgarry included Dalnaspidal,
    Dalnacardoch, Dalanfhraoich, Tom 'ic 'ille Donach, Dalantaruaine, Dalnamein,
    Drumachine, Drumchastail and Pitcastle.) Donald of Lochgarry married Isabel
    Gordon, daughter of John Gordon of Glenbucket. One of their sons, John,
    obtained the Lochgarry estate when it was restored; he also served in Fraser's
    Highlanders (78th) in 1757 and died in 1790 a lieutenant-colonel commanding
    the 76th Regiment. The other son, Alexander of Lochgarry, died a general in
    the Portuguese army. (*Clan Donald,* 3:328–31; and, for Lochgarry's holdings,
    Leneman, *Living in Atholl.*)

53 Stewart, *Sketches,* 2: 65.

54 Donald MacDonald, a unilingual Gael, is named as having been MacDonell's
    piper during King George IV's Edinburgh visit in 1822. (Prebble, *The King's
    Jaunt,* 135.)

55 McLean, *People of Glengarry.*

56 Johnston, letter to the *Oban Times & West Highland Times,* 3 September
    1919.

57 MacCulloch, *Highlands and Western Isles of Scotland,* 378.

58 Scotus, a small estate in Knoydart, was owned by a branch of the Glengarry
    family. It was neither forfeited nor annexed after Culloden. (McLean, *People of
    Glengarry,* 17.)

59 Monroe, *Chapters in the History of Delaware County, New York,* 65.

60 Whyte (Fionn), *Martial Music of the Clans,* 55.

61 Bearing in mind, for example, the large number of pipers from Morar who
    settled in Inverness County, Cape Breton, in the first two decades of the

nineteenth century, the average tacksman had an embarrassment of piping talent that must have seemed inexhaustible.

62 Lang, *Companions of Pickle.*

63 From his testimony at his treason trial in Edinburgh in 1754, he intimated that, on the strength of what he considered his strong case for his wrongful inclusion in the Act of Attainder, he had remained in Highland Scotland, where he had been ignored by officialdom because he had a pass granted him by Lord Albemarle in 1746. Archibald told his prosecutors that in June of that year (1746) he and his father, Coll, second Barisdale, had surrendered to Sir Alexander MacDonald, JP in Skye, before the cut-off date so as to avoid being attainted (Fraser-Mackintosh, "Minor Highland Septs").

64 "Selections from the Family Papers of the MacKays of Bighouse," *TGSI,* 21:120–71 (1896–97).

65 Executions in 1753 included Seumas a'Ghlinne (James Stewart) as accessory to Glenure's murder, Dr Archibald Cameron Jacobite agent, and the Sergeant Mór (Cameron, in the French service). Arrested and imprisoned that year were Alexander MacSorlie (Cameron of Glen Nevis), his bother Angus Cameron of Dunan in Rannoch, Cameron of Fassifern (who had judiciously stayed out of the '45), his lawyer Charles Stewart, Bàrasdal Og, John MacDonald, younger of Morar, Spanish John MacDonell, and others.

66 SRO E786/5/2, Mungo Campbell to D. Moncrieff, 12 June 1753, cited in McLean, *People of Glengarry,* 21, 22.

67 An Act to amend and enforce so much of an Act made in the nineteenth Year of his Majesty's Reign, as relates to the more effectual disarming the Highlands in Scotland (21 George 2, cap. 34), 1748.

68 21 George 2 Cap 34, An Act to Amend.

69 Citing the judicial rental of Barisdale in 1748 (SRO E741/1/1), McLean gives the apparent rental, after the losses of 1746, as £63, with the more reasonable figure being £133, since the tenants were paying rent to both Bàrasdal Og and the government. (McLean, *People of Glengarry,* 72, 227 n. 27.)

70 Fraser-Macintosh, "Minor Highland Septs," 93. Bàrasdal Og was sentenced to death for high treason (22 March 1754) but was granted a last-minute reprieve, the first of a number. He served several years of an indeterminate prison sentence in Edinburgh Castle until 29 March 1762, when he was released and took up a short-lived commission in the Queen's Highlanders (105th) under Col. David Graeme of Gorthy. Graeme of Gorthy's 105th Regiment had two battalions; it was embodied at Perth some time in 1762, served in Ireland, and was reduced in 1763. (Stewart of Garth, *Sketches,* 2:331, 332.)

71 Tearlach MacFarlane, Glenfinnan, wrote that there was doubt over who the progenitor of the Keppoch Inverlair MacDonald family was but that it was generally believed to have been a Clanranald MacDougal. (Personal correspondence to the author, 18 December 2000.)

72 McLean, *People of Glengarry,* 158.

73 If one works from Fraser-Mackintosh, "Donul nan Gleann," son of Eneas, third of Scotus, is counted the fourth, although he predeceased his father. If one accepts this numeration, Donul's son by his second marriage, Ranald Mac-Donell, is the fifth.

74 Fraser-Mackintosh, "The MacDonells of Scotos," 88, 89. The best treatment of the Knoydart emigrations is found in McLean, *People of Glengarry.* Marianne McLean suggested that the John MacDougall of Kinlochlochan was one of the two John MacDougalls who left Knoydart for Glengarry County, Ontario, in 1786. (Ibid., 109, 237 [citing emigrant list NA, MG29 C29]). To my knowledge, no record, written or otherwise, of MacDougall piping exists in Upper Canada.

75 MacAulay, "The Art and History of the MacDougalls of Aberfeldy," *Piping Times* 16, nos. 4 (7–10) and 5 (9–14). (January and February 1964). See also MacKenzie, *Sar-Obair,* 298–300.

76 "No longer does a Glengarry, with a numerous retinue, headed by Allan Dall, hold high festival in Glendulochan." (See Fraser-Mackintosh, "Minor Highland Septs," 102.) A Gleann an dubh Lochain is on the Inverie River.

77 Ordnance Survey, sheet 35, Loch Arkaig (revised to 1967), NG830(–832), 083(–085).

78 "Account of the competition of pipers," in MacKay, *Collection,* 16.

79 Tayler and Tayler, *1745 and After,* 65ff. (Note: The Taylers remarked that Lochgarry's honesty over the Loch Arkaig treasure had been questioned.)

CHAPTER TWO

1 In the 1740s MacDonell of Keppoch held his lands from MacIntosh and the duke of Gordon.

2 "Battle of Prestonpans – Sir John Cope's army," in Blaikie, *Itinerary of Prince Charles Edward Stewart,* 90 (citing Cope's trial, GCT 38–43, and *Scots Magazine,* 441).

3 MacMillan, *Bygone Lochaber,* 217–34. The claim, by Cameron of Lochiel, that in the prince's absence, he was leader of the Jacobite force in Scotland, would have ensured greater strictures on the estate and more sedulous policing after Culloden (J.S. Gibson, *Lochiel of the '45*).

4 See military disposition in Scotland in autumn 1747, *Scots Magazine,* September 1747, 453.

5 Forbes, *The Lyon in Mourning,* 3:91.

6 Ibid., 1:91, 92.

7 Queen Victoria wrote of pipers playing near Bridge of Roy, September 1873, but left no impressions of their music (Queen Victoria, *More Leaves from the Journal,* 244).

8 MacKenzie, "Lochaber Bards," in *Scottish Gaelic Studies,* vol. 10, part 1, 36 (August 1963); MacLean, *The Gaelic Bards from 1411 to 1715;* Campbell, *Songs Remembered in Exile,* 248; and Mac Gill-eain, *Ris a' Bhruthaich,*

211–34. Norman MacLeod appears to have used the term "Goistidh" in the sense of "old friend" (MacLeod, *Caraid nan Gaidheal,* 22).

9 The difficulties of fitting Dòmhnul Donn into the wider Keppoch MacDonell genealogical web is dealt with by Somhairle Mac Gill-eain in "Domhnall Donn of Bohuntin" (Mac Gill-eain, *Ris a' Bhruthaich*).

10 Campbell lore in the Mabou area of Inverness County, Cape Breton, confidently confirms this Campbell connection with the MacDonells of Keppoch. These Campbells were active Jacobites.

11 MacMillan, *Bygone Lochaber,* 157–8.

12 Dughalach, *Orain, Marbhrannan agus Duanan Ghaidhealach,* 2–4. See also MacDonald and MacDonald, *The Clan Donald,* 2:669, 670.

13 Whyte, *Martial Music of the Clans,* 97. Alexander MacDonell, known as Am Màidsear Mór (the Big Major), brother of Ronald, seventeenth of Keppoch, settled in Prince Edward Island in 1803, but I have no idea who accompanied him.

14 One difficulty regarding the Glenaladale emigrations to Île St-Jean in the early 1770s is that by no means all the names of the immigrants are known and, to my knowledge, no piper is identified among those whose names are known or among the immigrants of the earlier twenty-five years.

15 Archibald MacDonell was the fourteenth Keppoch, thus making Donald of Tirnadrish a first cousin of the sixteenth Keppoch.

16 MacDonald, *Back to Lochaber,* 286. I have not read the Borrow volume in question.

17 Keppoch was one of five MacDonald divisions (Sleat, Glengarry, Clanranald, Keppoch, and Glencoe) left to nurse their memories and hopes when the MacDonald Lordship of the Isles was suppressed in 1493. The idea that Keppoch chiefs were outlaws and thugs must be balanced against their own perception of Gaelic politics.

18 According to *The House of Gordon,* vol. 3, Alexander Gordon, fourth duke (1743–1827), raised a company for the 71st (Fraser's Highlanders) in 1775 to be captained by his wife's brother, a Maxwell. Stewart of Garth's list of officers of the 1st Battalion includes a Captain Hamilton Maxwell of Monreith (Stewart, *Sketches,* 2:89). The Gordons, until after Culloden, did not command the military fealty of the Keppochs.

19 MacDonald, *Highland Vocal Airs.*

20 MacKenzie, *History of the MacDonalds,* 498.

21 MacKenzie, *Sar-Obair,* 163, 164.

22 Matheson, *Songs of John MacCodrum,* 179, 304 nn.

23 Ibid., 304–5.

24 Comunn na Piobaireachd, *Piobaireachd,* 4:106. The date of Gardyne's interview with MacDonald is unknown.

25 The tune is also known as "MacQuarrie's Gathering" (*Piobaireachd,* 4:106). "An Tarbh Breac Dearg" was also attributed to Raonul MacAilein Oig by Arisaig folk c. 1950 (MacLean, *The Highlands,* 66). For later man-wrestles-bull

stories, see the adventures of Roualyn Gordon Cumming and the Borlum bull in Alexander MacDonald, *Story and Song from Loch Ness-side,* 137, 138, and Allan of Lathaig and the bull at Sloc Huimhligearraidh in Eigg, in *Tocher* 10, (1973): 51, 53.

26   MacPherson, "Notes on Antiquities from the island of Eigg," 582, 583.

27   Robertson, "Topography and Traditions of Eigg," 202; the article was read to the Gaelic Society of Inverness on 24 February 1898. Angus MacQuarrie (b. 1918), former warden of Antigonish County, who had visited Eigg and talked family with local historian Hugh MacKinnon (dec.), said that his (Angus's) paternal grandfather, the piper John MacQuarrie, was himself the descendant of an Eigg MacQuarrie who was known as "the big piper" and who flourished in MacCrimmon times. (John MacQuarrie emigrated and settled in Arasaig, Antigonish County, Nova Scotia, and died in 1874.)

28   MacKay, "Clanranald's Tacksmen of the Late 18th Century." See also MacDonald, *Moidart or among the Clanranalds.*

29   Necker de Saussure "minéralogiste et géologue réputé, fait une partie de ses études à l'Université d'Edimbourg pendant les années 1806, 1807 et 1808" (Bain, *Les voyageurs français en Ecosse).*

30   MacKay, "Clanranald's Tacksmen of the Late 18th Century"; and de Saussure, *Voyage to the Hebrides.* For lore dealing with Angus Lathaig MacDonald, see Hugh MacKinnon, "The MacDonalds of Laig," in *Tocher* 10.

31   Information from Hugh Cheape, assistant curator, National Museums of Scotland, 18 September 1992.

32   See "The Piper of Netherlorn," *Glasgow Herald,* 12 September 1834; also cited in Buisman, "More evidence on Colin Campbell."

33   MacKinnon, "Captain John MacDonald and the Glenaladale Settlers."

34   MacKay, "Glenalladale's settlement," 19.

35   Ibid., 20, 22.

36   Cameron, "A Romantic folly to Romantic folly," 888–91.

37   Ibid.

38   MacDonald, *Moidart or among the Clanranalds,* 215.

39   Queen Victoria, *More Leaves,* 272. According to "The Piper of Netherlorn" cited above, the grandson of Donald Campbell living in the Argyll-shire island of Luing showed the writer an old repaired pipe chanter given to his grandfather by Prince Charles a day or two after Culloden. (Buisman, "More evidence on Colin Campbell," part 1, appendix, 27, 28.

40   Canntaireachd was a singing system for transmitting ceòl mór (classical bagpiping) extra-instrumentally. It existed in the eighteenth and nineteenth centuries and is still used by some pipers. Many tunes were written down by Colin Campbell in the 1790s. Campbell must have anticipated the expiry of the old Gaelic memory-based foundation of piping. Notes and grace-notings are represented by otherwise meaningless vocables not dissimilar to, but more complicated than, the sol-fa system. In Campbell's earliest form, it is dependent on

the unambiguity of sound and singing. The reader is directed to the works of Frans Buisman and Barnaby Brown, both of whom have studied the subject minutely.

41 John MacCodrum's fidelity to the Presbyterian Church was less than unwavering. He once deserted the pews for seven years over an argument with the local minister.

42 Alexander MacDonald, known as Alasdair an Oir (Alexander of the Gold), was a son of MacDonald of Borrodale and, after he bought Captain John's estate, ninth of Glenaladale.

43 MacKay, "Glenalladale's Settlement," 17–20.

44 Blundell, *The Catholic Highlands of Scotland*, 199.

45 MacKay, "Clanranald's Tacksmen of the Late 18th Century," 65.

46 See "Allan MacCormack, Robert Brown and the leaving of South Uist," in MacCormack, *Highland Heritage & Freedom's Quest*, 63–8.

47 "Account," in MacKay, *Collection,* 16.

48 MacAulay, article in *Piping Times,* February 1963. MacAulay's work offers no references.

49 "The MacIntyres – Hereditary Pipers to Menzies of Menzies," in "Account of the Hereditary Pipers," in MacKay, *Collection,* 14.

50 The MacIntyre pipers in modern industrial Cape Breton may yet prove to be descendants of Robert MacIntyre, but so far no evidence links the Old and New World piping MacIntyres.

51 An illustration of the Bannockburn bagpipes has been published in Charles North, *The Book of the Club of True Highlanders*, vol. 2 (1881), plate 56, and these pipes have been discussed in print by D.P. Menzies ("Note on the 'Bannockburn Bagpipes of Menzies," in *Proceedings of the Society of Antiquaries of Scotland* [1894-94], 29:231–4, and A.A. MacGregor, *Land of the Mountain and the Flood,* 154–78).

52 MacDonald, "Pìobairean Smearcleit," 345.

53 Daiches, *Charles Edward Stuart,* 145–6. The tune under the same name appears in Nathaniel Gow's *Select Collection of Original Dances, Waltzes, Marches, Minuets and Airs*, 1815 and 1835 (posthumously). I am grateful to John Donald Cameron, Judique, for that information. John Donald, who has the immense repertoire of one of the last Gaelic-speaking Inverness County fiddlers, did not know the tune or the title. A commontime tune called "The King Shall Enjoy" is found in James Oswald's *Caledonian Pocket Companion*, NLS, Glen 203, book 2, p. 20.

54 Allardyce, *Historical Papers,* 2: 411.

55 Stewart and Stewart, *Cochruinneacha Taoghta,* 111.

56 The rebuilding of Achnacarry, at huge expense, contributed to Cameron's need to find more lucrative income from his lands than traditional Highland agriculture afforded. Allan Cameron in Meoble (South Morar) casually wrote to Archibald MacMillan in Montreal, early summer 1802: "The grand castle at

Achnacarry is going on with great speed, the estimate, [I] am told, is from 8 to £9,000 Sterling. He [Cameron of Lochiel] is in the country himself at present, but does not trouble any of his friends" (MacMillan, *Bygone Lochaber,* 181). The old Achnacarry house had been destroyed by Cumberland's forces. (Allan Cameron, somehow and at an undetermined time, displaced the old MacDonald family in South Morar, a member of which settled in Low Point, Inverness County, Nova Scotia, in the early nineteenth century.)

57 "Account of the Competition of Pipers," in MacKay, *Collection,* 16.

58 Clunes lies at the east end of Loch Arkaig overlooking Loch Lochy in the Great Glen.

59 MacMillan, *Bygone Lochaber,* 182.

60 Henry Thomas, Lord Cockburn (1779–1854). Probably born in Edinburgh; died in Bonaly, near Edinburgh.

61 Lord Cockburn, *Circuit Journeys of the Late Lord Cockburn,* 107–8.

62 "Account of the Competition of Pipers," in MacKay, *Collection,* 16.

63 Stewart calls this officer Cosmo Martin in his list of officers of the 77th (Stewart, *Sketches,* 2:60). MacMillan gives Cosmo Gordon (also known as Cosmo Martin and Cosmo MacMartin) as eighth of Letterfinlay, a farm on the Cameron of Lochiel estate (MacMillan, *Bygone Lochaber,* 18). Stewart earlier wrote that Cosmo Gordon "and 55 non-commissioned officers, pipers and privates" were killed at the second battle at Quebec, a battle that involved Fraser's Highlanders but not Montgomerie's (Stewart, *Sketches,* 1:319, 2:60).

64 Captain Cameron died of fever in August 1759; his final resting place is the old Protestant cemetery in Quebec.

65 MacMillan gives this officer as Ewen MacSorlie (Cameron), thirteenth of Glen Nevis, and names a private who joined Fraser's Highlanders, presumably with him, Ewen MacMillan (1736–1836) (MacMillan, *Bygone Lochaber,* 46, 92).

66 Stewart names Ensign Duncan Cameron "of Fassfern" among the wounded at the second battle of Quebec (David Stewart, *Sketches,* 1:319).

67 Stewart, *Sketches,* 2:89, 90.

68 Stewart gives no list of officers and only called this officer Cameron of Callart (Stewart, *Sketches,* 2:159). The detail of his family comes from MacMillan (MacMillan, *Bygone Lochaber,* 124).

69 Robertson, *The King's Bounty,* 209.

70 Stewart, *Sketches,* 2:251. MacMillan gives "Phillips Cameron" (MacMillan, *Bygone Lochaber,* 133) and dates his lieutenant-colonel's commission in his father's regiment (79th) at 19 April 1804. Another son of Col. Allan Cameron mentioned in MacMillan is Ewen Cameron, captain in the 79th and ADC to his father (ibid., 133). Nathaniel Cameron, yet another son, became lieutenant-colonel in the 2nd Battalion of the 79th in 1813 (ibid., 134). These sons of Erracht were born in England; their connections with Lochaber are not known.

71 Stewart, *Sketches,* 2:260. MacMillan describes John Cameron as born at Inverscaddle, 16 August 1771. He was fostered by "Ewen Bàn MacMillan at

Kinlocharkaig" and died a colonel at Quatre Bras (MacMillan, *Bygone Lochaber,* 140). The pipe(r)-major of the 92nd during the Peninsular War was Alexander Cameron, a Lochaber man ("Cameron, Alexander" in "Notices of Pipers," *Piping Times* 20 [January 1968]: 4, 6–7).

72 MacMillan was at pains to point out that there were a few tacksmen and rank and file who showed reluctance to fight for the Jamesian restoration, but after the property rape of Lochiel's estate after Culloden, there seems to have been no Cameron incentive to seek commissions in the Black Watch (MacMillan, *Bygone Lochaber,* 164–6).

73 Stewart, *Nether Lochaber,* 389.

74 For passenger lists and other information concerning the 1802 emigration of MacMillans, see Anderson, "Ships' Lists of Lochaber Immigrants 1802," 5–13; and Fleming, *Lochaber Emigrants to Glengarry,* passim.

75 MacMillan, *Bygone Lochaber,* 64.

76 Ibid., 88, 93.

77 Ibid., 87.

78 Comunn na Piobaireachd, *Pìobaireachd,* 10:290, 291.

79 There is no Dungallan on the old Ordnance Survey 1″ to 1 mile map but, according to Somerled MacMillan, Dungallan appears in the first half of the seventeenth century in association with John Cameron, first of Dungallon, son of Donald (tutor to Ewen Dubh, fifth Cameron of Lochiel [b. 1629]) (MacMillan, *Bygone Lochaber,* 136).

80 MacLeod, *Caraid nan Gàidheal,* 394–405.

81 Campsie, *MacCrimmon Legend,* 177.

82 Rev. Norman MacLeod's son, the Rev. Donald, in writing of his (Rev. Donald's) brother, Rev. Norman, noted: "Except to those immediately concerned, genealogies are uninteresting, and those of Highland families, with their endless ramifications, eminently unprofitable. It will be sufficient to state that I have before me a family 'tree' – such as used to be so common in the Highlands – in which are the names of the Camerons of Glendessary, scions of Lochiel" (MacLeod, *Memoir of Norman MacLeod, D.D.,* 2).

83 Malcolm MacQueen discovered that "the famous Highland minister, Roderick MacLeod (known as Maighstir Ruairidh)," visited Orwell in Prince Edward Island in the early pioneer days (MacQueen, *Skye Pioneers,* 71). MacQueen also described an instance of clerically inspired fiddle destroying in the Macdonaldite religious community (also of North Skye origin) in the same area of Prince Edward Island in the early nineteenth century (ibid, 84).

84 Ibid., 96 n, 109.

85 Fraser, *Some Reminiscences and the Bagpipe,* 291, 292.

86 David Daiches notes that "it was in Episcopalian households that the older traditions of music and poetry were more likely to be preserved, especially in the north-east" (Daiches, *Paradox of Scottish Culture*).

87 MacLeod, *Caraid nan Gàidheal,* 394–9.

88 "Litir o Fhionnladh Piobaire, mu Oidhche na Calluinn" (Letter from Finlay
    Piper concerning New Year's Day), in MacLeod, *Caraid nan Gàidheal,* 395.
89 Ibid.
90 Ibid., 396.
91 "Mac an Abraich" is the patronymic of the MacLeans of Coll (Dwelly, *Gael-
    ic-English Dictionary,* 1022).
92 MacLeod, *Caraid nan Gàidheal,* 384–90.
93 The order to pillage and destroy the property of the Jacobites in Athole had
    been given even earlier, on 13 February, to Sir Andrew Agnew of the Royal
    North British Fusiliers based in Blair.
94 "Lairds of the Central Inner Hebrides and adjacent mainland 1761–1771," cit-
    ing the "Valuation Roll for Argyllshire," in Timperley, *A Directory of
    Landownership in Scotland.*
95 Forbes, *The Lyon in Mourning,* 1: 293.
96 The information is contained in an official sworn list of losses sustained by
    Cameron of Lochiel's tenants from 1745 to 1747.
97 Fergusson, *Argyll in the Forty-five,* passim.
98 General John Campbell of Mamore, commander of HM's loyal Hanoverian
    forces in the West Highlands in 1745 and '46, was the duke of Argyll from 15
    April 1761 until 9 November 1770. He was succeeded in the dukedom by his
    son Col. John (Jack) Campbell, formerly of Loudon's Highlanders, also art
    and part of the devastating of the Jacobite areas of the Highlands in 1746 and
    a keen improver. Col. Jack died in 1806.
99 MacMillan, *Bygone Lochaber,* 181–2.
100 MacLeod, "Comhradh nan Cnoc," in MacLeod, *Caraid nan Gàidheal,* 79.
101 Through Finlay the Piper, MacLeod laid blame particularly at the door of the
    wives of the tacksmen: "O'n a sguir na mnathan uaisle de labhairt na Gàelic,
    o'n a thòisich iad ris na tighearnan òga 'chur do Shasunn a dh'fhaighinn an
    ionnsachaidh ... chaill mi mo thlachd dhiubh, cha-n aithnich iad mi." (Since
    the ladies gave up speaking Gaelic, since they began sending the young lairds
    to England for their education ... I've lost my pleasure in them, they don't
    know me.) (MacLeod, *Caraid nan Gàidheal,* 22.) Stewart of Garth, writing,
    generally, in 1822, remarked on the decline in the education of "the youth of
    the second order of Highland gentry [who] are more degenerated and more
    changed in every respect than the Highland peasantry." Stewart did not
    attribute this degeneration to educational policy but said that "three-fourths of
    the old respectable race of gentlemen tacksmen have disappeared, and have
    been supplanted by men totally different in manners, birth, and education"
    (Stewart, *Sketches,* 2; xxxi).
102 "Litir o Fhionnladh Pìobaire, mu Oidhche na Calluinn," in MacLeod, *Caraid
    nan Gàidheal,* 395.
103 "Litir o Fhionnladh Piobaire, mu'n Bhliadhn' Uir" (Letter from Finlay, about
    the New Year), in MacLeod, *Caraid nan Gàidheal,* 402.

104   Ibid., 404.

105   MacLeod acknowledged receipt of stories from his readership (MacLeod, *Caraid nan Gàidheal,* 40, 43).

106   Another suggestion that Caraid nan Gàidheal was intimately aware of the Glendessary area is found in this line in "Litir o Fhionnladh Pìobaire, mu oid-hche na Calluinne": "Thug am Brocair dhuinn Dàn a' Choin ghlais." (The vermin-destroyer gave us the Song of the grey Dog.) The grey dog, also known as the "Cù glas Mheoble" (The Grey Dog of Meoble), is a forerunner of death in the South Morar family that held Meoble, a farmable river-bottom acreage lying immediately west of Glen Pean and Glendessary.

107   The MacIntyres farmed a property known as Camas na h-Eirbhe (Bay of the Fence/Wall) near Callart on the north shore of Loch Leven. According to Somerled MacMillan, they were given the farm by the Stewarts of Appin some time after the latter were granted Mamore by King James IV in 1502. The question of its transference to the Camerons of Lochiel is untouched. These MacIntyres claimed descent from a Patrick MacIntyre, younger son of the MacIntyre chief of Glen Noe. During the '45 two sons of Duncan, ninth of Camas na h-Eirbhe, John and Donald, fought for Prince Charles, the latter dying at Culloden. John wrote an elegy for him. Later generations were known for their attachment to the Church of Scotland. MacMillan made no mention of instrumental musical talent in the family (MacMillan, *Bygone Lochaber,* 107–9).

CHAPTER THREE

1   That loyalty of many to King James also existed despite the fact that a Campbell of Argyll had long ago suborned the MacLeans' old ally Donald Cameron (1719–48), sixth of Locheil ("the gentle Lochiel of the '45"). His wife was Ann Campbell, daughter of the fifth Auchinbreck.

2   Many of them were Camerons whose chieftain, Cameron of Glendessary, held part of the Morvern estate that had once belonged to MacLean of Duart. It is also interesting to note that the Tiree people were solidly Jacobite in 1745.

3   Archibald Campbell was known to many in Scotland as the uncrowned king of Scotland. He was naturally angered that he could not control his tenants and sub-tenants.

4   Keltie, *History of the Scottish Highlands,* book 6, 227.

5   General John Campbell of Mamore (c. 1694–1770) became the fourth duke of Argyll in 1761, succeeding his uncle.

6   Fergusson, *Argyll in the Forty-five,* 217, citing Campbell to the duke of Cumberland, in Campbell of Mamore MSS 391.

7   One would have expected "Mac Cailein Mhóir" but the text gives Dwelly's usage (Dwelly, *Gaelic-English Dictionary,* 1005).

8   Cregeen, "The tacksmen and their successors."

9 A "kindly tenant" was one who held land hereditarily and customarily often by virtue of his or his ancestors' relationship to the chief or simply at the chief's indulgence.

10 SRO, GD 112/29/51/6, cited in Sanger, "MacCrimmon's Prentise," 17.

11 Archibald Campbell, third duke of Argyll, was an Etonian, a lawyer, and a resident of London. He was a stranger to Gaelic life and was treated as an alien by many of his tenants (Lindsay and Cosh, *Inveraray and the Dukes of Argyll*, 67, passim).

12 The Campbell gentlemen who were active Jacobites in 1745 were Alexander Campbell of Ardsliginish (in Ardnamurchan), known also as Am Pàpanach Mór (The Big Papist), and Archibald Campbell, younger son of Campbell of Glenlyon. The inactive member of the clan was the Jacobite agent Sir James Campbell of Auchinbreck (Donald Cameron, the "Gentle" Lochiel of the '45, was married to Ann Campbell, daughter of Auchenbreck). The Mac a'Ghlasraich Campbells in Lochaber were answerable only to Keppoch, ergo Jacobites.

13 The citation is taken from the General Register of Sasines, Scottish Record Office. I am indebted to Dr N.J. Mills for drawing my attention to this and other data concerning the last MacLean of Coll and his landholdings. The dates of his time as laird (1828–56) were given me by Dr Kenneth A. MacKinnon, Saint Mary's University, Halifax, Nova Scotia.

14 MacDougall, "The MacLeans of Foot Cape," in MacDougall, *History of Inverness County*, 336.

15 Ibid.

16 MacDougall, *History of Inverness County*, 517, 518; and Gibson, *Traditional Gaelic Bagpiping*, 246–8.

17 "Dìomoladh Pìoba Dhòmhnuill Bhàin" (The dispraising of Donald Ban's Pipes) made c. 1760, in Matheson, *Songs of John MacCodrum*.

18 Neil Rankin Morrison, from Kengharair in Mull, wrote that when Hector Rankin, of the Conduiligh family, left Mull for Greenock in 1804, "This was the first time, for 500 years at least, that Mull was without a Rankin who could play the pipes." (Morrison, "Clann Duiligh." A long-hand copy of this article was kindly given the author by Dr Kenneth A. MacKinnon, a descendant of the last Conduiligh Rankin who emigrated to Prince Edward Island in 1820.)

19 Ibid.

20 Whyte, *The Rankins – Pipers*, 4. Whyte cited Skene, *Celtic Scotland*, 3:481.

21 Ibid., 6; and Morrison, "Clann Duiligh."

22 Whyte, *The Rankins – Pipers*, 4, 5.

23 Johnson, *Journey to the Western Islands of Scotland*, 85.

24 "They told me during my stay in Mull that there had been beyond all time of memory in that island, a college or society of bagpipers which was not even entirely extinguished after the death of the famous Rankine, who had the direction of it about thirty years ago. M'Rimmon kept a similar school in the isle of Skye, and some of the principal families of the Hebrides always kept a piper,

whose office was hereditary" (Faujas de Saint Fond, *Journey through England and Scotland to the Hebrides in 1784*, 2; reproduced in *Piping Times* 26, no. 6 [March 1974]: 16–19).

25 Whyte, *The Rankins – Pipers*, 4. Whyte cited Skene, *Celtic Scotland*, 3:481.

26 MacDonald, "Compleat Theory of the Scots Highland Bagpipe." There is no evidence that Joseph MacDonald visited either Skye or Mull.

27 Morrison, "Clann Duiligh."

28 Ross, "Ceol Mor." Ross did not name any other colleges besides the MacCrimmons' and the Rankins'.

29 Both Ross and Johnston (Coll) managed to overlook the famous and prolific Blind Piper of Gairloch, or else considered him a product of Skye tuition.

30 Matheson, *Songs of John MacCodrum*, 2, 62–73, 250–61.

31 Although no relationship has been put forward, John MacCodrum almost certainly was related to the Trotternish Neil MacCodrum, piper to one of the MacDonald-led independent companies from Skye in 1746.

32 Matheson, *Songs of John MacCodrum*, 62.

33 Ibid.

34 The MacCrimmon believed to have been the most prominent in the 1760s was Dòmhnul Ruadh, Red Donald.

35 Matheson, *Songs of John MacCodrum*, 62, verse 4.

36 "A.M.S" (A MacLean Sinclair), "Clann Duilligh," in *MacTalla* 12, no. 2 (24 July 1903): 12–13.

37 Whyte's article is confirmed and enlarged upon by Neil Rankin Morrison, Kengharair, Isle of Mull, in "Clann Duiligh: Pipers to the Clan MacLean," referred to above. It is probable that Whyte's main informant, Condullie Rankin Morison, Dervaig, Mull, was closely related to Neil Rankin Morrison. The Rankin-Morrison relationship to the piping Rankin family springs from the marriage of Conduilligh mac Neill (emigrated 1820) to Mairearad Nic-Gilleathain (Margaret MacLean) in Ceanna gharair (Kengharair) in Mull in 1817 (see A.M.S., "Clann Duilligh," in *MacTalla*, 24 July 1903).

38 Whyte, *The Rankins – Pipers*, 13.

39 Yet another Coll John Johnston, John MacLean Johnston (Iain mac Alasdair 'ic Lachlainn 'ic Aonghuis 'ic Alasdair), was also a piper. His father's dates were 1843–97, so he was probably born c. 1865. An electrician, he emigrated to the United States, date unknown; no further information.

40 Cannon, *Bibliography*, 28.

41 In Cape Breton many people untrained in genetics believe that particular skills in music and dance are coded, carried, and transmitted genetically and not simply acquired through the richness of the family social environment.

42 This chorus, according to Neil Rankin Morrison, is all that remains of a song. (For an English translation, see, Morrison, "Clann Duiligh." Matheson cited the original Gaelic lines in "Dìmoladh Pìoba," 251.)

43 Whyte, *The Rankins – Pipers*, 8; and in Morrison, "Clann Duiligh." Although no occupations or vocations are given in Neill McNeill's "Census of the Small Isles 1764–65, at Canna 20th March 1765," a Duncan Rankin aged 30 is the head of the third family included in the "list of the people of Isle Muck protestants." Rankin's wife was Bess McCrimmon aged 27; his sons were "Allexr Rankin" and "Mallcum Rankin"; and the family had two servants, "Cathrina McLean" and "Caristina."

44 Whyte, *The Rankins – Pipers*, 10.

45 Ibid.

46 There was no Duncan MacLean, laird of Coll, in the eighteenth century, and while there are varying opinions concerning the twelfth of Coll, Neil Rankin Morrison, Kengharair, Mull, said that his name was Donald (Morrison, "Clann Duiligh," 73). Donald is given elsewhere as the tenth of Coll. Matheson gave Catherine, Neil the piper's wife, as Catrìona nighean Theàrlaich mhic Eachainn ("Dìomoladh," in Matheson, *Songs of John MacCodrum*, 251–2).

47 MacKinnon, "Rankin, Coun Douly (Con-duiligh MacRaing)."

48 The Duncan Rankin presumably of the story above is said to have met his future wife, Janet MacCrimmon, while receiving instruction with a MacCrimmon piper in Skye.

49 On the basis of an English translation of "an old song which was at one time very popular [regularly sung] among the people of Letter [Leitir/Lower] Torloisk, where Clan Duiligh lived," the son of "Robert the Smith" was "descended from Clann Duiligh and Patrick MacCrimmon." No date is given (Morrison, "Clann Duiligh," 37).

50 Unless there were a MacLean of Muck distinct from MacLean of Coll, this move to Grisipol must have taken place in or after 1857, when Muck was sold by the last Coll. This is not possible if they are the same people as mentioned in the census of the Small Isles referred to above.

51 "Account of the Hereditary Pipers," in MacKay, *Collection*, 13.

52 Dòmhnull Donn, in "Notices of Pipers," *Piping Times* 26, no. 9 (June 1974): 24. In Poulter's genealogy of the MacCrimmons, a Janet MacCrimmon, daughter of Iain Dubh MacCrimmon by his first wife, MacAskill, was married in America to a Ferguson (Poulter, *History of the Clan MacCrimmon*, part 1). John Johnston, Coll, said nothing about any MacCrimmon in Coll.

53 *TGSI*, op. cit.

54 "A.M.S." (A. MacLean Sinclair), "Clann Duiligh." This article, in Gaelic, marks the first appearance of the genealogy Nial mac Eachain 'ic Eoghain, 'ic Eachain 'ic Conduilligh.

55 MacLeod, *Memoir of Norman MacLeod, D.D.*, 19.

56 John MacDonald (Iain Lom), "Marbh-rann do Mhaistir Donull Mac Cuinn, Ministeir a bha ann an Cille Mhuire Throternis san Eilean-Sgiathanach Air fon, 'Slan gu'm faic mi thus Mharcuis,' le Iain Lom" (Death verse to Mr Donald MacQueen who was in Kilmore Troternish in the Island of Skye to the melody

'Health till I see you Mark' by Iain Lom [John MacDonald]), in Stewart and Stewart, *Cochruinneacha Taoghta de Shaothair nam Bard Gaëlach,* 25.

57 In some areas of Gaelic Scotland, in the leading Argyll family, perhaps also in the Munro chiefly family, this relationship of chief and piper had already disappeared.

58 Many non-Catholic chiefs continued as legal and military authorities in Gaelic Scotland, for varying lengths of time after the removal of the heritable jurisdictions. The chiefs became raisers of regiments (instead of clan levies), including pipers, from the 1750s. They took judicial appointments and became members of Parliament. Many, however modernized, showed sensitivity to their humble tenants.

59 Edinburgh University was the first in Scotland to establish a department of agriculture in the 1780s (Bryson, *Man and Society*).

60 Whyte, *The Rankins – Pipers,* 10.

61 MacLean, *History of Clan MacLean,* 290.

62 MacKinnon, "Rankin, Coun Douly (Con-duiligh MacRaing)," in *Dictionary of Canadian Biography,* 8:240, 241, 242.

63 Traditional classical piping certainly almost disappeared from Coll with the emigrations of the nineteenth century.

64 "Papers and correspondence of Seton Gordon, C.B.E.," in National Library of Scotland (NLS), Acc. 7451/1; and *Oban Times,* 3 September and 10 November 1919. See also Gordon, *Hebridean Memories.*

65 Allan MacFarlane, also known as "Allachan Aonghuis Dhuibh" (Little Allan Black Angus), was one of the last traditional dance-music pipers of Inverness County Cape Breton.

66 Morrison, "Clann Duiligh," 37.

67 Correspondence from Peter Cooke, School of Scottish Studies, University of Edinburgh, to John G. Gibson, 27 February 1987, and Gordon, *Hebridean Memories.*

68 "Account," in MacKay, *Collection,* 17, 18. See also *Pìobaireachd,* book 4, 106.

69 Court reporting of an abduction by the son of the piper to John Maclain of Lochbuy, *Scots Magazine,* August 1759, 441, 442 (SRO, "Register of Criminal Letters, 1751–80"). Boswell and Johnson visited Loch Buidhe 22 October 1773. James Boswell's father had been one of the panel of judges of the Court of Justiciary that fined John Maclain (Boswell, *Journal of a Tour,* 333–4).

70 According to "Lairds of the Central Inner Hebrides and adjacent mainland 1761–1771," "John Maclaine of Lochbuie" died in 1778. He was the son of Allan MacLean of Garmony and succeeded his uncle as Loch Buidhe in 1751. He transferred the estate to his son Archibald, "young Lochbuie," in 1775. (Data in "Lairds of the Central Inner Hebrides" were taken from the "Valuation Roll for Argyllshire," published in Timperley, *Directory of Landownership in Scotland c. 1770*.)

71 MacLean, *History of the Clan MacLean,* citing the Lochbuie Charter Room holdings.

72 Boswell, *Journal of a Tour,* 334.

73 At the time of Boswell and Johnson's visit to Mull in 1773 Archibald, Loch Buidhe's son, was away from Loch Buidhe driving cattle to the Falkirk fair (Boswell, *Journal of a Tour,* 334).

74 Archibald MacLean of Loch Buidhe's commission in the Royal Highland Emigrants was probably obtained through the offices of fellow-Mullman, Col. Allan MacLean of Torloisk (later general), who, along with Small, was one of the raisers of the Royal Highland Emigrants (84th).

75 In Capt. Patrick Sinclair's (and Lt Archibald MacLean's) company at Sorel, Quebec, between June and December of 1780, apart from Lt MacLean, there were no other MacLeans. Two drummers are named (Murray Logan, *Scottish Highlanders and the American Revolution,* 93) but no pipers were mentioned. (Two interesting names of privates are John Johnston and Donald McGregor [ibid., 93, 94].) There is evidence that there were pipers at least in the obviously Scotch companies. For example, in the muster records of the men of the 84th (RHE Regiment) who were mustered out in Nova Scotia in 1783, in the "5th Company – Commanded by Capt. Murdoch McLaine 25 December 1782–10 Oct. 1783," the following names were found by Sandy Lomas in 1975: "Israel Crone, James McDonald, Jacob Tuffard, *Drummers (2nd pipers 1782)* Johnathan Robertson, Alexr Ferguson, Nl McLean, Wm Forbus &c." (ibid., 130). Murray Logan did not indicate where the *"Drummers (2nd pipers 1782)"* began or ended in the list but normally there were two drummers per company and thus the second pipers almost certainly were Robertson and Ferguson.

76 For several years Ulva reverted to the ownership of Lachlan MacQuarrie, former governor of New South Wales, who retired to Britain in 1821. He finally sold the property in 1835.

77 Keltie reported that the MacQuarries were married into the MacLeans of Duart and of Loch Buidhe (Keltie, *History of the Scottish Highlands,* book 6, 264).

78 Stewart, *Sketches,* 2:157 n.

79 Gordon, National Library of Scotland, NLS Acc 7451/1.

80 Morrison, "Clann Duiligh," 37.

81 Scott, Letter to Joanna Baillie, 83.

82 Morrison, "Clann Duiligh," 37. The famous governor of New South Wales returned to his native Scotland in 1821 but may not have bought Staffa until at least 1825, since Ronald Macdonald was still styled as "of Staffa" in that year. Ulva passed from his hands in 1835. (Note: Iain Og Ile continued to be known as such long after his family had divested itself of land in Isla.)

83 "Account of the Competition of Pipers," in MacKay, *Collection,* 17.

CHAPTER FOUR

1 The Master of Lovat (Lord Lovat's son), Fraser of Foyers, Fraser of Avochna-cloy, Fraser of Little Garth, Fraser of Browich, and Fraser of Gortuleg (Keltie, *History of the Scottish Highlands,* book 4, 738).

2 The Braemar area was carefully occupied by the army after Culloden, since there was a Roman Catholic seminary at Scalan, near Shenval in the Cabrach (Dawson, *Catholics of Scotland,* 132).

3 Comunn na Piobaireachd, *Pìobaireachd,* book 9, 249. According to George Moss (1903–90), David Fraser had a brother named Uilleachan Ruadh (Red Willie) who was also a piper, trained at the MacCrimmon "piping school in Boreraig, Skye," and who was at Culloden. These brothers were genealogical antecedents of George Moss's grand-uncle "Alick Fraser (Aili Friseal), who emigrated to Australia ... He died in Melbourne in the late 1920s, age in the 90s. Therefore he was born around 1830" (Alick Fraser, the piper, was Mr Moss's mother's maternal uncle). (See Correspondence, George Moss, Kessock, by Inverness, Scotland, to the author, 4 May 1980.)

4 See the indenture between Lord Lovat and David Fraser, 1743, *Piping Times* 16, no. 5 (February 1964): 6–7; 21, no. 3 (December 1968): 20–1; and 44, no. 11 (August 1992): 52–3. See also Collinson, *The Bagpipe,* 213, 214; and Campsie, *MacCrimmon Legend,* 59, 60.

5 Fraser, *Papers from the Collection of Sir William Fraser, K.C.B., LL.D,* 45.

6 I have used the "Mackintosh" form only for the names of chiefs who used that spelling and "MacIntosh" elsewhere.

7 Mackintosh, *Notes Descriptive,* 35–6.

8 John Graham from Easter Ross served in the 71st during the American Revolutionary War, eventually settling in Judique, Cape Breton. Veterans of Tarleton's British Legion settled in Nova Scotia and Cape Breton (when the two were distinct), but through none of their descendants has any memory of piping by McCrumen or any other piper during that war come down to us.

9 Stewart, *Sketches;* and Harper, *Fraser Highlanders* (which cites the diary of Sergeant Thompson of Fraser's Highlanders, who fought at Quebec in 1759).

10 A captain-lieutenant took command of the commanding officer's company when called upon.

11 Stewart, *Sketches,* 2:65–6.

12 Minc, letter to *Piping Times* 44, no. 11 (August 1992): 55.

13 Keltie, *History of the Scottish Highlands,* 2:216.

14 Margaret Mackintosh of Mackintosh allows one to infer that the bulk of these recruits were from the Mackintosh estate (Mackintosh, *Clan Mackintosh,* 48).

15 Seton and Arnot, *Prisoners of the '45,* 1:295, 2:182, 183. Another Farquharson, John Farquharson of Aldlerg, a Jacobite prisoner, is cited in Keltie, *History of the Scottish Highlands,* book 4, 682 n. Keltie was citing "Forbes Papers, or Jacobite Memoirs of the Rebellion of 1745," 300.

16 The factor of the Lovat estate was Forbes of Newe in Aberdeenshire.

17 Keltie, *History of the Scottish Highlands,* book 6, 215–6.

18 Mackintosh, *Clan Mackintosh,* 65.

19 "Account of the Competition of Pipers," in MacKay, *Collection,* 18.

20 "The Aged Piper and his Bagpipe," *Perthshire Courier,* 1857 (no date given), reproduced in Burns, "John McGregor of Fortingall and his descendants," 105–9.

21 Queen Victoria, *Leaves from the Journal,* 129–30.

22 "Ingram, George," in "Notices of Pipers," *Piping Times* 21, no. 11 (August 1969): 17. The anonymous author cited the "Black Callendar of Aberdeen," 66.

23 John Roy Stuart described Anne Mackintosh as "ribhinn àilt nan ioma gràs, / a choisinn gràdh an t-sloigh" (noble young lady of the many graces / who won the love of the people). (See Stewart, "Cumha do Bhaintighearna Mhic-an-Toisich" (Lament for Lady Mackintosh), 269.) Margaret Mackintosh of Mackintosh wrote that the Hanoverian chief did not hinder his wife's raising his people as Jacobites (Mackintosh, *Clan Mackintosh,* 48).

24 MacKenzie, *Sar-Obair,* 269 (footnote by John MacKenzie subtending John Roy Stuart's song "Cumha do Bhaintighearna Mhic-an-Toisich").

25 Forbes, *Lyon in Mourning,* 1:219.

26 Tayler and Tayler, *1745 and After,* 130–1, citing the narrative of John William O'Sullivan.

27 Mackintosh, *Notes Descriptive,* 28.

28 I am uncertain as to what number of Clan Chattan chief he was. Angus Mackintosh (1755–1833), twenty-fifth chief of Clan Mackintosh, was twenty-sixth chief of Clan Chattan (he lived in America from the Revolutionary War times until 1827). See entry for Angus Mackintosh in *Dictionary of Canadian Biography* 6:473.

29 Mackintosh, *Notes Descriptive,* 35–6.

30 Ibid., 33.

31 Ibid.

32 Johnson, *Music and Society in Lowland Scotland,* 121.

33 MacFarlane (and MacDonald), "Tenants in Brae Lochaber."

34 Forbes, *Lyon in Mourning,* passim.

35 Stewart, *Sketches,* 1:263.

36 Ibid, 2:333, 334.

37 Fraser, *Airs and Melodies,* 2 (tune number 3).

38 MacDonald and MacDonald, *Clan Donald,* 2:465; MacDonald, *Story and Song from Loch Ness-side,* 98 (where John Grant is described as having been a great local bard).

39 For an idea of Bàrasdal Og's recruiting range, see Seton and Arnot, *Prisoners of the '45,* 1:314, 320.

40 Fraser, *Papers from the Collection of Sir William Fraser,* 17.

41 Finlay MacLeod was second in the Edinburgh competition of 1804.

42 Boswell, *Journal of a Tour to the Hebrides,* 118; and Johnson, *Journey to the Western Islands of Scotland,* 170, 171.

43 MacQueen didn't leave but it appears that his remark was not just a casual one; he was alluding to a major emigration from nearby Glenurquhart parish that took place in 1774. Lt William Grant (42nd Highlanders and possibly the independently raised companies before that), with his family and 150 people from the parish, sailed for America on the ship *Moore.*

44 Boswell, *Journal of a Tour to the Hebrides,* 118.

45 McLean listed 7 Cameron, 5 Grant, 2 Chisholm, and 4 MacDonell families that emigrated from Glenmoriston in 1773, which makes an average of 5 per family if 70 is the correct total of the "men" who emigrated. This average is typical for a family in the Glengarry emigrations. In the end, most, if not all, of these emigrants resettled in what is now Glengarry County, Ontario (McLean, *People of Glengarry,* 84).

46 For a contemporary idea of the relatively comfortable status of "a great number" of the emigrants aboard the ship *Pearl* which arrived in York Town (New York) in October 1773, see Mathews, *Mark of Honour,* 5, 179 n., citing the *New York Gazette,* 25 October 1773.

47 MacKay, *Urquhart and Glenmoriston,* 462 n. MacKay was citing "Lorimer's MS" of 1763.

48 "Grant, Patrick, of Sheughly, Glenurquhart," in "Notices of Pipers," *Piping Times* 21, no. 8 (May 1969): 24.

49 I do not know whether newcomers, Gaels or not, settled in Glenurquhart after this depopulating or, if there was a resettling, whether patterns of land use changed as they almost certainly should have.

50 Manuscripts by Rev. Dr D.B. Blair and Rev. A. MacLean Sinclair in "The Urquhart Settlement in Nova Scotia," *TGSI* 53 (1982-84): 444–63 (paper submitted by Hugh Barron on 4 May 1984); Patterson, *History of Pictou County;* Murray Logan, *Scottish Highlanders and the American Revolution;* and Duncanson, *Rawdon and Douglas.*

51 "Reverend Dr A. Maclean Sinclair's Manuscript – The Glen Urquhart settlers and others East River of Pictou, Nova Scotia," in "The Urquhart Settlement in Nova Scotia," *TGSI* 53: 454–62.

52 "The Urquhart Settlement in Nova Scotia," *TGSI* 53:462; identifying data for Lt Grant is incomplete. The additional note on pages 462–3 is attributed to "the Honorary Secretary" (of the Gaelic Society of Inverness), who cited "the *Scottish Highlander* 14/7/87" (462) for the Lt William Grant data.

53 "The Emigrant Ship – Glasgow," in Murray Logan, *Scottish Highlanders,* 48–52.

54 Pipers are found among the MacPhee descendants of 2nd Battalion 84th settlers.

55 George Moss, letter to J.G. Gibson, 4 May 1980.

56 Ibid.

57 Prebble, *Culloden,* 72. Elsewhere a "John Beag MacRae, Piper to the late Lord Seaforth" was named as the teacher of the Chisholm's last family piper, Kenneth Chisholm. See "Historical and Traditional Notes on the Piobaireachds," in MacKay, *Collection,* 7 (in appended notes to tune 16).

58 MacLennan, *History of the MacLennans,* 223.

59 Ibid.

60 Correspondence, George Moss to John G. Gibson, 4 May 1980.

61 "Historical and Traditional notes on the Piobaireachds," in MacKay, *Collection,* 7.

62 "Chisholm, Kenneth," in "Notices of Pipers," *Piping Times* 20, no. 11 (August 1968): 20.

63 Broader thinking must take into account the possibility of pipers to prominent families coming from the ranks of the ordinary Gael, especially after the social disruption attendant upon the tacksman emigrations that took people like Donald MacCrumen to North Carolina in the early 1770s. The accepted division, from what Joseph MacDonald wrote (*Compleat Theory*), appears to be artificial, and accepting it muddies the cultural waters.

64 MacLean, *History of Antigonish,* 1: 120 (under the rubric "Cape George" in chap. 41).

65 Correspondence, George Moss to John G. Gibson, 4 May 1980. The only Kenneth Chisholm mentioned by Alexander MacKenzie in *History of the Chisholms* who had fairly close ties to the chiefs is a great-grandson of Alexander Chisholm, seventeenth of Strathglass, and second cousin of Roderick, twenty-first Chisholm (1697-1767). Kenneth was son of Archibald Chisholm of Fasnakyle, son of Colin Chisholm first of Knockfin, son of Alexander (seventeenth of Strathglass). Kenneth had a brother Alexander and a half-brother who emigrated with his family to the Carolinas.

66 An Siosal Bàn was Alasdair (d. 1793), son of (unknown) (d. 1785), son of Rory (1697–1767). Rory was an active Jacobite in 1745–46 and his youngest son, Young Rory, uncle of Alasdair, was colonel of the Chisholms and was killed at Culloden.

67 Duncan Cameron had been a servant, in Boulogne, of Old Lochiel, John Cameron, who fought with Mar in 1715, was attainted, and died in Flanders in 1748.

68 Forbes, *Lyon in Mourning,* 1:204.

69 MacKenzie, *MacKenzies' History of Christmas Island Parish,* 113, 114.

70 The term "Piper" was probably used here to honour him or to distinguish this Hector from other Hector MacNeils. The nickname connotes being one of the famous piper's descendants and need not mean that he was a piper. That system of nomenclature is still common in Cape Breton.

71 Lt Roderick MacNeil of Fraser's Highlanders was "killed on the Heights of Abraham 1759" (Stewart, *Sketches,* 2:65).

72 MacPherson, *Tales from Barra,* 59. The Coddy's setting of Calum in Piper's Cove in Cape Breton ensures that the emigrant's last name was MacNeil.

73 The late Stephen Rory MacNeil, author of *All Call Iona Home,* told the author in 1972 that his MacNeil ancestor in the Iona area had first seen the area as one of Wolfe's soldiers and returned there much later as an immigrant, so the idea is not inconceivable.

74 Neill McNeill the catechist's "Census of the Small Isles 1764–1765" shows there to have been many Roman Catholic MacKinnon families in Eigg.

75 MacMillan, *To the Hill of Boisdale,* 313.

76· Cowan (Conn) Rankin MacKinnon (1860–1946) was a well-known piper in Prince Edward Island whose relationship to the Conduiligh Rankin family is obvious from his name.

77 In 1832 the (possibly a) piper to Col. (later Lt-Gen.) MacNeil of Barra (c. 1788–1863) was Donald MacInnes ("Account," in MacKay, *Collection,* 19).

78 MacPherson, *Tales from Barra,* 129.

CHAPTER FIVE

1 An initial source for the published and unpublished material dealing with the Raasay MacKays of Clann mhic Ruairidh is found in James R. McLeod's "John McKay's Black House at Eyre, Raasay."

2 Mac Ghille Chaluim, son of the servant of Malcolm, is the patronymic of the MacLeods of Raasay.

3 Boswell, *Journal of a Tour,* 147–61.

4 Rev. Donald MacQueen joined in the Gaelic chorus "Hatyin foam foam eri" to Captain Malcolm MacLeod's and the crew's singing of "an Erse song" (Boswell, *Journal of a Tour,* 145).

5 McLeod, "John McKay's Black House," part 2, 17.

6 Boswell, *Journal of a Tour,* 150. From the sixteenth century until 26 February 1726, Raasay fell within the parish of Kiltarlagain and Raasay. Raasay's fifty-foot-long church, dedicated to St Moluag, fell into ruin (presumably by 1726; Boswell and Johnson found it so in September 1773). The Court of Teinds in 1726 disjoined Kiltarlagain and Raasay, and the Kiltarlagain church was taken to Portree, which became the focus of the parish (Scott, *Fasti Ecclesiae Scotorum,* 7:173).

7 Ibid., 145.

8 Stewart, *Sketches,* 1:128. Donald Sage elsewhere noted that "the extension of the Church, too, although the plantation of kirks was enforced by law, could not ultimately be carried into effect until after a determined and almost sanguinary struggle with the adherents of Episcopacy ... Parishes in the north, and in Ross-shire particularly, were for many years kept vacant solely by the influence of Episcopacy." The same author wrote that the parishioners of Rev. Alexander Pope (d. 1782), minister of Reay, "when he was first settled among them [1734], were not only ignorant but flagrantly vicious. Like the people of Lochcarron, they were Episcopalians

in name, but heathens in reality" (Sage, *Memorabilia Domestica,* 2, 42, 43, 137).

9 Daiches, *Paradox of Scottish Culture,* 53. Where Skye is concerned, Norman MacLeod, the twenty-second chief of MacLeod at Dunvegan (d. 21 February 1772), was educated by a "MacRah" (MacRath or MacRae), the son of a non-juring (Episcopalian) minister from Kintail whose father's house and books were deliberately destroyed by General Wightman in the 1719 Jacobite rising (Grant, *MacLeods,* 385, 498).

10 McLeod, "John McKay's Black House," part 1, 18.

11 In the results of the 1835 piping competition, in which Angus MacKay won the "prize Pipe ... the highest prize among the ordinary competitors," he is described as "son of John MacKay Piper to Lord Willoughby d'Eresby" (three candidates, not including Angus MacKay, earlier had competed for the gold medal, the competition for which was limited to previous first-prize winners) ("Account of the Competition of Pipers," in MacKay, *Collection,* 20). Archibald Campbell wrote that John MacKay "ended his days some time after 1840 at Kyleakin in Skye" (Campbell, *Kilberry Book,* 9). Campbell's work is unannotated.

12 McLeod, "John McKay's Black House," part 2, 20. In his references, McLeod cited "Historical and Traditional Notes on Piobaireachd. Edinburgh: The Army School of Piping, 1964." In 1820 competitor Donald MacKay was described as "Piper to James MacLeod, Esq. of Rasay" and in 1821 as "Piper to R.G. Mac-Donald Esq. of Clanranald" ("Account," in MacKay, *Collection,* 19).

13 "It may not be out of place to mention that the editor's father, John MacKay, Piper to MacLeod of Rasay, to whom frequent reference has been made, received his first instructions from this worthy old Highlander and relates many anecdotes of old Malcolm and his contemporaries, who loved next to playing piobaireachd, to rehearse the transactions" ("Historical and Traditional Notes on the Piobaireachd," in MacKay, *Collection,* 14). For Capt. Malcolm MacLeod's family history, see Morrison, *MacLeods,* section 4. Although unlikely, Capt. Malcolm MacLeod may have learned piping as an adult, after Culloden.

14 Both men were married to sisters who were daughters of Angus MacQueen of Totaroam. Totaroam lies in the easterly shade of the Old Man of Storr to the south of Rigg in Trotternish (Morrison, *The MacLeods*).

15 MacKay, *Collection,* 169; and "Historical and Traditional Notes," in ibid., 13, 14. Angus MacKay's father, John MacKay, the Raasay herdboy, was a pupil of Fear Aire and for that reason the words in MacKay appear to be trustworthy.

16 MacLean, "Am Pìobaire Dall" (talk given 4 April 1952). I have not assessed the value of MacLean's statement that Malcolm MacLeod said that Ian Dall "added more to the conviviality of a company than any other man he knew." There is no trustworthy record of the Blind Piper's vital statistics and his burial place has not been found.

17 McLeod cites Archibald Campbell, "The History of Angus MacKay," 26–7, 32–7 (McLeod, "John McKay's Black House," part 2, 18, 22). Campsie cites "Angus MacKay MS vol, National Library of Scotland" (Campsie, *MacCrimmon Legend,* 10, 181).

18 McLeod, "John McKay's Black House," part 1, 21. McLeod cites MacKay, *Collection* (1838), although I have not found the line in the 1972 edition. Iain Dall MacKay is believed to have been born and to have died in Gairloch, son of Ruairidh (born in Reay).

19 Campsie, *MacCrimmon Legend,* passim.

20 Ibid., 93, 97, 99. Campsie adduced evidence from the contents in the Campbell Canntaireachd manuscript and in Angus MacKay's *Collection,* to reinforce his theory that MacKay plagiarized.

21 Ibid., 99, 156 (summary).

22 John Francis Campbell's honesty, interest in, and remarkable service to Scottish Gaelic studies in the mid-nineteenth century are undisputable. The author of *Popular Tales,* he was a Gaelic speaker whose childhood teacher was the Gaelic family piper at Isla, John Campbell, who died in 1831 aged 36 at Bellshill Lanarkshire. Campbell's father's Isla estate was sold in 1847 *(Lamplighter and Story-teller John Francis Campbell of Islay 1821–1885,* 7).

23 In July 1821 third prize at the Edinburgh competition was won by "John MacKenzie, Piper to Duncan Davidson, Esq. of Tulloch"; hence, if this is John Ban, his purpose in visiting Raasay is unlikely to have been to perfect fingering techniques ("Account," 19, in MacKay, *Collection*). He is known also to have been a reel-piper in 1819.

24 Cannon, *Bibliography of Bagpipe Music,* 134.

25 Ibid., 139.

26 Preface in MacKay, *Collection,* Like others I have assumed that Angus MacKay at least submitted information concerning his own family. That Rev. Patrick MacDonald would have countenanced the intrusion of fashionable but ignorant writing in *Highland Vocal Airs* (1784) had set the pattern for piping literature.

27 McLeod, "John McKay's Black House," part 1, 19, 22.

28 MacNeill, "Foreword" to the 1972 edition of MacKay, *Collection,* v.

29 Campsie, in his "References and bibliography," cited "Angus MacKay MS vol, National Library of Scotland, 10" (Campsie, *MacCrimmon Legend,* 181).

30 The case for Iain Ruadh, and not his father, Angus, having been the Gairloch piping teacher from the mid-1770s is found in Gibson, "Genealogical and Piping Notes."

31 Plagiarism and unscholarliness were common at the time, particularly in publications of violin music.

32 McLeod, "John McKay's Black House," part 2, 21, 22, citing " 'Piobaireachd,' " *Piping Times,* March 1953, 4–7. William MacLean was a neighbour of John MacKay's in Raasay and afterwards at Kyleakin in Skye, where John died in 1848.

33 Campbell, *Canntaireachd,* 33. Campbell had overheard John Ban MacKenzie talk to Duncan Ross, one of his pupils, about his (John Ban's) instruction with John MacKay, Raasay. The citation also appears in Neville T. MacKay, "Angus MacKay (1812–59)," 209.

34 "Account," in MacKay, *Collection,* 17. That the committee could admit that improvement was possible suggests that some of its competing pipers were novices or else clung unpleasantly to older, unsatisfactory fingering styles.

35 McLeod, "John McKay's Black House," part 1, 20. While McLeod seemed unable to penetrate what he imagined to be a shortcoming in Angus MacKay's way of counting his siblings, hinting even that his madness was hindering his lucidity, if one accepts that MacKay chose to ignore in his count the child who died in infancy, the detail is clear.

36 For treatment of piping on the Munro properties, see MacKenzie, *Piping Traditions of The North of Scotland.*

37 Dance-music bagpiping was popular in various parts of Skye and was observed by Rev. Roderick MacLeod in Dunvegan in 1823 (MacRae, "Revivals in the Highlands and the Islands in the 19th century," 67, cited in Laurie Stanley, *Well-Watered Garden,* 5).

38 Mac Gill-eain, *Ris a'Bhruthaich,* passim.

39 Somhairle's grandfather Eóghann had lost land for his part in Prince Charles Stuart's escape after Culloden (Mac Gill-eain, *Ris a'Bhruthaich,* passim). A Francis MacNicoll, Piper to the Scots Royals, was fifth in the Edinburgh piping competition in 1813 ("Account," in MacKay, *Collection,* 18).

40 Mac Gill-eain, *Ris a'Bhruthaich,* 298. Sorley MacLean told me in 1995 that Raasay had been almost 100 per cent Church of Scotland and all of those joined the Free Church in 1843. (Personal interview with Sorley MacLean, Edinburgh University, July 1995.)

41 Correspondence, Bridget MacKenzie to the author, 22 March 1997.

42 Buchan, *Massacre of Glencoe*; and Prebble, *Glencoe.*

43 Craven, *Journals of the Episcopal Visitations,* 348.

44 MacLean, *Discovering Invernesshire,* 146.

45 Correspondence from Tearlach MacFarlane to the author, 3 December 1985.

46 Prebble, *Glencoe,* 42, 74, 75, 222. Prebble cited James Philip of Almerieclose, "Panurgi Philocaballi Scoti Grameidos." The contemporary observation on the muster at Dalcomera is James Philip's *Grameid* and therein in *Scoti Grameidos,* book 4, 120, in which "Hic coiere duces, hic bella buccina signum / Dira dedit, Martemque ciens rauco ore pithaules / Inflarat plenis marsupia turgid buccis" is translated "Here gather the chiefs, here the trumpet gives the dread signal for war, here the piper, calling to the battle with hoarse note, blows up the swelling bags with inflated cheeks." In the same book, "Raucisonas sonuitque tubas" is translated "and has sounded the screaming pipes" (ibid., 118). Nowhere in Philip's book 4 is a piper named. ("Tuba" elsewhere is translated as "a trumpet, esp. a war-trumpet" [Smith, *Latin-English Dictionary*].)

47 MacLean, *The Highlands,* 47. Prebble wrote that a Duncan MacEanruig was listed below Ronald MacDonald of Inverrigan in a list of witnesses of the Glencoe massacre (1692) who presented themselves at Edinburgh (Prebble, *Glencoe,* 271). Campbell of Glenlyon was billetted at Inverrigan in 1692 (Keltie, *History of the Scottish Highlands*, book 2, 399).

48 MacDonald, *Mabou Pioneers,* 74. The author cites Buchan, *Massacre of Glencoe*; MacKenzie, *History of the MacDonalds*; and Drummond-Norie, *Loyal Lochaber.*

49 MacKenzie, *Sar-Obair,* 298–300.

50 Mamore was commander in chief of Scottish forces in the West Highlands and of the Argyll Militia.

51 Fergusson, *Argyll in the Forty-Five,* 247 n.

52 Glencoe had his son deliver the clan's weapons to Campbell of Skipness when the latter was stationed at Mingarry in Ardnamurchan (Fergusson, *Argyll in the Forty-Five,* 195–6, 204).

53 Ibid., 247ff.; and Seton and Arnot, *Prisoners of the '45,* passim.

54 See report of 17 August 1749, "Highland Reports, 1749–50," in Allardyce, *Historical Papers* 2:518. In 1750 Glencoe was part of the command of Capt. Patton of Guise's regiment. From the "Head of Glenco" three posts operated using one corporal and five private soldiers (ibid., 2:541).

55 Dughalach, *Orain, Marbhrannan agus Duanan Ghaidhealach,* passim.

56 MacFarlane, "Tenants in Brae Lochaber," no pagination. This Scottish Record Office material was taken from Fort William court records that are now (2001) in too poor condition to be read.

57 The Ardshiel estate was forfeited (1746) and factored initially by Colin Campbell of Glenure. Charles Stewart of Ardshiel was attainted along with John Roy Stewart and a number of other Stewarts, including Sir James Stewart of Good Trees (unidentified estate but probably Lowland), who was married to the Jacobite Lady Weemys, and Archibald Stewart, late provost of Edinburgh. Charles Stewart of Ardshiel, inasmuch as it lay in his power, left his estate in the hands of his half-brother Seumas a'Ghlinne, James Stewart of the Glen, the man hanged in chains at Bail' a' Chaolais (Ballachulish) for the murder of Colin Campbell of Glenure.

58 James Robertson of Blairfetty, George Robertson of Faskally, David Stewart of Kinnachin, and Charles Stewart of Balechallan were all declared guilty of treason and excepted from the General Pardon (20 Geo II, cap 52), (Seton and Arnot, *Prisoners,* 1:55, 56, 295, 296). Note: Charles Stewart of Bohallie, Stewart of Kinnachan, and Robertson of Faskally, all Jacobites, were still in their lands in 1751 (Leneman, *Living in Athol,* 235). Note also that a Patrick Stewart of Ballechan was baillie of Atholl in 1689 (Philip, *Grameid,* book 5).

59 Allan Breac Stewart, a man long suspected of some part in the Appin murder of Colin Campbell of Glenure in 1752, was a son of Domhnul mac Iain mhic Alasdair of Inverchomrie (Matheson, *Appin Murder,* 9). (Note: The secondary

source, John H.J. Stewart and Lt-Col. Duncan Stewart's *The Stewarts of Appin* was not available to the author.)

60 Benmore is in Strathfillan, Perthshire (Matheson, *Appin Murder,* 37, 58).

61 John Roy wrote, in English, "Upon the pipe I'll sound his praise," in "John Roy Stuart's Psalm" (MacKenzie, *Sar-Obair,* 268), which is probably formulaic. In "Oran Eile air Latha Chuilodair," the only other musical reference of John Roy's in *Sar-Obair* runs "Gun fhuaim clàrsaich, gun lasair chéire" (Without the sound of the clarsach, without the candle-light) (ibid., 267).

62 When James Stewart of Cluns, a Jacobite, during the 1746 Atholl Raid, apprehended the Campbells who had invested Kirkton of Strowan when the Jacobite army had been in England, included was James Stewart, late of Urrard and an officer in Lord Loudon's regiment, as well as an Alexander Stewart, minister of Blair Atholl. The capture was witnessed by MacKintosh, whose son signed the letter to Bishop Forbes (Forbes, *Lyon in Mourning,* 1:316).

63 Seton and Arnot, *Prisoners of the '45,* 3:334–48. Many of those listed were transported to Antigua, West Indies. Other Stewart prisoners included Lt Robert Stewart of Killichassie, Sir James Stewart of Burray, and Alexander Stewart, writer (lawyer) in Edinburgh (ibid., 299). Other families living on Stewart territory were various members of Clann mhic Sholla (given generally as Mac-Colls), Colquhouns and MacInneses (Matheson, *Appin Murder,* passim).

64 A "Dan. McFarlan, No 15" made a deposition at the trial of "Alexander Mac-Growther, senior," a lieutenant in the duke of Perth's regiment, in which he said that that regiment "marched ... with colours flying, drums beating, and pipes playing before them" (Allardyce, *Historical Papers,* 2:384). (MacGrowther had been left with the garrison at Carlisle. His defence showed that he had been forced into the Jacobite army, and although found guilty, he was reprieved.)

65 Ballantine was tried for treason at York, pleaded that he had been impressed, and was released (*Scots Magazine,* October 1746, 485).

66 Captain Charles Stewart was among the ten wounded in the Appin regiment at Culloden (where seventeen officers were killed). He was subsequently wounded at the second battle of Quebec, as a captain in Fraser's Highlanders. Listed with him in the regiment, 5 January 1757, was Lt Allan Stewart, son of Innernaheil (Invernhahyle) (Stewart, *Sketches,* 1:319, 319 n., and 2:65, 66). Who the Stewarts' piper was at Quebec is not known. A Stewart piping presence was almost certainly also found in Montgomerie's Highlanders (77th, 1757), where Ensign Allan Stewart, Adjutant Donald Stewart, and Surgeon Allan Stewart served (ibid., 2:61).

67 The descriptive "piper" does not exist in other contemporary British military records.

68 Public Archives of Canada holding, British Military and Naval Records "c" Series (RG8), microfilm c-4221, vol. 1883, 10, 15, 31, 37, 44. Note: "Lieut MacCrum[n]" enlisted a "Drummer Niel MacLeod" 21 September 1778 (ibid., 13). Microfilm c-4221, vol. 1884, 36, shows John McKay "Promoted to be

Serjeant 25th Dec 1780" in Miller's company, and vol. 1885, 94, lists Serjeant John McKay as "dead" 24 December 1782. Red Donald MacCrimmon signed himself in a British Legion muster as "Donald McCrummen Lt B. Legion."

69   Gibson, "Piper John MacKay and Roderick McLennan," 78.

70   There were two classical piping competitions in 1783 because at Falkirk the pipers thought that the judges' decisions were unjust.

71   In 1783, if he was still alive, James Stewart of Fasnacloich would have been about 60 years of age. (He was described as "younger of Fasnacloich" in 1752 when he was 29 [Matheson, *Appin Murder,* 59].)

72   In 1752 the ferryman at the Appin side of the Ballachulish narrows was Archibald MacInnes (Matheson, *Appin Murder,* 60).

73   "Account," in MacKay, *Collection,* 16. In 1783 he and another piper at Edinburgh won "an elegant Highland dress, with silver epaulettes, double silver loops, buttons, and feathers in their new bonnets, and money ... to defray their expenses" (ibid.). The famous piper John MacColl (1860–1943) was born at Ardshiel and, according to the *Piping Times,* was related to Paul MacInnes, piper from Fasnacloiche ("MacColl, John," in "Notices of Pipers," *Piping Times* 22, no. 8 [May 1970]: 20–1).

74   "Account," in MacKay, *Collection,* 20.

75   I know nothing about Lord Mountstuart in 1791.

76   "Reports of the Captains on the Different Highland Posts Sent to Mr. Fox" (chap. 37), in Allardyce, *Historical Papers,* 2:562. The Mr Stewart in question was Dougald Stewart, tenth of Appin.

77   Charles Stewart of Ardshiel escaped to France and died at Sens, 15 May 1757 (Matheson, *Appin Murder,* 3).

78   Bain, *Clans and Tartans of Scotland,* 278.

79   Glenure's nephew, Mungo Campbell, witnessed his uncle's murder in Appin in 1752 and cannot but have been even more influenced against the Jacobite Barasdal Og, young MacDonald of Barisdale, when he, Mungo Campbell, was factor for Barisdale.

80   Lord Cockburn, *Circuit Journeys,* 108.

81   Ibid.

82   Ibid., 275, 277.

83   Comunn na Piobaireachd, *Pìobaireachd,* 7:201.

84   Ibid., 202 nn.

85   Ross, *Binneas is Boreraig,* 5 vols.

86   John Buchan said that twenty pipers accompanied Lord George Murray and Cluny MacPherson at the Athole Raids (Buchan, *History of the Royal Scots Fusiliers,* 101).

87   I have not established yet (October 2001) if the family and estate records were destroyed or taken.

88   Stewart, *Sketches,* 1:60.

89 Cluny's wife tried to dissuade him from breaking his sacred oath. The shooting execution of three of Cluny's people as deserters from the 43rd Black Watch, on 12 July 1743, cannot have endeared him to King George.

90 A £1000 reward was offered for information about Cluny, and a promotion to any officer who caught him. As it was known that he was on his estate somewhere, "eighty men were constantly stationed there, besides the parties occasionally marching into the country, to intimidate his tenantry" (Stewart, *Sketches*, 1:59).

91 Stewart, *Sketches*, 1:59. Lt Hector Munro's detachment was removed from Badenoch to Rannoch in 1753 (ibid., 1:61). The 34th, Cholmondeley's, had been at Falkirk and at Culloden. Among its officers was Maj. Lockheart who had viciously killed a man in Glenmoriston in the immediate post-Culloden occupation. The 20th, which Wolfe commanded in Lord Bury's absence, also had been at Culloden (Blaikie, *Itinerary of Prince Charles*, 97, 98).

92 James Wolfe of the 20th Regiment of Foot, who many still believe was appalled at an order to murder a wounded man immediately after the action at Culloden, is seen now in a different light. In a letter to his friend Rickson in 1755, Wolfe wrote that he had sent a sergeant to find and capture Cluny MacPherson. The sergeant's strict orders were that, in the case of success, and were Cluny's clan to try to free their chief, he should kill Cluny immediately. Wolfe enlarged to say that this act would precipitate a violent reaction that would have given Wolfe "a sufficient pretext (without waiting for any instructions) to march into their country, où j'aurais fait main basse, sans miséricorde. Would you believe that I am so bloody?" (Wolfe to Rickson, Exeter, 7 March 1755, in Wright, *The Life of Major-General James Wolfe*, 307–11). Just returned to Britain from service in Nova Scotia, Rickson had been posted to Fort Augustus. MacPherson was still a wanted man and living locally.

93 Findlay, *Wolfe in Scotland*, 267–8. Capt. Trapaud married Annie, daughter of Mungo Campbell (son of Campbell of Barcaldine), Colin Campbell of Glenure's nephew and companion when the latter was murdered in Appin in 1752.

94 Forbes, *Lyon in Mourning*, 3:48.

95 Lang, *Companions of Pickle*, 154, citing the "Cumberland Papers" (ibid., 149).

96 Stewart, *Sketches*, vols. 1 and 2, passim.

97 Walter Scott reported that the descent occurred in 1396 before the battle of the North Inch of Perth (Logan, *Scottish Gaël*, 307).

98 Logan, *The Scottish Gaël*, 307, 308.

99 Ibid.

100 Stewart, *Sketches*, 2:89. Stewart also named a Capt. Duncan MacPherson as wounded 16 September 1776 at Bloomingdale, New York province, giving him, presumably incorrectly, as of the 42nd (ibid., 1:360; page 361 lists a piper of the 42nd wounded also). Fraser's Highlanders (71st) were with the 42nd in New York in 1776.

101 "Account," in MacKay, *Collection,* 18. The "Account" also gives a fifth prize
     to a James MacPherson in 1835 and fifth again to a Duncan MacKay in 1838,
     both pipers to MacPherson of Cluny.
102 Shaw, *Pigeon Holes,* 101 (from Eileanach's MS diary).

CHAPTER SIX

 1 The present and tenth MacCrimmon piper to MacLeod of MacLeod is a Cana-
    dian, Ian Norman MacCrimmon. A "Patrik Mcquhirryman, piper" is men-
    tioned in the *Register of the Privy Council,* vol. 5 (1592–99): 27, in connec-
    tion with a crime committed in Perthshire (*The Stewarts of Ardvorlich,* vol. 1,
    appendix XIV).
 2 In the foreword to Joseph MacDonald's *A Compleat Theory of the Scots High-
    land Bagpipe* (1971 edition), Seumas MacNeill wrote, "The book is full of
    puzzles. He [Joseph MacDonald] puts Mull before Skye, when we have
    always been accustomed to thinking of Skye first and the rest nowhere" (vi).
 3 Matheson, "Traditions of the Mathesons," 167.
 4 Campsie, *MacCrimmon Legend,* passim.
 5 Review of *The MacCrimmon Legend* in Alan Bruford, "Pipers, bards and
    other Gaels," *Tocher* 35 (1981): 348–50.
 6 Campsie was reported to have been a good piper. Donald MacPherson, lead-
    ing piper, wrote c. 1980 on hearing Campsie play that he wondered why they
    had never met in professional competition (MacPherson, "Urlar," in Campsie,
    MacCrimmon Legend, 1).
 7 From "Transcript of Will of Patrick McCrummen" (Donald MacCrummen's
    son) 1839, PCC Foreign Parts Prob 11, Piece 1915, 173 RH-174RH. Seton Gor-
    don wrote that when Campbell met Lt Donald MacCrimmon in late summer
    1814 the old veteran piper was "then nearly 70 years of age" (Gordon, "A
    Highland Journey," *Piping Times* 6?, no. 6? [March? 1954]: 9–10).
 8 A place called "Trein Gillan" supported thirty-five men in 1746 according to
    the local minister (Grant, *The MacLeods,* 550). On OS sheet 23, c. 1981
    (1:50,000, North Skye), Gillen is shown as having buildings.
 9 Poulter, *History of the Clan MacCrimmon,* part 1.
10 According to G. Huddy of the map library of the British Museum, the earliest
    Ordnance Survey reference to "Carn Cloinn Mhic Cruimein (on Glas Bheinn,
    National Grid reference NG 822 225) is the six-inch-to-the-mile scale of Inver-
    nesshire, sheets 47 and 47a, surveyed in 1872, published 31 March 1876. The
    first appearance of the place-name on the one-inch Ordnance Survey series
    appears in 1885, as cited in the text. The cairn is omitted from modern OS
    maps in the late twentieth century. I am unable to say if it remains.
11 For both data and speculation, see MacLeod, "Early MacCrimmon Records,"
    "The MacCrimmons and the '45," and "The End of the MacCrimmon
    College."

12 The twenty-third chief, Norman MacLeod of MacLeod (c. 1754–96), who probably knew Lt Donald MacCrimmon best, was a captain in the 1st batallion, Fraser's Highlanders (71st), both batallions of which served in the American campaign. At times the 71st fought with Col. Tarleton's British Legion, notably at Catawba River and Cowpens (Stewart, *Sketches,* 2:113, 115–17). MacLeod died a lieutenant-general in 1796.

13 The records of Norman MacLeod, twenty-second chief of MacLeod, show that in 1740 he patronized, among many others, pipers and a fiddler (John Munro) (Grant, *MacLeods,* 488–9). He was also an improver and increaser of rents.

14 Disdaining the force of reaction because it tended to strait-jacket a free tradition is best refuted by acknowledging the rapid losses to Gaelicness in Scotland over the critical years of the first four decades of the nineteenth century (the critical emigration decades). Among the many literate Scots who perceived the profoundness of the losses was John Dalyell, author of *Musical Memoirs* (1849). The subject of the modern so-called tradition is the main subject of William Donaldson, *The Highland Pipe and Scottish Society.*

15 MacLeod, "The End of the MacCrimmon College," 18. The document cited by MacLeod is SRO GD 170/629/97.

16 Ruairidh Halford MacLeod, Auchtermuchty, Fife, personal correspondence to the author, 6 September 1981. Whether or not Mackinnon was the piper's daughter-in-law's maiden name remains undiscovered.

17 MacLeod, " 'The best piper of his time' MacCrimmon," part 2, 68. Alexander Campbell's "A Slight Sketch" notes that the piper he heard at Fingal's Cave in 1814 was a favoured pupil of Lt Donald MacCrimmon. Seton Gordon wrote that this was "one of the MacArthurs" and that he was "Staffa's piper" (Gordon, "A Highland Journey," *Piping Times* 6?, no. 6? [March? 1954]). In 1804 Ronald MacDonald of Staffa's piper was John MacArthur, who placed third in the 1804 Edinburgh piping competition and declined second place in August 1806. (John Johnston heard "two of the very last [pipers] who studied under the great pipers of the day – one of the M'Arthurs, pipers to the M'Quarries of Ulva for generations. The last of them was John M'Arthur, and the other one was a Coll man" [Johnston, letter to the *Oban Times,* 10 November 1919].) In 1807 Lt MacCrimmon's pupil, the man Campbell heard and interviewed in Glenelg in 1814, Alexander Bruce (1777–1840, dates from *Piping Times* 20, no. 1 [October 1967]), MacLeod of Gesto's piper, was second ("Account," in MacKay, *Collection,* 17).

18 Lockhart, *Memoirs of the Life of Sir Walter Scott,* 3:231.

19 McCrummen's evidence given 15 February 1786 to commissioners appointed by Act of Parliament enquiring into losses and services of the American Loyalists in Halifax, Nova Scotia, shows the piper's claim to have "acted as Lieutenant in Kingsborough McDonald's Company" in the Loyalist force "who were defeated at Moore's Creek Bridge"; PRO A. O 35, vol. 35, (1785–88), 29, Microfilm copy PAC B1163. Mention of pipers at Moore's Creek Bridge is

found in PRO, Colonial Office 5, vol. 93, 287 (English records, box 12, folder 18), Capt. Alexr McLean, "A Narrative of the proceedings of a Body of Loyalists in North Carolina – Recd from Genl. 24th. March 1776 – In Genl Howe's Letter of the 25th April 1776 – 1." Filed in correspondence dated 25 April 1776.

20 Ruairidh Halford MacLeod, correspondence, 6 September 1981. In the Shelburne, Nova Scotia, record of christenings for 31 October 1791, a Jesse was registered as son of Peter and Hannah McCrimmon. No trace has yet been found of him or his descendants.

21 PCC Foreign Parts, Prob. 11, Piece 1915, p. 173, RH-174 RH, "Transcript of Will of Patrick McCrummen" (Donald MacCrummen's son), 1839.

22 Prebble, *Highland Clearances,* 243.

23 I.F. Grant, in scrutinizing MacLeods' bills, found in an account dated 1755, "To making a frok to the harper" (Grant, *MacLeods,* 489).

24 An argument from the literate record for a later advent of the bagpipe in Scotland than 1396 is presented in Cannon, *Highland Bagpipe,* 7–9. Cannon, citing, at second hand, Beague, *Histoire de la Guerre d'Ecosse* (1556), noted that the first record of the instrument is in a record of the battle of Pinkie (1549) (Cannon, *Highland Bagpipe,* 8).

25 Alexander Campbell allowed his reader to infer that Lt Donald MacCrimmon in Glenelg told him that he, MacCrimmon, was "the seventh in succession of the MacCrummons of Skye" (Campbell, "A Slight Sketch of a Journey made through parts of the Highlands and Hebrides; undertaken to collect materials for *Albyn's Anthology,*" cited in Collinson, *The Bagpipe,* 195–6).

26 MacLeod, *Memoir of Norman MacLeod,* 452.

27 Ibid.; Lockhart, *Memoirs of the Life of Sir Walter Scott,* 3:231. Campbell, "A Slight Sketch," Laing MS, Edinburgh University Library.

28 Campbell, *Albyn's Anthology,* 82–8. He collected "Pibroch of Donuil Dubh" in September 1815 (in that month he was in Rodel in Harris, in Skye and perhaps also in North Uist), but although he said he was aware of Joseph MacDonald's "Treatise," he presented the music in a different way (ibid., passim).

29 Campbell, "A Slight Sketch," in Collinson, *The Bagpipe,* 196.

30 Macdonald, *Back to Lochaber,* 184–208.

31 Dughalach, "Oran ... Do Mhac-Pharlain, Piobaire Mhic-Ic-Alastair" (Song ... to MacFarlane, Glengarry's Piper), in Dughalach, *Orain Ghàidhealacha.*

32 Campbell, *Albyn's Anthology,* 71 n.

33 Ibid., ix.

34 Lockhart, *Memoirs of the Life of Sir Walter Scott,* 3:231. Whether Scott meant to distinguish between tunes and pibrochs is unknown.

35 Grant, *The MacLeods,* 563 (citing Walter Scott's diary).

36 "Notices of Pipers," in *Piping Times* 22, no. 10 (July 1970).

37 MacLeod, "Early MacCrimmon Records."

38 Watson, *Orain agus Luinneagan Gàidhlig,* 34, lines 381–4.

39 Grant, *The MacLeods.*

40 Collinson, *The Bagpipe,* 143–4, 146. A modern expounding of the MacCrim-
    mons' religious philosophy and its cryptic manifestation in their bagpipe music
    is found in "The History and Religion of the MacCrimmons taken from notes
    and letters of Simon Fraser, from the Encyclopaedia Britannica and the Ameri-
    can Encyclopaedia." The author of this thesis attributed Joseph MacDonald's
    never including the MacCrimmon name in his manuscript to his holding of
    strong religious views, presumably of a contrary nature. The entire subject
    remains speculative. The speculative argument for an Italian place of origin for
    the MacCrimmons has been briefly summarized in Ronald Smith, letter to the
    editor, *Piping Times* 17, no. 7 (April 1965): 26–8.

41 MacKay, *Collection,* 99.

42 Ibid., tune 41, 10.

43 Comunn na Piobaireachd, *Pìobaireachd,* 3:86.

44 "Tutor" in Scots law meant guardian, representative, and administrator of an
    estate of a person legally incompetent, generally by reason of minority, the
    father being dead or incapable.

45 Glen, *Collection of Ancient Piobaireachd,* 4th ed.

46 Fergusson, *Fad air falbh as Innse Gall leis comh chruinneachadh Cheap
    Breatunn,* 109, 110.

47 Matheson, ed., *Songs of John MacCodrum,* 62–73, 250–61 (notes).

48 Vallay MacDonalds settled in Whycocomagh in Cape Breton (St Clair, "Vallay
    MacDonalds").

49 MacDonalds, *Clan Donald,* 3:85, 126–7.

50 Pennant, *Tour in Scotland 1769,* 2:301.

51 MacDonald and MacDonald, *Clan Donald,* 3:127.

52 Matheson, *Songs of John MacCodrum,* 252, 253.

53 Ibid.

54 "Notices of Pipers," *Piping Times* 22, no. 5 (February 1970).

55 "Notices of Pipers," *Piping Times* 22, nos. 5 and 6 (February and March
    1970).

56 Stewart, *Sketches,* 2:59.

57 A precedent for using gentlemen as private soldiers exists in the Life Guards
    which, from 1661 for a century enlisted "gentlemen of birth and education";
    into the last quarter of the nineteenth century, private soldiers in the regiment
    were styled "private gentlemen" of the Life Guards.

58 MacKenzie, *Sar-Obair,* 67.

59 The *sloinneadh* (genealogy) of Lachlan, the last of the MacVurichs (aged 58 in
    August 1800), given by himself to the Rev. Allan MacQueen, minister of North
    Uist (who wrote it down for him), is as follows: "Lachlunn mac Nèill, mhic
    Lachluinn, mhic Nèill, mhic Dhòmhnuill, mhic Lachuinn, mhic Nèill mhòir,
    mhic Lachuinn, Mhic Dhòmhnuill, do shloinne chlann Mhuirich" (MacKenzie,
    Sar-Obair, 62). In the footnote to the poem critical of John and Donald

MacArthur, the author is given as Niall mòr MacMhuirich. (See also Thomson, "The MacMhuirich Bardic Family.")

60 If this is the case, then the piper was in the ascendancy, at least in MacDonald country, much earlier than is generally believed.

61 A Neil MacArthur settled at Campbelltown (later Cross Creek), the thriving Highland market town in North Carolina, in 1764, with a modest stake that in eleven years he converted to "a handsome fortune" (Graham, *Colonists from Scotland,* 113).

62 Matheson, *Songs of John MacCodrum,* 254.

63 Alexander MacGregor was the secretary of Captain Neil MacLeod of Gesto (d. 1836), the collector of MacCrimmon piping from Iain Dubh MacCruimein. MacGregor was later minister of the West Parish Church in Inverness (*Celtic Monthly* 11, no. 10 [July 1903]: 183; and a letter from James E. Scott in *Piping Times* 16, no. 6 [March 1964]).

64 MacGregor, "John MacDonald."

65 NLS, "Accession 7451, Papers and Correspondence of Seton Gordon MBE," box 1, letter from John Johnston, Totamore, Coll, to Lieut Seton Gordon, RNVR, Kingstown, Ireland, 6 February 1918. See also letter to the *Oban Times* from John Johnston, Coll, 10 November 1919.

66 Gray, in *Piping Times* 25, no. 11 (August 1973).

67 MacDonald and MacDonald, *Clan Donald,* 3:127.

68 Calum MacCruimein (Malcolm MacCrimmon), father of Dòmhnul Ruadh and Iain Dubh, was piper to the senior company. As MacCodrum was not a common North Uist name, it is likely that Neil MacCodrum the piper was related to John MacCodrum the bard (Iain mac Fhearchair). According to William Matheson, Hugh MacDonald (Uisdean a' Bhaile Shear, d. 1769) commanded a company of Hanoverian militia at Kyleakin, Skye, during the '45 (Matheson, *Songs of John MacCodrum,* 309).

69 Nicolson, *History of Skye,* 255.

70 According to Stewart of Garth, the laird of Grant, in 1745, raised 1,100 men for King George of whom only 98 joined the duke of Cumberland (Stewart, *Sketches,* 2:334).

71 MacKay, *Urquhart and Glenmoriston,* 462 n.

72 It would have been unusual if he himself had not a family piper, but no trace of one has yet come to light.

73 MacDonald, *Story and Song from Loch Ness-side,* 21–4. Keltie; and Keltie, *History of the Scottish Highlands,* 2:253.

74 A study of the Cumming pipers is found in Cheape, "The Piper to the Laird of Grant," in *Proceedings of the Society of Antiquaries of Scotland,* vol. 125 (1995): 1163–73.

75 Logan, *The Scottish Gaël,* 268.

76 Forsyth, *In the Shadow of Cairngorm,* 276.

77 "Notices of Pipers," *Piping Times* 20, no. 12 (September 1968).

78 Cheape, "Portraiture in Piping."

79 Whoever played the small pipes that were held by a piper or pipers in Mont-gomerie's Highlanders in 1757 certainly fingered the chanter using the finger-tips to cover the holes. A photograph of Barnaby Brown playing a replica made by Julian Goodacre shows the phenomenon.

80 Unpublished report of Dr B.L.H. Horn of the Scottish Record Office, Edin-burgh, Scotland.

81 In 1795 Sir James Grant of Grant's piper was Peter MacNeil.

82 For the early kirk acts, see *The Principal Acts of the General Assembly, con-vened occasionally at Edinburgh, upon the 22 day of January, in the year 1645.* For early eighteenth-century data, see *Printed Acts of the General Assembly 1690–1717.*

83 MacDonald, *Story and Song from Loch Ness-side,* 113.

84 Logan, *Scottish Gaël,* 307, 308.

CHAPTER SEVEN

1 According to Keith Sanger's article, a "Donald Pypar M'Yndoir" bound him-self at Strathfillan, some time before 1561, to adopt Colin Campbell of Glenor-chy (*Notes and Queries of the Society of West Highland and Island Historical Research*, 30:4). Campbell of Auchinbreck's patrimony lay in the parish of Glassary, which abuts Inverary to the south and whence came the Mac a'Ghlas-raich Campbell pipers to Keppoch.

2 The kirk at Ardeonaig on Loch Tayside in Perthshire had a Gaelic-speaking minister (Iain Mac Caluim [John MacCallum]) until 1907.

3 Stewart, *Sketches,* 2:359.

4 There is a mountain in Argyllshire near Ardkinglass on Loch Fyne called Bin-nein an Fhìdhleir (the Fiddler's Pinnacle); see OS Landranger Series sheet 50 (Glen Orchy), 215 108.

5 At least two piping MacIntyre families emigrated to Cape Breton in the 1820s (Gibson, "MacIntyre Pipers and the Fairy Chanters;" Shears, *Gathering of the Clans Collection,* 1, 12; and MacMillan, *To the Hill of Boisdale*).

6 Stewart, *Sketches,* 1:77 n. (Note: In the family correspondences of the late Sandy MacIntyre [d. 1992], River Denys, Inverness County, there is evidence that MacIntyres were still employed on a Lorn estate in the early 1800s.)

7 I have used the spelling "Macintyre" only for Duncan Ban, following the usage employed by Angus MacLeod, editor and translator of *The Songs of Duncan Ban Macintyre.*

8 The MacIntyres of Camus na h-Eirbhe, on the north shores of Loch Leven in Cameron country, claimed also to be descended from the Glen Noe family. The Loch Leven MacIntyres are not known to have been pipers.

9 By letters patent signed on 20 September 1991, the Lord Lyon King of Arms

ratified and confirmed the arms of James Wallace MacIntyre of Glenoe, Chief
of the Name and Arms of MacIntyre.

10 MacIntyre, "Rainn Gearradh-Arm."

11 Later, in 1794, the Highland Society competition's second prize winner in
Edinburgh was one "Dugald MacIntyre from Lorne." In 1799 he won.

12 "Campbell of Mamore MSS," MSS nos. 249 and 262.

13 Stewart, *Sketches,* 1:77 n.; and Sinclair, "The MacIntyres of Glennoe."

14 Sanger, "MacCrimmon's Prentise," 16. Sanger cited SRO GD 112/29/31/24.

15 "Selections from the Family Papers of the MacKays of Bighouse," *TGSI* 21
(1896–97).

16 Sanger, "MacCrimmon's Prentise," 17.

17 MacLeod, "The End of the MacCrimmon College," 18. The document cited by
MacLeod is SRO GD 170/629/97. In duplicating it, Sanger omits the gemination
and the second half of the quotation.

18 Sanger, "MacCrimmon's Prentise," 17, citing SRO GD 112/29/51/6.

19 Records of the Highland Society piping competitions in the later eighteenth
century show that Breadalbane at times retained two pipers. The example found
in the Skye MacDonalds of the retention of several pipers was probably common to most of the larger Gaelic estates.

20 Sanger, "MacCrimmon's Prentise," 18, citing SRO GD 112/39/227/10. (The castle
at Caol a'Chùirn lies at the head of Loch Awe, at the mouth of the River Orchy.)

21 Buisman, "Expressive variability in canntaireachd and the phonology of Scottish Gaelic," unpublished MS, 1995 (citing Buisman, "From chant to script");
and Buisman, "More evidence on Colin Campbell."

22 Campsie, *MacCrimmon Legend,* 95, 96; and later Buisman, "More evidence on
Colin Campbell."

23 Comunn na Piobaireachd, *Pìobaireachd,* 10:v.

24 "Account of the Hereditary Pipers" in MacKay, *Collection,* 13.

25 For example, Donald Campbell's contemporary, David Fraser, piper to Simon,
Lord Lovat, in the late 1730s and early 1740s, presumably having learned his
piping from Lovat's piper, Evan MacGrigor, was sent by Lovat in 1743 to the
island of Skye to be "perfected as a Highland Pyper by the famous Malcolm
MacCrimon" (*inter alia,* Collinson, *The Bagpipe,* 156, 213, 214).

26 Mitchell, *Reminiscences of My Life in the Highlands,* 1:199 n.

27 Queen Victoria did not record having heard or seen any Culloden bagpipes on
her visit to Glenfinnan a decade before Mitchell's *Reminiscences* was written in
1883 (Queen Victoria, *More Leaves*).

28 "Account of the Hereditary Pipers," in MacKay, *Collection,* 13.

29 Keltie, *History of the Scottish Highlands,* 2:187–9.

30 In the Highland Society competitions held in Edinburgh in 1819, 1822, and
1824, Alexander Dewar "from the estate of Sir John MacGregor Murray,
Baronet" gained fifth and fourth prizes and, by default in 1824, an extra prize
("Account of the Hereditary Pipers," in MacKay, *Collection,* 18, 19).

31 Campsie, *MacCrimmon Legend,* 17.

32 MacMillan, *Bygone Lochaber,* 157.

33 Fergusson, *Argyll in the Forty-Five,* 205.

34 Ibid., 158.

35 MacAulay, "The Art and History of the MacDougalls of Aberfeldy."

36 McLean, *People of Glengarry,* 161.

37 Nowhere is there mention of the piper's having been replaced. Walter Frederick Campbell of Shawfield and Islay (1798–1855), MP, father of John Francis (Iain Og Ile), sold the Islay estate in 1847. In 1861 the new factor was a man from Stirling who had a partiality for Lowlander tenants.

38 Campbell, *Popular Tales,* 2:273, 274.

39 The man who won fifth prize in the 1819 piping competition was Alexander Dewar, who was from the estate of Sir John Murray MacGregor, Bart.

40 Campbell, *Popular Tales,* 1:xxi.

41 Logan, *Scottish Gaël,* 2:289.

42 Bain, *Voyages des français en Ecosse,* 46 (citing Chantreau, *Voyage dans les trois royaumes d'Angleterre, d'Ecosse et d'Irlande*).

43 Campbell, *Popular Tales,* 2:viii, 93.

44 The Argyll Justiciary Records show that a John McIlchonnel, a boat carpenter, was admitted a burgess of Inveraray in 1764. He was described further as "the Burgh piper" (Campbell and McWhannell, "The Macgillechonnels," citing Beaton and Macintyre, *Burgesses of Inveraray*). According to Alexander Fraser, at about the same time "[t]here was also the Town fiddler called MacPhee" (Fraser, *Royal Burgh of Inveraray,* 31).

45 MacAulay, "The Art and History of the MacDougalls of Aberfeldy."

46 Ross, *Binneas is Boreraig,* vol. 1, introduction.

47 Sanger, "MacCrimmon's Prentise," 18.

48 "Prefatory Notes by the Editor of the 'Northern Chronicle'" to "Contemporary Letters on the Rebellion of 1745," in "The Bighouse Papers," *TGSI* 21 (1896–97).

49 MacAulay's article on the MacIntyre pipers, reportedly published in the February 1963 *Piping Times,* has not been found in that issue.

CHAPTER EIGHT

1 See, MacKay, *Book of MacKay,* 216.

2 It is not inconceivable that this violin teaching was the primary source of the MacDonalds' musical literacy, and if so, one may be wise to comprehend, at least in some small degree, the later published musical works of Joseph and Patrick MacDonald as influenced by schooled attitudes to the playing of the violin (the same cannot be said of the bagpipes, for which at the time there were no literate standards or published technical methods). See Morrison, *Orain le Rob Donn,* in the note to the song "'S e do bhàs Choinnich Sutherlain," 28.

3 See Stewart and Stewart, *Cochruinneacha,* 1:65.

4 See Neville T. McKay, "Angus MacKay (1812–1859) and his contribution to Highland Music," *TGSI* 55 (1986–88): 203–16.

5 The song "Iseabail Nic-Aoidh" (air fonn "Failt' a'Phrionnsa") is divided into an *ùrlar* and *siubhal,* while the other song has no piping internal subdivisions but goes by the title "Pibroch of Aodh's wife" (see Morrison, *Orain le Rob Donn,* 181–3, 306–8).

6 See Morrison, *Orain le Rob Donn,* 288–92.

7 See MacKenzie, *Sar-Obair,* 208ff.

8 See MacKay, *Book of MacKay,* 156. The author was citing the Reay Papers.

9 See Gordon, *Highland Summer*; and MacKay, *Book of MacKay*, 414 ("No. 29. Remission to Donald McKy, fiar of Far, and many others for the slaughter of John Sinclair of Stirkoke ...").

10 See, MacKay, *Book of MacKay,* 213.

11 What may be a long-term MacLeod piping presence in Reay country is beginning to emerge, starting point unknown. Assuming Donald and George to be one and the same man and taking the bard's data as accurate, then the piper to George MacKay, Lord Reay, was George MacLeod. Then later, in 1822, a John and a George MacLeod are listed as Sutherland pipers in the Sutherland Estate Papers (NLS/313/3478). (See Henderson, *Highland Soldier,* 59.)

12 The interesting corollary is that the last MacKay piper to the MacKenzies of Gairloch, Red John MacKay, matured as a piper in a tradition other than the Blind Piper's.

13 See Conon House Archives 2/113.

14 According to Roy Wentworth, then curator of the Gairloch Heritage Museum, Cairbeg is now Kerrysdale. The peck was a land measure, a fourth part of a quarter, acreage unknown.

15 See Conon House Archives 3/105.

16 See Conon House Archives 9/114, Judicial Rental 1770.

17 The usual dates, Angus's birth c. 1725 and the Blind Piper's death c. 1754, leave Angus about thirty years to have absorbed his father's style and music (and presumably with it elements of the genius of the Blind Piper's putative teacher, Pàdruig Og Mac Cruimein). And yet, Dixon wrote that Angus MacKay, the piper and composer of several pieces of ceòl mór, got piping instruction in Edinburgh. Dixon gave no name for this Lowland-based piping teacher.

18 See Gibson, "Piper John MacKay and Roderick McLennan."

19 John H. Connan.

20 See MacKay, "Reminiscences of a Long Life," published by the *Oban Times* in the 1930s, MS held by the Public Archives of Nova Scotia (PANS), MG20 674 7, 1. Note: This portion was written in the 1860s in New Glasgow, Nova Scotia. See also Gibson, "Genealogical and Piping Notes."

21 See Conon House Archives 4/104.

22 See MacKay, "Reminiscences," 1.

23 See "Account of the Hereditary Pipers," in *Collection,* 12, 13.

24 The prevalent belief until recently was that Angus MacKay was John MacKay, Raasay's teacher of piping. The case against this may be found in *The Scottish Genealogist* 30, no. 3.

25 John MacKay's "Reminiscences" mention his father's having had a boat on Loch Maree.

26 Assynt was occupied in large part by MacLeods, and it is possible that the MacLeod pipers in Reay country in the eighteenth century were from there.

27 See MacKenzie, *Sar-Obair,* 361.

28 See ibid., 361 (in *"Aireamh Taghta de Shar-Obair nam Bard Gaelach"* [A choice number of the great works of the Gaelic bards]).

29 For a short study of the bard John MacRae, see MacDonell, *Emigrant Experience,* passim.

30 Angus MacKay's headings omit Gaelic long-vowel accents.

31 See "Historical and Traditional Notes," in MacKay, *Collection,* 8.

32 See Geikie, *The Life of Sir Roderick I. Murchison,* 2:110, 111.

33 See MacRae, "An Old Bagpipe."

34 See MacKay, *Collection,* 59.

35 "Historical and Traditional Notes on the Piobaireachds," in MacKay, *Collection,* 8.

36 After Culloden Lord George Sackville (1716–85) marched into Kintail via Glenaffric and plundered cattle and personal possessions, despite the clan's official loyalty.

37 Donald MacRae's dates will be touched upon again at the end of this chapter, where the story of the set of bagpipes he won in Edinburgh will be extended.

38 See "Account of the Hereditary Pipers – The MacCrummens," in MacKay, *Collection,* 10.

39 John MacRae (Iain mac Mhurchaidh) could not have been unaware of MacCrimmon piping. There had been MacCrimmons connected with neighbouring Glenelg for generations. In addition, the MacRae bard spent some of his childhood years at Gesto in Skye, a tacksman's home that produced Capt Niel MacLeod, whose canntaireachd versions of Iain Dubh MacCruimein's ceòl mór were published in 1828. "Ach 's truagh nach mise bha'n Geusdo nam bò, / Far an d'fhuair mi m'àrach 'nam phàisdean òg" (Ah 'tis sad I am not to be in Gesto of the cows, / Where I was raised as a young child), sang Iain mac Mhurchaidh Mac Raith. Also, the bard may have known of Lt Donald MacCrimmon in the Carolinas, whither they both went in the early 1770s.

40 See Dixon, *Gairloch,* 190.

41 Francis Rawdon-Hastings (1754–1826); Lord Rawdon, then [1793–1817] earl of Moira, then Marquis of Hastings) gave his name to the Nova Scotia Loyalist settlement of Rawdon founded in 1784. Nearby many disbanded Gaelic-speaking troops of the Royal Highland Emigrants were settled, including at least one piper, Alexander MacGregor.

42 See MacDougall, letter in *Celtic Monthly*, xi, 38–9; and Fionn (Henry Whyte), *Martial Music of the Clans,* 90, 92 (both quoted in Munro, "Archibald Munro, Piper to Glengarry").

43 Given the nearness of Glenelg to Ardintoul it is possible that the MacRas themselves sent Archibald Munro to Lt Donald MacCrimmon for tuition.

44 Sir John MacRa was never president of the Highland Society of London.

45 Gibson, *Traditional Gaelic Bagpiping,* 91–4.

46 Horn, unpublished research based on the records of the ducal Gordon family, held in the Historical Research Room, Scottish Record Office.

47 See Bulloch, *House of Gordon* 3:248. Lord Lewis Gordon, third son of the second duke of Gordon, escaped to France after Culloden and died at Montreuil of fever 15 July 1754.

48 See Campbell, *Two Hundred Years,* 76. Lord Adam Gordon as commander-in-chief at Edinburgh reviewed the 42nd (Black Watch) at Edinburgh in June 1791 (see *Sketches,* 1:392).

49 In 1806 the fourth duke styled himself "Alexander Duke of Gordon Marquis of Huntly and Enzie Lord Badenoch and Lochaber, etc. Superior of the Burgh Barony of Inverlochy called Gordonsburgh situated in the Lordship of Lochaber."

50 Citations to this point in this paragraph are taken from the unpublished researches of Dr B.L.H. Horn of the Scottish Record Office, supplied by Stuart Allan of the Historical Research Room (13 January 1994).

51 I cite correspondence from Bridget MacKay that in turn cites MacKay, *Autobiographical Journal of John MacDonald,* 34, to which I do not have access. The original John MacDonald MS, location unknown, was cited by its editor, Rev Angus MacKay in his *Book of MacKay*, 217–18. According to the latter source, MacDonald joined the company of the captain "Mr MacKay of Bighouse" (217) which stayed recruiting "in the country [presumably Reay country]" "till September" (217), then "all joined [as a company of 117, officers and men] at the Meikle Ferry" (218) on the Dornoch Firth. According to MacKay's paraphrasing in *The Book of MacKay* of the original MS, thence the company proceeded by stages to Elgin, where the regiment was embodied and quartered for some time, until November when they proceeded to Fort George. MacKay then cites the MS as saying, "We marched to Fort George in three divisions" (218).

52 See MacKay, *Book of MacKay*, 218, citing John MacDonald's original MS: "We marched to Fort George in three divisions." John MacDonald also is cited as having joined Bighouse as "pipe-major" (ibid., 217). Note: David Stewart of Garth wrote that the duke of Gordon's North Fencibles were raised on the duke's estates in Inverness, Moray, Banff, and Aberdeen and that they amounted to 960 men embodied in Aberdeen in 1778 (see Stewart, *Sketches,* 2:347). David Stewart may have been unaware of some bond of friendship or otherwise linking the duke of Gordon and MacKay of (Handa and) Bighouse (d. 1798).

53 See Bridget MacKenzie, letter to the author, 9 February 1999.

54 I am indebted to Allan C. Dunlop, retired assistant archivist of the province of Nova Scotia, for sending me a copy of this article in April 1999. In 1849 the *Globe*, in that year a tri-weekly, was operated by Alloa-born, Edinburgh-educated Scot George Brown (1818–80), grandson of George MacKenzie, "gentleman" of Stornoway (see *Dictionary of Canadian Biography*, 10:91–3).

55 See *Eastern Chronicle* (Halifax) 8 November 1849, 5, citing "[Globe" (*sic*).

56 In that year his captain's commission in the newly raised 89th Highland Regiment was turned down, at his mother's request, by George II (see Stewart, *Sketches*, 2:81).

57 See Wallace, [article's title missing], *Canadian Historical Review*, 1937, 137. Fraser of Inverallochy died of wounds received at the Battle of the Plains of Abraham. One of the other Simon Frasers was gazetted a lieutenant 8 January 1757, captain-lieutenant, 27 September 1758, and captain, 22 April 1759. The presence of Lt Cosmo Gordon in Fraser's Highlanders (gazetted 24 July 1757 and killed at the battle of Ste Foy, 28 April 1760) raises speculation as to why the bagpipes were lent to Simon Fraser.

58 See *Eastern Chronicle* (Halifax), 8 November 1849, 5, citing "[Globe" (*sic*). Note: A Donald MacRae from Applecross won the first prize at the annual Edinburgh piping competition (see "Account of the competition of Pipers," in MacKay, *Collection*, 16). MacKay notes that in 1792 the "preses" was "The Most Honourable the Marquis of Huntly" (ibid., 16). In the same year Campbell gives the president of the Highland Society of London as George Marquess of Lorne (later sixth of Argyll); the next year, 1793, the job came to George, duke of Huntly (probably George, fifth and last duke of Gordon) (see Campbell, *Two Hundred Years,* 76).

59 MacCrae probably took the prescribed option (three years or the duration of the war) of leaving the 78th and service in India in 1784. His service in the 42nd (Black Watch) probably began in or after 1790. In that year Alexander Gordon, seventh marquis of Huntly and later fourth duke of Gordon, raised a company for the Black Watch (see *Sketches*, 1:392).

60 David Stewart of Garth served as a major in 2nd Battalion of the 78th and was wounded at Maida; in describing the battle, he did not mention piping but said that it was one of the most efficiently conducted battles against a French enemy of higher numbers, for losses were only one in every 104 men (*Sketches*, 2:297–311, app. xciii).

61 According to Stewart's *Sketches* (2:292–329), neither the 1st nor 2nd Battalion of the 78th served in the Peninsula. However, when the 2nd returned from Egypt to Sicily, "the 78th joined an expedition under Sir John Moore intended for Lisbon, but they were afterwards ordered for England" (ibid., 320). The 42nd Regiment was at Corunna and it appears that MacCrae rejoined old comrades. It is unknown what company he served with in Egypt with the 78th, but a group of twenty MacRaes were at El Hamet in 1807; of these Ensign Christo-

pher MacRae, his sergeant John MacRae, and six other MacRaes were killed. Two officers of the 78th removed to the 42nd in 1808, David Stewart and Hercules Scott (*Sketches*, vol. 2, app. lxvi and app. lxvii), but the piper may have enjoyed some independence of movement.

62 See *Eastern Chronicle*, 8 November 1849, 5. Donald MacRae was said to be in his eightieth year in 1835 (see chapter 5).

63 See Bulloch, *House of Gordon,* 3:112–3.

64 See Whyte, *Martial Music of the Clans,* 7.

CHAPTER NINE

1 Pianos were used to give a starting note in the one mod I sang in in Fort William in the 1940s. The venue was not the traditional céilidh or a facsimile but an elevated stage in front of an audience. Gaelic choral music also was and is a remarkable departure from tradition. It too is normally presented in non-céilidh surroundings. The influence of the *eistoddfod* has been suggested as a model for the Gaelic mod.

2 Where the Reel is concerned, in comparison with the setting steps to strathspeys and reels found in Gaelic Cape Breton, the modern Scottish Reel setting steps represent radical simplifications.

3 Fletts, "Some Early Highland Dancing Competitions," *Aberdeen University Review*, Autumn 1956, 347.

4 C.I.N. MacLeod wrote among other things *Sgialachdan a Albainn Nuaidh* (1969) and *Bardachd a Albainn Nuaidh* (1970).

5 Calum MacLeod pounced on me with glee when I reported to him in 1972 that I had been at Frank MacInnis's wedding in Arasaig, Antigonish County, Nova Scotia. "And where do you think they got the dancing?" he asked when I told him it was strange to me.

6 Scottish Gaelic step-dancing is obviously a relation of Irish step-dancing and in historico-cultural terms is subtended by it. The question is how and when distinctions appeared between the two versions that were most closely related (presumably those found in the north of Eire and in the closest Hebridean islands and the southwest of Argyll). The Irish who settled near Antigonish were, in 1907, thorough-going Scotch Gaels (see Rev. Archibald Campbell, "Duthaich na Saorsa," in *Guth na Bliadhna,* book 5, no. 2 [Spring 1908]: 112, 113).

7 On 5 February 1908, under the heading "Scottish Organisations are Formed at Port Hood and Inverness [coal-mining communities in Inverness County]," the *Sydney Record* reported the formation of a Clan Macdonnell society at Port Hood and Clan Gordon at Inverness. "The degree work in Port Hood was conducted by Royal Deputy Macneil of Antigonish assisted by Clan Chisholm," and the new chief of the Macdonnells was a young rising barrister called J.D. Matheson. Clan Gordon's new chief was M.S. Beaton, mine manager for the

Inverness Railway and Coal Company. In keeping with modern "Scottish" fashion, both clans had pipers, the Macdonnells, Iain MacAllister, and the Gordons, D.M. Leslie (*Sydney Record* 11, no. 30 [5 February 1908]: 3). Insofar as past chiefs were mentioned, these societies already existed. The article's wording suggests that they were benevolent societies run along Masonic lines and in essence non-Gaelic.

8 The late James MacKay, Kingsville, local historian and remarkable informant and helper of all who were interested in Gaelic affairs, carried his resentment at the school system to his grave. He vividly remembered having to learn his first words of English suddenly, under threat of sanction, mockery, and force as a child going first to school.

9 Scottish studies at the University of Guelph, for example, are in essence studies of Saxon Scotland. An excellent library collection (built by W. Stanford Reid) serves this branch.

10 Since my time in Cape Breton (1972) I have known of many people who were still assembling collections of reel-to-reel and casette tapes and records of the older Gaelic-speaking fiddlers. Various organizations are at present accumulating what is available of what once was. At the professional level, St Francis Xavier University in Antigonish holds a collection of the work of Dr John Shaw, now of Edinburgh University's School of Scottish Studies.

11 The credit for first remarking on Alex Currie's traditional step-dance bagpiping belongs to Allister MacGillivray (*A Cape Breton Ceilidh*, 208, 209).

12 Barry Shears's three collections of pipe music include some of Alex Currie's music.

13 Malcolm MacDonald (1901–94), Long Point, Inverness County, pointed to the repeated mention of pipers in his grand-father's generation (born 1840–50) as evidence that the bagpipe was the dominant instrument in the Scottish and Nova Scotian Gàidhealtachds. He was aware of the fiddle's use in Gaelic Scotland but felt from his lack of knowledge of immigrant fiddlers that the instrument generally was more a latter-day adoption by New World Gaels in Nova Scotia (Malcolm MacDonald, personal interview, Long Point, September 1978, date unrecorded).

14 Modern pipers playing in the older step-dance style, however, often prefer to play with piano accompaniment despite the dissonances. Whether this preference comes from the violin-piano pairing or from an older bagpipe-organ/piano blending is unknown. Pipe chanters, by many reports, have been changing in their pitch.

15 When I revisited informants, I found, almost invariably, that there was simply no substitute for the initial spontaneity.

16 I don't think anyone was being secretive in not drawing my attention to the tapes, but there may have been a fear that I should overlook or denigrate the older style by applying critical modern technical standards to it.

17 The tape was loaned to me by Joseph Beaton (Eòs mac Dhòmhnuill 'ic

Aonghuis), Mabou, a first cousin once removed of Angus Campbell Beaton.

18 Since "step-dancing" and "dancing" were (and to an extent still are) synonymous terms and often required question and answer elaboration to establish that questioner and informant were discussing exactly the same thing, I often preferred to discuss the Scotch Four (sometimes simply Four, occasionally, if not different, Single Four) and the Square Set, post-1950. Both of the latter embodied step-dance setting steps (I strongly suspect that, while step-dance setting steps were not used in the Square Set from c. 1890 to 1950, the pipe and fiddle music that accompanied it was strictly traditional in speed and timing, with if anything an increase in speed).

19 By comparison, there would be a much greater tendency on the part of the modern piper to dismiss as substandard Alex "the Ridge" MacDonald's piping, or Alex Currie's for that matter. Old-style doublings on high A might generate interest, but other fingering anomalies would immediately be equated with incompetence. (I listened to a tape of Alex MacDonald's piping of "Seann Triubhais" at the office of Effie Rankin, interim professor of Celtic Studies at St Francis Xavier University, 16 April 1998.)

20 The well-mannered, almost prompted response of Inverness County Scottish audiences to Scottish Strathspey and Reel society violining, with its identical bowing, indicated to me that there was a sure awareness of what distinguished that music from the traditional Gaelic forms.

21 To complicate matters further, the same Gael, in discussing the fiddling of Sandy MacLean, told me that she enjoyed his music because it reminded her of piping. Sandy MacLean was a very popular Protestant Gaelic fiddler from Foot Cape south of Inverness whose ancestors had come from Rhum. He had started with the bagpipes but stopped playing early for health reasons; except over the radio, I never heard him fiddle.

22 Joe Neil MacNeil's *magnum opus* is *Tales until Dawn (Sgialachdan gu Latha)*.

23 Joe Neil travelled into his own memory with the utmost confidence, knowing that there he would find carefully accumulated memories. When I revisited Dan Angus Beaton, Blackstone (Inverness County), hoping to add to what he had told me twenty years earlier about the old piper Archibald Beaton from Mabou Coal Mines, I encountered the same rotishness of presentation and again I let it distress me.

24 Only once aside from my wonderful series of chats with Joe Neil had I felt the same way and that was in talking with Dan Angus Beaton, Blackstone, for the second time about Archibald and other Beaton pipers. Dan Angus was not long from death and I was surprised to recognize the conversation I had had a dozen years earlier. In the recitative nature (which I know I duplicate without realizing it) of what he told me again, I found myself wondering how many times he had told the same story and, had it been often, how much he may have formulized and distorted in so doing. For all that, I checked some of the central

points made by Dan Angus Beaton in a Charlottetown newspaper and found that his information was correct.

25 John Shaw wrote that "although literate in Gaelic, he always took care in our conversations to distinguish between oral and written sources of his tales" (*Tales until Dawn*, xvii). Almost any attitude Joe Neil might have had concerning the old hereditary piping families, particularly the MacCrimmons, likely sprang directly or indirectly from published accounts/imaginings in English. The subject never came up.

26 It was helpful in my gathering of personal memories that at no time was I receiving grant money or any wage for what I was doing.

27 Joe Neil MacNeil was awarded a doctoral degree by Saint Mary's University in Halifax.

28 Other personal glimpses of Neil R. MacIsaac are found in MacNeil, *Tales until Dawn*, and in MacInnes, *Journey in Celtic Music*.

29 The records of the MacGillivray Guest Home in Sydney show that Neil R. MacIsaac was born at Rear Big Pond, 25 September 1887, was admitted to the home 15 December 1970, and died there 23 August 1973. Sister Deveaux also spoke to Fr Angus J. MacLeod about Neil R. and was told that the piper was a "very stubborn Scotchman." Fr MacLeod had been approached to get Neil R. to pipe at an "entertainment" at Big Pond but Neil R. had turned him down (Sister Amelia Deveaux, MacGillivray Guest Home, telephone communication, 11 May 1998). Fr MacLeod wrote humorously about the occasion to me: "I was requested by the organizing committee to approach Neil R. with the request that he might participate in the program being planned. As a neophyte at the time I proceeded to visit Neil R. Much more preparation should have gone into the visit. While being the essence of courtesy and respect it became clear as the interview proceeded that Neil R. had no intention whatever of participating in the program and nothing that I could say or do seemed to change his mind ... More experience would have prompted me to approach the matter differently" (Fr Angus J. MacLeod, Sydney, personal correspondence, 22 May 1998).

30 Joe Neil MacNeil, telephone conversation, 19 September 1991. In 1980 Joe Neil said that MacIsaac had written down, or had had written down, 128 marches in one time (interview at Kingsville, Cape Breton, 27 July 1980).

31 Joe Neil's memory of pipe tunes was fixed best if he could see the musician's fingers although he never told me (and I may not have asked him) whether he played the chanter.

32 Interview at Kingsville, Cape Breton, 30 November 1979. When he later flipped through my copy of the *Skye Collection*, Joe Neil MacNeil identified "Christmas Carousing," "Bean Dhòmhnuil Bhig," "Chuir i glùn air a' bhodach," and "Peter Robertson's Strathspey" as some of the tunes that Neil R. MacIsaac played (interview at Kingsville, 27 July 1980).

33 The best book I have read on the subject of traditional musicians, musical

repertoires, spontaneity, and memories is Ciaran Carson's *Last Night's Fun*.

34 Joe Neil never told me that he played any instrument.

35 The late Dan Hughie MacEachern, Queensville, Inverness County, Cape Breton, fiddler/composer and compiler of two collections of traditional fiddle music, was a stickler for playing music the way it had been written, whether his own music, William Marshall's, Niel Gow's, or anyone's, but musical literacy is still no guarantee of fidelity to written music in Cape Breton. Erring from the document is a feature of traditional music and a sign of life, experiment, and change.

36 One of those whose name Joe Neil remembered from Neil R. was Little Angus MacKinnon, a piper and fiddler from the Woodbine area a few miles southeast of East Bay (interview at Kingsville, 27 July 1980).

37 Interview, 30 November 1979.

38 Ibid. A reproduction of a photograph of a mustachioed Rory Shim MacIsaac and his wife, Annie, appears on the cover of Barry Shears's *Gathering of the Clans Collection,* vol. 2.

39 Dannie Campbell, Alexandra Street, Sydney. Personal interview there, 9 May 1998. Dannie is the son of Mike Campbell, Iona, and Kate MacIsaac (Rory Shim's daughter). Kate cared for her father in his dotage.

40 Dannie Campbell, 9 May 1998.

41 Ibid.

42 Margaret (MacNeil) Gillis, 9 May 1998. Margaret Gillis was born in June 1918.

43 Telephone communication, 11 May 1998.

44 Joe Neil named "Struan Robertson's Rant," "Miss Drummond of Perth," and "Munlochy Bridge" as three strathspeys he often heard played on both the pipes and the fiddle (from interview at Kingsville, Cape Breton, 30 November 1979).

45 Joe Neil told John Shaw, "I never saw a foursome reel danced unless they danced it in a place where they were presenting a program of entertainment" (MacNeil, *Tales until Dawn*, 224).

46 In 1928, at the opening of the new parish hall in Big Pond, MacNeil remembered seeing the Scotch Four danced, followed by the even less durable Eight-Hand Reel, about which he never offered me detailed information.

47 I neglected to ask if there was a Gaelic equivalent for "break down," a term initially associated with the Quadrille in rural New England in the 1860s (OED). In Inverness county the term was not commonly used in description in the 1970s and '80s.

48 Joe Neil MacNeil, personal interview, Kingsville, 30 May 1982.

49 Joe Neil recollected particularly a "shower" in Irish Vale in 1950 for a woman he knew (or was related to) in which MacIsaac piped for the Square Set.

50 Joe Neil remembered MacIsaac piping for "five figures of the Square Set"; in this the dancers would take an inter-figure breather and MacIsaac went on non-

stop. MacNeil also recollected Joe MacIsaac from Rear Big Pond playing with Neil R. for Square Set dancing (interview at Kingsville, 11 May 1980).

51 MacGillivray, *Cape Breton Ceilidh,* 208, 209.

52 Interview at Frenchvale, 20 August 1991. Although Alex Currie has received, and is receiving, a great deal of attention in Nova Scotia and in Scotland, Joe Neil told me nothing about him or his piping.

53 Kempt Head, Boularderie, and Big Bras d'Or (where John Francis later settled) are in Victoria County (MacMillan, *To the Hill of Boisdale*), 217–24; see also MacDonald, *Mabou Pioneers,* 504.

54 Dannie Campbell, Alexandra Street, Sydney (b. 21 September 1913), did not know the Scots woman's name (Joe Neil gave me that) but said that she came to Vancouver. He was the first to mention Neil R.'s correspondence with a Scots piper and the only one to recollect Neil R.'s having subscribed to the *Oban Times.* Dannie Campbell was a son of Rory Shim's daughter Kate (married to Mike Campbell). Unluckily, when Neil R. was on his deathbed, his house in East Bay was broken into and then burnt down, so none of those records survived (interview, Dannie Campbell, 582 Alexandra Street, Sydney, 9 May 1998). From Margaret (MacNeil) Gillis on the same day, I learned that Neil R. had made a now-forgotten pipe tune for the MacIsaacs, which he wrote down and sent to an unnamed Scottish piper. Margaret Gillis is a granddaughter of a sister of Rory Shim's (Margaret Gillis, Lisgard Street, Sydney, 9 May 1998). Neil R. taught Dan Campbell's daughter Cecilia (Campbell) Cooke and Margaret Gillis's son Bernard to play the bagpipes.

55 There appears to be no above-average skill in mathematics associated with this traditional form of musicality.

56 Margaret (MacNeil) Gillis said that Rory Shim's mother's father was Hugh Gillis who settled at Ben Eoin, adding that Rory Shim got his land in Ben Eoin from Hugh (personal interview, 9 May 1998). Fr Allan MacMillan told me that Rory Shim got the "Shim" from his mother's brother's name, Simon (telephone communication, 11 May 1998).

57 John MacDonald's son Tony was also a piper. He could play by note. Joe Neil told me that he remembered seeing Tony MacDonald, George Sutherland (Soldier's Cove), and another Gaelic-speaking piper reading pipe music together (personal interview, 27 July 1980).

58 The names of other pipers whom Joe Neil MacNeil had heard in or near Big Pond and mentioned elsewhere were Alasdair a' Phìobaire MacPhee, Black Jack MacDonald, George Sutherland, Anthony MacDonald, Donald Austin (presumably the Dan Uisdein mentioned above), Peter MacKinnon, Joseph MacMullin, Joe MacIsaac, Peter Morrison, Donald MacLeod, Donald MacDonald (son of Charles), and Joe MacAdam (MacNeil, *Tales until Dawn,* 218, 221, 222).

59 Murdoch MacMillan left two daughters, one living in Florida in 1982 and another, Mrs Cameron, deceased (1981 or '82).

60 Joe Neil MacNeil, personal interview, Kingsville, 30 May 1982.

61 A Donald Stewart won second prize at the Edinburgh ceòl mór piping competition in 1824. He was described in Angus MacKay's "Account of the Competition of Pipers" as piper to the 79th Regiment (MacKay, *Collection,* 19).

62 Joe Neil MacNeil described Michael MacLean's father as "Eòs Pheadair Chaluim Ghobha," a man who married "a MacPhee woman from Big Pond, a daughter of Mìcheal Nìll Dhòmhnaill" (MacNeil, *Tales until Dawn,* 154). Mary MacPherson told me that Mike MacLean was son of Joe MacLean and Catherine MacPhee, daughter of Michael MacPhee. She died c. 1938 (interview at Big Pond, 9 May 1998). Joe Neil had known of my interest in learning about ceòl mór pipers from our earliest conversation in 1978, and it was clearly a subject he thought about, since he generously offered me most of these details unasked. No MacPhee piper appears in the Edinburgh competition winners lists from 1800.

63 Among the ceòl mór pipers Joe Neil mentioned, one was Cape Breton born, Stephen B. MacNeil (1851–1940), also known as "Am Pìobaire Mór" (Shears, *Gathering of the Clans Collection,* 1:21).

64 MacDonald, "Piping in Cape Breton."

65 A thoroughly researched description of the MacSweens is found in MacMillan, *To the Hill of Boisdale,* 541–61.

66 Joe Lawrence MacDonald was the paternal grandson of a South Uist-born Highlander (MacMillan, *To the Hill of Boisdale,* 202–7). Born in Ironville, he was a founding member of the Boisdale Gaelic Society, a local historian and genealogist, a teacher of his mother-tongue Gaelic, and a collector of Gaelic songs and stories for the Beaton Institute in Sydney (now part of University College of Cape Breton). Two index cards list seventy-one tape recordings of material recorded by or relating to Joe Lawrence, and another, T-3252, is devoted entirely to him (I am grateful to Dr Robert Morgan, UCCB, for this information).

67 Hugh's son Hector told me that, according to his father, the family had come originally from the Castle Sween area of Argyll. Of the two sons who emigrated, one retained his Presbyterian faith in Nova Scotia, while the other, Iain, was or became a Catholic. A number of descendants of both live in the Sydney area of Cape Breton (Hector MacSween, telephone conversation, 1 May 1998).

68 Maj. Allan MacNeil is unidentified. He is not mentioned in MacNeil, *All Call Iona Home.*

69 Shears, telephone interview with author.

70 MacMillan, *To the Hill of Boisdale,* 267.

71 Efforts to link these MacIntyres with the Robert MacIntyre who was Clanranald's piper in the early 1790s have been in vain.

72 Personal communication, Montreal, summer 1976. Fr Francis Cameron, Gaelic-speaking priest and fiddler, is styled Francis mac Fhionnlaidh 'ic Dhòmhnuil Mhóir 'ic Iain 'ic Aonghuis Dhuinn 'ic Aonghuis Dhuibh (MacMillan, *To the Hill of Boisdale,* 57).

73   A common Cape Breton version of the phrase "keep secret/hidden from" is "keep ahide on."

74   Joe Lawrence said that owing to the depth of the Rear Beaver Cove glen, late frosts discouraged farming and gardening and caused people to leave. His uncle and aunt are more likely to have been siblings of his mother, Margaret Gillis, who was from Rear Beaver Cove than of his father (likeliest members are named in MacMillan, *To the Hill of Boisdale*, 92).

75   MacMillan, citing an unspecified obituary, gives Calum Ruadh MacLean as dying in 1924 aged 106. He was in all likelihood a South Uist man (MacMillan, *To the Hill of Boisdale*, 370).

76   Information from Joe Lawrence MacDonald, 23 August 1980.

77   Sandy Nicolson's brother Angus (John Patrick) Nicholson and his family are described as coming from Barra and settling in Cape Mabou, Inverness County. An unnamed brother is acknowledged as having settled at Boisdale (see MacDougall, *History of Inverness County*, 614). Long Island in the text may mean Long Island Barrachois, which is nearby but in fact peninsular and more fertile. MacMillan's authoritative work on the Nicholsons is found in his *To the Hill of Boisdale*, 571–81.

78   MacMillan, *To the Hill of Boisdale*, 262, 266.

79   Ibid., 265.

80   Ibid., 66, 68–9. For a photograph of "Sleepy Mick Campbell," see Shears, *Cape Breton Collection of Bagpipe Music*, iii.

81   MacMillan, *To the Hill of Boisdale*, 129, 130.

82   Ibid., 63.

83   Ibid., 269. Name only given.

84   See Margaret MacDonell, "Na Sgeulaichean" in MacDonell and Shaw, *Luirgean Eachainn Nìll*.

85   Alex D. MacLean (1889–1974), Washabuck, was a great-grandson of the pipers' brother Neil MacLean. He was a source also for Stephen R. MacNeil, *All Call Iona Home*.

86   Personal telephone interview, Vincent MacLean to the author, 8 April 1999. Mr MacLean was not aware of the existence of a passenger list for the ship *Ann*. He did not have dates for Roderick MacLean but told me that Roderick's oldest son, Donald, was born in 1838 and died 1924 (telephone conversation, 14 April 1999).

87   It appears that Lachlann MacLean left a brother Hector in Barra who is believed to have been a blacksmith. Hector had three sons who emigrated c. 1818: Alexander (styled Alasdair Gobha) settled at Little Mabou, Malcolm (Calum Gobha) settled at Mabou Harbour while Charles (Tearlach Gobha) settled at Washabuck (see MacDonald, *Mabou Pioneers*, 727, 731). MacDougall described the family as "gow" (gobha) (see MacDougall, *History of Inverness County*, 276). Not only that but, according to Vincent MacLean (telephone conversation, 14 April 1999), when the wife of Neil, son of immigrant Lachlann (son of Hector) MacLean died, she told the priest (Fr Donald MacIsaac) that

she had been married to "Neil mac Lachlainn 'ic Eachainn Ghobha" (Neil, son of Lachlann, son of Hector the smith). Another Alexander MacLean, born in Barra in 1768, whose father and grandfather had been smiths to the "Laird of Barra," emigrated in 1818 to Pictou. Eventually he settled on eleven hundred acres at South Whycocomagh. There appears to be no relationship between the families. (See MacDougall, *History of Inverness County,* 462–3.)

88 A photograph of Roderick MacLean, with the Tobermory bagpipes, is used in Shears, *Gathering of the Clans Collection.*

89 Alex D. MacLean, unpublished MS ("Pioneers"), 16. Peter was being established as "piper for the family," which may also suggest some local prominence in Barra (ibid. 16).

90 See ibid., 17.

91 See Shears, *Gathering of the Clans Collection,* 1:18. The bagpipes appear to have two stocks and a bass and tenor drone. MacLean played left hand upper and with the instrument under his left shoulder. Barry Shears offered the opinion that the blow-pipe was usable by both right- and left-shoulder players (telephone conversation, 21 April 1999).

92 A.A. Johnston says that Alexander F. MacGillivray was born at Back Settlement of Knoydart (Dunmaglass), Antigonish County, N.S., in 1847, and ordained at Quebec, 8 June 1873 (see Johnston, *History of the Catholic Church,* 2:484). He arrived in Iona 23 August 1873 (ibid., 523–4). According to MacLean, Fr MacGillivray left Iona parish in 1880; he is buried in Boisdale, where, according to his gravestone, he had been pastor for a score of years, dying 29 October 1903 (personal telephone interview, 8 April 1999).

93 Alex D. MacLean, unpublished MS, 16.

94 Vincent MacLean told me that he did not speak Gaelic and while his parents knew a few words, it was his grandparents who last spoke it fluently in his family (personal interview, 8 April 1999). Gaelic is still spoken by several of the older people in Iona and the surrounding area, notably by Rod MacNeil, father of the step-dance piper Paul, and by Rod's brother James. It is also worthy of note that James Watson has for several years been teaching Gaelic at Iona's Highland Village in the summer.

95 John MacLean can and does play both forms of pipe music, traditional and modern.

96 Never having heard his piping, I cannot say if he indulges an (almost fashionable) interest in step-dance rhythm.

97 Nearly all the modern Scottish fiddlers in Nova Scotia are non-Gaelic speaking, but several among the grandparent generation, like Hugh A. MacMaster in Judique, and the late Bill Lamey of Glenora, and the late Dan Joe MacInnis of Sydney, though they too heard very little Gaelic from their parents (unfortunately this was often deliberate), play or played music that is the link to the older world. That is because these men were the last of the tradition from Gaelic-speaking contemporaries and parents.

98 Paul MacNeil and Jamie MacInnis made the first modern commercial recording to include reels played in the local idiom on the bagpipes.

99 See MacLean, "Traditional links to song & dance."

100 From a letter from Vincent MacLean, Washabuck, to the author, 20 March
1999, citing MacLean, unpublished MS, 10. Note the association of piping
with dress and regalia.

101 Ibid., citing MS, 25.

102 Alex D. MacLean, unpublished MS, 17. MacLean's overall impression of
funeral bagpiping in Mabou cannot but have been at least partially reliant on
memories, perhaps his own, of the funeral piping of Black Angus MacDonald
of Mount Young and probably that of Angus Johnnie Ranald Beaton as well.

CHAPTER TEN

1 MacFarlane (?) *Margaree.Doc* "The Parish of South-West Margaree Antigonish
Casket 1896," 13. The ending to MacFarlane's composite article reads "(There
are) about 120 families in the (parish with a) population of something less
(than a thous)and" (ibid., 13).

2 MacDougall, *History of Inverness County,* 405.

3 Copies of a lengthy article set in newspaper columns, 29 pages in length (arbi-
trarily cut), published in the Antigonish *Casket* in 1896 and attributed to D.D.
MacFarlane, p. 26. See Biographical and Genealogical file (B. and G. file), and
therein under "South West Margaree," in the Beaton Institute, University College of Cape Breton, Sydney, Cape Breton. (Also found in MacFarlane (?)
Margaree.Doc "The Parish of South-West Margaree Antigonish *Casket* 1896,"
14. This document reads "Peter Gillis and his brother Dan, Hugh McIsaac,
Angus and Patrick McFarlane, John and Charlie Jamieson [Neil's sons?], Jim
H. Gillis, Malcolm *(D?. McFarlane, ????McFarlane and ????-DMF)* McLellan." Insofar as only the D. of "Malcolm D. McFarlane" is slightly indistinct in
the first-mentioned source I am inclined to think that the *Margaree.Doc* was
taken from a handwritten manuscript. If so, I have been unable to discover it.

4 The decline of Gaelic was not perceived by everyone as a descent into cultural
anomie but rather as an ascent into a sophisticated world-dominant Victorian
consciousness bent on mental and material improvement. D.D. MacFarlane
mentions local debating societies and a world of great optimism; his regrets are
nostalgic, not outraged.

5 D.D. MacFarlane's diaries are held by the Archives at St Francis Xavier University, Antigonish, Nova Scotia.

6 MacDougall leaves his reader wondering if his listings of issue are chronologi-
cal; only a comparison with 1871 and later censuses where children's ages are
given resolves the matter. Perhaps in a work so large he was unimpressed by
the importance of the reallocation of grandparents' names to first and later sons
and daughters.

7   Joe Neil knew nothing about Allan MacFarlane.

8   Bernie MacNeil learned his Gaelic from age 11. He has been dead for some years, but when I visited him he showed me a medal that Allan MacFarlane had won in Sydney at a piping competition. MacNeil's thoughts about MacFarlane, especially the humorous ones, occurred to him first in Gaelic and he told me that he regretted having to talk to me about MacFarlane in English.

9   Fraser-Mackintosh, "The Macdonells of Scotos." Crowlin may be from *crodh* (cattle) and *linne* (pool, water by the shore).

10 At the time I thought that perhaps MacLean didn't realize that he was opening the door to an outsider on an aspect of Inverness County immigrant Gaelic music/dance culture that until then was unknown, unsuspected, and unstudied; had he known, he might have been silent. But that was quite unfair. In my time the best informants knew clearly that they were in a dwindling minority and took pleasure in reminiscing about their older world when they felt that the inquirer's motives were honourable and non-acquisitive.

11 Archie MacPhail, Scotsville, personal interview, 6 June 1979.

12 Ibid.

13 Peter MacMillan told me in the spring of 1998 that Clarence Moore's mother had married twice, her second husband being a rock expert, and that she had raised six children, five of whom were Clarence's older MacDonald half-brothers and -sisters. While his mother was alive, Clarence lived in what is now known as the MacDonald House. When he taught in Inverness, he lived with his half-sister Jessie. He married Alice MacKay, daughter of Angus. He and she are both dead (Peter MacMillan, East Lake, telephone conversation, 7 May 1998).

14 Headlake was a Presbyterian community at the south end of Lake Ainslie.

15 Clarence Moore described the hall's location as being where there was a laundromat in 1979, and George MacKinnon's as where the Van Larken's farm was in 1979. Both were at the south end of Lake Ainslie within a mile of John Neillie MacLean's home.

16 In Marble Mountain during the First World War, just as at East Lake Ainslie and Boisdale and Judique, when the dancers really wanted to dance and to show their virtuosity (i.e., to step-dance), they called for the Scotch Four because its setting steps were step-dance steps of the dancers' personal preferences. Bagpipes were not mentioned in the Marble Mountain example. At the time it was a thriving community on the Bras d'Or.

17 Walter Scott, interview in Inverness, Nova Scotia, 20 April 1977. Jack Collins, Scotsville, told me that his uncle Allan MacFarlane went to piping and fiddling competitions in Massachusetts and Maine.

18 I have permission to photograph the set, there being no likelihood of their changing hands or moving from the present owner's family, but so far I have chosen not to.

19 Jimmie MacLellan the ear piper was known locally as Seumas [mac] Dhòmhnuill ['ic] Fhearchair. According to a relative of Jimmie's, Allan gave the old set away.

20 I am indebted to Greg Smith for giving me Angus MacLellan's sloinneadh (whereby the family is traceable in MacDougall's *History*) and for suggesting I visit John Neillie MacLellan, Kempt Road, Richmond County.

21 Red Angus MacLellan died 17 April 1922 aged about 75 (Antigonish *Casket,* 11 May 1922, 8).

22 Walter Scott MacFarlane, Inverness, interview, 20 April 1977. Hughie Gillis was a brother of Angus Allan Gillis, the South West Margaree fiddler.

23 "Cumha. Le Aonghas Ban Mac Pharlain, Braighe Mhargairi," in Gillis, *Smeorach nan Cnoc 'S nan Gleann,* 123. Walter Scott MacFarlane composed an elegy for Allan MacFarlane called "Blow the Bugle."

24 *Soil Survey of Cape Breton Island Nova Scotia,* Report no. 12, southwest sheet.

25 Walter Scott MacFarlane said that Allan MacFarlane took his "Scotsville Reel" (see MacQuarrie, *The Cape Breton Collection of Scottish Melodies for the Violin,* 7) to a daughter of Dan John MacDonald to have her check his work. (Charles MacDonald of East Lake Ainslie believes [personal interview, July 1994] that this was Josie, daughter of Dan John MacDougall of East Lake.)

26 John Neillie MacLellan, personal interview at Kempt Road, 17 June 1998. Presumably "Gleann Mór" was the local designation for the Margaree Valley.

27 One of his legs was shorter than the other, his eyes seemed to roll in an oddly shaped head (of which one jealous neighbour said, "One side is full of music and the other's full of bad nature"), and he suffered from a speech impediment. Thoughtless children sometimes tormented him.

28 Alice (MacLean) Freeman, Inverness, has the words of a song made by Malcolm Gillis for Ann MacLean, granddaughter of the dancing master Calum MacLean from Mull, who settled at Scotsville. The gesture, for religious reasons, was pre-doomed. The air was the pipe tune "Bonnie Ann."

29 Bella (Gillis) MacIsaac, a pupil of the bard's, said that he taught the "tonic solfa" (MacIsaac, personal interview, Inverness, no date, 1972). Clara Dennis learned from the bard's widow that the bard "could play the bagpipes, accordion, mandolin, violin, organ and piano. His favourite was the violin. Many's the time when the children were little he'd take the violin at dusk and set them to dancing." Dennis was shown three cups the bard had won for fiddling, in River Denys, in Boston ("champion fiddler"), and another from the Intercolonial Club of Boston ("in appreciation of his artistic ability as an old-fashioned fiddler, 1926") (Dennis, *Cape Breton Over,* 236, 237).

30 Archie MacPhail, personal interview, Scotsville, 10 September 1994. MacPhail, a Presbyterian, was born in Scotsville but lived from 1922 to 1972 in the Boston area. When he was young he maintained many friendships with nearby musicians, both Protestant and Catholic, but notably with his Scotsville and Margaree Catholic neighbours. His admiration, for example, for the Margaree Gillises' musicality is matched only by his sorrow at its near disappearance today. He is a Gaelic speaker who learned from his Campbell grandparents, his father having died before he was born.

31 Francis MacDonald, telephone interview, 18 June 1998.

32 Cannon, *Bibliography,* 32.

33 There is no evidence that MacFarlane attended the famous fiddling contest in Maine in 1926 but at that event Scott Skinner the Scottish fiddler, nothing if not a modernist, failed to win.

34 George Sutherland, personal interview. Sutherland was a Gaelic speaker. He was a piping pupil of Black Jack MacDonald, also of Soldier's Cove, and learned from the beginning by note. (George Sutherland said that Black Jack was a note player who learned the *obair ùrlair* [ground work] of piping during the First World War.)

35 He is known to have offered the Highland Society the following tunes: "The Prince's Salute," "MacLachlan's March" and "Glas Mhuir" (Campbell, *Kilberry Book of Ceòl Mór,* 11).

36 There are no Jamiesons in the McNeill census of 1764/65, which includes twenty "Canna papists" families (to be cleared from the west of the island by Whit Sunday 1765 to make way for Protestants). Likewise there are no Jamiesons in the twenty-one families holding their land from "Mr McLeod" (Donald MacLeod, a Protestant whose tack was held of Clanranald) or among the "protestants of Canna" (McNeill, "Census").

37 I am grateful to Barry Shears for giving me Neil Jamieson's dates. Neil's brother James, "formerly of Piper's Glen," died 29 March 1918 aged 62 at Neil's Whitney Pier home (Antigonish *Casket* 66, no. 14 [4 April 1918]: 5). Another of the family, Donald Jamieson, died 21 February 1899 at Glen Campbell. His obituary said that he probably came from Canna some sixty-nine years earlier and that he emigrated with his parents. He left a wife and three daughters (Antigonish *Casket* 48, no. 25, March 1899: 5, 16.

38 The 1891 census gives Neil Jamieson (37), farmer and shoemaker, Ann (35), John (12), Jane (10), Catherine (8), Charles (7), Mary (5), Flory (4), Mary I (3), Charlot (1), and Mary (22), all born in Nova Scotia (Census of Nova Scotia, Inverness County, Young's Bridge section).

39 From a telephone conversation, 26 November 1976, between Greg Smith, Port Hawkesbury, and Gerry MacFarlane (now of Troy, Inverness County).

40 John Neillie MacLellan, telephone interview, 8 June 1998, and personal interview, 17 June 1998. J.L. MacDougall says that sixteen heads of MacLellan families settled in "South West of Margaree," several of whom were interrelated. Only Rory MacLellan was not from Morar, he being from the Clanranald island of Eigg (MacDougall, *History of Inverness County,* 389–94). The derivation given by Calder of mac 'ill' fhaolain (son of the little wolf) suggests some antiquity for the name but not enough to suggest it predates Clanranald MacDonalds in South Morar or other MacDonalds in North Morar.

41 John Neillie MacLellan, telephone interview, 8 June 1998. John Neillie also told me that Ruairidh had a brother Iain MacLellan who took up land on River

Denys Mountain and some of whose descendants are to be found in Inverness County yet.

42 John Neillie MacLellan, telephone interview, 8 June 1998. I am grateful also to John Archie and John James MacKenzie for earlier giving me Angus's mother's name, Margaret Stewart (John Archie MacKenzie, Belle Côte, telephone interview, 4 June 1998). This allowed me to identify Angus MacLellan the piper in MacDougall, *History of Inverness County* (391–2). The MacKenzies were originally from Piper's Glen, and although John Archie (64) told me that he was probably taught by Angus MacLellan at the Egypt school, it was his older brother John James, in his eighties, who retained clear memories.

43 John Neillie MacLellan, personal interview at Kempt Road, 17 June 1998.

44 These chanters were to my knowledge composed of one piece, with the reed being blown inside the mouth.

45 Angus MacLellan walked over the mountain to get some formal education from a Dr MacMillan at Twin Rock Valley (John Neillie MacLellan, 17 June 1998).

46 Angus MacLellan married and had a son, Jim A. MacLellan (now deceased), who lived in Brockton, Massachusetts, but he is not the same Jimmie MacLellan who had Allan MacFarlane's old bagpipes.

47 John Neillie MacLellan, 17 June 1998.

48 Ibid.

49 John Archie MacKenzie, Belle Côte, Inverness County, telephone conversation, 4 June 1998; and John James MacKenzie, South West Margaree, telephone interview, 15 June 1998. John James told the author that he thought that Angus MacLellan had played in a pipe band at some time (15 June 1998). In neither conversation did either man mention the piper Sandy MacDonell, although they were related to him through their mother.

50 Lauchie Dan N. MacLellan, interview at Dunvegan, 7 January 1980.

51 MacDougall, *History of Inverness County*, 391.

52 Greg Smith, Port Hawkesbury, Cape Breton, telephone interview, 8 June 1998.

53 Isabel (Cameron) MacMillan, personal interview at Twin Rock Valley (east side of Lake Ainslie), 29 October 1994. Mrs MacMillan (1903–98) specified two Presbyterian families among the seven (five Catholic) she talked about, her own Cameron family and John Lauchie MacKay's. She told me that a Catholic MacDonald family from Upper Margaree sent their children to school in Kiltarlity and that the first teacher was a Coady girl who boarded at the Cameron home. Later on a minister and then Malcolm H. Gillis, the bard (Calum Eoghainn), took the position. Gillis taught in English, instructing pupils who had no knowledge of the language (ibid).

54 MacDougall, *History of Inverness County,* 394–6.

55 Ibid., 394; and D.D. MacFarlane (?), "The Parish," 3.

56 Interview at the home of Jessie Alex Beag MacDonald, Duncan's sister, in "the glen," Kiltarlity, 1 September 1980. Duncan was home on vacation from St

John's, Newfoundland. Apart from the clan area of Keppoch in Lochaber, there is a Keppoch near Piper's Glen and one in Arisaig, Scotland, just south of South Morar.

57 That Jim (Seumas) and Sandy (Alasdair Mór) were brothers was confirmed by Jim's son Archie MacDonell, Broad Cove (interview, 17 August 1980).

58 Hughie Dan MacDonell told John Shaw that his MacDonells were from Keppoch (interview with John Shaw, Broad Cove, 27 July 1980). Shaw's description of Hughie Dan's storytelling technique is found in MacNeil, *Tales until Dawn*, xxxiii.

59 Jack Collins, interview at Scotsville, 17 August 1980.

60 Grantie MacDougall gave his sloinneadh as "Grannd mac Eoghainn, 'ic Mhurchaidh, 'ic Eachuinn, 'ic Dhùghail." The immigrant, whichever one he was, came from Haun in Mull.

61 Grantie MacDougall, personal interview, Scotsville, 3 November 1994.

62 Gibson, *Traditional Gaelic Bagpiping,* 218.

63 Interview with John Angie MacDonell, 307 MacKenzie Ave., Inverness, 5 July 1980. Another opinion of Sandy Russell's piping, long in retrospect, was given me by Donald Hugh MacDougall, Inverness, who included Russell in a short list of pipers who piped for step-dancing (others included the MacDonells, a MacLean, and Alex Dan MacKinnon). MacDougall also told me that he had "a vivid memory of piping [generally] for step-dancing" and that step-dance piping was strongly associated with the old Inverness picnics arranged by the Catholic parish priest as money-raisers (Donald Hugh MacDougall, Inverness, personal interview given on a car journey between Port Hastings and Antigonish [my car], 15 May 1978).

64 Sandy "Fly" MacNeil (b. 1905), a Square Set caller from Inverness, talked of five halls in Inverness in 1921: the Orange Hall, the Catholic Mutual Benefit Association Hall, the Provincial Workman's Association Hall (also known as "The Miners' Hall" and "The Labour Temple"), the Belgium Hall, and the Corner Hall.

65 Few Square Sets are called nowadays, and in the times that they were, every caller I learned about called in English.

66 Malcolm J. MacNeil (d. 1981 aged 72), a man who piped for Square Sets on the Benacadie Bridge in the 1930s, told me that he was aware of the "Single Four" or the Foursome Reel, which was popular before the Square Sets became the fashion. He was too young to remember a time before Square Sets (Malcolm J. MacNeil, Piper's Cove, personal interview, 13 July 1980).

67 Before Isabel MacMillan's time, which began c. 1907, it is conceivable that Calum Eoghainn (Malcolm H. Gillis) and his supplier D.D. MacFarlane taught in Gaelic at Kiltarlity. Jimmie Dubh Gillis, a piper, taught there in 1898 (Deacon, *Four Jameses,* 96).

68 John Angie MacDonell said that he met this Sandy MacDonell and that he died in the 1930s. No exact family relationship was established, but one was sup-

posed. Lauchie Dan N. MacLellan the storyteller told me in an interview at his home in Dunvegan, 7 January 1980, that Sandy MacDonell, Egypt, played step-dance music on the bagpipes.

69 Many unilingual English speakers in rural Inverness County in 1998 were capable of giving very much more detailed descriptions of their, and others', ancestors, often back to the immigrants.

70 John Angie MacDonell, personal interview at Inverness, 5 July 1980.

71 Gibson, "Pipers' styles in contrast at Broad Cove Concert."

72 Archie MacPhail, Scotsville, personal interview, 7 June 1979.

73 Antigonish *Casket* 53, no. 8 (23 February 1905): 5.

74 MacFarlane, diary entry of 25 January 1905. Hugh Piper's father was Donald (Irish) Gillis, who came to Scotsville c. 1830, from Antigonish, eight years after the MacFarlanes. Donald's MacGillivray wife is mentioned in MacDougall, *History of Inverness County,* 398; and MacFarlane, "The Parish," 3. In the Young's Bridge section of the 1891 census, Donald Gillis's age was 81 and his place of birth Ireland (Census of Nova Scotia, Inverness County, Young's Bridge).

75 Christie (Cameron) Gillis, Scotsville, telephone interview, 16 June 1998.

76 Archie MacPhail, Scotsville, personal interview, 6 June 1979. MacPhail spent about fifty years of his adult life in Boston but still speaks English with a Gaelic accent. He only began to learn English at school under the tutelage of Calum Eoghain (Malcolm Gillis), South West Margaree, and Archie Chisholm, father of Angus the fiddler and John Willie, Margaree Forks. He is a lover of piping.

77 Barry Fraser, personal interview, Kirkwood (East Lake Ainslie), 30 November 1994.

78 Information from Rev. A.D. MacKinnon's second wife, date and place misplaced or unrecorded.

79 Neil Allan MacLean, Scotsville, personal interview, 7 June 1979.

80 Ibid.

81 Hugh Don MacLean, Scotsville, personal interview, 7 June 1979.

CHAPTER ELEVEN

1 In the summer of 2001 Angus MacKenzie from Mabou taught "Traditional Piping" at Sabhal Mòr Ostaig in Skye. The subject is one of long standing in South Uist, where Hamish Moore introduced Cape Breton step-dance piping several years ago. (Sabhal Mòr Ostaig also offered a course in modern Scottish piping in summer 2001, under instructors pipe major Norman Gillies and pipe major John Burgess.)

2 The nub of the MacKay work was the assessment of two unpublished documents I found in Canada. Some of my findings were published in the *Nova Scotia Historical Review* (vol. 2, no. 2, December 1982) and the *Scottish Genealogist* (vol. 30, no. 3, September 1983). The more controversial work,

which entailed examining the unpublished Canadian MacKay family claim (made by Annie MacKay) that the Blind Piper was a grandson of "Lord Reay," has recently been published (see Gibson, "The Pedigree of the Blind Piper of Gairloch," *Royal Nova Scotia Historical Society Journal* 3 [2000]). This material in unpublished form was given to Bridget MacKenzie, who used it in her *Piping Traditions of the North of Scotland,* 148, 153.

3 My references to Lt Donald MacCrimmon's service in the British Legion and to his stay in Port Roseway/Shelburne, Nova Scotia, have been published (*Traditional Gaelic Bagpiping, 1745–1945*: *Nova Scotia Historical Review* 2, no. 2; and elsewhere), but unanswered questions, historical and genealogical, have halted my inquiry *pro tempore.*

4 Gibson, *Traditional Gaelic Bagpiping,* 219, 248, 254.

5 Many of Johnnie Williams's songs were recorded by Dr John Shaw for the archives of the Celtic Department at St Francis Xavier University in Antigonish. Johnnie told me on 21 May 1998 that a few days earlier he had made a tape of certain songs for Maxi MacNeil, Iona, who only had incomplete versions. He told me also that Angus, his father, had had a lot more songs than he himself had. Johnnie always felt a nostalgic closeness to Scotland from stories he heard from his MacLellan mother, who used to repeat stories of the homeland she had heard from one of her husband's maternal aunts, a Henderson. He said that the slightest improvement made to a property drove up the rent (telephone interview, 22 May 1998).

6 Neil Williams told me that in older days a *claigeann eich* (horse's skull) placed in the rafters of a home was propitious. He was not atypical in feeling the need to keep a horse, for whatever purpose.

7 Albert "Bornish" MacDonald is a grand-nephew of Bodach Bhornais, who settled in 1833 at Bornish on River Denys Mountain (telephone interview, 26 May 1998). For information about a small number of the Mountain families, see Read and Gillis, "Origins."

8 Albert MacDonald's set of bagpipes was one of a small number made by a man in Hillsdale in the parish of Judique, Inverness County.

9 Allan Dan MacInnis's sister Péigi Ruadh (Red Peggy) had married Angus Fortune c. 1895; Angus was of Irish extraction and lived at River Denys Mountain.

10 Nearly twenty years later, in 1998, Dan Fortune told me that after I'd left, Allan Dan had said in disgust that I knew nothing of Mùideart, which in his imaginings was rich and fertile farmland. The impressions that I gave him of Glenfinnan, Sheil Bridge, Kinlochmoideart, Glenuig, and then up through Alisary to Inverailort were not of sweeping meadows but of a rugged rocky beauty, of a wilder grandeur, with here and there good soils in valley bottoms (interview in Glendale, March/April 1998).

11 MacInnis, interview at Glendale, 2 May 1978. For a more thorough genealogy, see "MacInnis–MacInnis Road," in MacKay, *Genealogical History*. These MacInnises are known as "the Hennies," named for Henrietta MacLachlan,

immigrant wife of John MacInnis. The early West Bay Road Catholic church records are no longer extant.

12 MacKay's *Genealogical History* describes Donald, son of John MacInnis, as a maker of many songs long forgotten in 1975 (MacKay, *Genealogical History,* 57). The talent came down to his son Allan Dan, who made a vituperative song to commemorate his not having been invited to a party at Malcolm Sandy Mac-Donald's (John D. MacLeod, personal interview, Glendale, 17 April 1977).

13 The typed version of my notes of the interview give Domhnul Dubh Mac-Dhomhnuill (the manual typewriter had no grave accent), which I have given as Black Donald MacDonald. It is not impossible that this is an unjustified assumption and that the name should have been the sloinneadh, Dòmhnul Dubh Mac Dhòmhnuill (Black Donald, son of Donald), surname unknown. The problem of identifying the members of the family mentioned remains nonetheless.

14 Allan Dan MacInnis, interview, Glendale, 2 May 1978.

15 Neville T. McKay's "A History of the Office of Piper to the Sovereign" shows no Donald MacDonald holding any piping office in HRH Queen Victoria's household. He may have acted as piper to either George IV or William IV.

16 Allan Dan MacInnis, interview, Glendale, 5 May 1978. Albert "Bornish" Mac-Donald added that Lame Angus married Katie MacKay from Bornish, a neice of Bodach Bhornais and first cousin to Albert's mother, Sarah Catherine Mac-Donald. Lame Angus's old home was where Neil C. Gillis's was, and Albert had visited it as a boy. Where local mail driving was concerned, Albert MacDonald only remembered a man called Mullins driving the mail by horse and buggy to Victoria Line (Albert MacDonald, telephone interview, 26 May 1998).

17 The Boyds settled in what is now Glendale from South Uist. There is still a prominent Boyd family living in the community.

18 Patrick MacEachern, Glendale, telephone interview, 27 May 1998.

19 Dan Fortune (d. 2001) was one of the last people who remembered Marble Mountain when it was a going concern, before the Great War. Dan remembered a Campbell piper from Red Island who worked at the quarry and used to go out on a boat on the Bras d'Or to play. Dan said that he never heard him pipe for the weekly dances held at the Oddfellows' Hall in Marble Mountain (Dan Fortune, personal interview, Glendale, 2 August 1994).

20 A home-made chanter was owned by James MacKay, Kingsville. When a modern plastic chanter reed was put in it, no sound could be produced.

21 Joe Neil MacNeil told me that Steve Cameron, St Peter's, Richmond County, could describe pipe chanter making. Cameron had told Joe Neil that a small preliminary hole was drilled in a seasoned piece of wood and left for about two years. If this hole remained true after this time, the chanter was turned (Joe Neil MacNeil, interview, place unrecorded, 30 May 1982).

22 Albert MacDonald, telephone interview, 26 May 1998.

23 Big Jim's mother was a MacEachern, and Big Jim was a nephew of Angus and Sarah (Patrick MacEachern, personal interview conducted at Glendale, 2 July 1980).

24 MacKay, *Genealogical History*, 50, 51.

25 Sarah and Angus shared the old MacEachern Road home, she living into the 1940s (James MacKay, interview, Kingsville, 1 July 1980). According to D.R. MacEachern and Patrick MacEachern, Glendale, Sarah and Angus were aunt and uncle of Big Jim (interview, Glendale, 2 July 1980).

26 Patrick MacEachern, telephone interview, Glendale, 27 May 1998.

27 James MacKay, interview, Kingsville, 1 July 1980.

28 MacEachern's Collection, vols. 1 (1975) and 2 (1993). I am indebted to Margie Dunn, Lower South River, for her father's (John Willie MacEachern) and his brothers' dates. She mentioned that John Willie's paternal uncle Dan had three sons (John R., John Angus, and Dan Hughie) and two daughters (Ceitag Bhàn and Kate Jess) who were fiddlers, and this is only to touch upon the subject of fiddling in the wider MacEachern family.

29 MacDonell and Shaw, *Luirgean Eachainn Nìll*, xi.

30 The story went that a would-be married man was unfortunate enough to be a hopelessly poor dancer. For long he had put off the consummation of his passion because of his abiding fear of having to dance before the assembly the inevitable Scotch Four that every groom had to dance with his lovely new bride and the best man and lady. But after much encouragment he finally screwed his courage to the sticking place. Jimmie MacKay, who was there, said that throughout the Scotch Four ordeal the suffering groom had his eye immutably fixed on a knot-hole in the ceiling.

31 If the photograph of three pipers reproduced in *Traditional Gaelic Bagpiping* was taken at this picnic, then the Beaton was Angus Campbell Beaton (Angus Johnnie Ranald, Mabou); however, neither the Williamses nor Albert MacDonald mentioned that Black Angus MacDonald of Melrose Hill was there. (The photograph shows Black Angus MacDonald, Allan MacFarlane, and Angus Beaton.)

32 South West Margaree, while a mission, is one of the last communities I know of to have had a dancing master make an annual teaching visit. The building used was at the end of MacBain Road (Donald A. MacLellan, personal interview, 29 May 1979). Donald A.'s grand-uncle Big John MacLellan learned dancing there in the mid-nineteenth century. I asked Archie Dan MacLellan on 7 January 1980 if he knew the names of any of the dancing masters but he didn't.

33 The Antigonish *Casket* of the early years of the twentieth century and R.A. MacLean's *Bishop John Cameron,* 128, contain references to "round dancing." Question: Was prolonged body contact a spur to concupiscence? At least one *Casket* letter sang the praises of the old Scotch Four-Hand Reel; this dance did not include close body contact, but it suffered decline notwithstanding. The

temperance movement in northeastern Nova Scotia had of course much deeper roots in the nineteenth century.

34 My informant in early 1998 was Alex Hughie MacInnis, Kingsville, who has a copy of the newspaper in question and is a keen family historian.

35 I believe that Simon P. Gillis was a descendant of Alexander Gillis (Alasdair mac Iain 'ic Alasdair), who came to Inverness County in 1826 from Ardnamurach, North Morar, with his wife, Ann, the daughter of Capt. Donald Gillis, Stole, North Morar (MacDougall, *History of Inverness County*, 401). The name Simon suggests a Fraser connection, and indeed North Morar is still known as Mòrar MhicShimidh (Lovat's Morar). Simon P. Gillis's athletic achievements overseas were occasionally reported in the *Sydney Record*. The first such report appears in vol. 10, no. 60 (12 March 1907) when notice was given of his pending visit to Brazil to work as a carpenter on a dam at Rio de Janeiro. At the time he was "wearing the colors of the New York A.C." and was the junior hammer champion. In vol. 11, no. 163 (13 July 1908), "Simon P. Gillis, the great weight thrower, formerly of Margaree, C.B., and now representing the New York Athletic Club" was "Expected to Win Honors at London Olympic Games." J.L. MacDougall wrote that Simon Gillis had gone to the United States but nothing more than that (*History of Inverness County*, 401).

36 Alex MacEachern had moved to Marble Mountain to work, and the other local MacEachern relatives went to Montana, presumably in the late nineteenth century (Patrick MacEachern, Glendale, telephone interview, 24 June 1998).

37 Patrick MacEachern, Glendale, telephone interview, 24 June 1998.

38 MacDougall, *History of Inverness County*, 507.

39 "John MacDonald Esq" (Bodach Bhornais) died 14 June 1913 of "cancer in ear" (Glendale church death records, number 162). He is given in the 1861 census as head of a family that consisted in total of three males and five females. The 1871 census lists John (48) and his wife Sarah (46), both born in Scotland and Catholic, and seven daughters and three sons, all born between 1849 and 1869 (Sarah, Mary, Margaret, and John were born in 1861, '65, '67, and '69 respectively and do not figure in the 1861 census). (*Census of Nova Scotia, 1860–61*, Inverness Polling District 14, abstract 1; Census of 1871, District No. 203, Subdistrict "River Dennis" Division no. 1.)

40 Neil McNeill's "Census of the Small Isles" was made between November 1764 and March 1765. MacNeill was a Presbyterian catechist.

41 Johnnie Joe MacDonald, River Denys, personal interview, March 1982 (date misplaced).

42 MacDougall, *History of Inverness County*, 507.

43 MacKay, *Genealogical History*.

44 Carmeline's house stands where the River Denys Mountain road crosses the Trans-Canada Highway. Neil Williams said that once upon a time it was a place you could get rum and among the customers was a defrocked local Highland Catholic priest. On one occasion when the priest was gently chided over

his weakness, an argument developed over his powers; to put the fear into the less than faithful, he plunged two lighted candles into a bucket of water and drew them out still lit.

45· The 1861 census shows a Kenneth MacAskill among thirty-nine heads of families (his family consisted of three males and one female). The 1871 census lists Kenneth (75), his wife Isabella (70), both Catholics born in Scotland, and [their son?] "Rodric" (26) and daughter [-in-law?] Mary (26), both born in Nova Scotia. The 1871 census includes as its sixth family Malcolm MacAskill (28), his wife Flora (29), and their three children, all Catholics (*Census of Nova Scotia, 1860–61*, Inverness Polling District 14, abstract 1, no. 10; Census of 1871, District No. 203, Subdistrict "River Dennis" Division no 1, the fifth and sixth families). The MacAskills moved to Havre Boucher in Antigonish County (Albert MacDonald, telephone interview, 10 June 1998) and also to Auld's Cove (Patrick MacEachern to Alex Hughie MacInnis, telephone interview, 18 June 1998).

46 MacDougall, *History of Inverness County*, 507. This MacLeod family is distinct from the MacLeod family described by James MacKay in *Genealogical History,* 79, 80.

47 McNeill's census shows that there were Catholic MacLeods in Eigg in 1764–65 (McNeill, "Census of the Small Isles.")

48 Neil Williams, interview, Melford, 28 March 1977. John MacQuarrie's son Dan, a piper, was a member of a pipe and drum band in Boston. Margaret Sandy Malcolm MacDonald (1897–1966) also lived in Massachusetts at Chestnut Hill (Read and Gillis, 13).

49 Albert MacDonald, personal interviews 25 March 1977 and 6 August 1980. Hugh MacKinnon (1894-1972) included important notes on the last MacQuarries in Eigg in data given to Fr Anthony Ross O.P. in the summer of 1972. MacKinnon's material is in *Tocher* 10.

50 A large number of Protestant MacQuarries, many from Rhum, settled in the Port Hastings area and as far towards the north as Rhodena, in Inverness County. The census records do not substantiate the claim that there was at least one Catholic family living on River Denys Mountain. However, if they arrived after 1853 and were gone from the Mountain by 1861 and no land was granted to them there, there would be no record. Further, land grants often followed occupation by many years.

51 The 1861 census of Nova Scotia lists "Malcholm McDonald" as head of a family of four males and five females (Polling District 14, abstract no. 1).

52 Albert MacDonald, personal interview, Melford, 25 March 1977. Fr Duncan MacDonald and his brother Sandy Malcolm had a nephew, Little Malcolm MacDonald, who was born and raised on a property adjoining Malcolm Sandy Malcolm's on River Denys Mountain. Little Malcolm was a very good fiddler who played by ear. Dan Hughie MacEachern told me that "he was an ear player and he was good too. He had the style and the old tunes. He used to play for

dances around and if anyone tried to play with him he'd tune his fiddle up so that you couldn't play along with him. He did that to me once when I tried to play along with him" (Dan Hughie MacEachern, personal interview, 11 April 1977, place unknown, probably Kingsville or Melford). Little Malcolm died in the spring of 1967 in Sydney.

53 Catherine Effie (MacMillan) White, personal interview, Whiteside, Richmond County, Cape Breton, 8 August 1980. Catherine Effie (Mrs Malcolm White) told me that J.L. MacDougall was wrong in writing that all of immigrant Peter MacMillan's sons died unmarried (MacDougall, *History of Inverness County*, 479). She said that a son Joe Peter lived, married, and had two daughters, Julia and Minnie MacMillan. Catherine Effie, like her siblings, was a Gaelic speaker raised and schooled in Melford. She agreed with J.L. MacDougall that Peter MacMillan had left two spinster daughters and she added names and dates, describing Mary (d. 1947 aged 93) as "Màiri Pheadair" and her sister Peggy as "Peigi Pheadair" (d. 1926 aged 87) (ibid., 479).

54 Neil Williams, personal interview, Melford, 15 December 1976.

55 Mary (MacPherson) Matheson, wife of Billy Matheson the fiddler, told me that Dougal emigrated with his mother and siblings (Duncan, Donald and Catherine [twins], and Alex) and that they were preceded by their half-brothers, the children of their common father, Murdoch, from Scalpa (John Bàn, Roderick, and Kenneth) (personal interview, 2 July 1998).

56 Alex Matheson, Big Marsh, Inverness County, personal interview, 2 July 1998. It seems unlikely that Dougal Matheson was directly influenced in his piping by Col Sir John MacRa, KCH (1786–1847) of Ardintoul, patron to Archibald Munro, also a maker of bagpipes, because the colonel didn't retire to Kintail until 1826. However, there was a lively piping scene in nearby Glenelg where Donald MacCrumen was teaching one of the Bruces c. 1814.

57 See Gibson, "The two-drone bagpipe," a letter in *Am Bràighe*, winter 1998/99, 4, 6.

58 A right-shoulder, right-hand-upper piper played for the Pipes and Drums of the Scots Guards c. 1954 (see the frontispiece in *Scots Guards: Standard Settings of Pipe Music* [1954]. The photograph was reproduced from the magazine *The Field*).

59 This observation serves only to explain a little more fully the remarks made by Joseph MacDonald, c. 1760, that Highlanders indeed had a two-drone bagpipe, and by Dr Duncan A. Fraser (*Some Reminiscences and the Bagpipe*), c. 1890, that a two-drone bagpipe was used all over the West Highlands, from Assynt, to Skye, to Argyllshire, for dance-music piping. Any suggestion in the piping literature that the West Highlands preferred a two-drone bagpipe is a measure, in my opinion, of the strength of the céilidh in those parts of the Gàidhealtachd.

60 Alex Matheson, 2 July 1998. A few pieces of tartan, of unrecognized "sets," have turned up in Cape Breton, mainland Nova Scotia, and Prince Edward Island, but travellers' accounts of early Gaelic Nova Scotia have never recorded

the wearing of tartan. Immigration and hodden grey or its equivalent go together.

61 Alex Matheson, 2 July 1998.

62 Ibid. I must re-emphasize that I brought the subject up and led the conversation, and until I learn more of what Alex knows, I am unsure whether we were talking about "ceòl mór" or about slow airs.

63 Alex Matheson (2 July 1998) believed that Sandy Malcolm MacDonald's set of bagpipes was bought for him by a daughter in either Boston or Detroit.

64 Margaret A. (Blue) MacLean, Melford, personal interview, 16 March 1977.

65 MacLean, *God and the Devil at Seal Cove,* 108.

66 Ibid.

67 Bolliken could have belonged to the Catholic MacQuarrie family who for a few years settled on River Denys Mountain. The MacQuarrie family in Arasaig have never admitted relationship to this Kenneth. Otherwise, several immigrant MacQuarries settled in the Port Hastings–Queensville area (see MacDougall, *History of Inverness County,* 160–5 *inter alia).*

68 *Daily Record* 5, no. 195 (18 August 1902): 5.

CHAPTER TWELVE

1 There were probably no unilingual English speakers at all at West Lake Ainslie. Neither J.L. MacDougall (*History of Inverness County*) nor Fr Alexander D. MacDonald (*Mabou Pioneers*) mentions any English-speaking settlers over and above a number of Gaels who had been bilingual at the time they emigrated, like Capt. Angus "Tulloch" MacDonald and Capt. Angus MacLellan and his family. Peter MacMillan (1926–2001), East Lake Ainslie, told me unprompted that there were quite a few well-to-do settlers at West Lake Ainslie (personal interview at Eastern Counties Regional Libraries headquarters, Mulgrave, Nova Scotia, 22 November 1999).

2 Gibson, *History of Gaelic Bagpiping,* 240; and MacCormack, *Highland Heritage & Freedom's Quest.*

3 The South West Margaree church enjoyed the ministrations of a resident priest, Fr Aeneas MacIntyre, DD, for a few months in 1850 (Johnston, *History of the Catholic Church* 2:246).

4 Francis Dixie Walker, Captain's River, south of Harbourview, Inverness County, told me that his (late) father (b. 1901) remembered a visiting priest from Broad Cove crossing Lake Ainslie ice on horseback to say mass at the West Lake church (personal interview, 24 November 1999).

5 Lands and Forests land-grant folio 115, held by Eastern Counties Regional Library, Mulgrave, Nova Scotia.

6 Anon., "Immaculate Conception Church West Lake Ainslie – 125 Years 1871–1996," booklet (author credit given to Josephine Beaton, Brook Village, by Fr Bernard MacDonald, PP at Brook Village, 27 November 1999).

7 MacDonald's "Manuscript-book" lacks several pages; some probably contained rough drafts of personal letters.

8 Ibid., 71. The Nova Scotia Highland Brigade in the Great War was made up of the 85th, the 185th, the 193rd, and the 219th regiments.

9 MacDougall, *History of Inverness County*, 521.

10 MacDonald, "Manuscript-book," 48.

11 Ibid., 48. A.A. Johnston would not commit himself to a date for the building of the new (Immaculate Conception) church at West Lake Ainslie, by Fr Kenneth J. MacDonald. Johnston gave only the early 1870s (Johnston, *History of the Catholic Church*, 2:462).

12 The Brahan Seer, Coinneach Odhar/Dun Kenneth, was a famous Highland prophesier.

13 MacDonald, "Manuscript-book," 46 (MacDonald's translation included).

14 This citation occurs on the lower half of a detached page and appears to be in a different hand. Mac 'ic Ailein (son of the son of Allan) is the patronymic of MacDonald of Clanranald.

15 MacDonald, "Manuscript-book," 106. MacDonald takes his paternal line back to before the immigrant to Nova Scotia, which is much more helpful regarding the immigrant and earlier generations.

16 Land problems at West Lake Ainslie are dealt with by John R. MacCormack, *Highland Heritage & Freedom's Quest*, 69–89. Veterans of British military service appear uniformly to have had little difficulty in obtaining clear title.

17 Angus Tulloch MacDonald Sr (b. 1759), who is believed to have served in the 84th Royal Highland Emigrants Regiment, if commissioned, was either ensign or quarter-master (Murray Logan, *Scottish Highlanders*, 124, 126). He may have attained captaincy in the War of 1812; there is a claim that he had been granted two thousand acres in Nova Scotia (MacDonald, *Mabou Pioneers*, 588, citing PANS).

18 Capt. Angus MacDonald's older brother Ranald petitioned governor Ainslie for five hundred acres at Lake Ainslie, to be called "Tulloch." Under the heading "1819" he described himself as recently arrived from Scotland, aged 30, married with three children. He had served fourteen years in the 72nd Regiment (the 78th Seaforth Highlanders were renumbered the 72nd in 1786; they ceased to be kilted and to bear the title "Highland" in 1809) and the 7th Veterans and was a lieutenant on the retired list. At the end of the abstract is this note: "Note: Recommended. Name, 'Tulloch'" (Calendar of Cape Breton land papers 1787–1843, no. 2191; ECRL microfilm, 929.37169 Cal M-20; original documents held by Beaton Institute, UCCB, Sydney, Cape Breton).

19 It is probable that John Beaton was born at Achluachrach but nowhere is that written. However, the place-name Auch Lochart was applied in 1819 to a 250-acre lot (no. 3) situated between Cape Mabou and the river that had been occupied for the past eight years by an Alexander Beaton. Beaton was married with five children at the time (Calendar of Cape Breton land papers 1787–1843,

petition no. 2070). (MacDonald's *Mabou Pioneers* gives Alexander Beaton's date of arrival in Cape Breton as 1809.) He was probably Alasdair an Tàillear (Alexander the Tailor), brother of Finlay Beaton from Achluachrach in 1766 and paternal uncle of John Beaton.

20 Several Beatons, including Big Finlay and his brother Alexander and most of their children, like several other West Lake Ainslie pioneers, came to Cape Breton from Prince Edward Island, where getting clear title to land was exacerbated by a nastier brand of European landlordism.

21 Màiri nighean Alasdair 'ic Raonuil 'ic Alasdair Bhàin 'ic Alasdair an Tàillear (Peutanach): Mary, daughter of Alexander, son of Ranald, son of fair-haired Alexander, son of Alexander the Tailor (Beaton).

22 Gibson, "Mary MacDonald," 7, 8. The same data is found in a later source, MacGillivray, *Cape Breton Ceilidh*, 24.

23 A marriage by a Tulloch woman to a local Beaton has never been considered morganatic in the Mabou area, so presumably the Beatons may be considered as belonging to the same social level as the Tulloch MacDonalds.

24 MacDougall, *History of Inverness County,* 526.

25 Ibid., 527.

26 Ibid., 521, 522.

27 I am very grateful to Tearlach MacFarlane, Glenfinnan, for giving me information on the MacDougalls in Clanranald country and for exposing some current genealogical queries about them. He noted that the South Morar (Morar 'ic Dhùghail) tacksmen, although styled "MacDhùghail" (son of Dougal), never used the last name MacDougal and always went by MacDonald. This persists in the family in Low Point, Inverness County (personal correspondence from Tearlach MacFarlane, 18 December 2000).

28 MacFarlane correspondence, 18 December 2000.

29 The 1841 census shows that male MacDougall heads of families (14) and their respective families together total 83. They were all related if, as is believed (by local historian Josephine Beaton), there was only one immigrant MacDougall in West Lake Ainslie, namely Angus Bàn. All married women are hidden simply as numbers in the girls-over-14 list, and are unnamed in other families. Principally, because of the age distributions of Angus Bàn MacDougall's many grandchildren by his sons (20 [10/10] are given as over 14 in the 1841 census), Angus Bàn's year of birth is much more probably 1772 than 1778.

30 MacDonald, *History of Inverness County*, 522.

31 Ibid., 521.

32 A record of deaths in Nova Scotia for 1864–76 includes a Scots-born John MacDonald, a married man and son of Alexander (Alasdair) and Mary. John died 20 November 1873 at West Lake Ainslie aged 96 (i.e., John was born c. 1777 and was about 37 coming to Cape Breton).

33 MacDonald, *Mabou Pioneers*, 855. MacDougall (*History of Inverness County,*

528) said nothing about Walker being a bailiff and gave John Walker's wife as Catherine MacDougall from Mull.

34 Nova Scotia deaths 1864–76, O-Z, microfilm 929.3716, and microfilm 929.371691, Inv. M-36. The 1841 census for the western half of the Township of Ainslie gives a John Walker and family, total of eight people, including one male under 14, two males over 14, and four females over 14 (microfilm of 1838 census, RG1, vol. 449, no. 132). If the youngest son was 13 in 1841 then this John Walker fathered a son c. 1827.

35 Effie (d/o Angus Walker), born in Scotland, died a widow on 27 May 1927 aged 98 (Brook Village death records, no. 47). Frederick MacDonald's "Manuscript-book," confirming J.L. MacDougall's brief description of her (p. 528), gives her Gaelic styling: widow of "Domhul mac Ian mhor" (Donald, son of Big John).

36 MacDonald, *Mabou Pioneers*, 865. J.L. MacDougall wrote in 1922 that Angus Walker paid $80 for the MacEachen property "ninety years ago," presumably in 1832 (*History of Inverness County*, 528).

37 Deaths, microfilm 929.371691, p. 78.

38 A local genealogy ("Genealogy of John, Michael and Angus Walker"), which admits primary reliance on the other two, claims rightly that there were three Walker brothers involved one way or the other in the emigrations to Nova Scotia, John, Angus, and Michael. John and Angus emigrated; Michael stayed in Scotland, but three of his children, Angus, Malcolm, and Katie, emigrated to Rear West Lake Ainslie in 1842 ("Genealogy," 49). Frederick MacDonald's "Manuscript-book" mentions that a Catherine Walker (Michael's daughter) died in Cobalt, Ontario, on 26 March 1915 aged c. 89 (p. 29).

39 MacDonald and MacDonald, *Clan Donald*, 3:295–6. Walter Scott remarked in July 1810 that Staffa's Ulva home, his armed retainers, the entire atmosphere, smacked of "feudal splendour" (ibid., 3:295). Staffa's piper John MacArthur won third prize at the 1804 Edinburgh competition ("Account of the Competition of Pipers, in MacKay, *Collection*, 17). Staffa was every bit as much a caricature of the neo-chieftain as his contemporary Alasdair Ranaldson of Glengarry, another friend of Walter Scott.

40 MacDonald and MacDonald, *Clan Donald*, 3:295.

41 John Walker (Iain mac Alasdair 'ic Iain) of Hay's River, died 14 April 1925 aged 91 (MacDonald, "Manuscript-book," 39). If one consults all of the Walker family history sources, J.L. MacDougall, A.D. MacDonald, and Agnes Walker ("Genealogy of John, Michael and Angus Walker"), the only Alasdair, or Alexander, Walker who fits is a son of the immigrant John Walker, bailiff to Staffa.

42 The dispositions of the island of Staffa during the eighteenth century and later may be found in MacCulloch, *Islands – Staffa*, 30–6. A Donald MacCormick from Milton, South Uist, who emigrated to Leitches Creek, Cape Breton, in 1827 was married to an Isabella MacDonald, granddaughter of Colin of

Boisdale through a daughter (MacCormack, *Highland Heritage & Freedom's Quest*, 42), adding some plausibility to the Walker claim.

43 MacCormack, *Highland Heritage & Freedom's Quest*, 62, citing "Manuscript history of St. George's Parish preserved in the Catholic Rectory in St. Georges, P.E.I." (ibid., 159). This Angus Walker stayed in Prince Edward Island.

44 MacCormack, *Highland Heritage & Freedom's Quest*, 63.

45 Ibid., 159 n 167; for the date of emigration, ibid., 9.

46 Ibid., 128.

47 Ibid., 69.

48 Ibid., 9.

49 Deliberate economic abasement led to the emigrations from South Uist that John R. MacCormack enlarges on so well. In a listing of the tenants of the Clanranald estate, there is a note by Roderick Chisholm, the South Uist grounds officer, saying that many of the people employed in making kelp needed to be fed "a considerable quantity of meal" (PANS MG1, vol. 559, no. 462). Their deliberate diversion by the landowner from the older path of self-sufficiency is described in MacCormack, *Highland Heritage & Freedom's Quest*.

50 MacCormack, *Highland Heritage & Freedom's Quest*, 105, 118.

51 Albert MacDonald, personal interview, 6 August 1980.

52 Ainslie MacNeil, Inverness, Cape Breton, personal telephone communication, 14 July 1998. MacNeil is a son of John Colin MacNeil of Inverside and Janet D.F. MacDonald (1900–1988), sister of Angus and Frederick.

53 Ibid. Albert MacDonald had already mentioned that D.F.'s abrasive disposition caused his sons to leave home as soon as possible (personal interview, 6 August 1980).

54 Ainslie MaNeil, personal interview, 14 July 1998. MacNeil associated the piping of the old strathspey tune *"Calum Crubach"* with high-quality piping.

55 *Whig Standard* (Kingston), 9 August 1930.

56 In light of his Tulloch connection, one wonders how self-deprecatory Frederick D.F. had been on the radio; otherwise the listener's humour seems condescending. The first letter indicates that the piper had met Hugh MacPhee earlier than the radio recording visit.

57 MacCormack, *Highland Heritage & Freedom's Quest*, 111.

58 Francis "Dixie" Walker, personal interview at Harbourview, Inverness County, 23 November 1999.

59 "Immaculate Conception Church West Lake Ainslie 125 Years 1871–1996," under title "The Beginning."

60 Antigonish *Casket* 93, no. 12 (21 September 1944). Fr Angus Bernard MacEacharn was born in Kinlochmoidart. He emigrated to Prince Edward Island with the people quitting the Clanranald estate in the summer of 1790 and became bishop of Charlottetown in 1829. The passenger lists of the *Lucy* and the *Jane*, which left Druim an darraich (Oak Ridge) on Loch nan Uamh (Loch of the Caves) in Arasaig for Prince Edward Island on 12 July 1790, and

of the *British Queen*, which left from Arasaig for the same destination on 16 August 1790, do not include the priest's name.

61 A "Mrs James MacLellan (Black Smith) Centreville Brook Village" died Friday 29 November 1912 (MacDonald, "Manuscript-book," opposite p. 69).

62 In Colin S. MacDonald, "The Clanranald MacDonalds of Moidart," PANS MG1, vol. 559/11, no. 89.

63 One of the Denoon MacDonalds became professor of mathematics at St Francis Xavier University in the 1870s. His daughter married a MacKinnon nephew of Bishop MacKinnon (Ronald MacDonald, personal interview, 3 December 1999).

64 *Lucy*'s passenger list as duplicated from the original in the Scottish Catholic Archives, Oban Papers, in J.M. Bumsted, *The People's Clearance*, 241–1.

65 It is worth noting that the *Casket* writer seems to have had access to the *Lucy*'s passenger list. And, if one includes "Samlaman" and "Glenuis" as being part of Glenuig, then twenty-nine people (one single person and five families) left Glenuig in 1790 for Prince Edward Island aboard the *Lucy* and the *Jane*.

66 "The Clanranald MacDonalds of Kinlochmoidart," 1.

67 Ibid.

68 MacDonald, "Manuscript-book," 48. McLeod had been transferred to Antigonish before 1835, at his request, exhausted. On page 49 of the "Manuscript-book" Frederick MacDonald adds "or 1836" to the year 1835.

69 Ibid.

70 The piper is given as "Alexander MacDonald (Denoon) ... from Antigonish ... settled on the land now occupied by Allan and John MacKinnon [at West Lake Ainslie]" ("Immaculate Conception Church West Lake Ainslie 125 Years 1871–1996," under "The Beginning," no page). A Hugh Denoon is alleged to have chartered and overcrowded the ships *Dove* of Aberdeen and *Sarah* of Liverpool bound from Fort William to Pictou, Nova Scotia, in 1801 (Bumsted, *People's Clearance*, Appendix B, Passenger Lists VIII and IX citing SRO RH 2/4/87, 73–5 and 66–71).

71 Josephine Beaton, Brook Village, personal interview, November 1999.

72 These are particularly exemplified in the immigrant Beaton families in the Mabou area.

73 The author almost certainly was D.D. MacFarlane of South West Margaree (1861–1950), who wrote a series of articles on the parish history of South West Margaree in 1896 (Antigonish *Casket*, April and May 1896).

74 MacCormack, *Highland Heritage & Freedom's Quest*, 74.

75 I have been unable to find the citation in question, which appeared several years prior to the 1896 issues.

76 Stewart, *Sketches*, vol. 2, appendix, liii. J.F and T.M. Flett, in citing Stewart, expand on his mention of Rolt's work in 1753 to show that this sword-brandishing Sword Dance was done in or before 1739 (Flett and Flett, "Some Early Highland Dancing Competitions," *Aberdeen University Review* 36, no. 115 [Autumn 1956]).

77 Flett and Flett, "Some Early Highland Dancing Competitions," 354.

78 Ibid.

79 Ibid. After the 1835 piping competition an "Allan Cameron MacKay, dancer," from Strontian wrote to complain that a piper rather than an instrumental band should play the music for the "gillie Callum" (ibid.).

80 Another reference to the "Gillie Callum" appears in MacNeil, *Highland Heart of Nova Scotia* (153, 154) which is about the Gaelic community of Washabuckt settled mostly by Barra Gaels. Neil MacNeil's grandfather, Michael Eoin (b. c. 1825, in Cape Breton), apparently called for *"Callum Gille ... the tune for the Sword Dance"* when his old friend and contemporary, Black Dan the clock-maker-piper, made his annual visit. In his youth Michael Eoin had danced the Sword Dance and it seems highly improbable that the dance had reached him in any other than a Barra line. (He had also danced countless step-dance Four-Hand Reels to Black Dan's bagpipe music.) At the céilidhs at the MacNeil home Black Dan piped for the Scotch Four while the fiddler played for the "Square Dances." Black Dan used to sit to pipe; sometimes he used one foot, sometimes two, to keep time. He used to end his concert performance at the MacNeil home with "'McCrummen's Lament' its slow, sad melodies, the most woeful and weird sounds ever heard on earth" (154). Among the pioneers at Washabuck is a Donald "Piper" MacAulay (see "MacAulay-MacCormack" section in MacNeil, *All Call Iona Home*), but Black Dan remains unidentified.

81 George Ramsay, earl of Dalhousie, referred to his own Reel dancing in 1817 in what is now Antigonish County and implied that his "joyous expression of the Highland fling" was part of the Reel. Whether or not the Gaelic-speaking musicians involved called anything he danced the Highland Fling is unknown (*Traditional Gaelic Bagpiping*, 276, citing Whitelaw, *Dalhousie Journals*, 57).

CHAPTER THIRTEEN

1 *Guth na Bliadhna*, book 5, no. 2 (Spring 1908), and book 5, no. 3 (Summer 1908).

2 In fairness, Fr Campbell may have thought poorly of the elements of culture that he saw, or considered them inferior to Scottish forms, and simply was delicate and chose not to go into the subject in any detail; there is no hint of this, however.

3 The present priest, author Fr Allan MacMillan, is unusual inasmuch as he is a Gaelic speaker and singer of Gaelic songs. He replaced an older man who did not speak the language.

4 "Tha Ghàidhlig bheannaichte cho smiorail agus cho blasda 'sa tha i anns a'Ghàidhealtachd fhein, gu sonruichte ann an Ceap-Breatunn," in Campbell, "Dùthaich na Saorsa," 99. Campbell also wrote that there was no danger of Gaelic's dying out soon (ibid., 99).

5 Campbell, "Dùthaich na Saorsa," 98. The great-grandfather and his brother are unnamed. Later on Campbell found out that Rev. Donald, his brother Rev. Alexander, and the priest the Rev. Ronald at Saint Peter's, Cape Breton, were similarly related to him ("Tìr an Aigh," 205).

6 MacKenzie, "The Editor in Canada," *Celtic Magazine* 5, no. 49 (November 1879).

7 MacDougall, "Memorandum Page," unpublished, typed MS. I am grateful to Cyril MacDonald, Judique, who kindly gave me a copy of the page.

8 Ibid.

9 Stephen B. MacNeil was a literately trained bagpiper, but one might argue that the dictates of old step-dance speeds and rhythms for strathspeys and reels were dominant in his early days as a piper.

10 Robert Gillis (b. 10 July 1922), Hillsdale, personal telephone interview, 14 February 2000. Robert's sister Mary, Dannie Donald the piper MacLellan's god-daughter as well as his foster daughter, described the large Sunday meals that were made for Judique church-goers returning home from even further afield.

11 MacDougall, *History of Inverness County*, 217, 218.

12 Robert Gillis, Hillsdale Road, personal telephone interview, 14 February 2000.

13 Efforts to find a commissioned officer by that name in the British army have so far failed.

14 MacDougall, *History of Inverness County*, 217. The 1871 census confirms this, giving a John MacLellan (66), born in Scotland, and his wife Margaret (61), born in Nova Scotia, and their family. Listed last is a Margaret MacEachen (22), probably a domestic servant, possibly a daughter of neighbour John MacEachen (1871 Census of Inverness county, district 203, Judique, no. 16).

15 Marcella "Lella" (MacLellan) Dubuque, telephone interview, 17 February 2000. Catherine Kennedy was a daughter of John Kennedy from Glen Road in Antigonish County, Nova Scotia. The Antigonish *Casket* (76-1928-10-8) mentions her death, aged 94, in Judique North on 17 December 1927. She is given there simply as "Mrs Donald MacLellan [Piper] Judique" with no first name.

16 Robert Gillis, Hillsdale Road, Judique, 14 February 2000, telephone interview. Information confirmed by Robert's sister Mary (Gillis) MacIsaac, New Brunswick, on the same day (telephone interview). Mary was Dannie MacLellan's God-daughter as well as his foster daughter.

17 Mary (Gillis) MacIsaac, b. June 1925, lives in New Brunswick. Eleven days after her mother died on 3 February 1929 the piper's son Danny MacLellan and his wife, Marcella MacDonell, came to take her to their Hillsdale home, and I am grateful to her for her memories of Dannie Donald the piper MacLellan. (Personal interview, 12 February 2000). Note: Marcella MacDonell was a sister of Hughie Tàl MacDonell, Judique, and aunt of Alexander Hughie Tàl.

18 Donald A. MacLellan left a son Danny who has a son Donald A., so the latest generation will be known by the older Judique people as Donald A., Danny, Donald A., Danny, Donald A. the piper.

19   John D. MacMaster, personal interview at Long Point, Inverness County, Cape Breton, 24 October 1978. The words mean: "Put your nose in the black dog's arse / Put your nose in my own arse / And you'll get silver and gold." According to John Donald Cameron, Judique, the melody may not now be definitely identifiable, although when he tuned what he thought it might be, it was one I recognized as a 6/8 jig that my wife Patsy sings now and then, with different English words: "Have you a daughter Mr MacArthur? / Yes I have and a pretty one too / She went out for a bucket of water / She'll be back in a minute or two." This tune was used for the Newfoundland tune "Fellow from Fortune" (John Donald Cameron, telephone interview, 15 February 2000).

20   Jessica (Rankin) MacLellan, Hillsdale, personal telephone interview, 16 February 2000.

21   Antigonish *Casket*, no. 9 (1919): 5.

22   1871 Census for Inverness County, district 203, Judique, RG 31, vol. 1239, no. 83 (family no. 84).

23   1891 Census of Judique, Inverness County, district 36, pp. 17, 18, no. 62. The census of the Angus MacDougall family was made on 15 April 1891.

24   MacDougall, *History of Inverness County*, 209, 210. The census that Neill MacNeill the catechist made in 1764–65 of the Small Isles, including Eigg, shows no Patrick MacDougall (MacNeill, "Census of the Small Isles 1764–65").

25   MacDougall, *History of Inverness County*, 233.

26   1871 Census of Inverness County, no. 128, p. 48; 1891 Census of Inverness county, district 36, no. 89. Sister Margaret MacDonell gives Neil's dates as 1851–1923.

27   MacDonell, "Na Sgeulaichean," in MacDonell and Shaw, *Luirgean*, second page (unpaginated), wrote that according to family lore Charles Campbell left Muck in the 1840s following the potato crop failure. But, if the Catherine Campbell (36), born in Nova Scotia and listed in the family headed by Neil (24), number 128 in the 1871 census, was a sister, then she and her mother were in the province in 1835.

28   This piper Donald MacDonald may be the same Donald MacDonald mentioned in the Glendale section. Nothing is known about him.

29   MacDonell, "Na Sgeulaichean," third page.

30   See MacMillan, *To the Hill of Boisdale*, passim.

31   MacDonell, *"Na Sgeulaichean,"* first page.

32   1871 Census of Inverness County, no. 128, p. 48. Others living with him were Flora (22), Catherine (18), Isabella (32), Catherine (36), all born in Nova Scotia. Assuming that they were all sisters, then Catherine's age indicates that Charles Campbell emigrated in 1834 or 1835. Charles, Neil's father, must have been dead by 1871.

33   Albert MacDonald, personal interview at Melford, 6 August 1980.

34   Albert MacDonald has since parted with the old home-made set of drones.

35 Albert MacDonald, Melford, personal telephone interview, 16 February 2000.

36 1871 Census of Inverness County, sub-district e2, Judique, no. 131. The year's space between Hector and Frederick may have been filled by a daughter Margaret (22) in the John MacLellan household in Hillsdale (see text associated with note 13).

37 John A. MacLellan (1855–1937). See Mildred MacDonald and John Colin, *Fair Is the Place*, 404.

38 Peigi "the millar" (MacDonald) MacIsaac, Judique, was an excellent source for traditional dance and dancing information, having been good at it and having lived in conservative inland Glencoe.

39 Campbell, "Tìr an Aigh," 211.

40 Campbell, "Dùthaich na Saorsa," 104.

41 Jimmie MacKay, Kingsville, and his neighbour D.R. MacEachern, Glendale, knew him best (1980) as Am Pìobaire Mór.

42 Malcolm J. MacNeil, Piper's Cove, personal interview, 13 July 1980. If custom in naming is followed, then Murdoch was the immigrant.

43 Shears, *Gathering of the Clans Collection*, 20, 21.

44 Greg Gillis, personal conversation at Port Hawkesbury, 29 August 1980. The other was Fr Angus Beaton.

45 Greg Gillis, Port Hawkesbury, personal telephone interview, 19 February 2000. When his grandson Greg Gillis was a young man interested in learning fiddling, he asked his grandfather if he (his grandfather) could play. "Not too much," Stephen B. had said. Pressed a little, the piper eventually admitted that he only knew one fiddle tune, "Fire on the Mountain," and he proceeded to play it. He also told the story about how he learned the tune. As a young man at Gillis Point he had one day gone to a picnic at Grand Narrows or Christmas Island. At the picnic there was an Indian who played "Fire on the Mountain" over and over and over again. Later, when Stephen MacNeil walked home, the tune went on and on in his head. He never forgot it but it was the only tune he ever knew as a fiddle tune (Greg Gillis, Port Hawkesbury, telephone conversation, 19 February 2000). Mr Gillis (79) played it for me over the phone.

46 Shears, *Gathering of the Clans Collection*, 21.

47 Stephen MacNeil piped at the funeral of Captain John Gillis, Harborview, Inverness County, at the captain's specific request.

48 One day Stephen showed the book to Greg Gillis. Pointing to a Gaelic title, he asked his young grandson what it was in English. Greg didn't know any Gaelic and said he couldn't tell. "Piss but don't get the hair wet," the old piper told him (Gillis, 29 August 1980). Donald MacDonald in his first edition of *Collection of Quicksteps* (1828) gives the tune as "P*** and keep the hair dry" (see Cannon, *Bibliography of Bagpipe Music*, 126).

49 Fr Raymond MacDonald PP, Heatherton, Antigonish County, personal interview, 23 February 2000. Fr MacDonald retains the material that he obtained through the aegis of Rev. Dr Nicolson. He said that he had only had one

chanter lesson from his grandfather and that he sensed that his inability to produce a birl had slackened his teacher's interest (ibid). Nicolson held a doctorate in physics from Johns Hopkins University and had a very keen interest in Gaelic language and culture.

50 Raonul Màiri Bhàin (Beaton) owned what appears to be the only known second edition of William MacKay's *Complete Tutor for the great Highland bagpipe*, (n.d. – now minus the title and other introductory pages).

51 Campbell, "Dùthaich na Saorsa," 105.

52 I am grateful to Gordon MacAulay (87) of Baddeck, Vince MacLean of Washabuck, and James MacDonald of Baddeck for furnishing me with information about John E. Campbell, his wife, and family.

53 Campbell, "Dùthaich na Saorsa," 99.

54 "Tha iad so, cho gaolach air a'Chreideamh 'sa tha iad air Impearachd 'Bhreatunn'!" Campbell, "Dùthaich na Saorsa," 98.

55 Campbell, "Tìr an Aigh," 220 (citing Dr Alexander MacDonald).

CHAPTER FOURTEEN

1 From "Baptisms. Marriage & Burials …" for St Peter's Roman Catholic Church in South Ingonish. Rory McDougall died aged 83 on 17 July 1936, of senility. I am very grateful to Fr Peter Morison for generously allowing me access to the parish records. One of the Cape North museum records gives 1851 as his birth date but the more official record cites his date of birth as 1 November 1848. The earliest date would more readily present an answer to why so few memories of his piping exist today, especially if he was a long time senile.

2 St Peter's Church records used this spelling. The current spelling is "Whitty." Dan Rory's first wife was Christena (Christie) MacLean, who died in Ingonish in 1920. Bette (Donovan) MacDougall (b. 1923), the widow of Dannie the piper's step-dancing son Tim (1921–84), told me that her mother-in-law. Mary Ann Whitty, died in 1990 aged 96 (Bette MacDougall, personal interview, 20 June 2000).

3 Peggy MacDougall, personal interview, 13 June 2000.

4 Catholic MacDougalls also settled in the Clyburn valley, a fault which cuts dramatically into the granite massif to the west behind Ingonish Beach. The best land in the area is now occupied by an eighteen-hole golf-course, the land having been compulsorily purchased from the settlers/farmers. One of the MacDougalls was remembered by Marjorie (MacIntyre) Donovan (4 August 2000) and Maurice Donovan (24 June 2000) as having had a smithy on the hill near St Peter's Catholic Church. Another, a Capt. Dan, died as the result of an accident at age 90. He was buried 6 October 1918 (death records, St Peter's Church, Ingonish, from 30 December 1898, p. 60). And there was a John McDougall (Big Jack) who died in August 1899 aged 70 (death records, St

Peter's Church, Ingonish, 30 December 1898 forward, p. 50). A number of Irish Catholic families settled in the Clyburn valley. See Kenneth Donovan, "Mary Grace Barron and the Irish of Ingonish," 193.

5 I am fairly literate in Gaelic, but I do not speak the language fluently and I have found that stumbling and tentativeness discourage most native speakers from using the language.

6 Several people told me in the summer of 2000 that there was at least one old man from Black Point (in the Bay St Lawrence area), Alex Beag MacEachern (b. 1920), who spoke Gaelic. I met him at the Highland Manor in Neil's Harbour on 4 August 2000, and he told me that two strokes had deprived him of his mother tongue. (Alex Beag told me that he had been a fiddler and a piano and accordion player and that he step-danced.) The people who made the claim for Gaelic's survival did not speak the language and no one was even as able as I was to make the claim. I met Sarah (Fraser) Jennings (b. 1917), who had been a child in Lowland Cove and had a few sentences of Gaelic. I also met a middle-aged woman in MacKinnon's Hill to the north of White Point who had learned and still remembered a few Gaelic curses but no more. I also spoke to a MacGregor lady living in Dartmouth who certainly heard a lot of Gaelic spoken in the Pleasant Bay area as late as the 1950s. I asked her point blank if she spoke Gaelic. She paused before saying, "I would have to say I don't" (record misplaced). Gaelic may still exist but I did not find it and consider it dead north of the Chéticamp-Ingonish line.

7 An English-speaking woman working as an operator in the early 1950s picked up her receiver to catch a little of a local conversation only to be baffled by an instant change to Gaelic.

Note: Andrew "Allie" Timmons, Red River, stated that Dan MacGregor and his son John Kenneth were the last speakers of Gaelic in Pleasant Bay. Dan had lived in Big Intervale for six years before finally allowing his eviction to take effect; then he and his son moved to Pleasant Bay (Andrew "Allie" Timmons, 20 August 2000).

8 Andrew "Allie" Timmons (b. 1927), Hinkley Glen Road in Red River, called what is now the little depopulated community on the South Aspy River Road, Glen Nevis, pronouncing Nevis "Neevis," which is the Gaelic pronunciation of the original word Nibheis (as found in Beinn Nibheis/Ben Nevis, and Amhuinn Nibheis/ River Nevis, near Fort William, Scotland).

9 Genealogical records of the North Highlands Community Museum in Cape North.

10 MacNeil, *All Call Iona Home*, no pagination.

11 Ibid.

12 I have been unable to ascertain the place of origin of these MacDougalls in Scotland, but there are at least two strains of MacDougalls in Barra. Members of the group who are descendants of a John MacDougall (who had been a stonemason on Dunstaffnage Castle near Oban and who settled in Barra

c. 1770) are known to have left Barra and settled in Cape Breton c. 1820. They were known as "Na Muillearan" (The Millers). Although the date is too late for pioneer Donald mentioned above, I am grateful to the Very Reverend Angus John, Canon MacQueen, St Barr's, Castlebay, Barra, for the speculation.

13   MacNeil, *All Call Iona Home.* MacNeil numbered his families, he did not use pagination. Note: The 1871 census for Ingonish gives a Donald MacDougall, born 1841 in Nova Scotia. Next to his name is that of Mary MacKinnon, from Iona, daughter of Thomas MacKinnon and Elizabeth MacNeil. This is a different MacDougall family but is worth noting since the link with the Iona area is not unique to the musical MacDougalls (Szick, *Early Settlers*). Another man from Washabuck to move to the Ingonish area is Allan MacIntyre (b. c. 1848) (Brewer, *A Pioneer's Legacy*).

14   J.L. MacDougall gives the first settler "on the western side of the Ben Virich" as a Barra man called Hugh MacKinnon. MacDougall only named three sons of his family, but there is a MacKinnon's Brook in the area and three children would have made up a small family in those days (MacDougall, *History of Inverness County,* 604).

15   North Highlands Community Museum written record gives Michael Mac-Dougall as born in Aspy Bay, 1864, dying there in 1940; the computer record gives the same years but lists place of birth and death as Aspy Bay. Angus in the written record is given as b. 1855 in Bay St Lawrence, d. 1942 in Aspy Bay; in the computer file he is described as b. 1858 in Aspy Bay and d. 1942 in Aspy Bay. The computer file gives a sister Nancy Ann (b. 1847 in Sugarloaf), who married a Lang Chaisson. The written record shows her to have born in Bay St Lawrence in 1849; it adds that she died in Gloucester, Mass. The written record gives Elizabeth as "Little Betty", b. 1861; she never married and died in 1956 in Boston. Note: Angus MacDougall was married to a Mary Chaisson and another brother, Hector (b. 1844 or '46 in either Bay St Lawrence or Sugarloaf), was married to a Catherine Chaisson. Three Mac-Dougall siblings married Chaissons.

16   Joe Curtis, Bay St Lawrence, personal interview, 5 July 2000.

17   Ibid.

18   Mike MacDougall's widow, Peggy (b. 1929), told me that Mike was given Hector MacDougall's fiddle when he died (Margaret [Donovan] MacDougall, personal interview, Ingonish, 22 June 2000).

19   Donald MacDougall's first-born son, Alexander (b. 1840 or 1843), married a Margaret Burton (North Highlands Community Museum, Cape North).

20   Joe Curtis, Bay St Lawrence, personal interview, 5 July 2000.

21   William Budge, Ingonish, was a child on St Paul's Island, where his father kept the light in the mid-twentieth century. William, a professional photographer, is at present preparing a manuscript of his memories of the island. Suffice it to say that the place has no agricultural potential and invited no permanent settlement.

22 Joe named the participants: John J. MacNeil and his new wife, Janie, and Peter Sandy MacNeil, the best man, and Mary Joe MacNeil, the best man's partner (Joe Curtis, 5 July 2000). The North Highlands Community Museum records show a John J. MacNeil (1892–1976) who married a Janie MacNeil. John J. was son of James MacNeil, and Janie MacNeil (b. 8 August 1908) was a daughter of Murdoch (b. 1869), son of Roderick (b. Scotland, 1831). John J. and Janie MacNeil's first child, James Angus, was born 31 August 1931. No wedding date is given but the Scotch Four, or Wedding Reel, lasted in Bay St Lawrence into the late 1920s and early 1930s.

23 Joe Curtis, 5 July 2000. According to "Pioneer John MacNeil and wife Sarah MacKinnon and descendants," the early handwritten record of the family held by the North Highlands Community Museum in Cape North, John MacNeil was born in Scotland in 1798 and died 27 May 1886 at Bay St Lawrence. His wife was Sarah MacKinnon, born in Scotland in 1796, died 2 March 1873. Their issue included George MacNeil, born in Scotland in 1819. George's wife was Catherine MacNeil (b. 1816) and among their children were Alexander (Sandy George MacNeil, b. 1851) and Angus (b. 1856). Curtis enlarged on Angus George MacNeil; he was a very fluent Gaelic speaker who read and wrote Gaelic and made (Gaelic) songs. He didn't play an instrument. For a time he had been a lighthouse keeper on St Paul's Island (Curtis, 5 July 2000).

24 MacDonald, *Cape North and Vicinity Pioneer Families,* 137, 138.

25 This is challenged by the memories of Marjorie (MacIntyre) Donovan, see below.

26 Howard Chaisson told me that the Chaissons were originally from Chéticamp, Inverness County (Chaisson, personal interview, Aspey Bay, 24 June 2000).

27 Christena (Burton) Chaisson, Aspy Bay, telephone interview, 9 February 2001.

28 Chaisson remembered how "Gallic" "spilled out of them" (the older Aspy Bay residents) in the 1920s, but the language had been deliberately disallowed to their children and was used to keep secrets (Chaisson, 24 June 2000).

29 There is a story in Ingonish involving the Whittys and the MacDougalls that concerns the last hunt for caribou in the 1940s. The creature is believed to have become extinct in the Highlands in the 1920s, but George Whitty's father, Tim (1869–1957), clung to a belief that there were still a few on the barrens where he had hunted them years ago (George [b. 1907] remembered having eaten caribou). Tim convinced enough younger people and they set off in January on the two-day hike for "the Droke," a place near the edge of what George Whitty called "Chittican Lake" (he pronounced the "an" as in French). Chéticamp Lake could be gained from Power River (Tim Whitty farmed in those days on the Power River valley, on Whitty's Intervale). The party included the brothers Pius, George, Tom, and Maurice Whitty, Newman and Herb Donovan, Red Tim Whitty (George Whitty's nephew), John Hector Whitty (John James's son), and Charles Whitty (Jack's son) as well as Dannie MacDougall, at 57 the oldest man to go, and Dannie's son Tim MacDougall the step-dancer. There was no

music or dance on this adventure. In fact, the business nearly ended in disaster. George did not say anything about their first night at Ridge Camp but the second, at the Droke, was a nightmare. They dug down three feet in the snow to the ground and fashioned a cover from poles and boughs, but they had to huddle together to stay alive in the terrible cold. George had decided to go to sleep and was dozing off when Pius woke him, and he credits Pius with saving his life. He and Tom Whitty got pneumonia but didn't find the caribou. Both Mac-Dougalls survived (George Whitty, Ingonish Beach, interviews, 19 and 20 June 2000). Later attempts, in the 1960s, to reintroduce the caribou in the Cape Breton Highlands failed.

30 The informant's intended meaning was perfectly clear, but he could not think of the words. Thus, the term "kitchen racket," a fairly commonly used equivalent for "céilidh," is introduced by me (George Whitty, 19 June 2000).

31 A common custom in the Gaelic communities in Inverness County, and in others in Cape Breton, was to erect two stages at picnics, one exclusively for those who danced Scotch Fours.

32 The informant named two other local fiddlers, Alex Gillis, a Gaelic speaker born in Ingonish, and Murray Hawley, a fiddler and a piper. Both were Roman Catholics (Whitty, 19 June 2000).

33 George Whitty, 19 June 2000. Also present was the home-owner, George's son Maurice Whitty (b. 1938).

34 The slide collection of the Cape Breton Highlands National Park, held at Operations, Ingonish Beach, has a picture of the old Catholic church/hall.

35 George Whitty, 19 June 2000.

36 George Whitty, 20 June 2000.

37 Ibid.

38 Maurice Donovan told me on 24 June 2000 that he had a verse of "The Lobster Factory." I did not ask him to sing it because I had some difficulty understanding his normal speech.

39 George Whitty, 19 June 2000.

40 Maurice Donovan said that Dan Rory's best friend in "the Bay" was Joseph MacNeil, now long dead (Maurice Donovan, Highland Manor, Neil's Harbour, personal interview, 14 June 2000).

41 Ibid.

42 Ibid. Freddie Williams, retired schoolteacher and local historian, elaborated to say that an early park warden was called Farquharson. He added that it was possible that his parents had come here but that it was not a local name (Williams, 15 June 2000). (Note: Farquharson is a very rare Highland name in rural Cape Breton.)

43 Maurice Donovan, 24 June 2000. The politician, Rupert Curtis, is mentioned in two newspaper reports in connection with evading arrest for smuggling (*Sydney Record*, 15 August 1925 and 23 February 1926; see Fred Williams, *Up*

Country, arranged by date). Shaving the horse's tail might refer to the old practice of illegally obtaining hair for fiddle bows.

44 Allan MacIntyre, son of the immigrant Roderick MacIntyre, probably from Argyllshire, Scotland who settled in Washabuck.

45 Brewer, *A Pioneer's Legacy*.

46 Marjorie (MacIntyre) Donovan remembered the old Ingonish Ferry when it was running and reminisced about the MacLeods and MacKinnons, all Gaelic speakers, who lived there. She talked about a Murdoch MacLeod from Skye among them. None of them kept Gaelic up (Marjorie Donovan, 4 August 2000).

47 Marriage Register, St Peter's Roman Catholic Church, Ingonish Beach, from 6 September 1898, and deaths, from 30 December 1898, p. 15, entry no. 141. This entry shows that "John Thomas McDougall," who had been baptised in Iona in March 1910, married Elsie MacIntyre (bapt. Ingonish, 23 April 1921).

48 The pioneer MacKinnon families include pioneer Alexander, b. 1802 in Harris, and Joseph MacKinnon, b. 1826 in Margaree, Inverness County, who settled in Bay Road Valley. Pioneer MacKinnon folders, North Highlands Community Museum, Cape North (NHCM/f).

49 John A. MacKinnon, personal interview, Sugarloaf, 3 August 2000.

50 The NHCM data base material contains anomalies – the Archie born to the first wife is given a year of birth of 1890, while the David, first child of the second marriage, is given as born c. 1889 and Donald, the third, listed as born in 1890.

51 Ann Fraser, d/o Simon (b. c. 1800, Pictou County), s/o John (b. Scotland) (NHCM/db). Note: One of my informants, Sarah (Fraser) Jennings, was Sarah, d/o Angus, s/o Simon, s/o John Fraser. The Frasers were from Inverness, Scotland, and settled first in Mabou (Sarah Jennings, personal interview, 6 July 2000).

52 John A. MacKinnon, 3 August 2000. John A. referred to his grandfather's first wife as "Big Mary." He said that the children by her were Catholics while those of Lizzie Fraser were raised Protestants (ibid.).

53 The nearest word in Dwelly's Gaelic-English dictionary to "Ciosag" is "Ciosach," which conveys a sense of untidiness.

54 See Gibson, *Traditional Gaelic Bagpiping*, 246–8 and passim.

55 Sarah Jennings, 6 July 2000.

56 Ibid.

57 In 1927 there were between ten and fifteen families in Lowland Cove, Frasers and MacKinnons (Jim Wilkie, Sugarloaf, personal interview, 29 July 2000). (Jim Wilkie, through his mother, is a grandson of Jim Timmons, who kept the light from 1927 until the early 1940s. Timmons also built a school in Cape St Lawrence for the local children, including the youngsters from Lowland Cove. The school register is extant. Jim Wilkie is son of David, a prompter for the local Square Sets, who at times worked in the woods with Angus "Mossy-Face" MacKinnon.)

58 There has been litigation over misrepresentations in the media of the Black Point community before the people were cleared to Bay St Lawrence and St Margaret's Village as well as to Glen Nevis (south of Dingwall) and to Baddeck. One informant, who preferred to remain anonymous because the subject is still sensitive, told me in August 2000 that there had been at least thirty families in Black Point. The same source outlined two convenient justifications for doing to Black Pointers what had been done to countless Highland families during the Highland clearances: the first was that Cape Breton Highlands National Park was going to take over their land; and the second was poverty and unsanitary conditions in the community. The arguments still put forward against these are that the park did not take over the north of Cape Breton (although it later extended its mandate to ecological protection) and that the rural conditions at Black Point were little different from others in out-of-the-way places in Cape Breton and elsewhere in Canada. My informant put forward the nasty irony of religious discrimination as one of the dominant but unspoken reasons for breaking up Black Point. In this case, Black Point was a nest of Protestants in a Catholic parish.

59 Joe Curtis, Bay St Lawrence, 5 July 2000.

60 Mossy-Face was invariably described as a character and a great step-dancer. Joe Curtis said he was a Presbyterian not much touched by religiousness (Joe was not implying prescriptiveness on the part of local clergy). Joe said that Mossy-Face also had a sister who step-danced, but he did not name her (Joe Curtis, 5 July 2000). Joe, as well as Sarah Jennings and Lawrence Petrie, remembered Mossy-Face fiddling (Sarah Jennings and Lawrence Petrie, South Harbour, 6 July 2000).

61 Joe Curtis, 5 July 2000.

62 Douglas MacKinnon, Pleasant Bay, personal interview, 2 August 2000. Douglas is one of Rory's grandsons through his mother Tina MacKinnon. Rory's son John A. confirmed Otter Brook as his father's birthplace. Otter Brook is a deserted river mouth lying on the cliff shore south of Pollett's Cove.

63 Shears, *Cape Breton Collection*, viii.

64 Ibid., vii. If this is so, and if the data base is correct, then Red John was the John MacKinnon (son of "Big Mary") born at Pleasant Bay in 1871.

65 Andrew "Allie" Timmons, personal interview, Red River, Inverness County, 20 August 2000. See also Shears, *Cape Breton Collection*, vii.

66 Andrew "Allie" Timmons, 20 August 2000. (Note: My notes show this citation to be "nr verbatim"). Barry Shears's note that Creighton had recorded "previously unknown tunes as well as some unusual and 'tasty' settings of traditional tunes" hits the nail on the head (Shears, *Cape Breton Collection*, viii).

67 Andrew "Allie" Timmons, 20 August 2000.

68 Until adequate records are checked, I have to leave the confusion over brothers and half-brothers as it stands.

69 Rory's grandson Douglas MacKinnon, Pleasant Bay, said that Rory saved the money he earned from selling furs to buy the bagpipes and that on one occa-

sion when the family was needy he told Cassie he was going to dip into the savings. She wouldn't let him because she knew how much having professionally made bagpipes meant to him (Douglas MacKinnon, 2 August 2000). Christie Burchell has a photograph of her father in the red house opposite, all dolled up in a kilt, playing his new bagpipes.

70 Patrick Fraser, a commissioner for Parks Canada based in Chéticamp, is the son of the last Fraser born in Fishing Cove. Patrick is fluently bilingual, French-English.

71 With her husband Chester's prompting, Christie said that two Fraser brothers, Lame Alex and Donald, lived at Pollett's Cove at the time Rory fished from there (Christie [MacKinnon] Burchell, Sugarloaf, personal interview, 29 July 2000). J.L. MacDougall discusses Pollett's Cove's and Fishing Cove's early settlers in a section called "Pleasant Bay" in *History of Inverness County*, 614–27.

72 A telegraph line was run to Lowlands' Cove, date unspecified but pre-1922, which may have made a snowshoe journey not too difficult (MacDougall, *History of Inverness County*, 615).

73 John A. MacKinnon, 3 August 2000. The swordfishing industry was big business in the area in the 1920s and 1930s. Hickman Organ, Neil's Harbour, talked to me in the summer of 2000 about the water conditions that attracted the giant fish to harpoon range. Many fishermen in Neil's Harbour were involved in the industry.

74 Douglas MacKinnon, 2 August 2000.

75 John A. MacKinnon , 3 August 2000. A similar spell was used in Glendale involving spring water into which silver was placed. The water was known as "uisge airgid" or water of silver.

76 Christie Burchell, 9 August 2000.

77 Marie (MacIntosh) MacKinnon, Smelt Brook, 5 August 2000.

78 NHCM/f "Pioneer Alexander MacLellan and wife Mary Powers and descendants Meat Cove" gives Alexander b. 1836. Among their issue was a son called Alexander or Allan born "10 04 1883" at Meat Cove. Allie Timmons said that the pioneer must have left the north to find a Powers wife, there never having been any Powers living in the north of Cape Breton (Allie Timmons, 20 August 2000).

79 St Joseph's Roman Catholic Church, Bras d'Or, cemetery plan no. 554.

80 Robert Durando, s/o Hughie, s/o William Burton and Mary Theresa MacLellan (d/o the piper Sandy MacLellan), personal interview, August 2000 at Cape North.

81 NHCM/f "Pioneer Alexander MacLellan and wife Mary Powers and descendants Meat Cove."

82 Mary Theresa (Burton) MacLellan and Hughie Durando, personal interviews at Glen Nevis, 19 August 2000. Although she was quite sure Sandy piped for dancing at weddings, she never mentioned the Scotch Four and I chose not to mention the dance.

83 Hugh Durando, 19 August 2000.
84 Hugh Durando remembered being taken to an old farm in Benacadie Pond to visit Ann MacLean. He remembered seeing her laid out in her casket (Hugh Durando, 19 August 2000).
85 *Sydney Record* 17, no. 288 (7 December 1914):1. See also *Sydney Record* 17, no. 304 (26 December 1914):1, and 17, no. 271 (17 November 1914):1. All the robbers were captured but the intrepid agents had to go in with guns drawn.

CONCLUSION

1 See above (Andrew "Allie" Timmons, Hinkley Glen Road, Inverness County, personal interview, 20 August 2000).
2 Douglas MacKinnon, Pleasant Bay, 2 August, 2000.
3 Hugh Cheape, "Making Piped Music," book review in *Times Literary Supplement*, 11 August 2000.
4 See Shears's collections of pipe music.

Bibliography

ABBREVIATIONS

DCB   *Dictionary of Canadian Biography*
nfi   no further information
NHCM   North Highlands Community Museum, Cape Breton
NLS   National Library of Scotland
OS   Ordnance Survey
PANS   Provincial Archives of Nova Scotia
PRO   Public Record Office
SRO   Scottish Record Office
TGSI   *Transactions of the Gaelic Society of Inverness*
UCCB   University College of Cape Breton

ARCHIVAL MATERIAL

Archives nationales du Québec, Quebec City

"Journals of James Thompson Senior."

Beaton Institute, University College of Cape Breton

Biographical and Genealogical file (B. and G. file) and therein under "South West Margaree." Genealogical article attributed to D.D. MacFarlane and published in the Antigonish *Casket* in 1896.

Conan House Archives, Gairloch, Ross-shire

Tutorial Accounts 1704–1722 (first document recording of tenants' names), 2/113, 3/105, 9/114 (judicial rental 1770), 4/104 (minutes of the sett of 1780).

Eastern Counties Regional Library (Mulgrave, Nova Scotia)

Calendar of Cape Breton land papers 1787–1843, no. 2191. ECRL microfilm,
929.37169 Cal M-20. Original documents held by Beaton Institute, UCCB,
Sydney, Cape Breton.

Census of Inverness County, 1871 (RG31, vol. 1239). District 203 Inverness and
therein Judique, no. 83, p. 31 (Angus MacDougall); no. 128, p. 48 (Neil
Campbell); and no. 131, sub-district e2 Judique (John MacEachen).

Census of Inverness County, 1891. Judique, district 36, pp. 17 and 18, no. 62
(family of Angus MacDougall). The information was gathered on 15 April 1891;
and p. 26, no. 89 (family of Neil Campbell), enumerated 18 April 1891.

Lands and Forests land grant folio 115 (Lake Ainslie, Cape Breton), held by
Eastern Counties Regional Library, Mulgrave, Nova Scotia.

Edinburgh University Library

Campbell, Alexander. "A Slight Sketch of a Journey made through parts of the
Highlands and Hebrides; undertaken to collect materials for *Albyn's Anthology*"
(1815). MS La.111.577 and La.11.51, fol.172–6.

Fraser, Angus. "Ceol-Suaicheantas Morair Bhaidh'-Albainn. The distinguishing
Family Tune of The Lords of Breadalbane. An ancient Gaelic Melody." Unpublished MS in the Angus Fraser MSS (Gen. 614).

MacDonald, Joseph. "Compleat theory of the Scots Highland Bagpipe with all the
Terms of Art in which this instrument was originally taught by its first masters &
composers in the islands of Sky & Mull," c. 1760. Laing MS 111, 804.

MacGregor, Martin. "A political History of the MacGregors before 1751." PhD
thesis, Edinburgh University, 1989.

Glendale Parish Records (Glendale, Inverness County, Nova Scotia)

Including births, marriages and deaths from 1901, held at the Glebe-house,
St Francis de Sales Church, Lower River, Richmond County.

Lands and Forests, Nova Scotia

Index Sheet 109. Cadastral map of part of Inverness County, Nova Scotia.

Library of the Society of Antiquaries of Scotland

Cumming, James. Correspondence, 13 November 1781, from James Cumming of
the Society of the Antiquaries of Scotland in Edinburgh to Sir Alexander Dick of
Prestonfield.

National Library of Scotland (NLS)

Campbell of Mamore MSS. Manuscripts 249, 262, 391.

NLS/313/3478. Sutherland Estate Papers.

NLS Accession 7451. "Papers and Correspondence of Seton Gordon MBE," box 1, General Correspondence 1913–1939; letter from John Johnston, Totamore, Coll to Lieu^t Seton Gordon, RNVR, Naval Centre, Kingstown, Ireland, 6 February 1918.

North Highlands Community Museum, Cape North

Donald MacDougall [and his wife Mary], from computer files.

"Pioneer Donald MacDougall and his wife Mary."

"Pioneer John MacNeil and wife Sarah MacKinnon and descendants."

Parliamentary Acts

An Act for the more effectual disarming the Highlands in Scotland (Disarming Act), 19 Geo. 2, cap. 39, 1746.

An Act to amend and enforce so much of an Act made in the nineteenth Year of his Majesty's Reign, as relates to the more effectual disarming the Highlands in Scotland, 21 Geo. 2, cap. 34, 1748.

An Act to enlarge the Time limited by an Act of the last Session of Parliament, for restraining the Use of the Highland Dress, 20 Geo. 2, cap. 51, 1747 (cited in 21 Geo. 2, cap 34, section VII, 1748).

Public Archives of Nova Scotia

Census of Nova Scotia, 1860–61. Inverness Polling District 14, abstract no. 1, and Census [of Nova Scotia] of 1871, district no. 203, sub-district "River Dennis," division no. 1.

Christening records. Shelburne, Nova Scotia, October 1791.

Nova Scotia deaths 1864–1876, O–Z, microfilm 929.3716 and microfilm 929.371691, Inv. M-36, held by Eastern Counties Regional Library, Mulgrave, N.S.

PANS MGI 559/6, nos. 386, 388, 431, 458, 461, 462, which include (no. 458) "List of Tenants of South Uist as per Judicial Rental of 1798."

PANS MGI 559/11, no. 89. "The Clanranald MacDonalds of Moidart."

PANS MG20 674 7. "Squire" John MacKay's "Reminiscences of a Long Life."

PANS, newspapers. *The Eastern Chronicle*, November 1849, reel 4345.

PANS RGI vol. 449, 132. Census of Nova Scotia, 1841. "Return of the census for the western half of the Township of Ainslie in the County of Inverness, pursuant to the Act passed ..." in 1838.

Public Record Office, London, England (PRO)

British Military and Naval Records C Series (RG8). Microfilm copy held by PAC
(Public Archives of Canada) C-4221, vol. 1883, pp. 10, 15, 31, 37, 44.

PCC Foreign Parts Prob 11, Piece 1915, 173 RH–174RH. Transcript of the Will of
Patrick McCrummen (Lt Donald MacCrummen's son) 1839.

PRO A.O 12 35, vol. 35 (1785–88), p. 29, microfilm copy PAC B1163; American
Loyalist Claims, appeals and evidence made before "Commissioners appointed
by Act of Parliament enquiring into losses and services of the American Loyalists" in Halifax, Nova Scotia, 1785–88.

PRO Colonial Office 5, vol. 93: 287 (English records, box 12, folder 18). Capt.
Alex^r McLean, "A Narrative of the proceedings of a Body of Loyalists in North
Carolina – Rec^d from Genl 24th. March 1776 In Genl Howe's Letter of the 25th
April 1776 1." Filed in correspondence dated 25 April 1776.

PRO E768/41/1-43. Official sworn list of losses sustained by Cameron of Lochiel's
tenants from 1745 to 1747, and part of the records of the Forfeited Estates.

St Peter's Catholic Church Records
(Ingonish Beach, Victoria County, Cape Breton)

"Baptismal Register" from 28 October 1883 to 14 July 1918.

"Baptisms. Marriage & Burials."

Death records from 30 December 1898.

Marriage Register of St Peter's in Ingonish (6 September 1898–[unspecified]).

"Registrum Baptizatorum."

Scottish Record Office (SRO)

General Register of Sasines (GRS), Scottish Record Office.

Horn, Dr B.L.H. Unpublished researches in family records of the Gordon ducal
family and the Marchmont estate records, *inter alia*, held by Scottish Record
Office, made available by Stuart Allan, Historical Research Room.

"Register of Criminal Letters, 1751–80."

SRO E741/1/1. Judicial rental of Barisdale in 1748.

SRO E786/5/22. Correspondence, Mungo Campbell to D. Moncrieff, 12 June 1753.

SRO GD 112/29/31/24.

SRO GD 112/29/51/6. John Campbell, first earl of Breadalbane, account book,
1697.

SRO GD 170/629/97. Breadalbane estate records, 1696.

SRO RH 2/4/87, 73–5 and 66–71. Ships passenger lists of the *Dove of Aberdeen*
and *Sarah of Liverpool* bound from Fort William to Pictou, Nova Scotia, in
1801.

MANUSCRIPTS

Anonymous. Article dealing with Alexander Dubh MacDonald, Glenuig, in the Antigonish *Casket*, 21 September 1944.

Anonymous. "MacDonalds of Kinlochmoidart." N.p, n.d, n.p. Type-script, copies of the first two pages of which were given to the author by Fr Bernard Mac-Donald PP, Brook Village, Inverness County, Nova Scotia, 27 November 1999.

Anonymous. "Rìgh gur mór mo chuid mhulaid." No place but probably Edinburgh, no date but post-1989, no pagination.

Bruford, Alan. "Pipers, bards and other Gaels" (review of *The MacCrimmon Legend*). *Tocher* 35 (1981): 348–50.

– "The Rise of the Highland Piper." Unpublished, expanded version of a talk given to the International Celtic Congress, Oxford, 1983.

Buisman, Frans. "Expressive variability in canntaireachd and the phonology of Scottish Gaelic." Talk given 25 July 1995 to the 10th International Congress of Celtic Studies held at Edinburgh University.

MacDonald, Colin S. "The Alastair Dhu MacDonalds of West Lake Ainslie." In "The Clanranald MacDonalds of Moidart," PANS MGI 559/11 no. 89.

MacDonald, Frederick. "Manuscript-book of Frederick MacDonald, west side Lake Ainslie," begun September 1912.

MacDougall, Angus Innis. "Memorandum Page from the Diary of Angus Innis MacDougall, re Jesuit Mission in Judique, July 27th, 1907."

MacIntyre, Sandy (d. 1992). Nineteenth-century family correspondences from Scotland, held by the late Sandy MacIntyre, River Denys, Inverness County, Cape Breton, Nova Scotia.

MacLean, Alex D. "The Pioneers of Washabuckt." Unpublished, typed MS history of Washabuckt, Cape Breton, 15 September 1940.

MacLennan, John (1843–1923), and I.H. MacKay Scobie. "A Dictionary of Pipers and Piping, Notices of Scottish Highland Pipers and also Lowland Pipers, with Some of the other Countries and including those connected otherwise with piping Originally compiled by Lieutenant John MacLennan and Revised and Added to by Major I.H. MacKay Scobie, F.S.A. (Scot)," which is the source of "Notices" in *Piping Times* published at varying intervals from April 1967. The editor of *Piping Times* acknowledged permission to publish granted by D.R. MacLennan, and to include, from summer 1968, additional material submitted by Archibald Campbell of Kilberry (d. London 24 April 1963).

MacRae, Betty (Arinagour and Glasgow). Unpublished genealogical material: "Johnston Chart 1," "Johnston Chart 2," "Johnston Chart 3," and "Johnston/MacLean" chart.

Morrison, Neil Rankin. MS article "Clann Duiligh: Pipers to the Clan MacLean." Apparently read to the Gaelic Society of Inverness, 9 February 1934. The longhand article, with corrections and additions, is headed "Transactions of the Gaelic Society of Inverness (*TGSI*) Vol XXXVII, 1934–6."

Read, Donald E, and Allan J. Gillis. "Origins of Some Pioneers of River Denys Mtn. and Area, Inverness Co., Cape Breton Island, Nova Scotia: Bornish, South Uist to Bornish, Cape Breton," 1996.

Walker, Agnes. "Genealogy of John, Michael and Angus Walker. Book 1: Mabou Pioneers and research by Agnes Walker," 1990.

PERSONAL CORRESPONDENCE AND INTERVIEWS

Beaton, Josephine, Brook Village. Personal interview, November 1999.

Bruford, Alan, School of Scottish Studies' archivist, University of Edinburgh. Letter to Ann Heymann, Minneapolis, 1 March 1986.

Burchell, Christena Ellen (MacKinnon), and Chester Burchell, Sugarloaf, Victoria County, Cape Breton. Personal interview, 29 July and 9 August 2000.

Cameron, Francis, Cape Breton Gaelic-speaking priest. Interview in Montreal, summer 1976.

Cameron, John Donald, Judique. Telephone interviews, 14 and 15 February 2000.

Campbell, Dannie, 582 Alexandra Street, Sydney. Interview, 9 May 1998.

Chaisson, Christena (Burton), Aspy Bay, Victoria County, Cape Breton. Telephone interview, 9 February 2001.

Chaisson, Howard, Aspy Bay, Victoria County, Cape Breton. Personal interview, 24 June 2000.

Cheape, Hugh, assistant curator, National Museums of Scotland. Letter to Seamas MacNeill, 21 April 1987; letter to the author, 18 September 1992.

Collins, John Angus (Jack). Interviews at Scotsville, April 1977 and 17 August 1980.

Cooke, Peter, School of Scottish Studies, University of Edinburgh. Correspondence to the author, 27 February 1987.

Curtis, Joseph, "The island," Bay St Lawrence, Victoria County, Cape Breton. Personal interview, 5 July 2000.

Deveaux, Sr Amélia, administrator at MacGillivray Guest Home, Alexandra Street, Sydney. Telephone conversation, 11 May 1998.

Donovan, Marjorie (MacIntyre), South Ingonish Harbour, Victoria County, Cape Breton. Personal interview, 4 August 2000.

Donovan, Maurice Francis, Highland Manor, Neil's Harbour, Victoria County, Cape Breton. Personal interviews, 14 June and 5 July 2000.

Dubuque, Lala (MacLellan). Telephone conversations, 17 and 18 February 2000.

Dunn, Margaret, Lower South River. Telephone conversations, 31 May 1998.

Durando, Robert, Sydney, Cape Breton. Personal interview, August 2000 (date misplaced but either 17 or 18 August).

Dyker, Victoria (MacCrimmon), Kirriemuir, Angus. Correspondence to the author, 2 March 1998.

Fortune, Dan. Personal interviews at Glendale, 2 and 5 May 1978, 15 September 1991, 2 August 1994, and 21 January 1998.

Fraser, Barry. Personal interview, Kirkwood (East Lake Ainslie), 30 November 1994.

Gillis, Greg, Port Hawkesbury, N.S. Personal interview, 29 August 1980, and telephone interview, 19 February 2000.

Gillis, Margaret (MacNeil), Lisgard Street, Sydney. Personal interview, 9 May 1998.

Gillis, Robert, Hillsdale Road, Judique. Telephone interview, 14 February 2000.

Huddy, G(?), Map Library, British Library, London. Correspondence to the author, 7 January 1982.

Hussey, Roland, Ingonish Beach, Victoria County, Cape Breton. Personal interview, 13 June 2000.

Jennings, Sarah (Fraser). Personal interview, east of South Harbour, Victoria County, Cape Breton, 6 July 2000.

MacAulay, Gordon, Baddeck. Telephone conversation, 9 February 2000.

MacDonald, Albert, Melford, Inverness County, Cape Breton. Interviews conducted 1976–78, including 25 March 1977 and 6 August 1980, and telephone interviews, 26 May 1998, 10 June 1998, and 16 February 2000.

MacDonald, Angus "Bornish," personal interview in Inverness Consolidated Memorial Hospital, Inverness, Cape Breton, 5 July 1980.

MacDonald, Angus Tulloch, Colindale, Inverness County, Nova Scotia. Telephone interview, 4 December 1999.

MacDonald, Fr Bernard. Personal interview at Brook Village glebe house, Brook Village, Inverness County, Cape Breton, 27 November 1999.

MacDonald, Duncan Alex Beag. Interview at the home of Duncan's sister Jessie, at "the Glen," 1 September 1980.

MacDonald, Finlay Alex Beag. Interview at home on Scotsville-to-Gillisdale road on the west side of the Margaree River, 29 July 1980.

MacDonald, Francis, Inverness, Cape Breton. Telephone interview, 18 June 1998.

MacDonald, James, Baddeck. Telephone interview, 9 February 2000.

MacDonald, Joe Lawrence, Boisdale. Interview at Boisdale 23 and 26 August 1980.

MacDonald, Johnnie Joe, River Denys. Personal interview, March 1982 (date misplaced).

MacDonald, Joseph. Personal interview at Inverness Consolidated Memorial Hospital, Inverness, Cape Breton, 5 July 1980.

MacDonald, Malcolm. Personal interview at Long Point, September 1978, date unrecorded.

MacDonald, Ronald, Antigonish. Telephone interview, 3 December 1999.

MacDonald, Stanley, PP, Heatherton, Antigonish County, N.S. Interview, 23 February 2000.

MacDonell, Archie. Interview at Broad Cove, Cape Breton, 17 August 1980.

MacDonell, Hector. Interview at Main St, Inverness, Cape Breton, 14 November 1981.

MacDonell, John Angie. Interview at MacKenzie Ave., Inverness, Cape Breton, 5 July 1980.

MacDonell, Penelope. Interview at Forest St, Inverness, 14 November 1981.

MacDougall, Bette (Donovan), Ingonish Beach, Victoria County, Cape Breton. Personal interview, 20 June 2000.

MacDougall, Donald Hugh, Inverness. Personal interview given on a car journey between Port Hastings and Antigonish, 15 May 1978.

MacDougall, Grant. Personal interview at Scotsville, 3 November 1994.

MacDougall, Margaret (Peggy) (Donovan), Ingonish. Personal interview, 22 June 2000.

MacEachern, Catherine (Sister), Mabou Convent, Inverness County, Cape Breton. Telephone interviews, 15 June 1998.

MacEachern, D.R., Glendale, Cape Breton. Interview, 2 July 1980.

MacEachern, Dan Hughie. Personal interview, 11 April 1977, place unknown, probably Kingsville or Melford.

MacEachern, Patrick, Glendale, Cape Breton. Interview, Glendale, 2 July 1980; telephone interviews, 27 May and 24 June 1998; and Patrick MacEachern (Glendale) to Alex Hughie MacInnis (Kingsville), 18 June 1998, reported by the latter.

MacFarlane, Tearlach, Glenfinnan, Invernesshire, Scotland. Letters to the author, 3 December 1985 and 18 December 2000.

MacFarlane, Walter Scott. Interview in Inverness, Cape Breton, 20 April 1977.

MacInnes, Mrs Christie (MacIsaac), Big Pond, Cape Breton. Interview, 9 May 1998.

MacInnis, Allan Dan. Personal interviews at Glendale, 2 and 5 May 1978.

MacIsaac, Bella (Gillis). Personal interview, Inverness, 1972(?).

MacIsaac, Mary (Gillis), New Brunswick. Personal telephone interviews, 12 and 14 February 2000.

MacKay, James, Kingsville, Cape Breton. Interview, 1 July 1980.

MacKenzie, A.A, Merigomish, Pictou County, Nova Scotia. Telephone communication with the author, November 1997.

MacKenzie, Bridget, Lednabirichen, Dornoch, Sutherland. Letter to the author, 9 February, 1999 (includes citations from MacKay, *Autobiographical Journal of John MacDonald*).

MacKenzie, John Archie, Belle Côte, Inverness County. Telephone interview, 4 June 1998.

MacKenzie, John James, South West Margaree. Telephone interview, 15 June 1998.

MacKinnon, Douglas, Pleasant Bay, Cape Breton. Personal Interview, 2 August 2000.

MacKinnon, John A., Sugarloaf, Victoria County, Cape Breton. Personal interview, 3 August 2000.

MacKinnon, Marie (MacIntosh), MacKinnon's Hill, by Smelt Brook, Victoria County, Cape Breton. Personal interview, 5 August 2000.

MacLean, Hugh Don, Scotsville. Personal interview, 7 June 1979.

MacLean, Margaret A. (Blue), Melford. Personal interview, 16 March 1977.

MacLean, Neil Allan, Scotsville. Personal interview, 7 June 1979.

MacLean, Sorley. Personal interview at Edinburgh University, July 1995.

MacLean, Vincent, Washabuck, Victoria County. Letter to the author, 20 March 1999; and telephone conversations, 8 and 14 April 1999 and 11 and 13 February 2000.

MacLellan, Archie Dan. Personal interview, 7 January 1980.

MacLellan, Donald A., South West Margaree. Personal interview, 29 May 1979.

MacLellan, Jessica (Rankin), Hillsdale. Telephone interview, 16 February 2000.

MacLellan, John Neillie, Kempt Road, Richmond County, Cape Breton. Telephone interview, 8 June 1998; and personal interview at Kempt Road, 17 June 1998.

MacLellan, Lauchie Dan N. Interview at Dunvegan, 7 January 1980.

MacLeod, Fr Angus J., Sydney. Personal correspondence to the author, 22 May 1998.

MacLeod, Maj. C.I.N. Personal interview in Antigonish, summer 1972.

MacLeod, John D. Personal interview at Glendale, 17 April 1977.

MacLeod, Ruairidh Halford, Auchtermuchty, Fife. Letter to the author, 6 September 1981.

MacMillan, Fr Allan J., then at Petit de Grat, Cape Breton. Telephone conversation, 11 May 1998.

MacMillan, Peter. Personal interview at Mulgrave, N.S, 22 November 1999.

MacNeil, Ainslie, Inverness, Cape Breton. Telephone communication, 14 July 1998.

MacNeil, Joe Neil. Interview at Melford, Cape Breton, November 1978; interviews at Kingsville, Cape Breton, 30 November 1979, 11 May and 27 July 1980, and (place unrecorded) 30 May 1982; and telephone conversation, 19 September 1991.

MacNeil, Malcolm "Bernie." Interview at 105 MacRae, Sydney River, Cape Breton, 21 April 1977.

MacNeil, Malcolm J., Piper's Cove. Personal interview. 13 July 1980.

MacPhail, Archibald, Scotsville. Interviews, 6 and 7 June 1979 and 10 September 1994.

MacPhee, Hugh, BBC, Glasgow, Scotland. Letters to Piper Fred MacDonald, Glengarry Highlanders Pipe Band, Ninth Brigade, Third Division, Canadian Army Overseas, England, 19 January and 27 February 1942.

MacQuarrie, Murdock. Interview at Inveraray Manor, Inverness, Cape Breton, 1 September 1980.

MacQueen, Very Reverend Angus John, canon, St Barr's, Castlebay, Barra. Letter to the author, 23 October 2000.

MacRae, Betty. Correspondence to the author from Arinagour, 23 July and 13

August 1987, and from Hillhead, Glasgow, 27 September 1987 and 17 November 1991.

MacSween, Hector, Westmount, Sydney. Telephone interview, 1 May 1998; and interview at Westmount, 9 May 1998.

MacSween, Hugh, East Bay, Cape Breton. Personal interview, 25 August 1980.

Matheson, Alex. Personal interview at Big Marsh, Inverness County, Cape Breton, 2 July 1998.

Matheson, Mary (MacPherson). Personal interview at Big Marsh, Inverness County, 2 July 1998.

Moore, Clarence. Personal interview at Lake Ainslie, 9 May 1979.

Morgan, Robert J. Letter to the author, 6 May 1998.

Moss, George (1903–90), Kessock, by Inverness, Scotland. Correspondence to the author, 4 May 1980 and 15 February 1986.

Petrie, Lawrence, South Harbour, Victoria County, Cape Breton. Personal interview, 6 July 2000.

Shaw, John. Interview at Broad Cove, Inverness County, Cape Breton, 27 July 1980.

Shears, Barry. Telephone conversation, 21 April 1999.

Smith, Greg. Interview at Port Hawkesbury, Cape Breton, 26 November 1976, reporting a telephone conversation of that day between himself and Gerry MacFarlane (now of Troy, Inverness County), and telephone interview, 8 June 1998.

Sutherland, George. Interview at Soldier's Cove, Cape Breton, 25 August 1980.

Timmons, Andrew "Allie," Hinkley Glen Road, Red River, Inverness County, Cape Breton. Personal interview, 20 August 2000.

Walker, Felix, Launching, P.E.I. Personal telephone interview, 5 December 1999.

Walker, Francis J. "Dixie." Personal interview, 24 November 1999.

White, Catherine Effie (MacMillan), and her husband Malcolm. Personal interviews at Whiteside, Richmond County, Cape Breton, 8 August 1980.

Whitty, George, Ingonish Beach, Victoria County, Cape Breton. Personal interviews, 19 and 20 June 2000. Also Maurice Whitty, George's son, same place and dates.

Wilkie, Jim, Sugarloaf, Victoria County, Cape Breton. Personal interview, 29 July 2000.

Williams, Freddie, Ingonish, Victoria County, Cape Breton. Telephone interview, 15 June 2000.

Williams, John, Melford, Cape Breton. Telephone interview, 22 May 1998.

Williams, Neil. Personal interviews, Melford, 23 November 1976, 15 December 1976, 28 March 1977, 30 July 1980, *inter alia*.

OTHER SOURCES

Agnew, Sir Andrew, Bart, of Lochnaw. *The Hereditary Sheriffs of Galloway Their "forebears" and Friends their Courts and Customs of their Times with Notes of* the Early History, Ecclesiastical Legends, the Baronage and Place-names of the Province. 2 vols. Edinburgh, 1893.

Allardyce, Col. James, ed. Historical Papers Relating to the Jacobite Period 1699–1750. 2 vols. Aberdeen: New Spalding Club, 1895, 1896.

"A.M.S." (A. MacLean Sinclair). "Clann Duiligh." MacTalla 12, no. 2 (24 July 1903): 12–13.

Anderson, David G. "Ships' Lists of Lochaber Immigrants 1802." In Fleming, Lochaber Emigrants to Glengarry, 5–13.

Anonymous. "The life of Dr Archibald Cameron." Pamphlet, London, 1753. Cited in Chambers, History of the Rebellion of 1745–6.

Army Lists for 1791, 1800, 1810, 1814, and 1817; varying titles, including A List of the Officers of the Army and Marines; with an index: A Succession of Colonels; and a List of the Officers of the Army and Marines on Half-Pay; also with an index, 48th ed. (War Office, 1800).

Bain, Margaret I. Les Voyageurs français en Écosse 1770–1830 et leurs Curiosités Intellectuelles. Paris: H. Champion, 1931.

Bain, Robert. The Clans and Tartans of Scotland. Enlarged and re-edited by Margaret O. MacDougall. London and Glasgow: William Collins Son & Co., 1968.

Batson, Lewis E. "The Scale of the Highland Bagpipe." Piping Times 17, no. 11 (August 1965): 27–30.

Beaton, Elizabeth A., and Sheila W. Macintyre, eds. The Burgesses of Inverary, 1665–1963. Scottish Record Society, New Series 14. Edinburgh: Glasgow University Department of Scottish History, 1990.

Black, Ronald. "I got a Kiss of the King's Hand." Letter in Piping Times 19, no. 9 (June 1967): 26–9.

Blaikie, Walter Biggar. Itinerary of Prince Charles Edward Stuart from his landing in Scotland July 1745 to his departure in September 1746 Compiled from the Lyon in Mourning Supplemented and corrected from other contemporary sources. 1897; Edinburgh: Scottish Academic Press, 1975.

Blair, Reverend Dr D.B., and Reverend A. MacLean Sinclair. "The Urquhart Settlement in Nova Scotia." In Transactions of the Gaelic Society of Inverness (TGSI) 53 (1982–4): 444–63.

Blundell, Dom. Odo. The Catholic Highlands of Scotland. Edinburgh: Sands and Co., 1917.

Boswell, James. Journal of a Tour to the Hebrides with Samuel Johnson. 1773. Reprint, edited by Ernest Rhys, London and New York: Dent and Dutton, 1909.

Brewer, Tom. A Pioneer's Legacy: The Brewer Family Tree. No further information (nfi).

"Brown, George." In Dictionary of Canadian Biography, 10:91–3.

Bryson, Gladys. Man and Society: The Scottish Inquiry of the Eighteenth Century. New York: A.M. Kelley, 1968.

Buchan, John. The History of the Royal Scots Fusiliers (1678–1918). London, New York: T. Nelson and Sons, 1925.

– *The Massacre of Glencoe*. New York: G.P. Putnam's Sons, 1933.

Buisman, Frans. "From chant to script." *Piping Times* 39, no. 7 (April 1987).

– "More evidence on Colin Campbell and the development of the Campbell notation: SRO 112/1/803." *Piping Times* 47, nos. 11 and 12 (August and September 1995).

Bulloch, John Malcolm, ed. *The House of Gordon*. 3 vols. Aberdeen: New Spalding Club, 1903, 1908, and 1912.

Burns, David. "John McGregor of Fortingall and his descendants." *Scottish Genealogist* 29, no. 4 (December 1982).

Byrne, Cyril J.; Margaret Harry; and Pádraig Ó'Siadhail, eds. *Celtic Languages and Celtic Peoples*. Proceedings of the Second North American Congress of Celtic Studies. Halifax: Saint Mary's University, 1992.

Cameron, Neil. "A Romantic folly to Romantic folly: The Glenfinnan Monument reassessed." *Proceedings of the Society of Antiquaries of Scotland* 129 (1999): 887–907.

Campbell, Alastair, of Airds. *Two Hundred Years – The Highland Society of London*. London: Highland Society of London, 1983.

Campbell, Alastair, of Airds, and D.C. McWhannell. "The Macgillechonells – a Family of Hereditary Boatbuilders." *Notes and Queries of the Society of West Highland and Island Historical Research* 2, no. 14 (July 1995).

Campbell, Alexander. *Albyn's Anthology or a Select Collection of the Melodies & Vocal Poetry Peculiar to Scotland & The Isles Hitherto Unpublished*. Edinburgh: Oliver and Boyd, 1816; Norwood, Pa.: 1976.

Campbell, Archibald. "The History and Art of Angus MacKay." *Piping Times* 2, nos. 5–7 (February, March, and April 1950).

– "The History of Angus MacKay." *Piping Times* 37, no. 6 (March 1985).

– *The Kilberry Book of Ceòl Mór*. 3rd ed. Glasgow: John Smith & Son, on behalf of the Piobaireachd Society, 1969.

– "The MacGregor Pipers of the Clann an Sgeulaiche." *Piping Times* 2, no. 10 (July 1950).

Campbell, Archibald, SJ (An Ard-Urramach Gilleasbuig MacDhòmhnuill Ic Eoghain, CI). "Dùthaich na Saorsa," in *Guth na Bliadhna*, book 5, no. 2 (Spring 1908); and "Tìr an Aigh," in *Guth na Bliadhna*, book 5, no. 3 (Summer 1908).

Campbell, Duncan. *The Lairds of Glenlyon*. 2nd ed. Perth, 1984.

Campbell, J.L., ed. *Songs Remembered in Exile – Traditional Gaelic songs from Nova Scotia Recorded in Cape Breton and Antigonish County in 1937 with an Account of the Causes of Hebridean Emigration, 1790–1835*. Translated by S. Ennis. Aberdeen: Aberdeen University Press, 1990.

Campbell, John Francis. *Canntaireachd: Articulate Music, dedicated to the Islay Association, by J.F. Campbell, Iain Ileach. 14th August, 1880*. Glasgow: Archibald Sinclair, 1880. Facsimile edition, Edinburgh, 1989.

– *Popular Tales of the West Highlands Orally Collected with a Translation*. 4 vols. Edinburgh, 1860, 1862.

Campbell, John Gregorson. *Superstitions of the Highlands and Islands of Scotland Collected entirely from Oral Sources.* 1900. Reprint, York: Benjamin Blom, 1971.

Campsie, Alistair Keith. *The MacCrimmon Legend – The Madness of Angus Mac-Kay.* Edinburgh: Canongate Publishing, 1980.

Cann, D.B.; J.I. MacDougall; and J.D. Hilchey. *Soil Survey of Cape Breton Island Nova Scotia.* Report 12. Truro, N.S., 1963.

Cannon, Roderick D. *A Bibliography of Bagpipe Music.* Edinburgh: John Donald Publishers, 1980.

– *The Highland Bagpipe and Its Music.* Edinburgh: John Donald Publishers, 1988.

Carson, Ciaran. *Last Night's Fun about Music, Food and Time.* London: Pimlico, 1996.

Casket (Antigonish): 1928-10-8 (obituary of Mrs Donald MacLellan, 94); 1952-41-2 (obituary of Donald MacLellan, 79); and 1919-9-5 (obituary of Angus McDougal, 84). Also Antigonish *Casket*s for April and May 1896 and others.

Celtic Monthly. February 1911.

Chambers, Robert. *History of the Rebellion in Scotland in 1745–6.* 1827. 6th ed., Edinburgh, 1847.

Chantreau, Pierre-Nicolas. *Voyage dans les trois Royaumes d'Angleterre, d'Écosse et d'Irlande fait en 1788–1789.* Vol. 3. Paris, 1792.

Cheape. "Portraiture in Piping." *Scottish Pipe Band Monthly*, no. 6 (January 1988): 1163–73.

Church of Scotland. *Form of process in the Judicatories of the Church of Scotland; with relation to Scandals and censures* (1707 and the unchanged 1771 edition). N.p., n.d.

– *The Principal Acts of the General Assembly, convened occasionally at Edinburgh, upon the 22 day of January, in the year 1645.* Edinburgh, n.d.

– *Printed Acts of the General Assembly 1690–1717.* Edinburgh, n.d.

Cockburn, Lord (Henry Thomas). *Circuit Journeys by the Late Lord Cockburn.* Edinburgh: David Douglas, 1888.

Collinson, Francis. *The Bagpipe – The History of a Musical Instrument.* London and Boston: Routledge & Kegan Paul, 1975.

Comunn na Piobaireachd (Piobaireachd Society), ed. *Piobaireachd – A Fourth Book of 16 Tunes with a Preface and Explanatory Notes.* Glasgow: Bell, Aird & Coghill, 1968.

– *Piobaireachd – A Ninth Book of 16 Tunes with a Preface and Explanatory Notes.* Glasgow: Aird & Coghill, n.d. (Preface dated 1957.)

– *Piobaireachd – A Second Book of 12 Tunes in Staff and Canntaireachd Notations with a Preface and Explanatory Notes.* Glasgow: Aird & Coghill, 1963.

– *Piobaireachd – A Seventh Book of 16 Tunes with a Preface and Explanatory Notes.* Glasgow: Aird & Coghill, 1968.

– *Piobaireachd – A Tenth Book of 16 Tunes with a Preface and Explanatory Notes.* London: Lowe & Brydone (Printers), n.d.

– *Piobaireachd – A Third Book of 12 Tunes in Staff and Canntaireachd Notations with a Preface and Explanatory Notes*. Glasgow: Bell, Aird & Coghill, 1968.

– *Piobaireachd – 12 Tunes Edited by Comunn na Piobaireachd (The Piobaireachd Society) in Staff and Canntaireachd Notations with a Preface and Explanatory Notes – Book 1*. Glasgow: Bell, Aird & Coghill, 1968.

"Contemporary Letters on the Rebellion of 1745. Prefatory Notes by the Editor of the 'Northern Chronicle,'" from "Selections from the Family Papers of the MacKays of Bighouse." *TGSI* 21 (1896–97): 148–71.

Court report of an abduction by John Maclain of Lochbuy in section entitled "Scotland" in *Scots Magazine* 13 (August 1759): 441–2.

Craven, J.B. *Journals of the Episcopal Visitations of the Right Reverend Robert Forbes*. N.p., n.d.

Cregeen, E.R. "The tacksmen and their successors; a study of tenurial re-organisation in Mull, Morvern and Tiree in the early 18th century." *Scottish Studies* 13 (1969): 93–144.

Daiches, David. *Charles Edward Stuart: The Life and Times of Bonnie Prince Charlie*. London: Thames and Hudson, 1973.

– *The Paradox of Scottish Culture*. London: Oxford University Press, 1964.

Dalyell, Sir John Graham. *Musical Memoirs of Scotland, with Historical Annotations*. Edinburgh, 1849.

Deacon, W.A. *The Four Jameses*. MacMillan, 1974.

Dennis, Clara. *Cape Breton Over*. Toronto, 1942.

de Saussure, Necker. *Voyage to the Hebrides*. N.p., 1822.

Dixon, John H. *Gairloch in North-west Ross-shire – Its Records, Traditions, Inhabitants, and Natural History with a Guide to Gairloch and Loch Maree and a Map and Illustrations*. Edinburgh, 1886.

Donaldson, William. *The Highland Pipe and Scottish Society 1750–1950*. East Linton, Scotland: Tuckwell Press, 2000.

Donovan, Kenneth. "Mary Grace Barron and the Irish of Ingonish, Cape Breton 1822–1999." *Nashwaak Review,* nos. 6–7 (Fall 1999).

Drummond Norie, William. *Loyal Lochaber, Historical, Genealogical and Traditionary*. Glasgow: Morison Bros, 1898.

Dughalach, Ailean. *Orain Ghàidhealacha; maille ri co' chruinneachadh òran is dhàn le ùghdairibh eile*. Untranslated. N.p., 1798.

– *Orain, Marbhrannan agus Duanan Ghaidhealach*. Untranslated. N.p.: Alastair MacIntosh, 1829.

Duncanson, John Victor. *Rawdon and Douglas – Two Loyalist Townships in Nova Scotia*. Belleville, Ont.: Mika Publishing, 1989.

Dwelly, Edward. *The Illustrated Gaelic-English Dictionary*. 7th ed. Glasgow: Gairm Publications, 1971.

Eastern Chronicle, 8 November 1849, 5 ("A Celebrated Pair of Bagpipes," from the Toronto *Globe* [PANS Reel 4345]).

Eisenstadt, Maurice. "The Bagpipe Scale." *Piping Times* 18, no. 12 (September 1966): 6–19.

Ellis, Steven G. *Tudor Ireland: Crown, Community and the Conflict of Cultures, 1470–1603*. London and New York: Longman, 1985.

[Farquharson, John]. *Survey of Lochtayside 1769*. Edited by Margaret M. McArthur. Scottish History Society, series 3. Edinburgh: T. & A. Constable, 1936.

Faujas de Saint Fond, B. *A Journey through England and Scotland to the Hebrides in 1784*. Edited with notes by Archibald Geikie. Revised version of the English translation. N.p., 1907.

Fergusson, Donald A., ed. *Fad air falbh as Innse Gall leis comh chruinneachadh Cheap Breatunn (Beyond the Hebrides)*. Halifax: Printers Lawson Graphics Atlantic, 1977.

Fergusson, Sir James of Kilkerran. *Argyll in the Forty-five*. London: Faber and Faber, n.d. (1951?).

Findlay, J.T. *Wolfe in Scotland in the '45 and from 1749 to 1753*. London: Longmans, Green and Co., 1928.

Fleming, Rae, ed. *The Lochaber Emigrants to Glengarry*. Toronto: Natural Heritage/Natural History Inc., 1994.

Forbes, Robert, A.M. *The Lyon in Mourning or a Collection of Speeches Letters Journals etc. relative to the Affairs of Prince Charles Edward Stuart by the Rev. Robert Forbes A.M. Bishop of Ross and Caithness 1746–1775*. Edited by Henry Paton. 3 vols. Edinburgh: Scottish Academic Press, 1975.

Forsyth, Reverend W. *In the Shadow of Cairngorm – Chronicles of the United Parishes of Abernethy and Kincardine*. Inverness: Northern Counties Publishing Co., 1900.

Fraser, A. Duncan. *Some Reminiscences and the Bagpipe*. Edinburgh, 1907.

Fraser, Alexander. *The Royal Burgh of Inveraray*. Edinburgh: Saint Andrew Press, 1977.

Fraser, Master James. *Chronicles of the Frasers (Wardlaw MS) "Polichronicon seu Policratica Temporum or the true Genealogy of the Frasers."* Vol. 47. Edited by William Mackay. Scottish History Society, series 1. Edinburgh, 1905.

Fraser, Capt. Simon, ed. *The Airs and Melodies peculiar to the Highlands of Scotland and The Isles, communicated in an original pleasing & familiar style, having the lively airs introduced as medleys to form a sequence to each slower movement; with an admired plain harmony for the piano forte, harp, organ or violoncello, and Chiefly acquired during the interesting Period from 1715 to 1745, through the Authentic Source narrated in the Accompanying Prospectus*. 1816. Reprint, with introduction by Paul S. Cranford, Sydney, N.S., 1982.

Fraser, Sir William. *Papers from the Collection of Sir William Fraser K.C.B., LLD*. Edited by J.R.N. MacPhail. Edinburgh: Edinburgh University Press from T. & A. Constable, 1924.

Fraser-Mackintosh, Charles. *Antiquarian Notes*. Series 2. Inverness: n.p., 1897.
– "Glengarry – Coll MacDonell of Barisdale." In Fraser-Mackintosh, *Antiquarian Notes*.
– "Glengarry's piper and the canal commissioners in 1807, etc." In Fraser-Mackintosh, *Antiquarian Notes*, 149–55.
– "The MacDonells of Scotos." *TGSI* 16 (1889–90): 79–97.
– "Minor Highland Septs – the Mac-Donells of Barisdale." *TGSI* 13 (1886–7): 84–102.
Geikie, Archibald, ed. *The Life of Sir Roderick I. Murchison*. 2 vols. London, 1875.
Gibson, John G. "Genealogical and piping notes from 'Squire' John MacKay's 'Reminiscences of a Long Life (c. 1794–1884).'" *Scottish Genealogist: Quarterly Journal of the Scottish Genealogy Society* 30, no. 3 (September 1983): 94–8.
– "MacIntyre Pipers and the Fairy Chanters."*Clansman* (Halifax) 2, no. 4 (August 1988): 10–11.
– "Mary MacDonald ... One of the last of the old traditional [fiddle] players." *Fiddlers to the Fore* (a newspaper written and edited by the author), c. 1975.
– "The Pedigree of the Blind Piper." *Royal Nova Scotia Historical Society Journal* 3 (2000): 192–201.
– "Piper John MacKay and Roderick McLennan: a tale of two immigrants." *Nova Scotia Historical Review* 2, no. 2 (December 1982): 69–82.
– "Pipers' styles in contrast at Broad Cove Concert." *Oran* (Inverness, Cape Breton), 10 August 1994.
– *Traditional Gaelic Bagpiping, 1745–1945*. Montreal and Kingston: McGill-Queen's University Press, 1998.
– "The two-droned bagpipe." Letter in *Am Bràighe*, Winter 1998/99, 4, 6.
Gibson, John Sibbald. *Lochiel of the '45 – The Jacobite Chief and the Prince*. Edinburgh: Edinburgh University Press, 1994.
Glen, David. *A Collection of Ancient Piobaireachd compiled and arranged by David Glen. With Historic, Biographic and Legendary Notes regarding the Tunes by 'Fionn.'* 4th ed. Edinburgh: David Glen & Sons, n.d.
Gordon, Seton Paul. *Hebridean Memories*. London: Cassell & Co., 1923.
Graham, I.C.C. *Colonists from Scotland: Emigration to North America, 1707–1783*. Ithaca, N.Y.: Cornell University Press, 1956.
Grant, I.F. *The MacLeods: The History of a Clan 1200–1956*. London: Faber and Faber, 1959.
Grant, James. *Thoughts on the Origin and Descent of the Gael: with an Account of the Picts, Caledonians, and Scots; and Observations relative to the Authenticity of the Poems of Ossian*. Edinburgh: Archibald Constable and Co., 1814.
Gray, Pipe-Major W. Untitled article dealing with the MacArthur pipers. *Piping Times* 25, no. 11 (August 1973).
Gregory, Donald. *The History of the Western Highlands and Isles of Scotland from AD 80 to AD 1493*. 2nd ed. London, 1881.
Haldane, A.R.B. *The Drove Roads of Scotland*. London: Nelson, 1952.

Harper, J.R. *The Fraser Highlanders*. Montreal: Society of the Montreal Military and Maritime Museum, 1979.

Henderson, Diana M. *Highland Soldier – A Social Study of the Highland Regiments, 1820–1920*. Edinburgh: John Donald Publishers, 1989.

Hill Burton, John, and David Masson. *Register of the Privy Council of Scotland, first series (1545–1625)*. 14 vols. (1877–98). Vol. 5.

"Historical and Traditional Notes on Piobaireachd. Edinburgh: The Army School of Piping, 1964." Cited in McLeod, "John McKay's Black House." *Piping Times* 45, no. 6 (March 1993): 20.

Home, John, Esq. *The History of the Rebellion in Scotland in 1745*. Edinburgh, 1822.

Indenture between Lord Lovat and David Fraser, 1743. *Piping Times* 21, no. 3 (December 1969).

Johnson, David. *Music and Society in Lowland Scotland in the Eighteenth Century*. London: Oxford University Press, 1972.

Johnson, Samuel. *A Journey to the Western Island of Scotland*. Introduction and notes by J.D. Fleeman. Oxford, 1985.

Johnston, Rev. A.A. *Antigonish Diocese Priests and Bishops 1786–1925*. Edited by Kathleen M. MacKenzie. Antigonish, N.S.: Casket Printing, 1994.

– *A History of the Catholic Church in Eastern Nova Scotia*. 2 vols. Antigonish, N.S.: St Francis Xavier University Press, 1960, 1971.

Johnston, John, Coll. Letters to the editor of the *Oban Times & West Highland Times*, 3 September and 10 November 1919.

Kay's Edinburgh Portraits – A series of Anecdotal Biographies Chiefly of Scotchmen mostly written by James Paterson ... edited by James Maidment, Esq., Advocate. Popular Letterpress Edition, 2 vols. London: Hamilton, Adams and Co; Glasgow, Thomas D. Morison, 1885.

Keltie, Sir John Scott, ed. *A History of the Scottish Highlands, Highland Clans and Highland Regiments*. 2 vols. in 8 books. Edinburgh and London, 1875.

"Lairds of the Central Inner Hebrides and adjacent mainland 1761–1771." In Timperley, *Directory of Landownership in Scotland 1770*.

Lang, Andrew. *The Companions of Pickle – being a Sequel to 'Pickle the Spy.'* London, 1898.

– *Pickle the Spy, or the Incognito of Prince Charles*. 3rd ed. London, 1897.

Le Moine, J.M. (Sir James Macpherson). *Quebec Past and Present – A History of Quebec 1628–1876*. In 2 parts. Quebec: Augustin Coté Printers, 1876.

Leneman, Leah. *Living in Atholl – A Social History of the Estates 1685–1785*. Edinburgh: Edinburgh University Press, 1986.

Lindsay, Ian G., and Mary Cosh. *Inverary and the Dukes of Argyll*. Edinburgh: Edinburgh University Press, 1973.

Lockhart, John Gibson. *Memoirs of the Life of Sir Walter Scott*. 7 vols. Edinburgh, 1837, 1838.

Logan, James. *The Scottish Gaël; or, Celtic Manners, as preserved among the Highlanders.* 2 vols. London, 1831.

MacAulay, Alexander. "The Art and History of the MacDougalls of Aberfeldy." *Piping Times* 16, nos. 4, 5 (January and February 1964).

MacCormack, John R. *Highland Heritage & Freedom's Quest: Three Centuries of MacCarmaics in Ireland, Scotland, Prince Edward Island and West Lake Ainslie, Nova Scotia.* 2nd ed. Halifax: Kinloch Books, 1999.

MacCulloch, Donald B. *Islands – Staffa.* London: David & Chanos, 1975.

MacCulloch, John. *The Highlands and Western Isles of Scotland containing Descriptions of their Scenery and Antiquities, with an Account of the Political History and Ancient Manners, and of the Origin, Language, Agriculture, Economy, Music, Present Condition of the People &c. &c. &c. founded on a Series of Annual Journeys between the Years 1811 and 1821, and forming an Universal Guide to that Country, in letters to Sir Walter Scott, Bart.* 4 vols. London, 1824.

MacDonald, Rev. A., and Rev. A. MacDonald. *Clan Donald.* 3 vols. Inverness: Northern Counties Publishing Co., 1900.

MacDonald, Alexander. *Story and Song from Loch Ness-side.* 1914. Reprint, Inverness: Gaelic Society of Inverness, 1982.

MacDonald, Alexander D. *The Mabou Pioneers.* Reissue. Antigonish, N.S.: Formac Publishing Company, n.d.

MacDonald, Allan. "Pìobairean Smearcleit." From the MSS of the late Rev. Fr Allan Macdonald. *Celtic Review* 5 (July 1908–April 1909): 345–7.

MacDonald, Rev. Charles. *Moidart or Among the Clanranalds.* Oban: Duncan Cameron, 1889. Reprint, Edinburgh: James Thin, 1989.

MacDonald, Rev. Donald. *Cape North and Vicinity Pioneer Families History and Chronicles including Pleasant Bay, Bay St. Lawrence, Aspy Bay, White Point, New Haven and Neil's Harbour.* 1933. Nfi.

MacDonald, J.M. "Piping in Cape Breton." *Piping Times* 21, no. 2 (November 1968).

MacDonald, John (Iain Lom). "Marbh-rann do Mhaistir Donull Mac Cuinn, Ministeir a bha ann an Cille Mhuire Throternis san Eilean-Sgiathanach Air fon [*sic*], 'Slan gu'm faic mi thus Mharcuis,' le Iain Lom." (Death verse to Mr Donald MacQueen who was in Kilmore Troternish in the Island of Skye to the melody 'Health till I see you Mark.') In Stewart and Stewart, *Cochruinneacha Taoghta de Shaothair nam Bard Gaëlach*, 20–8.

MacDonald, Joseph. *A Compleat Theory of the Scots Highland Bagpipe.* 1803. Reprint, Wakefield, U.K.: S.R. Publishers, 1971.

MacDonald, Mildred, and John Colin Big John. *Fair is the Place, An Account of Two Clanranald Families at Judique, Cape Breton.* Sydney, N.S.: City Printers, n.d. (late 1980s).

Macdonald, Stuart. *Back to Lochaber – A Search for Historic Events, Travels, Tales and Customs.* Edinburgh, Cambridge, and Durham: Pentland Press, 1994.

McDonell Dawson, Aeneas. *The Catholics of Scotland – From 1593, and the Extinction of the Hierarchy in 1603, till the Death of Bishop Carruthers in 1852.* London, Ont., 1890.

MacDonell, Col. John, of Scottos. *Spanish John; being a Narrative of the Early Life of Colonel John McDonell of Scottos, Written by Himself.* Edinburgh and London: Blackwood & Sons, 1931.

MacDonell, Margaret. *The Emigrant Experience: Songs of Highland Emigrants in North America.* Toronto: University of Toronto Press, 1982.

MacDonell, Margaret, and John Shaw, eds. *Luirgean Eachainn Nìll: A collection of folktales told by Hector Campbell, transcribed and translated from the original Gaelic.* Inverness: John G. Eccles Printers, n.d. [1970].

MacDougall, D. Letter cited by Fionn (Henry Whyte) in "Martial Music of the Munros," in Fionn's serial "The Martial Music of the Clans." *Celtic Monthly: A Magazine for Highlanders* 11, nos. 38–39 (1903).

MacDougall, J.L. *History of Inverness County.* Canadiana Reprint Series, no. 43. Belleville, Ont.: Mika Publishing, 1922, 1976.

MacFarlane, D.D.(?) *Margaree.Doc* "The Parish of South-West Margaree Antigonish Casket 1896," from Beaton Institute (UCCB) biographic folder of D.D. MacFarlane, including bracketed, italicized glosses by Don MacFarlane and by person unknown, presumably D.D. MacFarlane. Folder includes material from the following issues of the Antigonish *Casket*: 45, no. 13 (16 April 1896): 6; 45, no. 15 (30 April 1896): 2; 45, no. 17 (14 May 1896): 3; 45, no. 18, (21 May 1896): 3; and other material.

MacFarlane, Robert. "Tenants in Brae Lochaber." Unpublished MS, c. 1995 (primary source research by Dr Iain S. MacDonald, Falkirk).

MacGill, William. *Old Ross-shire and Scotland from the Tain and Balnagown Documents.* Inverness: Northern Counties Newspaper and Printing and Publishing Co., 1909.

Mac Gill-eain, Somhairle. "Domhnall Donn of Bohuntin." In Somhairle Mac Gill-eain, *Ris a' Bhruthaich – The Criticism and Prose Writings of Sorley MacLean by Somhairle Mac Gill-eain.* Edited by William Gillies. Stornoway: Acair, 1985.

MacGillivray, Allister. *A Cape Breton Ceilidh*, Sydney, Cape Breton, N.S.: Sea Cape Music, 1988.

MacGillivray, Rev. Ronald (Sagairt Arasaig). "A History of the County of Antigonish, Nova Scotia." Published serially in Antigonish *Casket*, 1890–92. Reprint, *History of Antigonish.* Edited by R.A. MacLean. Antigonish, N.S.: Casket Printing and Publishing Co., 1976.

MacGregor, Alasdair Alpin. *Land of the Mountain and the Flood.* London: Michael Joseph, 1965.

MacGregor, Alexander. "John MacDonald – An Adherent of Prince Charles." *Celtic Magazine* 3, no. 36 (October 1878): 462–6.

MacGregor, James Roy. Letters in *Blackwood's Magazine*, December 1817.

MacInnes, Sheldon. *A Journey in Celtic Music*. Sydney, Cape Breton, N.S.: UCCB Press, 1997.

MacIntyre, Duncan Ban. "Rainn Gearradh-arm." In MacIntyre, *Songs of Duncan Ban MacIntyre*, 236, 237.

– *The Songs of Duncan Ban MacIntyre*. Edited and translated by Angus MacLeod. Scottish Gaelic Texts Society, 4. Edinburgh: Oliver & Boyd, 1952.

MacKay, Rev. Angus. *Autobiographical Journal of John MacDonald schoolmaster and soldier 1770–1830 – with introduction, illustrations, and notes*. Edinburgh, Norman MacLeod; Caithness, Forbes, Halkirk; and Canada, MacKay, Madoc, Ont., 1906.

– *The Book of MacKay*. Privately printed by William Rae, Wick, Scotland, 1906.

MacKay, Angus. *A Collection of Ancient Piobaireachd or Highland Pipe Music, many of the pieces being adapted to the piano forte with full instructions for those desirous of qualifying themselves in performing on the National Instrument. to which are prefixed some sketches of the principal HEREDITARY PIPERS and their ESTABLISHMENTS with historical & traditional notes respecting the origin of the various pieces. Dedicated by permission to the Highland Society of London*. Includes no author(s) "A Circumstantial Account of the Competitions for the Prizes given by the Highland Society in London, to the best Performers on the Great Highland Bagpipe, from the year 1781," 15–20; "Account of the Hereditary Pipers," 7–14; and "Historical and Traditional Notes on the Piobaireachds," 1–14. Wakefield, U.K.: EP Publishing, 1972.

– *The piper's assistant, a collection of marches, quicksteps, strathspeys, reels & jigs – Consisting of 155 tunes. By Angus MacKay, piper to Her Majesty. Author of clan pibrachd. &c.* Edinburgh: Alexander Glen, 1843.

MacKay, Annie. "All We Know about our Grandparents." Holograph longhand MS privately held by Sandy MacKay, Lyon's Brook, Pictou County, N.S. N.d.

MacKay, Iain. "Clanranald's Tacksmen of the late 18th Century." *TGSI* 44 (1964–66): 61–93.

MacKay, Iain R. "Glenalladale's settlement, Prince Edward Island." *Scottish Gaelic Studies* (University of Aberdeen) 10, part 1 (August 1963): 16–24.

MacKay, James. *Genealogical History – St. Mary's Parish Glendale, N.S.* Glace Bay: Brodie Printing Company, n.d. [1975].

McKay, Neville T. "Angus MacKay (1812–1859) and his contribution to Highland Music." *TGSI* 55 (1986–88): 203–16.

– "A History of the Office of Piper to the Sovereign." *Folk Music Journal* (English Folk Dance and Song Society) 7, no. 2 (1996): 188–204.

MacKay, William. *The complete tutor for the great Highland bagpipe with a compendious selection of marches, quick steps, strathspeys, reels & jigs. Amounting to one hundred – The whole selected and arranged for the Instrument by William MacKay piper to the Celtic Society of Scotland*. Edinburgh: Alexander Glen, 1840.

McKay, William. *The Tutor for the Highland Bagpipe – with a Selection of March-*

es *Quicksteps Strathspeys Reels and Jigs – amounting to one hundred tunes by William McKay in 1841–1843 corrected and improved by Angus McKay piper to Her Majesty.* Edinburgh: Alexander Glen, 1871.

MacKay, William. *Urquhart and Glenmoriston.* Inverness, 1893.

MacKellar, Mary. "Unknown Lochaber Bards." *TGSI* 12 (1885–86): 211–26.

MacKenzie, Alexander. *History of the Chisholms – with Genealogies of the Principal Families of the Name.* Inverness, 1891.

– *History of the MacDonalds and Lords of the Isles.* Inverness, 1881.

MacKenzie, Annie H. "Lochaber Bards." *Scottish Gaelic Studies* (University of Aberdeen) 10, part 1 (August 1963): 25–43.

MacKenzie, Archibald A. *The MacKenzies' History of Christmas Island Parish. 1926.* Revised and updated by author's son Archibald A. MacKenzie, Sudbury, Ont.: Mackenzie Rothe Publishers, 1984.

MacKenzie, Bridget Gordon. "On the relation of Norse skaldic verse to Irish syllabic poetry." In Dronke, Helgadóttir, Weber, and Bekker-Nielsen, eds., *Speculum Norroenum – Norse studies in memory of Gabriel turville-Petre.* Odense: Odense University Press, 1981.

– *Piping Traditions of The North of Scotland.* Edinburgh: John Donald Publishers, 1998.

MacKenzie, John, Esq. *Sar-Obair nam Bard Gaelach: or, The Beauties of Gaelic Poetry, and Lives of the Highland bards; with Historical and Critical Notes, and a Comprehensive glossary of Provincial Words.* New edition. Edinburgh: N. MacLeod, 1904.

MacKenzie, Osgood Hanbury. *A Hundred Years in the Highlands.* New edition. London: Geoffrey Bles, 1952.

MacKinnon, Rev. Dr Donald, and Alick Morrison. *The MacLeods – The Genealogy of a Clan.* Section one: "MacLeod Chiefs of Harris and Dunvegan." Edinburgh: Clan MacLeod Society, 1969.

MacKinnon, Hugh. "The MacDonalds of Laig." *Tocher* (University of Edinburgh) 10 (1973): 41–80.

MacKinnon, Kenneth A. "Captain John MacDonald and the Glenaladale Settlers: The Proprietor as Community Leader." In *Celtic Languages and Celtic Peoples*, edited by Cyril J. Byrne et al., 661–81. Proceedings of the Second North American Congress of Celtic Studies. Halifax: Saint Mary's University, 1992.

– "Rankin, Coun Douly (Con-duiligh MacRaing)." *Dictionary of Canadian Biography* 8: 240–2.

Mackintosh, Sir Aeneas, Bart. *Notes Descriptive and Historical Principally Relating to the Parish of Moy in Strathdearn and the Town and Neighbourhood of Inverness.* N.p., 1892.

Mackintosh, Margaret. *The Clan Mackintosh and the Clan Chattan.* Edinburgh and London: W. and A.K. Johnston, 1948.

MacLean, Angus Hector. *God and the Devil at Seal Cove.* Halifax: Petheric Press, 1976.

MacLean, Calum. *The Highlands*. London: B.T. Batsford, 1959.

MacLean, John. "Am Piobaire Dall." *TGSI* 41 (1951–52): 283–306.

MacLean, John. "Traditional Links to song & dance" (review of Gibson, *Tradition-al Gaelic Bagpiping*) and Editor's Note. *Celtic Heritage* 13, no. 1 (February/March 1999): 18, 19.

MacLean, Loraine. *Discovering Invernesshire*. N.p., n.d.

McLean, Marianne. *The People of Glengarry, Highlanders in Transition, 1745–1820*. Montreal and Kingston: McGill-Queen's University Press, 1991.

MacLean, R.A. *Bishop John Cameron: Piety & Politics*. Antigonish, N.S.: Casket Printing and Publishing Co., 1991.

– , ed. *History of Antigonish* (the work of Sagairt Arasaig, Rev. Ronald MacGillivray [1835–92]). Antigonish, N.S.: Casket Printing and Publishing Co., 1976.

MacLennan, Ronald George. *The History of the MacLennans*. Inverness: John G. Eccles Printers, 1978.

MacLeod, C.I.N. *Bardachd a Albainn Nuaidh*. Glasgow: Gairm, 1970.

– *Sgialachdan a Albainn Nuaidh*. Glasgow: Gairm, 1969.

MacLeod, Rev. Donald. *Memoir of Norman MacLeod, D.D.* Toronto, 1876.

McLeod, James R. "John McKay's Black House at Eyre, Raasay." Part 1, *Piping Times* 45, no. 5 (February 1993); and Part 2, *Piping Times* 45, no. 6 (March 1993).

MacLeod, Neil. "Donnachadh Ban Mac-an-t-Saoir." *TGSI* 12 (1885–86), 94–8.

MacLeod, Niel (Gesto). *Pibereach or pipe tunes, as taught verbally by the McCrimmen pipers in Skye to their apprentices. The following as taken from John McCrimmon, piper to the old Laird of MacLeod, and his grandson the late General McLeod of McLeod, at Dunvegan*. Edinburgh: Lawrie & Co., 1828.

MacLeod, Norman. *Caraid nan Gàidheal (The Friend of the Gael.) A choice selec-tion of the Gaelic Writings of the late Norman MacLeod, D.D., of St. Columba Parish, Glasgow ... with a memoir of the author by his son, the late Norman MacLeod, D.D., of the Barony Parish, Glasgow, selected and edited by Rev. A. Clerk, LL.D (minister of Kilmallie)*. New edition. Edinburgh: Norman MacLeod, 1899.

– *Teachdaire Gaelach (Gaelic Messenger)*. Monthly publication between 1830 and 1832.

MacLeod, Ruairidh Halford. "'The best piper of his time' MacCrimmon." *Clan MacLeod Magazine* 9, nos. 54 (part 1) and 55 (part 2) (1982): 66–73.

– "Early MacCrimmon Records." *Piping Times* 29, no. 5 (February 1977).

– "The end of the MacCrimmon College." *Piping Times* 29, no. 8 (May 1977).

– "The MacCrimmons and the '45." *Piping Times* 29, no. 6 (March 1977).

MacMillan, Rev. Allan J. *To the Hill of Boisdale: A Short History and a Genealogi-cal Tracing of the Pioneer Families of Boisdale, Cape Breton, and the Surround-ing Areas*. Sydney, N.S.: City Printers, 1986.

MacMillan, Somerled. *Bygone Lochaber – Historical and Traditional.* Glasgow: K. and R. Davidson, Printers, 1971.

Mac Neil, Rev. Angus. Letter to Dr Blair concerning the authenticity of James MacPherson's Ossianic poems. In Grant, *Thoughts on the Origin*, 389–92.

MacNeil, Joe Neil. *Tales until Dawn – the World of a Cape Breton Gaelic Story-Teller. Sgeul gu Latha le Eòs (Eòs Nìll bhig MacNill).* Translated and edited by John Shaw. Montreal and Kingston: McGill-Queen's University Press, 1987.

MacNeil, Stephen R. *All Call Iona Home.* Antigonish, N.S.: Formac Publishing, 1979.

– "Centenary of the first landing of a Catholic Bishop on the Shores of the Bras d'Or Lakes, Cape Breton (1815–1915)." Booklet. N.d., n.p.

McNeill, F. Marian. *An Iona Anthology.* New edition. Glasgow: Iona Community, 1952.

McNeill, Neill. "Census of the Small Isles 1764–65, at Canna 20th March 1765." Appendices 2 and 3 transcribed by Catherine MacInnes and Catherine and Alan Blair. Used as part of Daniel W. MacInnes's talk at Saint Mary's University, Halifax, Nova Scotia, 26–29 September 1996. The census is unpublished and has no pagination.

MacNeill, Seumas. "Foreword." In MacKay, *Collection of Ancient Piobaireachd*, 1972 edition.

– , and John M.A. Lenihan. "The Scale of the Highland Bagpipe." *Piping Times* 13, no. 2 (November 1960): 6–10, and no. 4 (January 1961): 8–11.

MacPherson, Donald. "Urlar." In Campsie, *MacCrimmon Legend*, 1–2.

MacPherson, John. *Tales from Barra, Told by the Coddy (John MacPherson, Northbay, Barra, 1876–1955).* Foreword by Compton MacKenzie. Introduction and notes by J.L. Campbell. Edinburgh: W. and A.K. Johnston and G.W. Bacon, 1960.

MacPherson, Norman. "Notes on Antiquities from the island of Eigg." *Proceedings of the Society of Antiquaries of Scotland* 12, part 2 (1876–78): 577–97.

MacQuarrie, Gordon F., compiler and arranger. *The Cape Breton Collection of Scottish Melodies for the Violin Consisting of Marches, Slow Airs, Strathspeys, Reels, Jigs, Hornpipes, Etc, Mostly Original, and Containing 152 Selections.* Edited by J. Beaton. Originally printed in 1940. 2nd printing. Medford, Mass.: J. Beaton, 1975.

MacQueen, Malcolm A. *Skye Pioneers and "The Island."* Winnipeg: Stovel Co., 1929.

MacRae, Rev. Alexander. *History of the Clan MacRae with Genealogies.* Dingwall, Scotland, 1899.

MacRae, Alexander, *Revivals in the Highlands and in the Islands in the 19th Century.* Stirling: Eneas McKay, n.d. (1906?).

MacRae, Finlay. "An Old Bagpipe." *Piping Times* 30, no. 5 (May 1978): 25.

McWhannell, Donald C., and Alastair Campbell, of Airds. "The Macgillechonnels – a family of hereditary boatbuilders." Unpublished MS. Dundee and Inveraray, 1995.

Marshall's Scottish Melodies Airs Strathspeys, Reels, Jigs &c for the Violin. (The work includes *Marshall's Scottish Airs.* Edinburgh: Alex Robertson, 1822; *A Collection of Strathspeys, Reels* ... Edinburgh: Neil Stewart, 1781; *Volume 2nd of a Collection* ... Edinburgh: Alex Robertson, 1845; and *Kinrara.* Edinburgh: Urbani and Liston, 1800). Harrisville, N.H.: Fiddlecase Books, 1978.

Matheson, Angus. *The Appin Murder – A Traditional Account Reprinted from Vol. XXXV of the Transactions of the Gaelic Society of Inverness.* Inverness: Club Leabhar, 1975.

Matheson, William. "Traditions of the Mathesons." *TGSI* 42 (1953–59): 153–81.

– , ed. *The Songs of John MacCodrum, Bard to Sir James MacDonald of Sleat.* Vol. 2. Edinburgh: Scottish Gaelic Texts Society, Oliver and Boyd, 1938.

Mathews, Hazel C. *The Mark of Honour.* Toronto: University of Toronto Press, 1965.

Menzies, D.P. *The "Red and White" Book of Menzies – Leabhar dearg 'us geal na Meinerich – The History of Clan Menzies.* Glasgow, 1894.

Military disposition in Highland Scotland in Autumn 1747. *Scots Magazine*, September 1747, 453.

Minc, Henryk. Letter to *Piping Times* 44, no. 11 (August 1992): 51–5.

Mitchell, Joseph. *Reminiscences of My Life in the Highlands.* Vol. 1. 1883. Reprint, Newton Abbott, Devon: David and Charles, 1971.

Monroe, John D. *Chapters in the History of Delaware County, New York.* N.p.: Delaware County Historical Association, 1949.

Morrison, Alick. *The MacLeods – The Genealogy of a Clan.* Edinburgh: Clan MacLeod Society, 1974.

Morrison, Hew, ed. *Orain le Rob Donn bard ainmeal na h-Ard Tuath.* Untranslated. 3rd edition, revised and enlarged, with a history of Rob Donn in English. Edinburgh: John Grant, 1899.

Munro, R.W. "Archibald Munro, piper to Glengarry." *Clan Munro Magazine*, no. 9 (1965).

Murphy, Gerard, ed. *Early Irish Lyrics – Eighth to Twelfth Century.* London: Oxford University Press, 1956.

Murray Logan, G. *Scottish Highlanders and the American Revolution.* Halifax: McCurdy Printing Co., 1976.

National Library of Scotland. *Lamplighter and Story-teller, John Francis Campbell of Islay 1821–1885.* Exhibition catalogue 25. Edinburgh, 1985.

Nicolson, Alexander. *History of Skye – a Record of the Families, the Social Conditions, and the Literature of the Island.* Glasgow: A. Maclaren & Sons, 1930.

"Notices of Pipers." *Piping Times* 20, no. 4 (January 1968); 20, no. 12 (September 1960); 22, nos. 5 and 6 (February and March 1970).

Ordnance Survey (OS). Sheet 35, Loch Arkaig (revised to 1967); *OS* Landranger Series, sheet 19 (Gairloch and Ullapool).

Ó Riada, Seán. *Our Musical Heritage.* Edited by Thomas Kinsella. Music editor

Tomás Ó canainn. Portlaoise, Ireland: Dolmen Press and Fundúireacht an Riadaigh, 1982.

Oxford University Press. *The Compact Edition of the Oxford English Dictionary.* Oxford, 1971.

Patterson, Rev. George. *A History of the County of Pictou, Nova Scotia.* Montreal, 1877. Reprint, Toronto: James Campbell and Son, 1977.

Pennant, Thomas. *A Tour in Scotland 1769.* 3rd ed. 3 vols. Warrington: W. Eyres (Printer), 1774–76.

Philip, James (of Almerieclose). *The Grameid, an Heroic Poem descriptive of the Campaign of Viscount Dundee in 1689 and Other Pieces.* Vol. 3. Edited by Alexander D. Murdoch. Edinburgh: Scottish History Society, 1888.

– *Scoti Grameidos.* Book 4. In Philip, *The Grameid.*

Piobaireachd Society. *See* Comunn na Piobaireachd.

Poulter, G.C.B. *History of the Clan MacCrimmon, compiled by G.C.B. Poulter.* Camberley, England: Clan MacCrimmon Society, 1938.

Prebble, John Ross. *Culloden.* London: Secker and Warburg, 1961.

– *Glencoe: The Story of the Massacre.* New York: Holt, Reinhart and Winston; London: Secker and Warburg, 1966.

– *The Highland Clearances.* London, 1963.

– *The King's Jaunt – George IV in Scotland, August 1822: 'One and twenty daft days.'* London: Collins, 1988.

Rankin, Rev. Duncan J. *A History of the County of Antigonish, Nova Scotia.* Toronto, 1929.

Rea, F.G. *A School in South Uist, Reminiscences of a Hebridean School-master.* Edited by John Lorne Campbell. London: Routledge and Kegan Paul, 1964.

Rearick, Charles. *Beyond the Enlightenment – Historians and Folklore in Nineteenth Century France.* Vol. 27. Folklore Monograph Series. Bloomington and London: Indiana University Press, 1974.

Reay Papers, also referred to as the Reay Charter Chests. Unpublished source material used in Reverend Angus MacKay, *The Book of MacKay,* 1906.

Register of the Privy Council (RPC). First Series, 5:28.

Report of the piping competition held in Edinburgh in October 1784. *Scots Magazine* 46 (October 1784): 552–3.

Robertson, Rev. C.M. "Topography and Traditions of Eigg." *TGSI* 22 (1897–98): 202.

Robertson, Marion. *The King's Bounty: A History of Early Shelburne, Nova Scotia.* Halifax, 1983.

Rogers, Rev. Charles. *The Scottish Minstrel – the Songs of Scotland Subsequent to Burns – with Memoirs of the Poets.* Edinburgh: William P. Nimmo, 1873.

Ross, Neil. "Ceol Mor – The Classical Music of the Bagpipes." *TGSI* 32 (1924–25): 158–71.

Ross, Roderick. *Binneas is Boreraig.* 5 vols. Edinburgh: MacDonald Printers, 1959–67.

Sage, Rev. Donald. *Memorabilia Domestica or, Parish life in the North of Scotland.* Edinburgh: W. Rae, Wick and John Menzies and Co., 1889.

St Clair, Jim. "The Vallay MacDonalds in Whycocomagh." *Participaper* 6, no. 12 (April 1985). Port Hood, Inverness County, N.S.

Sanger, Keith. "Auchinbreck's Harper, a Donald Pypar M'Yndoir." *Notes and Queries of the Society of West Highland and Island Historical Research*, vol. 30 (February 1987).

– "MacCrimmon's Prentise – A Post Graduate Student Perhaps." *Piping Times* 44, no. 6 (March 1992): 16–19.

– , and Alison Kinnaird. *Tree of Strings – crann nan teud.* Temple, Midlothian, Scotland: Kinmor Music, 1992.

Scobie, I.H. MacKay. *Pipers and Pipe Music in a Highland Regiment – A record of Piping in the 1st Seaforth Highlanders, originally the Earl of Seaforth's or 78th (Highland) regiment, afterwards the 72nd or Duke of Albany's Own Highlanders.* Dingwall: Ross-shire Printing and Publishing Company, 1924.

Scott, Hew. *Fasti Ecclesiae Scoticanae.* New edition. 8 vols. Edinburgh: Oliver and Boyd, 1915–50.

Scott, James E. Letter to *Piping Times* 16, no. 6 (March 1964).

Scott, Walter. Letter to Joanna Baillie, dated Ulva House, 19 July 1810, in McNeill, *An Iona Anthology*, 83–4.

– *Rob Roy.* Preface by W.M. Parker. London: Everyman's Library, 1966.

Seton, Sir Bruce, and Jean Gordon Arnot, eds. *Prisoners of the '45.* 3 vols. Vol. 14 of the 3rd Scottish History series. Edinburgh: Constable, 1928, 1929.

Shaw, Christina Byam. *Pigeon Holes of Memory – The Life and Times of Dr John Mackenzie (1803–1886) edited from his Manuscript Memoirs.* London: Constable, 1988.

Shears, Barry. *The Cape Breton Collection of Bagpipe Music.* Halifax: Taigh a' Chiuil, 1995.

– *The Gathering of the Clans Collection.* Vol. 1. Privately published. Halifax: Bounty Press, 1991.

– *The Gathering of the Clans Collection: A Collection of Music, Photographs and Historical Essays Compiled and Collected by Barry W. Shears.* Vol. 2. Halifax: Bounty Press, 2001.

Sinclair, Rev. A. MacLean. "Clann Duilligh." *MacTalla* 2, no. 2 (24 July 1903): 12–13.

– "The Gaelic Bards and the Collectors of their Works." *TGSI* 24 (1899–1901): 259–77.

– *The Gaelic Bards from 1411 to 1715.* Charlottetown: Haszard & Moore, 1890.

– "The MacIntyres of Glennoe." *TGSI* 18 (1891–92): 289–95.

Skelton, Constance Oliver, and John Malcolm Bulloch. *The House of Gordon.* Vol. 3. Aberdeen: New Spalding Club, 1912.

Skene, W.F. *Celtic Scotland.* Edinburgh, 1880.

Smith, William, and Theophilus D. Hall. *A Smaller Latin-English Dictionary.* London: John Murray, Albemarle Street, 1886.

Splatt, Les. "The Scale of the Highland Bagpipe." *Piping Times* 18, no. 3 (December 1965): 8–13.

Stanley, Laurie. *The Well-Watered Garden: The Presbyterian Church in Cape Breton, 1798–1860,* Sydney, N.S.: UCCB Press, 1983.

Statistical Account of Scotland (Old Statistical Account), 1790s.

Stewart(?). *The Stewarts of Ardvorlich.* Vol. 1, app. 14.

Stewart, Rev. Alexander. *Nether Lochaber: The Natural History, Legends, and Folk-lore of the West Highlands.* Edinburgh, 1883.

Stewart, Alexander, and Donald Stewart. *Cochruinneacha Taoghta de Shaothair nam Bard Gaëlach.* Edinburgh, 1804.

Stewart, Col. David, of Garth. *Sketches of the character, Manners, and Present State of the Highlanders of Scotland: with Details of the Military Service of the Highland Regiments.* 2 vols. Edinburgh, 1822.

Stuart, John Roy (Iain Ruadh Stiubhart). "Cumha do Bhaintighearna Mhic-an-Toisich." In MacKenzie, *Sar-Obair nam Bard,* 264–9.

Sydney Record 10, no. 60 (12 March 1907), taken from National Library of Canada microfilms, N-68931 (January–June 1907); and vol. 11, no. 163 (13 July 1908).

Szick, Lark B. *Early Settlers of Ingonish 1800–1994.* Nfi.

Tayler, Alistair, and Henrietta Tayler. *1745 and After.* In essence, "Narrative: of John William O'Sullivan, one of the seven men of Moidart." London: Thomas Nelson and Sons, 1938.

Thomason, C.S. *Ceol Mor: written in a new and abbreviated system of musical notation for the piobaireachd as played on the Highland bagpipe.* Part 3. Glasgow: John MacKay, 1897.

Thomson, Derick S. "The MacMhuirich Bardic Family." *TGSI* 43 (1960–63): 276–304.

– "Niall Mor MacMhuirich." *TGSI* 49 (1974–76): 9–25.

Timperley, Loretta R., ed. *A Directory of Landownership in Scotland 1770.* Edinburgh: Scottish Record Society, 1976.

Unacknowledged. "Immaculate Conception Church West Lake Ainslie 125 Years 1871–1996," no pagination, n.d, n.a (credit given to Josephine Beaton, Brook Village, by Fr Bernard MacDonald, PP Brook Village, 27 November 1999).

United Kingdom. *The Statutes at Large, from the Ninth Year of the Reign of King George the Second to the Twenty-fifth Year of the Reign of King George the Second.* Vol. 6. London, 1786.

Victoria Regina. *More Leaves from the Journal of a Life in the Highlands from 1862 to 1883.* 4th ed. Toronto: A.H. Hovey & Co, 1884.

Watson, J.G. *Orain agus Luinneagan Gàidhlig, le Màiri nighean Alasdair Ruaidh.* (Gaelic Songs and Poems, by Mary daughter of Red Alasdair.) Edinburgh: Scottish Gaelic Texts Society, 1965.

Watson, William J. "Place names of Perthshire: The Lyon Basin." *TGSI* 35 (1929–30): 277–96.

Whig Standard (Kingston), 9 August 1930.

Whitelaw, Marjorie, ed. *Dalhousie Journals.* Ottawa: Oberon Press, 1978.

Whyte, Henry (Fionn). *The Martial Music of the Clans with Historic, Biographic, & Legendary Notes regarding the Origin of the Music, also portraits of Highland chiefs & Distinguished Clansmen, with their Seats, Arms, etc. etc.* Glasgow: J. MacKay, 1904.

– *The Rankins – Pipers to the MacLeans of Duart, and later to the MacLeans of Coll.* Glasgow, 1907.

Wimberley, Capt. D. "Papers from the Bighouse Charter Chest." Published in part I under heading "Selections from the family papers of the MacKays of Bighouse, consisting mainly of letters addressed to John Campbell of Barcaldine, some time one of the government factors on the forfeited estates after the '45." *TGSI* 21 (1896–97): 120–71.

Wright, Robert. *The life of Major-General James Wolfe founded on Original Documents and illustrated by his Correspondence including numerous Unpublished Letters contributed from the Family Papers and Noblemen and Gentlemen, Descendants of his Companions.* London, 1864.

Wrong, George M. *A Canadian Manor and Its Seigneurs – The Story of a Hundred Years 1761–1861.* 2nd ed. Toronto: MacMillan of Canada, 1926.

Youngson, A.J. *After the Forty-Five – The Economic Impact on the Scottish Highlands.* Edinburgh: Edinburgh University Press, 1973.

Index

Note: Nearly everyone listed below as a "Cape Breton piper" was a step-dance piper – the only exceptions are those Cape Breton pipers who took up the bagpipes in the later twentieth century when literate learning had supplanted the traditional ear-learned method. I have chosen not to make that distinction. Where pipers are given as step-dance and/or Scotch Four pipers, they were so described to me and learned in traditional times. Thus I obviate the difficulty of classifying modern, literately taught pipers who have managed to play step-dance music.